Financial Statement Analysis

CFA® PROGRAM CURRICULUM • VOLUME 3

LEVEL I
2007

PEARSON

Custom
Publishing

Cover photograph courtesy, Hewlett-Packard Development Company, L.P.

Printed in the United States of America

10 9 8 7 6 5 4

ISBN 0-536-17615-9

2005160771

BK/JS

Please visit our web site at *www.pearsoncustom.com*

PEARSON CUSTOM PUBLISHING
75 Arlington Street, Suite 300, Boston, MA 02116
A Pearson Education Company

CONTENTS

4⅛ 4¹¹/₁₆ ⅜

5½ 5½ —

5½ 21¹³/₁₆ — ¹/₁₆

20⅝ 21¹³/₁₆ 18⅛ + ⅞

17³/₈ 18⅛ +

6½ — ½

6½ 6½ —

7¼ 6½ 3¹/₃₂ — ⅛

15/16 ⁹/₁₆

1 9/16

19/32 7¹⁵/₁₆

7¹⁵/₁₆ 7¹³/₁₆ 7¹⁵/₁₆

2½ +

2⅝ 2¹¹/₃₂ 2½ +

2¾ 2¼ 2¼

11¼ +

5⅝ 12¹/₁₆ 11⅜ 11¼ +

87 33¾ 33 33¼ —

602 25⅝ 24⁹/₁₆ 25⅝ +

833 12 11⅝ 11⅞ +

16 10½ 10½ 10½ —

78 15⅝ 15¹³/₁₆ 15⅝ —

4608 9¹/₁₆ 8¼ 8⅜ +

130 11¼ 10⅛

HOW TO USE THE CFA PROGRAM CURRICULUM

Congratulations on your decision to enter the Chartered Financial Analyst (CFA®) Program. This exciting and rewarding program of study reflects your desire to become a serious investment professional. You are embarking on a program noted for its requirement of ethics and breadth of knowledge, skills, and abilities.

The credential you seek is respected around the world as a mark of accomplishment and dedication, and each level of the program represents a distinct achievement in professional development. Successful completion of the program is rewarded with membership in a prestigious global community of investment professionals. CFA charterholders are dedicated to life-long learning and maintaining currency with the ever-changing dynamics of a challenging profession.

Curriculum Development

The CFA Program curriculum is grounded in the practice of the investment profession. CFA Institute regularly conducts a practice analysis survey of investment professionals around the world to determine the knowledge, skills, and abilities that are relevant to the profession. The survey results define the Candidate Body of Knowledge (CBOK™), an inventory of knowledge and responsibilities expected of the investment management professional at the level of a new CFA charterholder. The survey also determines how much emphasis each of the major topic areas receives on the CFA examinations.

A committee made up of practicing charterholders, in conjunction with CFA Institute staff, designs the CFA Program curriculum to deliver the CBOK to candidates. The examinations, also written by practicing charterholders, are designed for you to demonstrate mastery of the CBOK as set forth in the CFA Program curriculum. As you structure your personal study program, you should emphasize mastery of the CBOK and the practical application of that knowledge. For more information on the practice analysis, CBOK, and development of the CFA Program curriculum, please visit www.cfainstitute.org/course.

Organization

The 2007 Level I CFA Program curriculum is organized into 10 topic areas. Each topic area begins with a topic level learning outcome that summarizes the broad objective of the material to follow and indicates the depth of knowledge expected. Each topic area is then divided into one or more study sessions, each devoted to a sub-topic (or group of sub-topics) within that topic area. The 2007 Level I curriculum is organized into 18 study sessions. Each study session begins with a purpose statement defining the content structure and objective of that session. Finally, each study session is further divided into reading assignments. *The outline on the inside front cover of each volume should further illustrate this important hierarchy.*

The reading assignments are the basis for all examination questions. The readings are selected or developed specifically to teach candidates the CBOK. Readings are drawn from textbook chapters, professional journal articles, research analyst reports, CFA Program-commissioned content, and cases. Many readings include problems and solutions as well as appendices to help you learn.

Reading-specific Learning Outcome Statements (LOS) are listed in the study session opener page as well as prior to each reading. Reading-specific LOS indicate what you should be able to accomplish after studying the reading. It is important, however, not to interpret LOS narrowly by focusing on a few key sentences in a reading. Readings, particularly CFA Program-commissioned readings, provide context for the learning outcome and enable you to apply a principle or concept in a variety of scenarios. Thus, you should use the LOS to guide and focus your study, as each examination question is based explicitly on one or more LOS. We encourage you to thoroughly review how to properly use LOS and the list and descriptions of commonly used LOS command words at www.cfainstitute.org/toolkit. The command words signal the depth of learning you are expected to achieve from the reading.

Features for 2007

▶ **Required vs. Optional segments** - Several reading assignments use only a portion of the original source textbook chapter or journal article. In order to allow you to read the assignment within its full context, however, we have reprinted the entire chapter or article in the curriculum. When an optional segment begins, you will see an icon. A vertical solid bar in the outside margin will continue until the optional segment ends, symbolized by another icon. Unless the material is specifically noted as optional, you should assume it is required. Keep in mind that the optional material is provided strictly for your convenience and will not be tested. *You should rely on the required segments and the reading-specific LOS in preparing for the examination.*

▶ **Problems/Solutions** - When appropriate, we have developed and assigned problems after readings to demonstrate practical application and reinforce understanding of the concepts presented. The solutions to the problems are provided in an appendix at the back of each volume. Candidates should consider all problems and solutions required material as your ability to solve these problems will prepare you for exam questions.

▶ **Margins** - We have inserted wide margins throughout each volume to allow for easier note taking.

▶ **Two-color format** - To enrich the visual appeal and clarity of the exhibits, tables, and required vs. optional treatments, we have printed the curriculum in two-color format.

▶ **Six- volume structure** - To improve the portability of the curriculum, we have spread the material over six volumes versus the four we had last year.

▶ **Glossary and Index** - For your convenience, we have printed a comprehensive glossary and index in each volume. Throughout the curriculum, a **bolded blue** word in a reading denotes a glossary term.

Designing your personal study program:

Create a schedule - An orderly, systematic approach to preparation is critical to successful completion of the examination. You should dedicate a consistent block of time every week to reading and studying. Complete all reading assignments and the associated problems and solutions in each study session. Review the LOS both before and after you study each reading to ensure that you have mastered the applicable content and can complete the action(s) specified. Upon completion of each study session, review the session's purpose statement and confirm that you thoroughly understand the subject matter. When you complete a topic area, review the topic level learning outcome and verify that you have mastered the objectives.

CFA Institute estimates that you will need to devote a minimum of 10-15 hours per week for 18 weeks to study the assigned readings. Allow a minimum of one week for each study session spread over several days, with completion scheduled for at least 30-45 days prior to the examination. This schedule will allow you to spend the final four to six weeks before the examination reviewing the assigned material and taking multiple on-line sample examinations. At CFA Institute, we believe that candidates need to commit to a *minimum* of 250 hours reading and reviewing the curriculum and taking online sample exams to master the material. This recommendation, however, may substantially underestimate the hours needed for appropriate exam preparation depending on individual circumstances and academic background.

You will undoubtedly adjust your study time to conform to your own strengths and weaknesses and academic background, and you will probably spend more time on some study sessions than on others. You should allow ample time for both in-depth study of all topic areas and additional concentration on those topic areas for which you feel least prepared.

Preliminary Readings - The reading assignments in Economics and Financial Statement Analysis assume candidates already have a basic mastery of the concepts typically presented in introductory university-level economics and accounting courses. Information on suggested readings to improve your knowledge of these topics precedes these study sessions.

Candidate Preparation Toolkit - We have created the online toolkit to provide a single comprehensive location for resources and guidance for candidate preparation. In addition to in-depth information on study program planning, the CFA Program curriculum, and the online sample exams, the toolkit also contains curriculum errata, printable study session outlines, sample exam questions, and more. We encourage you to use the toolkit as your central preparation resource during your tenure as a candidate. Visit the toolkit at www.cfainstitute.org/toolkit.

Online Sample Exams - After completing your study of the assigned curriculum, use the CFA Institute online sample exams to measure your knowledge of the topics and improve your exam-taking skills. After each question, you will receive immediate feedback noting the correct response and indicating the assigned curriculum for further study. The sample exams are designed by the same people who create the actual CFA exams, and reflect the question formats, topics, and level of difficulty of the actual CFA examinations, in a timed environment. Aggregate data indicate that the CFA examination pass rate was higher among candidates who took one or more online sample examinations than for candidates who did not take the online sample exams. For more information on the online sample exams, please visit www.cfainstitute.org/toolkit.

Review Programs - After you enroll in the CFA Program, you may receive numerous solicitations for preparatory courses and review materials. Although preparatory courses and notes may be helpful to some candidates, you should view these resources as *supplements to the assigned CFA Program curriculum*. The CFA exams reference *only* the 2007 CFA Institute assigned curriculum; no preparatory course or review course materials are consulted or referenced.

Furthermore, CFA Institute does not endorse, promote, review, or warrant the accuracy of the products or services offered by preparatory organizations. CFA Institute does not verify or endorse the pass rates or other claims made by these organizations.

Feedback

At CFA Institute, we are committed to delivering a comprehensive and rigorous curriculum for the development of competent, ethically grounded investment professionals. We rely on candidate and member feedback as we work to incorporate content, design, and packaging improvements. You can be assured that we will continue to listen to your suggestions. Please send any comments or feedback to curriculum@cfainstitute.org. Ongoing improvements in the curriculum will help you prepare for success on the upcoming examinations, and for a lifetime of learning as a serious investment professional.

FINANCIAL STATEMENT ANALYSIS

STUDY SESSIONS

TOPIC LEVEL LEARNING OUTCOME

The candidate should be able to demonstrate a thorough knowledge of financial accounting procedures and the rules that govern disclosure. Emphasis is on basic financial statements and how alternative accounting methods affect those statements and the analysis of financial statement relationships.

Supplemental Materials

Please note that the original publisher of the primary readings in the Financial Statement Analysis Study Sessions, John Wiley & Sons, Inc., continues to make available a supplementary study tool for your use. In Study Session 7 (Readings 33, 34, and 36), Study Session 9 (Readings 40, 42, and 43), and Study Session 10 (Readings 44, 45, and 46), there are examples and assigned problems that illustrate important points through use of actual corporate financial statements, or portions of financial statements. For the full context of the example or problem, candidates may find it helpful to refer to the financial statements, which are provided on the website. The financial statements can be found on the Wiley website at he-cda.wiley.com/WileyCDA/HigherEdTitle/productCd-0471375942.html. On the right side of this page, under *Students,* click on the *Student Companion Site* link. This will open a new page; on the left side under *Browse by Resource,* click on *Annual Reports.*

Preparing to Study the CFA Curriculum Materials on Financial Statement Analysis

Before beginning the Reading Assignments, candidates should have a basic mastery of the concepts typically presented in introductory university-level accounting courses. The primary source of Reading Assignments in the CFA Curriculum is *The Analysis and Use of Financial Statements*, 3rd edition, by White, Sondhi, and Fried.

These Reading Assignments assume candidates are already knowledgeable in accounting practices, and understand the following important subjects:

▶ the accounting equation and the mechanics of journal entries (debits and credits)

▶ accounting terms and definitions

▶ practices for measuring and reporting business and financial activities

▶ basic principles and rules of financial reporting, as required by U.S. and IASB GAAP

▶ the relationship between management decisions and financial reporting

▶ the construction of and interrelationships among the balance sheet, income statement, and statement of cash flows

▶ basic accounting and business vocabulary related to the use and construction of financial statements and financial reporting.

If you have not taken an introductory accounting course during the past few years, we strongly encourage you to consider additional study of introductory course material. Although examination questions are drawn only from the Reading Assignments, studying the additional introductory material will strengthen candidates' understanding of the required concepts. A good basic accounting textbook, *Financial Accounting*, 9th edition, by Needles and Powers is available from Houghton Mifflin. At a minimum, we recommend that you study the following chapters:

▶ Chapter 3 – Measuring Business Income

▶ Chapter 4 – Financial Reporting and Analysis (pp. 224-246)

▶ Chapter 6 – Inventories

▶ Chapter 7 – Cash and Receivables

▶ Chapter 8 – Current Liabilities and the Time Value of Money (pp. 416-434)

▶ Chapter 11 – Contributed Capital (pp. 576-590)

▶ Chapter 12 – The Corporate Income Statement and the Statement of Stockholders' Equity (pp. 626-634)

Many accounting textbooks and courses provide similar coverage and will enable you to master the concepts and principles discussed in the Needles and Powers text.

Before you begin your study program, take some time to review the Reading Assignments in the textbook by White, Sondhi and Fried. If you find the material too difficult, it may be an indication that you would benefit from first studying basic accounting concepts and practices.

4⅛ 4¹¹⁄₁₆ — ⅜
5½ 5½ — ¼
20⅝ 21¹³⁄₁₆ — ⅛
17³⁄₈ 18⅛ + ⅞
6½ 6½ — ½
7¼ 15⁄₁₆ 31⁄₃₂ — ⅛
9⁄₁₆ 9⁄₁₆
1⅓₂ 7¹³⁄₁₆ 7¹⁵⁄₁₆
7¹⁵⁄₁₆ 2⁵⁄₈ 2¹¹⁄₃₂ 2½ +
2¾ 2¼ 2¼
12¹⁄₁₆ 11⅜ 11¼ +
33¾ 33 33¼ —
25⅝ 24⁹⁄₁₆ 25⅜ +
12 11⅝ 11⅞ +
16 10½ 10½ 10½ —
78 15⅞ 15¹³⁄₁₆ 15⅞ +
9¹⁄₁₆ 8¼ 8⅞ +
11¼ 10⅛

STUDY SESSION 7
FINANCIAL STATEMENT ANALYSIS:
Basic Concepts, Cash Flow Analysis and IASB GAAP

READING ASSIGNMENTS

Reading 33 Framework for Financial Statement Analysis
Reading 34 Accounting Income and Assets: The Accrual Concept
Reading 35 The Statement of Cash Flows
Reading 36 Analysis of Cash Flows
Reading 37 Worldwide Accounting Diversity

The readings in this study session discuss and illustrate the general principles of the financial reporting system and the critical role of financial statement analysis (including cash flow analysis) to the investment decision making process.

Financial statements provide accounting data and information about a company's income, cash flows, assets, and liabilities. Financial statement information may be deficient of economic reality because, first, it often uses alternative accounting policies and estimates (making company investment comparability difficult) and, second, it is prepared under a selective economic event reporting system that must comply with accounting regulatory standards and principles.

The primary purpose of a cash flow statement is to provide information about a company's cash receipts and cash payments during a financial reporting period. A secondary objective is to provide cash flow information about the company's operating, investing, and financing activities.

Note:
Some of the accounting concepts in the Financial Statement Analysis study sessions (Session 7 through Session 10) may have been superseded by updated rulings and/or pronouncements issued after a reading was published. Candidates are expected to be familiar with the overall analytical framework contained in the study session readings, as well as the implications of alternative accounting methods for financial analysis and valuation, as provided in the assigned readings.

LEARNING OUTCOMES

Reading 33: Framework for Financial Statement Analysis
The candidate should be able to:

a. discuss the general principles of the financial reporting system and explain the objectives of financial reporting according to the Financial Accounting Standards Board (FASB) conceptual framework;

Note:
For purposes of the Level I Examination, candidates should assume that U.S. GAAP (Generally Accepted Accounting Principles) applies unless otherwise noted.

b. identify the two primary qualities of accounting information (i.e., relevance and reliability), the ingredients of relevance (i.e., predictive value, feedback value and timeliness), the ingredients of reliability (i.e., verifiability, neutrality and representational faithfulness), the two secondary qualities of accounting information (i.e., comparability and consistency), and discuss how these qualities provide useful information to an analyst;

c. describe and explain the purposes of the five principal financial statements (i.e., Balance Sheet, Income Statement, Statement of Comprehensive Income, Statement of Cash Flows and Statement of Stockholders' Equity) and discuss the additional sources of information accompanying the financial statements, including the financial footnotes, supplementary schedules, Management Discussion and Analysis (MD&A) and proxy statements;

d. discuss the role of the auditor and the meaning of the audit opinion.

Reading 34: Accounting Income and Assets: The Accrual Concept
The candidate should be able to:

a. describe the format of the income statement and discuss the components of net income;

b. describe the criteria for revenue and expense recognition and discuss major issues in revenue and expense recognition including the affect on reported earnings and their implications for financial analysis;

c. compare the percentage-of-completion method with the completed contract method and contrast the effects of the two methods on the income statement, balance sheet, statement of cash flows and selected financial ratios;

d. describe the types and analysis of unusual or infrequent items, extraordinary items, discontinued operations, accounting changes, and prior period adjustments;

e. discuss managerial discretion in areas such as classification of good news/bad news, income smoothing, big bath behavior and accounting changes, and explain how this discretion can affect the financial statements;

f. describe the format and the components of the balance sheet and the format, classification, and use of each component of the statement of stockholders' equity.

Reading 35: The Statement of Cash Flows
The candidate should be able to:

a. identify the principal purposes and uses of the statement of cash flows;

b. compare and contrast the three major classifications (i.e., cash provided or used by operating activities, investing activities, and financing activities) in a statement of cash flows, and describe how noncash investing and financing transactions are reported;

c. calculate and analyze, using the indirect method, the net cash flow provided or used by operating activities, investing activities and financing activities.

Reading 36: Analysis of Cash Flows

The candidate should be able to:

a. classify a particular transaction or item as cash flow from 1) operations, 2) investing, or 3) financing;

b. compute and interpret a statement of cash flows, using the direct method and the indirect method;

c. convert an indirect statement of cash flows to a direct basis;

d. explain the two primary factors (i.e., acquisitions/divestitures and translation of foreign subsidiaries) that may cause discrepancies between balances of operating assets and liabilities reported on the balance sheet and those reported in the cash flow statement;

e. describe and compute free cash flow;

f. distinguish between U.S. GAAP and IAS GAAP classifications of dividends paid or received and interest paid or received for statement of cash flow purposes.

Reading 37: Worldwide Accounting Diversity and International Standards

The candidate should be able to:

a. discuss the factors influencing and leading to diversity in accounting and reporting practices throughout the world and explain why worldwide accounting diversity causes problems for capital market participants;

b. discuss the importance of the hierarchical model of accounting diversity;

c. discuss the arguments for and against harmonization and discuss the role of the International Accounting Standards Board (IASB).

4⅝ 4¹¹/₁₆
5½ 5½ — ³/₈
5½ 5½ — ³/₈
20⅝ 21³/₁₆ — ¹/₁₆
17⅜ 18⅛ + ⅞
6½ 6½ — ½
7¼ 6½ 6½ — ¹/₈
15/16 31/32 —
9/16 9/16
7⁵/₁₆ 7¹³/₁₆ 7¹⁵/₁₆
2⅝ 2¹¹/₃₂ 2½ +
2¾ 2¼ 2¼
6¹/₆ 12¹/₁₆ 11⅜ 11¼ +
87 33¾ 33 33¼ —
602 25⅝ 24⁹/₁₆ 25⅝ +
833 12 11⅝ 11⅞ +
16 10½ 10½ 10½ —
78 15⅞ 15¹³/₁₆ 15⅞ +
4608 9¹/₁₆ 8¼ 8½ +
430 11¼ 10⅛

FRAMEWORK FOR FINANCIAL STATEMENT ANALYSIS

by Gerald I. White, Ashwinpaul C. Sondhi, and Dov Fried

LEARNING OUTCOMES

The candidate should be able to:

a. discuss the general principles of the financial reporting system and explain the objectives of financial reporting according to the Financial Accounting Standards Board (FASB) conceptual framework;

b. identify the two primary qualities of accounting information (i.e., relevance and reliability), the ingredients of relevance (i.e., predictive value, feedback value and timeliness), the ingredients of reliability (i.e., verifiability, neutrality and representational faithfulness), the two secondary qualities of accounting information (i.e., comparability and consistency), and discuss how these qualities provide useful information to an analyst;

c. describe and explain the purposes of the five principal financial statements (i.e., Balance Sheet, Income Statement, Statement of Comprehensive Income, Statement of Cash Flows and Statement of Stockholders' Equity) and discuss the additional sources of information accompanying the financial statements, including the financial footnotes, supplementary schedules, Management Discussion and Analysis (MD&A) and proxy statements;

d. discuss the role of the auditor and the meaning of the audit opinion.

INTRODUCTION   1

Why are financial statements useful? Because they help investors and creditors make better economic decisions. The goal of this book is to enhance financial statement users' understanding of financial reporting in order to facilitate improved decision making. We will examine the impact of the differential application of accounting methods and estimates on financial statements, with particular emphasis on the effect of accounting choices on reported earnings, stockholders' equity, cash flow, and various measures of corporate performance (including, but not limited to, financial ratios). We will also stress the use of cash flow analysis to evaluate the financial health of an enterprise.

Financial statements are, at best, only an approximation of economic reality because of the selective reporting of economic events by the accounting system, compounded by alternative accounting methods and estimates. The tendency to delay accounting recognition of some transactions and valuation changes means that financial statements tend to lag behind reality as well.

This reading provides a framework for the study of financial statement analysis. This framework consists of the users being served, the information system available to them, and the institutional structure within which they interact.

2 NEED FOR FINANCIAL STATEMENT ANALYSIS

The United States has the most complex financial reporting system in the world. Detailed accounting principles are augmented by extensive disclosure requirements. The financial statements of large multinationals add up to dozens of pages, and many of these firms voluntarily publish additional "fact books" for dissemination to financial analysts and other interested users.

Financial reporting in other major developed countries and many emerging markets has also evolved substantially in recent years, with an increasing emphasis on providing information useful to both domestic and foreign creditors and equity investors. International Accounting Standards have become a credible **rival** to U.S. standards.

In an ideal world, the user of financial statements could focus only on the bottom lines of financial reporting: net income and stockholders' equity. If financial statements were comparable among companies (regardless of country), consistent over time, and always fully reflecting the economic position of the firm, financial statement analysis would be simple, and this text a very short one.

The financial reporting system is not perfect. Economic events and accounting entries do not correspond precisely; they diverge across the dimensions of timing, recognition, and measurement. Financial analysis and investment decisions are further complicated by variations in accounting treatment among countries in each of these dimensions.

Economic events and accounting recognition of those events frequently take place at different times. One example of this phenomenon is the recognition of capital gains and losses only upon sale in most cases. Appreciation of a real estate investment, which took place over a period of many years, for example, receives income statement recognition only in the period management chooses for its disposal.[1]

Similarly, long-lived assets are written down, most of the time, in the fiscal period of management's choice. The period of recognition may be neither the period in which the impairment took place nor the period of sale or disposal.

---

[1] However, in countries (such as the United Kingdom) where periodic asset revaluation is permitted, balance sheet recognition of market value changes may occur much sooner.

Accounting for discontinued operations, in the same manner, results in recognition of a loss in a period different from when the loss occurred or the disposal is consummated.[2]

In addition, many economic events do not receive accounting recognition at all. Most contracts, for example, are not reflected in financial statements when entered into, despite significant effects on financial condition and operating and financial risk. Some contracts, such as leases and hedging activities, are recognized in the financial statements by some companies but disclosed only in footnotes by others. Disclosure requirements for derivatives and hedging activities are in place in many jurisdictions, but recognition and measurement is only recently required[3] in the United States.

Further, **generally accepted accounting principles (GAAP)** in the United States and elsewhere permit economic events that do receive accounting recognition to be recognized in different ways by different financial statement preparers. Inventory and depreciation of fixed assets are only two of the significant areas where comparability may be lacking.

Financial reports often contain supplementary data that, although not included in the statements themselves, help the financial statement user to interpret the statements or adjust measures of corporate performance (such as financial ratios) to make them more comparable, consistent over time, and more representative of economic reality. When making adjustments to financial statements, we will seek to discern substance from form and exploit the information contained in footnotes and supplementary schedules of data in the annual report and SEC filings. The analytic treatment of "off-balance-sheet" financing activities is a good example of this process. We also illustrate the use of reconciliations to U.S. GAAP in foreign registrants' Form 20-F filings.

Finally, information from outside the financial reporting process can be used to make financial data more useful. Estimating the effects of changing prices on corporate performance, for example, may require the use of price data from outside sources.

FOCUS ON INVESTMENT DECISIONS 3

This reading is concerned with the concepts and techniques of financial analysis employed by users of financial statements who are external to the company. Principal emphasis is on the financial statements of companies whose securities are publicly traded. The techniques described are generally applicable to the analysis of financial statements prepared according to U.S. GAAP. However, we will also discuss the pronouncements of the International Accounting Standards Board (IASB) and standard setters in other countries, compare them to U.S. GAAP, and analyze financial statements prepared in accordance with these other reporting standards.

The common characteristic of external users is their general lack of authority to prescribe the information they want from an enterprise. They depend on general-purpose external financial reports provided by management. The Financial Accounting Standards Board (FASB) in its Statement of Financial

---

[2] In the United States, Statement of Financial Accounting Standards (SFAS) No. 121, Accounting for the Impairment of Long-Lived Assets and for Long-Lived Assets to Be Disposed of, as amended by SFAS No. 144, Accounting for the Impairment or Disposal of Long-Lived Assets, constrains but does not eliminate management control over the timing of recognition and the measurement of impairments. In most foreign countries there are few, if any, guidelines governing the accounting for impaired assets.

[3] SFAS 133, Accounting for Derivative Instruments and Hedging Activities, became effective in 2000.

Accounting Concepts (SFAC) 1, Objectives of Financial Reporting by Business Enterprises, aptly describes the objectives of these external users:

Information Useful in Investment and Credit Decisions

Financial reporting should provide information that is useful to present and potential investors and creditors and other users in making rational investment, credit, and similar decisions. The information should be comprehensible to those who have a reasonable understanding of business and economic activities and are willing to study the information with reasonable diligence.[4]

Classes of Users

External users of financial information encompass a wide range of interests but can be classified into three general groups:

1. Credit and equity investors
2. Government (executive and legislative branches), regulatory bodies, and tax authorities
3. The general public and special interest groups, labor unions, and consumer groups

Each of these user groups has a particular objective in financial statement analysis, but, as the FASB stated, the *primary users are equity investors and creditors.* However, the information supplied to investors and creditors is likely to be generally useful to other user groups as well. Hence, financial accounting standards are geared to the purposes and perceptions of investors and creditors. That is the group for whom the analytical techniques in this reading are intended.

The underlying objective of financial analysis is the comparative measurement of risk and return to make investment or credit decisions. These decisions require estimates of the future, be it a month, a year, or a decade. General-purpose financial statements, which describe the past, provide one basis for projecting future earnings and cash flows. Many of the techniques used in this analytical process are broadly applicable to all types of decisions, but there are also specialized techniques concerned with specific investment interests or, in other words, risks and returns specific to one class of investors or securities.

The equity investor is primarily interested in the long-term earning power of the company, its ability to grow, and, ultimately, its ability to pay dividends and increase in value. Since the equity investor bears the residual risk in an enterprise, the largest and most volatile risk, the required analysis is the most comprehensive of any user and encompasses techniques employed by all other external users.

Creditors need somewhat different analytical approaches. Short-term creditors, such as banks and trade creditors, place more emphasis on the immediate liquidity of the business because they seek an early **payback** of their investment. Long-term investors in bonds, such as insurance companies and pension funds, are primarily concerned with the long-term asset position and earning power of the company. They seek assurance of the payment of interest and the capability of retiring or refunding the obligation at maturity. Credit risks are usually smaller than equity risks and may be more easily quantifiable.

More subordinated or junior creditors, especially owners of "high-yield" debt, however, bear risks similar to those of equity investors and may find analytic

---

[4] SFAC 1, para. 34.

techniques normally applied to equity investments more relevant than those employed by creditors.

Financial Information and Capital Markets

The usefulness of accounting information in the decision-making processes of investors and creditors has been the subject of much academic research over the last 35 years. That research has examined the interrelationship of accounting information and reporting standards in financial markets in great detail. At times, the research conclusions are highly critical of the accounting standard-setting process and of the utility of financial analysis. This criticism is based on research performed in a capital market setting. These findings do not negate the usefulness of financial analysis of individual securities that may be mispriced or of decisions made outside a capital market setting.[5]

Some researchers argue that financial data are useful to investors only for prediction of a firm's risk characteristics. To a great extent, this line of reasoning is influenced by the finance literature and the prevalent acceptance of the **efficient market** hypothesis. Others argue that the impact of accounting is not so much in its information content per se, but rather in the "economic consequences" to the firm resulting from contracts (implicit or explicit) that are based on or driven by accounting-determined variables.[6]

By and large, the early conclusions of the academic literature have proven to be somewhat premature. More recent research demonstrates that the interplay between markets and information is richer and more sophisticated than originally thought. In fact, the trend in research is now to incorporate techniques of fundamental analysis in model development and research design.

THE FINANCIAL REPORTING SYSTEM   **4**

An understanding of the conceptual bases of the financial reporting system and of the preparation of financial statements are essential prerequisites to financial analysis. Corporate management issues financial statements and is responsible for their form and content. It is management that selects accounting methods, compiles accounting data, and prepares the financial statements. For smaller companies, auditors may carry out portions of the preparation work.

The accounting process or financial reporting system, which generates financial information for external users, encompasses five principal financial statements:

1. Balance sheet (statement of financial position)
2. Income statement (statement of earnings)
3. Statement of comprehensive income
4. Statement of cash flows
5. Statement of stockholders' equity

---

[5] Examples include acquisitions and credit decisions made by banks or other institutional lenders.

[6] Management compensation contracts and covenants contained in debt agreements are two examples of such contracts.

These five financial statements, augmented by footnotes and supplementary data, are interrelated. Collectively, they are intended to provide relevant, reliable, and timely information essential to making investment, credit, and similar decisions, thus meeting the objectives of financial reporting.

General Principles and Measurement Rules

Financial statements provide information about the assets (resources), liabilities (obligations), income and cash flows, and stockholders' equity of the firm. The effects of transactions and other events are recorded in the appropriate financial statement(s). The income statement reports revenues, expenses, and gains and losses. The balance sheet shows assets, liabilities, and stockholders' equity; the statement of stockholders' equity reports capital transactions with owners. The statement of comprehensive income reports changes in certain balance sheet accounts[7] that bypass the income statement. The **statement of cash flows** includes operating, investing, and financing inflows and outflows. Many transactions are reflected in more than one statement so that the entire set is required to evaluate the firm.

The financial reporting system is based on data generated from *accounting events and selected economic events*. The financial statements recognize events and transactions meeting certain criteria, primarily exchange transactions (the exchange of cash or another asset for a different asset or to create or settle a liability). Other events recognized in the financial reporting system include the passage of time (e.g., accrual of interest), the use of services (e.g., insurance) or assets (e.g., depreciation), estimates such as bad debts or accruals for warranties, and the impact of some contracts (e.g., capital leases). Selected external or economic events, including some market value changes, are also recognized. However, many contractual arrangements and market value changes are disclosed only in the footnotes or in supplementary schedules, if at all.

The emphasis on reporting exchange transactions does not mean that the exchange of cash is necessary for the recognition of revenue and expense events. Under *accrual accounting*, revenues are recognized when goods are delivered or services are performed and expenses are recorded as services are used, rather than when cash is collected or expenditures are incurred for these transactions. Accrual accounting rests on the *matching principle*, which says that performance can be measured only if the related revenues and costs are accounted for in the same period.

Financial statements are prepared using a monetary unit to quantify (measure) the operations of the firm. Transactions are generally measured at their *historical cost*, the amount of cash or other resources exchanged for the asset or liability; changes in value subsequent to acquisition are usually ignored. The advantage of historical cost is that it is objective and verifiable. Its utility declines as specific prices or the general price level changes; as a result, the SEC, FASB, and non-U.S. standard setters have added disclosure and accounting standards for financial instruments.

Financial reporting also relies on the *going concern assumption*, that the firm will continue in operation indefinitely. The alternative assumes liquidation or sale of the firm, which requires different measures of assets and liabilities. Only by assuming normal future operations is it possible, for example, to depreciate fixed assets over their useful life rather than valuing them at their estimated disposal value.

---

[7] Pfizer shows currency translation adjustments, changes in the market value of marketable securities, and a minimum pension liability.

THE U.S. FINANCIAL REPORTING SYSTEM

5

In the United States, the Securities and Exchange Commission (SEC) through its regulation S-X governs the form and content of the financial statements of companies whose securities are publicly traded. Although the SEC has delegated much of this responsibility to the FASB, it frequently adds its own requirements. The SEC functions as a highly effective enforcement mechanism for standards promulgated in the private sector.

Securities and Exchange Commission

As stated previously, while financial reporting standards are developed primarily in the private sector, the SEC often augments the FASB's work. For example, the SEC-mandated Management Discussion and Analysis (MD&A) provides helpful information regarding past operating results and current financial position. In such areas as segment data, leases, the effects of changing prices, and disclosure of oil and gas reserves, SEC-required disclosures preceded FASB action.

Audited financial statements, related footnotes, and supplementary data are presented in both annual reports sent to stockholders and those filed with the SEC. The SEC filings often contain other valuable information not presented in stockholder reports. Exhibit 33-1 contains a listing of SEC-required filings. Quarterly financial reports and SEC 10-Q filings, both of which contain abbreviated financial statements, may be reviewed by auditors but are rarely audited.

As the SEC reviews the financial statements of public companies, and those wishing to issue securities in the U.S. capital markets, its views on proper financial reporting carry great weight. It promulgates these views through Staff Accounting Bulletins (SAB) and through participation in the FASB's Emerging Issues Task Force (see next section) as well as through the review process and enforcement actions. SABs and EITFs are discussed where appropriate throughout this text.

Financial Accounting Standards Board

The FASB is a nongovernmental body with seven full-time members. The board sets accounting standards for all companies issuing audited financial statements. Because of Rule 203 of the American Institute of Certified Public Accountants (AICPA), all FASB pronouncements are considered authoritative; new FASB statements immediately become part of GAAP. Prior to creation of the FASB in 1973, the Accounting Principles Board (APB), an AICPA committee, set accounting standards. Unless superseded, APB opinions remain part of GAAP.[8]

Because the SEC recognizes FASB statements as authoritative (as it recognized APB opinions prior to 1973), there is only one body of GAAP applicable to the United States. There are a few instances (e.g., earnings per share) in which nonpublic companies are exempted from certain GAAP requirements. Generally

---

[8] FASB statements and interpretations, Accounting Principles Board (APB) opinions, and AICPA accounting research bulletins constitute the highest level of authority in the hierarchy of accounting principles. These are followed in descending order of authority by FASB technical bulletins, cleared AICPA industry audit guides, and AICPA statements of position at level B. ("Cleared" means that the FASB has not objected to the issuance of the guide or the statement of position.) Positions of the FASB Emerging Issues Task Force and cleared AcSec practice bulletins constitute level C, followed by AICPA accounting interpretations, question-and-answer guides published by the FASB staff, uncleared AICPA statements of position, and uncleared AICPA industry audit and accounting guides. The lowest authoritative level includes FASB concepts statements, APB statements, AICPA issues papers, and IASB statements.

EXHIBIT 33-1	Corporate Filings: Securities and Exchange Commission

10-K Annual Report

Contents   (partial listing):
Business of Company
Properties
Legal Proceedings
Management Discussion and Analysis
Changes or Disagreements with Auditors
Financial Statements and Footnotes
Investee Financial Statements (where applicable)
Parent Company Financial Statements (where applicable)

Schedules:
  I.   Condensed Financial Information
  II.   Bad Debt and Other Valuation Accounts
  III.   Real Estate and Accumulated Depreciation
  IV.   Mortgage Loans on Real Estate
  V.   Supplementary Information Concerning Property-Casualty Insurance Operations

Due Date: 3 months following end of fiscal year.

10-Q Quarterly Report

Contents   Financial Statements
Management Discussion and Analysis

Due Date: 45 days following end of fiscal quarter. Not required for fourth quarter of fiscal year.

8-K Current Reports

Contents   (used to report important events):
Change in Control
Acquisitions and Divestitures
Bankruptcy
Change in Auditors
Resignation of Directors

Due Date: 15 days following event.

Source: Adapted from SEC Regulation S-X.

speaking, however, all audited statements are prepared using the same financial reporting framework.

The FASB is an independent body whose members are required to sever all ties with previous employers. Although historically most board members have been former auditors, others have come from the corporate world, government service, and academia. The analyst community is currently represented on the board by Gary Schieneman; Frank Block, CFA, served from 1979 to 1985, and Anthony Cope, CFA, from 1993 to 2000.

Before issuing a new Statement of Financial Accounting Standards (SFAS), the FASB staff often works with a task force—composed of public accountants, representatives from industry, academics, regulators, and financial statement users—to develop a discussion memorandum. After public comments are received and hearings held, the staff prepares an exposure draft (a proposed standard) for public comment.[9] The FASB also collaborates with other standard-setting authorities. For example, recent standards on earnings per share and segment reporting were developed in conjunction with the IASB and the Canadian Accounting Standards Board.

The Board's due process rules necessitate extensive dissemination of its agenda. SEC rulemaking is also normally preceded by a request for comments on a proposed set of rules. Thus, it is possible to anticipate new accounting and disclosure standards well in advance of their issuance and implementation.

After new standards are issued, and in areas where standards are nonexistent or ambiguous, there may be a need for guidance as to proper accounting. The FASB staff sometimes issues such documents, especially after major new standards (such as the one on hedging). The Emerging Issues Task Force (EITF), with members from auditing firms, preparers, and the SEC (but under FASB purview) tries to achieve consensus on technical issues. Some projects, especially those that are industry specific, are handled by the AICPA's Accounting Standards Committee (AcSec); these Statements of Position (SOPs) must be cleared by the FASB to become effective.

FASB Conceptual Framework

The conceptual basis for U.S. GAAP stems from FASB concepts statements that create a "constitution" or conceptual framework used by the board to set standards. Many critics of the FASB view the conceptual framework as a failure.[10] They state that the definitions are unduly vague and that the board has repeatedly deferred difficult decisions (such as how to measure income). Others believe that the conceptual framework has helped the board set better standards.

For the analyst, the conceptual framework is an important building block in understanding the information provided by financial statements. The conceptual framework delineates the characteristics accounting information must possess to be useful in investment and other economic decisions.

We have already addressed Statement of Financial Accounting Concepts (SFAC) 1, which sets forth the objectives of financial reporting. SFAC 2 is concerned with the Qualitative Characteristics of Accounting Information. These characteristics are shown in Figure 33-1, which is reproduced from the statement. A brief discussion follows.

Qualitative Characteristics of Accounting Information. Analysts' concern with the qualitative characteristics of accounting information derives from the need for information that facilitates comparison of firms using alternative reporting methods and is useful for decision making. Although some of these characteristics are self-evident, others require some explanation. We start with relevance and reliability, key characteristics from the analyst point of view.

---

[9] The FASB sometimes issues an intermediate document, labeled *preliminary views or tentative conclusions,* to obtain comment on difficult issues.

[10] For example, see David Solomons, "The FASB's Conceptual Framework: An Evaluation," *Journal of Accountancy* (June 1986), pp. 114–124.

FIGURE 33-1   A Hierarchy of Accounting Qualities

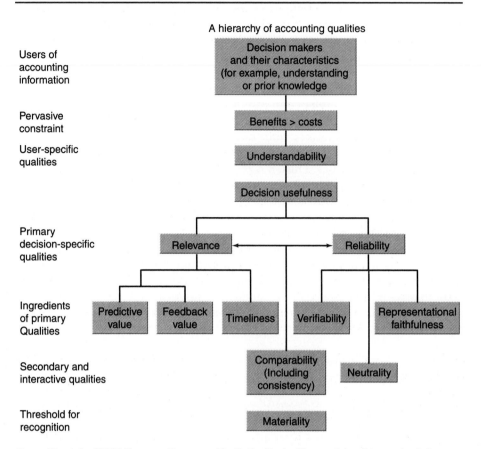

Source: Figure 1 of FASB Concepts Statement No. 2, *Qualitative Characteristics of Accounting Information,* copyright by Financial Accounting Standards Board, Norwalk, CT.

Relevance is defined as "the capacity of information to make a difference in a decision. . . ."[11] In practice, of course, the relevance of information depends on the decision maker. To a technical analyst (chartist), all financial data are irrelevant. For fundamental analysts, the relevance of information varies with the method of analysis (emphasis on income statement, cash flow, balance sheet, etc.).

Timeliness is an important aspect of relevance. Information loses value rapidly in the financial world. Market prices are predicated on estimates of the future; data on the past are helpful in making projections. But as time passes and the future becomes the present, past data become increasingly irrelevant.

Reliability encompasses *verifiability, representational faithfulness,* and *neutrality.* The first two elements (verifiability and representational faithfulness) are concerned with whether financial data have been measured accurately and whether they are what they purport to be. Data without these characteristics cannot be relied on in making investment decisions.

Neutrality is concerned with whether financial statement data are biased. FASB proposals are frequently the object of complaints that companies will be adversely affected by the new standard. The principle of neutrality states that the board should consider only the relevance and reliability of the data, not any possible economic impact.

---

[11] SFAC 2, Glossary.

Unfortunately, relevance and reliability tend to be opposing qualities. For example, the audit process improves the reliability of data, but at the cost of timeliness. For that reason, financial statement users have generally not supported the auditing of quarterly data, believing that the time delay does not compensate for any improved data quality.

Relevance and reliability also clash strongly in a number of accounting areas. Market value data are probably the best example. Information on the current market value of assets such as real estate and agricultural properties may be highly relevant but may be accurate (reliable) only to a limited extent. Yet historical cost, although highly reliable, may have little relevance. It is the old argument as to whether it is better to be "precisely wrong" or "approximately right."

Analysts have generally opted for approximately right. They have supported the disclosure of supplementary data in such areas as natural resources (SFAS 69, Reading 42), off-balance-sheet financing (Reading 46), and segment data (SFAS 131). Auditors and preparers, more concerned with reliability (and legal liability), have often opposed the inclusion of less reliable data in the financial statements.

Consistency and *comparability* are also key characteristics of accounting information from the analyst perspective. Consistency refers to use of the same accounting principles over time. A broader term, comparability, refers to comparisons among companies.

Consistency is affected by new accounting standards and voluntary changes in accounting principles and estimates. Accounting changes hinder the comparison of operating results between periods when the accounting principles used to measure those results differ. As the transition provisions of new accounting standards vary, it is frequently difficult to obtain a consistent time series of earnings properly adjusted for such changes. For voluntary changes (such as depreciation methods and lives), the effect of the change is generally disclosed only for the year of the change.

Comparability is a pervasive problem in financial analysis. Companies are free to choose among different accounting methods and estimates in a variety of areas, making comparisons of different enterprises difficult or impossible. Although the FASB (and to some extent, the IASB) has narrowed these differences somewhat in recent years, new types of transactions (such as securitization of assets) create new sources of noncomparability. Even when accounting differences do not exist, however, comparability may be elusive because of real differences between the firms (e.g., one has foreign operations and the other does not).

Materiality is paradoxically the most elusive accounting quality and arguably the most important. As shown in Figure 33-1, materiality is the threshold for financial statement recognition. FASB statements routinely state that they do not apply to immaterial items.

We define information to be material when it would make a difference in the valuation of the firm. While some use quantitative measures of materiality (e.g., 5% of income), even very small items can affect valuation. For example:

▶ A firm makes sales (just prior to the end of the quarter) under unusually favorable conditions (to the buyer) to meet sales expectations for the quarter.

▶ A firm realizes capital gains on long-term investments to achieve projected earnings growth for the period.

In Staff Accounting Bulletin (SAB) 99,[12] the SEC provided additional guidance regarding materiality because of perceived abuses. The SEC stated that financial

---

[12] August 12, 1999.

statement issuers and auditors must consider qualitative factors as well as quantitative rules of thumb. These qualitative factors include:

1. Obscuring changes in earnings trend
2. Hiding the failure to achieve analyst forecasts
3. Changing a reported loss to income or vice versa
4. Obscuring changes in significant business segments
5. Increasing management compensation
6. Affecting compliance with regulatory requirements, loan covenants, or other contracts
7. Concealing unlawful acts

Materiality is best defined in a firm context. The analyst should always be wary of firms that use "materiality" to hide significant data.

In addition to concept statements 1 and 2, which we have just reviewed, there are four others. SFAC 3, Elements of Financial Statements of Business Enterprises, has been superseded by SFAC 6, Elements of Financial Statements, which is discussed in subsequent sections of this reading. The topics covered by SFAC 4, Objectives of Financial Reporting by Nonbusiness Organizations, are beyond the scope of this text. SFAC 5, Recognition and Measurement in Financial Statements of Business Enterprises, is referenced in Reading 34. SFAC 7, Using Cash Flow Information and Present Value in Accounting Measurement, is discussed in Box 33-1.

6   INTERNATIONAL ACCOUNTING STANDARDS

Growing international trade, multinational industrial and financial enterprises, and increasingly global capital markets have significantly expanded investment opportunities. Creditors and equity investors need to analyze both domestic and foreign companies. Yet differences in accounting and reporting standards make it difficult to compare domestic companies with those in other countries. Furthermore, as accounting standards are established separately in each country, it is difficult to generalize about those differences.

Financial reporting requirements are a function of tax regulations, corporate law, the comparative significance of capital markets and financial institutions in industrial development, and cultural differences. However, as capital markets and international investments expand, the need for global accounting standards is obvious.

Two questions arise: Who should develop such standards, and who would enforce them?

This section provides a brief discussion of the International Organization of Securities Commissions (IOSCO), the International Accounting Standards Board (IASB), and European financial reporting standards; a review of SEC reporting requirements for foreign registrants follows. These discussions review the significant recent progress toward harmonization of international reporting requirements.

International Organization of Securities Commissions

IOSCO is an organization of securities regulators from more than 65 countries, including the SEC from the United States. IOSCO's Technical Committee

BOX 33-1   SFAC 7: USING CASH FLOW INFORMATION AND PRESENT VALUE IN ACCOUNTING MEASUREMENT

SFAC 7 (2000) deals only with measurement. It does not state when assets or liabilities must be measured using these principles. While present values are widely used in financial reporting (e.g., retirement plans), the FASB is expected to extend their use in the future. The statement says:

> The objective of using present value as an accounting measurement is to capture, to the extent possible, the economic difference between sets of future cash flows.*

Capturing the economic difference requires consideration of the following elements of the present value calculation:

1. Estimation of future cash flows

2. Expectations regarding the timing and amounts of those cash flows

3. Time value of money, measured by the risk-free interest rate

4. The effect of uncertainty on the required rate of return

5. Other factors, such as liquidity, that affect the required rate of return

In traditional present value calculations, factors 2 through 5 are rolled up into a single interest rate. SFAC 7, however, requires that each of these factors be considered separately, using the *expected cash flow* approach. We illustrate this method using the following example:†

Cash flow = $10,000 due in 10 years
Probability of collection = 80%
Risk-free rate (10 years) = 5%
Risk premium = $500

The initial step is to compute the expected cash flow:

($10,000 × 80% + $0 × 20%) = $8,000

Second, deduct the risk premium that a risk-averse investor would demand to assume the default risk:

$8,000 − $500 = $7,500

Finally, discount by the risk-free rate:

Present value at 5% of $7,500 due in 10 years = $4,604

Under this approach, the carrying value would be $4,604. This works out to an effective interest rate of 8.065%, which can be broken down into the following components:‡

Risk-free rate	5.000%
Adjustment for expectations	2.370
Adjustment for risk	.695
Total	8.065%

After initial measurement, the asset (or liability) would increase (accrete) at that 8.065 interest rate. Thus, after one year (assuming annual compounding), the carrying amount would be:

$4,604 (1 + .08065) = $4,975

(continued)

BOX 33-1 *(continued)*

At the end of 10 years, the carrying amount would be $10,000. Depending on the amount actually paid, there would be a gain or loss recognized at that time.

The extent to which SFAC 7 is applied to more assets and liabilities in the future may depend on whether preparers, auditors, and users become convinced that the expected value method provides better information. Auditors are especially concerned that the SFAC 7 method is less auditable than the historical approach of applying a composite discount rate to management's best estimate.

---

*Para. 20.

†Asset D from Appendix 1 of SFAC 7; see that appendix for comparison with other variations.

‡This example ignores factor 5 (liquidity or other factors).

OPTIONAL SEGMENT ENDS

investigates regulatory issues related to international securities transactions and is charged with developing solutions to problems in these areas.

IOSCO is also involved in standard setting through the Technical Committee's Working Party 1 on Multinational Disclosure and Accounting, which is charged with advocating financial reporting regulation that facilitates cross-border securities offerings and promotes effective and efficient international capital markets.

The Technical Committee's Working Party established a comprehensive core set of international accounting standards that could be recognized by IOSCO members for use in cross-border offerings and global multiple listings. However, each country's regulatory agency must approve these standards. It appears that enforcement would also remain a country-by-country matter.

International Accounting Standards Board

The IASB was established in 1973 to harmonize (conform) the accounting standards of different nations. In 2001, the IASB adopted a new structure, moving away from its "consensus" model[13] to one more like the FASB.

The new IASB structure provides for 19 trustees, headed by Paul Volcker, former chair of the U.S. Federal Reserve Board. The trustees, most of whom are not Americans, perform the functions of a corporate board of directors. The new IASB Board consists of 14 members; its chairman is David Tweedie, former head of the UK Accounting Standards Board. Anthony Cope, CFA, a former analyst and FASB member, is an IASB Board member. The IASB is maintaining its Standing Interpretations Committee (similar to the FASB's EITF), which deals with questions that arise after a new standard is adopted. There is a new Standards Advisory Council, which (like the similar FASB body) provides input from constituents.

As of December 31, 2001, the IASB has issued 41 international accounting standards (IAS) as well as a Framework for the Preparation and Presentation of Financial Statements, similar to the FASB conceptual framework, used to review existing standards and develop future IAS. This framework is also used to promote harmonization of regulations and standard setting by providing a

---

[13] The prior IASC had representatives from national accounting federations, stock exchanges, financial institutions, and other groups (including the International Coordinating Committee of Financial Analysts Associations). Because of a supermajority approval requirement a broad consensus was required to adopt a new standard.

basis for reducing the number of alternative accounting treatments permitted by the IASB.

The IASB has largely "caught up" with the FASB. In October 1993, IOSCO endorsed IAS 7, Cash Flow Statements, and published a list of core standards that would form the basis for a reasonably complete set of global standards. IASB completed work on these "core standards" and the SEC and other IOSCO members are evaluating their suitability for "global GAAP."

As capital markets become more international in scope, the need for global accounting standards and the demand for multiple listings grow. Discussion of financial reporting in Europe will be followed by an examination of the SEC's efforts to facilitate foreign listings.

European Financial Reporting Standards

Financial reporting requirements in Europe differ from those in the United States and other countries because of differences in their economies, relevance of local commercial law to the development of reporting standards, comparative importance of capital markets and banks as a source of financing, and the degree to which tax laws influence financial reporting.

Because of their desire to access other capital markets, a number of European multinational firms have adopted either U.S. standards (Daimler adopted U.S. GAAP even before it merged with Chrysler) or IASB GAAP. Despite occasional talk about "European GAAP," cultural differences and the existence of the IASB model suggest that large European companies will continue to gravitate toward either U.S. or IASB standards, depending on the outcome of the SEC decision concerning the acceptability of IASB standards for U.S. capital markets.

SEC REPORTING REQUIREMENTS FOR FOREIGN REGISTRANTS

7

Foreign issuers that wish to sell securities in the United States must register with the SEC and are subject to substantially the same reporting requirements as their domestic counterparts. Foreign issuers may elect to file the registration and reporting forms used by domestic issuers (see Exhibit 33-1). Alternatively, foreign filers may elect to file the generally less stringent Forms 20-F (similar to 10-K) and 6-K (similar to 8-K). Issuers of American Depositary Receipts (ADRs)[14] may register either Form F-6 or 20-F and are exempt from Form 8-K requirements.

Foreign issuers commonly use Form 20-F filings, thereby exempting them from requirements to file proxies and insider trading reports. Form 20-F annual reports are due six months after the fiscal year-end, quarterly reports are optional, and relatively little business and segment data disclosure is required.

Form 20-F filers must identify both the reporting principles used and the material variations from U.S. GAAP and reconcile reported income and stockholders' equity to U.S. GAAP. These reconciliations provide insights into the differences in reporting requirements across countries and the tasks involved in developing universal financial reporting standards. The data provided in Form 20-F reconciliations are used to illustrate accounting differences throughout the text.

---

[14] ADRs are depositary shares representing a specified number of shares and are issued against the deposit of a foreign issuer's securities. ADRs must be registered on Form F-6 unless another registration form is more appropriate.

Staff Accounting Bulletin 88 (August 1990) clarified the disclosures and quantitative reconciliations required by Item 17 of Form 20-F. The new guidance requires some additional disclosures regarding pension obligations (SFAS 87) and financial instruments (SFAS 105) in the MD&A. However, SAB 88 does not mandate those disclosures required by U.S. GAAP or the SEC but not required by the foreign issuer's local GAAP.[15]

The SEC no longer requires foreign issuers to reconcile to U.S. GAAP for differences stemming from the use of:

▶ IAS 7, Cash Flow Statements

▶ IAS 21, The Effects of Changes in Foreign Exchange Rates

▶ IAS 22, Business Combinations

These changes reflect two parallel developments. First, some IAS standards are considered equivalent to U.S. GAAP and are deemed acceptable for filings in the United States. Second, U.S. filing requirements for foreign registrants have affected requirements for U.S. entities. FRR 44 (December 13, 1994) eliminated the requirement for domestic issuers to file schedules with data on marketable securities, property, plant, and equipment, accumulated depreciation, and short-term borrowings. Although these amendments "leveled the field" for domestic and foreign filers, they also eliminated a significant amount of information useful in financial analysis.[16]

8 PRINCIPAL FINANCIAL STATEMENTS

The preceding sections described the general principles and measurement rules of the basic accounting process applicable to financial reporting in the United States. They also examined the role of international and domestic standard-setting bodies (the SEC and FASB) and the latter's conceptual framework that guides this process, along with the qualitative characteristics of accounting information. This section provides a detailed discussion of the output of this system: the different financial statements, footnotes, and supplementary data.[17]

The Balance Sheet

The balance sheet (statement of financial position) reports major classes and amounts of assets (resources owned or controlled by the firm), liabilities (external claims on those assets), and stockholders' equity (owners' capital contributions and other internally generated sources of capital) and their interrelationships at specific points in time.

Assets reported on the balance sheet are either purchased by the firm or generated through operations; they are, directly or indirectly, financed by the creditors and stockholders of the firm. This fundamental accounting relationship

---

[15] See R. Dieter and J. A. Heyman, "Implications of SEC Staff Accounting Bulletin 88 for Foreign Registrants," *Journal of Accountancy* (August 1991), pp. 121–125.

[16] In 1999, the SEC proposed reinstating disclosure requirements relating to bad debt and other valuation reserves and property, plant, and equipment.

[17] The requirements of IAS standards are very similar; differences are discussed in Readings 34 and 36.

provides the basis for recording all transactions in financial reporting and is expressed as the balance sheet equation:

$$\text{Assets (A)} = \text{Liabilities (L)} + \text{Stockholders' Equity (E)}$$

In the United States, firms issue balance sheets at the end of each quarter and the end of the fiscal year. Annual or semiannual reporting is the norm in most other countries.

Elements of the Balance Sheet

SFAC 6 discusses the elements of financial statements. Although this statement also deals with nonprofit organizations, we restrict our comments to business enterprises.

Assets are defined in SFAC 6 as

> probable future economic benefits obtained or controlled by a particular entity as a result of past transactions or events. (para. 25)

This definition seems to be noncontroversial. Its weakness is its lack of reference to risk. It seems to us that an enterprise that retains the risks of ownership still "owns" the asset. This issue is important, for example, as it relates to the sale of assets (such as accounts receivable, loans, and mortgages; see Reading 46) when the seller retains some risk of loss.

Liabilities are defined, similarly, as

> probable future sacrifices of economic benefits arising from present obligations of a particular entity to transfer assets or provide services to other entities in the future as a result of past transactions or events. (para. 35)

Again, the definition reads well. Yet it permits the nonrecognition of contractual obligations such as operating leases (see Reading 46). The interpretation of "present obligation" and "result of past transactions or events" is key to accounting for all such contracts; some believe that only payments immediately due as a consequence of completed transactions create liabilities.[18] Others believe that all long-term contracts should be recognized as long-term liabilities. Another important problem area is the derecognition of liabilities that have been prefunded but remain outstanding (see the discussion of defeasance in Reading 45).[19]

As required by the fundamental accounting equation, *stockholders' equity* is therefore

> the residual interest in the net assets of an entity that remains after deducting its liabilities. (para. 49)

In practice, some financial instruments have characteristics of both liabilities and equities, making them difficult to categorize. Convertible debt and redeemable preferreds are two common examples examined in Reading 45. That reading also discusses the FASB Exposure Draft (ED) on recognition and measurement of instruments with equity and liability characteristics.

---

[18] The capitalization of all executory contracts was advocated in the AIMR position paper "Financial Reporting in the 1990s and Beyond" (1993).

[19] SFAS 125 (1996), Accounting for Transfers and Servicing of Financial Assets and Extinguishments of Liabilities, prohibits derecognition of liabilities using in-substance defeasance.

The Income Statement

The income statement (statement of earnings) reports on the performance of the firm, the result of its **operating activities**. It explains some but not all of the changes in the assets, liabilities, and equity of the firm between two consecutive balance sheet dates. Use of the accrual concept means that income and the balance sheet are interrelated.

The preparation of the income statement is governed by the matching principle, which states that performance can be measured only if revenues and related costs are accounted for during the same time period. This requires the recognition of expenses incurred to generate revenues in the same period as the related revenues. For example, the cost of a machine is recognized as an expense (it is depreciated) over its useful life (as it is used in production) rather than as an expense in the period it is purchased.[20]

Elements of the Income Statement

Revenues are defined in SFAC 6 as

> inflows . . . of an entity . . . from delivering or producing goods, rendering services, or other activities that constitute the entity's ongoing major or central operations. (para. 78)

Expenses are defined as

> outflows . . . from delivering or producing goods, rendering services, or carrying out other activities that constitute the entity's ongoing major or central operations. (para. 80)

These definitions explicitly exclude *gains (and losses)*, defined as

> increases (decreases) in equity (net assets) from peripheral or incidental transactions. . . . (para. 82)

Gains or losses are, therefore, nonoperating events. Examples would include gains and losses from asset sales, lawsuits, and changes in market values (including currency rates).

These definitions are, like the others in SFAC 6, easy to accept as stated. The difficulties come in practice. For example, investment activities may be "central" to a financial institution but "peripheral" to a manufacturing company. Similarly, sales of assets such as automobiles may be "incidental" to a retailer but "central" to a car rental firm. The writedown of inventories due to **obsolescence** is more difficult to characterize: Is this an operating expense or a loss? To some extent, the distinction between revenue and expense on the one hand and gains and losses on the other is a precursor of the controversies over the characterizations of "recurring versus nonrecurring activities," "operating versus nonoperating activities," and "extraordinary items." From the analyst point of view, disclosure is more important than classification; analysts prefer to make their own distinctions between operating and nonoperating events in many instances. From the point of view of database users, however, the outcome of the debate is important.

---

[20] Note that no depreciation would be recorded if the products manufactured were not sold in the period the machine was used; the cost of using the machine would be added to work-in-process or finished goods inventories and carried on the balance sheet as an asset until the goods were sold.

Even more important is the decision on when to recognize revenues and expenses. The recognition decision can be a major determinant of reported income, especially for technology and other "new economy" enterprises. This issue is discussed in Reading 34.

Statement of Comprehensive Income

Comprehensive income is defined as:

> the change in equity of a business enterprise during a period from transactions and other events and circumstances from nonowner sources. It includes *all changes in equity during a period except those resulting from investments by owners and distributions to owners*.[21]

Thus, comprehensive income includes both net income and direct-to-equity adjustments such as:

▶ Cumulative translation adjustments under SFAS 52

▶ Minimum pension liability under SFAS 87

▶ Unrealized gains and losses on available-for-sale securities under SFAS 115

▶ Deferred gains and losses on cash flow hedges under SFAS 133

These adjustments are collectively known as *other comprehensive income*. SFAS 130 (1997) requires that firms with items of other comprehensive income report:

▶ The closing balance of each such item. Their total is reported as a separate component of equity called *accumulated other comprehensive income.*

▶ The change (either pretax or after-tax) in each item; the change can be reported either gross (showing both additions and subtractions) or net.

▶ Reclassification adjustments to avoid double counting. For example, realized investment gains that include unrealized gains from prior years would be double counted unless those unrealized gains are deducted from other comprehensive income in the year of realization.[22]

▶ Total comprehensive income in condensed financial statements provided for interim periods.

Alternative displays are permitted. For example, firms can provide a separate statement of comprehensive income or can combine that statement with the income statement. Some data can be reported either on the statement face or in footnotes. IAS 1 (1997), with similar requirements, also permits alternative formats.[23]

Illustration: Pfizer. The shareholders' equity section of Pfizer's balance sheet has a line item: accumulated other comprehensive income. Note 5 shows the

---

[21] SFAC 6 (1985), para. 70, emphasis added.

[22] Reclassification adjustments are not required for the minimum pension liability. Such adjustments for the cumulative translation adjustment are limited to translation gains and losses realized upon sale or liquidation of the investment in foreign subsidiaries. Reclassification adjustments in comparative statements provided for earlier periods are encouraged, but not required.

[23] IAS 1 does not use the term comprehensive income; its example is titled "Statement of Recognized Gains and Losses."

Statement of Comprehensive Income, with annual changes and balances for the currency translation adjustment, net unrealized gain on available-for-sale securities, and minimum pension liability.[24] All items are presented net of tax with the tax benefit shown as a single annual total. The individual items will be discussed in the appropriate readings.

Statement of Cash Flows

The statement of cash flows reports cash receipts and payments in the period of their occurrence, classified as to operating, investing, and financing activities. It also provides supplementary disclosures about noncash investing and financing activities. Cash flow data also help explain changes in consecutive balance sheets and supplement the information provided by the income statement.

SFAS 95, Statement of Cash Flows (1987), defines investing cash flows as those resulting from:

▶ Acquisition or sale of property, plant, and equipment
▶ Acquisition or sale of a subsidiary or segment
▶ Purchase or sale of investments in other firms

Similarly, financing cash flows are those resulting from:

▶ Issuance or retirement of debt and equity securities
▶ Dividends paid to stockholders

The standard requires gross rather than net reporting of significant investing and financing activities, thereby providing improved disclosure. For example, cash flows for property acquisitions must be shown separately from those related to property sales.

Enterprises with foreign currency transactions or foreign operations must report the effect of exchange rate changes on cash and cash equivalents as a separate component of the reconciliation of cash and cash equivalents for the period.

Significant noncash investing and financing activities (such as capitalized leases) must be disclosed separately within the cash flow statement or in a footnote elsewhere in the financial statements. Complex investment and financing transactions sometimes involve combinations of cash, debt, and other resources—these diverse but related components must be reported separately.

Cash from Operations. This key performance measure includes the cash effects of all transactions that do not meet the definition of investing or financing. This measure, moreover, excludes the effect of changes in exchange rates. In effect, it includes the cash flow consequences of the revenue-producing activities of the firm. Cash from operations may be reported either directly, using major categories of gross cash receipts and payments, or indirectly by providing a reconciliation of net income to net cash flow from operating activities. Both methods require separate disclosure of the cash outflows for income taxes and interest within the statement or elsewhere in the financial statements.

---

[24] These same amounts are shown in Pfizer's statement of shareholders' equity, which follows the balance sheet.

Statement of Stockholders' Equity

This statement reports the amounts and sources of changes in equity from capital transactions with owners and may include the following components:

- ▶ Preferred shares
- ▶ Common shares (at par or stated value)
- ▶ Additional paid-in capital
- ▶ Retained earnings
- ▶ Treasury shares (repurchased equity)
- ▶ Employee Stock Ownership Plan (ESOP) adjustments

and as components of other comprehensive income:

- ▶ Minimum pension liability
- ▶ Unrealized gains and losses on available for sale securities
- ▶ Cumulative translation adjustment (foreign operations)
- ▶ Unrealized gains and losses on cash flow hedges

Equity events and transactions are generally recognized as they occur, but capital market developments have created significant measurement and classification problems in transactions with owners.

The firm usually records the issuance of preferred and common stock at par (or stated) value and the amounts received in excess of par as additional paid-in capital. Repurchases or retirements of common stock may be reported as Treasury shares, a contra account, which reflects a reduction in common stock outstanding. Retained (reinvested) earnings, which increase with income and decline with dividend declarations, are also reported. Finally, this statement also includes adjustments related to ESOPs.

The minimum pension liability results when the accounting liability for pensions is less than the accumulated benefit obligation. The unrealized gains and losses on available for sale securities and the cumulative foreign currency translation adjustment result from selective recognition of market value changes and exchange rate changes. Unrealized gains and losses on cash flow hedges result from the provisions of SFAS 133.

Footnotes

Information provided in the financial statements is augmented by footnotes and other supplementary disclosures. Footnotes are an integral part of the financial statements and provide data on such subjects as business segments, the financial position of retirement plans, and off-balance-sheet obligations. These data are required by either GAAP (FASB standards) or regulatory authorities (the SEC). The financial statements and footnotes in the annual report and the SEC 10-K filings are audited.

Supplementary schedules, some required by the SEC in 10-K filings (see Exhibit 33-1), provide additional useful information. Some of these supplementary data are unaudited.

Footnotes provide information about the accounting methods, assumptions, and estimates used by management to develop the data reported in the financial statements. They are designed to allow users to improve assessments of the amounts, timing, and uncertainty of the estimates reported in the financial statements. Footnotes provide additional disclosure related to such areas as:

- ▶ Fixed assets
- ▶ Inventories
- ▶ Income taxes
- ▶ Pension and other postemployment benefit plans
- ▶ Debt (interest rates, maturity schedules, and contractual terms)
- ▶ Lawsuits and other loss contingencies
- ▶ Marketable securities and other investments
- ▶ Hedging and other risk management activities
- ▶ Business segments
- ▶ Significant customers, sales to related parties, and export sales

Contingencies

Footnotes often contain disclosures relating to contingent[25] losses. Firms are required to accrue a loss (recognize a balance sheet liability) when *both* of the following conditions are met:

1. It is probable that assets have been impaired or a liability has been incurred.

2. The amount of the loss can be reasonably estimated.

If the loss amount lies within a range, the most likely amount should be accrued. When no amount in the range is a better estimate, the firm may report the minimum amount in the range.[26]

SFAS 5 defines *probable* events as those "more likely than not" to occur, suggesting that a probability of more than 50% requires recognition of a loss. However, in practice, firms generally report contingencies as losses only when the probability of loss is significantly higher.

Footnote disclosure of (unrecognized) loss contingencies is required when it is *reasonably possible* (more than remote but less than probable) that a loss has been incurred or when it is probable that a loss has occurred but the amount cannot be reasonably estimated. The standard provides an extensive discussion of loss contingencies.

The recognition and measurement of loss contingencies are problematic because they involve judgment and are subjective at best. External analysis is hampered by the paucity of data, as disclosures are often vague. Footnote disclosures and the SEC-mandated MD&A are the best sources of information.

Significant problem areas include environmental remediation liabilities, litigation, expropriation, self-insurance, debt guarantees, repurchase agreements, take-or-pay contracts, and throughput arrangements. In later readings we provide discussion of analytical techniques applicable to many of these contingencies and examples of losses recognized in the financial statements as well as others disclosed only in footnotes.

---

[25] The FASB defines a contingency as an "existing condition, situation, or set of circumstances involving uncertainty as to possible gain or loss" (SFAS 5, para. 1).

[26] See FASB Interpretation 14, Reasonable Estimation of the Amount of a Loss.

Pfizer's Note 18, Litigation, includes substantial disclosures regarding legal and governmental actions affecting the company. As the drug industry is heavily regulated and patents are important assets,[27] most of the note concerns these two areas. Although the note contains considerable uninformative "boilerplate," it does tell us that:

▶ Pfizer pleaded guilty to price fixing in 1999, and class action suits have been filed against the company.

▶ In 1999, a jury awarded $143 million in damages against Pfizer in the Trovan case.

▶ Pfizer is paying claims resulting from settlement of the Shiley lawsuits concerning defective heart valves.

▶ The company has been designated a "potentially responsible party" for certain waste sites and may be responsible for the cost of environmental remediation.

▶ A Pfizer subsidiary sold products containing asbestos, and many personal injury claims are pending against the company. The company expects the cost of such claims to be largely covered by insurance.

There is no indication, however, what provision Pfizer has made (if any) for losses from these suits. There are a couple of clues:

1. The Management Discussion and Analysis discloses (under Net Income) that 1998 includes $126 million "other" expense, mainly for legal settlements.

2. Note 8 shows provisions for the cost of antitrust litigation of $2 million and $57 million for 1999 and 1998, respectively.

Footnote and MD&A disclosures of contingencies should be read carefully, as they provide clues about possible future expense provisions and cash outflows.[28] While firms making acquisitions are generally careful to examine environmental and other risks of the acquired company, liability may emerge years later.[29] In extreme cases (asbestos, for example), environmental claims have driven firms into bankruptcy. Lawsuits and claims are, in addition, sometimes indicators of illegal acts or poor management practices.

Case 33-1 shows the effect on Bristol Myers, another drug company, of breast implant litigation that took a number of years to be fully reflected in its financial statements.

Risks and Uncertainties

In 1994, the AICPA issued Statement of Position (SOP) 94-6, Disclosure of Certain Significant Risks and Uncertainties.[30] Although most AICPA SOPs are narrow in scope, applying to only one industry or narrow category of transactions,

---

[27] Self-developed patents are not recognized in the financial statements, however. Reading 42 discusses patents and other intangible assets.

[28] See M. E. Barth and M. F. McNichols, "Estimation and Valuation of Environmental Liabilities." *Journal of Accounting Research* (Supplement 1994), pp. 177–209.

[29] In 2000, Aventis (a large French chemicals and pharmaceutical firm) agreed to pay up to $916 million to clean up a defunct copper mine. The mine was owned by Stauffer Chemical, which was acquired by Rhone-Poulenc, which merged with Hoechst to form Aventis in 1999. (*New York Times*, October 22, 2000, p. 32.)

[30] One of the authors of this text was a member of the task force that prepared the SOP.

SOP 94-6 has broad application. It requires that audited financial statements report the following information:

1. *Nature of operations.* Description of the firm's major business activities and markets.

2. *Use of estimates.* Statement that financial statements use estimates.

3. *Certain significant estimates.* When it is reasonably possible that an estimate used to prepare financial statements will change in the near term, and such change would have a material impact on those statements, then disclosures must be made regarding the nature of the uncertainty involved. Examples include the effect of technological obsolescence on operating assets, capitalized costs that might not be recoverable from operations, and contingent liabilities for environmental remediation or litigation.

4. *Current vulnerability due to certain concentrations.* Firms must disclose concentrations when it is reasonably possible that there could be a severe impact in the near term. Examples include concentrations in customers, suppliers, or markets.

For companies subject to SEC reporting requirements, the SOP has limited effect,[31] although it was intended to help firms (and their auditors) understand the application of SFAS 5 (Contingencies). The major effect of the SOP is on nonpublic companies, whose disclosures are not governed by the SEC; their disclosures were inadequate to analysts accustomed to reviewing the financial statements of public companies.

Supplementary Schedules

In some cases, additional information about the assets and liabilities of a firm is provided within the financial statement footnotes, or as supplementary data outside the financial statements. Examples include:

▶ Oil and gas companies provide additional data on their exploration activities, quantities and types of reserves, and the present value of cash flows expected from those reserves (Reading 42).

▶ Supplemental disclosures of the impact of changing prices.

▶ Disclosure of sales revenue, operating income, and other data for major business segments and by geographic areas. Firms also provide information about export sales.

▶ Disclosures related to financial instruments and hedging activities.

9   OTHER SOURCES OF FINANCIAL INFORMATION

Stockholder reports often contain useful supplementary financial and statistical data as well as management comments. In some cases, the stockholder report is included ("incorporated by reference") in the SEC filing, or vice versa. The MD&A required by the SEC may appear in either reports to stockholders or SEC

---

[31] SFAS 14 requires more detailed segment data. The SOP permits the use of imprecise language such as "approximately."

filings. A brief discussion of the contents of the MD&A is followed by a discussion of other sources of financial data.

Management Discussion and Analysis

Companies with publicly traded securities have been required since 1968 to provide a discussion of earnings in the MD&A section. The MD&A included in the financial statements of Pfizer is one example. In 1980, the SEC expanded the requirements to a comprehensive, broad-based discussion and analysis of the financial statements to encourage more meaningful disclosure.

The MD&A is required to discuss:

▶ Results of operations, including discussion of trends in sales and categories of expense

▶ Capital resources and liquidity, including discussion of cash flow trends

▶ Outlook based on known trends

In 1989, the SEC issued an interpretive release providing additional guidance on compliance in the following areas:

1. Prospective information and required discussion of significant effects of currently known trends, events, and uncertainties; for example, decline in market share or impact of inventory obsolescence. Firms may voluntarily disclose forward-looking data that anticipate trends or events.

2. Liquidity and capital resources: Firms are expected to use cash flow statements to analyze liquidity; provide a balanced discussion of operating, financing, and investing cash flows; and discuss transactions or events with material current or expected long-term liquidity implications.

3. Discussion of discontinued operations, extraordinary items, and other "unusual or infrequent" events with current or expected material effects on financial condition or results of operations.

4. Extensive disclosures in interim financial statements in keeping with the obligation to periodically update MD&A disclosures.

5. Disclosure of a segment's disproportionate need for cash flows or contribution to revenues or profits. Also, disclosure of any restrictions on a free flow of funds between segments.

On January 22, 2002, the SEC issued a statement reinforcing its views on the importance of MD&A disclosures. The release reminds registrants that disclosure "must be both useful and understandable."

Topics addressed include:

1. Liquidity and capital resources, including the impact of off-balance-sheet arrangements on liquidity and capital resources,

2. Disclosures about contractual obligations and commercial commitments (that is, off-balance-sheet arrangements),

3. Disclosures about trading activities, including non-exchange traded contracts, and

4. The effects of transactions with related parties, including persons (such as former employees) that may fall outside of the technical definition of a related party.

Other Data Sources

Companies that issue securities to the public are required to publish a registration statement, including a prospectus. For large companies, the 10-K and other SEC filings are "incorporated by reference" and little new information is provided. For initial public offerings (IPOs) and smaller companies, however, the prospectus will contain a detailed discussion of the enterprise as well as full financial statements.

Proxy statements, issued in connection with shareholder meetings, contain information about board members and management, executive compensation, stock options, and major stockholders.

Many companies prepare periodic "fact books" containing additional financial and operational data. Corporate press releases also provide new information on a timely basis. Computerized services (e.g., the Dow Jones News Retrieval System) and various on-line services provide databases of corporate releases and other business news. In addition, many companies hold periodic meetings or conference telephone calls to keep the financial community apprised of recent developments regarding the company. In between or in lieu of such meetings, a company officer may be designated to answer questions and provide additional data to analysts following the company.

Industry data and other information about a company also may be obtained from sources outside the company. Trade publications, the general business press, computerized databases, investment research reports, and the publications of competitors are among the sources that may supplement company-originated financial data.

The growth of the Internet has greatly improved access to data relevant to investment decisions. Given the rapid change in Internet offerings, we have not attempted to compile a specific list. Examples include:

▶ Company home pages that contain financial, product, and other data
▶ EDGAR, which contains corporate filings with the SEC
▶ Market data from exchanges and private data providers
▶ Tax regulations
▶ Economic data
▶ Industry data

A comprehensive analysis of a company requires the use of all of these sources of information.

When reviewing corporate reports to stockholders and other publications, it is important to remember that management writes them. Management often views annual reports as public relations or sales materials, intended to impress customers, suppliers, and employees, as well as stockholders. As a result, these reports must be read with at least some degree of skepticism. Only the financial statements (including footnotes and other disclosures labeled "audited") are independently reviewed and attested to by outside auditors.

10   ROLE OF THE AUDITOR

The auditor (independent certified public accountant) is responsible for seeing that the financial statements issued conform with generally accepted accounting principles. Thus, the auditor must agree that management's choice of accounting principles is appropriate and any estimates are reasonable. The auditor also examines the company's accounting and internal control systems, confirms assets and liabilities, and generally tries to ensure that there are no material errors in the financial statements. The auditor will often review interim reports and "unaudited" portions of the annual report. Although hired by the company (often through the audit committee of the board of directors), the auditor is supposed to be independent of management and to serve the stockholders and other users of the financial statements.

Audited financial statements are always accompanied by the auditor's report, often referred to as an "opinion." Because of the boilerplate nature of these reports, there is a tendency to skip over them when reviewing financial statements. Failure to read this report, however, may cause the financial analyst to miss significant information.

Exhibit 33-2 is the independent auditor's report issued by Ernst & Young, LLP after its 1999 audit of Amerada Hess. The first three paragraphs of the report are standard and are required by Statement of Auditing Standards (SAS) 58, Reports on Audited Financial Statements,[32] which addresses the audit report in which auditors express their opinion on the financial statements developed by management. It clarifies the scope of the assurance provided by the auditors and briefly describes the audit work. The report tells us the following:

1. Although the financial statements are prepared by Amerada management and are the responsibility of management, the auditor has performed an independent review of the statements.

2. The audit has been conducted using generally accepted auditing standards (GAAS) that require the auditor to provide "reasonable assurance" that there are no material errors in the financial statements. The auditor does not guarantee that the statements are free from error or no fraud is present. The auditor has performed tests of the company's accounting system designed to ensure that the statements are accurate.

3. Amerada's financial statements are prepared in accordance with GAAP. The auditor is satisfied that the accounting principles chosen and the estimates employed are reasonable.

An auditor's report on GAAP-based financial statements will always include these three claims.

SAS 58 also requires the addition of an explanatory paragraph to the auditor's report when accounting methods have not been used consistently among periods. For Amerada, the final paragraph tells us that the company changed its method of accounting for inventories in 1999 (a change discussed in Reading 40).

Reporting on Uncertainties

In some cases, the SAS requires the addition of an explanatory paragraph (following the "opinion" paragraph) that reports and describes material uncertainties affecting the financial statements, such as:

▶ Doubt concerning the "going concern" assumption that underlies the preparation of financial statements

---

[32] Auditing Standards Board of the American Institute of Certified Public Accountants, 1989.

▶ Uncertainty regarding the valuation or realization of assets or liabilities

▶ Uncertainty due to litigation

For the second and third cases, the opinion references the footnote(s) to the financial statements that further detail those uncertainties. The auditor's report

---

| **EXHIBIT 33-2** | Audit Report: Amerada Hess |

Report of Ernst & Young LLP, Independent Auditors

The Board of Directors and Stockholders
Amerada Hess Corporation

We have audited the accompanying consolidated balance sheet of Amerada Corporation and consolidated subsidiaries as of December 31, 1999 and 1998 and the related consolidated statements of income, retained earnings, cash flows, changes in common stock and capital in excess of par value and comprehensive income for each of the three years in the period ended December 31, 1999. These financial statements are the responsibility of the Corporation's management. Our responsibility is to express an opinion on these financial statements based on our audits.

We conducted our audits in accordance with auditing standards generally accepted in the United States. Those standards require that we plan and perform the audit to obtain reasonable assurance about whether the financial statements are free of material misstatement. An audit includes examining, on a test basis, evidence supporting the amounts and disclosures in the financial statements. An audit also includes assessing the accounting principles used and significant estimates made by management, as well as evaluating the overall financial statement presentation. We believe that our audits provide a reasonable basis for our opinion.

In our opinion, the financial statements referred to above present fairly, in all material respects, the consolidated financial position of Amerada Hess Corporation and consolidated subsidiaries at December 31, 1999 and 1998 and the consolidated results of their operations and their consolidated cash flows for each of the three years in the period ended December 31, 1999, in conformity with accounting principles generally accepted in the United States.

As discussed in Note 3 to the consolidated financial statements, in 1999 the Corporation adopted the last-in, first-out (LIFO) inventory method for valuing its refining and marketing inventories, and in 1998 the Corporation adopted AICPA Statement of Position 98-1, Accounting for the Costs of Computer Software Developed or Obtained for Internal Use.

/s/ Ernst & Young LLP

New York, NY
February 24, 2000

Source: Amerada Hess, 1999 Annual Report.

on material uncertainties depends on the probability of material loss due to uncertainty. If the probability of a loss is remote, the auditor issues a standard, unqualified opinion. When a material loss is probable and the amount of the loss cannot be reasonably estimated, an explanatory paragraph is required.

The first category is the most serious. A "going concern" qualification conveys doubt that the firm can continue in business. It may be that the firm requires financing due to losses or a lack of liquidity. This paragraph should be viewed as the equivalent of a flashing red light.[33]

Exhibit 33-3 contains the auditors' report on the financial statements of Read-Rite, a producer of magnetic recording heads for computer disk drives. It indicates that the company was not in compliance with financial covenants of its loan agreements and that "these conditions raise substantial doubt about the Company's ability to continue as a going concern." The paragraph then references the paragraph in Note 1, which discusses the conditions that warranted the going concern qualification and management's plans to remedy them.[34]

The other two categories suggest problems that are significant, but may not threaten the firm's existence. In these cases, the analyst should examine the uncertainty and incorporate any concerns in the investment decision.

Whenever the auditor's report contains any of the three types of disclosures just listed, or the consistency exception, the financial statements should be examined closely. Note that "subject to" and "except for" disclosures no longer appear in auditors' reports; they were replaced in 1989 by the language (SAS 58) discussed previously.

Other Auditor Services

The auditor also performs other services less visible to readers of financial statements. The auditor examines the internal control system of the company and reports any weaknesses to management or the audit committee of the board of directors. The report to the audit committee sometimes also contains information regarding significant audit adjustments, unusual transactions, disagreements with management, or serious audit difficulties. This report is generally not available to outside financial statement users. In 1989, the Auditing Standards Board (ASB) of the American Institute of Certified Public Accountants issued two standards dealing with these reports.

U.S. companies are required to report in their proxy statement the amount paid to the auditor for audit services and (separately) for other services (such as consulting).[35] The intent of this SEC requirement is to alert investors that the auditor's nonaudit fees may be material enough to affect the independence of the audit.

---

[33] Empirical studies [e.g., Carcello et al. (1995) and Rama et al. (1995)] have indicated that approximately 60% of bankrupt firms received a prior going-concern modified audit report and approximately 10% of firms receiving a first-time going-concern qualification entered into bankruptcy within one year of the date of the financial statements. Similarly, Holder-Webb and Wilkins (2000), with respect to SFAS 59, report evidence that resultant going-concern qualifications were useful in "warning" the market of imminent bankruptcies.

[34] In fact, Read-Rite did take steps to reduce its debt and, with the help of improved industry conditions, regained stability. It received a "clean" audit opinion at September 30, 2000. Case 10-1 is concerned with the restructuring of Read-Rite debt.

[35] In July, 2002 U.S. legislation restricted the non-audit services that auditors are permitted to perform for firms that they audit.

EXHIBIT 33-3	Audit Opinion: Read-Rite

Report of Ernst & Young LLP, Independent Auditors

The Board of Directors and Stockholders
Read-Rite Corporation

We have audited the accompanying consolidated balance sheets of Read-Rite Corporation as of September 30, 1999 and 1998, and the related consolidated statements of operations, cash flows and stockholders' equity for each of the three years in the period ended September 30, 1999. Our audits also included the financial statement schedule listed in the index at item 14(a). These financial statements and schedule are the responsibility of the Company's management. Our responsibility is to express an opinion on these financial statements and schedule based on our audits.

We conducted our audits in accordance with generally accepted auditing standards. Those standards require that we plan and perform the audit to obtain reasonable assurance about whether the financial statements are free of material misstatement. An audit includes examining, on a test basis, evidence supporting the amounts and disclosures in the financial statements. An audit also includes assessing the accounting principles used and significant estimates made by management, as well as evaluating the overall financial statement presentation. We believe that our audits provide a reasonable basis for our opinion.

In our opinion, the consolidated financial statements referred to above present fairly, in all material respects, the consolidated financial position of Read-Rite Corporation at September 30, 1999 and 1998, and the consolidated results of its operations and its cash flows for each of the three years in the period ended September 30, 1999, in conformity with generally accepted accounting principles. Also, in our opinion, the related financial statement schedule, when considered in relation to the basic financial statements taken as a whole, presents fairly in all material respects the information set forth therein.

The accompanying financial statements have been prepared assuming that Read-Rite Corporation will continue as a going concern. As more fully described in Note 1, the Company has incurred operating losses and is out of compliance with certain financial covenants of loan agreements with its lenders. These conditions raise substantial doubt about the Company's ability to continue as a going concern. Management's plans in regard to these matters are also described in Note 1. The financial statements do not include any adjustments to reflect the possible future effects on the recoverability and classification of assets or the amounts and classification of liabilities that may result from the outcome of this uncertainty.

/s/ Ernst & Young LLP

San Jose, California
October 22, 1999, except for the
sixth paragraph of Note 1, as to
which the date is December 29, 1999.

Source: Read-Rite Annual Report, September 30, 1999.

Changing Auditors

Changes in auditors have become more frequent in recent years. In many cases, changes are due to an effort to reduce audit costs or to personality issues. Some changes, however, result from disagreements regarding the application of accounting principles. When an auditor is willing to lose a client because of such a disagreement, the financial analyst should exercise extreme caution with respect to the financial statements of the company in question.

Auditing Outside of the United States

The role of the auditor is determined by auditing standards that vary, as do accounting standards, from one jurisdiction to another. Aracruz, while a Brazilian company, follows U.S. GAAP and its audit opinion is based on U.S. auditing standards.

Reviewing the Report of Group Auditors shown in Roche's annual report, we see that:

1. Roche financial statements are prepared in accordance with International Accounting Standards.
2. These statements also comply with Swiss law (Roche is a Swiss company).
3. The audit was conducted in accordance with International Standards on Auditing, issued by the International Federation of Accountants.

Reviewing Note 1 of Roche's financial statements, we see that the company adopted a number of new IAS standards in 2000. The auditor's opinion makes no reference to these changes. This is one example of how standards applied to the audit of non-U.S. companies may differ from those that readers of U.S. GAAP financial statements are used to. Thus it is especially important to read the accounting principles note of the financial statements of non-U.S. companies to determine the accounting and auditing principles followed.

SUMMARY

Reading 33 provided an informational background for the study of financial statement analysis. It examined the sources of financial data and the institutional framework in which accounting and disclosure standards are set. In addition, it provided a general guide to the contents of the financial statements and the roles played by statement preparers and auditors. In Readings 34 and 36, we build on this informational framework by addressing the financial statements— the raw material of analysis.

ACCOUNTING INCOME AND ASSETS: THE ACCRUAL CONCEPT

by Gerald I. White, Ashwinpaul C. Sondhi, and Dov Fried

LEARNING OUTCOMES

The candidate should be able to:

a. describe the format of the income statement and discuss the components of net income;

b. describe the criteria for revenue and expense recognition and discuss major issues in revenue and expense recognition, including the affect on reported earnings and their implications for financial analysis;

c. compare the percentage-of-completion method with the completed contract method and contrast the effects of the two methods on the income statement, balance sheet, statement of cash flows and selected financial ratios;

d. describe the types and analysis of unusual or infrequent items, extraordinary items, discontinued operations, accounting changes, and prior period adjustments;

e. discuss managerial discretion in areas such as classification of good news/bad news, income smoothing, big bath behavior and accounting changes, and explain how this discretion can affect the financial statements;

f. describe the format and the components of the balance sheet and the format, classification, and use of each component of the statement of stockholders' equity.

INTRODUCTION 1

The primary objective of this book is to help users of financial statements develop the skills needed to analyze financial statement data and use these data when making rational investment, credit, and similar decisions. Such decisions require comparison of the risk and return characteristics of alternative investments. Risk and return projections depend on income and cash flow forecasts and assessments of firm assets and liabilities.

Financial statements are the starting point for analysis as they report data about income, cash flows, and assets and liabilities that users can tailor to their specific needs. To do so, they need to understand the information provided by financial statements and the shortcomings of those data. In addition, financial statement users must be able to rearrange the information provided in a manner consistent with their objectives.

The first question is, How should income and cash flow be defined and measured? Are they simply the amounts provided by financial statements or should reported amounts be adjusted? Reporting methods, measurement techniques, and the presentation of financial information can all be criticized in many cases; good analysis requires skepticism.

Comprehensive financial analysis, therefore, requires a thorough understanding of the financial reporting system and its output. Reading 33 provided a general overview of the accounting process, the reporting system, and their product: the financial statements. We are now ready for the next step. This reading deals with the income statement and balance sheet—products of the accrual system of accounting. Reading 36 considers the statement of cash flows. For exposition purposes, we use Pfizer's financial statements.

2 INCOME, CASH FLOWS, AND ASSETS: DEFINITIONS AND RELATIONSHIPS

As background for the discussion of net income and cash flows in this and in Reading 36, we first examine conceptual definitions of "income." We will then explore the relationship between these concepts of income and "accounting income" reported by the current financial reporting system. We use insights from this discussion to delve into the relationship among income, cash flows, and assets as the first stage of the development of our understanding of "return" in our study of comparative risk–return analyses. Later readings will broaden our understanding of the analysis and use of financial statement information in the evaluation of different elements of risk and return.

This section introduces several conceptual definitions of income, measured in terms of cash flows and changes in the market values of assets.

In a world of certainty,[1] the interrelationship among income, cash flow, and assets is captured by the concept of *economic earnings*, defined as net cash flow plus the change in market value of the firm's net assets. The market value of the firm's assets in this certain world is equal to the present value of their future cash flows discounted at the (risk-free) rate r.

We illustrate this concept using a two-period model with the following assumptions:

---

[1] This would include perfect financial markets.

▶ The entity has a single asset, an investment with zero liquidation value.

▶ The entity has no debt; the asset is 100% equity financed.

▶ The investment generates a return of $100 at the end of each of two years.

▶ The $100 received at the end of year 1 is distributed to the owners and not reinvested in the firm.

▶ The (risk-free) rate r equals 5%.

Because the cash received at the end of each period equals $100 and $r = 5\%$, the value of the firm's assets is

Beginning of period 1 = $100/(1.05) + \$100/(1.05)^2$ = $185.94
Beginning of period 2 = $100/(1.05)$ = $95.24

and economic earnings equals cash flow plus the change in **net asset value**:[2]

Period 1: $100 + ($95.24 − $185.94) = $9.30
Period 2: $100 + ($0 − $95.24) = $4.76

Note that economic income in each year is equal to the rate of return times the opening value of the assets:

Period 1: $0.05 \times \$185.94$ = $9.30
Period 2: $0.05 \times \$95.24$ = $4.76

Equivalently, the market value at the beginning of the period is equal to a (constant) multiple of earnings equal to $1/r$. In this example, the price/earnings multiple is 20 $(1/0.05)$.

However, future cash flows and interest rates are uncertain in the real world, and the interrelationships are not as neat. Therefore, market prices of assets are also uncertain;[3] available prices may be difficult to relate to the present value of generally unknown, estimated future cash flows discounted at estimated interest rates. These estimates of future cash flows and interest rates and their interrelationships depend on the expectations of different decision makers.

Moreover, the market value of an asset may be measured with different levels of reliability using various (often inconsistent) methods, for example, at its replacement cost or liquidating value. *In this world of uncertainty, income (however measured) is, at best, only a proxy for economic income.* Thus, economists, analysts, and others have developed a number of analytic and practical definitions of earnings to serve as proxies for economic earnings.

Distributable earnings are defined as the amount of earnings that can be paid out as dividends without changing the value of the firm. This concept is derived from the Hicksian definition of income:

The amount that a person can consume during a period of time and be as well off at the end of that time as at the beginning.[4]

---

[2] The change in net asset value in this example is often referred to as economic depreciation (see Reading 43).

[3] Some assets are heavily traded on regulated markets (common stock of companies like Pfizer and Sears), others may be thinly traded (stocks of small companies), and still others have limited secondary markets from which verifiable prices can be obtained (most manufacturing equipment).

[4] J. R. Hicks, *Value and Capital*, 2nd ed. (Oxford: Chaundon Press, 1946), p. 176.

A related measure, *sustainable income*, refers to the level of income that can be maintained in the future given the firm's stock of capital investment (e.g., fixed assets and inventory).

Another measure, *permanent earnings*,[5] used by analysts for valuation purposes is the amount that can be normally earned given the firm's assets and equals the market value of those assets times the firm's required rate of return. Similar to economic earnings, it is the base to which a multiple is applied to arrive at a "fair price."[6]

All these definitions are attempts to capture the concept of economic earnings. Box 34-1 provides a discussion of the difficulties associated with applying these concepts in practice due to measurement and asset valuation problems.

As a result of these difficulties, the financial reporting concept of income—*accounting income*—is often quite different. The analyst, therefore, needs to relate accounting income to the economic income concepts just discussed.

Accounting income is measured using the accrual concept and provides information about the ability of the enterprise to generate future cash flows. It is not, *a priori*, equivalent to any of the definitions discussed earlier.

3   THE ACCRUAL CONCEPT OF INCOME

Accounting and economic income both define income as the sum of cash flows and changes in net assets. However, in financial reporting, the determination of

▶ Which cash flows are included in income and when

▶ Which changes in asset and liability values are included in income

▶ How and when the selected changes in asset and liability values are measured

are based on accounting rules and principles that make up generally accepted accounting principles (GAAP). With a few exceptions, the accounting process only recognizes value changes arising from actual transactions.

Accounting income represents a *selective* recognition of both current period actual cash flows and changes in asset values. Reported income under the accrual concept provides a measure of current operating performance[7] that is not solely based on actual current period cash flows. Cash inflows and outflows (past, present, and future) are recognized in income in the "appropriate" accounting periods, that is, as goods and services are provided and used rather than as cash is collected and expenditures incurred. *The selected period "best" indicates the firm's present and continuing ability to generate future cash flows.*

The accrual concept of accounting income assumes that forecasts of future cash flows require more than historical cash flow data:

> Information about enterprise earnings based on accrual accounting generally provides a better indication of an enterprise's present and continuing ability to generate cash flows than information limited to the financial effects of cash receipts and payments.[8]

---

[5] Normalized earnings and earnings power are similar concepts.

[6] The price/earnings ratio used by analysts represents this conceptual relationship.

[7] However, see the discussion of nonrecurring items later in this reading.

[8] SFAC 1. Objectives of Financial Reporting by Business Enterprises (November 1978), p. ix.

BOX 34-1   ELABORATION OF CONCEPTUAL INCOME, CASH FLOW, AND ASSET RELATIONSHIPS

The following discussion assumes that all income is paid out as dividends, allowing us to avoid considering reinvestment of income in the firm.

Case A

Assume that a firm purchases an asset at the beginning of each period for $10 and sells it for $12 at the end of each period. Further, assume that this markup of 20% is equivalent to the interest (discount) rate.* Under these conditions, the market value of the firm at the beginning of the period equals the $10 paid for the asset.

The market value of $10 can be derived in a single- or multiperiod context. For a single period, the present value of the end-of-period cash flow is $12/1.20 = $10. If we use a multiperiod model, the firm will earn $2 ($12 sale price less $10 cost of asset). The present value of $2 per period earned for an infinite period equals $2/0.20 = $10.

The economic earnings of the firm equal the cash flow of $2 ($12 − $10), the expected level of earnings in the future; the market value of the firm is a constant $10. Based on this same calculation, the distributable income is also $2, since paying out $2 will not change the value of the firm. Similarly, sustainable income is also $2, as that amount can be distributed without altering the firm's level of operations (buying and selling one asset per period). Finally, since the value of the firm is $10, permanent earnings equal $2 (0.2 × $10). Thus, economic, distributable, sustainable, and permanent earnings are all identical in this simplified case.

However, introducing uncertainty and changing one assumption make the problem much more complex.

Case B

Now assume that the sale price of the asset suddenly increases to $13.20. Accordingly, the purchase price of the asset should also increase as its one-period present value is now $13.20/1.20 = $11.00. Thus, if the firm replaces the asset at the end of that period, economic earnings are the sum of the cash flow of $2.20 ($13.20 − $11.00) and an increase in the market value of the firm of $1.00 (from $10.00 to $11.00), for a total of $3.20.

What are the expected earnings of the firm, given the change in the value of the asset? The answer is clearly not $3.20. It depends on the assumption one makes as to the level of operations the firm maintains.

Maintenance of Physical Level of Assets

If the firm retains the original level of *physical* assets, now valued at $11.00, the expected earnings are $2.20 (20% of $11.00). Note that economic earnings now have two components: operating earnings of $2.20 and a *holding gain* of $1.00. The holding gain results from owning an asset while its market value increases. This "one-time" occurrence cannot be expected to recur. Expected earnings would be the operating earnings as this amount can be expected to continue into the future given the level of physical assets.

Maintenance of Monetary Level of Assets

If we assume that the asset is divisible and the firm does not replace the entire asset but only maintains its *monetary* level of assets by purchasing $10.00 of the now more expensive asset, economic earnings for the current period will still be $3.20.

(continued)

> ### BOX 34-1 *(continued)*
>
> Net cash flow will be $3.20 ($13.20 sales proceeds − $10.00 reinvestment). Since the market value of assets remains $10.00, economic earnings are $3.20 as above. Expected earnings, however, differ. If the firm retains the original level of monetary assets of $10.00, expected earnings are $2.00 (20% of $10.00).
>
> What happens to the other definitions of income under this scenario? Distributable income is $3.20, which maintains the initial wealth level of $10.00, equivalent to economic earnings. However, sustainable income, the achievable earnings level of the firm in the future, is only $2.00 (if we assume that $3.20 is distributed).
>
> However, if the firm maintains the same physical level of assets and we consider the Hicksian definition of income in terms of the physical measure of assets, both distributable and sustainable income equal $2.20. Similarly, permanent earnings depend on whether the firm retains its original physical asset base (whose value is now $11.00), or whether it retains its original monetary asset base of $10.00. In the former case, permanent earnings are $2.20; in the latter, they will be $2.00.
>
> Under real-world conditions, income measures become judgmental. The neat mappings from one definition to another no longer hold as they become situation specific.
>
> ──────────
>
> * Under conditions of certainty, the rate of return earned on the asset (the 20% markup) equals the prevailing interest rate.

The accrual basis of accounting thus allocates (recognizes as revenue and expense) many transactions and events producing cash flows to time periods other than those in which the cash flows occur. Accrual accounting principles are, fundamentally, the decision rules that tell preparers of financial statements when to recognize the revenue and expense consequences of cash flows and other events.

The recognition of revenues and expenses in periods other than when cash is actually received or spent has a corollary effect on the balance sheet. *Under accrual accounting, both the recognition and measurement of certain assets and liabilities are results of the application of the accrual concept of income.* The differences between the income recognized and actual cash flows for the period are *accrued* as assets or liabilities.

In case A in Box 34-1, we assume that an item purchased for $10 at the beginning of period 1 is sold for $12 at the end of that period and replaced at the start of the next period at a cost of $10. If we further assume that the sale is made on credit and cash will be collected in the following period, the actual cash outflow in period 1 is $10, the cost of acquiring the asset at the beginning of period 1.

Under accrual accounting, revenue (expected future cash flow) is recognized at the time of sale, and is reported as an increase of $12 in the asset "accounts receivable." Income is measured as the change in assets plus actual cash flows:

Income = $12 Increase in accounts receivable − $10 Cash outflow = $2

Which is a better indicator of the earning power of the firm and its ability to generate future cash flows: the cash outflow of $10 or the income of $2? The accrual accounting concept reports income of $2, providing better forward-looking information than pure cash flow accounting.

The Matching Principle. Revenue and expense recognition are also governed by the *matching principle*, which states that operating performance can be measured only if related revenues and expenses are accounted for during the same time period. It is the matching principle that requires the expense (cost of goods sold) of inventory to be recognized in the same period in which the sale of that inventory is recorded. This facilitates measurement of the periodic income, that is, operating performance generated by selling inventories during the period regardless of when collections or expenditures occur. In the previous example, if we assume that the item also was purchased on credit in period 1 with payment expected in the following period, accrual accounting would still recognize income of $2 in period 1:

Income = $12 Increase in accounts receivable −
$10 Increase in accounts payable = $2

Over the life of the firm, income and cash flows converge. They differ only as to timing of recognition. The recognition of revenues and expenses in "appropriate" accounting periods is both the strength and the weakness of the accrual method. It is a strength in that it results in more meaningful measurement of current operating performance (income statement) and is a better indicator of future operating performance and earnings power. If accrual accounting did not exist, financial analysts would have to invent it.[9] The weakness is that the amount and timing of accruals are subject to management discretion and are based on assumptions and estimates that can and do change over time. Analysts need to differentiate between real events and accruals stemming from management choice.

Overall, as the empirical evidence in Box 34-2 indicates, the accrual process does provide information and enhances the predictive ability of cash flows. However, as the evidence also indicates (and as we elaborate on in Reading 36), it does not mean that cash flows are not relevant. They provide information as to the *quality* of accounting earnings and can be used to mitigate the weaknesses of the accrual process.

The determination of accounting earnings is also governed by:

▶ General principles and measurement rules underlying all accounting transactions and events

▶ Specific rules to determine revenue, expense, gain, and loss recognition

For example, the *historical cost-based* approach underlying GAAP results in rules that exclude from income *many* unrealized holding gains or losses (increases/decreases in the market value of certain assets and liabilities held by the firm). Recognition of these gains/losses must await the disposal of the assets and the retirement or settlement of the liabilities.

However, some nontransaction-related changes in asset values *can* affect reported income. For example,

▶ Current assets must be evaluated at each financial statement date and any estimated declines in asset values recognized as losses.

▶ SFAS 121, Accounting for the Impairment of Long-Lived Assets and for Long-Lived Assets to Be Disposed of, extended this requirement to most classes of fixed assets. The amount and timing of loss recognition remain substantively discretionary because these assets must be evaluated for declines only when certain impairment criteria are present.[10]

---

[9] This occasionally happens. Because of the deficiencies of (cash-based) regulatory accounting in the insurance industry, analysts developed methods of analysis in the 1960s that eventually were adopted as GAAP by the industry. More recently, German analysts developed their own method of adjusting tax-based income statements.

[10] See Reading 43 for a discussion of this standard.

▶ Certain investments in securities are marked to market and changes in market value are reported as a component of income.[11]

Generally, although changes in market values of assets and liabilities may occur over a number of periods, they are recognized in income either in the period of sale or disposal or when certain impairment criteria are met. The result is current period income that may be distorted and may not be indicative of normal earning power. As an initial step, one needs to understand the components that make up the income statement.

BOX 34-2   ACCURAL INCOME VERSUS CASH FLOW: SOME EMPIRICAL EVIDENCE

A number of empirical studies have compared the benefits of accrual income with those of cash flows. Some of these studies asked whether one of the measures provided incremental information, given the other measure. Those studies* offer consistent evidence that, given cash flows from operations (CFO), accruals give incremental information, and given accrual income, CFO provides incremental information.

Bernard and Stober (1989) noted that the variation in cash flow results found by some studies may be caused by using models that do not capture the specific implications of any particular company or situation. That is, in many cases the relative benefits of accruals versus cash flows may be firm-, industry-, and/or situation-specific; they suggest that "further progress in this line of research will require a better understanding of the economic context in which the implications of detailed earnings components are interpreted."†

Livnat and Zarowin (1990) found that, although aggregate CFO did not provide additional informational content, individual components from both CFO and financing cash flows did add incremental information. This, however, does not mean that cash flow information is superior to accrual information as the relevant comparison would have to be with individual components of accrual income.

Dechow (1994) compared accrual income directly with CFO showing that accrual income more closely measured *firm performance as reflected in stock returns*. Moreover, she found that the "superiority" of accrual income as a predictor of stock returns was more likely to occur when cash flows have significant timing and matching problems. That is, accrual income performed better:

▶ The shorter the interval over which performance is measured

▶ The more volatile the working capital requirements and investment and financing activities

▶ The longer the operating cycle of the firm‡

Dechow, Kothari, and Watts (1998) showed (consistent with our conjecture in the chapter) that accrual income is a *better predictor of future (operating) cash flows* than current (operating) cash flows (CFO) themselves. Barth, Cram, and Nelson (2001) extended Dechow et al.'s model and found that disaggregating accrual income into its

(continued)

---

[11] Other investments in securities also are reported at fair value with the unrealized gains and losses accumulated in "other comprehensive income"; these changes are moved to income when the investments are sold.

Income Statement

Format and Classification

U.S. GAAP do not specify the format of the income statement. Actual formats vary across companies, especially in the reporting of the gain or loss on sale of assets, equity in earnings of affiliates, and other nonoperating income and expense. In some cases, income statement detail appears in financial statement footnotes. Consequently, the sample format presented below should be viewed in a generic sense rather than as a strict rendition of how an income statement is laid out:

Sample Income Statement Format

	Revenues from the sales of goods and services:
+	Other income and revenues
−	Operating expenses
−	Financing costs
+/−	Unusual or infrequent items
=	Pretax earnings from continuing operations
−	Income tax expense
=	Net income from continuing operations*
+/−	Income from discontinued operations (net of tax)*
+/−	Extraordinary items (net of tax)*
+/−	Cumulative effect of accounting changes (net of tax)*
=	Net income*

*Per share amounts are reported for each of these items.

IAS Presentation Requirements

IAS 1 (revised 1997) governs the presentation of financial statements prepared in accordance with IAS GAAP. The requirements are broadly similar to those under U.S. GAAP in that financial statement preparers are permitted considerable flexibility as to format as long as all required information is disclosed either on the face of the financial statements or in the financial statement notes. IAS 1 specifically allows for presentation of the income statement in either of two formats:

1. Classification of expenses by function (the format shown above).
2. Classification of expenses based on their nature. Under this alternative, the company reports expenditures using categories such as raw materials, employees, and changes in inventories.

Components of Net Income

The format typically found in actual statements may not be the most useful for analytical purposes. It is important for the analyst to be cognizant of the various categories or groupings into which the income statement components *can* be combined. These groupings do not necessarily coincide with the classifications presented in actual financial statements (or our sample income statement above). In our discussion of the income statement components, we shall follow the suggested groupings presented below. These groupings provide information about different aspects of a firm's operations:

Suggested Format

	Revenues from the sales of goods and services
−	Operating expenses
=	Operating income from continuing operations
+	Other income and revenues
=	Recurring income before interest and taxes from continuing operations
−	Financing costs
=	Recurring (pretax) income from continuing operations
+/−	Unusual or infrequent items
=	Pretax earnings from continuing operations
−	Income tax expense
=	Net income from continuing operations
+/−	Income from discontinued operations (net of tax)
+/−	Extraordinary items (net of tax)
+/−	Cumulative effect of accounting changes (net of tax)
=	Net income

The income statement reports revenues generated by the sales of goods and services from a firm's continuing operations. The costs and expenses incurred to generate these revenues follow. The costs of manufacturing or purchasing the goods sold are normally listed first since they are directly related to the period's revenues. Indirect costs of selling and administrative activities and expense categories such as research and development are reported next. The excess of revenues over these costs and expenses (excluding interest expense) measures the firm's *operating income from continuing operations*, which is independent of its capital structure.

In addition to its core business, a firm may have income (loss) from other activities, such as interest or dividends from investments, equity in (share of) the income of its unconsolidated affiliates, and gains or losses on sales or disposal of assets. *Recurring earnings before interest and taxes from continuing operations* usually include these items and are also independent of the firm's capital structure. Deducting financing costs (interest expense) results in *recurring (pretax) income from continuing operations*.

Unusual or infrequent items, such as pretax gains and losses from the sale or impairment of assets or investments,[12] are often shown as separate line items yielding *pretax income from continuing operations*. Income tax expense is usually the final deduction before arriving at *net income from continuing operations*.

The income statement effects of discontinued operations (discussed later in this reading) are segregated and reported net of income tax to emphasize the fact that these operations will not contribute to future revenues and income. The net of tax effect of "extraordinary items" is also reported separately because they are incidental to the firm's operating activities, unusual in nature, and not expected to be a normal, recurring component of income and cash flows.

Finally, the income statement separately reports the cumulative effect of accounting changes adopted during the period since they are unrelated to the period's income or operating activities and rarely have any cash flow consequences.[13] Footnotes provide detailed information on both mandatory and voluntary changes in accounting methods, which must be analyzed to evaluate the impact on present and future reported earnings.

A more detailed description and discussion of an income statement and related footnotes, using Pfizer, Inc. as an example, are provided in Box 34-3.

Changes in Income Statement Presentation. Companies sometimes change their income statement presentation in order to obscure unfavorable trends. IBM provides an instructive example. Through 1999, the company listed revenues and various expenses in its income statement separately, showing gross profit, operating income, and net income. Using the 1999 format, the analyst could compute the following trends in operating income and net income.

	Years Ended December 31		
	1997	1998	1999
Percentage change in operating income	5.84%	0.73%	30.15%
Percentage change in net income	12.23%	3.87%	21.87%

---

[12] The appropriate income statement classification of such items and their analytic significance are discussed later in this reading.

[13] Actual cash flows are not affected by accounting changes unless the firm also changes the method used for income tax reporting (e.g., LIFO, discussed in Reading 40). However, changes in accounting methods may affect the classification of cash flows, as discussed in Reading 36.

BOX 34-3   PFIZER, INC. INCOME STATEMENT COMPONENTS

Pfizer's 1997–1999 income statements illustrate the format used by a manufacturing company. Comments on the individual line items are provided in this box. In addition, we provide below an index listing the readings containing detailed discussions of selected components of the income statement:

Income Statement Component	Curriculum Reading
Net sales–revenue recognition	34
Alliance revenues	34
Costs and operating expenses, which include:	
Cost of sales (Note 1-C)	40
Employee benefits	NA
Amortization of goodwill and other intangibles (Note 8)	NA
Depreciation expense (Note 1-D)	43
Research and development	42
Other income (Note 8), which includes:	
Interest Income	34
Interest expense (net of capitalized interest)	42, 45
Asset impairments	43
Restructuring charges	34
Gain (loss) on foreign currency transactions	NA
Legal settlements	34
Other "nonrecurring" items	34
Minority interests	NA
Income taxes	44
Discontinued operations	34
Earnings per share	NA

Net sales include proceeds from human and animal pharmaceutical product sales. Pfizer also reports alliance revenues (generally, a percentage of partners' sales) from co-promoted products developed by other companies. Reported revenue may not be comparable across firms because it depends on management's choice of revenue recognition methods and significant estimates and assumptions.

Costs and operating (*selling, informational, and administrative*) *expenses* include the majority of the costs of producing the medical products that constitute Pfizer's operations. Cost of sales includes the cost of raw materials, supplies, and manufacturing outlays. Pfizer's 1999 cost of sales also includes a $310 million write-off of excess inventories of a suspended drug (Note 1-C) and a $6.6 million benefit of a change to the first-in, first-out (FIFO) inventory costing method (Note 6).

Depreciation expense reflects the allocation of past expenditures for property, plant, and equipment. Goodwill amortization (reported in the other deductions—net component) represents a systematic allocation of the excess purchase price (over fair value) of net assets acquired. Pfizer's expenditures for *research and development* are expensed in the period incurred as required by U.S. GAAP.

(continued)

> ## BOX 34-3   *(continued)*
>
> *Selling, general, and administrative expenses* (SG&A)* include operating expenses not reported as components of costs of goods sold. The division between costs of goods sold and SG&A depends on the company's accounting choices, and the breakdown may not be comparable among firms. SG&A expenses are not always directly related to sales levels as they contain fixed components. In Note 1-H, Pfizer separately reports its accounting policies and annual expense for advertising and promotional activities.
>
> In *other deductions* (see Note 8) Pfizer reports interest income, interest expense (net of capitalized interest), and costs of legal settlements. The company also incurred a loss on foreign currency transactions.
>
> Note 8 also shows that, in 1998, the company recorded $177 million of restructuring charges and $213 million in asset impairments for workforce reductions and plant and product lines rationalizations. These restructuring plans were substantially completed in 1999. In 1998, Pfizer recorded large expenses for co-promotion payments to Searle and for a contribution to the Pfizer Foundation.
>
> *Interest expense* reflects financing charges net of capitalized interest. The recognition of minority interest in consolidated subsidiaries and a *provision for income taxes* completes the computation of income from continuing operations.
>
> Note 2, Discontinued Operations, reports a 1999 payment of $20 million to settle antitrust charges concerning a business group divested in 1996. *Earnings per share* are reported separately for income from continuing operations, loss from discontinued operations, and net income. Note 15, earnings per common share, discloses and reconciles the number of shares used to compute both basic and diluted per-share amounts. The note also reports the effect of dilutive securities.
>
> _____
>
> *Unlike most companies, Pfizer uses the term *selling, informational, and administrative (SI&A)* expenses.

OPTIONAL SEGMENT ENDS

In 2000, IBM changed its income statement format to exclude the line item, "operating income," from its income statement. The company continued to report all other line items included in income statements in prior years. This permits us to extend the table through 2000:

	Years Ended December 31			
	1997	**1998**	**1999**	**2000**
Percentage change in operating income	5.84%	0.73%	30.15%	−2.46%
Percentage change in net income	12.23%	3.87%	21.87%	4.94%

Why did IBM change the income statement format? We assume that the company did not wish to highlight the decline in operating income. The lesson is that analysts should use their own formats, allowing them to see trends that management may wish to conceal. Using the same format for all companies within an industry also facilitates comparisons.

Recurring versus Nonrecurring Items

Reported net income is only loosely related to the concept of *comprehensive income* discussed in Reading 33. It contains income from operations as well as all realized (but only some unrealized) changes in the market value of assets and liabilities.

From an analyst's perspective, however, it may not be the most informative measure of the income and cash-generating ability of the firm. Generally, income from a firm's recurring operating activities is considered the best indicator of future income. The predictive ability of reported income is enhanced if it excludes the impact of transitory or random components, which are not directly related to operating activities and are generally more volatile. The economic concepts of income discussed earlier (and elaborated on in Box 34-1) tell us that transitory gains or losses should not be regarded as components of permanent or sustainable income. The concept of recurring income is similar to permanent or sustainable income in the sense that it is persistent; that is, its level or rate of growth is relatively predictable, and cash flows will eventually follow at the predicted levels and growth rates.

If we use the terminology above, *recurring income (pretax or post tax[14]) from continuing operations* should be the primary focus of analysis.

Segregation of the results of normal, recurring operations from the effects of nonrecurring items facilitates the forecasting of future earnings and cash flows. Financial reporting defines nonrecurring by the *type of transaction or event*. However, depending on the firm, the nature of the event, and to some extent management discretion, similar transactions may be included in operating income or reported below the line. Operational definitions of "operating," "nonrecurring," and "extraordinary" are elusive and both accounting standards setters and analysts have struggled with this issue for decades.

More recently, companies have increasingly provided early indications of their results for a period by announcing earnings in advance of scheduled annual or quarterly release dates. The nature of these early announcements has further blurred the distinctions between "operating," "nonrecurring," and "extraordinary" components of income. We elaborate on this issue elsewhere in this reading.

For purposes of analysis, however, the important issue is whether each item classified by management as nonrecurring income or loss in a given year is a good predictor of future income or loss. For example, for some firms, a material gain or loss from the sale of fixed assets will be rare; the transaction reported has no predictive value. Other firms retire fixed assets each year and regularly report gains or losses (e.g., consider a car rental company that retires part of its fleet of cars annually). In the latter case, the analytic issue is whether this year's income or loss from the sale of retired property is higher or lower than the "normal" amount.

Ultimately, the analyst must evaluate the significance of nonrecurring items, regardless of whether they are reported in the extraordinary, unusual, or some other category, in the prediction of earnings power. The goal of analysis of the income statement is to derive an effective measure of future earnings and cash flows. Therefore, analysts often exclude components of reported income (regardless of their accounting labels) that may reduce its predictive ability.

Fairfield et al. (1996) examined whether the classification scheme used in financial statements can improve predictive ability. Their results indicated that the forecasting of one-year-ahead profitability, that is, return on equity (ROE), was improved by disaggregating previous year's ROE into the separate compo-

---

[14] Recurring income on a post-tax basis can be arrived at by either (1) adding back to net income from continuing operations the after-tax consequences of unusual or infrequent items, that is,

Net income from recurring operations = Net income from continuing
operations + / − [unusual or infrequent items × (1 − tax rate)]

or (2) adjusting recurring income from continuing operations directly for taxes:

Net income from recurring operations = Recurring income from continuing
operations × (1 − tax rate)

nents discussed earlier. They found that extraordinary items and discontinued operations were not useful in predicting bottom-line ROE or ROE from continuing operations *although unusual and infrequent items were*. This latter result implies that unusual or infrequent items often contain a recurring element.

The predictive ability objective does not mean that financial analysis of the income (or other financial) statements is simply the extrapolation of previous trends. Rather, all financial statement information should be viewed as part of a database that provides limited information about future prospects and opportunities facing the firm. For example, an increase in the sale of semiconductors also provides useful information about the demand for equipment used for their manufacture.

Nonrecurring items can also provide such information, but in a different fashion. The implication of the sale of an operating asset, for example, depends on the utilization of the cash generated by the sale, and how its productive capacity will be replaced.

We return to nonrecurring items later in this reading. First, however, we look at the revenue and expense recognition rules used to report a firm's recurring operations.

Accounting Income: Revenue and Expense Recognition

When accrual accounting is used to prepare financial statements, two revenue and expense recognition issues must be addressed:

1. *Timing.* When should revenue and expense be recognized?

2. *Measurement.* How much revenue and expense should be recognized?

The responses to these questions determine the amount and timing of periodic revenue and expense. In practice, there is considerable scope for management discretion with respect to both revenue and expense recognition. At this point, however, the focus of our discussion is revenue recognition and how the application of the *matching principle* relates expense recognition to revenue recognition.[15] Other issues of expense recognition are discussed, on an issue-by-issue basis, in the readings that follow.

Statement of Financial Accounting Concepts (SFAC) 5, Recognition and Measurement in Financial Statements of Business Enterprises, specifies *two conditions that must be met for revenue recognition to take place*. These conditions are:

1. Completion of the earnings process

2. Assurance of payment

To satisfy the first condition, the firm must have provided all or virtually all the goods or services for which it is to be paid, and it must be possible to measure the total expected cost of providing the goods or services; that is, the seller must have no remaining significant contingent obligation. If the seller is obligated to provide future services, for example, warranty protection for equipment or

---

[15] Direct costs, such as cost of goods sold, are recognized as related revenue as recognized under accrual accounting. Note that the cost of goods sold often includes depreciation expense or capitalized overhead. However, other expenses cannot be directly related to revenues and must be recognized using different principles. Some, called period costs (e.g., advertising costs), are expensed as incurred. Other costs are recognized as time passes, for example, interest costs. Finally, some costs may be based on other criteria, for example, taxes on income.

upgrades and enhancements for software, but cannot estimate the cost of doing so, this condition is not satisfied.

Revenue recognition also requires a second condition: the quantification of cash or assets expected to be received for the goods or services provided. Reliable measurement encompasses the realizability (collectibility) of the proceeds of sale. If the seller cannot reasonably estimate the probability of non-payment, realization is not reasonably assured, and the second condition is not satisfied.

The general rule for revenue recognition includes this concept of realizability: Revenue, measured as the amount expected to be collected, can be recognized when goods or services have been provided and their cost can be reliably determined.

The amount of revenue recognized at any given point in time is measured as

$$\frac{\text{Goods and services provided to date}}{\text{Total goods and services to be provided}} \times \text{Total expected revenue}$$

This equation measures the amount of revenue recognized *cumulatively* to date. Revenue reported for the current period is the *cumulative total less revenue recognized in prior periods.*

The most common case is revenue recognition at the time of sale. Goods or services have been provided, and the sale is for cash or to customers whose ability to pay is reasonably assured.[16]

In some cases, payment is received prior to the delivery of goods or services. Examples include:

▶ Magazine publishers receive subscription payments in advance; the receipts represent an obligation to provide periodic delivery of the publication. Revenues are recognized in proportion to issues delivered.

▶ Credit card fees are recognized as advances from customers; revenue is recorded as the right to use the cards expires over time.

▶ Revenue from leased equipment is recognized as time passes or based on usage (copier rental is sometimes based on a per-copy charge).

These examples show that revenue recognition can be measured by cash expenditures, the passage of time, or the provision of service (measured in physical units) to the customer.

Departures from the Sales Basis of Revenue Recognition

Revenue may be recognized *prior* to sale or delivery when the earnings process is substantially complete and the proceeds of sale can be reasonably measured. For example, revenue is recognized at the completion of production in the case of commodities (such as oil or agricultural products) with highly organized and liquid markets or, in the case of long-term construction contracts, as production takes place.

---

[16] In some cases, the buyer has a right to return unsold goods. If the risks or benefits (or both) of ownership are retained by the "seller," the transaction is, in economic substance, a consignment rather than a completed sale. SFAS 48, Revenue Recognition When Right of Return Exists, governs such sales. See also SFAS 49, Accounting for Product Financing Arrangements.

Alternatively, revenues may not be recognized even at the time of sale if there is significant uncertainty regarding the seller's ability to collect the sales price or to estimate remaining costs. Either the installment method or the more extreme cost recovery method, both discussed shortly, must be used in such cases.

Percentage-of-Completion and Completed Contract Methods

The *percentage-of-completion* method recognizes revenues and costs in proportion to and as work is completed; production activity is considered the critical event in signaling the completion of the earnings process rather than delivery or cash collections. This method is used for long-term projects when there is a contract, and reliable estimates of production completed, revenues, and costs are possible.

The percentage-of-completion method measures progress toward completion using *either*:

▶ Engineering estimates (or physical milestones such as miles of road completed), or

▶ Ratios of costs incurred to expected total costs.

This method may overstate revenue and gross profit if expenditures made are recognized before they contribute to completed work, for example, when the costs of raw materials and advance payments to subcontractors are included in the determination of work completed.

When estimates of revenue or costs change, a catch-up effect is included in the earnings of the period in which the change in estimate is made. Earnings of prior periods are not restated because it is a change in accounting estimate. When a loss is expected on the contract, it must be recognized in the period the amount of the loss can be estimated.

The *completed contract method* recognizes revenues and expenses only at the end of the contract. It must be used when any one of the conditions required for the use of the percentage-of-completion method is not met, generally when no contract exists or estimates of the selling price or collectibility are not reliable. It must be used for short-term contracts.[17]

Comparison of Percentage-of-Completion and Completed Contract Methods

Exhibit 34-1 compares the percentage-of-completion and completed contract revenue recognition methods. Part A compares the revenues, expenses, and income reported under each method for each year. Computations for the percentage-of-completion method use the ratio of costs (assumed to provide a reliable measure of actual work performed) incurred each period to expected total costs. In 2001, 16.67% of estimated costs are incurred, so that revenue recognized for that year equals 16.67% of the **contract price**. As a result, if we use the matching principle, the same percentage (16.67%) of expected total expenses and total income is recognized for 2001. This pattern is repeated as long as actual results closely mirror expectations.

---

[17] SFAS 56 (1982) emphasizes that the percentage-of-completion and the completed contract method are not "intended to be free-choice alternatives under either Accounting Research Bulletin No. 45 (ARB 45) or AICPA SOP 81-1." ARB 45 states that the percentage-of-completion method is preferable when estimates of costs and degree of completion are reliable. SOP 81-1 reiterates this position.

Under the completed contract method, revenues, expenses, and income are recognized only at the end of the contract period; no revenue, expense, or income is reported during the first two years.

As a result, the two different revenue recognition methods produce different patterns of reported revenue, expense, and income, although total revenue, expense, and income over the life of the contract are identical under both methods.

EXHIBIT 34-1	Comparison of Percentage-of-Completion and Completed Contract Revenue Recognition Methods

In 2001, Justin Corp. entered into a construction project with a total contract price of $6 million and expected costs to complete of $4.8 million resulting in expected profits of $1.2 million.

Actual production costs and cash flow information over the duration of the contract are provided as follows (in $thousands):

	2001	2002	2003
Costs incurred: Current year	$ 800	$2,800	$1,200
Cumulative	800	3,600	4,800
Estimated *remaining* costs to complete (as of December 31)	4,000	1,200	0
Amounts billed and cash received			
Current year	$1,300	$2,500	$2,200
Cumulative	1,300	3,800	6,000

A. Income Statement (in $ thousands)

	Percentage-of-Completion				Completed Contract			
	2001	2002	2003	Total	2001	2002	2003	Total
Revenue*	$1,000	$3,500	$1,500	$6,000	$0	$0	$6,000	$6,000
Expense	(800)	(2,800)	(1,200)	(4,800)	(0)	(0)	(4,800)	(4,800)
Income	$ 200	$ 700	$ 300	$1,200	$0	$0	$1,200	$1,200

$$*2001: \frac{\$800}{\$4,800} \times \$6,000 = \$1,000$$

$$2002: \frac{(\$800 + \$2,800)}{\$4,800} \times \$6,000 = \$4,500 - \$1,000 = \$3,500$$

$$2003: \frac{(\$800 + \$2,800 + \$1,200)}{\$4,800} \times \$6,000 = \$6,000 - \$4,500 = \$1,500$$

(Exhibit continued on next page ...)

EXHIBIT 34-1	(continued)

B. Balance Sheet (in $ thousands)

	Percentage-of-Completion			Completed Contract		
	2001	**2002**	**2003**	**2001**	**2002**	**2003**
Assets						
Cash	$500	$200	$1,200	$500	$200	$1,200
Construction in progress	0	700	0	0	0	0
Total assets	$500	$900	$1,200	$500	$200	$1,200
Liabilities and equity						
Advance billings	$300	$ 0	$ 0	$500	$200	$ 0
Retained earnings	200	900	1,200	0	0	1,200
Total liabilities and equity	$500	$900	$1,200	$500	$200	$1,200

Explanation:

Cash: Identical for both methods and equivalent to cumulative cash received less costs incurred.

Retained earnings: Cumulative earnings since inception of project.

Construction in progress and advance billings: *Net* amount of following table where advance billings represent cumulative cash received and construction in progress is based on cumulative costs incurred plus profit recognized:

	Percentage-of-Completion			Completed Contract		
	2001	**2002**	**2003**	**2001**	**2002**	**2003**
Costs incurred	$ 800	$3,600	$4,800	$ 800	$3,600	$4,800
Profit recognized	200	900	1,200	0	0	1,200
Construction in progress	**$1,000**	**$4,500**	**$6,000**	**$800**	**$3,600**	**$6,000**
Advance billings	(1,300)	(3,800)	(6,000)	(1,300)	(3,800)	(6,000)
Net asset (liability)	$ (300)	$ 700	$ 0	$ (500)	$ (200)	$ 0

C. Change in Estimated Costs to Complete

On December 31, 2002, Justin Corp. determines that the total cost of the project will be $5,400, making remaining costs to complete $1,800, an increase of $600 from the original estimate. This changes *both* revenue and income for 2002 under the percentage-of-completion method. The adjustment is made on a cumulative basis; revenue and expense reported for previous years are *not* restated.

Cumulative revenue recognized is

$$\frac{\$3,600 \ (\text{cumulative costs incurred})}{\$5,400 \ (\text{revised total costs})} \times \$6,000$$

= $4,000, of which $1,000 was recognized as revenue in 2001.

(*Exhibit continued on next page...*)

EXHIBIT 34-1	(continued)

Therefore, $3,000 ($4,000 − $1,000) is recognized as revenue for 2002.
Cumulative expense recognized is $3,600, the total incurred. Expense recognized for 2002 remains unchanged at $1,800. As a result, income recognized in 2002 is $3,000 − $2,800 = $200.

The revised income statements for percentage of completion are presented below in panel I. (For completed contract, the revision would all be reflected in year 2003.)

Panel II shows what percentage of completion income would have been had Justin known the actual costs at the beginning of the project.

Percentage-of-Completion

	I. Revised				**II. Foreknowledge of Actual Costs**			
	2001	**2002**	**2003**	**Total**	**2001**	**2002**	**2003**	**Total**
Revenue	$1,000	$3,000	$2,000	$6,000	$889	$3,111	$2,000	$6,000
Expense	(800)	(2,800)	(1,800)	(5,400)	(800)	(2,800)	(1,800)	(5,400)
Income	$ 200	$ 200	$ 200	$ 600	$ 89	$ 311	$ 200	$ 600

The percentage-of-completion method provides both a better measure of operating activity and a more informative disclosure of the status of incomplete contracts. For a firm with constant revenues the two methods produce identical results.[18] However, since the business world is rarely in a steady state of equilibrium, *the percentage-of-completion method reports income earlier and is a better indicator of trends in earning power.* Although better disclosure of contracts in progress under the completed contract method would help analysts forecast future operating results and cash flows, the percentage-of-completion method is more informative.

The choice of method also affects the reported assets and liabilities on the balance sheet. Part B shows the balance sheet effects of the two methods.

Under the completed contract method, expenditures prior to completion are reported as inventory (*construction-in-progress*) and cash receipts as advances from customers.

Using the percentage-of-completion method,

► Costs incurred are also accumulated in an asset account titled *construction-in-progress*. However, *gross profit (income) for the period is also accumulated in the construction-in-progress account.* (Periodic gross profit is not recognized under the completed contract method.)

► Amounts billed to customers are recorded as a liability (*advance billings*) and an asset (accounts receivable). When cash is received, the receivable is reduced. The difference between cash received and billings is treated as accounts receivable.[19]

---

[18] This statement assumes that, with a large number of contracts, income recognized from contracts completed in each period would be equal to the income recognized from the partial completion of contracts in process.

[19] In our example, amounts billed and cash received were identical, leaving a zero receivables balance.

Example 34-1

Chicago Bridge & Iron is a global engineering and construction firm. Its 10-K report for the year ended December 31, 1999 lists, among significant accounting policies:

REVENUE RECOGNITION: Revenues are recognized using the percentage of completion method. Contract revenues are accrued based generally on the percentage that costs-to-date bear to total estimated costs.

Footnote 3 contains the following table:

Contracts in Progress	1999	1998
Revenues recognized on contracts in progress	$808,312	$871,100
Billings on contracts in progress	(813,140)	(896,506)
Shown on balance sheet as:		
Contracts in progress with earned revenues exceeding related progress billings (asset)	$48,486	$ 51,953
Contracts in progress with progress billings exceeding related earned revenues (liability)	(53,314)	(77,359)
	$(4,828)	$(25,406)

For financial reporting purposes, construction-in-progress and advance billings are netted. For example, at the end of 2001 (percentage of completion method), Justin's balance sheet will show (a liability of) $300 as "amounts billed in excess of contract costs." At the end of 2002 (percentage of completion method), Justin will report (an asset of) $700 as "contract costs in excess of amounts billed." For a company with many contracts in process, it is typical to find both net asset and net liability amounts on the balance sheet. The gross amounts will be reported in footnotes.

At the end of the contract period, under both methods, the construction-in-progress and advance billings accounts are eliminated. Thus, at contract completion under both methods, the only remaining balance sheet amounts are cash and retained earnings. Both amounts equal $1,200, which is the profit on the contract.

As can be seen from the above table, the **netting** process reduces very large activities to relatively small net amounts on the balance sheet. As Chicago Bridge had total assets of $337 million at December 31, 1999, reporting revenues and billings gross would have greatly increased total assets and liabilities.

Returning to part B of the Justin example, the only difference in the balance sheet effects of the two methods is that, under the percentage-of-completion method, there is an additional accrual of gross profit in construction-in-progress. When there is an excess of advance billings over costs (e.g., 2001), reported total assets are identical under both methods. When construction-in-progress exceeds billings (e.g., 2002), total assets will be higher under the percentage-of-completion method. For all years, liabilities are lower and retained earnings (equity) higher under the percentage-of-completion method, reflecting the higher level of construction-in-progress.

Generalizing these effects for a company with a continuing flow of profitable contracts, under the percentage-of-completion method:

► Total assets are higher, reflecting the accrual of gross profit during the contract period.

► Liabilities are lower as the higher level of construction-in-progress provides a larger offset.

► Stockholders' equity is higher due to the earlier accrual of gross profit.

► The ratio of liabilities to equity is lower, reflecting lower liabilities and higher equity.

Part C shows the impact of a change in estimate: The estimated cost to complete is increased at the end of the second year (2002). This increase is recognized in 2002, and that year's income reflects the income on work completed during the period offset by the impact of the change in estimate. Note that the cumulative income correctly reflects the degree of completion using the revised cost estimate.[20]

Installment Method of Revenue Recognition

Revenues should not be recognized at the time of sale or delivery when there is no reasonable basis to estimate collectibility of the sales proceeds. The installment method recognizes gross profit in proportion to cash collections, resulting in delayed recognition of revenues and expenses as compared with full recognition at the time of sale. This method is sometimes used to report income from sales of noncurrent assets and real estate transactions.

Cost Recovery Method

Revenue recognition on sale or delivery is also precluded when the costs to provide goods or services cannot be reasonably determined, for example, in the development of raw land. This occurs when completion of the sale is dependent on expenditures to be made in the future (e.g., road construction) and it is impossible to estimate the amount of those expenditures (which may depend on zoning or environmental factors).

In many cases, there is also substantial uncertainty about revenue realization since only small down payments may be required with nonrecourse financing provided by the seller. With both future costs and collection uncertain, the cost recovery method requires that all cash receipts be first accounted for as a recovery of costs. Only after all costs are recovered can profit be recognized under this method.[21]

---

[20] The firm has completed two-thirds ($3,600 of costs incurred to date out of total expected costs of $5,400) of the work on the project and at the end of the year will have recognized $400 or two-thirds of expected income of $600 ($200 in 2001 and $200 in 2002).

Similarly, if the firm estimated the remaining cost to complete the project at $2,750 at the end of 2002 (rather than the original $1,200), the expected loss of $350 (on the entire contract) would be recognized in that year. The previously recognized earnings would be offset and the full contract loss would be recognized in 2002, the year in which it can be estimated, even though some of that loss will be incurred in 2003.

[21] When a company markets, sells, or leases software originally developed for internal use, SOP 98-1, Accounting for the Costs of Computer Software Developed for Internal Use, requires the application of the cost recovery method until all unamortized costs have been recovered.

The installment and cost recovery methods may be used to recognize franchise revenues[22] when revenue is collectible over an extended period and there is no reasonable basis to estimate that collectibility. These methods may also be used, under specific circumstances, in real estate sales and retail land sales.[23]

Issues in Revenue and Expense Recognition

While the theoretical basis for revenue and expense recognition appears to be straightforward, the application of these principles has been inconsistent in practice, especially in those areas where GAAP itself lacks definitive standards. Companies have strong incentives to accelerate the recognition of revenues and delay the recording of expense. The significant growth in (1) technology and (2) the use of revenue and gross margin to value companies without earnings have increased the incentives to use accounting methods that increase reported revenues. The result has been new guidelines (a series of consensuses from the Emerging Issues Task Force (EITF) and the U.S. Securities and Exchange Commission). SEC Staff Accounting Bulletin 101, Revenue Recognition in Financial Statements, and Frequently Asked Questions and Answers related to SAB 101[24] forced many companies (including many "old economy" firms) to change their reported revenue and expense.

The accounting issues can be categorized as follows:

1. Revenue recognition
2. Expense recognition
3. Classification

We discuss each of these in turn. The end-of-reading problems illustrate the financial statement effects of some of these accounting methods. While some of these issues relate primarily to technology companies, virtually any company's income statement may be affected.

Revenue Recognition

Some accounting issues affect the amount and/or timing of revenue recognition. Examples include:

▶ Sales incentives (such as discounts or the granting of stock options to customers) to achieve revenue goals. Such incentives may become especially important when a company nears the end of a reporting period and wishes to meet its preannounced revenue goals. In extreme cases, companies may provide rights of return or other privileges that violate the realization principle (and may not be recorded or disclosed to auditors).

▶ Barter arrangements under which a firm provides goods or services to another in exchange for that firm's goods or services. Barter revenues may be recorded at "list prices" rather than the lower prices that would pertain to arm's-length transactions.

▶ Recording license fees or membership fees when an agreement is signed, rather than over the term of the agreement.

---

[22] See SFAS 45, Accounting for Franchise Fee Revenue, para. 6 (FASB, 1981).

[23] See SFAS 66, Accounting for Sales of Real Estate (FASB, 1982).

[24] http://www.sec.gov/info/accountants/sab101faq.htm.

- ► Recording revenues based on estimated usage, even when bills have not been sent out.[25]

- ► Companies that act as agents (e.g., advertising agencies or sales intermediaries) record the gross amount billed as revenue rather than their commission income.

- ► Recognition of all revenue from a contract even when the customer has not yet agreed that the project is fully installed and operational.

- ► Reporting shipping and handling costs charged to customers as revenues.

These and other practices vary among companies, making comparisons of revenue levels and growth difficult. When analysts use revenues to value company shares, the incentive to use accounting methods that maximize reported revenues is very high.

When companies are forced to change their revenue recognition policies, the consequences for shareholders can be dire. Consider the example of MicroStrategy [MSTR], a provider of business software, which was required to restate its operating results for 1997 through 1999. Exhibit 34-2 contains an extract from MSTR's 10-K report, showing the effect of the restatement and explaining the accounting changes. Note the significant changes in revenues (1998 and 1999), net income (all three years), accounts receivable, deferred revenues, and stockholders' equity.

MicroStrategy shares, which reached a price of $333 on March 10, 2000 (ten days prior to announcement of the restatement) fell to less than $17 in late May. One year later the share price was below $4.

Expense Recognition

The following accounting issues affect the amount and/or timing of expense recognition:

- ► Deferral of marketing expenses and sales commissions
- ► Accrual or deferral of the cost of periodic major maintenance projects
- ► Bad debt expense
- ► Warranty expense

Deferral of Marketing Expenses and Sales Commissions. When marketing costs or sales commissions are deferred, reported income increases. While deferred expenses must be recognized sooner or later, the deferral of expenses by growth companies may exceed the recognition of previously deferred costs for extended time periods.

Example 34-2

Sears defers direct marketing expenses associated with catalog and other sales activities. Note 1 states that such capitalized costs rose from $131 million at January 2, 1999 to $180 million at January 1, 2000. If all costs had been expensed, Sears' pretax income would have been $49 million ($180 − $131) lower.

---

[25] Many utility companies report "unbilled revenues" as sales.

EXHIBIT 34-2 **Microstrategy: Restatement for Change in Revenue Recognition Policies**

Notes to Consolidated Financial Statements

(3) Restatement of Financial Statements

Subsequent to the filing of a registration statement on Form S-3 with the SEC which included the Company's audited financial statements for the years ended December 31, 1999, 1998 and 1997 the Company became aware that the timing and amount of reported earned revenues from license transactions in 1999, 1998 and 1997 required revision.

These revisions primarily addressed the recognition of revenue for certain software arrangements which should be accounted for under the subscription method or the percentage of completion method, which spread the recognition of revenue over the entire contract period. For example, when fees are received in a transaction in which the Company is licensing software and also performing significant development, customization or consulting services, the fees should be recognized using the percentage of completion method and, therefore, product license and product support and other services revenue are recognized as work progresses. Revenue from arrangements where the Company provides hosting services is generally recognized over the hosting term, which is generally two to three years. The effect of these revisions is to defer the time in which revenue is recognized for large, complex contracts that combine both products and services. These revisions also resulted in a substantial increase in the amount of deferred revenue reflected on the Company's balance sheet at the end of 1999 and 1998. Additionally, these revisions include the effects of changes in the reporting periods when revenue from certain contracts are recognized. In the course of reviewing its revenue recognition on various transactions, the Company became aware that, in certain instances, the Company had recorded revenue on certain contracts in one reporting period where customer signature and delivery had been completed, but where the contract may not have been fully executed by the Company in that reporting period. The Company subsequently reviewed license agreements executed near the end of the years 1999, 1998 and 1997 and determined that revisions were necessary to ensure that all agreements for which the Company was recognizing revenue in a reporting period were executed by both parties no later than the end of the reporting period in which the revenue is recognized. The total effect of all revisions to revenue was to reduce revenues by $54.0 million, $10.9 million and $1.0 million for the years ended December 31, 1999, 1998 and 1997, respectively.

The Company also made certain revisions to our balance sheet as of December 31, 1999.

Accordingly, such financial statements have been restated as follows:

	1999		1998		1997	
Statements of Operations Data	**Reported**	**Restated**	**Reported**	**Restated**	**Reported**	**Restated**
Revenues:						
Product licenses	$143,193	$85,797	$72,721	$61,635	$36,601	$35,478
Product support and other services	62,136	65,461	33,709	33,854	16,956	17,073
Income (loss) from operations	18,319	(34,533)	9	(2,549)	372	(634)
Provision for income taxes	7,735	1,246	3,442	—	—	—
Net income (loss)	12,620	(33,743)	6,178	(2,255)	121	(885)
Balance sheet data						
Accounts receivable, net	61,149	37,586	33,054	25,377	16,085	15,121
Deferred revenue and advance payments (current and noncurrent)	16,782	71,283	11,478	13,048	9,387	9,429
Retained earnings (deficit)	17,849	(37,953)	5,229	(4,210)	(634)	(1,640)

Source: MicroStrategy 10-K, December 31, 1999.

Expensing Periodic Major Maintenance Projects.   Some fixed assets require periodic major overhauls. Firms can either accrue the costs in advance (and charge the actual expenditure against the accrued liability) or defer recognizing the expense until it is actually incurred. The latter method delays expense recognition, increasing reported earnings.[26] A third alternative is to capitalize the actual expenditure and amortize it against earnings in subsequent years (as will be discussed in Reading 42).

Example 34-3

Airborne Freight [ABF] stated in its 2000 annual report:

Effective January 1, 2000, the Company changed its method of accounting for major engine overhaul costs on DC-9 aircraft from the accrual method to the direct expense method where costs are expensed as incurred. Previously, these costs were accrued in advance of the next scheduled overhaul based upon engine usage and estimates of overhaul costs.

The change resulted in a cumulative effect (for prior periods) of $14.2 million and increased earnings for 2000 by $3.7 million. Adding the two components together, the change accounted for 63% of Airborne's total earnings for the year of $28.5 million.

Bad Debt Expense.   Credit losses affect reported income only indirectly and not at the time they actually occur. The timing of the expense recognition for bad debts and the actual receivable write-off do not coincide. Each year a company makes a provision for bad debt expense reflecting its estimate of the proportion of its credit customers who will default. In making this estimate, the company sets up a reserve for bad debts (allowance for doubtful accounts). When an actual write-off occurs (i.e., it becomes certain that the customer will not pay), the charge is made to the reserve, not earnings.

The procedure is illustrated in the example below. The example also indicates that the estimation process for bad debts can be used to smooth earnings and/or delay the reporting of bad news. Analysts should watch the level of the reserve relative to receivables (considering economic conditions within the industry) as well as the provision against earnings.

Warranty Expenses.   Many firms provide warranties—guarantees to fix or replace defective products. Expense recognition is similar to that of bad debts. GAAP requires that firms estimate the cost of providing warranties, and deduct that expense from income at the time of sale. A corresponding reserve (liability)

---

[26] For example, a company anticipating a $3 million overhaul in three years would, under the accrual method, recognize an expense (and accrued liability of) $1 million in each of the three years in advance of the overhaul. At the time of the overhaul, the $3 million expenditure would reduce the liability. Recognizing the expense only when incurred would result in a $3 million expense in the year of the overhaul and no expense (or liability) in the years leading up to the overhaul.

Example 34-4

Lucent

The Lucent [LU] 1999 financial statements show the following data ($millions):

	September 30 1998	1999
Sales	$31,806	$38,303
Receivables (net of allowance)	7,405	10,438
Allowance for doubtful accounts	416	362
Add back the allowance to get gross receivables	$ 7,821	$10,800
Allowance as % of gross receivables	5.32%	3.35%

There are two red flags here. One is the decline in the allowance relative to gross receivables. The second is the 38% increase in gross receivables, compared with a 1999 sales increase of only 20%.

Lucent's 1999 10-K reveals the following additional data relating to the changes in its bad debt reserve:

	Years Ended September 30 1998	1999
Allowance for doubtful accounts (beginning balance)	363	416
Bad debt expense	132	68
Write-offs	(20)	(159)
Other changes	(59)	37
Allowance for doubtful accounts (ending balance)	416	362

As the above table indicates, the timing of the expense for bad debt and the actual write-off do not coincide. In 1998 Lucent recorded bad debt expense of $132 million, increasing the allowance for doubtful accounts. The actual accounts receivable written off as uncollectible was only $20 million. That amount was not expensed but charged against the reserve.[27] In 1999, the situation reversed, as the amount expensed ($68 million) was considerably less than the amount actually written off ($159 million).

---

[27] Lucent's entries in 1998 were:

Bad debt expense $132		and	Allowance for doubtful accounts	$20
Allowance for doubtful accounts $132			Accounts receivable	$20

> *Lucent reduced its provision for bad debts in 1999 although actual credit losses rose substantially from the 1998 level. Had Lucent made a provision sufficient to bring the allowance relative to gross receivables up to the fiscal 1998 level ($10,800 × .0532 = $575 million), its pretax income would have been ($575 − $362) $213 million (4%) lower.*
>
> It should be noted that in the years 2000 and 2001, Lucent wrote off approximately $1 billion of receivables, evidence that the 1999 year-end provision (of $362 million) was insufficient.
>
> In September 1999, a Lucent subsidiary sold $625 million of accounts receivable to a nonconsolidated entity and the company itself transferred $700 million of accounts receivable as collateral to that entity. Thus, Lucent removed $1,325 million of receivables (but not the related allowance for doubtful accounts).[28] Without these transactions, on September 30, 1999, Lucent's receivables balance would have been $12,125 million (instead of the reported $10,800 million). The actual increase in receivables was 55%, much higher than the 20% increase in sales. The company would have needed an allowance for doubtful accounts balance of $645 million to reflect an allowance comparable to that reported in 1998 and its pretax income would have been ($645 − $362) $283 million (5.4%) lower. *During December 1999, Lucent repurchased $408 million of the $625 million receivables sold in September 1999.*

is set up on the balance sheet.[29] Such estimates are inherently difficult, especially for new products. The analyst should watch the trend in warranty reserves, as they can be used to smooth reported income.

Capitalizing current period expenditures can also reduce reported expenses. Reading 42 discusses the capitalization of interest, research and development, and software development expense.

Classification Issues

Many analysts use gross margin (revenues less cost of goods sold) and gross margin percentage (gross margin as a % of sales) to evaluate companies, especially those that have negative earnings. Some reporting methods boost gross margins without affecting operating income:

▶ Including costs such as discounts and marketing costs as operating expense rather than cost of goods sold

▶ Recording shipping and handling costs (included in revenue) as operating expense rather than cost of goods sold

Classification issues and changes in classification may not be explicitly disclosed in financial statements. However, differences in classification for the same firm over time and among competing firms may distort analyses and comparisons of gross margin levels, percentages, and growth rates.

---

[28] See Reading 46 for our discussion of the financial statement impact of sales of receivables.

[29] The reserve is reduced when an actual warranty cost is incurred.

Example 34-5

AT Cross

AT Cross [ATX] produces pens with a lifetime warranty. In 2000, the company's fourth successive loss year, it reduced its warranty reserve "reflecting lower cost trends among the several factors that impact the company's cost to service the warranty." The data follow ($thousands):

| | Years Ended December 31 | | |
	1998	1999	2000
Sales	$152,783	$126,994	$130,548
Warranty expense	881	720	(761)
% sales	0.6%	0.6%	−0.6%
Warranty reserve			
Opening balance	$ 5,821	$ 5,821	$ 5,821
Expense	881	720	(761)
Costs paid	(881)	(720)	(367)
Closing balance	$ 5,821	$ 5,821	$ 4,693

The accounting change increased operating profit margins by 1.2%. If Cross had recorded sufficient warranty expense to maintain its existing reserve (as in 1998 and 1999), the expense would have been $367,000; if it had accrued expense equal to .6% of sales, the expense would have been $783,000. Either amount would have increased the operating loss further.

The analyst should question companies regarding their revenue and expense recognition practices, and the classification of revenues and expense. Intercompany comparisons may require adjustment for reporting differences.

Software Revenue Recognition

Transactions in the software industry range from the sale or license of a single software product to complex contractual arrangements that involve delivery, significant subsequent production, modification, or customization of the software. The latter complex arrangements generally must be accounted for in accordance with Accounting Research Bulletin (ARB) 45, Long-Term Construction-Type Contracts, and SOP 81-1, Accounting for the Performance of Construction-Type Contracts and Certain Production-Type Contracts.

SOP 97-2, Software Revenue Recognition, and SOP 98-9, Modification of SOP 97-2, Software Revenue Recognition, With Respect to Certain Transactions, apply to software transactions that do not require significant subsequent production, modification, or customization of the software. SOP 97-2 stipulates four criteria that must *all* be satisfied to recognize revenue for single- or multiple-element software transactions:

1. Persuasive evidence of an arrangement

2. Delivery

   3. A fixed or determinable fee

   4. Assurance of collectibility

SOP 97-2 requires that revenue be allocated among the components of a multiple-element arrangement based on fair values of the individual elements. In the absence of fair value data, all revenue must be deferred until completion of the project. However, vendor-specific objective evidence (VSOE)[30] of the fair value of the elements can be used to recognize revenue for individual elements.

   SOP 98-9 amends SOP 97-2 to require the use of the "residual method" of revenue recognition when:

   ▶ VSOE of the fair values of all the undelivered elements is available,

   ▶ VSOE of one or more delivered elements is not available, and

   ▶ All other revenue recognition criteria of SOP 97-2 are met.

The residual method requires that the total fair value of the undelivered elements be deferred; only the excess of the total sales price over the amount deferred is recognized as revenue. SOP 97-2 applies to the subsequent revenue recognition for the undelivered elements.

Illustration.   Assume that a software company agrees to sell a product for $950, including one year of customer support. The company separately sells customer support for $150 a year (providing VSOE for the price of customer support). If the company does not have VSOE for the software, customer support ($150) revenue would be deferred and recognized over the one-year term. Under SOP 98-9, the remaining $800 would be recognized when the software product is delivered (assuming all other requirements of SOP 97-2 are met).

   However, absent VSOE for the customer support price, the entire $950 would be deferred and recognized over the one-year term. The deferral method would apply even if there were VSOE regarding the software product price. In other words, to recognize the revenue related to one or more elements of a multi-element sale, there must be VSOE to support the revenue allocated to the undelivered elements.

Other Issues

The software industry is not the only one that has particular revenue recognition issues. We have examined it at length given its richness and current relevance. Four examples of other industries and situations follow:

   1. In the broadcast industry, television stations buy the rights to show a film for a given period of time. Should the revenue be recognized by the film's owner:

   ▶ When the agreement is signed?

   ▶ When the film is physically transferred to the television station?

   ▶ Over time as the film is shown?

   2. Mortgage issuers charge a fee, *origination points*, that is, in effect, interest paid in advance. Points are not refundable even if the mortgage is repaid before its due date. Should the fee be recognized as income:

   ▶ Over time?

   ▶ At the time of origination?

---

[30] VSOE means the price charged when the element is sold separately or the price established by the vendor for that element.

Example 34-6

Microsoft provides an instructive example of revenue recognition issues in the software industry.[31] Starting in 1996, Microsoft deferred increasing amounts of revenue (designated as unearned revenue), recognizing the deferred revenue in future time periods. The company adopted SOP 97-2 in the fourth quarter of fiscal 1999. Concurrently, Microsoft extended the life cycle of its principal product from two to three years. Maintenance and subscription revenue, based on the average sales prices of each element, are recognized ratably (straight-line basis) over the product's life cycle.

Exhibit 34-3 shows that the company has reported declining revenue growth rates since 1996. The growth rate of cash collections also steadily declined, from 53% in fiscal 1996 to less than 11% in fiscal 2000. However, Microsoft changes accounting methods and estimates as the products mature and as the undelivered components of the products are developed or delivered. Although Microsoft discloses the various components of unearned or deferred revenues, the disclosures do not enable the user to forecast the rate and amount of unearned revenues that will be recognized over the products' life cycles.

EXHIBIT 34-3	Microsoft Corporation					
	Years Ended June 30 (amounts in $millions)					
	1995	**1996**	**1997**	**1998**	**1999**	**2000**
Revenues	$5,937	$8,671	$11,936	$15,262	$19,747	$22,956
Unearned revenue*	69	983	1,601	3,268	5,877	6,177
Recognition of prior period unearned revenue*	(54)	(477)	(743)	(1,798)	(4,526)	(5,600)
Change in accounts receivable			(58)	(341)	(480)	(785)	(1,005)
Cash collections	$5,952	$9,119	$12,453	$16,252	$20,313	$22,528
Cash collections growth rate (%)		53.21%	36.56%	30.51%	24.99%	10.90%
Unearned revenue (year-end balance sheet)	$ 54	$ 560	$ 1,418	$ 2,888	$ 4,239	$ 4,816
Prior period revenue as % of reported revenue		5.50%	6.22%	11.78%	22.92%	24.39%
Reported revenue growth rate (%)		46.05%	37.65%	27.87%	29.39%	16.25%

*From statement of cash flows.

Source: Microsoft *Annual Reports, 1996–2000.*

---

[31] See the footnote on revenue recognition under Accounting Policies in Microsoft's *Annual Report* for the year ended June 30, 2000.

3. An exercise club charges a refundable annual membership fee, payable quarterly. Should revenue be recognized:

   ▶ When the membership is sold?

   ▶ When payments are received?

   ▶ Over one year?

   Should the answer change if payment is made when the contract is signed? What if it is nonrefundable?

4. A company offers price incentives or preferential access to goods to induce customers to purchase future period requirements in advance.[32] The result is an increase in current period revenues. Should all sales be recognized in the current period?

These are but a few examples of complex revenue recognition issues. Others are provided in the problems at the end of this reading. It should be clear, however, that the analyst must have a thorough understanding of the nature of the business and its relationship to revenue recognition. *When valuation is based on revenue or gross margin, pay careful attention to accounting methods that affect these measures, even when net income is unaffected.*

Summary of Revenue Recognition Methods

The preceding sections discuss the conceptual bases and financial statement effects of different revenue recognition methods. The analyst must be aware of the assumptions underlying these methods both for interfirm comparisons and because questionable revenue is a poor predictor of future cash flows.

Furthermore, revenue recognition abuses may also indicate more serious problems. Richard H. Walker, the SEC head of enforcement, stated that:

> . . . the most common type of accounting fraud has been improper recording of revenue. This can occur when a company books revenue for sales that never took place, accelerates or defers revenue to another quarter, or books sales before they are confirmed. . . . Investors have lost billions of dollars in the last few years when companies dropped in market value after restating earnings. . . . [33]

Although the United States has a rich (and growing) body of revenue and expense recognition rules, IAS standards and those of most foreign countries provide little or no guidance. For example, Sir David Tweedie, chairman of the UK Accounting Standards Board, acknowledged the deficiency in UK standards: "It seems ridiculous, we have no rules."[34]

Revenue and expense recognition rules will change as global standard setters respond to the need for improved guidelines. Whichever reporting method is used, the analyst needs to monitor the income statement and its relationship to the cash flow statement. As discussed in the next reading, the statement of cash flows can warn the financial statement user when overly aggressive revenue recognition methods are being used.

---

[32] In 2002, Bristol-Myers [BMY] reported that it had offered sales incentives to wholesalers in 2000 and 2001 that resulted in approximately $1.5 billion of wholesaler inventory buildup. The required inventory workdown significantly reduced earnings in 2002 and 2003.

[33] Interview with Neil Roland of Bloomberg, February 27, 2001.

[34] Quoted in *The Financial Times* (London), December 1, 2000, p. 24. In January 2001, Tweedie became chairman of the reconstituted IASB.

NONRECURRING ITEMS 4

Nonrecurring items affect the analysis of the income- and cash-generating ability of most firms. As companies have increased their effort to explain earnings variations, they have made greater use of the "unusual" and "nonrecurring" labels, especially for items that reduce reported income. Many new economy firms have taken this practice to new depths. These firms often announce *pro forma earnings* amounts that exclude goodwill amortization, stock compensation expense, and other selected accruals. We have previously noted that, when estimating a firm's earning power, analysts should exclude items that are unusual or nonrecurring in nature. However, this does not mean that everything management labels nonrecurring should be ignored. In this section, we discuss the extent to which such items provide useful information and how they should be treated in financial analysis.

Types of Nonrecurring Items

The income statement contains four categories of nonrecurring income:

1. Unusual or infrequent items
2. Extraordinary items
3. Discontinued operations
4. Accounting changes

Unusual or infrequent items are reported "above the line" as part of "income from continuing operations" and are presented on a pretax basis. The other three categories are "below the line," excluded from "income from continuing operations," and presented net of tax.[35] We first describe these classifications and then discuss their analytical implications.

Unusual or Infrequent Items

Transactions or events that are *either unusual in nature or infrequent in occurrence but not both* may be disclosed separately (as a single-line item) as a component of income from continuing operations. These items must be reported pretax in the income statement; the tax impact (or the net-of-tax amount) may be disclosed separately. Common examples are:

▶ Gains or losses from disposal of a portion of a business segment
▶ Gains or losses from sales of assets or investments in affiliates or subsidiaries
▶ Provisions for environmental remediation
▶ Impairments, write-offs, writedowns, and restructuring costs
▶ Expenses related to the integration of acquired companies

Texaco has reported several "special items" every year for the last several years. The 1999 Management Discussion and Analysis (MD&A) reported write-

---

[35] The fact that some nonrecurring items are presented pretax (and included in income from continuing operations) but others are reported after tax (excluded from income from continuing operations) hampers analysis. Attention to detail and a little thought, however, can conquer the inconsistent presentation of nonrecurring items.

downs of assets in both domestic and international business segments and gains (losses) on major assets sales in each year, 1997 through 1999. These amounts were recorded as components of depreciation, **depletion**, and amortization expense. Texaco has also reported:

▶ Reorganizations, restructurings, and employee separation costs

▶ Inventory valuation adjustments

▶ Settlements of royalty valuation issues

▶ Environmental liabilities

The company provides extensive disclosures for the reorganizations, restructurings, and employee separation programs including the amount and location (in the income statement) of the expenses recorded each year, changes in provisions, cash payments made during the year, amounts transferred to long-term obligations, and the remaining obligations at the end of each year. Note that many of these charges should be considered normal operating charges for a company of the size and complexity of Texaco. While it may be helpful for near-term earnings projections for Texaco to disclose these items, we cannot assume that similar items will not appear in future years. In 2000, for example, Texaco again reported **asset impairment** and employee separation costs. Thus, while such disclosures are useful adjuncts to the income statement, the analyst should carefully consider case-by-case whether valuation should be based on earnings that exclude "nonrecurring" items.

The Texaco example shows us that nonrecurring items are not always disclosed as separate line items in the income statement. They may be included in the catchall "other income" classification or may be buried in COGS or SG&A. Both footnote disclosures and the MD&A should be scrutinized for events and transactions that may have had a material impact on earnings, but that management has either chosen to treat as normal, recurring items or classified as nonrecurring transactions or events.

Extraordinary Items

APB 30 (1973) created the U.S. GAAP income statement format discussed earlier. It defines *extraordinary items* as transactions and events that are *unusual in nature and infrequent in occurrence and are material in amount*. Extraordinary items must be reported separately, net of income tax. Firms are also required to report per-share amounts for these items and encouraged to provide additional footnote disclosures. Extraordinary items are intended to be rare; based on APB 30, such events as losses due to a foreign government's expropriation of assets qualify as an extraordinary item, whereas gains or losses on the sale of noncurrent assets do not.

In the early 1970s, high interest rates and an economic recession led firms with depressed profits to refinance low coupon debt, whose market value was below the face amount, with high coupon debt, reporting an accounting gain.[36] SFAS 4 (1975) broadened the classification of extraordinary items by requiring that *gains or losses on qualifying early retirement of debt*[37] be classified as extraordinary.

In April 2002, SFAS 145 rescinded SFAS 4. As a result, gains or losses on the early retirement of debt are extraordinary items only when the requirements of APB 30 are met.

---

[36] See Reading 45 for a comparison of the accounting and economic consequences of refinancing.

[37] Gains and losses on early retirement of debt were considered extraordinary, except for those related to sinking fund requirements (SFAS 4, 1975).

In recent years, firms have refinanced high coupon debt, whose market value exceeded face amount after sharp declines in interest rates, and these debt retirements have resulted in reported extraordinary losses. Of the sample of 600 companies in the 2000 *Accounting Trends and Techniques*, 61 companies reported 62 extraordinary items and 56 (10 at a gain and 45 at a loss) of these represented the early retirement of debt. The other items included casualty losses and gains from asset disposals.

Discontinued Operations

The discontinuation or sale of a component of a business may indicate that it:

▶ Has inadequate or uncertain markets or prospects

▶ Has an unsatisfactory contribution to earnings and cash flows

▶ Is no longer considered by management to be a strategic fit

▶ Can be sold at a significant profit

Operating income from discontinued operations and any gains or losses (net of taxes) from their sale are segregated in the income statement, since these activities will not contribute to future income and cash flows. As in the case of extraordinary items, this segregation makes the reported information more useful for analysis.

A component of business is defined by SFAS 144 (2001) as any business component with separately identifiable operations, assets, and cash flows that has been disposed of or is held for sale. Subsidiaries and investees also qualify as separate components.

To qualify for treatment as discontinued operations, the assets, results of operations, and investing and financing activities of a component must be separable from those of the firm. SFAS 144 states that the separation must be possible physically and operationally, and for financial reporting purposes.

Once management develops or adopts a formal plan for the sale or disposal of a component (the *measurement date*), the operating results of the component are segregated within the income statement. The income statement will report the income or loss from operations of the discontinued component only on a net-of-tax basis. A condensed income statement for the component is usually shown in a footnote. Prior-period income statements are restated as well.

In the period in which a component of an entity is classified as held for sale or has been disposed of, the results of operations of the component and any gain or loss recognized[38] must be reported as discontinued operations in the income statement for current and prior periods.

Pfizer (see Note 2 to 1999 annual report) sold four businesses in 1998, treating them as discontinued operations. The significant effects include:

▶ The 1997 balance sheet shows a single line item—net assets of discontinued operations.

▶ The revenues and expenses of the discontinued operations have been removed from the income statement. The operating earnings from these

---

[38] A component classified as held for sale must be reported at the lower of its carrying amount or fair value less cost to sell. A loss must be recognized for any initial or subsequent writedown to fair value less cost to sell. Subsequent gain recognition is limited to the cumulative loss recognized. Only a previously unrecognized gain or loss must be recognized on date of sale or disposal.

businesses are combined with the net gain on disposal as earnings from discontinued operations, reported separately on the income statement. Note 2 contains a summarized income statement for these operations.

▶ The operating cash flow from discontinued businesses is *not* shown separately.[39]

Accounting Changes

Accounting changes fall into two general categories: those undertaken voluntarily by the firm and those mandated by new accounting standards. Generally, accounting changes do not have direct cash flow consequences.

The change from one acceptable accounting method to another acceptable method is reported in the period of change. Any cumulative impact on *prior period* earnings is reported net of tax after extraordinary items and discontinued operations on the income statement.[40] Firms are required to provide footnote disclosure of the impact of the change on current period operations (and on each prior period, if restated) and their justification for the change. However, accounting changes also affect future operating results. That impact is rarely disclosed but can sometimes be estimated. Accounting changes are dealt with frequently in the remaining readings of the text.

APB 20 (1971) identifies four exceptions to the general treatment of accounting changes. These are:

1. Change from LIFO to another inventory method (see Reading 40)
2. Change to or from the full cost method (see Reading 41)
3. Change to or from the percentage-of-completion method
4. Change in accounting methods prior to an initial public offering

These exceptions require retroactive restatement of all years presented.

Example 34-7

In 1999, Lucent changed its method for calculating the market-related value of pension plan assets. The cumulative (net-of-tax) effect of the accounting change was $1,308 million (net of income taxes of $842 million) or $0.42 per diluted share, shown as a separate line item in the income statement. Note 10, Employee Benefit Plans, also reports that the accounting change increased reported 1999 income by $260 million (net of taxes of $167) or $0.08 per diluted share. Lucent reported 1999 net income of $1.52 per diluted share of which nearly one-third ($0.50 per diluted share) came from this accounting change.

---

[39] Separate disclosure of the cash flows from discontinued operations is optional under U.S. GAAP. However, IAS 35 (1998) requires (para. 6) separate disclosure of "the net cash flows attributable to the operating, investing, and financing cash flows of the discontinuing operation."

[40] In most cases, prior period results are not restated. The cumulative impact is computed under the assumption that the new method had been used in all past periods and is therefore the difference between reported income and what income would have been if the new method had been applied.

In some cases, prior period results are restated; the portion of the cumulative impact applicable to periods preceding those for which an income statement is presented is shown as an adjustment to retained earnings.

Prior Period Adjustments

A change from an incorrect to an acceptable accounting method is treated as an error, and its impact is reported as a *prior period adjustment*. On occasion, newly available information clarifies transactions that were accounted for in prior periods. In some cases, the appropriate adjustment is not reported as a component of current period income, but recorded directly to retained earnings. SFAS 16, Prior Period Adjustments, restricts this treatment to accounting errors. In most cases, however, these adjustments are included in reported income of the period in which the new information becomes available.

IAS Standards for Nonrecurring Items

IAS 8 (revised 1993) governs the treatment of nonrecurring items under IAS GAAP. While these standards are similar to U.S. GAAP, there are several significant differences:

▶ The IAS definition of extraordinary differs slightly from the U.S. definition, allowing for the possibility of different treatments of the same item.

▶ IAS 8 does not require the separate presentation of earnings from continuing operations, earnings from discontinued operations, and income before extraordinary items.

▶ For accounting changes, IAS 8 permits *either* the cumulative change method *or* the restatement of prior periods.[41]

▶ Errors can be corrected by *either* restating prior periods *or* including the item in current period results.

IAS 35 (1998), which provides standards for discontinued operations, also differs slightly from U.S. GAAP. The most important differences are:

▶ IAS GAAP requires the estimated losses from a discontinued unit to be reported as incurred, rather than accrued as under U.S. GAAP.

▶ Impairment losses associated with discontinued operations may be reported as part of the loss from continued operations under IAS GAAP, even if recognized prior to the announcement date.

▶ Under IAS 35, the "discontinuation" date may differ from that under SFAS 144.

Example 34-8

In 1999, Roche announced plans to spin off its flavors and fragrances division, Givaudan (see Note 7 to Roche annual report). Yet the results of Givaudan are included in the Roche income statement for 1999 and its assets and liabilities remain on Roche's December 31, 1999 balance sheet. Givaudan's operating results and cash flows were included in those of Roche through the spinoff date (June 8, 2000).

---

[41] IAS standards do not require the restatement of prior period results in deference to the prohibition against restatement in the GAAP of many countries.

Analysis of Nonrecurring Items

The preceding discussion of unusual items, extraordinary items, and discontinued operations illustrates the difficulty presented by nonrecurring items. Accounting standard setters cannot draw "bright lines" that are adequate to separate clearly unusual items. In practice, gains tend to be buried in continuing operations, whereas losses are often shown separately; disclosure is not always sufficient. In some cases, the MD&A provides more information about unusual items than the financial statements themselves.

When estimating a firm's "earning power," analysts normally exclude items that are unusual or nonrecurring in nature. Yet such events seem to recur, more so in some companies than others. Some companies seem to be "accident prone," although each "accident" is different. Nonrecurring items are not all alike. Although the sale of assets, divisions, or segments may not be part of continuing operations, such sales may recur, albeit sporadically. Recurring and nonrecurring are not two distinct categories but rather a continuum. The objective, therefore, is to place each item in its appropriate place on the spectrum. *When determining the earnings amount used for firm valuation, the analyst must classify income and expenses between operating and nonrecurring using the preceding discussion rather than relying on the classification provided by the company.*

Income Statement Impact of Nonrecurring Items

The current period income statement effect of nonrecurring items is generally clearly stated. However, such items also have implications for previously reported income and future earnings.

Some nonrecurring items are, in effect, a correction of prior period income. A common example is asset writedowns, frequently included in "restructuring" provisions. Such writedowns suggest that prior period depreciation or amortization changes were insufficient and reported income for these periods was overstated. The recognition of liabilities for environmental remediation is another indication that prior year earnings were overstated.

Asset impairment and "restructuring" charges result in increases in future reported income. To the extent that assets are written down, future depreciation and amortization expense will be lower than would otherwise have been the case. The accrual of future lease rental expense and employee severance costs also affects future earnings, which will no longer be saddled with these costs. The restructuring charges recorded by Texaco contain asset writedowns that reflect on both past and future reported earnings.

These implications for previous and future earnings must be carefully considered. *If nonrecurring charges are really prior year expenses taken too late or future expenses charged off early, then the practice of ignoring nonrecurring charges and focusing on recurring operating income results in an overestimation of the firm's earnings trend.*

Some commentators have criticized the ever-increasing spate of restructurings and special charges (e.g., Texaco reports several in each of the years 1997 to 2000) as being motivated by the desire to paint a better earnings picture:

> How can repeated write-offs be nonrecurring or extraordinary? *How can investors believe that reported earnings are real and won't be canceled by subsequent write-offs?* . . .
> Here's how this kind of charge can boost earnings. Say Company XYZ reports rising profits of $1 million in year 1 and $1.2 million in year 2; in year 3, XYZ takes a restructuring charge of $5 million for the cost of closing a few businesses. The charge turned year 3's net into a loss of $3.5 million—but XYZ says profit would have been $1.5 million before the charge. The next year, year 4, the upward trend resumes as XYZ reports profits of $1.8 million. But the results are helped because $2 million of the company's year 4 expenses—say, for severance

payments and plant closings—can be counted against the charge already taken in year 3. . . .

> *The most obvious way restructuring charges make companies' earnings look better is if the companies can convince investors that operating earnings—before the charges—provide a more meaningful indication of trends. . . .*

Wall Street analysts often use some version of operating earnings—not counting charges—to track a company's earnings trend. Thus, many analysts and research services that follow AT&T show a tidy growth track for the company: $3.13 a share for 1994, $3.45 for 1995, and $3.95 for 1996. But that doesn't include AT&T's 1995 charges of $5.4 billion, or $3.35 a share. . . . [42]

We believe that the need to assess "nonrecurring" charges has increased since these words were written. Moreover, the increased use of pro forma earnings for valuation purposes (discussed in Box 34-4) has made these issues even more pressing.

BOX 34-4   PRO FORMA EARNINGS

An increasing number of companies are reporting pro forma earnings in press releases announcing their earnings before filing quarterly reports with the SEC. Companies use varying definitions of "pro forma earnings" and some companies report more than one category of such earnings. Unlike GAAP-based earnings, pro forma earnings exclude one or more of the following expenses and gains or losses:

- ▶ Goodwill amortization
- ▶ Other intangible-asset amortization
- ▶ Stock-compensation expense
- ▶ Writedowns of impaired assets
- ▶ Restructuring charges
- ▶ Severance pay and early or involuntary termination benefits
- ▶ Interest expense
- ▶ Marketing expenses
- ▶ Results of Internet operations (and other wholly or majority-owned subsidiaries, and equity-method investees)
- ▶ Gain or loss on sale of stock in subsidiaries, investees, or other affiliates

Companies have advanced several reasons to justify reporting pro forma earnings:

- ▶ Users of financial statements and analysts prefer "cash earnings" that exclude amortization of goodwill and other noncash charges.
- ▶ Management's breakdown of earnings and cash flows enhances the transparency of financial statements and is more informative.
- ▶ Restructuring charges, impairments, and other one-time or nonrecurring charges are not relevant as they are not expected to contribute to future earnings and cash flows.
- ▶ The results of operations of Internet operations and other subsidiaries or affiliates may not be relevant if the company plans to spin off the operations at some unspecified or uncertain future date.

(continued)

OPTIONAL SEGMENT BEGINS

---

[42] Quotations are excerpted from "Are Companies Using Restructuring Costs to Fudge the Figures?: A Repeated Strategic Move Makes Future Earnings Seem Unrealistically Rosy," *Wall Street Journal* (January 30, 1996), emphasis added.

BOX 34-4   *(continued)*

The SEC has expressed concern about but has no authority to specify what companies say in press releases. Unfortunately, some analysts have acceded to management demands to forecast pro forma earnings rather than GAAP-based earnings.

In 2001, Financial Executives International (FEI) proposed guidelines for press releases intended to reflect best practices and reduce abusive practices.

Example 34-9

In a January 30, 2001 press release, Amazon.com announced its fourth quarter 2000 results, with the following headline:

**Fourth-Quarter 2000 Pro Forma Operating Loss Improves
from 26 Percent to 6 Percent of Net Sales**

The release reported a pro forma operating loss for the fourth quarter of 2000 of $60 million, or 6% of net sales. The reported pro forma net loss was $90 million. Later in the press release the company reported that its fourth-quarter GAAP loss from operations was $322 million and the GAAP-based net loss was $545 million, including charges of $339 million for impairment of goodwill and equity investments. Stock-based compensation charges and equity in losses of equity-method investees were among the other items excluded from the pro forma operating loss.

When a company has truly nonrecurring gains or losses, or has made a large acquisition or divestiture, data that remove the effects of these distortions may be very informative. However, in most cases, the reporting of pro forma operating results is an effort to persuade analysts to ignore certain expenses or categories of expense and thereby improve the valuation of the firm's securities. Thus it is important to cast a skeptical eye on such reports; the analyst should use reported GAAP data (after appropriate adjustments by the analyst) for valuation decisions.

Cash Flow and Valuation Impact

Nonrecurring items with cash flow consequences do affect the wealth of the firm. However, they should still be segregated because their valuation implications differ from those for recurring income. As outlined in Box 34-4, (true) nonrecurring components of income have only a onetime dollar-for-dollar effect on valuation, whereas the multiple for changes in recurring income (the price-earnings multiple) is greater.

The analyst must distinguish among items that:

▶ Have no cash flow implications (e.g., asset writedowns)

▶ Affect current period cash flow only (e.g., employee severance costs)

▶ Have future cash flow effects (e.g., lease payments for closed facilities)

Careful attention must be paid to footnote disclosures to ascertain the cash flow effects of "restructuring" provisions in particular. In some cases, the cash drain from such provisions extends years into the future.

The 1995 pretax business restructuring charges of $2,467 million and asset impairment and other charges of $188 million reported by Lucent are a good example of the continuing income and cash flow consequences of such announcements. Its 1999 annual report shows deductions from business restructuring reserves, noncash charges, and cash payments continuing through fiscal 1999. In 1999, Lucent reversed $141 million of the business restructuring charges due to favorable experience in employee separation and lower costs of other restructuring projects announced in 1995.

Implications for Continuing Operations

Nonrecurring events, even those without cash flow effects, may also provide useful information about the firm. A plant closing and the write-off of its book value are one example. The actual cash outflows occurred in the past and are only now being expensed. The value implication of the gain or loss reported on the income statement may be nonexistent. The plant closing itself may, however, help forecast the firm's future sales, earnings, and cash flows. Similarly, Lucent's 1995 restructuring charge included employee severance costs. Future reported earnings should be higher than previously expected because its employment costs are reduced. The reduced number of employees also will affect benefit accruals.

Management Discretion and Earnings Manipulation

When estimating earnings trends, the analyst must also be wary of the discretionary nature of the income statement. Items requiring separate disclosure on the income statement may be discretionary with respect to the:

► Timing of the occurrence (e.g., the disposal of an asset or the discontinuation of a segment)
► Classification of the item (ordinary, unusual, or extraordinary)

In addition, changes in accounting methods can alter reported income statement trends. In many cases, there is no disclosure (except in the aggregate) of the effects of the accounting change on income reported in individual prior periods, making adjustment difficult.

The discretionary nature of income recognition permits an examination of the degree of management manipulation of earnings under one or more of the following guises:

► Classification of good news/bad news
► Income smoothing
► Big-bath behavior
► Accounting changes

Classification of Good News/Bad News. Management prefers to report good news "above the line" as part of continuing operations and bad news "below the line" as extraordinary or discontinued operations. For example, management determines whether the component of the firm sold meets the definition of a discontinued operation and hence is given below-the-line treatment as income from discontinued operations. As SFAS 131 notes, the

> management approach (to segmentation) is based on the way the management organizes the segments within the enterprise for making operating decisions and assessing performance.[43]

This discretion permits management to report unusual items most favorably.[44]

Income Smoothing.   Some firms reduce earnings in good years (defer gains or recognize losses) and inflate earnings in bad years (recognize gains or defer losses) in order to report stable earnings. Empirical evidence indicates that managements can and do engage in such behavior by engaging in two types of smoothing. *Intertemporal smoothing* refers to either:

▶ Timing expenditures such as research and development, repairs and maintenance, and asset disposals, or

▶ Choosing accounting methods (e.g., capitalization or expensing) that allocate the expenditure over time.

Classificatory smoothing is smoothing by choosing to classify an item as either income from continuing operations, or extraordinary income. The implicit assumption is that analysts focus on ordinary income and ignore nonrecurring/extraordinary items. Thus, by shifting items above or below the line, management can report a desired trend.

Asset sales are an example of a nonrecurring item that has been used as both an intertemporal and classificatory smoothing instrument. Bartov (1993) showed that such sales have been *timed* to smooth income. Furthermore, as there is discretion in how a segment is defined, the sale of a portion of a business can be classified as part of continuing operations or as a discontinued operation. Fried et al. (1996) showed that the *classification* choices made by their sample of firms were consistent with smoothing.

Ronen and Sadan (1981) have argued that smoothing is not necessarily bad. Rather, by engaging in smoothing, management may be aiding the predictive ability of reported earnings by conveying information about the future prospects of the firm. Moses (1987) made similar arguments. Possible incentives for earnings manipulation are varied [see the discussion in Bartov (1993) and the survey paper by Healy and Wahlen (1999)] and not necessarily limited to the desire to show stable earnings and/or aid predictive ability. A number of authors [e.g., Healy (1985), Holthausen et al. (1995), and Gaver et al. (1995)] examined executive bonus plans and showed that depending on the structure of such plans, management may be motivated to engage in discretionary accruals, manipulating earnings in an upward or downward direction. Jones (1991) showed that firms that would benefit from import relief (e.g., tariff increases and quota reductions) decrease income through earnings manipulation in order to influence the U.S. International Trade Commission. Bartov, on the other hand, demonstrated that firms attempt to manipulate earnings in an upward direction in order to escape possible restrictions imposed by their bond covenant agreements.

---

[43] SFAS 131, para. 4.

[44] Rapacciolli and Schiff (1991) show that in their sample of about 500 disposals, approximately 60% of the cases were accorded the more favorable treatment, with 61% of gains reported above the line and 57% of losses reported below the line.

More recently, research has focused on earnings management geared to meet (or just beat) analysts' expectations. Burgstahler and Eames (1998) found that managers manage earnings upward to avoid missing analyst expectations.[45] In this spirit, Bradshaw, Moberg, and Sloan (2000) broaden the definition of earnings management to include "management of the 'perception' of earnings" and argue that managers have taken earnings management a step further by encouraging analysts to focus on (management defined) pro forma earnings (discussed in Box 34-4) rather than GAAP earnings.

Big-Bath Accounting.   In contrast to income smoothing, the big-bath hypothesis suggests that management will report additional losses in bad years in the hope that, by taking all available losses at one time, they will "clear the decks" once and for all. The implicit assumption is that future reported profits will increase.

This hypothesis is more widely accepted in the financial press than in the academic literature. Francis, Hanna, and Vincent (1996) and Elliott and Shaw (1988) found that analyst forecasts following large write-offs are not consistent with the big-bath theory. Rather than increasing following a write-off, indicating a clearing of the deck, forecast earnings tended to decrease. Fried et al. (1989) reported that a firm taking an asset writedown in one year is likely to take another one soon after. This is inconsistent with big-bath behavior, which argues that firms would overestimate rather than underestimate the size and amounts of write-offs.[46]

Accounting Changes.   Regardless of whether accounting changes are voluntary or mandatory, they typically have no direct cash flow consequences for a U.S. company.[47] Thus, such changes can be viewed as a form of earnings manipulation. Empirical research has studied accounting changes extensively, focusing on both managerial motivations and stock market reaction. We shall refer to many of these studies in later readings.

Elliott and Philbrick (1990) examined the effects of accounting changes on earnings predictability. Not surprisingly, they found that analysts had difficulty forecasting earnings for the year of the change. That difficulty was more pronounced for mandatory changes, for which there was no prior information regarding the change. Moreover, they found that when analysts had no prior information about the change, the effect of the accounting change tended to be in the *opposite* direction of forecast revisions made by analysts in the latter part of the fiscal year (fourth quarter). For example, accounting changes that *increased* income were associated with *downward* forecast revisions; that is, when income was lower than originally expected (causing downward forecast revisions), accounting changes were adopted that raised reported income. This behavior, the authors concluded, was consistent with management's use of accounting changes to manipulate or smooth earnings.

Quality of Earnings

The term "quality of earnings" is used in two different senses. We use it to mean the use of accounting methods and assumptions that tend not to overstate reported revenues and earnings. The discussion of revenue and expense recognition earlier in this reading should already have provided a sense of how accounting methods and assumptions can affect reported operating results.

---

[45] Similar evidence was found by Kaznick (1999) with respect to meeting management's own earnings forecasts.

[46] See the discussion of impairment in Reading 43 for more details of these results.

[47] The FIFO to LIFO change is the major exception in the United States (see Reading 39).

However, some use the term to indicate consistency of reported earnings (lack of volatility). The two meanings are somewhat contradictory. Firms that report "consistent" earnings growth often do so by managing earnings in ways that the external analyst cannot see. Earnings management may include the use of aggressive accounting assumptions when required to meet analyst expectations. Companies that stretch the financial reporting system to meet unattainable expectations may also cross the line into financial fraud. Companies that use conservative methods are unlikely to commit fraud, as they can change accounting methods and assumptions first.

5   THE BALANCE SHEET

The balance sheet (statement of financial position) reports the categories and amounts of assets (firm resources), liabilities (claims on those resources), and stockholders' equity at specific points in time. In the United States, balance sheets are generally issued at the end of each quarter and the end of the fiscal year; outside of the United States, annual or semiannual reporting is the general rule.

Format and Classification

The definitions of assets, liabilities, and stockholders' equity are discussed in Reading 1. We now discuss the format and classification prevalent in most companies. IAS standards are similar to those used by firms in the United States. Box 34-5 lists and discusses Pfizer's balance sheet components.

Assets and liabilities are classified according to liquidity, that is, their expected use in operations or conversion to cash in the case of assets and time to maturity for liabilities. Assets expected to be converted to cash or used within one year (or one operating cycle, if longer than one year) are classified as current assets. Current liabilities include obligations the firm expects to settle within one year (or one operating cycle, if longer).

Assets expected to provide benefits and services over periods exceeding one year and liabilities to be repaid after one year are classified as **long-term assets** and liabilities. **Tangible assets** and liabilities are generally reported before intangibles and other assets and liabilities whose measurement is less certain.

This classification scheme can be used to develop ratios employed in financial analysis. The current–noncurrent distinction can be used to measure liquidity, for example. In recent years, however, that distinction has become somewhat arbitrary as differences between short-term and long-term investments and debt are sometimes difficult to discern.

The most liquid assets, cash and cash equivalents, precede marketable equity securities, receivables, inventories, and prepaid expenses in the current asset section of the balance sheet. Long-lived assets, including property, plant, and equipment, investments in affiliated companies, and intangible assets such as brand names, patents, copyrights, and goodwill, are reported as noncurrent assets.

Short-term bank and other debt, the current portion of long-term debt and capitalized leases, accounts payable to suppliers, accrued liabilities (amounts owed to employees and others), interest, and taxes payable are classified as current liabilities. Long-term debt, capitalized lease obligations, pension obligations, and other "liabilities" (such as deferred income taxes and minority interest in the net assets of consolidated affiliates) are commonly observed noncurrent liabilities.

Stockholders' equity (the residual interest in the firm) lists components in order of their priority in liquidation with any preference (preferred) stock listed before common stock, Treasury stock, and reinvested earnings. This section may also include the additional components shown in Box 34-5.

Measurement of Assets and Liabilities

Most components of the balance sheet are reported at historical cost, that is, the exchange price at their acquisition date. As noted earlier in this reading, in the discussion of the accrual concept of income, the nature (and amount) of a recognized asset is a function of the firm's revenue recognition method.

In some cases (e.g., accounts receivable), valuation allowances (reserve for uncollectible receivables) adjust the originally recorded amount to an approximation of net realizable value. The reserve for uncollectibles is an estimate of bad debts, reported as a deduction from the gross receivables balance; this is called a *contra* account. (Accumulated depreciation is also a contra account since it reduces the carrying value of long-lived assets to reflect their use.)

Changes in some other assets or liabilities are accumulated in *adjunct* accounts, such as the premium on bonds payable that records the excess of the bond's issue price over its face value. These contra and adjunct accounts allow firms to report both the original, historical cost (e.g., gross plant assets) and the net carrying amount (plant assets net of accumulated depreciation). They also reflect management's estimate of realizable values of the underlying assets, for example, receivables net of the allowance for uncollectibles. However, these are accounting estimates of net realizable values and not market values.[48]

Lower of cost or market and impairment rules[49] may, however, require writedowns to fair or market values when they are below cost. In most cases, however, market values are not reflected in the balance sheet prior to realization, and recoveries (reversal of previous writedowns) to the original acquisition cost are not allowed under U.S. GAAP.[50] The exception to this rule is the accounting for investments in securities.[51]

Finally, the assets and liabilities of foreign affiliates or those denominated in other currencies are reported at amounts translated from other currencies at the exchange rate prevailing on the financial statement date or a combination of this current rate and specific historical rates for certain components.

The balance sheet does not report all assets and liabilities of the firm, but reflects only those meeting specific recognition criteria.[52] Some assets and liabilities meet these criteria, but are not reported because they cannot be reliably measured (see the discussion of contingencies in Reading 33).

---

[48] The level and trend of the allowance for uncollectible receivables may, however, help assess the market value of receivables, as well as the firm's credit policies and revenue recognition method.

[49] See Reading 43.

[50] Under IASB standards, however, writedowns of fixed and intangible assets can be written back up to the original carrying amount if conditions change (see Reading 43).

[51] Companies also record acquired assets and liabilities at fair market value when the purchase method is used.

[52] SFAC 5, Recognition and Measurement in Financial Statements of Business Enterprises (FASB 1984), requires financial statement recognition when four basic criteria are met:

Definition. The item qualifies as an element (e.g., asset or liability) of financial statements.

Measurability. It can be reliably measured.

Relevance. The information provided by the item can make a difference in user decisions.

Reliability. The information is representationally faithful, verifiable, and neutral.

Recognition is subject to cost/benefit and materiality constraints.

BOX 34-5   PFIZER, INC. BALANCE SHEET COMPONENTS

Although every firm's financial statements are unique, we can use Pfizer's 1997–1999 balance sheets* to review the components of the balance sheet. These components are discussed in greater detail in various readings as listed below:

Assets	Curriculum Reading
Cash and cash equivalents	36
Investments and Loans	NA
Accounts receivable	34
Inventories	40
Deferred income taxes	44
Prepaid expenses	34
Deferred taxes	44
Current assets	NA
Net assets of discontinued operations	34
Fixed assets	42
(Accumulated depreciation)	43
Capital leases	46
Investments in affiliates	NA
Prepaid pension costs	NA
Intangible assets†	42

Liabilities	
Accounts payable	NA
Income tax liability	44
Advance billings	34
Current liabilities	45
Debt—short- and long-term	45
Capital leases	46
Pensions and other postretirement benefits	NA
Deferred income tax	44
Minority Interests	NA
Stockholders' equity	34
Cumulative translation adjustment	NA
Minimum pensions liability	NA
Unrealized gains and losses	NA
Treasury stock	34

In the discussion that follows, all "Note" references are to the financial statement footnotes of Pfizer.

(continued)

BOX 34-5   *(continued)*

Assets

SFAS 95 defines *cash and cash equivalents* as risk-free assets with original maturities of 90 days or less. Examples include bank accounts, U.S. Treasury Bills, and similar assets. The net change in cash and cash equivalents for the period is reported in the statement of cash flows. Other investments (Note 4-A), which do not meet the criteria for reporting as cash equivalents, are shown separately (broken out into short-term and long-term components).

Accounts receivable may contain both trade receivables (which may include loans to customers) and notes receivable (e.g., from asset sales or loans to management). The distinction is important. Trade receivables are a result of credit sales of products and services and they are important indicators of liquidity and the soundness of revenue recognition methods. The maturity and collectibility of notes receivable may have important implications for the future cash flow and the liquidity of the firm. As Pfizer shows loans separately, its accounts receivable may be trade-only.

The accounting method used for *inventories* (Notes 1-C and 6) can significantly affect the measurement of this important operating asset as well as the level and trend of reported income. As noted in Box 34-3, Pfizer wrote off $310 million of excess inventories of a suspended drug and it switched to the first-in, first-out inventory costing method in 1999, recording a pretax benefit of $6.6 million.

Deferred income taxes represent deferred tax debits. Note 9 provides details regarding the firm's income tax position. Prepaid expenses and taxes (some companies use the "other current assets" caption) may include prepaid expenses such as tax and insurance prepayments, items that will be reported as expenses in future income statements.

Total current assets include all of Pfizer's assets that are expected to generate cash (or reduce cash outflows) within one year or one operating cycle. However, most of these assets revolve; new receivables and inventories arise as old ones are used in the manufacturing process and turned into cash. Thus, current assets alone are not a forecast of future cash flow.

As required by U.S. GAAP, Pfizer shows the assets of discontinued operations net of liabilities.

Property, plant, and equipment (PPE) is the largest asset category for many industrial and manufacturing companies. The stated amount is a function of accounting policies regarding the capitalization, depreciation, and impairment. Note 7 contains a breakdown of Pfizer's fixed assets and Note 11 tells us that a small amount of operating properties have been leased. Assets under operating leases are not included in the PPE totals; Note 11 provides data on Pfizer's operating leases.

We assume that Pfizer has included prepaid pension cost (Note 10) in its "other assets, deferred taxes, and deferred charges" category. Pfizer reports *goodwill and other acquired intangibles* reflecting the excess of the purchase price over the fair value of identifiable net assets acquired in purchase method business acquisitions.

"Other assets, deferred taxes, and deferred charges" may contain long-term deferred tax debits, investments in securities, and intangible assets such as goodwill. Unlike some firms, Pfizer does not provide complete footnote disclosure of the components of this category, although Note 9 does report the location of all deferred tax accruals.

Liabilities

Total current liabilities include *accounts payable* (trade payables represent amounts owed to the suppliers of operating assets such as inventories), *payroll and benefit-related liabilities* (obligations to employees for services received), debt maturing within one year (amounts expected to be repaid during the next year; see Notes 4-B and C), and the relatively significant (15% of current liabilities) other current liabilities.

(continued)

BOX 34-5   *(continued)*

Note 10 provides necessary detail for *postretirement and benefit-related liabilities.* *Long-term debt* (Notes 4-C and 11 for operating leases) reflects amounts to be paid after one year. Note 9 lists the sources of *deferred income taxes—net*, and the poorly explained *other noncurrent liabilities* rounds out the long-term liabilities.

Stockholders' Equity

Pfizer has authorized but never issued *preferred stock*. When issued, preferred stock would represent a claim senior to that represented by the outstanding *common stock*. The *additional paid-in capital* and common stock in total represent the total amount received by the firm from issuance or other sales of stock. Pfizer reports adjustments to additional paid-in capital due to employee stock option and benefit trust transactions. Pfizer, as most companies, separately reports Treasury stock, representing expenditures incurred to repurchase common stock. Pfizer also reports shares held by its employee benefit trusts (Note 14).

Retained earnings report the accumulated earnings that were not paid as dividends to stockholders. For most companies, the distinction between these three components of capital is unimportant. In rare cases, however, a low level of (or absence of) retained earnings may affect the firm's ability to declare dividends or the tax treatment of those dividends. The *employee benefit trusts* reflects transactions with or commitments to those plans.

Accumulated other comprehensive income (loss) includes (Note 5):

▶ Foreign currency translation adjustment,

▶ Minimum pension liability, and

▶ Unrealized holding gains (or losses) on investments carried at market value.

---

* Pfizer reports three consecutive balance sheets, facilitating analysis. Most companies report only two years.

† Not shown in these years.

Some intangible assets have extremely uncertain or hard-to-measure benefits, for example, customer lists or brand names, and they are recognized only when acquired in a purchase method acquisition. Others, such as research and development, are never recognized as assets under U.S. GAAP. Similarly, liabilities may exist as a result of legal action, but because they are not reliably measurable, only footnote disclosure may be required (see, e.g., Note 18 on litigation in Pfizer's 1999 financial statements).

Thus, a balance sheet does not report the market value of a firm's assets, liabilities, or equity, although the information provided can be useful when estimating the market value of the firm or its securities.

Uses of the Balance Sheet

The reported balance sheet is one starting point for the analysis of a firm. It provides information about a firm's resources (assets) and obligations (liabilities), including liquidity and solvency. For creditors, the balance sheet provides information about the nature of assets that the firm uses as debt collateral.

The balance sheet also reports on a firm's earnings-generating ability in two ways. First, assets are defined as economic resources that are expected to provide future benefits. Consistent with the long-run going concern perspective of the firm, these future benefits are not only cash flows but also the ability to generate earnings.

Receivables are forecasts of cash collections. Fixed assets and inventory, on the other hand, are assets that generate future sales. Increases and decreases in such assets assist forecasts of the firm's sales and profitability.

Second, proper evaluation of a firm's profitability must consider the amount of resources, that is, the level of investment, required for a specified level of sales or profitability. The balance sheet provides such data and (together with the income statement) can be used to measure the efficiency of a firm's operations and its return on investment.

The balance sheet can also generate forecasts about a firm's future cash flow needs. The asset levels needed to generate certain operating levels as well as the age of the firm's assets are useful inputs in assessing when a firm may have to replace its assets.

Finally, the reported balance sheet is the starting point for the preparation of an adjusted balance sheet and book value using current cost data.

Limitations of the Balance Sheet.   The usefulness of the balance sheet is limited by the following three factors:

1. *Selective reporting*. Important assets and liabilities may be omitted from the balance sheet because GAAP does not require their inclusion. One example is operating leases and other off-balance-sheet financing techniques (see Reading 46). Some included assets may have no economic value.

2. *Measurement*. Some assets and liabilities are carried at historical cost, others at market value. Historical costs may bear little relationship to their real market value. Inventories (Reading 40) and long-lived assets (Reading 42) are good examples.

3. *Delayed recognition*. GAAP permits companies to delay recognition of value changes. An important example is employee benefit plans.

Fortunately, footnote and supplementary data are often used by analysts to adjust reported balance sheets and thereby improve their usefulness. Starting with Reading 40, we discuss the adjustments that can be made to prepare a current cost balance sheet that provides a better measure of a firm's resources and obligations.

STATEMENT OF STOCKHOLDERS' EQUITY   6

This statement reports components of stockholders' equity or the investment of the owners in the firm, the earnings reinvested in the business, and various accounting adjustments that reflect selected market value changes in certain investments in securities, any minimum pension liability, certain unrealized gains and losses on cash flow hedges, and the effect of exchange rate changes on certain foreign subsidiaries. U.S. and IAS GAAP have similar requirements for the presentation of stockholders' equity.

Format, Classification, and Use

Companies generally report components of stockholders' equity in order of preference upon liquidation. For each class of shares, firms report the number of shares authorized, issued, and outstanding at each balance sheet date.

Preferred (preference) stock has priority for liquidation and dividends. Common characteristics and related disclosure requirements include but are not limited to:

▶ Cumulative rights to dividends that may be:
  ▶ Fixed.
  ▶ Floating rate.
  ▶ Tied to amounts declared for common stock.
▶ Callable by issuer; call price must be disclosed.
▶ Convertible into common stock at option of holder; specified prices must be disclosed.
▶ Mandatory conversion into common shares at a specified date or under certain conditions; terms must be disclosed.

These features must be evaluated to determine the treatment of different classes of preferred stock in the analysis of leverage, capital structure, and earnings per share.

Redeemable preferred stock is redeemable at the option of the holder or according to a fixed time schedule. Such issues must be excluded from stockholders' equity, and reported after liabilities but before the equity section of the balance sheet.[53] The liquidation preference or redemption price should be used in the computation of book value per share, leverage, and capital ratios.

Common stock represents the owners' residual interest in the firm after all other claims have been met. Firms may issue one or more classes of common stock. The balance sheet or related footnotes generally disclose the various rights (such as voting rights and dividends) of the different classes of common stock. The par (or stated) value of common stock is normally reported separately from any additional paid-in capital. The latter represents the cumulative difference between the par value of common and the amount received when issued.

Firms often purchase their own common stock on the open market when management thinks it is undervalued, for reissue, or to prevent hostile takeovers. Treasury stock is usually reported as a contra account within stockholders' equity.[54] Although such repurchases were largely a U.S. phenomenon, they have become increasingly common in other countries.

The statement of stockholders' equity also reconciles the beginning and ending balance of retained earnings reinvested in the firm. This reconciliation reports the net income for the period, preferred and common dividends declared during the year, and any adjustments for stock splits, stock dividends, and acquisitions or quasi-reorganizations.

The statement must also report changes in comprehensive income (see Reading 33 for presentation and discussion). There may be changes in the:

▶ Minimum liability recognized for underfunded pension plans
▶ Market values of noncurrent investments
▶ Unrealized gains and losses on cash flow hedges

---

[53] Rule 5-02(28) of Regulation S-X requires the exclusion of mandatorily redeemable preferred stock from the equity section of the financial statements. Preferred stocks that are not redeemable or are redeemable only at the option of the issuer and common stock should be included in the equity section. Staff Accounting Bulletin 64 details the accounting treatment of redeemable preferred.

[54] Some companies report the difference between the purchase price of Treasury stock and the price at subsequent reissuance of that Treasury stock as a component of additional paid-in capital. Other firms reflect this difference as an adjustment to retained earnings.

► Cumulative effect of exchange rate changes

► Unearned shares issued to employee stock ownership plans (ESOPs)

However, these items are sometimes different under IAS standards than under U.S. GAAP.

The valuation allowance for changes in the carrying amount of investment securities and the cumulative translation adjustment are examples of reserves permitted by U.S. or IAS GAAP. For many foreign companies, the statement of stockholders' equity includes reserve accounts that are required or discretionary under financial reporting standards or tax rules. Some foreign firms appropriate some percentage of earnings to preserve liquidity by limiting earnings available for dividends. The use of conservative accounting rules can achieve the same goal.

Some foreign countries permit firms to account for selected transactions as direct charges to the additional paid-in capital account. These include debt and equity issue and repurchase costs (including premiums and discounts on debt) and organization costs. Finally, some countries allow the revaluation of assets with the resulting gain or loss reported in a revaluation reserve. UK GAAP (SSAP 6) requires a statement or a separate footnote on changes in reserves.

The growth of international capital markets has increased the transparency of reserves reported by foreign multinationals. Examples are provided and analyzed in various readings in the text.

Example 34-10

Pfizer's 1999 Consolidated Balance Sheet and Statement of Shareholders' Equity report the:

1. Number of preferred shares authorized (none are outstanding).

2. Par value and number of common shares authorized and issued as of year-end.[55]

3. Additional paid-in capital.

4. Retained earnings and changes due to net income and common dividends declared.

5. Accumulated other comprehensive income (expense) and changes in each of its after-tax components.

6. Deduction for shares held by employee benefit trusts, and the annual changes (see Note 14 for discussion).

7. Deduction for Treasury stock repurchased (see Note 12 for details).

When a company has preferred shares outstanding, careful attention should be paid to their terms. When shares are convertible into common, the analyst should consider treating them as common shares when conversion is highly likely. When computing book value per common share, preferred shares should be stated at their redemption value when higher than the par or stated *amount.*

---

[55] Note that the 1999 stock split increased par value by $138 million and reduced APIC by an equal amount.

Example 34-11

Hecla Mining reported the following in its annual report for the year ended December 31, 2000:

Shareholders' Equity

December 31 Amounts in $thousands	2000	1999
Preferred stock, $0.25 par value, authorized 5,000,000 shares; issued and outstanding— 2,300,000 shares, liquidation preference $119,025	575	575
Common stock, $0.25 par value, authorized 100,000,000 shares; issued 2000—66,859,752 shares, issued 1999—66,844,575 shares	16,715	16,711
Capital surplus	400,236	400,205
Accumulated deficit	(366,523)	(278,533)
Accumulated other comprehensive loss	(4,858)	(4,871)
Less stock held by grantor trust; 2000—139,467 common shares, 1999—132,290 common shares	(514)	(500)
Less treasury stock, at cost; 2000—62,114 common shares, 1999—62,111 common shares	(886)	(886)
Total shareholders' equity	44,745	132,701

Note 11: **Shareholders' Equity**
Preferred Stock

Hecla has 2.3 million shares of Series B Cumulative Convertible Preferred Stock (the Preferred Shares) outstanding. Holders of the Preferred Shares are entitled to receive cumulative cash dividends at the annual rate of $3.50 per share payable quarterly, when and if declared by the Board of Directors. As of January 31, 2001, Hecla has failed to pay the equivalent of two quarterly dividends of $4.0 million.

The Preferred Shares are convertible, in whole or in part, at the option of the holders thereof, into shares of common stock at an initial conversion price of $15.55 per share of common stock. The Preferred Shares were not redeemable by Hecla prior to July 1, 1996. After such date, the shares are redeemable at the option of Hecla at any time, in whole or in part, initially at $52.45 per share and thereafter at prices declining ratably on each July 1 to $50.00 per share on or after July 1, 2003.

While the preferred shares are shown at their carrying amount (575,000) they should be valued at their liquidating preference of $119 million [(2.3 million shares × $50 per share) + $4 million of unpaid dividends].[56] Correctly valuing the preferred shows that Hecla's common stockholders' equity was negative. As the market price of Hecla's common shares was $.50 at December 31, 2000, clearly the conversion feature had insignificant value at that date.

---

[56] One can also argue for a liquidating value of $121.4 million [(2.3 million shares × $51.05 per share) + $4 million of unpaid dividends], where $51.05 is the redemption price at December 31, 2000.

SUMMARY

This introduces the balance sheet, the income statement, and the accrual concept that links them together. Financial statements are interrelated and good financial analysis requires the use of all available information. Our introduction, therefore, is incomplete.

The next reading discusses the use of the cash flow statement and cash flow data in the assessment of the firm. It begins with the cash flow statement and the information it contains, and then develops the relationship between cash flow and income. Reading 36 concludes our introduction to a firm's financial statements—the raw material of analysis.

PROBLEMS FOR READING 34

1. [Revenue recognition criteria] Describe the conditions under which revenue would be recognized:

   a. At the time of production, but prior to sale

   b. At the time of sale, but prior to cash collection

   c. Only when cash collection has occurred

2. [Contract accounting; CFA© adapted] On December 31, 1999, LAS1 Construction entered into a major long-term construction with the following terms:

   Total contract price $3,000,000

   Total expected cost $2,400,000

   Construction is expected to take three years. Production costs and cash flows are shown in the following table:

   Projected Production Costs and Cash Flows

Year	Costs Incurred	Cash Received
2000	$ 900,000	$1,000,000
2001	800,000	1,000,000
2002	700,000	1,000,000
Totals	$2,400,000	$3,000,000

   a. Show the revenue and pretax income for each year under *both* the percentage-of-completion and completed contract methods.

   b. Show the balance sheet accounts at December 31, 2000 resulting from the contract under the

      (i) Percentage-of-completion method

      (ii) Completed contract method

   c. Assume that total projected costs increase by $100,000 and the change in estimate is made at December 31, 2001. Compute the revenue and pretax income for 2001 under the revised assumption.

3. [Balance sheet effects of revenue recognition methods] Lucent's balance sheet shows the following accounts:

   ▶ Contracts in process (current assets)

   ▶ Advance billings (current liabilities)

   a. Describe the nature of the two accounts listed above.

   b. State the other accounts on the company's balance sheet to which these accounts are similar.

   c. Determine the accounting method that Lucent uses to account for its long-term construction projects.

4. [Provision for bad debts] Nucor [NUE], a large U.S. steel producer, reported the following (amounts in $millions):

| | Years Ended December 31 | | | |
	1997	1998	1999	2000
Allowance for Doubtful Accounts				
Opening balance	$ 14.6	$ 18.0	$ 16.3	$ 21.1
Charged to earnings	4.2	(1.4)	5.3	
Write-offs (net of recoveries)	(0.8)	(0.3)	(0.5)	
Closing balance	$ 18.0	$ 16.3	$ 21.1	$ 27.6
Other Financial Data				
Accounts receivable (net)	$ 386.4	$ 299.2	$ 393.8	$ 350.2
Sales	4,184.5	4,151.2	4,009.3	4,586.1
Pretax income	460.2	415.3	379.2	478.3

a. Compute the following ratios (in %):
   (i) Ending balance of reserves to gross receivables for all years
   (ii) Accounts written off to revenues for 1997 to 1999

b. Assuming that Nucor had expensed accounts written off rather than accruing a reserve for bad debts, compute pretax income for 1997 through 2000.

c. Assuming that Nucor had maintained its bad debt reserve at the 1997 ratio of gross receivables, compute the effect on pretax income for 1998 through 2000.

d. Discuss two reasons that might explain the level of reserve accrual by Nucor for 1998 through 2000.

Nucor did not disclose the charge to earnings and writeoffs in 2000. Nucor's CFO told one of the authors that: "the amounts are clearly immaterial, bad debt writeoffs for the last six years averaged .02% of sales, and in no year were more than .03% of sales."

e. Evaluate the CFO's statement that the amounts are immaterial, stating one argument that supports his statement and one argument against it.

f. Explain why a chief financial officer would prefer not to disclose the charge to earnings and writeoffs.

g. Explain why a financial analyst would want those disclosures.

$4\frac{5}{8}$ $4\frac{11}{16}$ — $\frac{3}{8}$

$5\frac{1}{2}$ $5\frac{1}{2}$ — $\frac{3}{8}$

$20\frac{5}{8}$ $21\frac{3}{16}$ — $\frac{1}{16}$

$17\frac{3}{8}$ $18\frac{1}{8}$ + $\frac{7}{8}$

$15\frac{1}{2}$ $6\frac{1}{2}$ $6\frac{1}{2}$ — $\frac{1}{2}$

$7\frac{1}{4}$ $6\frac{1}{2}$ $31\frac{1}{32}$ — $\frac{1}{8}$

$15/16$

$9/16$

$\frac{9}{32}$

$7\frac{15}{16}$ $7\frac{13}{16}$ $7\frac{15}{16}$

$7\frac{15}{16}$ $7\frac{13}{16}$

$2\frac{5}{8}$ $2\frac{11}{32}$ $2\frac{1}{2}$ +

$2\frac{3}{4}$ $2\frac{1}{4}$ $2\frac{1}{4}$

$12\frac{1}{16}$ $11\frac{3}{8}$ $11\frac{3}{4}$ +

$33\frac{3}{4}$ 33 $33\frac{1}{16}$ —

602 $25\frac{5}{8}$ $24\frac{9}{16}$ $25\frac{3}{8}$ +

833 12 $11\frac{5}{8}$ $11\frac{7}{8}$ +

16 $10\frac{1}{2}$ $10\frac{1}{2}$ $10\frac{1}{2}$ —

78 $15\frac{7}{8}$ $15\frac{13}{16}$ $15\frac{7}{8}$ —

$9\frac{1}{16}$ $8\frac{1}{4}$ $8\frac{5}{8}$

430 $11\frac{1}{4}$ $10\frac{5}{8}$

THE STATEMENT OF CASH FLOWS

by Belverd E. Needles and Marian Powers

LEARNING OUTCOMES

The candidate should be able to:

a. identify the principal purposes and uses of the statement of cash flows;

b. compare and contrast the three major classifications (i.e., cash provided or used by operating activities, investing activities, and financing activities) in a statement of cash flows, and describe how noncash investing and financing transactions are reported;

c. calculate and analyze, using the indirect method, the net cash flow provided or used by operating activities, investing activities and financing activities.

INTRODUCTION   1

Cash flows are the lifeblood of a business. They enable a company to pay expenses, debts, employees' wages, and taxes, and to invest in the assets it needs for its operations. Without sufficient cash flows, a company cannot grow and prosper. Because of the importance of cash flows, one must be alert to the possibility that items may be incorrectly classified in a statement of cash flows and that the statement may not fully disclose all pertinent information. This reading identifies the classifications used in a statement of cash flows and explains how to analyze the statement.

OVERVIEW OF THE STATEMENT   2
OF CASH FLOWS

The **statement of cash flows** shows how a company's operating, investing, and financing activities have affected cash during an accounting period. It explains the net increase (or decrease) in cash during the period. For purposes

Note:
U.S. GAAP permits either the direct method or the indirect method in the operating activities section of the cash flows statement. Though FASB expressed a preference for the direct method, more than 99% of all U.S. companies report by using the indirect method. Accountants (e.g., Needles and Powers) generally believe that the indirect method is the best approach (their argument is that it is easier and less costly to prepare); while financial analysts (e.g., White, Sondhi and Fried) generally believe that the direct method conveys better information about operating cash flows. Consequently, the analyst must know how to recast indirect cash flow information to the direct method.

DECISION POINT A USER'S FOCUS

Marriott International is a world leader in lodging and hospitality services. The company believes that maintaining strong cash flows is very important to its future. Its emphasis on cash flows is reflected in its compensation plan for top executives, which gives the greatest weight to cash flows. Why does Marriott place such emphasis on cash flows?

Strong cash flows are critical to achieving and maintaining liquidity. If cash flows exceed the amount a company needs for operations and expansion, it will not have to borrow additional funds. It can use its excess cash to reduce debt, thereby lowering its debt to equity ratio and improving its financial position. That, in turn, can increase the market value of its stock, which will increase shareholders' value.

The statement of cash flows provides information essential to evaluating a company's liquidity. The Financial Highlights below summarize key components of Marriott's statement of cash flows.[1]

MARRIOT'S FINANCIAL HIGHLIGHTS:
Consolidated Statement of Cash Flows
(In millions)

	2004	2003	2002
Net cash provided by operating activities	$891	$403	$ 516
Net cash provided by investing activities	287	311	317
Net cash used in financing activities	(637)	(683)	(1,447)
Increase (decrease) in cash and equivalents	$541	$ 31	($ 614)

> **Study Note**
> Money market accounts, commercial paper (short-term notes), and U.S. Treasury bills are considered cash equivalents because they are highly liquid, temporary (90 days or less) holding places for cash not currently needed to operate the business.

of preparing this statement, **cash** is defined as including both cash and cash equivalents. **Cash equivalents** are investments that can be quickly converted to cash; they have a maturity of 90 days or less when they are purchased. They include money market accounts, commercial paper, and U.S. Treasury bills. A company invests in cash equivalents to earn interest on cash that would otherwise be temporarily idle.

Suppose, for example, that a company has $1,000,000 that it will not need for 30 days. To earn a return on this amount, the company could place the cash in an account that earns interest (such as a money market account), lend the cash to another corporation by purchasing that corporation's short-term notes (commercial paper), or purchase a short-term obligation of the U.S. government (a Treasury bill).

Because cash includes cash equivalents, transfers between the Cash account and cash equivalents are not treated as cash receipts or cash payments. On the statement of cash flows, cash equivalents are combined with the Cash account. Cash equivalents should not be confused with short-term investments, or marketable securities. These items are not combined with the Cash account on the statement of cash flows; rather, purchases of marketable securities are treated as cash outflows, and sales of marketable securities are treated as cash inflows.

Purposes of the Statement of Cash Flows

The primary purpose of the statement of cash flows is to provide information about a company's cash receipts and cash payments during an accounting period.

---

[1] Marriott International, Inc., *Annual Report,* 2004.

A secondary purpose is to provide information about a company's operating, investing, and financing activities during the accounting period. Some information about those activities may be inferred from other financial statements, but the statement of cash flows summarizes *all* transactions that affect cash.

Uses of the Statement of Cash Flows

The statement of cash flows is useful to management, as well as to investors and creditors.

▶ Management uses the statement of cash flows to assess liquidity, to determine dividend policy, and to evaluate the effects of major policy decisions involving investments and financing. Examples include determining if short-term financing is needed to pay current liabilities, deciding whether to raise or lower dividends, and planning for investing and financing needs.

▶ Investors and creditors use the statement to assess a company's ability to manage cash flows, to generate positive future cash flows, to pay its liabilities, to pay dividends and interest, and to anticipate its need for additional financing.

Classification of Cash Flows

The statement of cash flows has three major classifications: operating, investing, and financing activities. The components of these activities are illustrated in Figure 35-1 and summarized below.

1. **Operating activities** involve the cash inflows and outflows from activities that enter into the determination of net income. Cash inflows in this category include cash receipts from the sale of goods and services and from the sale of *trading securities*. Trading securities are a type of marketable security that a company buys and sells for the purpose of making a profit in the near term. Cash inflows also include interest and dividends received on loans and investments. Cash outflows include cash payments for wages, inventory, expenses, interest, taxes, and the purchase of trading securities. In effect, accrual-based income from the income statement is changed to reflect cash flows.

2. **Investing activities** involve the acquisition and sale of property, plant, and equipment and other long-term assets, including long-term investments. They also involve the acquisition and sale of short-term marketable securities, other than trading securities, and the making and collecting of loans. Cash inflows include the cash received from selling marketable securities and long-term assets and from collecting on loans. Cash outflows include the cash expended on purchasing these securities and assets and the cash lent to borrowers.

3. **Financing activities** involve obtaining resources from stockholders and providing them with a return on their investments, and obtaining resources from creditors and repaying the amounts borrowed or otherwise settling the obligations. Cash inflows include the proceeds from stock issues and from short- and long-term borrowing. Cash outflows include the repayments of loans (excluding interest) and payments to owners, including cash

Study Note
Operating activities involve the day-to-day sale of goods and services, investing activities involve long-term assets and investments, and financing activities deal with stockholders' equity accounts and debt (borrowing).

FIGURE 35-1   Classification of Cash Inflows and Cash Outflows

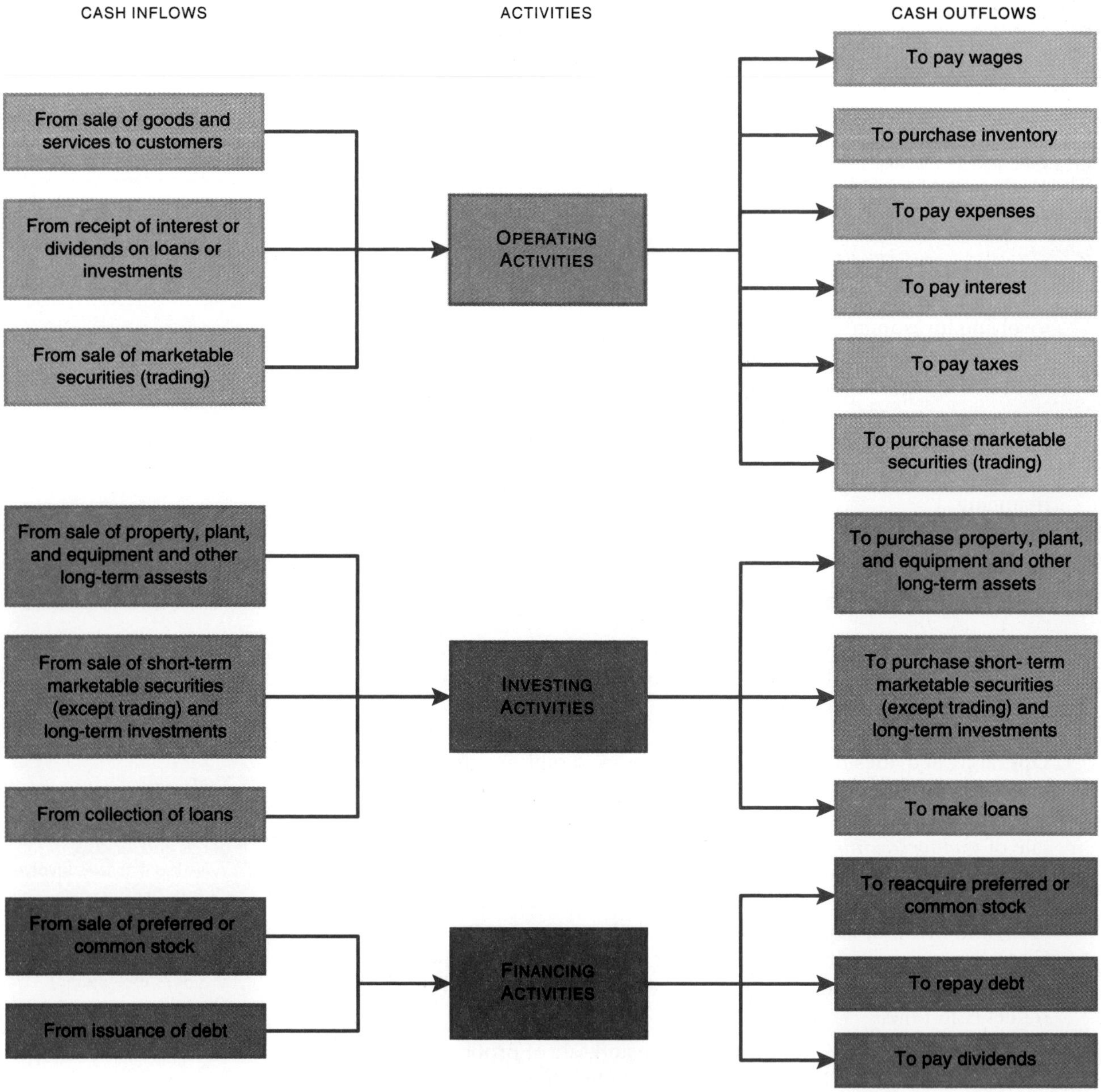

CASH INFLOWS	ACTIVITIES	CASH OUTFLOWS
From sale of goods and services to customers	OPERATING ACTIVITIES	To pay wages
From receipt of interest or dividends on loans or investments		To purchase inventory
From sale of marketable securities (trading)		To pay expenses
		To pay interest
		To pay taxes
		To purchase marketable securities (trading)
From sale of property, plant, and equipment and other long-term assests	INVESTING ACTIVITIES	To purchase property, plant, and equipment and other long-term assets
From sale of short-term marketable securities (except trading) and long-term investments		To purchase short- term marketable securities (except trading) and long-term investments
From collection of loans		To make loans
From sale of preferred or common stock	FINANCING ACTIVITIES	To reacquire preferred or common stock
From issuance of debt		To repay debt
		To pay dividends

dividends. Treasury stock transactions are also considered financing activities. Repayments of accounts payable or accrued liabilities are not considered repayments of loans; they are classified as cash outflows under operating activities.

Noncash Investing and Financing Transactions

Companies occasionally engage in significant **noncash investing and financing transactions**. These transactions involve only long-term assets, long-term liabilities, or stockholders' equity. For instance, a company might exchange a long-term asset for a long-term liability, settle a debt by issuing capital stock, or take out a long-term mortgage to purchase real estate. Noncash transactions represent significant investing and financing activities, but they are not reflected on the statement of cash flows because they do not affect current cash inflows or outflows. They will, however, affect future cash flows. For this reason, they are disclosed in a separate schedule or as part of the statement of cash flows.

Format of the Statement of Cash Flows

The Financial Highlights at the beginning of the reading summarize the key components of **Marriott's** statement of cash flows. Exhibit 35-1 presents the full statement.

▶ The first section of the statement of cash flows is cash flows from operating activities. When the **indirect method** is used to prepare this section, it begins with net income and ends with cash flows from operating activities. This is the method most commonly used; we discuss it in detail later in the reading.

▶ The second section, cash flows from investing activities, shows cash transactions involving capital expenditures (for property and equipment) and loans. Cash outflows for capital expenditures are usually shown separately from cash inflows from their disposal, as they are in Marriott's statement. However, when the inflows are not material, some companies combine these two lines to show the net amount of outflow.

▶ The third section, cash flows from financing activities, shows debt and common stock transactions, as well as payments for dividends and treasury stock.

▶ A reconciliation of the beginning and ending balances of cash appears at the bottom of the statement. These cash balances will tie into the cash balances of the balance sheets.

Ethical Considerations and the Statement of Cash Flows

Although cash inflows and outflows are not as subject to manipulation as earnings are, managers are acutely aware of users' emphasis on cash flows from

FOCUS ON BUSINESS PRACTICE

How Universal Is the Statement of Cash Flows?

Despite the importance of the statement of cash flows in assessing the liquidity of companies in the United States, there has been considerable variation in its use and format in other countries. For example, in many countries, the statement shows the change in working capital rather than the change in cash and cash equivalents. Although the European Union's principal directives for financial reporting do not address the statement of cash flows, international accounting standards require it, and international financial markets expect it to be presented. As a result, most multinational companies include the statement in their financial reports. Most European countries will adopt the statement of cash flows by 2006, when the European Union will require the use of international accounting standards.

EXHIBIT 35-1	Consolidated Statement of Cash Flows

Marriott International, Inc., and Subsidiaries
Consolidated Statement of Cash Flows

	For the Years Ended		
(In millions)	2004	2003	2002
OPERATING ACTIVITIES			
Net income	$ 594	$ 476	$ 439
Adjustments to reconcile to cash provided by operations:			
Income from discontinued operations	2	7	9
Discontinued operations—gain (loss) on sale/exit	—	19	(171)
Depreciation and amortization	166	160	187
Minority interest in results of synthetic fuel operation	(40)	55	—
Income taxes	(63)	(171)	(105)
Timeshare activity, net	113	(111)	(63)
Other	(77)	(73)	223
Working capital changes:			
Accounts receivable	(6)	(81)	(31)
Other current assets	(16)	11	60
Accounts payable and accruals	218	111	(32)
Cash provided by operations	$ 891	$ 403	$ 516
INVESTING ACTIVITIES			
Capital expenditures	$(181)	$(210)	$ (292)
Dispositions	402	494	729
Loan advances	(129)	(241)	(237)
Loan collections and sales	276	280	124
Other	(81)	(12)	(7)
Cash provided by investing activities	$ 287	$ 311	$ 317
FINANCING ACTIVITIES			
Commercial paper, net	$ —	$(102)	$ 102
Issuance of long-term debt	20	14	26
Repayment of long-term debt	(99)	(273)	(946)
Redemption of convertible subordinated debt	(62)	—	(347)
Issuance of Class A common stock	206	102	35
Dividends paid	(73)	(68)	(65)
Purchase of treasury stock	(664)	(373)	(252)
Earn-outs received, net	35	17	—
Cash used in financing activities	$(637)	$(683)	$(1,447)
(DECREASE) INCREASE IN CASH AND EQUIVALENTS	$ 541	$ 31	$ (614)
CASH AND EQUIVALENTS, beginning of year	229	198	812
CASH AND EQUIVALENTS, end of year	$ 770	$ 229	$ 198

Source: Marriott International, Inc., *Annual Report,* 2004.

operations as an important measure of performance. Thus, an incentive exists to overstate these cash flows.

By treating operating expenses of about $10 billion over several years as purchases of equipment, **WorldCom** reduced reported expenses and improved reported earnings. In addition, by classifying payments of operating expenses as investments on the statement of cash flows, it was able to show an improvement in cash flows from operations. The inclusion of the expenditures in the investing activities section did not draw special attention because the company normally had large capital expenditures.

Another way a company can show an apparent improvement in its performance is through lack of transparency, or lack of full disclosure, in its financial statements. For instance, securitization—the sale of batches of accounts receivable—is clearly a means of financing, and the proceeds from it should be shown in the financing section of the statement of cash flows. However, because the accounting standards are somewhat vague about where these proceeds should go, some companies net the proceeds against the accounts receivable in the operating section of the statement and bury the explanation in the notes to the financial statements. By doing so, they make collections of receivables in the operating activities section look better than they actually were. It is not illegal to do this, but from an ethical standpoint, it obscures the company's true performance.

ANALYZING CASH FLOWS   3

Like the analysis of other financial statements, an analysis of the statement of cash flows can reveal significant relationships. Two areas on which analysts focus when examining a company's statement of cash flows are cash-generating efficiency and free cash flow.

Cash-Generating Efficiency

Managers accustomed to evaluating income statements usually focus on the bottom-line result. While the level of cash at the bottom of the statement of cash flows is certainly an important consideration, such information can be obtained from the balance sheet. The focal point of cash flow analysis is on cash inflows and outflows from operating activities. These cash flows are used in ratios that measure **cash-generating efficiency**, which is a company's ability to generate cash from its current or continuing operations. The ratios that analysts use to compute cash-generating efficiency are cash flow yield, cash flows to sales, and cash flows to assets. In this section, we compute these ratios for **Marriott** in 2004 using data from Exhibit 35-1 and the following information from Marriott's 2004 annual report. (All dollar amounts are in millions.)

	2004	**2003**	**2002**
Net Sales	$10,099	$9,014	$8,415
Total Assets	8,668	8,177	8,296

Cash flow yield is the ratio of net cash flows from operating activities to net income:

$$\text{Cash Flow Yield} = \frac{\text{Net Cash Flows from Operating Activities}}{\text{Net Income}}$$

$$= \frac{\$891}{\$594}$$

$$= 1.5 \text{ times}$$

Marriott's cash flow yield of 1.5 times means that its operating activities were generating about 50 percent more cash flow than net income. At a minimum, cash-flow yield should be 1.0, which is the level typical for a service enterprise. However, a firm with significant depreciable assets should have a cash flow yield greater than 1.0 because depreciation expense is added back to net income to arrive at cash flows from operating activities. If special items, such as discontinued operations, appear on the income statement and are material, income from continuing operations should be used as the denominator.

Cash flows to sales is the ratio of net cash flows from operating activities to sales:

$$\text{Cash Flows to Sales} = \frac{\text{Net Cash Flows from Operating Activities}}{\text{Sales}}$$

$$= \frac{\$891}{\$10,099}$$

$$= 8.8\%$$

Thus, Marriott generated positive cash flows to sales of 8.8 percent.

Cash flows to assets is the ratio of net cash flows from operating activities to average total assets:

$$\text{Cash Flows to Assets} = \frac{\text{Net Cash Flows from Operating Activities}}{\text{Average Total Assets}}$$

$$= \frac{\$891}{(\$8,668 + \$8,177) \div 2}$$

$$= 10.6\%$$

Marriott's cash flows to assets ratio is higher than its cash flows to sales ratio because of its good asset turnover ratio (sales ÷ average total assets) of 1.2 times (10.6% ÷ 8.8%). Cash flows to sales and cash flows to assets are closely related to the profitability measures of profit margin and return on assets. They exceed those measures by the amount of the cash flow yield ratio because cash flow yield is the ratio of net cash flows from operating activities to net income.

Free Cash Flow

Free cash flow is the amount of cash that remains after deducting the funds a company must commit to continue operating at its planned level. If free cash flow is positive, it means that the company has met all of its planned cash commitments and has cash available to reduce debt or to expand. A negative free cash flow means that the company will have to sell investments, borrow money, or issue stock in the short term to continue at its planned level; if a company's free cash flow remains negative for several years, it may not be able to raise cash by issuing stocks or bonds. On the statement of cash flows, cash commitments for current and continuing operations, interest, and income taxes are incorporated in cash flows from current operations.

FOCUS ON BUSINESS PRACTICE

Cash Flows Tell All.

In early 2001, the telecommunications industry began one of the biggest market crashes in history. Could it have been predicted? The capital expenditures that telecommunications firms must make for equipment, such as cable lines and computers, are sizable. When the capital expenditures (a negative component of free cash flow) of 41 telecommunications companies are compared with their cash flows from sales over the six years preceding the crash, an interesting pattern emerges. In the first three years, both capital expenditures and cash flows from sales were about 20 percent of sales. In other words, free cash flows were neutral, with operations generating enough cash flows to cover capital expenditures. In the next three years, cash flows from sales stayed at about 20 percent of sales, but the companies' capital expenditure increased dramatically, to 35 percent of sales. Thus, free cash flows turned very negative, and almost half of capital expenditures had to be financed by debt instead of operations, making these companies more vulnerable to the downturn in the economy that occurred in 2001.[2]

Free cash flow for **Marriott** is computed as follows (in millions):

Free Cash Flow = Net Cash Flows from Operating Activities − Dividends −
(Purchases of Plant Assets − Sales of Plant Assets)
= $891 − $73 − ($181 − $402)
= $1,039

Study Note
The computation for free cash flow sometimes uses *net capital expenditures* in place of *(purchases of plant assets = sales of plant assets).*

Purchases of plant assets (capital expenditures) and sales (dispositions) of plant assets appear in the investing activities section of the statement of cash flows. When sales of plant assets are small or immaterial, companies can subtract the sales amount from the purchases of plant assets and refer to the result as "net capital expenditures." Dividends appear in the financing activities section. Marriott's positive free cash flow of $1,039 million was due primarily to its strong operating cash flow of $891 million and the $402 million cash it received from the disposition of assets. Cash was used in financing activities in all three years

FOCUS ON BUSINESS PRACTICE

What Do You Mean, "Free Cash Flow"?

Because the statement of cash flows has been around for less than 20 years, no generally accepted analyses have yet been developed. For example, the term *free cash flow* is commonly used in the business press, but there is no agreement on its definition. An article in *Forbes* defines *free cash flow* as "cash available after paying out capital expenditures and dividends, but *before taxes and interest*"[3] [emphasis added]. An article in *The Wall Street Journal* defines it as "operating income less maintenance-level capital expenditures."[4] The definition with which we are most in agreement is the one used in *BusinessWeek:* free cash flow is net cash flows from operating activities less net capital expenditures and dividends. This "measures truly discretionary funds—company money that an owner could pocket without harming the business."[5]

---

[2] "Deadweight on the Markets," *BusinessWeek*, February 19, 2001.

[3] Gary Slutsker, "Look at the Birdie and Say: 'Cash Flow,'" *Forbes*, October 25, 1993.

[4] Jonathan Clements, "Yacktman Fund is Bloodied but Unbowed." *The Wall Street Journal*, November 8, 1993.

[5] Jeffery Laderman, "Earnings, Schmearnings—Look at the Cash," *BusinessWeek*, July 24, 1989.

Telecommunications firms must make large capital expenditures for plant assets, such as the radio tower shown here. These expenditures are a negative component of free cash flow, which is the amount of cash that remains after deducting the funds a company needs to operate at its planned level. Between 1998 and 2000, negative free cash flows forced a number of telecommunications firms to rely heavily on debt to finance their capital expenditures, thus increasing their vulnerability to the economic downturn of 2001.

Courtesy of Hartmut Schwarzbach/Peter Arnold, Inc.

primarily because of debt repayments and the purchase of treasury stock. The company relied mainly on the increased cash provided by operations to make up for these cash outflows.

Because cash flows can vary from year to year, analysts should look at trends in cash flow measures over several years. Marriott's management sums up its approach to managing cash flows as follows:

Cash from Operations

We consider [our borrowing] resources, together with cash we expect to generate from operations, adequate to meet short-term and long-term liquidity requirements, finance our long-term growth plans, meet debt service and fulfill other cash requirements.[6]

4   OPERATING ACTIVITIES

To demonstrate the preparation of the statement of cash flows, we will work through an example step by step. The data for this example are presented in Exhibit 35-2, which shows Amir Corporation's income statement for 20x7, and in Exhibit 35-3, which shows Amir's balance sheets for December 31, 20x7 and 20x6. Exhibit 35-3 shows the balance sheet accounts that we use for analysis and whether the change in each account is an increase or a decrease.

---

[6] Marriott International, Inc., *Annual Report*, 2004.

EXHIBIT 35-2	Income Statement

Amir Corporation
Income Statement
For the Year Ended December 31, 20×7

Sales		$349,000
Cost of goods sold		260,000
Gross margin		$ 89,000
Operating expenses (including depreciation expense of $18,500)		73,500
Operating income		$ 15,500
Other income (expenses)		
Interest expense	($11,500)	
Interest income	3,000	
Gain on sale of investments	6,000	
Loss on sale of plant assets	(1,500)	(4,000)
Income before income taxes		$ 11,500
Income taxes expense		3,500
Net income		$ 8,000

The first step in preparing the statement of cash flows is to determine cash flows from operating activities. The income statement indicates how successful a company has been in earning an income from its operating activities, but because that statement is prepared on an accrual basis, it does not reflect the inflow and outflow of cash related to operating activities. Revenues are recorded even though the company may not yet have received the cash, and expenses are recorded even though the company may not yet have expended the cash. Thus, to ascertain cash flows from operations, the figures on the income statement must be converted from an accrual basis to a cash basis.

There are two methods of accomplishing this:

▶ The **direct method** adjusts each item on the income statement from the accrual basis to the cash basis. The result is a statement that begins with cash receipts from sales and interest and deducts cash payments for purchases, operating expenses, interest payments, and income taxes to arrive at net cash flows from operating activities.

▶ The **indirect method** does not require the adjustment of each item on the income statement. It lists only the adjustments necessary to convert net income to cash flows from operations.

Study Note
The direct and indirect methods relate only to the operating activities section of the statement of cash flows. They are both acceptable for financial reporting purposes.

The direct and indirect methods always produce the same net figure. The average person finds the direct method easier to understand because its presentation of operating cash flows is more straightforward than that of the indirect method. However, the indirect method is the overwhelming choice of most companies and accountants. A survey of large companies shows that 99 percent use this method.[7]

---

[7] American Institute of Certified Public Accountants, *Accounting Trends & Techniques* (New York: AICPA, 2004).

EXHIBIT 35-3	Comparative Balance Sheets Showing Changes in Accounts

Amir Corporation
Comparative Balance Sheets
December 31, 20×7 and 20×6

	20×7	20×6	Change	Increase or Decrease
Assets				
Current assets				
Cash	$ 23,000	$ 7,500	$ 15,500	Increase
Accounts receivable (net)	23,500	27,500	(4,000)	Decrease
Inventory	72,000	55,000	17,000	Increase
Prepaid expenses	500	2,500	(2,000)	Decrease
Total current assets	$119,000	$ 92,500	$ 26,500	
Investments	$ 57,500	$ 63,500	($ 6,000)	Decrease
Plant assets	$357,500	$252,500	$105,000	Increase
Less accumulated depreciation	(51,500)	(34,000)	(17,500)	Increase
Total plant assets	$306,000	$218,500	$ 87,500	
Total assets	$482,500	$374,500	$108,000	
Liabilities				
Current liabilities				
Accounts payable	$ 25,000	$ 21,500	$ 3,500	Increase
Accrued liabilities	6,000	4,500	1,500	Increase
Income taxes payable	1,500	2,500	(1,000)	Decrease
Total current liabilities	$ 32,500	$ 28,500	$ 4,000	
Long-term liabilities				
Bonds payable	147,500	122,500	25,000	Increase
Total liabilities				
	$180,000	$151,000	$ 29,000	
Stockholders' Equity				
Common stock, $5 par value	$138,000	$100,000	$ 38,000	Increase
Additional paid-in capital	107,000	57,500	49,500	Increase
Retained earnings	70,000	66,000	4,000	Increase
Treasury stock	(12,500)	0	(12,500)	Increase
Total stockholders' equity	$302,500	$223,500	$ 79,000	
Total liabilities and stockholders' equity	$482,500	$374,500	$108,000	

FIGURE 35-2   Indirect Method of Determining Net Cash Flows from Operating Activities

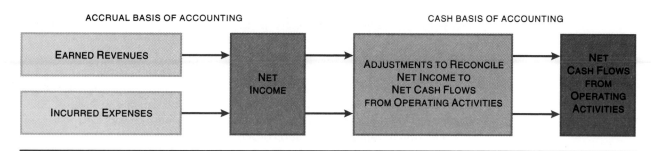

From an analyst's perspective, the indirect method is superior to the direct method because it begins with net income and derives cash flows from operations; the analyst can readily identify the factors that cause cash flows from operations. From a company's standpoint, the indirect method is easier and less expensive to prepare. For these reasons, we use the indirect method in our example.

As Figure 35-2 shows, the indirect method focuses on adjusting items on the income statement to reconcile net income to net cash flows from operating activities. These items include depreciation, amortization, and depletion; gains and losses; and changes in the balances of current asset and current liability accounts. The schedule in Exhibit 35-4 shows the reconciliation of Amir Corporation's net income to net cash flows from operating activities. We discuss each adjustment in the sections that follow.

EXHIBIT 35-4	Schedule of Cash Flows from Operating Activities: Indirect Method

Amir Corporation
Schedule of Cash Flows from Operating Activities
For the Year Ended December 31, 20×7

Cash flows from operating activities		
Net income		$ 8,000
Adjustments to reconcile net income to net cash flows from operating activities		
Depreciation	$18,500	
Gain on sale of investments	(6,000)	
Loss on sale of plant assets	1,500	
Changes in current assets and current liabilities		
Decrease in accounts receivable	4,000	
Increase in inventory	(17,000)	
Decrease in prepaid expenses	2,000	
Increase in accounts payable	3,500	
Increase in accrued liabilities	1,500	
Decrease in income taxes payable	(1,000)	7,000
Net cash flows from operating activities		$15,000

Depreciation

The investing activities section of the statement of cash flows shows the cash payments that the company made for plant assets, intangible assets, and natural resources during the accounting period. Depreciation expense, amortization expense, and depletion expense for these assets appear on the income statement as allocations of the costs of the original purchases to the current accounting period. The amount of these expenses can usually be found in the income statement or in a note to the financial statements. As you can see in Exhibit 35-2, Amir Corporation's income statement discloses depreciation expense of $18,500, which would have been recorded as follows:

A	= L +	SE
−18,500		−18,500

Depreciation Expense	18,500	
Accumulated Depreciation		18,500
To record annual depreciation on plant assets		

Study Note
Operating expenses on the income statement include depreciation expense, which does not require a cash outlay.

Even though depreciation expense appears on the income statement, it involves no outlay of cash and so does not affect cash flows in the current period. Thus, to arrive at cash flows from operations on the statement of cash flows, an adjustment is needed to increase net income by the amount of depreciation expense shown on the income statement.

Gains and Losses

Study Note
Gains and losses by themselves do not represent cash flows; they are merely bookkeeping adjustments. For example, when a long-term asset is sold, it is the *proceeds* (cash received), not the gain or loss, that constitute cash flow.

Like depreciation expense, gains and losses that appear on the income statement do not affect cash flows from operating activities and need to be removed from this section of the statement of cash flows. The cash receipts generated by the disposal of the assets that resulted in the gains or losses are included in the investing activities section of the statement of cash flows. Thus, to reconcile net income to cash flows from operating activities (and prevent double counting), gains and losses must be removed from net income.

For example, on its income statement, Amir Corporation shows a $6,000 gain on the sale of investments. This amount is subtracted from net income to reconcile net income to net cash flows from operating activities. The reason for doing this is that the $6,000 is included in the investing activities section of the statement of cash flows as part of the cash from the sale of the investment. Because the gain has already been included in the calculation of net income, the $6,000 gain must be subtracted to prevent double counting.

Amir's income statement also shows a $1,500 loss on the sale of plant assets. This loss is already reflected in the sale of plant assets in the investing activities section of the statement of cash flows. Thus, the $1,500 is added to net income to reconcile net income to net cash flows from operating activities.

Changes in Current Assets

Decreases in current assets other than cash have positive effects on cash flows, and increases in current assets have negative effects on cash flows. A decrease in a current asset frees up invested cash, thereby increasing cash flow. An increase in a current asset consumes cash, thereby decreasing cash flow. For example, look at Amir Corporation's income statement and balance sheets in Exhibits 35-2 and 35-3. Note that net sales in 20x7 were $349,000 and that Accounts Receivable decreased by $4,000. Thus, collections were $4,000 more than sales recorded for the year, and the total cash received from sales was $353,000 ($349,000 + $4,000 = $353,000). The effect on accounts receivable can be illustrated as follows:

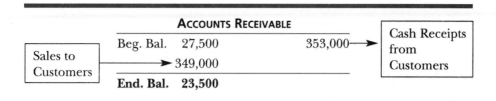

To reconcile net income to net cash flows from operating activities, the $4,000 decrease in Accounts Receivable is added to net income.

Inventory can be analyzed in the same way. For example, Exhibit 35-3 shows that Amir's Inventory account increased by $17,000 between 20x6 and 20x7. This means that Amir expended $17,000 more in cash for purchases than it included in cost of goods sold on its income statement. Because of this expenditure, net income is higher than net cash flows from operating activities, so $17,000 must be deducted from net income. By the same logic, the decrease of $2,000 in Prepaid Expenses shown on the balance sheets must be added to net income to reconcile net income to net cash flows from operations.

Changes in Current Liabilities

The effect that changes in current liabilities have on cash flows is the opposite of the effect of changes in current assets. An increase in a current liability represents a postponement of a cash payment, which frees up cash and increases cash flow in the current period. A decrease in a current liability consumes cash, which decreases cash flow. To reconcile net income to net cash flows from operating activities, increases in current liabilities are added to net income, and decreases are deducted. For example, Exhibit 35-3 shows that from 20x6 to 20x7, Amir's accounts payable increased by $3,500. This means that Amir paid $3,500 less to creditors than the amount indicated in the cost of goods sold on its income statement. The following T account illustrates this relationship:

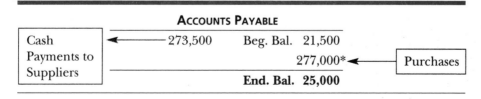

*Purchases = Cost of Goods Sold ($260,000) + Increase in Inventory ($17,000)

Thus, $3,500 must be added to net income to reconcile net income to net cash flows from operating activities. By the same logic, the increase of $1,500 in accrued liabilities shown on the balance sheets must be added to net income, and the decrease of $1,000 in income taxes payable must be deducted from net income.

FOCUS ON BUSINESS PRACTICE

What Is EBITDA, and Is It Any Good?

Some companies and analysts like to use EBITDA (an acronym for Earnings Before Interest, Taxes, Depreciation, and Amortization) as a short-cut measure of cash flows from operations. But recent events have caused many analysts to reconsider this measure of performance. For instance, when **WorldCom** transferred $3.8 billion from expenses to capital expenditures in one year, it touted its EBITDA; at the time, the firm was, in fact, nearly bankrupt. The demise of **Vivendi**, the big French company that imploded when it did not have enough cash to pay its debts and that also touted its EBITDA, is another reason that analysts have had second thoughts about relying on this measure of performance.

Some analysts are now saying that EBITDA is "to a great extent misleading" and that it "is a confusing metric. . . . Some take it for a proxy for profits and some take it for a proxy for cash flow, and it's neither."[8] Cash flows from operations and free cash flow, both of which take into account interest, taxes, and depreciation, are better and more comprehensive measures of a company's cash-generating efficiency.

Schedule of Cash Flows from Operating Activities

In summary, Exhibit 35-4 shows that by using the indirect method, net income of $8,000 has been adjusted by reconciling items totaling $7,000 to arrive at net cash flows from operating activities of $15,000. This means that although Amir's net income was $8,000, the company actually had net cash flows of $15,000 available from operating activities to use for purchasing assets, reducing debts, and paying dividends.

The treatment of income statement items that do not affect cash flows can be summarized as follows:

	Add to or Deduct from Net Income
Depreciation expense	Add
Amortization expense	Add
Depletion expense	Add
Losses	Add
Gains	Deduct

The following summarizes the adjustments for increases and decreases in current assets and current liabilities:

	Add to Net Income	Deduct from Net Income
Current assets		
Accounts receivable (net)	Decrease	Increase
Inventory	Decrease	Increase
Prepaid expenses	Decrease	Increase
Current liabilities		
Accounts payable	Increase	Decrease
Accrued liabilities	Increase	Decrease
Income taxes payable	Increase	Decrease

---

[8] Martin Peers and Robin Sidel, "WorldCom Causes Analysts to Evaluate EBITDA's Role," *The Wall Street Journal,* July 15, 2002.

INVESTING ACTIVITIES   5

To determine cash flows from investing activities, accounts involving cash receipts and cash payments from investing activities are examined individually. The objective is to explain the change in each account balance from one year to the next.

Although investing activities center on the long-term assets shown on the balance sheet, they also include any short-term investments shown under current assets on the balance sheet and any investment gains and losses on the income statement. The balance sheets in Exhibit 35-3 show that Amir had no short-term investments and that its long-term assets consisted of investments and plant assets. The income statement in Exhibit 35-2 shows that Amir had a gain on the sale of investments and a loss on the sale of plant assets.

The following transactions pertain to Amir's investing activities in 20x7:

1. Purchased investments in the amount of $39,000.

2. Sold investments that cost $45,000 for $51,000.

3. Purchased plant assets in the amount of $60,000.

4. Sold plant assets that cost $5,000 and that had accumulated depreciation of $1,000 for $2,500.

5. Issued $50,000 of bonds at face value in a noncash exchange for plant assets.

In the following sections, we analyze the accounts related to investing activities to determine their effects on Amir's cash flows.

Investments

Our objective in this section is to explain Amir Corporation's $6,000 decrease in investments. We do this by analyzing the increases and decreases in Amir's Investments account to determine their effects on the Cash account.

Item **1** in the list of Amir's transactions states that its purchases of investments totaled $39,000 during 20x7. This transaction, which caused a $39,000 decrease in cash flows, is recorded as follows:

Investments	39,000	
Cash		39,000
Purchase of investments		

A	= L +	SE
+39,000		
−39,000		

Item **2** states that Amir sold investments that cost $45,000 for $51,000. This transaction resulted in a gain of $6,000. It is recorded as follows:

Cash	51,000	
Investments		45,000
Gain on Sale of Investments		6,000
Sale of investments for a gain		

A	= L +	SE
+51,000		+6,000
−45,000		

The effect of this transaction is a $51,000 increase in cash flows. Note that the gain on the sale is included in the $51,000. This is the reason we excluded it in computing cash flows from operations. If it had been included in that section, it would have been counted twice.

Study Note
Investing activities involve long-term assets and short- and long-term investments. Inflows and outflows of cash are shown in the investing activities section of the statement of cash flows.

We have now explained the $6,000 decrease in the Investments account during 20x7, as illustrated in the following T account:

INVESTMENTS			
Beg. Bal.	63,500	Sales	45,000
Purchases	39,000		
End. Bal.	**57,500**		

The cash flow effects of these transactions are shown in the investing activities section of the statement of cash flows as follows:

Purchase of investments	($39,000)
Sale of investments	51,000

Notice that purchases and sales are listed separately as cash outflows and inflows to give readers of the statement a complete view of investing activity. However, some companies prefer to list them as a single net amount.

If Amir Corporation had short-term investments or marketable securities, the analysis of cash flows would be the same.

Plant Assets

For plant assets, we have to explain changes in both the Plant Assets account and the related Accumulated Depreciation account. Exhibit 35-3 shows that from 2006 to 2007, Amir Corporation's plant assets increased by $105,000 and that accumulated depreciation increased by $17,500.

Item **3** in the list of Amir's transactions in 2007 states that the company purchased plant assets totaling $60,000. The following entry records this cash outflow:

A   = L + SE
+60,000
−60,000

Plant Assets	60,000	
Cash		60,000
Purchase of plant assets		

Item **4** states that Amir Corporation sold plant assets that cost $5,000 and that had accumulated depreciation of $1,000 for $2,500. Thus, this transaction resulted in a loss of $1,500. The entry to record it is as follows:

A   = L + SE
+2,500   −1,500
+1,000
−5,000

Cash	2,500	
Accumulated Depreciation	1,000	
Loss on Sale of Plant Assets	1,500	
Plant Assets		5,000
Sale of plant assets at a loss		

Note that in this transaction, the positive cash flow is equal to the amount of cash received, $2,500. The loss on the sale of plant assets is included in the investing activities section of the statement of cash flows and excluded from the operating activities section by adjusting net income for the amount of the loss. The amount of a loss or gain on the sale of an asset is determined by the amount of cash received and does not represent a cash outflow or inflow.

The investing activities section of Amir's statement of cash flows reports the firm's purchase and sale of plant assets as follows:

Purchase of plant assets	($60,000)
Sale of plant assets	2,500

Cash outflows and cash inflows are listed separately here, but companies sometimes combine them into a single net amount, as they do the purchase and sale of investments.

Item **5** in the list of Amir's transactions is a noncash exchange that affects two long-term accounts, Plant Assets and Bonds Payable. It is recorded as follows:

Plant Assets	50,000	
Bonds Payable		50,000
Issued bonds at face value for plant assets		

A	=	L	+ SE
+50,000		+50,000	

Although this transaction does not involve an inflow or outflow of cash, it is a significant transaction involving both an investing activity (the purchase of plant assets) and a financing activity (the issue of bonds payable). Because one purpose of the statement of cash flows is to show important investing and financing activities, the transaction is listed at the bottom of the statement of cash flows or in a separate schedule, as follows:

Schedule of Noncash Investing and Financing Transactions
Issue of bonds payable for plant assets $50,000

We have now accounted for all the changes related to Amir's plant asset accounts. The following T accounts summarize these changes:

PLANT ASSETS

Beg. Bal.	252,500	Sale	5,000
Cash Purchase	60,000		
Noncash Purchase	50,000		
End. Bal.	**357,500**		

ACCUMULATED DEPRECIATION

Sale	1,000	Beg. Bal.	34,000
		Dep. Exp.	18,500
		End. Bal.	**51,500**

Had the balance sheet included specific plant asset accounts (e.g., Equipment and the related accumulated depreciation account) or other long-term asset accounts (e.g., Intangibles), the analysis would have been the same.

6   FINANCING ACTIVITIES

Determining cash flows from financing activities is very similar to determining cash flows from investing activities, but the accounts analyzed relate to short-term borrowings, long-term liabilities, and stockholders equity. Because Amir Corporation does not have short-term borrowings, we deal only with long-term liabilities and stockholders' equity accounts.

The following transactions pertain to Amir's financing activities in 20x7:

1. Issued $50,000 of bonds at face value in a noncash exchange for plant assets.

2. Repaid $25,000 of bonds at face value at maturity.

3. Issued 7,600 shares of $5 par value common stock for $87,500.

4. Paid cash dividends in the amount of $4,000.

5. Purchased treasury stock for $12,500.

Bonds Payable

Exhibit 35-3 shows that Amir's Bonds Payable account increased by $25,000 in 20x7. Both items **1** and **2** in the list above affect this account. We analyzed item **1** in connection with plant assets, but it also pertains to the Bonds Payable account. As we noted, this transaction is reported on the schedule of noncash investing and financing transactions. Item **2** results in a cash outflow, which is recorded as follows:

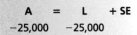

Bonds Payable	25,000	
Cash		25,000
Repayment of bonds at face value at maturity		

This appears in the financing activities section of the statement of cash flows as

Repayment of bonds   ($25,000)

The following T account explains the change in Bonds Payable:

BONDS PAYABLE			
Repayment	25,000	Beg. Bal.	122,500
		Noncash Issue	50,000
		End. Bal.	**147,500**

If Amir Corporation had any notes payable, the analysis would be the same.

How Much Cash Does a Company Need?

Some kinds of industries are more vulnerable to downturns in the economy than others. Historically, because of the amount of debt they carry and their large interest and loan payments, companies in the airline and automotive industries have been hard hit by economic downturns. But research has shown that high-tech companies with large amounts of intangible assets are also hard hit. Biotechnology, pharmaceutical, and computer hardware and soft-ware companies can lose up to 80 percent of their value in times of financial stress. In contrast, companies with large amounts of tangible assets, such as oil companies and rail-roads, can lose as little as 10 percent. To survive during economic downturns, it is very important for high-tech companies to use their cash-generating efficiency to build cash reserves. It makes sense for these companies to hoard cash and not pay dividends to the extent that companies in other industries do.[9]

Common Stock

Like the Plant Asset account and its related accounts, accounts related to stock-holders' equity should be analyzed together. For example, the Additional Paid-in Capital account should be examined along with the Common Stock account. In 20x7, Amir's Common Stock account increased by $38,000, and its Additional Paid-in Capital account increased by $49,500. Item **3** in the list of Amir's transactions, which states that the company issued 7,600 shares of $5 par value common stock for $87,500, explains these increases. The entry to record the cash inflow is as follows:

Cash	87,500	
Common Stock		38,000
Additional Paid-in Capital		49,500
Issued 7,600 shares of $5 par value common stock		

A	= L +	SE
+87,500		+38,000
		+49,500

This appears in the financing activities section of the statement of cash flows as

Issue of common stock $87,000

The following analysis of this transaction is all that is needed to explain the changes in the two accounts during 20x7:

COMMON STOCK			ADDITIONAL PAID-IN CAPTIAL		
	Beg. Bal.	100,000		Beg. Bal.	57,500
	Issue	38,000		Issue	49,500
	End. Bal.	**138,000**		**End. Bal.**	**107,000**

---

[9]Richard Passov, "How Much Cash Does Your Company Need?" *Harvard Business Review,* November 2003.

High-tech companies with large amounts of intangible assets, such as PharmaMar, a pharmaceutical firm based in Madrid, can lose up to 80 percent of their value in times of financial stress. As a hedge against economic downturns, these companies need to build cash reserves, and they may therefore choose to hoard cash rather than pay dividends.

Courtesy of AFP/Getty Images, Inc.

Retained Earnings

At this point, we have dealt with several items that affect retained earnings. The only item affecting Amir's retained earnings that we have not considered is the payment of $4,000 in cash dividends (item **4** in the list of Amir's transactions). At the time it declared the dividend, Amir would have debited its Dividends account. After paying the dividend, it would have closed the Dividends account to Retained Earnings and recorded the closing with the following entry:

A = L + SE
−4,000
+4,000

Retained Earnings	4,000	
Dividends		4,000
To close the Dividends account		

Study Note
It is dividends paid, not dividends declared, that appear on the statement of cash flows.

Cash dividends would be displayed in the financing activities section of Amir's statement of cash flows as follows:

Payment of dividends   ($4,000)

The following T account shows the change in the Retained Earnings account:

RETAINED EARNINGS			
Dividends	4,000	Beg. Bal.	66,000
		Net Income	8,000
		End. Bal.	**70,000**

Treasury Stock

Many companies buy back their own stock on the open market. These buybacks use cash, as this entry shows:

Treasury Stock	12,500	
Cash		12,500

A	= L +	SE
−12,500		−12,500

This use of cash is classified in the statement of cash flows as a financing activity:

Purchase of treasury stock   ($12,500)

Study Note
The purchase of treasury stock qualifies as a financing activity, but it is also a cash outflow.

The T account for this transaction is as follows:

TREASURY STOCK
Purchase   12,500

We have now analyzed all Amir Corporation's income statement items, explained all balance sheet changes, and taken all additional information into account. Exhibit 35-5 shows how our data are assembled in Amir's statement of cash flows.

EXHIBIT 35-5	Statement of Cash Flows: Indirect Method

Amir Corporation
Statement of Cash Flows
For the Year Ended December 31, 20×7

Cash flows from operating activities		
Net income		$ 8,000
Adjustments to reconcile net income to net cash flows from operating activities		
Depreciation	$18,500	
Gain on sale of investments	(6,000)	
Loss on sale of plant assets	1,500	

(Exhibit continued on next page ...)

EXHIBIT 35-5	Statement of Cash Flows: Indirect Method (continued)

Amir Corporation
Statement of Cash Flows
For the Year Ended December 31, 20×7

Changes in current assets and current liabilities		
Decrease in accounts receivable	4,000	
Increase in inventory	(17,000)	
Decrease in prepaid expenses	2,000	
Increase in accounts payable	3,500	
Increase in accrued liabilities	1,500	
Decrease in income taxes payable	(1,000)	7,000
Net cash flows from operating activities		$15,000
Cash flows from investing activities		
Purchase of investments	($39,000)	
Sale of investments	51,000	
Purchase of plant assets	(60,000)	
Sale of plant assets	2,500	
Net cash flows from investing activities		(45,500)
Cash flows from financing activities		
Repayment of bonds	($25,000)	
Issue of common stock	87,500	
Payment of dividends	(4,000)	
Purchase of treasury stock	(12,500)	
Net cash flows from financing activities		46,000
Net increase (decrease) in cash		$15,500
Cash at beginning of year		7,500
Cash at end of year		$23,000

Schedule of Noncash Investing and Financing Transactions

Issue of bonds payable for plant assets	$50,000

FOCUS ON BUSINESS

MARRIOTT INTERNATIONAL, INC.

As we pointed out in this reading's Decision Point, strong cash flows are a basic ingredient in **Marriott's** plans for the future. Strong cash flows enable a company to achieve and maintain liquidity, to expand, and to increase the value of its shareholders' investments. A company's statement of cash flows provides information essential to evaluating the strength of its cash flows and its liquidity. A user of Marriott's statement of cash flows would want to ask the following questions:

▶ **Are operations generating sufficient operating cash flows?**

▶ **Is the company growing by investing in long-term assets?**

▶ **Has the company had to borrow money or issue stock to finance its growth?**

Using data from Exhibit 35-1, which presents Marriott's statements of cash flows, we can answer these questions. We can gauge Marriott's ability to generate cash flows from operations by calculating its cash flow yields in 2003 and 2004:

Cash Flow Yield		2004	2003
$\dfrac{\text{Net Cash Flows from Operating Activities}}{\text{Net Income}}$	=	$\dfrac{\$891}{\$594}$	$\dfrac{\$403}{\$476}$
	=	1.5 times	0.8 times

As you can see, Marriott's cash flow yield almost doubled over the two years. The 1.5 cash yield in 2004 surpassed the 1.0 level normally considered the minimum acceptable level of cash flows from operations. Because of the increase in cash provided by operations, Marriott's cash flows to sales and assets would also show improvement over the two-year period.

Free cash flow measures the sufficiency of cash flows in a different way. The following computations show that in 2004, Marriott's free cash flow was over $400 million greater than in 2003:

Free Cash Flow		2004	2003
Net Cash Flows from Operating Activities − Dividends − (Purchases of Plant Assets − Sales of Plant Assets)	=	$891 − $73 − ($181 − $402)	$403 − $68 − ($210 − $494)
	=	$1,039	$619

Marriott's statement of cash flows shows that the company was investing in long-term assets ($210 million in 2003 and $181 million in 2004) but that its sales of assets exceeded its capital expenditures. Thus, the company did not have to rely on borrowing money or issuing stock to finance its growth. In fact, it repaid much more long-term debt than it borrowed and purchased more than three times as much treasury stock as it issued in common stock. Financing activities totaled $683 million in 2003 and $637 million in 2004; the sum of these expenditures was less than the sum of Marriott's free cash flows in the two years.

SUMMARY

The statement of cash flows shows how a company's operating, investing, and financing activities have affected cash during an accounting period. For the statement of cash flows, *cash* is defined as including both cash and cash equivalents. The primary purpose of the statement is to provide information about a firm's cash receipts and cash payments during an accounting period. A secondary purpose is to provide information about a firm's operating, investing, and financing activities. Management uses the statement to assess liquidity, determine dividend policy, and plan investing and financing activities. Investors and creditors use it to assess the company's cash-generating ability.

The statement of cash flows has three major classifications: (1) operating activities, which involve the cash effects of transactions and other events that enter into the determination of net income; (2) investing activities, which involve the acquisition and sale of marketable securities and long-term assets and the making and collecting of loans; and (3) financing activities, which involve obtaining resources from stockholders and creditors and providing the former with a return on their investments and the latter with repayment. Non-cash investing and financing transactions are also important because they affect future cash flows; these exchanges of long-term assets or liabilities are of interest to potential investors and creditors.

In examining a firm's statement of cash flows, analysts tend to focus on cash-generating efficiency and free cash flow. Cash-generating efficiency is a firm's ability to generate cash from its current or continuing operations. The ratios used to measure cash-generating efficiency are cash flow yield, cash flows to sales, and cash flows to assets. Free cash flow is the cash that remains after deducting the funds a firm must commit to continue operating at its planned level. These commitments include current and continuing operations, interest, income taxes, dividends, and capital expenditures.

The indirect method adjusts net income for all items in the income statement that do not have cash flow effects (such as depreciation, amortization, and gains and losses on sales of assets) and for changes in liabilities that affect operating cash flows. Generally, increases in current assets have a negative effect on cash flows, and decreases have a positive effect. Conversely, increases in current liabilities have a positive effect on cash flows, and decreases have a negative effect.

Investing activities involve the acquisition and sale of property, plant, and equipment and other long-term assets, including long-term investments. They also involve the acquisition and sale of short-term marketable securities, other than trading securities, and the making and collecting of loans. Cash flows from investing activities are determined by analyzing the cash flow effects of changes in each account related to investing activities. The effects of gains and losses reported on the income statement must also be considered.

Determining cash flows from financing activities is almost identical to determining cash flows from investing activities. The difference is that the accounts analyzed relate to short-term borrowings, long-term liabilities, and stockholders' equity. After the changes in the balance sheet accounts from one accounting period to the next have been explained, all the cash flow effects should have been identified.

ANALYSIS OF CASH FLOWS

by Gerald I. White, Ashwinpaul C. Sondhi, and Dov Fried

LEARNING OUTCOMES

The candidate should be able to:

a. classify a particular transaction or item as cash flow from 1) operations, 2) investing, or 3) financing;

b. compute and interpret a statement of cash flows, using the direct method and the indirect method;

c. convert an indirect statement of cash flows to a direct basis;

d. explain the two primary factors (i.e., acquisitions/divestitures and translation of foreign subsidiaries) that may cause discrepancies between balances of operating assets and liabilities reported on the balance sheet and those reported in the cash flow statement;

e. describe and compute free cash flow;

f. distinguish between U.S. GAAP and IAS GAAP classifications of dividends paid or received and interest paid or received for statement of cash flow purposes.

STATEMENT OF CASH FLOWS 1

Cash flow data supplement the information provided by the income statement as both link consecutive balance sheets. The statement of cash flows reports all the cash inflows and outflows (classified among operating, investing, and financing activities) of the firm for a specified period. It also includes disclosures about that period's noncash investing and financing activities.

The classification of cash flows among operating, financing, and investing activities is essential to the analysis of cash flow data. Net cash flow (the change in cash and cash equivalents during the period) has little informational content by itself; it is the classification and individual components that are informative.

Cash flow from operating activities (cash from operations or CFO) measures the amount of cash generated or used by the firm as a result of its production and sales of goods and services. Although deficits or negative cash flows from operations are expected in some circumstances (e.g., rapid growth), for most firms positive operating cash flows are essential for long-run survival. Internally generated funds can be used to pay dividends or repurchase equity, repay loans, replace existing capacity, or invest in acquisitions and growth.

Investing cash flow (*CFI*) reports the amount of cash used to acquire assets such as plant and equipment as well as investments and entire businesses. These outlays are necessary to maintain a firm's current operating capacity and to provide capacity for future growth. CFI also includes cash received from the sale or disposal of assets or segments of the business.

Financing cash flow (*CFF*) contains the cash flow consequences of the firm's capital structure (debt and equity) decisions, including proceeds from the issuance of equity, returns to shareholders in the form of dividends and repurchase of equity, and the incurrence and repayment of debt.

Firms with significant foreign operations separately report a fourth category, *the effect of exchange rate changes on cash*, which accumulates the effects of changes in exchange rates on the translation of foreign currencies. This segregation is essential to accurately report the cash flow consequences of operating, investing, and financing decisions, unaffected by the impact of changes in exchange rates.

Direct and Indirect Method Cash Flow Statements

SFAS 95, Statement of Cash Flows (1987), and IAS 7 (1992) govern the preparation of cash flow statements under U.S. and IAS GAAP, respectively. Both standards permit firms to report cash from operations either *directly* by reporting major categories of gross cash receipts and payments, or *indirectly* by reconciling accrual-based net income to CFO.[1] Both investing and financing cash flows are usually computed identically under the two methods. However, there are reporting options under IAS 7 that can create noncomparability between cash flow statements prepared under the two standards.[2]

Exhibit 36-1 contrasts the direct and indirect cash flow statements of the WSF Company. These statements are generated from the company's balance sheet (Exhibit 36-2) and income statement (Exhibit 36-3).

Under the indirect method, CFO is computed by adjusting net income[3] for all:

1. Noncash revenues and expenses (for example, depreciation expense)

2. Nonoperating items included in net income (for example, gains from property sales)

3. Noncash changes in operating assets and liabilities (operating changes in receivables, payables, etc.)

Enterprises using the direct method must also provide this reconciliation. Firms using either method must disclose the cash outflows for income taxes and interest within the statement or elsewhere in the financial statements (e.g., in the footnotes).[4]

---

[1] Para. 19 of IAS 7 encourages use of the direct method.

[2] See table in "Cash Flow Statements: An International Perspective," later in this reading.

[3] Income from continuing operations may be used when the cash flows from discontinued operations are shown separately. IAS 35 (1998) requires separate disclosure of cash flows from discontinued operations; SFAS 95 does not.

[4] Required by para. 29 of SFAS 95. The AICPA's 2000 *Accounting Trends and Techniques* reports that 33 of the 600 firms surveyed did not disclose interest payments and 22 firms did not disclose income tax payments.

EXHIBIT 36-1	The WSF Company Statement of Cash Flows for Year Ended December 31, 2001

A. Direct Method

Cash collections		$ 2,675,000
Less: Cash inputs	$(1,750,000)	
Cash expenses (rent, operating)	(430,000)	
Cash interest	(125,000)	(2,305,000)
Cash flow from operations		**$370,000**
Capital expenditures	(500,000)	
Investment in affiliate	(710,000)	
Cash flow from investing		**(1,210,000)**
Short-term borrowing	500,000	
Dividends paid	(35,000)	
Cash flow from financing		**465,000**
Net cash flow		**$ (375,000)**
Cash balance, as of December 31		
2001	$ 3,625,000	
2000	4,000,000	
Net change		**$ (375,000)**

B. Indirect Method

Net income		78,870
Add: Noncash expenses		
Depreciation expense		175,000
		$ 253,870
Changes in operating accounts		
(Increase) in receivables	(224,500)	
Decrease in inventories	425,000	
(Decrease) in accounts payable	(475,000)	
Increase in accrued liabilities	50,000	
Increase in interest payable	125,000	
Increase in taxes payable	40,630	
Increase in advances from customers	175,000	116,130
Cash flows from operations		**$ 370,000**

Note: Cash flow from investing and financing identical to that shown on direct method. The firm would also provide a separate footnote on cash payments for interest and taxes. The WSF Company paid $125,000 in interest, but it made no tax payments during the year ended December 31, 2001.

Cash flow statements prepared using the indirect method have a significant drawback. Because the *indirect format reports the net cash flow from operations, it does not facilitate the comparison and analysis of operating cash inflows and outflows by function with the revenue and expense activities that generated them, as is possible from direct method cash flow statements.* In the absence of acquisitions, divestitures, and significant foreign operations, the indirect method simply recasts the income statement

EXHIBIT 36-2	The WSF Company Balance Sheets at December 31, 2000 and 2001		
		2000	**2001**
Assets			
Cash		$4,000,000	$3,625,000
Accounts receivable		0	224,500
Inventory		850,000	425,000
Current assets		$4,850,000	$4,274,500
Investment in affiliates		0	710,000
Buildings		3,500,000	4,000,000
Less: Accumulated depreciation		0	(175,000)
Long-term assets		$3,500,000	$4,535,000
Total assets		$8,350,000	$8,809,500
Liabilities			
Short-term debt		$ 0	$500,000
Advances from customers		0	175,000
Accounts payable		850,000	375,000
Accrued liabilities		0	50,000
Interest payable		0	125,000
Taxes payable		0	40,630
Dividends payable		0	35,000
Current liabilities		$ 850,000	$1,300,630
Bonds payable		2,500,000	2,500,000
Total liabilities		$3,350,000	$3,800,630
Common stock		1,000,000	1,000,000
Additional paid-in capital		4,000,000	4,000,000
Retained earnings		0	8,870
Stockholders' equity		$5,000,000	$5,008,870
Total liabilities and equities		$8,350,000	$8,809,500

and the balance sheet, providing little new information on or insight into the specific components of a firm's cash-generating ability. As a majority of firms prepare the SoCF using the indirect method,[5] it is often necessary to convert an indirect statement into a direct one.

Preparation of a Statement of Cash Flows

The cash flow statement combines cash flows for events that are reported on the balance sheet (e.g., purchases of inventories) and the income statement (e.g., the cost of goods sold). The process is complicated by timing differences

[5] Of the 600 firms surveyed by the AICPA in the 2000 *Accounting Trends and Techniques*, only 7 report using the direct method.

EXHIBIT 36-3	The WSF Company Income Statement for Year Ended December 31, 2001	

Net sales		$ 2,724,500
Less: Cost of goods sold		(1,700,000)
Gross margin		$ 1,024,500
Less: Operating expense	$360,000	
Depreciation expense	175,000	
Rent expense	120,000	
Interest expense	250,000	(905,000)
Income before taxes		119,500
Tax expense		(40,630)
Net income		$ 78,870

Statement of Retained Earnings

Beginning balance, January 1, 2001		$ 0
Net income		78,870
Dividends declared		(70,000)
Ending balance, December 31, 2001		$ 8,870

between when cash flows occur and when they are recognized as revenues, expenses, assets, or liabilities. The next section discusses methods used to prepare direct and indirect method cash flow statements.

Transactional Analysis

Transactional analysis[6] is a technique that can be used to create a cash flow statement for firms that do not prepare such statements in accordance with SFAS 95 and IAS 7.[7] It can also be used to convert indirect method cash flow from operations to the direct method.

One objective of transactional analysis is to understand the relationship between the accruals of revenues, expenses, assets, and liabilities and their cash flow consequences. Another goal is to facilitate analysis by classifying gross cash flows between operating, financing, and investing activities.

The method reconciles line-item changes in the balance sheet with their related income statement components to derive the cash flow consequences of the reported transactions and events. These changes are grouped according to whether they are operating,

---

[6] See Ashwinpaul C. Sondhi, George H. Sorter, and Gerald I. White, "Transactional Analysis," *Financial Analysts Journal* (September/October 1987), pp. 57–64. "Cash Flow Redefined: FAS 95 and Security Analysis," *Financial Analysts Journal* (November/December 1988), pp. 19–20 by the same authors links the transactional analysis method of preparing cash flow statements to those required by SFAS 95.

[7] The number of non-U.S. companies preparing statements of cash flows is on the increase. Firms using IAS 7 are not required to reconcile their cash flow statements to U.S. GAAP. Despite the increased use of IAS GAAP by non-U.S. firms, many foreign firms do not report any cash flow statement or report changes in funds (see "Cash Flow Statements: An International Perspective," near the end of this reading).

investing, or financing in nature. The classification and cash flow description for a typical firm follow:

Changes in Balance Sheet Accounts	Income Statement Items	Cash Flow Description
Cash Flow from Operating Activities (CFO)		
Accounts receivable	Net sales	Cash received from customers
Advances from customers	Net sales	Cash received from customers
Inventories and accounts payable	COGS	Cash paid for inputs
Prepaid expenses	SG&A expense	Cash operating expenses
Rent payable	Rent expense	Cash operating expenses
Accrued expenses	SG&A expense	Cash operating expenses
Interest payable	Interest expense	Interest paid
Income tax payable and deferred income taxes	Income tax expense	Income tax paid
Cash Flow from Investing Activities (CFI)		
Property, plant, and equipment	Depreciation expense	Capital expenditures
Intangible assets	Amortization expense	Capital expenditures
Investment in affiliates	Equity in income of affiliates	Cash paid for and received from investments in affiliates
Short and long-term investments and gains (losses) on certain investments	Realized gains or losses on investments	Cash paid for and received from investments
Assets and liabilities resulting from acquisitions and divestitures		Cash paid for acquisitions or received from divestitures
Cash Flow from Financing Activities (CFF)		
Dividends payable		Dividends paid
Notes payable		Increase or decrease in debt
Short-term debt		Increase or decrease in debt
Long-term debt		Increase or decrease in debt
Bonds payable		Increase or decrease in debt
Common stock and APIC		Increase or decrease in equity
Retained earnings		Dividends paid

The relationship between balance sheet changes and cash flows can be summarized as follows:

▶ Increases (decreases) in assets represent net cash outflows (inflows). If an asset increases, the firm must have paid cash in exchange.

▶ Increases (decreases) in liabilities represent net cash inflows (outflows). When a liability increases, the firm must have received cash in exchange.

While these points are simple (they ignore payments or receipts other than cash), they are useful in practice.

Two examples clarify the application of these points to transactional analysis:

1. When accounts receivable increase, the period's credit sales (revenues) must have exceeded cash collections. Thus, the increase in receivables must be deducted from the accrued sales revenue to derive the cash collected from customers during the period.

2. When interest payable increases, the firm has not paid all the interest expense accrued during the period. Hence, the increase in interest payable must be deducted from the interest expense to compute the amount of interest paid during the period.

Preparation of a Direct Method Statement of Cash Flows

Exhibit 36-4 illustrates the use of transactional analysis to prepare a direct method statement of cash flows for the WSF Company. We use the data from Exhibits 36-2 and 36-3 to explain the method without the complications present in most actual financial statements. A brief discussion of the most critical problems in the preparation of cash flow statements is provided later.

Cash Flows from Operations

Cash Collections.   The principal component of CFO is the cash collections for the period. To derive this amount, we start with WSF net sales of $2,724,500 in 2001. The increase of $224,500 in the balance of accounts receivable means that cash has not yet been collected for all the sales recognized. In addition, the firm received cash advances ($175,000) for which revenue has not yet been recognized.

We modify net sales by deducting the increase in accounts receivable and adding the increase in advances, to arrive at cash collections. This is the amount of cash actually received during the period as a result of sales activities, regardless of when the related revenues are recognized.

Cash Outflows.   The next stage involves the computation of operating cash outflows incurred to generate the cash collections. The first component is the cash outflow for inputs into the manufacturing or retailing process. The decrease in inventory balances[8] (cash outflow occurred in the prior period) is subtracted from, and the decrease in accounts payable (cash outflow in the current period for goods received in a prior period) is added to the cost of goods sold to determine the cash inputs or outflow for the manufacturing process.

---

[8] The cash outflow for inputs is not affected by the inventory valuation method used by the firm, facilitating comparison across firms.

EXHIBIT 36-4	The WSF Company Transactional Analysis ($000)

Balance Sheet

	Income Statement	12/31/00	12/31/01	Change	Cash Effect	Cash	
Cash Collections							
Net sales	2,724.5				Increase	2,724.5	
Accounts receivable	—		224.5	224.5	(Decrease)	(224.5)	
Advances	—		175.0	175.0	Increase	175.0	**2,675.0**
Cash Inputs							
COGS	(1,700.0)				(Decrease)	(1,700.0)	
Inventory		850.0	425.0	(425.0)	Increase	425.0	
Accounts payable		850.0	375.0	(475.0)	(Decrease)	(475.0)	**(1,750.0)**
Cash Expenses							
Operating expense	(360.0)				(Decrease)	(360.0)	
Rent expense	(120.0)				(Decrease)	(120.0)	
Accrued liabilities	—		50.0	50.0	Increase	50.0	**(430.0)**
Cash Taxes Paid							
Tax expense	(40.63)				(Decrease)	(40.63)	
Taxes payable		0	40.63	40.63	Increase	40.63	—
Cash Interest paid							
Interest expense	(250.0)				(Decrease)	(250.0)	
Interest payable		0	125	125	Increase	125.0	**(125.0)**
Operating Cash Flow							**370.0**
Capital Expenditures							
Depreciation	(175.0)				(Decrease)	(175.0)	
Buildings—Net		3,500	3,825	325.0	(Decrease)	(325.0)	**(500.0)**
Cash Invested in Affiliates							
Investment in affiliates	—		710.0	710.0	(Decrease)		**(710.0)**
Investing Cash Flow							**(1,210.0)**
Cash from Borrowing							
Short-term debt	—		500.0	500.0	Increase	500.0	
Bonds payable		2,500	2,500	—		—	**500.0**
Equity Financing							
Common stock		1,000	1,000	—			
Additional paid-in capital		4,000	4,000	—			
Net income	78.87						
Dividends							
Dividends declared					(Decrease)	(70.0)	
Dividends payable	—		35.0		Increase	35.0	**(35.0)**
Financing Cash Flow							**465.0**
Change in cash							**(375.0)**

The remaining income statement accounts and their related balance sheet accounts are similarly modified to their cash analogs to determine the cash outflows for operating expenses, interest, and taxes. In each case, the goal is to link the income statement account with related balance sheet accounts. By related, we mean the balance sheet account that contains cash flows that either have been recognized in that income statement account (accruals and payables) or will be recognized in the future (prepayments).

In many cases, disclosures are inadequate to do this precisely. Educated guesses and approximations may be necessary. For example, we assume that accounts payable reported by WSF relate only to the purchase of inventory for operating purposes although they may also be related to other operating expenses.

A careful reading of footnote data is necessary to obtain additional information on aggregated balance sheet accounts, permitting finer breakdowns of assets and liabilities. For example, in addition to trade accounts receivable, the amounts reported on the balance sheet may include notes and loans receivable, which represent investment cash flows.

Additionally, balance sheet and income statement accounts may require reallocation of some components. For example, when depreciation expense is not reported separately in the income statement, we must reduce COGS by the amount of depreciation expense to accurately reflect cash inputs and create a "depreciation expense" account to correctly estimate cash invested in property. The depreciation expense may be disclosed separately in footnotes, or in the indirect cash flow statement.

Cash flows that are considered nonrecurring[9] or peripheral to the basic activities of the firm are combined in the miscellaneous category, which also includes the cash impact of transactions for which the financial statements and the footnotes do not provide information enabling more precise classification.

Investing Cash Flow

Capital expenditures for long-term assets such as plant and machinery are usually the primary component of investing cash flow. As depreciation changes (net) property, plant, and equipment, the calculation of capital expenditures requires the amount of depreciation, depletion, and amortization expense in addition to the changes in all related long-term asset accounts.[10]

Capital expenditures may be calculated net or gross of proceeds on the sales of these assets. The cash flows from such sales are considered investment cash flows, regardless of whether they are netted in capital expenditures. Trends in gross capital expenditures contain useful insights into management plans.

Other components of cash flows from investing activities include cash flows from investments in joint ventures and affiliates and long-term investments in securities.[11] The cash flow consequences of acquisitions and divestitures must also be reported in this category. Footnote disclosures (when available) should be used to segregate operating assets and liabilities obtained (relinquished) in acquisitions (divestitures). This analysis, as discussed later, may be necessary to calculate CFO.

---

[9] However, the transaction should be analyzed to determine whether it is best classified as operating, investing, or financing.

[10] The deduction for depreciation expense is not taken because depreciation represents a cash flow; rather, it is needed to calculate the cash capital expenditures.

[11] The nature of the relationship between parent and subsidiary or joint venture affiliate should be periodically reviewed to ensure proper classification; in some cases, affiliates may be more accurately considered part of operations. However, contractual arrangements may constrain the parent's control over or access to cash flows from affiliates.

Financing Cash Flow

Components of financing cash flow include inflows from additional borrowing and equity financing, and outflows for repayment of debt, dividend payments, and equity repurchases. Debt financing for the period is the sum of the changes in short- and long-term debt accounts.

The calculation of equity financing cash flows requires analysis of the change in stock-holders' equity, separating:

▶ Net income.

▶ Dividends declared.

▶ Shares issued or repurchased.

▶ Changes in valuation accounts included in equity (each of these may require reallocation to appropriate operating or investing cash flow categories[12]).

Once this is done, every change in the balance sheet has been included (net income is included by incorporating each of its components) except cash. The net cash flow must, by definition, be equal to the change in cash. This identity provides a check on computations.[13]

The last step is to summarize the cash flows from operations, financing, and investing activities. The result is a direct method statement of cash flows, as shown in Exhibit 36-1A.

Indirect Method

Exhibit 36-1B presents the indirect method statement of cash flows for the WSF Company. The reporting of investing and financing activities is identical to the direct method. *The reporting of cash flow from operations, however, is quite different.* Under the indirect method, the starting point is the period's net income. Two types of adjustments are then made to net income to arrive at the CFO:

1. All "noncash" expense (revenue) components of the income statement are added (subtracted).

2. Changes in operating accounts are added/subtracted as follows:

▶ Increases (decreases) in the balances of operating asset accounts are subtracted (added).

▶ Increases (decreases) in the balances of operating liability accounts are added (subtracted).

The second type of adjustment represents the same balance sheet changes that were used to derive individual components of cash from operations under the direct method. As these adjustments are provided by the reconciliation in the indirect cash flow method, they can be used to derive a direct method cash flow statement from an indirect one.

In Box 36-1, we demonstrate this process using Pfizer's indirect method statement of cash flows. As the discussion in the box indicates, careful analysis of footnote information is required to make the necessary adjustments.

---

[12] For example, the change in the unrealized gains (losses) on investments account must be reflected as a component of investment cash flows.

[13] As an additional check, make sure that the income statement components used in the transactional analysis add up to net income.

BOX 36-1   PFIZER: DERIVATION OF DIRECT METHOD CFO ($ IN MILLIONS)

1999 Income Statement

Net sales	$14,133
Alliance revenue	2,071
Total revenues	$16,204
Costs and expenses:	
Cost of sales	(2,528)
Selling, informational, and administrative expenses	(6,351)
Research and development expenses	(2,776)
Other deductions—net	(101)
Income from continuing operations before provision for taxes on income and minority interests	$ 4,448
Provision for taxes on income	(1,244)
Minority interests	(5)
Income from continuing operations	$ 3,199

Indirect CFO from SoCF

Income from continuing operations	$ 3,199
Adjustments:	
Depreciation and amortization	542
Trovan inventory write-off	310
Deferred taxes and other	286
Changes in assets and liabilities:	
Accounts receivable	(978)
Inventories	(240)
Prepaid and other assets	68
Accounts payable and accrued liabilities	61
Income taxes payable	(179)
Other deferred items	7
Net cash provided by operating activities	$ 3,076

(continued)

Two important requirements of SFAS 95 must, however, be explained before proceeding to Box 36-1:

1. *Changes in operating accounts shown on Pfizer's statement of cash flows do not equal the balance sheet changes.* For example, in the 1999 cash flow statement, accounts receivable are reported to *increase by $978*; the balance sheet shows an *increase of $950*. What accounts for this and similar discrepancies in other operating assets and liabilities?

BOX 36-1   *(continued)*

Derivation of Direct Method CFO

Cash collections from customers		
Net sales (excluding alliance revenues)	$14,133	
Change in accounts receivable	(978)	**$13,155**
Cash from alliance revenues		**2,071**
Cash payments for inputs		
COGS	(2,528)	
Depreciation and amortization	542	
Trovan inventory write-off	310	
Change in inventories	(240)	
Change in accounts payable	61	**(1,855)**
Cash payments for SI&A		
Selling, informational, and administrative expenses	(6,351)	
Prepaid and other assets	68	**(6,283)**
Cash for research and development		**(2,776)**
Cash taxes paid		**(1,293)**
Cash interest paid		**(238)**
Miscellaneous cash flows (including minority interest)		**295**
Cash flow from operations		**$ 3,076**

Discussion

The direct method CFO is derived from the income statement and indirect method CFO.* Unlike many other companies, Pfizer does not provide details for most balance sheet categories. A number of assumptions were used to develop the direct method cash flow statement.

Cash collections are derived by deducting the $978 million increase in accounts receivable [see the reported indirect method statement of cash flows (SoCF)] from reported net sales of $14,133 million.

Pfizer reported cost of sales of $2,528 million; depreciation and amortization expense of $542 and the $310 million inventory write-off are added back as they reflect noncash portions of COGS.† We also adjust for the changes in inventory and accounts payable. This latter adjustment requires the simplifying assumption that the accounts payable are related primarily to inventories.

To derive cash expenses, we add the $68 million of prepaid expenses to the reported selling, informational, and administrative expenses of $6,351 million. Research and development expenses are taken directly from the income statement. Pfizer discloses cash tax payments of $1,293 million and cash interest payments of $238 million.

The miscellaneous amount of $295 million is a "plug" amount used to arrive at the reported CFO of $3,076 million.

---

*Note that the CFI and CFF portions of the SoCF are identical under the direct and indirect methods. Thus we need only adjust the CFO portion.

† Many companies disclose depreciation as a separate item on the income statement. For those companies, depreciation on the SoCF equals the depreciation expense shown on the income statement. For companies that do not disclose depreciation separately, an assumption has to be made as to whether the depreciation is (primarily) included in COGS or SG&A. The rule of thumb is to assume COGS for manufacturing firms and SG&A for other firms.

2. Pfizer's statement of cash flows contains the *effect of exchange rate changes on cash* (in addition to the three cash flow categories: operating, investing, and financing). The 1999 amount is $26 million. What does it represent?

We address both issues later in this reading.

Reported versus Operating Changes in Assets and Liabilities

The discrepancies between the changes in accounts reported on the balance sheet and those reported in the cash flow statement are primarily due to two[14] factors:

▶ Acquisitions and divestitures
▶ Foreign subsidiaries

Acquisitions and Divestitures

Changes in reported balances of operating asset and liability accounts may include the effects of both operating activities and acquisitions or divestitures. For example, the inventory account may have increased as a result of:

1. Purchase of inventory from a supplier (an operating activity)
2. Acquisition of (merger with) another firm that has inventory as a component of its balance sheet (an investing activity)

SFAS 95 requires that CFO include only operating transactions and events. Thus, for firms that acquire the operating assets and liabilities of another company, the changes reported in the statement of cash flows as adjustments to income to arrive at CFO will not match the increase or decrease reported on the balance sheet.

The difference between the changes reported in the two statements provides useful information to the analyst. If the difference for any balance sheet account represents the amount of that component acquired through a merger, *the analyst can reconstruct the assets and liabilities obtained by the firm through an acquisition.*[15] This information is generally not provided anywhere else.

Although the reporting requirements accomplish the necessary segregation in the period of the acquisition (or divestiture), cash flows for subsequent periods may be distorted. For example, cash paid for the accounts receivable of an acquired firm is reported as an investment cash outflow. However, collection of the acquired receivable in a subsequent period will be reported as a component of operating cash flows. The result is overstated cash flows from operations, as the cost of acquiring the accounts receivable was never reflected in cash outflows

---

[14] As previously discussed, balance sheet accounts may include both operating and nonoperating (investing or financing) items. The cash flow statement must allocate balance sheet changes to the appropriate activity.

[15] This can be done if we assume that the confounding effect of exchange rate changes (discussed next) is not significant. Thus, ignoring that issue for the moment, one would estimate that Pfizer's accounts receivable increased by $978 million and the balance sheet change reflects a divestiture of $28 million ($978 − $950).

for operations.[16] *Acquisitions, divestitures, and continuing corporate reorganizations can therefore distort trends in both cash flows from operations and investing cash flows.*

Translation of Foreign Subsidiaries

The second difference between the changes reported on the cash flow statement and those reported on the balance sheet relates to foreign operations. The assets and liabilities of foreign subsidiaries must be translated into the reporting currency (i.e., U.S. dollars) upon preparation of consolidated financial statements. This process generates a U.S. dollar balance for each asset and liability account that includes both operating changes (representing real cash flow effects) and exchange rate effects that have no current cash flow consequences.

For example, assume a firm has a foreign subsidiary that has an opening and closing accounts receivable balance of £10,000. Assume further that at the beginning of year 1, the pound is worth $1.00, but at the end of the year a pound is worth $1.10. Upon consolidation, the parent's balance sheet will include

Opening accounts receivable from foreign subsidiary (£10,000 × opening exchange rate of £1 = $1)	$10,000
Closing accounts receivable from foreign subsidiary (£10,000 × closing exchange rate of £1 = $1.1)	11,000
Increase	$ 1,000

This $1,000 increase is included in accounts receivable shown on the balance sheet. However, it will not appear as a component of cash collections for the period because it is not a change resulting from operations. Thus, CFO does not include the effects of the translation process.

Translation gains and losses resulting from exchange rate changes are excluded from cash flows from operating, investing, and financing activities. The effect of these excluded gains and losses is reported as the effect of exchange rate changes on cash (see the next section). The $28 million discrepancy between the balance sheet increase in receivables ($950 million) and that reported in Pfizer's cash flow statement ($978 million) most likely reflects the impact of changes in exchange rates as the $U.S. appreciated during 1999, reducing the $U.S. equivalent of foreign currency receivables.

Effect of Exchange Rate Changes on Cash

An explanation of the *effect of exchange rate changes on cash* follows directly from our previous discussion. Suppose the foreign subsidiary in our previous example had a cash balance of £4,000 at the beginning and end of the year. Upon consolidation, the parent's reported cash balance includes $4,000 at the beginning of the year and $4,400 (£4,000 × 1.10) at the end of the year. This increase of $400 needs to be reported as it does not appear as an operating, investing, or financing activity.

---

[16] Similarly, cash received for accounts receivable of a divested business is reflected as an investment cash inflow, whereas the cash outflow required to generate the receivable (purchase of inventory, selling costs) was previously reported as a component of CFO. However, the CFI characterization is correct since the divested business will no longer contribute to cash flows from continuing operations. Prior period receivables (and CFO) would also exclude balances related to the divested business.

In Pfizer's case, the $26 million reported as "effect of exchange rate on cash" reflects the effect of exchange rate changes on the firm's foreign currency cash holdings.

Example 36-1

Pfizer

We examine each component of Pfizer's cash flow statement, in turn, to demonstrate the use and analysis of cash flow statements.

Cash from Operations. Pfizer reports cash flows using the *indirect method*. As a result, the company provides a reconciliation of the difference between income from continuing operations[17] and CFO. The reconciling adjustments fall into three categories:

1. Noncash expenses
2. Nonoperating cash flows
3. Changes in operating assets and liabilities

Noncash expenses consist mostly of the amortization of past investment outflows. Although the matching principle requires amortization when computing net income, it is not a current-period cash flow. Pfizer adds back depreciation and amortization expense. The company also adjusts the income from continuing operations for the noncash effect of the Trovan inventory write-off.[18]

Nonoperating cash flows relate to investment and financing activities. For example, gains and losses from the sales of investments result from investment activities (discussed below) and must be excluded from the CFO. Similarly, extraordinary losses relate to the early extinguishment of debt, a financing activity, and must also be excluded from the computation of the cash flows from operations.

Finally, cash from operations reports changes in balance sheet accounts that are operating in nature. Such accounts include inventories, accounts receivable and payable (excluding amounts relating to investing and financing activities), and accruals for such operating items as interest,[19] income taxes, and employee benefits.

The reconciliation uses only the changes due to operating activities and, as discussed in the preceding section, excludes two other sources of changes in operating assets and liabilities: acquisitions/divestitures and the impact of changes in exchange rates.

---

[17] Net cash used in (provided by) discontinued operations is separately reported for each year from 1997 to 1999. This distinction is important for the analysis of current CFO and future forecasts of CFO because the discontinued operations will no longer contribute to cash flows.

[18] Other examples of noncash expenses include the cumulative effect of adopting new accounting standards when those standards have no cash flow consequences.

[19] In a subsequent section of this reading, we argue that cash flows for interest represent financing rather than operating activities.

Investing Cash Flow. Pfizer's **net investment in** property, plant, and equipment (PPE) grew steadily each year from $831 million (purchases of $878 million less disposal proceeds of $47 million) in 1997 to $1,490 million in 1999. Pfizer received cash inflows from the sale of businesses, most significantly proceeds of $3,059 million from the sale of the medical technology segment (see Note 2 for details). The company also reports significant transactions in short-term financial instruments, purchases of long-term investments, and other investing activities.

The separate disclosure of cash outflows for acquisitions is an important feature of the cash flow statement. These amounts reflect the assets purchased less liabilities assumed in acquisitions accounted for using the purchase method. *The cash outflows for the acquisitions of operating assets and liabilities of the acquired firm are excluded from CFO but included in CFI.*

Pfizer's transactions in short-term investments require some discussion. These investments are not considered "cash equivalents" because they do not meet the SFAS 95 definition (risk-free with maturities of less than three months). Nonetheless, from a practical point of view, they may be little different. If their risk is low and liquidity high, they should be treated analytically as cash equivalents as they represent additional short-term liquidity. Note that changes in the level of these investments may be reported net, one of the exceptions to the "gross" reporting requirements of SFAS 95. Under that standard, changes in balance sheet assets and liabilities that turn over frequently (another example is credit card receivables) may be reported net. Investments that are long-term, less liquid, and riskier (e.g., stocks or long-term bonds) must be treated differently.

Financing Cash Flow. This category contains cash flows between the firm and suppliers of its debt and equity capital. Pfizer reports a net increase in short-term debt and repayment of long-term debt. CFF also includes dividends paid to shareholders, purchases of common stock, cash effects of stock option transactions, and cash received from the sale of common stock.

Effect of Exchange Rate Changes on Cash. Pfizer has foreign subsidiaries and cash balances denominated in foreign currencies. Changes in exchange rates create translation gains and losses that are not cash flows, but must be reported for the cash flow statement to balance. The $26 million reported by Pfizer captures, in a single number, the effect of exchange rate changes on the firm's foreign cash holdings.

Change in Cash and Cash Equivalents. The net reconciling number is the period's change in the balance of cash and equivalents, equal to the sum of the three major cash flow components (CFO, CFI, and CFF) and any exchange rate effects. This number is necessarily equal to the difference between cash at the beginning of the year and the amount at the end of the year. However, although this number is easy to measure, it has no analytic value. Firms can influence the net change by accelerating or delaying payments, or by making use of short-term financing facilities.

OPTIONAL SEGMENT
ENDS

ANALYSIS OF CASH FLOW INFORMATION   2

The cash flow statement is intended to help predict the firm's ability to sustain (and increase) cash from current operations. In doing so, the statement provides more objective information about:

▶ A firm's ability to generate cash flows from operations

▶ Trends in cash flow components and cash consequences of investing and financing decisions

▶ Management decisions regarding such critical areas as financial policy (leverage), dividend policy, and investment for growth

Neither the statement of cash flows nor the income statement alone contains sufficient information for decision making. (See Box 36-2 for some empirical evidence in this respect.) Income statement and balance sheet data must be combined with cash flows for insights into the firm's ability to turn its assets into cash inflows, repay its liabilities, and generate positive returns to shareholders. All three financial statements are needed to value the firm appropriately.

Free Cash Flows and Valuation

An important but elusive concept often used in cash flow analysis is *free cash flow* (FCF). It is intended to measure the cash available to the firm for discretionary uses after making all required cash outlays. The concept is widely used by analysts and in the finance literature as the basis for many valuation models. The basic elements required to calculate FCF are available from the cash flow statement. In practice, however, the definition of FCF varies widely, depending on how one defines required and discretionary uses.

The basic definition used by many analysts is cash from operations less the amount of capital expenditures required to maintain the firm's *present* productive capacity.[20] Discretionary uses include growth-oriented capital expenditures and acquisitions, debt reduction, and payments to stockholders (dividends and stock repurchase). The larger the firm's FCF, the healthier it is, because it has more cash available for growth, debt payment, and dividends.

The argument for this definition is similar to Hicks's argument regarding the computation of net income, discussed in the previous reading. If historical cost depreciation provided a good measure of the use of productive capacity, then FCF would equal CFO less depreciation expense. However (as discussed in Reading 43), historical cost depreciation is arbitrary and measures the cost to replace operating capacity only by coincidence.

The obvious alternative to depreciation is the amount of capital expenditures made to maintain current capacity, excluding capital expenditures for growth. In practice, however, it is difficult to separate capital expenditures into expansion and replacement components. Lacking better information, all capital expenditures are subtracted from CFO to obtain FCF.

Subtracting all capital expenditures from CFO to arrive at FCF brings the definition of FCF closer to the one used in finance valuation models. In these models, required outflows are defined as operating cash flows less capital expenditures to replace current operating capacity *as well as capital expenditures necessary to finance the firm's*

---

[20] IAS 7 recommends this disclosure.

growth opportunities. Growth opportunities are defined as those in which the firm can make "above-normal" returns. It is difficult to determine *a priori* the amount of capital expenditures required to maintain growth and the discretionary portion of these expenditures; pragmatically, FCF is generally measured as CFO less capital expenditures.

Valuation models do, however, differ as to whether FCF is measured as *FCF available to the firm* [*i.e., all providers of capital (debt and equity)*] or as *FCF available to equity shareholders.* In the former case, required payments *do not* include outlays for interest and debt. In the latter case, they do. Thus, for FCF to the firm, one cannot use reported CFO (less capital expenditures) because CFO includes outlays for interest expense. We return to this issue later in this reading.

Relationship of Income and Cash Flows

When periodic financial statements are prepared, estimates of the revenues earned and expenses incurred during the reporting interval are required. As discussed in the previous reading, these estimates require management judgment and are subject to modification as more information about the operating cycle becomes available. Accrual accounting can therefore be affected by management's choice of accounting policies and estimates. Furthermore, accrual accounting *by itself* fails to provide adequate information about the liquidity of the firm and long-term solvency. Some of these problems can be alleviated by the use of the cash flow statement in conjunction with the income statement.

Cash flow is relatively (but not completely) free of the drawbacks of the accrual concept. It is less likely to be affected by variations in accounting principles and estimates, making it more useful than reported income in assessing liquidity and solvency.

Figure 36-1 compares the level and trend of net income, cash from operations, and two measures of free cash flow for three different companies: Kmart, Westvaco, and Intel. Reported income and CFO were taken directly from the firms' financial statements. Two measures of free cash flow are used:

> FCF1 equals CFO minus (net) capital expenditures.
>
> FCF2 equals CFO minus CFI and thus includes expenditures (receipts) for acquisitions (divestitures) and other investments.

Note that CFO exceeds income for all three companies because CFO is not reduced by the cost of productive capacity.[21] Depreciation is usually the largest component of the adjustment from income to CFO. When the cost of productive capacity is included, as in FCF1, the relationship is company specific and varies from year to year.

Intel is a "growth" company; its income[22] and CFO (except 1998) show steady growth from 1997 to 2000. FCF1 is below income in each period (except 1999), reflecting capital expenditures for expansion as well as for replacement. FCF1 is positive in each year, a healthy sign given rapid growth. FCF2 is also positive each year. FCF patterns have to be monitored carefully for growth companies to ensure that they are not growing too fast, which can cause liquidity problems.

---

[21] This point is elaborated on further in the section entitled "Cash Flow Classification Issues."

[22] Although Intel reported increasing income, one source of that increase was gains on investments in new technology companies, which proved to be ephemeral. Net income was also increased by substantial interest income. Since management has considerable discretion over the amount and timing of realized gains on investments, and the measurement of unrealized gains, the analyst needs to be wary of income growth stemming from nonoperating sources.

FIGURE 36-1 Comparison of Patterns of Income, CFO, and Free Cash Flows

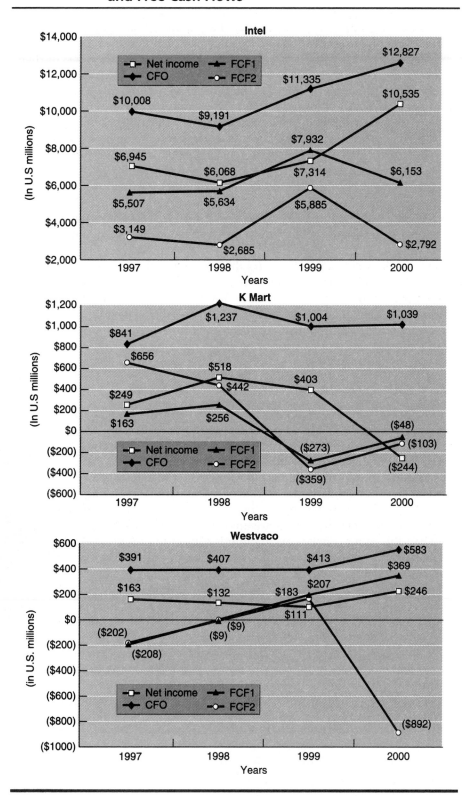

While the 1998 and 1999 increases in free cash flow (due to declines in Intel's CFI) are surprising for a **growth company**, the decrease may simply mean that Intel avoided overexpansion during those years. The 2000 declines in FCF1 and FCF2 are the result of increased capital expenditures and acquisitions.

Kmart reported increases in both income and cash flow from 1997 to 1998, lower CFO in 1999 and 2000, and a decline in income in 1999 and a loss in 2000. CFO remained positive despite a loss in 2000. Both FCF1 and FCF2 deteriorated over the four-year period as capital expenditures and CFI increased. Investments in operating assets, new businesses, and the acquisition of leases of other companies explain the difference between the income and cash flow measures.

Westvaco is an example of a **cyclical company**. Income declined from 1997–1999 with significant improvement in 2000. Debt and interest costs increased every year. After peaking in 1997, capital expenditures declined every year. Net operating assets declined as well until 2000. The result was high and increasing (relative to income) CFO every year from 1997 to 2000. FCF1 was positive in 1999 and 2000 but FCF2 was positive only in 1999. The 2000 decline in FCF2 reflects significant global acquisitions as the company expanded its packaging business.

The previous discussion illustrates the use of cash flow statements together with information from the income statement, the balance sheet, and footnotes to assess the cash-generating ability of a firm. This assessment should consider the firm's liquidity, the viability of income as a predictor of future cash flows, and the effect of timing and recognition differences. We elaborate on these points in the next sections.

Income, Cash Flow, and the Going-Concern Assumption

As noted earlier, income statement amounts based on accrual accounting are generally presumed to be good predictors of future cash flows. That predictive ability is subject to a number of implicit assumptions, including the going-concern assumption. For example, the classification of inventories as assets rather than expenses implicitly assumes that they will be sold in the normal course of business. Similarly, the accrual of revenue from credit sales and the valuation of receivables assume that the firm will continue to operate normally; failing firms may find that customers are unwilling to pay.

When the going concern assumption is subject to doubt, revenue recognition and asset valuation can no longer be taken for granted. The value of inventory and receivables declines sharply when they must be quickly liquidated. Long-term assets (especially intangibles and other assets with little or no value in a nonoperating framework) also must be reexamined when the going-concern assumption is questioned. In this respect, *the statement of cash flows serves as a check on the assumptions inherent in the income statement.*

To find out why income can fail as a predictor of cash-generating ability (uncollected receivables or unsold inventories) requires a comparison of amounts recorded as sales and cost of goods sold on the income statement with the pattern of cash collections from customers and cash paid for inventories on the cash flow statement. A direct method cash flow statement is helpful in this regard.

Income, Cash Flow, and the Choice of Accounting Policies

Consider the income statements for the three hypothetical companies presented in Exhibit 36-5. They are based on the example illustrated in Exhibit 36-1. Their income patterns differ only because of the choice of accounting policy. The policies selected convey information about management expectations. In case A,

EXHIBIT 36-5	Derivation of Cash from Operations Under Alternative Accounting Methods			

		Year		
Indirect Method	**1**	**2**	**3**	**Total**
Company A: Percentage of Completion				
Revenue	$1,000	$3,500	$1,500	$6,000
Expense	(800)	(2,800)	(1,200)	(4,800)
Net income	$ 200	$ 700	$ 300	$1,200
Add (deduct): Increase (decrease in advances)	300	(300)	—	—
Add (deduct): Decreases (increases) in construction in progress	—	(700)	700	—
Cash from operations	$ 500	$ (300)	$1,000	$1,200
Company B: Completed Contract				
Revenue	$ —	$ —	$6,000	$6,000
Expense	—	—	(4,800)	(4,800)
Net income	$ —	$ —	$1,200	$1,200
Add (deduct): Increase (decrease in advances)	500	(300)	(200)	—
Cash from operations	$ 500	$ (300)	$1,000	$1,200
Company C: Cost Recovery				
Revenue	$ 800	$2,800	$2,400	$6,000
Expense	(800)	(2,800)	(1,200)	(4,800)
Net income	$ —	$ —	$1,200	$1,200
Add (deduct): Increase (decrease in advances)	500	(300)	(200)	—
Cash from operations	$ 500	$ (300)	$1,000	$1,200
Direct Method: Identical for All Three Companies				
Cash collections	$1,300	$2,500	$2,200	$6,000
Cash disbursements	(800)	(2,800)	(1,200)	(4,800)
Cash from operations	$ 500	$ (300)	$1,000	$1,200

income is positive each year as management expects to complete the project within budget. In case B, a more conservative management recognizes income only when the project is completed. The annual income statement reports no activities during the first two years. Finally, in case C, management assumes that the eventual collectibility of the revenues is uncertain and thus does not recognize profit until collections are sufficient to recover all costs.

The periodic net income differs because accounting methods and assumptions of managers differ, not because their economic activities differ. *The cash flow statement allows the analyst to distinguish between the actual events that have occurred and the accounting assumptions that have been used to report these events.* This is not to say that the assumptions made by management are wrong. These assumptions may provide useful information. The user of financial statements needs to understand the interrelationship between these events and financial reporting choices.

The cash flow statement shows that the cash collected, cash disbursed, and the cash flow from operations is identical for all three companies because the economic activities of these companies are identical. The three companies differ only with respect to reported income, which is a function of different accounting assumptions and policies.

Income, Cash Flow, and Liquidity

Companies can grow too fast, resulting in liquidity problems. Although Intel, discussed above, does not suffer from liquidity problems, its cash flow pattern can be a prelude to such problems. Another fast-growing company, The Discovery Zone, an operator of children's indoor entertainment facilities, provides such an example. The company filed for bankruptcy reorganization under Chapter 11 in 1995. At that time, its CEO stated:

> A successful Chapter 11 reorganization will address the problems caused by the company's *rapid expansion* and put Discovery Zone on stronger financial footing.

Rapid growth is often accompanied by increases in capital expenditures and negative free cash flows. Moreover, growth companies may also report weak operating cash flows because they must finance growth in current operating assets. As firms usually pay for inventories before they are sold and collect sales proceeds subsequent to sale, there may be a long time lag between payments to suppliers and receipts from customers.

The cash flow statement provides information about the firm's liquidity and its ability to finance its growth from internally generated funds. It can highlight potential liquidity problems, such as an increasing need for operating capital or lagging cash collections.

However, reliance on the cash flow statement is insufficient for a complete assessment of the underlying strength of the company. Trends in sales and earnings must be evaluated from income statement data to determine whether there is a strong growth pattern that indicates a sustainable ability to generate cash flows in the future.

Analysis of Cash Flow Trends

The data contained in the statement of cash flows can be used to:

1. Review individual cash flow items for analytic significance.

2. Examine the trend of different cash flow components over time and their relationship to related income statement items.

3. Consider the interrelationship between cash flow components over time.

We examine each of these uses continuing with Pfizer as an example. A summary of Pfizer's cash flow statements for 1997–1999 is presented below:

Pfizer Statement of Cash Flows			
	1997–1999 (in $millions)		
	1997	**1998**	**1999**
Cash from operations (CFO)	$1,580	$3,282	$3,076
Investing cash flow (CFI)	(963)	(335)	(2,768)
Financing cash flow (CFF)	(981)	(2,277)	(1,127)
Cash provided by (used in) discontinued operations	118	4	(20)
Effect of exchange rate changes	(27)	1	26
Change in cash and equivalents	$ (273)	$ 675	$ (813)

The CFI portion of Pfizer's cash flow statement shows a significant increase in investment[23] in property, plant, and equipment from $831 million in 1997 to $1,490 million in 1999. Pfizer's segment data (Note 19) tell us that more than 90% of the investment has been made in the pharmaceutical segment. The company derives most of its revenues and profits from that segment. Pfizer's merger with the Warner-Lambert Company indicates a continuing emphasis on pharmaceuticals. Revenues are nearly unchanged and profits have been erratic in the only other segment of operations, animal health.

The CFF component reports significant and increasing payments to stockholders; net repurchases of stock and dividend payments were $1,467, $2,888, and $3,586 million in 1997, 1998, and 1999 respectively. Pfizer's free cash flow (CFO—capital expenditures) was not sufficient to meet the demands of its capital structure choices in 1997 and 1999. The company borrowed (short-term debt) $2,083 million in 1999 and Note 4B tells us that weighted-average interest rate on those borrowings during that year was 4.3%. Note that the company reports significant investments in securities during these three years while it increased both Treasury stock and short-term debt. These actions raise the following questions:

▶ Why is the company borrowing and investing short-term?

▶ What do the share repurchases say about the company's investment opportunities?

For an example of the second type of analysis, we look at cash from operations. Because CFO is subject to random and cyclical influences, it should be analyzed over long periods (three to five years). In general, CFO should be positive and increase over time because it provides the resources to service debt, invest in growth, and reward shareholders.

Pfizer's CFO grew by $1,496 million or 95% from 1997–1999. Given the company's sales growth (47%) and increasing profitability (44%), higher CFO is a healthy sign. Significant growth often results in negative CFO for brief periods, as the required increase in working capital more than offsets growth in income. This is not the case for Pfizer, which reports improved CFO despite an increase in operating assets.[24]

---

[23] The capital expenditures are calculated net of disposals. In 1997, for example, there were purchases of $878 million less disposal proceeds of $47 million.

[24] The ratio analysis of Pfizer provides further insight into this issue.

In other cases, however, weak CFO may reflect operating problems such as unrealistic revenue recognition accounting policies or the inability to collect receivables. A comparison of revenue and expense trends with the pattern of cash collections from customers and cash payments should reveal the causes of lower CFO and suggest whether the trend is likely to reverse.

Direct method statements allow analysts to make such comparisons because they provide information better suited to trend analysis. Direct method statements reveal, for example, whether CFO is increasing because cash collections are increasing or payments to suppliers are decreasing. The discussion of Pfizer uses the 1999 data derived in Box 36-1, and 1997 and 1998 data derived using the same method.

First, we compute a "cash gross margin" percentage and compare it to one based on income:

Pfizer: Cash and Income-based Gross Margins

	1997 to 1999 (in $millions)		
	1997	**1998**	**1999**
Cash Flow Statement			
Cash collections	$10,262	$11,912	$13,155
Cash inputs	(2,189)	(1,905)	(1,855)
Cash gross margin	$8,073	$10,007	$11,300
Percent	78.7%	84.0%	85.9%
Income Statement			
Sales	$10,739	$12,677	$14,133
COGS	(1,776)	(2,094)	(2,528)
Gross margin	$ 8,963	$10,583	$11,605
Percent	83.5%	83.5%	82.1%
Other Ratios			
Cash collections/sales	95.6%	94.0%	93.1%
Cash inputs/COGS	123.3%	91.0%	73.4%

Pfizer's cash gross margin increased by $3,227 million (40%) over the 1997–1999 period, more than twice the $1,496 million improvement in CFO. Pfizer has reported increases in both cash expenses and research and development expenditures. Cash gross margin improved in both 1998 and 1999. The income statement–based gross margin held steady at 83.5% in 1997 and 1998, falling to 82.1% in 1999.[25] Future pricing pressures combined with required increases in expenditures may limit growth in Pfizer's CFO.

The cash collections/sales ratio has declined marginally as receivables have increased 74% while sales rose only 32% during this period. *The major improve-*

---

[25] Excluding the Trovan inventory write-off, this gross margin would have risen to 84.3%.

ment over time derives from cash inputs. The cash for inputs/COGS ratio declined, as inputs declined despite rising COGS. Inventories have generally increased, with 1999 inventories declining partly because of the Trovan inventory write-off. The cash for inputs/COGS ratio would be 84% if we exclude the write-off from COGS.

The third type of analysis of cash flow components looks at the relationship among those components over time. An example is provided by Pfizer's free cash flows defined here as CFO less capital expenditures.

Pfizer Free Cash Flows			
	1997 to 1999 (in $millions)		
	1997	**1998**	**1999**
Cash from operations	$1,580	$3,282	$3,076
Capital expenditures	(831)	(1,119)	(1,490)
Free cash flow	$ 749	$2,163	$1,586
CFF	(981)	(2,277)	(1,127)

Pfizer's FCF increased significantly (by $837 million or nearly 112%) over the 1997–1999 period. This increase reflects the improvement in CFO despite higher capital expenditures. As noted in a preceding section, Pfizer did not generate sufficient free cash flow to fund its dividend and share repurchase programs. In 1999, the stockholder payments (share repurchases and dividend payments) were offset by a significant increase in short-term borrowing.

Trend analysis of cyclical companies requires more than the evaluation of data for individual years; aggregated data should be evaluated as well. In Box 36-2, we provide an analysis of A. M. Castle (a cyclical company) over the five-year period 1996 through 2000.

Cash Flow Classification Issues

Although the classification of cash flows into the three main categories is important, we must recognize that classification guidelines can be arbitrary. The resulting data may require selective adjustment before they are used to make investment decisions. The classification guidelines of SFAS 95 often create problems for users of the cash flow statement in the following areas:

- ▶ Cash flows involving property, plant, and equipment
- ▶ Differences due to some accounting methods
- ▶ Interest and dividends received
- ▶ Interest paid
- ▶ Noncash transactions

Some of these issues have been touched on earlier in this reading. We discuss each in greater detail now.

BOX 36-2   A. M. CASTLE

Analysis of Cash Flows, 1996–2000 (in $thousands)

	1996	1997	1998	1999	2000	Total
Cash collections	$675,236	$742,275	$802,283	$710,024	$736,235	$3,666,053
Cash inputs	(479,343)	(555,006)	(617,401)	(431,424)	(537,847)	(2,621,021)
Cash expenses	(142,596)	(164,214)	(188,791)	(190,856)	(197,972)	(884,429)
Cash joint ventures and minority interest					(2,547)	(2,547)
Cash taxes	(15,268)	(13,729)	(10,134)	(3,302)	(5,402)	(47,835)
Cash interest	(2,997)	(4,209)	(7,987)	(11,353)	(10,992)	(37,538)
Miscellaneous	(117)	48	(1,498)	508	(81)	(1,140)
CFO	$ 34,915	$ 5,165	$(23,528)	$ 73,597	$(18,606)	$ 71,543
Capital expenditures	$ (22,544)	$(16,182)	$(30,236)	$(17,770)	$(13,231)	$ (99,963)
Proceeds from sales of PPE	2,521	2,470	9,640	7,399	8,264	30,294
Investments and acquisitions	(17,984)	(29,265)	(26,171)	(3,129)	(4,050)	(80,599)
CFI	(38,007)	$(42,977)	$(46,767)	$(13,500)	$ (9,017)	$ (150,268)
CFF	4,230	38,782	70,474	(60,473)	27,124	80,137
Change in cash	$ 1,138	$ 970	$ 179	$ (376)	$ (499)	$ 1,412
Beginning balance	667	1,805	2,775	2,954	2,578	10,779
Ending balance	$ 1,805	$ 2,775	$ 2,954	$ 2,578	$ 2,954	$ 13,066
Cash inputs/cash collections	70.99%	74.77%	76.96%	60.76%	73.05%	
CFO/cash collections	5.17%	0.70%	-2.93%	10.37%	-2.53%	
COGS/net sales*	71.58%	71.57%	70.52%	68.29%	70.23%	
Operating expense/net sales*	20.84%	21.81%	23.35%	26.73%	26.26%	

*These ratios are based on income statement data not shown.

BOX 36-2   *(continued)*

Discussion

A direct method cash flow statement for A. M. Castle (Castle) for the five years from 1996 to 2000 is presented. These statements were derived from the reported indirect method statements using the methodology depicted in Box 36-1.

Castle is a metal wholesaler. Its revenues and earnings are heavily influenced by the business cycle. Because of the cyclicality, we start by reviewing cash flows over the entire five-year period.

Aggregate cash from operations was approximately $71.5 million, although CFO was negative for two of the five years. Net capital expenditures were nearly $70 million (capital expenditures of $100 million less proceeds from sales of $30 million). The company also reported investment and acquisition outflows of $80.5 million during the same period. Even if we assume that the capital expenditures reflect replacement of productive capacity, free cash flow of $1.5 million would have been inadequate for expansion. Sales have risen from $672 million in 1996 to $745 million in 2000, peaking at $793 million in 1998.

Castle has paid its stockholders nearly $50 million in dividends over the five-year period and borrowed nearly $130 million to finance its investments and acquisitions. Total balance sheet debt has grown from $43 million in 1996 to $164.5 million in 2000 with the debt-to-equity ratio rising from about 36% in 1996 to 127% in 2000.

During this five-year period, cash for inputs (production costs) ranged from 61% in 1999 to as much as 77% in 1998 while the COGS as a percentage of net sales remained comparatively stable (68% to 71.6%). The difference is due to swings in inventory levels and prices

ENDS

Classification of Cash Flows for Property, Plant, and Equipment

Consider the components of cash flow from operations in the following simple example:

Net income	$30,000
Noncash expense: depreciation	5,000
	$35,000
Change in operating accounts: decrease in inventory	15,000
= Cash from operations	$50,000

The cash flow statement adds both depreciation expense (a noncash expense) and the decrease in inventory (change in an operating asset) to net income to arrive at cash from operations for the current period. Their differing classifications suggest that the reason for these addbacks is not identical. Both adjustments reflect prior-period cash outflows that are recognized in income in the current period. Depreciation allocates the cost of fixed assets to the period in which they are used. Similarly, the cost of goods sold allocates the cost of inventory to the period in which the inventory is actually sold.

The difference between the two adjustments is the classification of the initial cash outlays. In one sense, both initial outlays were for investments. In one case, the firm invested in fixed assets; in the other, it invested in inventories. The latter, however, is classified as an operating cash outflow,[26] deducted from CFO in the period of the initial outlay and added back to income when expensed to avoid double counting.

---

[26] An exception occurs, as previously discussed, when inventory is acquired as part of an acquisition.

The original investment in fixed assets was reported as an investment cash outflow, and its allocation (depreciation expense) is added back to income and never classified as an operating flow, but always as an investment flow.[27]

The implications of this classification issue follow:

1. Cash from operations does not include a charge for use of the firm's operating capacity. Cash required to replace the productive capacity or physical plant used during operations is not included in CFO.

2. Firms reporting positive CFO may not thrive unless the CFO (generated and retained) is sufficient to replace the productive capacity used to generate the operating cash flow.

3. Identical firms with equal capital intensity will report different CFOs when one firm leases plant assets and the other owns its assets. The firm that leases reports lower CFO because lease rentals are operating expenditures (operating cash flows), whereas the other firm's expenditures are reported as investment cash flows.

4. Cash payments for operating assets and obligations to pay operating liabilities may also be excluded from CFO. For example, the cash paid for an acquired firm's inventories is included in investing cash flow. However, the proceeds from the sale of such "purchased" inventory in subsequent periods are included in CFO, distorting reported CFO because its purchase cost is never reported in CFO. Similarly, cash paid to settle acquired operating liabilities would be reported in CFO in subsequent periods.

5. An additional problem is that "investment" is not precisely defined. Two examples follow:

   ▶ Hertz classifies its investment in rental cars as inventory, and purchases are included in CFO. In this case, CFO is understated relative to a firm that classifies its operating assets as property.

   ▶ Media companies consider programming purchases as long-term fixed assets. Although amortization impacts reported earnings, purchase costs are never reported in CFO. Yet financial markets seem to value such firms based on multiples of CFO per share rather than earnings per share!

Free cash flow, which deducts capital expenditures (however defined) from CFO, is generally free from the classification issue. However, the classification decision can have a significant impact on reported CFO.

Effect of Differences in Accounting Methods

We previously demonstrated that CFO is not affected by the timing differences generated by revenue and expense recognition methods. In that sense, CFO is less affected by differing accounting policies. However, *CFO is affected by reporting methods that alter the classification of cash flows among operating, investing, and financing categories.* If one accounting method results in the classification of a cash flow as investing and an alternative results in its classification as operating, then the reported CFOs will differ. Moreover, unlike revenue and expense differences in accounting policies that reverse over time, *the differences in CFO classification caused by reporting methods are permanent.*[28]

---

[27] As discussed later in this reading, this applies to all expenditures that are capitalized and amortized rather than expensed.

[28] The effects on the calculation of free cash flows must also be considered. If the classification difference is just between CFO and CFI, then Free Cash Flow = CFO − CFI will not be affected. However, if the classification difference results in a shift between CFO and CFF (as in the case of leasing), FCF is affected as well.

The capitalization of expenditures such as internal-use computer software leads to the classification of cash outflows as investing cash flows. However, they are reported as operating cash flows when expensed immediately.[29] Reading 42 contains an extensive discussion of this issue. Lease classification (discussed in Reading 46) also affects cash flow components for both lessors and lessees. We shall demonstrate other examples throughout the book.

Example 36-2

On July 1, 2000, Amazon.com, Inc. adopted the consensus of Emerging Issues Task Force Issue 00-2, Accounting for Web Site Development Costs. For the year ended December 31, 2000, the company capitalized costs of $3.0 million, reported as a component of fixed assets, and amortized over a period of two years. The company also capitalized the cost of internal-use software including the costs of operating the company's website. *None of these capitalized costs will ever be reported as components of CFO.*

Interest and Dividends Received

Interest income and dividends received from investments in other firms are classified under SFAS 95 as operating cash flows. *As a result, the return on capital is separated from the return of capital.*[30] Combining these two returns to report cash flow to and from investees facilitates analysis. More important, the reclassification of after-tax dividend and interest from operating to investing cash flows has the advantage of reporting operating cash flows that reflect only the operating activities of the firm's core business.[31]

Interest Paid

Interest payments are classified as operating cash outflows under SFAS 95. Such payments are the result of capital structure and leverage decisions and they reflect financing rather than operating risk. The reported CFOs of two firms with different capital structures are not comparable because returns to creditors (interest) are included in CFO, whereas returns to stockholders (dividends) are reported as financing cash flows. For analytical purposes, therefore, interest payments (after tax to reflect the cash flow benefits of tax deductibility) should be reclassified as financing cash flows. The resulting operating cash flow is independent of the firm's capitalization, facilitating the comparison of firms with different capital structures.

The treatment of interest payments in cash flow statements has an important valuation impact. The telecommunications company Sprint has issued two tracking stocks. One is the wireless unit, Sprint PCS, and the other is Sprint FON, comprised of the local, long-distance, and data businesses. Sprint allocated $14 billion

---

[29] This effect depends on the cash flow classification of the capitalized amount. Overhead capitalized in inventory, for example, will not change reported CFO because changes in inventory are also included in CFO. Overhead capitalized in fixed assets, however, will result in reclassification of the outflow from operating to investing cash flow.

[30] Only the nominal (cash) return (dividend or interest received) is reported as an operating cash flow: the real (total) return (which includes capital gain or loss) is split between operating and investing cash flow.

[31] However, some investments and joint ventures are operating in nature. Such investments may assist in current and future operations, require significant financing commitments, and provide some control over the cash flows generated by the investee.

of debt to Sprint PCS and $4 billion to Sprint FON. Sprint PCS pays nearly 8% interest (2% more than the actual cost) on its debt. In its 10-Q filings, Sprint says that the difference between actual interest cost and the amount charged to Sprint PCS is reported as a deduction from Sprint FON's interest expense.

The August 6, 2001 issue of *Barron's* suggests a reason: Sprint PCS (as a start-up, without earnings) is valued on pretax cash flow before interest by the financial markets whereas Sprint FON is valued on after-tax earnings.

Noncash Transactions

Some investing and financing activities do not require direct outlays of cash. For example, a building may be acquired by assuming a mortgage. Under current disclosure rules, such transactions do not appear as cash from financing or investing activities but are given separate footnote disclosure as "significant non-cash financing and investment activities."

For analytical purposes, however, this transaction is identical to the issuance of a bond to a third party, using the proceeds to acquire the building. *The "noncash" transaction reflects both a financing and investing activity and should be included in each category.* Knowledge of the firm's cash requirements for investing activities is as important as the method of financing. The latter provides information about future cash flow needs for interest and the repayment of principal.

The classification issues discussed in this section should provide the reader with an awareness that the cash flow statement is based on assumptions, definitions, and (somewhat arbitrary) accounting rules. Knowledge of these assumptions and rules allows the analyst to make informed adjustments that may be better suited for analytical purposes.

3   CASH FLOW STATEMENTS: AN INTERNATIONAL PERSPECTIVE

As discussed earlier in this reading, the requirements of IAS 7 are quite similar to those of SFAS 95. The following table highlights the most significant differences:

Issue	US GAAP (SFAS 95)	IAS GAAP (IAS 7)
Bank overdrafts	Shown as liability; changes are shown in cash flow statement	May be shown as part of cash equivalents, in countries where it is customary to use overdrafts as part of cash management programs; changes *not* shown in cash flow statement
Interest and dividends received	Cash from operations (CFO)	May be shown as *either* CFO *or* cash from investing (CFI)
Interest paid	Cash from operations (CFO)	May be shown as *either* CFO *or* cash from financing (CFF)
Dividends paid	Cash from financing (CFF)	May be shown as *either* CFO *or* cash from financing (CFF)
Reconciliation from net income to CFO	Always required	Not required when direct method used

The cash flow classification differences are especially significant for companies using IAS GAAP that choose the alternative that differs from U.S. GAAP. For example, the cash flow statement in the 2000 annual report of Roche includes interest and dividends received in cash flows from investing activities and interest paid in financing activities. Financial statement users must watch for such differences and adjust for them to make cash flow measures comparable.

The International Organization of Securities Commissions (IOSCO) has endorsed IAS 7 in financial statements used in cross-border offerings; the U.S. SEC does not require reconciliation when foreign issuers prepare cash flow statements using IAS 7.

Although income statements and balance sheets are required as part of the periodic financial statements virtually around the world, there is no cash flow statement requirement in many countries. For example, Germany and The Netherlands have no requirement; in Japan, it is only required of listed companies as part of an unaudited schedule. Takeda includes a cash flow statement in its English language reports (as explained in Note 1) although Japanese GAAP do not require it. Holmen's cash flow statement uses a quite different format. When no cash flow statement is provided, the analyst should use the transactional analysis method (Exhibit 36-4) to generate a direct method cash flow statement.

When cash flow statements are required, their format varies greatly across countries. Australian GAAP require the use of the direct method. In the United Kingdom, interest and dividends paid (returns to providers of capital) are grouped in a separate category, not included as part of either CFO or CFF. Although we believe this format is superior to the SFAS 95 format, reported cash flows are not comparable without adjustment.[32]

Cash flow analysis is an important tool for international comparisons because of significant accounting differences across countries. As noted, cash flows (CFO and FCF) are generally less susceptible than income to variations resulting from differences in accounting methods. However, differences in accounting methods do affect cash flow classifications. Thus, international comparisons may require the adjustment of reported cash flows.[33]

---

[32] A few countries still present a statement of changes in funds (working capital). The focus on working capital ignores changes in operating accounts. Such statements do not add informational value to net income..

[33] See, for example, Kenneth S. Hackel and Joshua Livnat, "International Investments Based on Free Cash Flow: A Practical Approach," *Journal of Financial Statement Analysis* (Fall 1995), pp. 5–14, where such an approach is applied to a sample of firms. See also Chapter 10 of *Cash Flow and Security Analysis*, 2nd ed. (Irwin, 1995) by the same authors

PROBLEMS FOR READING 36

1. [Cash flows; CFA © adapted] Cash flow data of Palomba Pizza Stores for the year ended December 31, 2000 follow:

Cash payment of dividends	$(35,000)
Acquisition of real estate	(14,000)
Cash payments for interest	(10,000)
Cash payments for salaries	(45,000)
Sale of equipment	38,000
Retirement of common stock	(25,000)
Purchase of equipment	(30,000)
Cash payments to suppliers	(85,000)
Cash collections from customers	250,000
Cash at December 31, 1999	50,000

   a. Prepare a statement of cash flows for Palomba for 2000. Classify cash flows as required by SFAS 95.

   b. Discuss, from an analyst's viewpoint, the purpose of classifying cash flows into the three categories used in part a.

   c. Discuss whether any of the cash flows should be classified differently.

   d. Discuss the significance of the change in cash during 2000 as an indicator of Palomba's performance.

   e. Calculate Palomba's *free cash flow*.

   f. In your calculation of free cash flow, justify your treatment of cash payments for interest and cash paid for acquisitions.

2. [Revenue and expense recognition: cash flow analysis] The Stengel Company showed the following pattern of sales, bad debt expense, and net receivables for 1997 through 2001 (in $ millions):

	1997	1998	1999	2000	2001
Sales	$140	$150	$165	$175	$195
Bad debt expense	7	7	8	10	10
Net receivables*	40	50	60	75	95
Net receivables* at 1996 = 30					

*At year-end.

   a. Calculate the cash collected from customers each year from 1997 to 2001.

   b. For each year presented, calculate the following ratios:

      (i) Bad debt expense/sales

      (ii) Net receivables/sales

      (iii) Cash collections/sales

c. Based on the patterns of sales, net receivables, and cash collections in part A and ratios calculated in part B, discuss the adequacy of the provision for bad debts.

3. [Cash flow: transactional analysis; CFA© adapted] The following financial statements are from the *2001 Annual Report* of the Niagara Company:

Income Statement for Year Ended December 31, 2001

Sales	$1,000
Cost of goods sold	(650)
Depreciation expense	(100)
Sales and general expense	(100)
Interest expense	(50)
Income tax expense	(40)
Net income	$ 60

Balance Sheets at December 31, 2000 and 2001

	2000	2001
Assets		
Cash	$ 50	$ 60
Accounts receivable	500	520
Inventory	750	770
Current assets	$1,300	$1,350
Fixed assets (net)	500	550
Total assets	$1,800	$1,900
Liabilities and Equity		
Notes payable to banks	$ 100	$ 75
Accounts payable	590	615
Interest payable	10	20
Current liabilities	$ 700	$ 710
Long-term debt	300	350
Deferred income tax	300	310
Capital stock	400	400
Retained earnings	100	130
Total liabilities and equity	$1,800	$1,900

Use the direct method to prepare a statement of cash flows for the year ended December 31, 2001.

4. [Preparation of cash flow statement—direct and indirect methods; CFA © adapted] The balance sheet and income statement for the Green Company are presented in Exhibit 36P-1.

 a. Based on the financial statements provided, prepare a statement of cash flows for 2001 using the

   (i) Indirect method

   (ii) Direct method

 b. Calculate the company's free cash flow.

EXHIBIT 36P-1	The Green Company Balance Sheet and Income Statement

Balance Sheet As of December 31	2000	2001	Income Statement for the Year Ending December 31, 2001	
Assets			Sales	$10,000
Cash	$ 1,000	$ 1,100	Cost of goods sold	6,000
Accounts receivable	1,500	1,650	Depreciation	600
Inventory	2,000	2,200	Selling, general, and	
Total current assets	$ 4,500	$ 4,950	administrative expenses	1,000
Fixed assets—at cost*	11,000	12,150	Interest expense	600
Accumulated depreciation	4,500	5,100	Taxable income	$ 1,800
Net fixed assets	6,500	7,050	Taxes	720
Total assets	$11,000	$12,000	Net income	$ 1,080
Liabilities and Equity				
Accrued liabilities	$ 800	$ 880		
Accounts payable	1,200	1,320		
Notes payable	5,500	6,050		
Total current liabilities	7,500	8,250		
Long-term debt	2,000	1,602		
Common stock	1,000	1,000		
Retained earnings	500	1,148		
Total liabilities and equity	$11,000	$12,000		

*No fixed assets were sold during 1996.

WORLDWIDE ACCOUNTING DIVERSITY AND INTERNATIONAL STANDARDS

by Joe Hoyle, Thomas Schaefer, and Timothy Doupnik

LEARNING OUTCOMES

The candidate should be able to:

a. discuss the factors influencing and leading to diversity in accounting and reporting practices throughout the world and explain why worldwide accounting diversity causes problems for capital market participants;

b. discuss the importance of the hierarchical model of accounting diversity;

c. discuss the arguments for and against harmonization and discuss the role of the International Accounting Standards Board (IASB).

INTRODUCTION 1

Considerable differences exist across countries in the accounting treatment of many items. Goodwill is an asset subject to annual impairment testing in the United States; however, it must be amortized over a period not to exceed 20 years in Brazil. For the most part, U.S. companies are not allowed to report assets at amounts higher than historical cost. Mexican companies, on the other hand, must write up their assets on the balance sheet to inflation-adjusted amounts. Research and development costs must be expensed as incurred in the United States, but development costs must be capitalized in European Union countries when certain criteria are met. Numerous other differences exist across countries. In its 2004 annual report, the Dutch electronics firm Philips described six significant differences between U.S. and Dutch accounting rules.[1] If Philips had used U.S. GAAP in 2004, its net income would have been 21 percent higher than the amount the firm actually reported in conformity with Dutch GAAP. In its 2004 annual report,

---

[1] The adjustments related to differences in accounting for goodwill, gains on sale of securities, impairment charges, and other items.

the British beverage company Cadbury Schweppes listed 11 significant differences between U.S. and U.K. GAAP.[2] If Cadbury Schweppes had used U.S. accounting rules, its 2004 net income would have been 12 percent higher than the amount the firm actually reported in accordance with U.K. GAAP, and its shareholders' equity would have been 32 percent higher.

This reading is divided into three parts. Part 1 presents evidence of accounting diversity, explores the reasons for accounting diversity, and describes international patterns or models of accounting. Part 2 discusses and evaluates accounting harmonization efforts. Regarding harmonization, we concentrate on the effort undertaken in the European Union and, more importantly, on the standards developed by the International Accounting Standards Board. We also describe current efforts to converge IASB standards with U.S. GAAP. Part 3 provides a description of the accounting environment in several major countries. We focus on the accounting profession and the presentation of financial statements in those countries.

2   EVIDENCE OF ACCOUNTING DIVERSITY

Exhibit 37-1 presents the 2004 balance sheet for the British company Imperial Chemical Industries PLC (ICI). A quick examination of this statement reveals several differences in format and terminology used between statements in the United Kingdom and the United States. Noncurrent assets in general are called *fixed assets* in the United Kingdom, whereas property, plant, and equipment are referred to as *tangible assets.* Liabilities are called *creditors,* and accounts receivable are *debtors.* Unless one is fluent in the language of U.K. accounting, stocks might be thought to be marketable securities, when actually stocks are *inventories.* Called Up Share Capital is the par value, and Share Premium Account is the Paid-In Capital in Excess of Par on Common Stock. Retained earnings are not reported separately but are included in the item labeled Profit and Loss Account. Rather than being treated as an asset, goodwill is included in the Profit and Loss Account as a negative item. Goodwill written off to shareholders' equity exceeds the amount of retained earnings, resulting in a negative balance in the Profit and Loss Account.

From the perspective of U.S. financial reporting, the U.K. balance sheet has an unusual structure. Rather than the U.S. norm of Assets = Liabilities + Shareholders' Equity, ICI's balance sheet is presented as Total Assets − Current Liabilities = Long-Term Liabilities + Shareholders' Equity. Listed in reverse order of liquidity, assets start with tangible assets and move down to cash. Current liabilities follow current assets to arrive at net working capital.

All of these superficial differences would probably cause a financial analyst no problem in analyzing the company's financial statements. More important than the format and terminology differences are the differences in measurement rules employed to value assets and calculate income. Because ICI's common stock is listed on the New York Stock Exchange, the company is required to be registered and file financial statements with the U.S. Securities and Exchange Commission (SEC). For foreign registrants, the SEC requires income and stockholders' equity reported under foreign GAAP to be reconciled with U.S. GAAP. ICI's 2004 reconciliation to U.S. GAAP is in Exhibit 37-2. This reconciliation provides

---

[2] The accounting difference requiring the largest adjustment was related to goodwill/intangibles amortization.

Balance Sheets at 31 December 2004

	Notes	Group 2004 £m	Group 2003 £m	Company 2004 £m	Company 2003 £m
Assets employed					
Fixed assets					
Intangible assets—goodwill	11	**480**	532	—	—
Tangible assets	4,12	**1,659**	1,794	**66**	68
Investments					
Subsidiary undertakings	13	—	—	**11,854**	10,489
Participating and other interests	14	**61**	57	**1**	1
		2,200	2,383	**11,921**	10,558
Current assets					
Stocks	15	**648**	626	**37**	27
Debtors	16	**1,587**	1,605	**2,187**	2,438
Investments and short-term deposits	17	**105**	345	—	—
Cash	33	**396**	249	**9**	9
		2,736	2,825	**2,233**	2,474
Total assets		**4,936**	5,208	**14,154**	13,032
Creditors due within one year					
Short-term borrowings	18	**(137)**	(29)	—	—
Current installments of loans	20	**(165)**	(534)	**(105)**	—
Other creditors	19	**(1,775)**	(1,663)	**(5,877)**	(4,725)
		(2,077)	(2,226)	**(5,982)**	(4,725)
Net current assets (liabilities)		**659**	599	**(3,749)**	(2,251)
Total assets less current liabilities	4	**2,859**	2,982	**8,172**	8,307
Financed by					
Creditors due after more than one year					
Loans	20	**1,117**	1,353	**26**	133
Other creditors	19	**20**	18	**3,335**	3,450
		1,137	1,371	**3,361**	3,583
Provisions for liabilities and charges	21	**914**	1,092	**185**	207
Minority interests—equity		**87**	69	—	—
Shareholders' fund—equity					
Called-up share capital	23	**1,191**	1,191	**1,191**	1,191
Reserves					
Share premium account		**933**	933	**933**	933
Associates' reserves		**15**	13	—	—
Profit and loss account		**(1,418)**	(1,687)	**2,502**	2,393
Total reserves	24	**(470)**	(741)	**3,435**	3,326
Total shareholders' funds		**721**	450	**4,626**	4,517
		2,859	2,982	**8,172**	8,307

	2004 £m	2003 £m	2002 £m
Net income (loss) after exceptional items—U.K. GAAP	210	20	179
Continuing operations	224	23	166
Discontinued operations	(14)	(3)	13
Adjustments to conform with U.S. GAAP			
Pension expense	(24)	(7)	(14)
Purchase accounting adjustments			
Amortisation/impairment of goodwill and amortisation of intangibles	(10)	(249)	(117)
Disposals and other adjustments	(67)	72	(31)
Capitalisation of interest less amortisation and disposals	(4)	(5)	(5)
Derivative instruments and hedging activities	(10)	(15)	(41)
Restructuring costs	(47)	46	(6)
Share compensation expense	(7)	(7)	(3)
Others	—	—	(2)
Tax effect of U.S. GAAP adjustments	64	(21)	49
Total U.S. GAAP adjustments	(105)	(186)	(170)
Net income (loss)—U.S. GAAP	105	(166)	9
Continuing operations	129	(181)	(124)
Discontinued operations	(24)	15	133

	Pence	Pence	Pence
Basic and diluted net earnings (net loss) per Ordinary Share in accordance with U.S. GAAP	8.9	(14.0)	0.8
Continuing operations	10.9	(15.3)	(11.1)
Discontinued operations	(2.0)	1.3	11.9

	2004 £m	2003 £m
Shareholders' funds—equity, as shown in the Group balance sheet—U.K. GAAP	721	450
Adjustments to conform with U.S. GAAP		
Pension costs	(510)	(482)
Pension costs—minimum pension liability	(582)	(601)
Purchase accounting adjustments, including goodwill and intangibles	2,489	2,778
Disposal accounting adjustments	(100)	(29)
Capitalisation of interest less amortisation and disposals	27	31
Derivative instruments and hedging activities	24	25
Restructuring—contract terminations	(2)	8
Restructuring—asset impairment	2	39
Ordinary dividends	46	42
Deferred taxation and tax effects of U.S. GAAP adjustments	(225)	(421)
Deferred taxation and tax effects of U.S. GAAP adjustments	389	519
Total U.S. GAAP adjustments	1,558	1,909
Shareholders' equity in accordance with U.S. GAAP	2,279	2,359

significant insight into the major differences in accounting principles between the United States and the United Kingdom. Note that although only eight items required adjustments, the aggregate effect on income and stockholders' equity was highly significant. Net income in 2004 under U.K. GAAP was twice as high as under U.S. GAAP. Stockholders' equity under U.K. GAAP was less than one-third the amount reported under U.S. accounting rules.

Magnitude of Accounting Diversity

Although it is generally assumed that accounting diversity results in significant differences in the measurement of income and equity across countries, until the 1990s there was very little systematic empirical documentation of the effect that these differences have on published financial statements. In 1993, the SEC published a survey that examined the U.S. GAAP reconciliations made by 444 foreign entities from 36 countries.[3] The results of that survey indicate that approximately two-thirds of the foreign companies showed material differences between net income and owners' equity reported on the basis of home GAAP and U.S. GAAP. Of those with material differences, net income would have been lower under U.S. GAAP for about two-thirds of the companies (higher using U.S. GAAP for about one-third). Similar results were found with regard to owners' equity. At the extremes, income was 29 times higher under U.S. GAAP for one foreign entity, and 178 times higher using British GAAP for another entity. In addition, the study found that significant differences are spread relatively evenly across countries. In other words, material differences are as likely to exist for a British or Canadian company as for a company in South America, Asia, or Continental Europe.

Focusing on the U.S. GAAP reconciliations of British companies, a separate study found that all 39 companies examined reported material differences in income or equity. Over 90 percent reported lower income under U.S. GAAP and approximately 60 percent reported higher equity. The average difference in income, even after including those with higher U.S. GAAP income, was a 42 percent reduction in income when reconciling to U.S. GAAP.[4] It is clear that differences in accounting principles can have a material impact on amounts reported in financial statements.

REASONS FOR ACCOUNTING DIVERSITY 3

Why do differences in financial reporting practices exist across countries? Accounting scholars have hypothesized numerous influences on a country's accounting system, including factors as varied as the nature of the political system, the stage of economic development, and the state of accounting education and research. A survey of the relevant literature identified the following five items as commonly accepted factors influencing a country's financial reporting practices: (1) legal system, (2) taxation, (3) providers of financing, (4) inflation, and (5) political and economic ties.[5]

3 United States Securities and Exchange Commission, *Survey of Financial Statement Reconciliations by Foreign Registrants* (Washington, D.C., 1993).

4 Vivian Periar, Ron Paterson, and Allister Wilson, *UK/US GAAP Comparison*, 2nd ed. (London: Kogan Page Limited, 1992), pp. 384–93.

5 Gary K. Meek and Sharokh M. Saudagaran, "A Survey of Research on Financial Reporting in a Transnational Context," *Journal of Accounting Literature*, 1990, pp. 145–82.

Legal System

The two major types of legal systems used around the world are common law and codified Roman law. Common law began in England and is found primarily in the English-speaking countries of the world. Common law countries rely on a limited amount of statute law that is interpreted by the courts. Court decisions establish precedents, thereby developing case law that supplements the statutes. A system of code law, followed in most non-English-speaking countries, originated in the Roman *jus civile* and was developed further in European universities during the Middle Ages. Code law countries tend to have relatively more statute or codified law governing a wider range of human activity.

What does a country's legal system have to do with accounting? Code law countries generally have a corporation law (sometimes called a *commercial code* or *companies act*) that establishes the basic legal parameters governing business enterprises. Corporation law often stipulates which financial statements must be published in accordance with a prescribed format. Additional accounting measurement and disclosure rules are included in an accounting law that has been debated and passed by the national legislature. The accounting profession tends to have little influence on the development of accounting standards. In countries with a tradition of common law, although a corporation law laying the basic framework for accounting might exist (such as in the United Kingdom), the profession or an independent, nongovernmental body representing a variety of constituencies establishes specific accounting rules. Thus, the type of legal system in a country determines whether the primary source of accounting rules is the government or the accounting profession.

In code law countries, the accounting law is rather general; it does not provide much detail regarding specific accounting practices and may provide no guidance at all in certain areas. Germany is a good example of a code law country. The German accounting law passed in 1985 is only 47 pages in length and is silent with regard to issues such as leases, foreign currency translation, and a cash flows statement.[6] In those situations where no guidance is provided in the law, German companies must refer to other sources, including tax law and opinions of the German auditing profession, to decide how to do their accounting. Common law countries, where a nongovernment organization is likely to develop accounting standards, have much more detailed rules. The extreme case might be the FASB in the United States. The Board provides very specific detail in its Statements of Financial Accounting Standards about how to apply the rules and has been accused of producing a standards overload.

Taxation

In some countries, published financial statements form the basis for taxation, whereas in other countries, financial statements are adjusted for tax purposes and submitted to the government separately from the reports sent to stockholders. Continuing to focus on Germany, its so-called conformity principle (*Massgeblichkeitsprinzip*) requires that, in most cases, an expense also must be used in calculating financial statement income to be deductible for tax purposes. Well-managed German companies attempt to minimize income for tax purposes, for example, through the use of accelerated depreciation to

---

[6] Jermyn Paul Brooks and Dietz Mertin, *Neues Deutsches Bilanzrecht* (Düsseldorf: IDW-Verlag GmbH, 1986).

reduce their tax liability. As a result of the conformity principle, accelerated depreciation also must be taken in the calculation of accounting income.

In the United States, on the other hand, conformity between the tax statement and financial statements is required only for the use of the LIFO inventory cost-flow assumption. U.S. companies are allowed to use accelerated depreciation for tax purposes and straight-line depreciation in the financial statements. All else being equal, a U.S. company is likely to report higher income than its German counterpart.

Providers of Financing

The major providers of financing for business enterprises are family members, banks, governments, and shareholders. In those countries in which company financing is dominated by families, banks, or the state, there is less pressure for public accountability and information disclosure. Banks and the state often are represented on the board of directors and therefore are able to obtain information necessary for decision making from inside the company. As companies depend more on financing from the general populace through the public offering of shares of stock, the demand for more information made available outside the company increases. It simply is not feasible for the company to allow the hundreds, thousands, or hundreds of thousands of shareholders access to internal accounting records. The information needs of those financial statement users can be satisfied only through extensive disclosures in accounting reports.

There also can be a difference in orientation, with stockholders more interested in profit (emphasis on the income statement) and banks more interested in solvency and liquidity (emphasis on the balance sheet). Bankers prefer companies to practice rather conservative accounting with regard to assets and liabilities.

Inflation

Countries with chronically high rates of inflation have been forced to adopt accounting rules that require the inflation adjustment of historical cost amounts. This has been especially true in Latin America, which as a region has had more inflation than any other part of the world. For example, prior to economic reform in the mid-1990s, Brazil regularly experienced annual inflation rates exceeding 100 percent. The high point was reached in 1993 when annual inflation was nearly 1,800 percent. Double- and triple-digit inflation rates render historical costs meaningless. This factor primarily distinguishes accounting in Latin America from the rest of the world.

Political and Economic Ties

Accounting is a technology that can be borrowed relatively easily from or imposed on another country. Through political and economic linkages, accounting rules have been conveyed from one country to another. For example, through previous colonialism, both England and France have transferred their accounting frameworks to a variety of countries around the world. British accounting systems can be found in countries as far-flung as Australia and Zimbabwe. French accounting is prevalent in the former French colonies of western Africa. More recently, economic ties with the United States have had an impact on accounting in Canada, Mexico, and Israel.

Correlation of Factors

Whether by coincidence or not, there is a high degree of correlation between the legal system, tax conformity, and source of financing. Common law countries separate taxation from accounting and rely more heavily on the stock market as a source of capital. Code law countries link taxation to accounting statements and rely less on financing provided by shareholders.

4 PROBLEMS CAUSED BY DIVERSE ACCOUNTING PRACTICES

The diversity in accounting practices across countries causes problems that can be quite serious for some parties. One problem relates to the preparation of consolidated financial statements by companies with foreign operations. Consider The Coca-Cola Company, which has subsidiaries in more than 100 countries around the world. Each subsidiary incorporated in the country in which it is located is required to prepare financial statements in accordance with local regulations. These regulations usually require companies to keep books in the local currency and follow local accounting principles. Thus, Coca-Cola Italia SRL prepares financial statements in euros using Italian accounting rules, and Coca-Cola Amatil Ltd. prepares financial statements in Australian dollars using Australian standards. To prepare consolidated financial statements in the United States, in addition to translating the foreign currency financial statements into U.S. dollars, the parent company must also convert the financial statements of its foreign subsidiaries into U.S. GAAP. Each foreign subsidiary must either maintain two sets of books prepared in accordance with both local and U.S. GAAP or, as is more common, make reconciliations from local GAAP to U.S. GAAP at the balance sheet date. In either case, considerable effort and cost are involved; company personnel must develop an expertise in more than one country's accounting standards.

A second problem relates to companies gaining access to foreign capital markets. If a company desires to obtain capital by selling stock or borrowing money in a foreign country, it might be required to present a set of financial statements prepared in accordance with the accounting standards in the country in which the capital is being obtained. Consider the case of the Swedish appliance manufacturer Electrolux. The equity market in Sweden is so small (there are fewer than 9 million Swedes) and Electrolux's capital needs are so great that the company has found it necessary to have its common shares listed on foreign stock exchanges in London and Frankfurt and on NASDAQ in the United States. To have their stock traded in the United States, foreign companies must reconcile financial statements to U.S. accounting standards. This can be quite costly. To prepare for a New York Stock Exchange (NYSE) listing in 1993, the German automaker Daimler-Benz estimated it spent $60 million to initially prepare U.S. GAAP financial statements; it planned to spend $15 to 20 million each year thereafter.[7]

A third problem relates to the lack of comparability of financial statements between companies from different countries. This can significantly affect the analysis of foreign financial statements for making investment and lending decisions. In 2001 alone, U.S. investors bought nearly $95 billion in debt

---

[7] Allan B. Afterman, *International Accounting, Financial Reporting, and Analysis* (New York: Warren, Gorham & Lamont, 1995), pp. C1-17 and C1-22.

and equity of foreign entities while foreign investors pumped approximately $408 billion into U.S. entities through similar acquisitions.[8] In recent years there has been an explosion in mutual funds that invest in the stock of foreign companies—from 123 in 1989 to 534 at the end of 1995.[9] T. Rowe Price's New Asia Fund, for example, invests exclusively in stocks and bonds of companies located in Asian countries other than Japan. The job of deciding which foreign company to invest in is complicated by the fact that foreign companies use accounting rules that differ from those used in the United States, and those rules differ from country to country. It is very difficult, if not impossible, for a potential investor to directly compare the financial position and performance of chemical companies in Germany (BASF), China (Sinopec), and the U.S. (DuPont) because these three countries have different financial accounting and reporting standards. According to Ralph E. Walters, former chairman of the steering committee of the International Accounting Standards Committee, "Either international investors have to be extremely knowledgeable about multiple reporting methods or they have to be willing to take greater risk."[10]

A lack of comparability of financial statements also can have an adverse effect on corporations when making foreign acquisition decisions. As a case in point, consider the experience of foreign investors in Eastern Europe. After the fall of the Berlin Wall in 1989, officials invited Western companies to acquire newly privatized companies in Poland, Hungary, and other countries in the former communist bloc. The concept of profit and accounting for assets in those countries under communism was so much different from accounting practice in the West that most Western investors found financial statements useless in helping them determine the most attractive acquisition targets. Many investors asked the then Big 5 public accounting firms to convert financial statements to a Western basis before acquisition of a company could be seriously considered.

Because of the problems associated with worldwide accounting diversity, attempts to reduce accounting differences across countries have been ongoing for more than three decades. This process is known as *harmonization*. The ultimate goal of harmonization is to have all companies around the world follow one set of international accounting standards.

ACCOUNTING CLUSTERS   5

Given the discussion regarding factors influencing accounting practice worldwide, it should not be surprising to learn that clusters of countries share common accounting practices. One classification scheme identifies four major accounting models: British—American, Continental, South American, and Mixed Economy.[11] **British-American** describes the approach used in the United Kingdom and United States where accounting is oriented toward the decision needs of large numbers of investors and creditors. Dutch accounting is quite similar. This model is used in most of the English-speaking countries, and other

---

[8] U.S. Department of Commerce, *Survey of Current Business,* January 2003, p. 38.

[9] James L. Cochrane, James E. Shapiro, and Jean E. Tobin, "Foreign Equities and U.S. Investors: Breaking Down the Barriers Separating Supply and Demand," NYSE Working Paper 95-04, 1995.

[10] Stephen H. Collins, "The Move to Globalization, *Journal of Accountancy,* March 1989, p. 82.

[11] Gerhard G. Mueller, Helen Gernon, and Gary Meek, *Accounting—An International Perspective,* 3rd ed. (Burr Ridge, Ill.: Richard D. Irwin, 1994), pp. 8–12.

countries heavily influenced by the United Kingdom or United States. Most of these countries follow a common law legal system. Most of continental Europe and Japan use the **Continental** model. Companies in this group usually are tied quite closely to banks that serve as the primary suppliers of financing. Because these are code law countries, accounting is legalistic, designed to provide information for taxation or government planning purposes. The **South American** model resembles the Continental model in its legalistic, tax, and government planning orientation. This model distinguishes itself, however, through the extensive use of adjustments for inflation. The **Mixed Economy** model describes the approach recently developed in Eastern Europe and the former Union of Soviet Socialist Republics that combines elements of the former planned economic system and the recent market economy reforms.

Concentrating on the British-American and Continental model countries, Professor Chris Nobes has developed a more refined classification scheme that shows how the financial reporting systems in 14 developed countries relate to one another. An adaptation of Nobes's classification is in Exhibit 37-3.[12]

A Hypothetical Model of Accounting Diversity

The terms *micro-based* and *macro-uniform* describe the British-American and Continental models, respectively. Each of these classes is divided into two subclasses

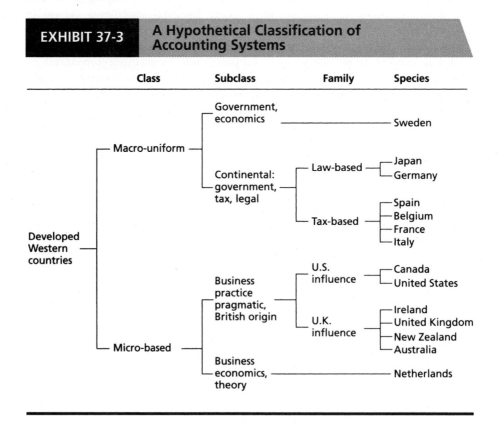

EXHIBIT 37-3   **A Hypothetical Classification of Accounting Systems**

---

[12] Source: C. W. Nobes, "A Judgemental International Classification of Financial Reporting Practices," *Journal of Business Finance and Accounting*, Spring 1983, p. 7.

that are further divided into families. Within the micro-based class of accounting system is a subclass heavily influenced by business economics and accounting theory. The Netherlands is the only country in this subclass. One manifestation of the influence of theory is that Dutch companies may use current replacement cost accounting in their primary financial statements. The other micro-based subclass is of British origin and is more pragmatic and oriented toward business practice, relying less on economic theory in the development of accounting rules. The British origin subclass can be split into two families: one dominated by the United States and one dominated by the United Kingdom. Nobes does not indicate how these two families differ.

On the macro-uniform side of the model, a government, economics subclass has only one country, Sweden. Swedish accounting distinguishes itself from the other macro-uniform countries in being closely aligned with national economic policies. For example, income smoothing is allowed to promote economic stability, and social accounting has developed to meet macroeconomic concerns. The Continental government, tax, legal subclass contains Continental European countries divided into two families. Led by Germany, the law-based family includes Japan. The tax-based family consists of several Romance-language countries. The major difference between these families is that the accounting law is the primary determinant of accounting practice in Germany, whereas the tax law dominates in the Southern European countries.

The importance of this hierarchical model is that it shows the comparative distances between countries and could be used as a blueprint for determining where financial statement comparability is likely to be greater. For example, comparisons of financial statements in the United States and those in Canada (which are in the same family) are likely to be more valid than comparisons between those in the United States and in the United Kingdom (which are not in the same family). However, the United States and the United Kingdom (which are in the same subclass) are more comparable than are the United States and the Netherlands (which are in different subclasses). Finally, comparisons between the United States and the Netherlands (which are in the same class) might be more meaningful than comparisons between the United States and any of the macro-uniform countries.

The hypothetical model in Exhibit 37-3 was empirically tested in 1993.[13] Data gathered on 100 financial reporting practices in 50 countries (including the 14 countries in Exhibit 37-3) were analyzed using the statistical procedure of hierarchical cluster analysis. The significant clusters arising from the analysis are in Exhibit 37-4.

The large size of the U.K. influence cluster (Cluster 1) clearly shows the influence of British colonialism on accounting worldwide. In contrast, Cluster 2, which includes the United States, is quite small. The emergence of Cluster 4, which includes several Latin American countries, is evidence of the importance of inflation as a factor affecting accounting practice.

The two classes of accounting reflected in Exhibit 37-4 differ significantly on 66 of the 100 financial reporting practices examined.[14] Differences exist for 41 of the 56 disclosure practices studied. In all but one case, the micro class of

---

[13] Timothy S. Doupnik and Stephen B. Salter, "An Empirical Test of a Judgemental International Classification of Financial Reporting Practices," *Journal of International Business Studies,* First Quarter 1993, pp. 41–60.

[14] Ibid., 1993, p. 56.

| EXHIBIT 37-4 | Results of Cluster Analysis on 100 Financial Reporting Practices |

Micro Class		Macro Class		
Cluster 1	**Cluster 2**	**Cluster 3**	**Cluster 5**	**Cluster 7**
Australia	Bermuda	Costa Rica	Colombia	Finland
Botswana	Canada		Denmark	Sweden
Hong Kong	Israel	**Cluster 4**	France	
Ireland	United States	Argentina	Italy	**Cluster 8**
Jamaica		Brazil	Norway	Germany
Luxembourg		Chile	Portugal	
Malaysia		Mexico	Spain	**Cluster 9**
Namibia				Japan
Netherlands			**Cluster 6**	
Netherlands Antilles			Belgium	
Nigeria			Egypt	
New Zealand			Liberia	
Philippines			Panama	
Papua New Guinea			Saudi Arabia	
South Africa			Thailand	
Singapore			United Arab Emirates	
Sri Lanka				
Taiwan				
Trinidad and Tobago				
United Kingdom				
Zambia				
Zimbabwe				

Source: Timothy S. Doupnik and Stephen B. Salter, "An Empirical Test of a Judgemental International Classification of Financial Reporting Practices," *Journal of International Business Studies,* First Quarter 1993, p. 53.

countries provided a higher level of disclosure than the macro class of countries. There were also significant differences for 25 of the 44 practices examined affecting income measurement. Of particular importance is the item asking whether accounting practice adhered to tax requirements. The mean level of agreement with this statement among macro countries was 72 percent, whereas it was only 45 percent among micro countries. To summarize, companies in the micro-based countries provide more extensive disclosure than do companies in the macro-uniform countries, and companies in the macro countries are more heavily influenced by taxation than are companies in the micro countries. These results are consistent with the relative importance of equity finance and relatively weak link between accounting and taxation in the micro countries.

INTERNATIONAL HARMONIZATION OF FINANCIAL REPORTING

6

The preceding sections make clear the significant, systematic differences in accounting practices across countries. As noted in the introduction, these differences cause complications for those preparing and using financial statements. Several organizations around the world are involved in an effort to harmonize financial reporting practices.

Harmonization is the process of reducing differences in financial reporting practices across countries, thereby increasing the comparability of financial statements. Ultimately, harmonization implies the development of a set of international accounting standards that would be applied in all countries.

Arguments for Harmonization

Proponents of accounting harmonization argue that comparability of financial statements worldwide is necessary for the globalization of capital markets. Financial statement comparability would make it easier for investors to evaluate potential investments in foreign securities and thereby take advantage of the risk reduction possible through international diversification. It also would simplify the evaluation by multinational companies of possible foreign takeover targets. From the other side, with harmonization, companies could gain access to all capital markets in the world with one set of financial statements. This would allow companies to lower their cost of capital and would make it easier for foreign investors to acquire the company's stock.

One set of universally accepted accounting standards would reduce the cost of preparing worldwide consolidated financial statements and would simplify the auditing of these statements. Multinational companies would find it easier to transfer accounting staff to other countries. This would be true for the international auditing firms as well.

Arguments against Harmonization

One obstacle to harmonization is the magnitude of the differences between countries and the fact that the political cost of eliminating those differences could be quite high. As stated by Dennis Beresford, former chairman of the FASB, "High on almost everybody's list of obstacles is nationalism. Whether out of deep-seated tradition, indifference born of economic power, or resistance to intrusion of foreign influence, some say that national entities will not bow to any international body."[15] Arriving at principles that satisfy all of the parties involved throughout the world seems an almost Herculean task.

Harmonization is difficult to achieve, and the need for such standards is not universally accepted. As Richard Karl Goeltz stated, "Full harmonization of international accounting standards is probably neither practical nor truly valuable. . . . It is not clear whether significant benefits would be derived in fact. A well-developed global capital market exists already. It has evolved without uniform accounting standards."[16] Opponents of harmonization argue that it is

---

[15] Dennis R. Beresford, "Accounting for International Operations," *CPA Journal*, October 1988, pp. 79–80.

[16] Richard Karl Goeltz, "International Accounting Harmonization: The Impossible (and Unnecessary?) Dream," *Accounting Horizons*, March 1991, pp. 85–86.

unnecessary to force all companies worldwide to follow a common set of rules. The international capital market will force those companies that benefit from accessing the market to provide the required accounting information without harmonization.

Another argument against harmonization is that because of different environmental influences, differences in accounting across countries might be appropriate and necessary. For example, countries at different stages of economic development or that rely on different sources of financing perhaps should have differently oriented accounting systems.

Regardless of the arguments against harmonization, substantial effort to reduce differences in accounting practice and to develop a set of international accounting standards has been ongoing for several decades. The question is no longer *whether* harmonization should be strived for, but *to what extent* accounting practices can be harmonized and *how fast.*

7   MAJOR HARMONIZATION EFFORTS

While numerous organizations are involved in harmonization on either a regional or worldwide basis, the two most important players in this effort have been the European Union on a regional basis and the International Accounting Standards Board on a global basis.

European Union

The major objective embodied in the Treaty of Rome that created the European Economic Community in 1957 (now called the *European Union*) was the establishment of free movement of persons, goods and services, and capital across member countries. To achieve a common capital market, the **European Union (EU)** has attempted to harmonize financial reporting practices within the community. To do this, the EU issues directives that must be incorporated into the laws of member nations. Two directives have helped harmonize accounting. The Fourth Directive, issued in 1978, deals with valuation rules, disclosure requirements, and the format of financial statements. The Seventh Directive, issued in 1983, relates to the preparation of consolidated financial statements.

The Seventh Directive requires companies to prepare consolidated financial statements and outlines the procedures for their preparation. This directive has had a significant impact on European accounting because consolidations were previously uncommon on the Continent.

The Fourth Directive provides considerable flexibility with dozens of provisions beginning with the expression "member states may require or permit companies to"; these allow countries to choose from among acceptable alternatives. One manifestation of this flexibility is that under Dutch and British law, companies may write up assets to higher market values, whereas in Germany this is strictly forbidden. Notwithstanding this flexibility, implementation of the directives into local law caused extensive change in accounting practice in several countries.

Given that EU countries are in four of the nine clusters in Exhibit 37-4, the Fourth and Seventh Directives clearly did not create complete harmonization within the European Union. As an illustration of the effects of differing principles within the EU, the profits of one case study company were measured in European currency units (ECUs) using the accounting principles of various member states. The results are almost startling:

Most Likely Profit—Case Study Company	
Country	**ECUs (millions)**
Spain	131
Germany	133
Belgium	135
Netherlands	140
France	149
Italy	174
United Kingdom	192

Source: Anthony Carey, "Harmonization: Europe Moves Forward," *Accountancy,* March 1990, pp. 92–93.

Part of the difference in profit across EU countries is the result of several important topics not being covered in the directives including lease accounting, foreign currency translation, accounting changes, contingencies, income taxes, and long-term construction contracts. In 1990, the EU Commission indicated that there would be no further accounting directives. Instead, the Commission indicated in 1995 that it would associate the EU with efforts undertaken by the International Accounting Standards Committee toward a broader international harmonization of accounting standards. We will return to the EU harmonization effort later in this reading.

INTERNATIONAL ACCOUNTING STANDARDS COMMITTEE   8

In hopes of eliminating the diversity of principles used throughout the world, the International Accounting Standards Committee (IASC) was formed in June 1973 by accountancy bodies in Australia, Canada, France, Germany, Japan, Mexico, the Netherlands, the United Kingdom and Ireland, and the United States. The IASC operated until April 1, 2001, when it was succeeded by the International Accounting Standards Board (IASB).

Based in London, the IASC's primary objective was the development of international accounting standards (IASs). The IASC had no power to require the use of its standards, but member accountancy bodies pledged to work toward adoption of IASs in their countries. IASs were approved by a board consisting of representatives from 14 countries. The part-time board members normally met only three times a year for three or four days. The publication of a final IAS required approval of at least 11 of the 14 board members.

Early IASs tended to follow a lowest common denominator approach and often allowed at least two methods for dealing with a particular accounting issue. For example, IAS 2, originally issued in 1975, allowed the use of specific identification, FIFO, LIFO, average cost, and the base stock method for valuing inventories, effectively sanctioning most of the alternative methods in worldwide use. For the same reason, the IASC initially allowed both the traditional U.S. treatment of expensing goodwill over a period of up to 40 years and the U.K. approach of writing off goodwill directly to stockholders' equity. Although perhaps necessary from a political perspective, such compromise brought the IASC under heavy criticism.

A study conducted by the IASC in 1988 found that all or most companies listed on the stock exchange in the countries in Exhibit 37-3 (except Italy and Germany) were in compliance with IASC standards.[17] Given that research has shown that these countries were following at least four significantly different models of accounting at that time, it is obvious that IASC standards existing in 1988 introduced little if any comparability of financial statements across countries.

9   THE IOSCO AGREEMENT

In 1987, the International Organization of Securities Commissions (IOSCO) became a member of the IASC's Consultative Group. IOSCO's membership is composed of the stock exchange regulators in more than 100 countries, including the U.S. SEC. As one of its objectives, IOSCO works to facilitate cross-border securities offerings and listings by multinational issuers. To this end, IOSCO has supported the IASC's efforts at developing IASs that could be used by foreign issuers in lieu of local accounting standards when entering capital markets outside of their home country. "This could mean, for example, that if a French company has a simultaneous stock offering in the United States, Canada, and Japan, financial statements prepared in accordance with international standards could be used in all three nations."[18]

IOSCO supported the IASC's Comparability Project (begun in 1987), the purpose of which was "to eliminate most of the choices of accounting treatment currently permitted under International Accounting Standards."[19] As a result of the Comparability Project, 10 revised IASs were approved in 1993 to become effective in 1995. In 1993, IOSCO and the IASC agreed upon a list of "core" standards for use in financial statements of companies involved in cross-border securities offerings and listings. Upon their completion, IOSCO agreed to evaluate the core standards for possible endorsement for cross-border listing purposes.

The IASC accelerated its pace of standards development, issuing or revising 16 standards in the period 1997–1998. With the publication of IAS 39 in December 1998, the IASC completed its work program to develop the core set of standards. In 2000, IOSCO's Technical Committee recommended that securities regulators permit foreign issuers to use IASC standards to gain access to a country's capital market as an alternative to using local standards. The Technical Committee consists of securities regulators representing the 14 largest and most developed capital markets including Australia, France, Germany, Japan, the United Kingdom, and the United States.

---

[17] International Accounting Standards Committee, *Survey of the Use and Application of International Accounting Standards* (1988), p. 5.

[18] Stephen H. Collins, "The SEC on Full and Fair Disclosure," *Journal of Accountancy,* January 1989, p. 84.

[19] International Accounting Standards Committee, *International Accounting Standards* 1990 (London: IASC, 1990), p. 13.

INTERNATIONAL ACCOUNTING STANDARDS BOARD

Upon completion of its core set of standards, the IASC proposed a new structure that would allow it and national standard setters to better work together toward global harmonization. The restructuring created the International Accounting Standards Board (IASB). In April 2001, the IASB assumed accounting standard-setting responsibilities from its predecessor body, the IASC.

The IASB consists of 14 members—12 full-time and 2 part-time. To ensure independence of the IASB, all full-time members are required to sever their employment relationships with former employers and are not allowed to hold any position giving rise to perceived economic incentives that might call their independence into question. Seven of the full-time IASB members have a formal liaison responsibility with one or more national standard setters; the other seven do not have such a responsibility. A minimum of five IASB members must have a background as practicing auditors, three must have a background as preparers of financial statements and three as users of financial statements, and at least one member must come from academia. The most important criterion for selection as an IASB member is technical competence. The initial IASB members came from nine countries: Australia, Canada, France, Germany, Japan, South Africa, Switzerland, the United Kingdom (4), and the United States (3).

International Financial Reporting Standards (IFRSs)

In April 2001, the IASB adopted all international accounting standards issued by the IASC and announced that its accounting standards would be called *international financial reporting standards* (IFRSs). *IAS 1*, "Presentation of Financial Statements," was amended in 2003 and defines IFRSs as standards and interpretations adopted by the IASB. The authoritative pronouncements that make up IFRSs consist of these:

▶ International Financial Reporting Standards issued by the IASB.

▶ International Accounting Standards issued by the IASC (and adopted by the IASB).

▶ Interpretations originated by the International Financial Reporting Interpretations Committee (IFRIC).

Under the new structure, the IASB has sole responsibility for establishing IFRSs.

The IASC issued 41 IASs from 1975 to 2001, and the IASB had issued five international financial reporting standards (IFRSs) as of January 1, 2005. Several IASs have been withdrawn or superseded by subsequent standards. For example, later standards dealing with property, plant, and equipment, and intangible assets have superseded *IAS 4*, "Depreciation Accounting," originally issued in 1976. Other IASs have been revised one or more times since their original issuance. For example, *IAS 2*, "Inventories," was originally issued in 1975 and then revised as part of the comparability project in 1993. As part of an improvements project undertaken by the IASB, *IAS 2* was again updated in 2003. Unlike the U.S. FASB, which creates a uniquely numbered statement of financial accounting standards to amend a previous standard the IASC and IASB recycle existing numbers.[20] Of 41 IASs issued by the IASC, only 31 were still in force as of January 1, 2005. The IASB issued the first IFRS in 2003; it deals with the important question of how a company should restate its financial statements when it adopts IFRSs for the first time.

Exhibit 37-5 provides a complete list of the 36 IASs and IFRSs in force as of January 1, 2005. Together these two sets of standards create what the IASB refers to as *IFRSs* and what can be thought of as IASB GAAP. IFRSs constitute a comprehensive set of financial reporting standards that cover the major accounting issues. In addition, the IASB's Framework for the Preparation and Presentation of Financial Statements, which is very similar in scope to the FASB's Conceptual Framework, provides a basis for determining the appropriate accounting treatment for those items not covered by a specific standard or interpretation. As was true for its predecessor, the IASB does not have the ability to enforce its standards. It develops IFRSs for the public good and makes them available to any organization or nation that might wish to use them.

Use of IFRSs

A country can use IFRSs in a number of different ways. For example, a country could (1) adopt IFRSs as its national GAAP, (2) require domestic listed companies to use IFRSs in preparing their consolidated financial statements, (3) allow domestic listed companies to use IFRSs, and/or (4) require or allow foreign companies listed on a domestic stock exchange to use IFRSs. See Exhibit 37-6 for a summary of the extent to which IFRSs are required or permitted to be used by domestic listed companies in countries around the world.

Of the 132 countries included in Exhibit 37-6, 66 require all domestic listed companies to use IFRSs. Perhaps most significant among this group are the 25 countries of the European Union. All publicly traded companies in the EU have been required to use IFRSs to prepare their consolidated financial statements since January 1, 2005. The only exceptions are those companies that were already using U.S. GAAP, which several jurisdictions allowed, or that have publicly traded debt securities only.[21] These companies will begin using IFRSs in 2007. EU companies continue to use domestic GAAP to prepare parent company financial statements, which often serve as the basis for taxation.

In addition to the EU, many developing countries require the use of IFRSs. This is especially true for countries in Eastern Europe and the former Union of Soviet Socialist Republics (USSR), which may have found adoption of IFRSs an inexpensive means of switching from a Soviet-style accounting system to one oriented toward a free market.

Few countries in the Western Hemisphere require or permit domestic listed companies to use IFRSs in preparing their financial statements, and those that do tend to be the smaller economies. None of the largest economies in the Americas—the United States, Canada, Brazil, Mexico, Argentina, Chile—allows the use of IFRSs by domestic companies. This situation is unlikely to continue for very long. In March 2005, the Accounting Standards Board in Canada issued an invitation to comment on a strategic plan for converging Canadian GAAP with IFRSs. The plan proposes to converge Canadian standards with IFRSs over a

---

[20] In December 2004, the FASB broke with its tradition of using new numbers for revisions to standards when it issued *SFAS 123* (revised 2004) to supersede *SFAS 123*, originally issued in 1995.

[21] One of the best-known examples of a European company using U.S. GAAP prior to the introduction of IFRSs in the EU was Daimler-Chrysler, the largest manufacturing firm in Germany.

EXHIBIT 37-5	International Financial Reporting Standards as of January 2005	
	Title	**Issued**
IAS 1	Presentation of Financial Statements	1975 (revised 1997, 2003)
IAS 2	Inventories	1975 (revised 1993, 2003)
IAS 7	Cash Flow Statements	1977 (revised 1992)
IAS 8	Net Profit or Loss for the Period, Fundamental Errors and Changes in Accounting Policies	1978 (revised 1993, 2003)
IAS 10	Events after the Balance Sheet Date	1978 (revised 1999, 2003)
IAS 11	Construction Contracts	1979 (revised 1993)
IAS 12	Accounting for Taxes on Income	1979 (revised 1997, 2000)
IAS 14	Segment Reporting	1981 (revised 1997)
IAS 16	Property, Plant, and Equipment	1982 (revised 1993, 1998, 2003)
IAS 17	Leases	1982 (revised 1997)
IAS 18	Revenue	1982 (revised 1993)
IAS 19	Employee Benefits	1983 (revised 1997, 2000)
IAS 20	Accounting for Government Grants and Disclosure of Government Assistance	1983
IAS 21	The Effects of Changes in Foreign Exchange Rates	1983 (revised 1993, 2003)
IAS 23	Borrowing Costs	1984 (revised 1993)
IAS 24	Related Party Disclosures	1984 (revised 2003)
IAS 26	Accounting and Reporting by Retirement Benefit Plans	1987
IAS 27	Consolidated Financial Statements and Accounting for Investments in Subsidiaries	1989 (revised 2003)
IAS 28	Accounting for Investments in Associates	1989 (revised 1998, 2003)
IAS 29	Financial Reporting in Hyperinflationary Economies	1989
IAS 30	Disclosures in the Financial Statements of Banks and Similar Financial Institutions	1990
IAS 31	Financial Reporting of Interests in Joint Ventures	1990 (revised 1998, 2003)
IAS 32	Financial Instruments: Disclosure and Presentation	1995 (revised 2003)
IAS 33	Earnings per Share	1997 (revised 2003)
IAS 34	Interim Financial Reporting	1998
IAS 36	Impairment of Assets	1998 (revised 2004)
IAS 37	Provisions, Contingent Liabilities and Contingent Assets	1998
IAS 38	Intangible Assets	1998 (revised 2004)
IAS 39	Financial Instruments: Recognition and Measurement	1998 (revised 2000, 2003)
IAS 40	Investment Property	2000 (revised 2003)
IAS 41	Agriculture	2001
IFRS 1	First-Time Adoption of IFRS	2003
IFRS 2	Share-Based Payment	2004
IFRS 3	Business Combinations	2004
IFRS 4	Insurance Contracts	2004
IFRS 5	Non-Current Assets Held for Sale and Discontinued Operations	2004

period of five years, and at the end of that period, "Canadian GAAP will cease to exist as a separate, distinct basis of financial reporting for public companies."[22]

A number of countries that do not allow domestic listed companies to use IFRSs nevertheless allow *foreign* companies listed on domestic stock exchanges to use them as recommended by IOSCO. For example, Japan allows foreign companies listing on the Tokyo Stock Exchange to prepare IFRS-based financial

| EXHIBIT 37-6 | Use of IFRSs in Preparing Consolidated Financial Statements |

IFRSs Required for All Domestic Listed Companies

Armenia	Finland*	Kyrgyzstan	Peru
Austria*	France*	Latvia*	Poland*
Bahamas	Georgia	Lebanon	Portugal*
Barbados	Germany*	Liechtenstein	Slovak Republic*
Bangladesh	Greece*	Lithuania*	Slovenia*
Belgium*	Guatemala	Luxembourg*	South Africa
Bosnia & Herzegovina	Guyana	Macedonia	Spain*
Bulgaria	Haiti	Malawi	Sweden*
Costa Rica	Honduras	Malta*	Tajikistan
Croatia	Hungary*	Mauritius	Tanzania
Cyprus*	Iceland	Nepal	Trinidad & Tobago
Czech Republic*	Ireland*	Netherlands*	Ukraine
Denmark*	Italy*	Nicaragua	United Kingdom*
Dominican Republic	Jamaica	Norway	Venezuela
Ecuador	Jordan	Oman	Yugoslavia
Egypt	Kenya	Panama	
Estonia*	Kuwait	Papua New Guinea	

IFRSs Required for Some Domestic Listed Companies

Bahrain	Kazakhstan	Russian Federation	United Arab Emirates
China	Romania		

IFRSs Permitted for Domestic Listed Companies

Aruba	Dominica	Myanmar	Turkey
Bermuda	El Salvador	Namibia	Uganda
Bolivia	Gibraltar	Netherlands Antilles	Uruguay
Botswana	Hong Kong†	Sri Lanka	Virgin Is. (British)
Brunei	Laos	Swaziland	Zambia
Cayman Islands	Lesotho	Switzerland	Zimbabwe

(Exhibit continued on next page ...)

---

[22] Accounting Standards Board (Canada), "Accounting Standards in Canada: Future Directions Draft Strategic Plan," page i, accessed at www.acsbcanada.org, May 6, 2005.

EXHIBIT 37-6	(continued)

IFRSs Not Permitted for Domestic Listed Companies

Argentina	Cote d'Ivoire	Mali	Singapore‡
Australia#	Fiji	Mexico	Syria
Benin	Ghana	Moldova	Taiwan
Bhutan	India	Mozambique	Thailand
Brazil	Indonesia	New Zealand#	Togo
Burkina Faso	Israel	Niger	Tunisia
Canada	Japan	Pakistan	United States
Chile	Korea (S)	Philippines†	Uzbekistan
Colombia	Malaysia	Saudi Arabia	Vietnam

*Denotes EU membership.

†Hong Kong and Philippines have adopted national standards that are identical to IFRSs.

‡Singapore has adopted many IFRSs word for word but has changed several IFRSs when adopting them as national standards.

#Australia and New Zealand have national standards described as IFRS equivalents; some options permitted in IFRSs are not available under the equivalent national standard.

Source: Deloitte Touche Tohmatsu, "Use of IFRSs for Reporting by Domestic Listed Companies, by Country—Status as of 2005," www.iasplus.com. accessed May 5, 2005.

statements without reconciling them to Japanese GAAP. The SEC in the United States also allows foreign registrants to prepare their financial statements in accordance with IFRSs, or any other non-U.S. GAAP for that matter. However, in those cases, the foreign company must also provide a reconciliation of net income and stockholders' equity to U.S. GAAP in the notes to the financial statements included in its annual report filed on Form 20-F with the SEC. The SEC has been under pressure for a number of years to eliminate its GAAP reconciliation requirement for those foreign registrants that use IFRSs. With the adoption of IFRSs in the EU in 2005, pressure from Europe has intensified.

As the IASC was completing its core set of standards under the IOSCO agreement in the 1990s, the SEC put the IASC and the rest of the world on notice that it would not necessarily approve the use of IASs simply because IOSCO recommended that it do so. In 1996, the SEC announced that to be acceptable for cross-listing purposes, IASs would have to meet three key criteria. The core set of standards would have to

► Constitute a comprehensive, generally accepted basis of accounting.
► Be of high quality, resulting in comparability and transparency, and providing for full disclosure.
► Be rigorously interpreted and applied.

The SEC began its assessment of the IASC's core set of standards in 1999 and issued a Concept Release in 2000 to solicit comments on whether it should modify its GAAP reconciliation requirement. The GAAP reconciliation requirement has not yet been changed, but in April 2005, SEC Chairman Donaldson discussed a road map with EU Internal Market Commissioner McCreevy to eliminate the U.S. GAAP reconciliation requirement "as early as possible between now and 2009 at the latest."[23] The extent to which EU companies are faithful and consistent in their application and interpretation of IFRSs in preparing their financial statements from 2005 on will be of great interest to the SEC.

11   FASB–IASB CONVERGENCE

At a joint meeting in Norwalk, Connecticut, in September 2002, the FASB and IASB agreed to "use their best efforts to (a) make their existing financial reporting standards fully compatible as soon as is practicable and (b) to coordinate their work program to ensure that once achieved, compatibility is maintained."[24] Both the SEC chairman and the EU's commissioner for the internal market immediately welcomed the so-called Norwalk Agreement.

The six key FASB initiatives to further convergence[25] between IFRSs and U.S. GAAP follow:

1. *Short-term convergence project.* The objective of the short-term convergence project is to eliminate those differences between U.S. GAAP and IFRSs in which convergence is likely to be achievable in the short term. Convergence is expected to occur by selecting either existing U.S. GAAP or IASB requirements as the high-quality solution.

2. *Joint projects.* Joint projects involve sharing FASB and IASB staff resources and working on a similar time schedule.

3. *The convergence research project.* The FASB staff embarked on a project to identify all of the substantive differences between U.S. GAAP and IFRSs and catalog differences based on the FASB's strategy for resolving them.

4. *Liaison IASB member on site at the FASB officers.* To facilitate information exchange and foster cooperation, a full-time IASB member is in residence at the FASB offices. Former FASB Vice-Chair James Leisenring was the first IASB member to serve in this capacity.

5. *Monitoring IASB projects.* The FASB monitors IASB projects based on the level of interest in the topic being addressed.

6. *Explicit consideration of convergence potential in board agenda decisions.* As part of the process for considering topics to add to its agenda, the FASB explicitly considers the potential for cooperation with the IASB.

Short-Term Convergence Project

The short-term convergence project is intended to remove a variety of individual differences between IFRSs and U.S. GAAP that are not covered in broader projects and for which a high-quality solution appears to be achievable in a short

---

[23] SEC Press Release, "Chairman Donaldson Meets with EU Internal Market Commissioner McCreevy," April 21, 2005, available at www.sec.gov.

[24] FASB-IASB, Memorandum of Understanding, "The Norwalk Agreement," available at www.iasplus.com.

[25] Extensive information on the FASB's international convergence project can be found on the organization's Web site at www.fasb.org.

period of time. The short-term convergence project already has resulted in several changes to U.S. GAAP. Topics covered under this project include these:

1. *Inventory costs.* The FASB issued *SFAS 151,* "Inventory Costs—An Amendment of ARB 43, Chapter 4," in December 2004, to converge with the IASB's treatment of items such as idle facility expenses, excessive spoilage, double freight, and rehandling costs as current period expenses.

2. *Asset exchanges.* APB *Opinion 29* provided an exception to the general rule that asset exchanges should be measured at fair value. That exception related to nonmonetary exchanges of similar assets. To converge with IFRSs, *SFAS 153,* "Exchanges of Nonmonetary Assets—An Amendment of APB Opinion 29," issued in December 2004, eliminates this exception.

3. *Accounting changes.* The FASB issued *SFAS 154,* "Accounting Changes and Error Corrections—A Replacement of APB Opinion No. 20 and FASB Statement No. 3," in May 2005. This statement changes the reporting of certain accounting changes to be consistent with their treatment under IFRSs. Reporting the cumulative effect of a change in accounting principle in current period net income is no longer permissible. Instead, retrospective application of the new accounting principle is required.

4. *Earnings per share.* In December 2003, the FASB issued the Exposure Draft, "Earnings per Share—An Amendment of FASB Statement No. 128," which would amend the guidance for computing earnings per share. The FASB indicates that this proposed standard would improve financial reporting by enhancing the comparability of financial statements prepared under U.S. GAAP and IFRSs.

Although not formally a part of the short-term convergence project, the issuance of *SFAS 123* (revised 2004), "Share-Based Payment," in December 2004, which requires share-based payments to be measured at fair value, was at least partially justified through convergence with IFRSs. As one of the principal reasons for issuing this statement, the FASB provided the following explanation:

Converging with international accounting standards   This Statement will result in greater international comparability in the accounting for share-based payment transactions. In February 2004, the International Accounting Standards Board (IASB), whose standards are followed by entities in many countries, issued International Financial Reporting Standard (IFRS) 2, *Share-Based Payment.* IFRS 2 requires that all entities recognize an expense for all employee services received in share-based payment transactions, using a fair-value-based method that is similar in most respects to the fair-value-based method established in Statement 123 and the improvements made to it by this Statement. Converging to a common set of high-quality financial accounting standards for share-based payment transactions with employees improves the comparability of financial information around the world and makes the accounting requirements for entities that report financial statements under both U.S. GAAP and international accounting standards less burdensome.[26]

---

[26] FASB, *Statement of Financial Accounting Standards No. 123* (revised 2004), "Share-Based Payment," page ii.

Joint Projects

The IASB and FASB are jointly working on several projects that deal with broader issues expected to take longer to resolve than those topics covered by the short-term project. We describe four of these projects.

Business Combinations Project

After separately eliminating the pooling of interests method, the FASB and IASB developed common exposure drafts to revise existing guidance on the application of the purchase method. As a result of this project, the two boards developed common solutions with respect to the measurement at full fair value of an acquired company's assets and liabilities and the measurement and presentation of noncontrolling interests.

Performance Reporting Project

This project deals with the presentation of information in the financial statements. The objective is to enhance the usefulness of information in assessing the financial performance of the reporting enterprise. The FASB issued an initial proposal related to this project in August 2001. In April 2004, the FASB and IASB agreed to work together on this project in the future. Issues being considered in this project include whether a single statement of comprehensive income should be required to be presented as a primary financial statement, whether the direct method should be mandated for reporting cash flow from operations in the statement of cash flows, how many years should be included in comparative financial statements, and which totals and subtotals should be reported on each required financial statement.

Revenue Recognition Project

This project's objective is to develop a common, comprehensive standard on revenue recognition that is grounded in conceptually based principles. More than 140 authoritative pronouncements in the United States relate to revenue recognition.[27] Finding the answer to a specific revenue recognition question can be difficult, and gaps exist. Unlike U.S. GAAP, IFRSs contain a single, general standard on revenue recognition (*IAS 19*, "Revenue"). However, this standard is of limited use in determining the appropriate recognition of revenue in many cases. This project is expected to result in a single standard that will (1) eliminate inconsistencies in existing literature, (2) fill the gaps that have developed in recent years as new business models have emerged, and (3) provide a conceptual basis for addressing issues that arise in the future.

Conceptual Framework Project

This project seeks to develop a common conceptual framework that both boards could use as a basis for future standards. Although the IASB Framework and the FASB's Conceptual Framework (as embodied in its *Statements of Financial Accounting Concepts*) are substantially similar, differences do exist. More importantly, the existing frameworks have internal inconsistencies and are not comprehensive.

---

[27] FASB, "The Revenue Recognition Project," *The FASB Report*, December 24, 2002.

DIFFERENCES BETWEEN IFRSS AND U.S. GAAP   12

In a comparison of IFRSs and U.S. GAAP conducted in January 2005, Deloitte Touche Tohmatsu identified some 120 key differences in the two sets of standards. A few of these differences are summarized in Exhibit 37-7. Note that a number of these differences are within the scope of the FASB-IASB convergence projects and therefore are likely to be eliminated over time.

The types of differences that exist between IFRSs and U.S. GAAP can be generally classified as follows:

1. Recognition differences.

2. Measurement differences.

3. Presentation and disclosure differences.

Examples of each type of difference are described next.

Recognition Differences

Several differences between IFRSs and U.S. GAAP relate to (1) whether an item is recognized or not, (2) how it is recognized, or (3) when it is recognized. A good example of this type of difference relates to the accounting for research and development costs. Under U.S. GAAP, research and development costs must be expensed immediately. The only exception relates to costs incurred in developing computer software, which must be capitalized when several restrictive criteria are met. *IAS 38*, "Intangible Assets," also requires immediate expensing of all research costs. Development costs, on the other hand, must be recognized as an internally generated intangible asset when certain criteria are met. Deferred development costs are amortized over their useful life but not to exceed 20 years. Development costs include all costs directly attributable to or that can be reasonably allocated to development activities including personnel costs, materials and services costs, depreciation on fixed assets, amortization of patents and licenses, and overhead costs other than general administration. The types of development costs that might qualify as an internally generated intangible asset under *IAS 38* include computer software costs, patents and copyrights, customer or supplier relationships, market share, fishing licenses, and franchises. Brands, advertising costs, training costs, and customer lists are specifically excluded from recognition as an intangible asset.

Other recognition differences relate to (1) gains on sale and leaseback transactions, (2) past service costs related to vested pension benefits, (3) deferred tax assets, (4) purchased in-process R&D, and (5) negative goodwill.

Measurement Differences

Measurement differences result in the recognition of different amounts in the financial statements under IFRSs and U.S. GAAP. In some cases, these differences result from different measurement methods required under the two sets of standards. For example, although both IFRSs and U.S. GAAP require the use of a lower-of-cost-or-market rule in valuing inventory, the two sets of standards measure "market" differently. Under U.S. GAAP, market value is measured as *replacement cost* (with net realizable value as a ceiling and net realizable value minus a normal profit as a floor). *IAS 2*, "Inventory," requires inventory to be carried on the balance sheet at the lower of cost or *net realizable value*.

Accounting Item	IFRSs	U.S. GAAP
Inventory		
Cost-flow assumption	LIFO not allowed	LIFO Fallowed
"Market" in lower-of-cost-or-market rule	Net realizable value	Replacement cost (with ceiling and floor)
Reversal of inventory writedown	Required if certain criteria are met	Not allowed
Property, plant, and equipment		
Measurement subsequent to acquisition	Based on historical cost or a revalued amount	Based on historical cost
Major inspection or overhaul costs	Generally capitalized	Generally expensed
Capitalization of interest on qualifying assets	Permitted but not required	Required
Asset impairment		
Indication of impairment	Asset's carrying value exceeds the greater of its (1) value in use (discounted expected future cash flows) or (2) fair value less costs to sell	Asset's carrying value exceeds the undiscounted expected future cash flows from the asset
Subsequent reversal of an impairment loss	Required if certain criteria are met	Not allowed
Construction contracts		
Method used when percentage of completion not appropriate	Cost recovery method	Completed contract method
Research and development costs		
Development costs	Capitalized if certain criteria are met	Expensed immediately (except computer software development)
Leases		
Recognition of gain on sale and leaseback on an operating lease	Recognized immediately	Amortized over the lease term
Pensions		
Recognition of past service costs related to benefits that have vested	Recognized immediately	Amortized over the remaining service period of life expectancy
Recognition of minimum liability	No minimum liability requirement	Unfunded accumulated benefit obligation must be recognized as a minimum
Income taxes		
Recognition of deferred tax assets	Recognized only if realization of tax benefit is probable	Always recognized but a valuation allowance is provided

(Exhibit continued on next page ...)

EXHIBIT 37-7 Some Key Differences between IFRSs and U.S. GAAP at January 2005

EXHIBIT 37-7	(continued)	

Accounting Item	IFRSs	U.S. GAAP
Consolidated financial statements		
Different accounting policies of parent and subsidiaries	Must conform policies	No requirement to conform policies
Presentation of minority interest	In equity	Between liabilities and equity
Purchased in-process R&D	Recognized as intangible asset if separately measurable, otherwise as part of goodwill	Expensed immediately
Negative goodwill	Recognize immediately as a gain	Allocate on a pro rata basis as reduction in certain acquired nonfinancial assets, with any excess recognized as an extraordinary gain
Presentation of "extraordinary" items	Not allowed	Required when certain criteria are met
Definition of a "discontinued operation"	A reportable business or geographic segment	A reportable segment, operating segment, reporting unit, subsidiary, or asset group
Interim reporting	Interim period is treated as discrete accounting period	Interim period treated as integral part of full year
Segment reporting	Disclosures required for both industry and geographic segments, one of which is "primary" and the other "secondary"	Disclosures required for operating segments, plus certain "enterprise-wide" disclosures

Source: Deloitte Touche Tohmatsu, "Status of Some Key Differences between IFRSs and U.S. GAAP as of January 2005." www.iasplus.com, accessed May 5, 2005.

In other cases, measurement differences can exist because of alternatives allowed by one set of standards but not the other. Permitting the use of LIFO under U.S. GAAP but not allowing its use under IFRSs is an example of this type of difference. Another example can be found in *IAS 23*, "Borrowing Costs", which establishes a benchmark and an allowed alternative treatment for the accounting for interest and other costs associated with borrowings. The benchmark treatment is to expense all borrowing costs immediately. This treatment is inconsistent with U.S. GAAP, which requires the capitalization of interest on qualifying selfconstructed assets. A company using the benchmark treatment under *IAS 23* would measure the cost of its qualifying self-constructed assets differently from a company using U.S. GAAP. However, as an allowed alternative, companies may capitalize interest as part of the cost of a qualifying asset in much the same manner as is required under U.S. GAAP.

One of the greatest potential differences between the application of IFRSs and U.S. GAAP is found in *IAS 16*, "Property, Plant, and Equipment." In measuring fixed assets subsequent to acquisition, *IAS 16* establishes cost less accumulated depreciation and impairment losses as the benchmark treatment. This is consistent with U.S. GAAP. The allowed alternative provided in *IAS 16* allows fixed assets to be measured and reported on the balance sheet subsequent to acquisition at a revalued amount, which is measured as fair value at the date of revaluation less any subsequent accumulated depreciation and impairment losses. If a company elects to follow the allowed alternative, it must make revaluations regularly enough that the carrying value reported on the balance sheet does not differ materially from fair value. Companies following the allowed alternative need not adopt this treatment for all classes of property, plant, and equipment. However, they must apply it to all items within a class of assets. A company could choose to revalue land but not buildings, for example, but it would need to revalue each and every parcel of land it owns at the same time.

Presentation and Disclosure Differences

Presentation and disclosure differences relate to the manner in which items are presented on the financial statements or disclosed in the notes to the financial statements. Presentation of certain gains and losses as *extraordinary items* under U.S. GAAP, which is not allowed under IFRSs, is one example. The difference between the two sets of standards in what is considered a discontinued operation and therefore presented separately in the income statement is another example. The definition of a discontinued operation is less restrictive under U.S. GAAP.

Differences exist in the reporting of segments under the two sets of standards. U.S. GAAP requires a management approach in which extensive disclosures must be made for operating segments, which can be based on either product line or geography. If operating segments are based on product line, additional disclosures must be provided for all foreign operations and for each material foreign country. *IAS 14*, "Segment Reporting," requires disclosures to be provided for both industry segments and geographic segments, one of which is designated as the primary reporting format and for which more extensive information must be provided. Geographic segments typically are defined as regions of the world rather than as individual countries.

U.S. GAAP Reconciliations

A good source of information for understanding the differences between IFRSs and U.S. GAAP and their impact on financial statements are the U.S. GAAP reconciliations prepared by foreign companies listed on U.S. stock exchanges in compliance with SEC regulations. Studying these reconciliations was instrumental in determining which were the most important issues to address in the FASB-IASB convergence project.[28] Exhibit 37-8 provides an excerpt from the U.S. GAAP reconciliation included in the 2003 Form 20-F of China Eastern Airlines Corporation Limited (CEA). CEA is one of several Chinese companies listed on the New York Stock Exchange that prepares its consolidated financial statements in accordance with IFRSs.

Note 40, "Significant Differences between IFRS and U.S. GAAP", indicates that CEA made four adjustments to both net income and owners' equity as stated under IFRSs to reconcile to U.S. GAAP. Adjustments (a) and (b) relate to the fact that CEA uses the allowed alternative treatment of *IAS 16*, "Property, Plant,

---

[28] International Accounting Standards Committee Foundation (IASCF), Annual Report 2003, p. 5. The IASCF oversees, funds, and selects the members of the IASB.

Note 40. Significant Differences between IFRS and U.S. GAAP

Differences between IFRS and U.S. GAAP which have significant effects on the consolidated profits/(loss) attributable to shareholders and consolidated owners' equity of the Group are summarized as follows:

Consolidated profit/(loss) attributable to shareholders

(Amounts in thousands except per share data)

| | | Year Ended December 31, | | | |
	Note	2001 RMB	2002 RMB	2003 RMB	2003 US$ (note 2a)
As stated under IFRS		541,713	86,369	(949,816)	(114,758)
U.S. GAAP adjustments:					
Reversal of difference in depreciation charges arising from revaluation of fixed assets	(a)	94,140	20,370	63,895	7,720
Reversal of revaluation deficit of fixed assets	(a)	—	171,753	—	—
Gain/(loss) on disposal of aircraft and related assets	(b)	5,791	(26,046)	(10,083)	(1,218)
Others	(c)	(11,295)	23,767	6,860	829
Deferred tax effect on U.S. GAAP adjustments	(d)	(155,877)	(28,477)	(9,101)	(1,100)
As stated under U.S. GAAP		474,472	247,736	(898,245)	(108,527)

Consolidated owners' equity

(Amounts in thousands)

| | | December 31, | | |
	Note	2002 RMB	2003 RMB	2003 US$ (note 2a)
As stated under IFRS		7,379,103	6,382,151	771,099
U.S. GAAP adjustments:				
Reversal of net revaluation surplus of fixed assets	(a)	(908,873)	(908,873)	(109,811)
Reversal of difference in depreciation charges and accumulated depreciation and loss on disposals arising from the revaluation of fixed assets	(a), (b)	637,423	691,235	83,516
Others	(c)	29,111	35,971	4,346
Deferred tax effect on U.S. GAAP adjustments	(d)	20,844	9,225	1,115
As stated under U.S. GAAP		7,157,608	6,209,709	750,264

Notes:

(a) Revaluation of fixed assets
Under IFRS, fixed assets of the Group are initially recorded at cost and are subsequently restated at revalued amounts less accumulated depreciation. Fixed assets of the Group were revalued as of June 30, 1996, as part of the restructuring of the Group for the purpose of listing. In addition, as of December 31, 2002, a revaluation of the Group's aircraft and engines was carried out and difference between the valuation and carrying amount was recognized. Under U.S. GAAP, the revaluation surplus or deficit and the related difference in depreciation are reversed since fixed assets are required to be stated at cost.

(b) Disposals of aircraft and related assets
This represents the loss on disposals of aircraft and related assets during the years. Under U.S. GAAP, fixed assets are required to be stated at cost. Accordingly, the accumulated depreciation and the gain or loss on disposals of aircraft is different between IFRS and U.S. GAAP, which is attributable to the surplus or deficit upon valuation associated with the assets disposed of.

(c) Other U.S. GAAP adjustments
The application of U.S. GAAP differs in certain other respects from IFRS, mainly relating to sale and leaseback transactions, post retirement benefits and goodwill. Under US GAAP: (i) recognition of gain on sale and leaseback transactions is deferred and amortized, (ii) transitional obligation for post retirement benefits is amortized over the average remaining service period of active plan participants, and (iii) goodwill is reviewed for impairment and is not amortized.

(d) Deferred tax effect
These represent the corresponding deferred tax effect as a result of the adjustments stated in (a), (b), and (c) above.

and Equipment," to revalue fixed assets subsequent to initial recognition. CEA revalued fixed assets in 1996 as part of the process of transforming from a state-owned enterprise to a publicly traded company. An additional revaluation of assets occurred in 2002. The net result of these revaluations was an increase in the carrying value of fixed assets accompanied by an increase in owner's equity. The revaluation of fixed assets also resulted in an increase in the amount of annual depreciation expense.

Adjustment (a) reverses the additional depreciation taken under IFRSs on the revaluation amount that would not be allowed under U.S. GAAP. In 2003, this resulted in an increase in net income of US$7,720 to reconcile to U.S. GAAP. Also in 2003, IFRS-based owner's equity is decreased by US$109,811 to remove the revaluation surplus that was recognized under IFRSs.

The profit(loss) effect of adjustment (b) relates to the difference in the amount of loss recognized on the disposal of aircraft and related assets because of different carrying values under IFRSs and U.S. GAAP. Due to revaluation, fixed assets have a larger carrying value under IFRSs, which results in a smaller loss being recognized upon disposal. To reconcile to U.S. GAAP, an additional amount of loss based on the original cost of the assets must be subtracted from net income. The owners' equity account affected by adjustment (b) is retained earnings. Because additional depreciation expense on the revaluation amount has been taken under IFRSs, net income has been smaller in each year since 1996 under IFRSs than it would have been if U.S. GAAP had been used. The cumulative amount of the difference in income must be added back to retained earnings to reconcile to a U.S. GAAP basis.

The company explains that adjustment (c) is composed of adjustments related to the difference between IFRSs and U.S. GAAP in the accounting for (1) gains on sale and leaseback transactions, (2) post-retirement benefit obligations, and (3) goodwill. Prior to the publication of *IFRS 3*, "Business Combinations", in 2004, a difference existed between IFRSs and U.S. GAAP in the accounting for goodwill. Under IFRSs, goodwill was capitalized and amortized systematically over its useful life, whereas goodwill is not amortized but instead is subject to annual impairment under U.S. GAAP. *IFRS 3* removed this difference, converging IFRSs with U.S. GAAP.

Adjustment (d) arises because of the difference in reported profit(loss) under IFRSs and U.S. GAAP. This adjustments reflects the net deferred tax effect of adjustments (a), (b), and (c).

Exhibit 37-9 presents the net income reconciliation provided by Swiss pharmaceutical giant Novartis AG in its 2004 Form 20-F. Novartis made 12 adjustments to convert net income under IFRSs to a U.S. GAAP basis. Net income in 2004 on a U.S. GAAP basis was 13.5 percent smaller than under IFRSs; this difference was 24.5 percent the previous year.

Three adjustments made in 2004 relate to the use of the pooling method and the manner in which goodwill was recognized and amortized prior to 2004 under IFRSs. These differences from U.S. GAAP were removed with the issuance of *IFRS 3* in late 2004. Another adjustment arising from business combinations relates to in-process research and development, which is expensed immediately under U.S. GAAP but treated as an asset under IFRSs. This type of adjustment is likely to continue in the future because neither the IASB nor the FASB has yet addressed this difference.

Adjustment (j) pertains to a portion of the cumulative translation adjustment in equity being transferred to net income under IFRSs as a result of the partial repayment of the capital of a foreign subsidiary. Under U.S. GAAP, the cumulative translation adjustment is recognized in income only upon disposal of a subsidiary.

| EXHIBIT 37-9 | Novartis AG 2004 Form 20-F Excerpt from Note 32 |

32. Significant Differences between IFRS and United States Generally Accepted Accounting Principles (U.S. GAAP) ($ millions)

	Notes	2004	2003	2002
Net income under IFRS		5,767	5,016	4,725
U.S. GAAP adjustments:				
Purchase accounting: Ciba-Geigy	a	(366)	(339)	(294)
Purchase accounting: other acquisitions	b	17	(175)	(298)
Purchase accounting: IFRS goodwill amortization	c	170	172	140
Available-for-sale securities and derivative financial instruments	d	(183)	(240)	(273)
Pension provisions	e	(6)	(18)	27
Share-based compensation	f	(326)	(273)	(120)
Consolidation of share-based employee compensation foundation	g	(4)	(3)	(20)
Deferred taxes	h	100	(63)	(93)
In-process research and development	i	(55)	(260)	(11)
Reversal of currency translation gain	j	(301)		
Other	l	13	(20)	(95)
Deferred tax effect on U.S. GAAP adjustments		163	(9)	141
Net income under U.S. GAAP		**4,989**	**3,788**	**3,829**

THE ACCOUNTING PROFESSION AND FINANCIAL STATEMENT PRESENTATION

13

As discussed earlier in this reading, accounting has evolved differently in different countries in response to environmental factors such as the nature of the legal system, the relationship between financial reporting and taxation, and the importance of the equity market as a source of financing. The final section of this reading describes the accounting environment in three key countries, focusing on the accounting profession and the presentation of financial statements in these countries.

United Kingdom

"The United Kingdom has the oldest accounting profession in the world today, and its reputation is second to none."[29] As this quotation indicates, no discussion of world accounting principles would be complete without a study of the United

---

[29] Geoffrey Alan Lee, "Accounting in the United Kingdom," *International Accounting* (New York: Harper & Row, 1984), p. 261.

Kingdom, a world leader in commerce and accounting. The legal foundation for accounting is provided by the Companies Acts, a series of legislation culminating in the Companies Act of 1989. The Companies Acts are basic commercial legislation designed to provide legal rules for U.K. corporations concerning issues dealing with management, administration, and dissolution. However, these laws also cover the issuance and content of financial statements. Prior to the 1980s, the law provided little more than a framework within which the accounting profession could set more detailed principles.[30] In 1981, the Companies Act was amended to incorporate the European Union's Fourth Directive, and in 1989 it was amended to implement the Seventh Directive, thereby increasing the importance of legislation in determining GAAP. Although the law prescribes some specific accounting procedures consistent with the EU directives, the law also requires companies to present a "true and fair view" of their results and financial position. This principle overrides the detailed requirements of the law. That is, if strict compliance with legislated accounting rules (or professional accounting standards) would not allow for a true and fair view to be presented, U.K. companies should deviate from the rules. A survey of some 450 U.K. companies in 1993 found that 10 percent used the true and fair view override.[31] The EU adopted the concept of true and fair view in its accounting directives.

In the United Kingdom, professional accounting organizations are quite important; membership now nears 200,000. A person may be a chartered accountant only through membership in the Institutes of Chartered Accountants in England and Wales, of Scotland, or in Ireland. Normally, once required exams have been passed, a license to practice is available to members after two years of approved experience.

In total, six different professional groups exist; and the largest is the Institute of Chartered Accountants in England and Wales. Until 1990, these organizations collectively controlled the accounting standard-setting process. Together, they formally created the Consultative Committee of Accountancy Bodies. A subcommittee of this group, the Accounting Standards Committee (ASC), produced 25 statements of standard accounting practice (SSAPs) between 1971 and 1990.

The ASC was originally created "to reduce and regularize the range of permissable accounting treatments applicable to comparable transactions and situations."[32] Over the years, the ASC gradually branched into a standard-setting role. However, the committee experienced difficulty because its pronouncements had to be accepted by each of the six professional organizations before being issued. Thus, the creation of accounting standards was agonizingly slow at times.

Consequently, the Accounting Standards Board (ASB) was formed on August 1, 1990, to replace the ASC as the standard-setting organization in the United Kingdom. The ASB is an independent body styled somewhat along the lines of the FASB in the United States. The ASB issues financial reporting standards (FRSs) on its own authority. The ASB has sanctioned all of the SSAPs and has issued several FRSs, including one that requires cash flow information. Any deviation from the ASB's standards must be explained and the financial effects disclosed.

A second body, the Financial Reporting Review Panel (FRRP), was created along with the ASB. The FRRP monitors compliance with the accounting standards. This panel has the authority to seek a court order against companies producing financial statements that fail to provide a true and fair view.

---

[30] Lee H. Radebaugh and Sidney J. Gray, *International Accounting and Multinational Enterprises*, 3rd ed. (New York: John Wiley and Sons, 1993), p. 83.

[31] J. M. Samuels, R. E. Brayshaw, and J. M. Cramer, *Financial Statement Analysis in Europe* (London: Chapman and Hall, 1995), p. 361.

[32] Emile Woolf, "The ASC at the Crossroads," *Accountancy*, September 1988, p. 72.

Financial statements must be submitted to the shareholders at the annual meeting. They include a directors' report describing the directors' activities for the period, post-balance sheet events, the business year in general, research and development activities, and a host of other information. The financial statements themselves are normally the balance sheet, profit and loss account, and cash flows statement. In addition, a statement of total recognized gains and losses often is presented that among other things reports the amount of translation adjustments included in stockholders' equity but not in income. In contrast to practice in the United States, separate parent company financial statements are provided along with the consolidated statements.

For the balance sheet and profit and loss account, two different formats (allowed under the EU's Fourth Directive) are available: a vertical and a horizontal presentation. Most British companies provide a vertical balance sheet; an example is that of Imperial Chemical Industries PLC in Exhibit 37-1. An example of a British profit and loss account is in Exhibit 37-10.

In the United Kingdom, the group profit and loss account is the equivalent of a consolidated income statement. The statement begins with *turnover* (the British term for *net sales*) followed by operating expenses, interest, and then taxes. Exceptional items related to continuing operations and discontinued operations appear in separate columns. Exceptional items primarily consist of restructuring costs (operating costs) and gains on closure of operations. Similar to the U.S. practice, British companies must report earnings per share at the bottom of the profit and loss account. Also as in the United States, reported figures tend to be highly condensed with much of the information provided in the notes to the statements. On the face of the financial statements, specific references relate the notes to particular line items.

Germany

Accounting principles in Germany are set by the national legislature. Currently, these mandatory principles are outlined in detail in the Third Book of the Commercial Code. Tax laws have had a significant influence on the reporting principles established by the code. In addition, because the code is silent with regard to many accounting issues, German companies refer to tax law, professional pronouncements, academic commentaries, and international accounting standards to fill in the gaps. Actual changes in the accounting laws are rare because they must be passed by the legislature. A major change to the accounting law was passed in December 1985 to bring German accounting principles in line with the directives of the European Union. Although this law introduced the notion of a true and fair view into German accounting practice, application of this principle differs from that in the United Kingdom. Günter Seckler found, "It still seems to be the dominant opinion in Germany that compliance with legal requirements ensures a true and fair presentation."[33] Financial statements must be prepared in accordance with the code. If this does not result in a true and fair view, additional information must be presented in the notes to the financial statements.

As in many countries where legislated accounting rules exist, German accounting is considered quite conservative. This is true for two major reasons. One is the so-called tax conformity principle that is not found in many other countries. In Germany, commercial financial statements are the basis for taxation. Thus, for an item to be deducted for tax purposes, it must be recorded

---

[33] Günter Seckler, "Germany," in *European Accounting Guide,* 3d ed., ed. David Alexander and Simon Archer (New York: Harcourt Brace & Company, 1998), p. 361.

EXHIBIT 37-10   United Kingdom Income Statement

IMPERIAL CHEMICAL INDUSTRIES PLC
Group Profit and Loss Account for the Year Ended 31 December 2004

	Notes	Continuing Operations — Before Exceptional Items £m	Exceptional Items £m	Discontinued Operations £m	Total £m
Turnover	4,5	5,601	—	—	5,601
Operating costs	3,5	(5,192)	(5)	—	(5,197)
Other operating income	5	35	—	—	35
Trading profit (loss)	3,4,5	444	(5)	—	439
After deducting goodwill amortisation	4	(35)	—	—	(35)
Share of operating profits less losses of associates	6	4	—	—	4
		448	(5)	—	443
Profits less losses on sale or closure of operations	3		(23)	(20)	3
Profits less losses on disposals of fixed assets	3		(1)	—	(1)
Amounts written off investments	3	—	—	—	—
Profit (loss) on ordinary activities before interest	4	448	17	(20)	445
Net interest payable	7				
Group		(86)	—	—	(86)
Associates		—	—	—	—
		(86)	—	—	(86)
Profit (loss) on ordinary activities before taxation		362	17	(20)	359
Taxation on profit (loss) on ordinary activities	8	(111)	11)	6	(116)
Profit (loss) on ordinary activities after taxation		251	6	14	243
Attributable to minorities		(27)	(6)	—	(33)
Net profit (loss) for the financial year		224	—	(14)	210
Dividends	9				(86)
Profit (loss) retained for the year	24				124
Earnings (loss) per £1 Ordinary Share	10				
Basic		18.9p	—	(1.1)p	17.8p
Diluted		18.8p	—	(1.1)p	17.7p

as an expense in calculating income in the financial statements. Companies interested in taking advantage of provisions in the tax law to reduce taxable income are required to report lower financial income as well. The second is that German accounting "is greatly influenced by the German banks, because they provide the major investment and mandate the reporting requirements for many industries in Germany.... When individuals in other countries analyze the financial statements, they generally write up the figures because of the extreme conservatism of German policies and procedures."[34] In fact, the German Association of Financial Analysts (DVFA) has developed a standardized procedure for adjusting reported earnings to assess the real profitability of German companies. The adjustments include adding back to income special depreciation allowed for tax purposes and excess amounts transferred to provisions.

The accounting profession in Germany is well established. The *Wirtschaftsprüfer* is the equivalent of a certified public accountant. A person can use this designation only after passing a series of difficult examinations and gaining six years of relevant experience. Only college graduates with degrees in economics, law, or a related subject may sit for the exams. "Because of the comprehensive requirements for entry to the profession, it is almost impossible to fulfill all of them before the age of 30, and most are 35 before they are admitted."[35] The profession's self-governing body is the *Wirtschaftsprüferkammer,* which enforces strict rules on independence and ethics.

In Germany, companies must produce a balance sheet each year as well as an income statement and notes to the financial statements. Also required is a management report to discuss issues such as current business position, significant subsequent events, future prospects, and research and development activities. Many companies fulfill a disclosure requirement regarding changes in fixed assets by providing a statement of fixed assets in addition to the balance sheet and income statement. A law passed in 1998 requires publicly traded companies to prepare a statement of cash flows.

The income statement must be produced according to one of two formats. The cost of sales approach, which has increased in popularity in recent years with Germany's larger multinationals, is similar to the structure of the income statement typically found in the United States. In contrast, the type-of-cost statement is more traditional in Germany. The consolidated statement of income for Brau und Brunnen AG for the year ending December 31, 2003, is an example of this format (see Exhibit 37-11).

In the traditional cost of sales format used in the United States, manufacturing costs (materials, labor, overhead) are included in the cost of sales line item in the income statement, and administrative costs are reported in a separate line. Under this approach, the total wages and salaries paid by a company are disaggregated into two parts: Manufacturing wages are reported in cost of sales, and administrative wages are reported in administrative expense. The same is true for depreciation and other operating expenses. Using the type-of-cost approach, Brau und Brunnen reports total wages and salaries (manufacturing and administrative) in a single line. Similarly, it reports total depreciation and amortization as well as total other operating expenses in one line. Brau und Brunnen reports the materials component of cost of sales in two parts: Purchases are reported as an expense in cost of materials, and the difference between beginning and ending Work in Process and Finished Goods Inventory is treated as an adjustment to sales. Although quite unique in appearance when compared to a

---

[34] Roger K. Doost and Karen M. Ligon, "How U.S. and European Accounting Practices Differ," *Management Accounting,* October 1986, p. 40.

[35] Thomas G. Evans, Martin E. Taylor, and Robert J. Rolfe, *International Accounting and Reporting,* 3d ed. (Houston, Texas: Dame Publications, 1999), p. 38.

EXHIBIT 37-11 **German Income Statement**

BRAU UND BRUNNEN AG
Consolidated Profit and Loss Account
For the Year Ended December 31, 2003

		2003 (EUR)
Sales revenues		647,810,090.56
Decrease in work-in-process, finished goods, and uninvoiced services		−1,448,721.92
		646,361,368.64
Other manufacturing costs capitalised		536,047.73
Other operating income		99,373,867.52
		746,271,283.89
Cost of materials		
Expenses for raw materials, supplies, and merchandise purchased	131,426,366.79	
Expenses for services purchased	10,262,787.12	
		141,689,173.91
Staff expenses		
Wages and salaries	123,161,388.42	
Social security levies and cost of pension schemes and related benefits	43,200,577.32	
of which for pension schemes EUR 19,260,172.47		
		166,361,965.74
Depreciation and amortisation		
Depreciation and amortisation of intangible fixed assets and of tangible assets		74,343,753.87
Other operating expenses		269,491,754.64
		94,384,635.73
Income from profit transfer agreements		6,274.78
Income from equity interests		178,493.63
of which from affiliated companies EUR 91,977.72		
Income from other securities and from loans forming part of the financial assets		1,328,218.96
Other interest and similar income		782,502.50
of which from affiliated companies EUR 3,626.55		
		96,680,125.60
Depreciation of financial assets and of securities held as current assets		10,011,559.19
Expenses for the assumption of losses		68,891.69
Losses from shares in associated companies		51,421.26
Interest and similar expenses		8,272,004.58
of which for affiliated companies EUR 2,685,267.02		
Results from ordinary activities		78,276,248.88
Extraordinary income	6,442,269.00	
Extraordinary expenses	12,337,349.28	
Extraordinary results		−5,895,080.28
		72,381,168.60
Taxes on income and profit		209,017.00
Other taxes		64,699,005.52
NET PROFIT FOR THE YEAR		7,473,146.08

U.S. income statement, the type-of-cost approach and the cost of sales approach result in the same calculation of earnings. One analytical limitation of this approach, however, is that it is not possible to calculate the cost of sales; therefore, gross profit cannot be determined.

Note the 2004 consolidated balance sheet for the chemical company BASF AG in Exhibit 37-12. Similar to the financial reporting in the United Kingdom, the German balance sheet begins with noncurrent assets followed by current assets. Deferred taxes and prepaid expenses are not classified as either current or noncurrent. Stockholders' equity usually appears next before the reporting of any liabilities, and minority interest is specifically included in equity.

German companies do not classify obligations on the balance sheet as current and noncurrent. Instead, they classify obligations as either provisions or liabilities. The major distinction between the two is that provisions are generally estimated whereas liabilities are of a fixed, contractual nature. German companies have traditionally considered liabilities due within the next five years as short term. However, the 1985 accounting law requires companies to disclose in the notes the amount of liabilities due within one year; many companies also continue to indicate those liabilities due in more than five years.

BASF's provisions include estimates for items such as pensions, taxes, warranties, and other identifiable risks. In addition to being extremely conservative, German companies are notorious for their use of provisions to conceal profits and create hidden reserves. In profitable years, provisions are created for items such as deferred repairs (that is, repairs the company plans to make sometime in the future) and for undetermined obligations resulting from general business risks that might occur in the future. The counterpart to the balance sheet provision is an expense or loss reported in income. In years in which profits are below expectations, provisions are released with an offsetting increase to income. This income smoothing is an acceptable practice, done within the law, and very much a part of German business culture.

One of the most dramatic examples of the use of hidden reserves was carried out by Daimler-Benz AG in 1989. In 1988, the company reported income of 1.7 billion deutschemarks (DM). Because 1989 was a bad year for automobile sales, analysts expected Daimler-Benz's 1989 income to be somewhat lower than the year before. It created quite a stir in the German business community when the company reported 1989 income as DM6.8 billion, a fourfold increase over the prior year. The notes to the 1989 financial statements provide the following explanation:

> Provisions for old-age pensions and similar obligations are actuarially computed in accordance with the tax regulation of Section 6a of the Income Tax Act, at an interest rate of 6 percent per annum. Previously, a rate of 3.5 percent was used. Using the higher interest rate resulted in higher income of about DM4.9 billion and is shown in the income statement under "Other Operating Income."

Through the selection of a low (and therefore more conservative) discount rate from a range accepted by tax law, Daimler-Benz was able to report higher expenses in years prior to 1989 and thus establish hidden reserves. The release of those reserves in 1989 through a change in the discount rate significantly affected net income. Without the change, income would have been only DM1.9 billion.

In 1992, Daimler-Benz reported net income of DM1.45 billion after creating provisions for loss contingencies of DM774 million. Otherwise, 1992 profit would have been DM2.22 billion. In 1993, reported income was DM615 million but included the release of previous provisions of DM4.26 billion, thus masking a loss of some DM3.65 billion.

EXHIBIT 37-12	German Balance Sheet

BASF AG
Consolidated Balance Sheets
December 31, 2004

Million EUR	Explanations in Note	2004	2003
Assets			
Intangible assets	(11)	3,338.1	3,793.2
Property, plant, and equipment	(12)	12,444.2	13,069.9
Financial assets	(13)	1,911.9	2,599.6
Fixed assets.................................		**17,694.2**	**19,462.7**
Inventories	(14)	**4,626.4**	**4,151.1**
Accounts receivable, trade....................		5,511.0	4,954.0
Receivables from affiliated companies		443.9	575.5
Miscellaneous receivables and other assets.......		2,008.4	2,069.5
Receivables and other assets	(15)	**7,963.3**	**7,599.0**
Marketable securities	(16)	162.8	146.9
Cash & cash equivalents......................		2,085.9	480.6
Liquid funds		**2,248.7**	**627.5**
Current assets................................		**14,838.4**	**12,377.6**
Deferred taxes	(8)	**1,210.9**	**1,247.0**
Prepaid expenses	(17)	**172.1**	**514.3**
Total assets		**33,915.6**	**33,601.6**
Stockholders' Equity and Liabilities			
Subscribed capital............................	(18)	1,383.5	1,425.0
Capital surplus	(18)	3,021.8	2,982.4
Retained earnings.............................	(19)	12,252.7	12,054.8
Currency translation adjustment................		(1,224.8)	(971.9)
Minority interests	(20)	331.8	388.1
Stockholders' equity..........................		**15,765.0**	**15,878.4**
Provisions for pensions and similar obligations ...	(21)	3,866.3	3,862.4
Provisions for taxes...........................		1,303.9	1,078.8
Other provisions.............................	(22)	4,557.7	4,246.2
Provisions		**9,727.9**	**9,187.4**
Bonds and other liabilities to capital market	(23)	2,525.0	2,610.6
Liabilities to credit institutions	(23)	778.3	896.1
Accounts payable, trade.......................		2,220.1	2,056.3
Liabilities to affiliated companies		381.0	400.6
Miscellaneous liabilities	(23)	2,167.4	2,202.4
Liabilities....................................		**8,071.8**	**8,166.0**
Deferred income		**350.9**	**369.8**
Total stockholders' equity and liabilities		**33,915.6**	**33,601.6**

Perhaps the ultimate in income smoothing was done by the electrical equipment manufacturer AEG, which reported net income of exactly zero in each of the three years 1985, 1986, and 1987. The odds of a company generating net income of zero in any given year, let alone three years in a row, without the help of income smoothing are extremely small.

Recently, German accounting has undergone considerable change. German law was amended in 1998 to allow German companies to use IASs in their consolidated financial statements. In fact, German companies could choose to use U.S. GAAP, U.K. GAAP, or any other internationally accepted standards in lieu of German law in preparing consolidated statements. Also in 1998, the German Accounting Standards Committee was created to develop standards for consolidated financial reporting, represent German interests in international meetings, and advise the Ministry of Justice on accounting legislation. Since 2005, German publicly traded companies have been required to use IFRSs in preparing consolidated financial statements. Parent company financial statements continue to be prepared in accordance with German GAAP.

Japan

In Japan and most other code law countries, basic accounting principles are set primarily by the government. The Japanese Commercial Code requires annual audited financial statements of joint stock corporations (known as *Kabushiki Kaisha,* or KK) that have stated capital of at least 500 million yen or total liabilities of 20 billion yen or more. The Securities and Exchange Law imposes a similar reporting requirement on companies listed on Japanese stock exchanges as well as companies issuing stocks and bonds in the amount of 100 million yen or more. Consequently, many Japanese companies must produce two sets of financial statements: one to fulfill the requirements of the Commercial Code and the other based on the securities law. The two sets of statements are very similar except that the securities law requires more disclosure, and its requirements are more precisely defined.

The Commercial Code prescribes a few basic accounting principles (valuation of assets and liabilities, recording of deferred assets, and the like). These rules are supplemented by the *Financial Accounting Standards for Business Enterprises* developed by the Business Accounting Deliberation Council (BADC). The BADC is, therefore, the single most important source of accounting principles in Japan. The BADC is made up of individuals drawn from the government, business, education, and the accounting profession. Membership in this council is by appointment of the Ministry of Finance, which, therefore, allows government control.

In 2001, a private sector accounting standard-setting body was established. The Accounting Standards Board of Japan (ASBJ) is modeled on the U.S. FASB and derives its standard-setting authority from the BADC. The BADC reserves the right, however, to override ASBJ pronouncements.

Tax laws quite heavily influence financial reporting in Japan. Companies usually follow the tax guidelines in producing their statements unless absolutely prohibited from doing so. Fortunately, the tax laws are written so that actual differences with official accounting pronouncements are few.

The Japanese Institute of Certified Public Accountants (JICPA) has not been a powerful force in establishing accounting principles. The Audit Committee of the JICPA, though, does issue papers describing preferable accounting practices.

More recently, the JICPA has been involved in standard setting through members serving on the ASBJ and its various technical committees.

To become a certified public accountant in Japan, applicants must pass three examinations: the first (from which college graduates are exempted) consists of mathematics, the Japanese language, and a thesis. The second comprises accounting, cost accounting, auditing, management, economics, and commercial law. Passing this second test qualifies one as a Junior CPA. Then, after three years of experience, a third examination is required to become a CPA. This final test is made up of accounting practice, auditing practice, and financial analysis. Although the population of Japan is about one-third the size of the population in the United States, Japan has only about one-sixteenth as many CPAs.

Financial statements required by the Japanese Commercial Code consist of the following:

▶ Balance sheet.

▶ Income statement.

▶ Proposal of appropriation of profit or disposition of loss.

▶ Business report.

Although a statement of cash flows is not specifically required, companies must provide extensive cash flow information in supplementary information filed with the Ministry of Finance. It is not uncommon for companies to voluntarily provide a cash flows statement in their annual reports.

Large Japanese companies commonly prepare an English language version of their annual report, known as *convenience translations*. (The same is true for the larger European companies.) In their English language convenience translations, Japanese companies usually translate yen amounts into U.S. dollars for the benefit of foreign readers. Note 2 to Nippon Light Metal's financial statements indicates how this is carried out.

The rate of ¥133.25 = U.S. $1, the approximate current rate prevailing at March 31, 2002, has been used to present the U.S. dollar amounts in the accompanying consolidated financial statements. These amounts are included solely for convenience and should not be construed as representations that the yen amounts actually represent or have been or could be converted into U.S. dollars. The amounts shown in U.S. dollars are not intended to be computed in accordance with generally accepted accounting principles.

Because each financial statement item is translated using the same rate, no translation adjustment arises.

The Japanese balance sheet is similar in appearance to that used in the United States. Assets and liabilities usually are classified as current or long term.

The Japanese income statement is divided into two sections to arrive at income before income taxes: ordinary income and special items. The income statement of Nippon Light Metal Company, Ltd., in Exhibit 37-13 is an example of this structure. The first part of this statement includes operating revenues and expenses as well as nonoperating items such as interest and equity method income. The definition of a special item in Japan is not as restrictive as the definition of an extraordinary item in the United States. Japanese companies are required to report earnings per share calculated as net income divided by the weighted average number of shares outstanding during the period. There is no requirement to present earnings per share on a fully diluted basis.

EXHIBIT 37-13 Japanese Income Statement

NIPPON LIGHT METAL COMPANY, LTD.
Consolidated Statement of Income
For the Year Ended March 31, 2004

	Millions of Yen	Thousands of U.S. Dollars (Note 2)
	2004	2004
Net sales	¥532,201	$5,035,490
Cost of sales (Note 13)	419,908	3,973,015
Gross profit	112,293	1,062,475
Selling, general, and administrative expenses (Note 13)	85,938	813,114
Operating profit	26,355	249,361
Nonoperating income:		
Interest income	80	757
Amortization of negative goodwill	1,409	13,332
Equity in earnings of associates	304	2,876
Other	3,484	32,964
Total nonoperating income	5,277	49,929
Nonoperating expenses:		
Interest expense	5,438	51,452
Amortization of transition obligation for employee retirement benefits (Note 7)	2,130	20,153
Loss on disposal of inventories	1,292	12,224
Other	6,680	63,204
Total nonoperating expenses	15,540	147,033
Ordinary profit	16,092	152,257
Special gains:		
Gain on sale of fixed assets	3,699	34,999
Gain on sale of investment securities (Note 5)	1,231	11,647
Total special gains	4,930	46,646
Special losses:		
Loss on devaluation of investment securities	1,914	18,110
Additional retirement allowance for early retirement program (Note 7)	—	—
Loss on disposal of fixed assets	—	—
Prior years' severance costs for directors and statutory auditors	—	—
Total special losses	1,914	18,110
Income before income taxes and minority interest	19,108	180,793
Income taxes (Note 8)—current	4,562	43,164
—deferred	2,309	21,847
	6,871	65,011
Minority interest in income of consolidated subsidiaries	712	6,737
Net income	¥ 11,525	$ 109,045

Per share of common stock:	Yen	U.S. dollars (Note 2)
Net income	¥ 21.24	$ 0.20
Cash dividends	¥ 2.50	$ 0.02

DISCUSSION QUESTION

WHICH ACCOUNTING METHOD REALLY IS APPROPRIATE?

In this era of rapidly changing technology, research and development expenditures represent one of the most important factors in the future success of many companies. Organizations that spend too little on R&D risk being left behind by the competition. Conversely, companies that spend too much may waste money or not be able to make efficient use of the results.

In the United States, all research and development expenditures are expensed as incurred. Mexico uses this same treatment. However, expensing all research and development costs is not an approach used in much of the world. Firms using IFRSs must capitalize development costs as an intangible asset when they can demonstrate (1) the technical feasibility of completing the project, (2) the intention to complete the project, (3) the ability to use or sell the intangible asset, (4) how the intangible asset will generate future benefits, (5) the availability of adequate resources to complete the asset, and (6) the ability to measure development costs associated with the intangible asset. Similarly, Canadian companies must capitalize development costs when certain criteria are met. Japanese accounting allows research and development costs to be capitalized if the research is directed toward new goods or techniques, development of markets, or exploitation of resources. Korean businesses capitalize their research and development costs when they are incurred in relation to a specific product or technology, when costs can be separately identified, and when the recovery of costs is reasonably expected. Brazil also allows research and development costs to be capitalized under certain conditions.

Should any portion of research and development costs be capitalized? Is the expensing of all research and development expenditures the best method of reporting these vital costs? Is the U.S. system necessarily the best approach? Which approach provides the best representation of the company's activities?

In March 2005, the ASBJ and the IASB held an initial meeting to discuss a project with a goal of converging their respective standards. Subsequent to that meeting, the chairman of the U.S. SEC and the Japan Minister of State for Financial Services met to discuss convergence between the United States and Japan. Japan appears to be firmly committed to international convergence of financial reporting.

SUMMARY

1. The world is rapidly developing a global economy with numerous multinational corporations. U.S. companies are expanding into other countries while foreign investors are acquiring businesses in the United States. Thus, a knowledge of the accounting principles applied throughout the world is necessary to be an efficient decision maker, especially when dealing with international capital markets. The wide diversity of these accounting principles can make understanding reported financial information and comparing companies a difficult task.

2. Accounting rules differ significantly across countries partially because of environmental factors such as the type of legal system followed in the country, the importance of equity as a source of capital, and the extent to which accounting statements serve as the basis for taxation. The two major classes of accounting systems in the world are the macro-uniform and the micro-based classes. Each class is composed of several families, the largest of which is heavily influenced by accounting development in the United Kingdom.

3. The International Accounting Standards Committee (IASC) was formed in 1973 to develop accounting standards universally acceptable in all countries. In 2001, the International Accounting Standards Board (IASB) replaced the IASC. As a private organization, the IASB does not have the ability to require the use of its standards. However, an increasing number of countries either require or allow the use of IFRSs for domestic companies. All publicly traded companies in the EU began using IFRSs in 2005. The International Organization of Securities Commissions (IOSCO) recommends that securities regulators permit foreign issuers to use IAS for cross-listing. Most major stock exchanges comply with this recommendation.

4. In 2002 the FASB and the IASB announced the Norwalk Agreement to converge their financial reporting standards as soon as practicable. The FASB's initiatives to further convergence include a short-term project to eliminate those differences in which convergence is likely to be achievable in the short term by selecting either existing U.S. GAAP or IASB requirements. The FASB and IASB also are jointly working on several projects that deal with broader issues, including a project to converge the two boards' conceptual frameworks. In addition, a full-time member of the IASB serves as a liaison with the FASB.

5. Numerous differences exist between IFRSs and U.S. GAAP. These differences can be categorized as relating to (a) recognition, (b) measurement, or (c) presentation and disclosure. Recognizing development costs as an asset when certain criteria are met under IFRSs while requiring they be expensed immediately under U.S. GAAP is an example of a recognition difference. Writing inventory down to net realizable value under IFRSs versus replacement cost under U.S. GAAP when applying the lower-of-cost-or-market rule is a measurement difference. Presenting certain gains and losses in the income statement as extraordinary items in accordance with U.S. GAAP, which is not allowed by IFRSs, is an example of a presentation difference. The U.S. GAAP reconciliations prepared by foreign companies that have securities registered with the SEC are a good source of information about the practical importance of differences between IFRSs and U.S. GAAP.

6. The accounting standards in Japan, Germany, and other macro-uniform countries are based on government regulation and are quite conservative. Financial institutions and tax authorities are considered the primary users of published financial data. In the United Kingdom, a micro-based country, individual investors are the main users of statements. Accounting standards are set by the accounting profession, and measurement rules are less conservative. The financial statements of each of these countries exhibit a number of unique characteristics when viewed from the perspective of a U.S. company. For example, the profit and loss statement in Japan labels a wide variety of transactions as extraordinary (or special). In both Germany and the United Kingdom, the balance sheet begins with fixed assets.

STUDY SESSION 8
FINANCIAL STATEMENT ANALYSIS:
FINANCIAL RATIOS AND EARNINGS PER SHARE

READING ASSIGNMENTS

Reading 38 Analysis of Financial Statements
Reading 39 Dilutive Securities and Earnings per Share

The readings in this study session discuss and illustrate the earnings analysis of financial statements and the critical role that financial ratio analysis plays in making investment or credit decisions through the measurement of financial performance and risk.

Financial ratios may be used to compare the risk and return of a company with that of other companies of different sizes. A significant hurdle in applying ratio analysis is the difficulty of comparing companies that use alternative accounting policies and estimates. To achieve appropriate comparability, the accounting differences must be identified and then the financial statement balances adjusted for those differences.

Basic and **diluted earnings per share** are important and widely used performance statistics for publicly traded companies. Unlike other ratios presented in this study session, the measurement and calculation of the earnings per share ratio is strictly determined by the regulatory requirements of U.S. GAAP.

LEARNING OUTCOMES

Reading 38: Analysis of Financial Statements
The candidate should be able to:

a. interpret common-size balance sheets and common-size income statements, and discuss the circumstances under which the use of common-size financial statements is appropriate;

b. discuss the purposes and limitations of financial ratios and why it is important to examine a company's performance relative to the economy and its industry;

Note:
For Level I examination purposes on Financial Statement Analysis, when a ratio is defined and calculated differently in various texts, candidates should use the definition given in the Reilly and Brown text. Such differences are part of the nature of practical financial analysis. For example, some practitioners call "efficiency" ratios "activity" ratios or "turnover" ratios.

201

c. calculate, interpret and discuss the uses of measures of a company's internal liquidity, operating performance (i.e., operating efficiency and operating profitability), risk analysis, and growth potential;

d. calculate and interpret the various components of the company's return on equity using the original and extended DuPont systems and a company's financial ratios relative to its industry, to the aggregate economy, and to the company's own performance over time.

Reading 39: Dilutive Securities and Earnings per Share
The candidate should be able to:

a. differentiate between simple and complex capital structures for purposes of calculating earnings per share (EPS), describe the components of EPS, and calculate a company's EPS in a simple capital structure;

b. calculate a company's weighted average number of shares outstanding;

c. determine the effect of stock dividends and stock splits on a company's weighted average number of shares outstanding;

d. distinguish between dilutive and antidilutive securities and calculate a company's basic and diluted EPS in a complex capital structure, and describe and determine the effects of convertible securities, options and warrants on a company's EPS;

e. compare and contrast the requirements for EPS reporting in simple versus complex capital structures.

ANALYSIS OF FINANCIAL STATEMENTS

by Frank K. Reilly and Keith C. Brown

LEARNING OUTCOMES

The candidate should be able to:

a. interpret common-size balance sheets and common-size income statements, and discuss the circumstances under which the use of common-size financial statements is appropriate;

b. discuss the purposes and limitations of financial ratios and why it is important to examine a company's performance relative to the economy and its industry;

c. calculate, interpret and discuss the uses of measures of a company's internal liquidity, operating performance (i.e., operating efficiency and operating profitability), risk analysis, and growth potential;

d. calculate and interpret the various components of the company's return on equity using the original and extended DuPont systems and a company's financial ratios relative to its industry, to the aggregate economy, and to the company's own performance over time.

INTRODUCTION 1

Y ou have probably already noted that this is a fairly long reading with several financial statements and numerous financial ratios. The reason for this extensive discussion of how to analyze financial statements is that our ultimate goal is to construct a portfolio of investments that will provide rates of return that are consistent with the risk of the portfolio. In turn, to determine the expected rates of return on different assets we must *estimate the future value* of each asset since a major component of the rate of return is the change in value for the asset over time. Therefore, the crux of investments is *valuation.* Although we will consider various valuation models for common stocks in Reading 59, you are already aware that the value of any earning asset is the present value of the expected cash flows generated by the asset. To estimate the value of an asset we must derive an estimate of the discount rate for the asset (the required rate of return) and its expected cash flows. The main source of the information needed to make these two estimates is the financial statements. To derive an estimate of the required rate of return, we need to understand the business and financial risk of the firm. To estimate future cash flows, we must understand the composition of cash flows and what will contribute to the short-run and long-run growth of these cash flows. Financial statements, business and financial risk, and analysis of the composition and growth of cash flow are all topics of this reading. In other words, a primary purpose of this reading is to help you understand how to estimate the variables in valuation models.

Financial statements are also the main source of information when deciding whether to lend money to a firm (invest in its bonds) or to buy warrants or options on a firm's stock. In this reading, we first introduce a corporation's major financial statements and discuss why and how financial ratios are useful. We also provide example computations of ratios that reflect internal liquidity, operating performance, risk analysis, and growth analysis. In addition, we address four major areas in investments where financial ratios have been effectively employed.

Our example company in this reading is Walgreens Co., the largest retail drugstore chain in the United States. It operates 4,582 drugstores in 44 states and Puerto Rico. Pharmacy prescription sales generate over 63 percent of total sales. The firm leads its industry (retail drugstores) in sales, profit, and store growth. The firm's goal is to be America's most convenient and technologically advanced health-care retailer. It takes great pride in its steady sales and earnings growth that have been reflected in outstanding stock performance—e.g., dividends have increased in each of the past 29 years and since 1980 the stock has been split two-for-one seven times.

MAJOR FINANCIAL STATEMENTS

Financial statements are intended to provide information on the resources available to management, how these resources were financed, and what the firm accomplished with them. Corporate shareholder annual and quarterly reports include three required financial statements: the balance sheet, the income statement, and the statement of cash flows. In addition, reports that must be filed with the Securities and Exchange Commission (SEC) (for example, the 10-K and 10-Q reports) carry detailed information about the firm, such as information on loan agreements and data on product line and subsidiary performance. Information from the basic financial statements can be used to calculate financial ratios and to analyze the operations of the firm to determine what factors influence a firm's earnings, cash flows, and risk characteristics.

Generally Accepted Accounting Principles

Among the input used to construct the financial statements are **generally accepted accounting principles (GAAP),** which are formulated by the Financial

Accounting Standards Board (FASB). The FASB recognizes that it would be improper for all companies to use identical and restrictive accounting principles. Some flexibility and choice are needed because industries and firms within industries differ in their operating environments. Therefore, the FASB allows companies some flexibility to choose among appropriate GAAP. This flexibility allows the firms managers to choose accounting standards that best reflect company practice. On the negative side, this flexibility can allow firms to appear healthier than they really are.[1] Given this possibility, the financial analyst must rigorously analyze the available financial information to separate those firms that *appear* attractive from those that actually are in good financial shape.

Fortunately, the FASB requires that financial statements include footnotes that indicate which accounting principles were used by the firm. Because accounting principles frequently differ among firms, the footnote information assists the financial analyst in adjusting the financial statements of companies so the analyst can better compare "apples with apples."

Balance Sheet

The **balance sheet** shows what resources (assets) the firm controls and how it has financed these assets. Specifically, it indicates the current and fixed assets available to the firm *at a point in time* (the end of the fiscal year or the end of a quarter). In most cases, the firm owns these assets, but some firms lease assets on a long-term basis. How the firm has financed the acquisition of these assets is indicated by its mixture of current liabilities (accounts payable or short-term borrowing), long-term liabilities (fixed debt and leases), and owners' equity (preferred stock, common stock, and retained earnings).

The balance sheet for Walgreens in Exhibit 38-1 represents the *stock* of assets and its financing mix as of the end of Walgreen Co.'s fiscal year, August 31, 2002, 2003, and 2004.

Income Statement

The **income statement** contains information on the operating performance of the firm during some *period of time* (a quarter or a year). In contrast to the balance sheet, which is at a fixed point in time, the income statement indicates the *flow* of sales, expenses, and earnings during a period of time. The income statement for Walgreens for the years 2002, 2003, and 2004 appears in Exhibit 38-2. We concentrate on earnings from operations after tax as the relevant net earnings figure. For Walgreens, this is typically the same as net income because the firm generally has no nonrecurring or unusual income or expense items.

---

[1] The recent Enron fiasco clearly makes this point. For a general discussion on this topic, see Byrnes and Henry (2001), Henry (2001), and McNamee (2002).

EXHIBIT 38-1	Walgreen Co. and Subsidiaries Consolidated Balance Sheet ($ Millions), Years Ended August 31, 2002, 2003, and 2004

	2004	2003	2002
Assets			
Current assets			
Cash and cash equivalents	$ 1,696	$ 1,268	$ 450
Accounts receivable, net of allowances	1,169	1,018	955
Inventories	4,739	4,203	3,645
Other current assets	161	121	117
Total current assets	7,765	6,610	5,167
Property, plant, and equipment, gross	7,094	6,362	5,918
Less accumulated depreciation and amortization	1,648	1,422	1,327
Property, plant, and equipment, net	5,446	4,940	4,591
Other noncurrent assets	131	108	121
Total assets	$ 13,342	$ 11,658	$ 9,879
Liabilities and shareholders' equity			
Current liabilities			
Short-term borrowings	$ 0	$ 0	$ 0
Current maturities of long-term debt	0	0	0
Trade accounts payable	2,642	2,408	1,836
Total accrued expenses and other liabilities	1,370	1,158	1,018
Accrued expenses and other liabilities	0	0	0
Income taxes payable	66	106	101
Total current liabilities	4,078	3,672	2,955
Deferred income taxes	328	228	177
Long-term debt, net of current maturities	0	0	0
Other noncurrent liabilities	709	562	517
Preferred stock, $0.0625 par value; authorized 32 million shares; none issued	0	0	0
Common shareholders' equity			
Common stock, $0.078125 par value; authorized 3.2 billion shares; issued and outstanding 1,205,400,000 in 2004 1,204,908,276 in 2003, 2002	80	80	80
Paid-in capital	632	698	748
Retained earnings	7,591	6,418	5,402
Treasury stock at cost, 2,107,263 shares in 2004	(76)	0	0
Total shareholders' equity	8,227	7,196	6,230
Total liabilities and common shareholders' equity	$ 13,342	$ 11,658	$ 9,879

Source: Reprinted with permission from Walgreen Co., Deerfield, IL.

EXHIBIT 38-2	Walgreen Co. and Subsidiaries Consolidated Statement of Earnings and Shareholders' Equity ($ Millions, Except per Share Data), Years Ended August 31, 2002, 2003, and 2004

	2004	2003	2002
Net sales	$ 37,508	$ 32,505	$ 28,681
Cost of sales	27,310	23,706	21,076
Gross profit	10,198	8,799	7,605
Selling, occupancy, and administrative expense	8,055	6,951	5,981
Operating profit (EBIT)	2,143	1,848	1,624
Interest income	17	11	7
Interest expense	0	0	0
Other income	16	30	6
Operating income before income taxes	2,176	1,889	1,637
Provision for income taxes	816	713	618
Reported net income	1,360	1,176	1,019
Reported net income available for common	1,360	1,176	1,019
Net earnings (loss) per share	$ 1.33	$ 1.14	$ 0.99
Dividends per common share	$ 0.18	$ 0.16	$ 0.15
Average number of common shares outstanding (millions)	1,032	1,032	1,032

Source: Reprinted with permission from Walgreen Co., Deerfield, IL.

EXHIBIT 38-3	Walgreen Co. and Subsidiaries Consolidated Statement of Cash Flows for Fiscal Years Ended August 31, 2002, 2003, and 2004 ($ Millions)

	2004	2003	2002
Cash flow from operating activities			
Net income	$ 1,360	$ 1,176	$ 1,019
Adjustments to reconcile net income to net cash provided by operating activities:			
Cumulative effect of accounting changes	0	0	0
Depreciation and amortization	403	346	307
Deferred income taxes	72	59	23
Income tax savings from employee stock plans	50	24	57
Other net income adjustments	31	29	(9)
Changes in operating assets and liabilities (used in) provided from continuing operations:			
(Increase) decrease in inventories	(536)	(558)	(163)
(Increase) decrease in accounts receivable	(172)	(57)	(171)
Increase (decrease) in trade accounts payable	234	295	254
Increase (decrease) in accrued expenses and other liabilities	208	136	141
Income taxes	(40)	5	14
Other operating assets and liabilities	42	48	31
Net cash flows from operating activities	$ 1,653	$ 1,504	$ 1,504

(Exhibit continued on next page ...)

EXHIBIT 38-3	(continued)		
	2004	**2003**	**2002**
Cash flows from investing activities:			
Additions to property and equipment	(940)	(795)	(934)
Disposition of property and equipment	6	85	368
Net proceeds from corporate-owned life insurance	10	8	14
Net (purchase) sales of marketable security	0	0	0
Net cash flows from investing activities	$ (923)	$ (702)	$ (552)
Cash flows from financing activities:			
(Payments of) proceeds from short-term borrowing	0	0	(441)
Cash dividends paid	(177)	(152)	(147)
Stock purchases	(299)	(149)	(25)
Proceeds from employee stock plans	145	82	137
Other	29	(3)	(12)
Net cash flows from financing activities	$ (302)	$ (222)	$ (488)
Net increase (decrease) in cash and cash equivalents	428	580	463
Cash and cash equivalents at beginning of year	1268	688	225
Cash and cash equivalents at end of year	$ 1,696	$ 1,268	$ 688

Source: Reprinted with permission from Walgreen Co., Deerfield, IL.

Statement of Cash Flows

Our earlier discussion on valuation indicates that cash flows are a critical input. Therefore accountants now require firms to provide such information. The **statement of cash flows** integrates the information on the balance sheet and income statement to show the effects on the firm's cash flow of income flows (based on the most recent year's income statement) and changes on the balance sheet (based on the two most recent annual balance sheets) that imply an effect on cash flows. Analysts use these cash flow values to estimate the value of a firm and to evaluate the risk and return of the firm's bonds and stock.

The statement of cash flows has three sections: cash flows from operating activities, cash flows from investing activities, and cash flows from financing activities. The total cash flows from the three sections is the net change in the cash position of the firm that should equal the difference in the cash balance between the ending and beginning balance sheets. The statements of cash flow for Walgreens for 2002, 2003, and 2004 appear in Exhibit 38-3.

Cash Flows from Operating Activities   This section of the statement lists the sources and uses of cash that arise from the normal operations of a firm. In general, the net cash flow from operations is computed as the net income reported on the income statement including changes in net working capital items (i.e., receivables, inventories, and so on) plus adjustments for non-cash revenues and expenses (such as depreciation), or:

$$\text{Cash Flow from Operating Activities} = \text{Net Income} + \text{Noncash Revenue and Expenses} + \text{Changes in Net Working Capital Items} \qquad \textbf{(38-1)}$$

Consistent with our previous discussion, the cash account is not included in the calculations of cash flow from operations. Notably, Walgreens has been able to generate consistently large and growing cash flows from operations even after accounting for consistent substantial increases in receivables and inventory required by the firm's growth.

Cash Flows from Investing Activities   A firm makes investments in both its own noncurrent and fixed assets and the equity of other firms (which may be subsidiaries or joint ventures of the parent firm. They are listed in the "investment" account of the balance sheet). Increases and decreases in these noncurrent accounts are considered investment activities. The cash flow from investing activities is the change in gross plant and equipment plus the change in the investment account. The changes are positive if they represent a source of funds (e.g., sale of some plant and/or equipment); otherwise they are negative. The dollar changes in these accounts are computed using the firm's two most recent balance sheets. Most firms (including Walgreens) experience negative cash flows from investments due to significant capital expenditures.

Cash Flows from Financing Activities   Cash inflows are created by increasing notes payable and long-term liability and equity accounts, such as bond and stock issues. Financing uses (out-flows) include decreases in such accounts (that is, paying down liability accounts or the repurchase of common shares). Dividend payments are a significant financing cash outflow. For Walgreens and for many firms, the repurchase of shares has also been a major outflow in recent years.

The total cash flows from operating, investing, and financing activities are the net increase or decrease in the firm's cash. The statement of cash flows provides cash flow detail that is lacking in the balance sheet and income statement.

Measures of Cash Flow

There are several cash flow measures an analyst can use to determine the underlying health of the corporation.

Traditional Cash Flow   The traditional measure of cash flow equals net income plus depreciation expense and deferred taxes. But as we have just seen, it is also necessary to adjust for changes in operating (current) assets and liabilities that either use or provide cash. These changes can add to or subtract from the cash flow estimated from the traditional measure of cash flow: net income plus noncash expenses.

The table below compares the cash flow from operations figures (Exhibit 38-3) to the traditional cash flow figures for Walgreens from 2002 to 2004.

	Traditional Cash Flow Equals Net Income + Depreciation + Change in Deferred Taxes	Cash Flow from Operations from Statement of Cash Flows
2004	1,863	1,653
2003	1,581	1,504
2002	1,349	1,504

In two of the three years the cash flow from operations was less than the traditional cash flow estimate because of the several adjustments needed to arrive at cash flow from operations. Therefore, using this more exact measure of cash flow for these two years, the Walgreens ratios would not have been as strong. For many firms, this is fairly typical because the effect of working capital changes is often a large negative cash flow due to necessary increases in receivables or inventory to support sales growth (especially for high-growth companies).

Free Cash Flow   Free cash flow modifies cash flow from operations to recognize that some investing and financing activities are critical to the firm. It is assumed that these expenditures must be made before a firm can use its cash flow for other purposes such as reducing debt outstanding or repurchasing common stock. Two additional items are considered: (1) capital expenditures (an investing expenditure) and (2) the disposition of property and equipment (a divestment source of cash). These two items are used to modify Walgreen Co.'s cash flow from operations as follows (most analysts only subtract net capital expenditures, but conservative analysts also subtract dividends).

	Cash Flow from Operations	−	Capital Expenditures	+	Disposition of Property and Equipment	=	Free Cash Flow
2004	1,653	−	940	+	6	=	719
2003	1,504	−	795	+	85	=	794
2002	1,504	−	934	+	368	=	938

For firms involved in leveraged buyouts, this free cash flow number is critical because the new owners typically want to use the firm's free cash flow as funds available for retiring outstanding debt. It is not unusual for a firm's free cash flow to be a negative value. For Walgreens, the free cash flow value has been positive but has declined because of significant capital expenditures related to store growth. Notably, this free cash flow value or a variation of it will be used in the subsequent cash flow valuation models.[2]

EBITDA   The EBITDA (earnings before interest, taxes, depreciation, and amortization) measure of cash flow is extremely liberal. This very generous measure of operating earnings does not consider any of the adjustments noted previously. Specifically, it adds back depreciation and amortization (as in the traditional measure) along with both interest expense and taxes, but does not consider the effect of changes in working capital items (such as additions to receivables and inventory) or the significant impact of capital expenditures. The following table, which compares this measure to the other three measures of cash flow for Walgreens, demonstrates the large differences among these measures.

Year	EBITDA	Traditional Cash Flow	Cash Flow from Operations	Free Cash Flow
2004	2,579	1,863	1,653	719
2003	2,235	1,581	1,504	794
2002	1,944	1,349	1,504	938

---

[2] As we will show in Reading 59, small modifications of this free cash flow—called free cash flow to equity (FCFE), free cash flow to the firm (FCFF), and net operating profits less applicable taxes (NOPLAT)—are used in valuation models and also the economic value added (EVA) model.

Some analysts have used EBITDA as a proxy for cash flow and a metric for valuation similar to earnings—that is, they refer to EBITDA multiples as other analysts would refer to price-earnings (P/E) multiples. Yet given what this measure does not consider, this is a very questionable practice and is *not* recommended by the authors.[3]

Purpose of Financial Statement Analysis

Financial statement analysis seeks to evaluate management performance in several important areas, including profitability, efficiency, and risk. Although we will necessarily analyze historical data, the ultimate goal of this analysis is to provide insights that will help us to project *future* management performance, including pro forma balance sheets, income statements, cash flows, and risk. It is the firm's *expected future* performance that determines whether we should lend money to a firm or invest in it.

ANALYSIS OF FINANCIAL RATIOS

3

Analysts use financial ratios because numbers in isolation typically convey little meaning. For example, knowing that a firm earned a net income of $100,000 is not very informative unless we also know the sales figure that generated this income ($1 million or $10 million) and the assets or capital committed to the enterprise. Thus, ratios are intended to provide meaningful *relationships* between individual values in the financial statements.

Because the major financial statements report numerous individual items, it is possible to produce a vast number of potential ratios, many of which will have little value. Therefore, we limit our examination to the most relevant ratios and group them into categories that will provide information on important economic characteristics of the firm.

Importance of Relative Financial Ratios

Just as a single number from a financial statement is of little use, an individual financial ratio has little value except in relation to comparable ratios for other entities. That is, *only relative financial ratios are relevant*. Therefore, it is important to compare a firm's performance relative to

- ▶ The aggregate economy
- ▶ Its industry or industries
- ▶ Its major competitors within the industry
- ▶ Its past performance (time-series analysis)

The comparison to the aggregate economy is important because almost all firms are influenced by economic fluctuations. For example, it is unreasonable to expect an increase in the profit margin for a firm during a recession; a stable margin might be encouraging under such conditions. In contrast, a small increase in a firm's profit margin during a major business expansion may

---

[3] For a detailed discussion of the problems with using EBITDA, see Greenberg (2000).

be a sign of weakness. Thus, this analysis that considers the economic environment helps investors understand how a firm reacts to the business cycle and *estimate* the future performance of the firm during subsequent business cycles.

Probably the most significant comparison relates a firm's performance to that of its industry. Different industries affect the firms within them differently, but this relationship is always significant. The industry effect is strongest for industries with homogeneous products such as steel, rubber, glass, and wood products, because all firms within these industries experience coincidental shifts in demand. In addition, these firms employ fairly similar technology and production processes. For example, even the best-managed steel firm experiences a decline in sales and profit margins during a recession. In such a case, the relevant question is not whether sales and margins declined, but how bad was the decline relative to other steel firms? In addition, investors should examine an industry's performance relative to the economy to understand how the industry responds to the business cycle, as discussed in Reading 60.

When comparing a firm's financial ratios to industry ratios, investors may not want to use the average (mean) industry value when there is wide variation among firms in the industry. Alternatively, if we believe that a firm has a unique component, a **cross-sectional analysis** in which we compare the firm to a subset of industry firms comparable in size or characteristics, may be appropriate. As an example, we would compare the performance of Kroger to that of other national food chains rather than regional food chains or specialty food chains.

Another practical problem with comparing a firm to its industry is that many large firms are multi-industry. Inappropriate comparisons can arise when a multi-industry firm is evaluated against the ratios from a single industry. To mitigate this problem, we can use a cross-sectional analysis that compares the firm against a rival that operates in many of the same industries. Alternatively, we can construct composite industry average ratios for the firm. To do this, we use the firm's annual report or 10-K filing to identify each industry in which the firm operates and the proportion of total firm sales derived from each industry. The composite industry ratios would be the weighted-average ratios based on the proportion of firm sales derived from each industry.

Finally, **time-series analysis,** in which we examine a firm's relative performance over time to determine whether it is progressing or declining, is helpful when estimating future performance. Calculating the five or ten year average of a ratio without considering the time-series trend can result in misleading conclusions. For example, an average rate of return of 10 percent can be the result of rates of return that have increased from 5 percent to 15 percent over time or the result of a series that declined from 15 percent to 5 percent. Obviously, the difference in the trend for these series would have a major impact on our estimate for the future. Ideally, we would examine a firm's time series of *relative* financial ratios compared to its industry and the economy.

4   COMPUTATION OF FINANCIAL RATIOS

In the following discussion, we divide the financial ratios into five major categories that underscore the important economic characteristics of a firm. The five categories are

1. Common size statements
2. Internal liquidity (solvency)

3. Operating performance
   a. Operating efficiency
   b. Operating profitability
4. Risk analysis
   a. Business risk
   b. Financial risk
   c. External liquidity risk
5. Growth analysis

Common Size Statements

Common size statements normalize balance sheet and income statement items to allow easier comparison of different sized firms. A common size *balance sheet* expresses all balance sheet accounts as a *percentage of total assets*. A common size *income statement* expresses all income statement items as a *percentage of sales*. Exhibit 38-4 is the common size balance sheet for Walgreens, and Exhibit 38-5 contains the common size income statement. Common size ratios are useful to quickly compare two different sized firms and to examine trends over time within a single firm. Common size statements also give insight into a firm's financial condition, for example, the proportion of liquid assets or the proportion of short-term liabilities, and the percentage of sales consumed by production costs or interest expense. In the case of Walgreens, the common size balance sheet shows a consistent increase in the percent of current assets (due to a cash increase), and an increase followed by a decline in the proportion of net property. Alternatively, the common size income statement shows that Walgreen Co.'s cost of goods sold and its selling and administrative expenses were quite stable from 2000 to 2004 in proportion to sales. As a result of this stability, the firm has experienced virtually a constant operating profit margin before and after taxes. The ability of Walgreens to experience strong growth in sales (over 14 percent a year) *and* a constant profit margin during a period that included a recession is very impressive.

EVALUATING INTERNAL LIQUIDITY   5

Internal liquidity (solvency) ratios are intended to indicate the ability of the firm to meet future short-term financial obligations. They compare near-term financial obligations, such as accounts payable or notes payable, to current assets or cash flows that will be available to meet these obligations.

Internal Liquidity Ratios

Current Ratio   Clearly the best-known liquidity measure is the current ratio, which examines the relationship between current assets and current liabilities as follows:

$$\text{Current Ratio} = \frac{\text{Current Assets}}{\text{Current Liabilities}} \qquad \textbf{(38-2)}$$

EXHIBIT 38-4	Walgreen Co. and Subsidiaries Common Size Balance Sheet ($ Millions), Years Ended August 31, 2000, 2001, 2002, 2003, and 2004

	2004	2003	2002	2001	2000
Assets					
Current assets					
Cash and cash equivalents	12.71%	10.88%	4.56%	0.19%	0.18%
Accounts receivable, net of allowances	8.76	8.73	9.67	9.04	8.65
Inventories	35.52	36.05	36.90	39.42	39.85
Other current assets	1.21	1.04	1.18	1.09	1.30
Total current assets	58.20	56.70	52.30	49.74	49.98
Property, plant, and equipment, gross	53.17	54.57	59.90	62.30	62.22
Less accumulated depreciation and amortization	12.35	12.20	13.43	13.11	13.96
Property, plant, and equipment, net	40.82	42.37	46.47	49.19	48.26
Other noncurrent assets	0.98	0.93	1.22	1.07	1.77
Total assets	100.00%	100.00%	100.00%	100.00%	100.00%
Liabilities and shareholders' equity					
Current liabilities					
Short-term borrowings	0.00%	0.00%	0.00%	4.99%	0.00%
Current maturities of long-term debt	0	0	0	0	0
Trade accounts payable	19.80	20.66	18.58	17.51	19.20
Total accrued expenses and other liabilities	10.27	9.93	10.30	10.61	11.93
Income taxes payable	0.49	0.91	1.02	0.98	1.30
Total current liabilities	30.57	31.50	29.91	34.09	32.43
Deferred income taxes	2.46	1.96	1.79	1.55	1.43
Long-term debt, net of current maturities	0	0	0	0	0
Other noncurrent liabilities	5.31	4.82	5.23	5.41	6.54
Preferred stock, $0.0625 par value; authorized 32 million shares; none issued	0	0	0	0	0
Common shareholders' equity					
Common stock, $0.078125 par value; authorized 3.2 billion shares; issued and outstanding 1,205,400,000 in 2004 1,204,908,276 in 2003, 2002	0.60	0.69	0.81	0.90	1.11
Paid-in capital	4.74	5.99	7.57	6.75	5.17
Retained earnings	56.90	55.05	54.68	51.29	53.32
Treasury stock at cost, 2,107,263 shares in 2004	0.57	0	0	0	0
Total shareholders' equity	61.66	61.73	63.06	58.95	59.60
Total liabilities and common shareholders' equity	100.00%	100.00%	100.00%	100.00%	100.00%

Source: Information calculated using publicly available data of Walgreen Co. Reprinted with the permission of Walgreen Co.

EXHIBIT 38-5

Walgreen Co. and Subsidiaries Common Size Statement of Income ($ Millions, Except per Share Data), Years Ended August 31, 2000, 2001, 2002, 2003, and 2004

	2004	%	2003	%	2002	%	2001	%	2000	%
Net sales	$ 37,508	100.00	$ 32,505	100.00	$ 28,681	100.00	$ 37,508	100.00	$ 32,505	100.00
Cost of sales	27,310	72.81	23,706	72.93	21,076	73.48	27,310	72.81	23,706	72.93
Gross profit	10,198	27.19	8,799	27.07	7,605	26.52	10,198	27.19	8,799	27.07
Selling, occupancy, and administrative expense	8,055	21.48	6,951	21.38	5,981	20.85	8,055	21.48	6,951	21.38
Operating profit (EBIT)	2,143	5.71	1,848	5.69	1,624	5.66	2,143	5.71	1,848	5.69
Interest income	17	0.05	11	0.03	7	0.02	17	0.05	11	0.03
Interest expense	0	0.00	0	0	0	0	0	0	0	0
Other income	16	0.04	30	0.09	6	0.02	16	0.04	30	0.09
Operating income before income taxes	2,176	5.80	1,889	5.81	1,637	5.71	2,176	5.80	1,889	5.81
Provision for income taxes	816	2.18	713	2.19	618	2.15	816	2.18	713	2.19
Reported net income	1,360	3.63	1,176	3.62	1,019	3.55	1,360	3.63	1,176	3.62

Source: Information calculated using publicly available data of Walgreen Co. Reprinted with the permission of Walgreen Co.

For Walgreens, the current ratios (in thousands of dollars) were:

$$2004: \quad \frac{7,764}{4,078} = 1.90$$

$$2003: \quad \frac{6,609}{3,671} = 1.80$$

$$2002: \quad \frac{5,167}{2,955} = 1.75$$

These current ratios experienced a consistent increase during the three years and are consistent with the typical current ratio. As always, it is important to compare these values with similar figures for the firm's industry and the aggregate market. If the ratios differ from the industry results, we need to determine what might explain it. (We will discuss comparative analysis in a later section.)

Quick Ratio   Some observers question using total current assets to gauge the ability of a firm to meet its current obligations because inventories and some other current assets might not be very liquid. They prefer the quick ratio, which relates current liabilities to only relatively liquid current assets (cash items and accounts receivable) as follows:

$$\text{Quick Ratio} = \frac{\text{Cash + Marketable Securities + Receivables}}{\text{Current Liabilities}} \qquad \textbf{(38-3)}$$

Walgreen Co.'s quick ratios were

$$2004: \quad \frac{2,865}{4,078} = 0.70$$

$$2003: \quad \frac{2,286}{3,672} = 0.62$$

$$2002: \quad \frac{1,405}{2,955} = 0.48$$

These quick ratios were respectable and increased over the three years. As before, we should compare these values relative to other firms in the industry and to the aggregate economy.

Cash Ratio   The most conservative liquidity ratio is the cash ratio, which relates the firm's cash and short-term marketable securities to its current liabilities as follows:

$$\text{Cash Ratio} = \frac{\text{Cash and Marketable Securities}}{\text{Current Liabilities}} \qquad \textbf{(38-4)}$$

Walgreens Co.'s cash ratios were

$$2004: \quad \frac{1,696}{4,078} = 0.42$$

$$2003: \quad \frac{1,268}{3,672} = 0.35$$

$$2002: \quad \frac{450}{2,955} = 0.15$$

The cash ratios grew substantially from 2002 to 2004, to a point that they were almost excessive for a fast-growing retailer with inventories being financed by accounts payable to its suppliers. In addition, the firm has strong lines of credit at various banks.

Receivables Turnover   In addition to examining total liquid assets, it is useful to analyze the quality (liquidity) of the accounts receivable by calculating how often the firm's receivables turn over, which implies an average collection period. The faster these accounts are paid, the sooner the firm gets the funds to pay off its own current liabilities. Receivables turnover is computed as

$$\text{Receivable Turnover} = \frac{\text{Net Annual Sales}}{\text{Average Receivables}} \qquad \textbf{(38-5)}$$

The average receivables figure is typically equal to the beginning receivables figure plus the ending value divided by two. Receivables turnover ratios for Walgreens were

$$2004: \quad \frac{37{,}508}{(1{,}169 + 1{,}018)/2} = 34.30 \text{ times}$$

$$2003: \quad \frac{32{,}505}{(1{,}018 + 955)/2} = 32.95 \text{ times}$$

We cannot compute a turnover value for 2002 because the tables used do not include a beginning receivables figure for 2002 (that is, we lack the ending receivables figure for 2001).

Given these annual receivables turnover figures, the average collection period is

$$\text{Average Receivable Collection Period} = \frac{365 \text{ Days}}{\text{Annual Receivables Turnover}} \qquad \textbf{(38-6)}$$

For Walgreens,

$$2004: \quad \frac{365}{34.30} = 10.6 \text{ days}$$

$$2003: \quad \frac{365}{32.95} = 11.1 \text{ days}$$

These results indicate that Walgreens currently collects its accounts receivable in about 11 days, on average. To determine whether these account collection numbers are good or bad, it is essential that they be related to the firm's credit policy and to comparable numbers for other firms in the industry. The point is, the receivables collection period value varies dramatically for different firms (e.g., from 10 to over 60), and it is mainly due to the product and the industry. An industry comparison would indicate similar rapid collection periods for other drugstore chains, since most sales are for cash. The reason for a small increase in the collection period over several years (since 2000) is that a significant change has occurred in pharmacy sales: about 92 percent of pharmacy sales are now to a third party (i.e., they are reimbursed by a managed-care or insurance company), which has caused the increase in receivables.

The receivables turnover is one of the ratios in which a firm *does not want to deviate too much from the norm*. In an industry where the norm is 40 days, a collection period of 80 days would indicate slow-paying customers, which increases the capital tied up in receivables and the possibility of bad debts. Therefore, the firm wants to be somewhat below the norm (for example, 35 days vs. 40 days), but a figure *substantially below* the norm (e.g., 20 days) might indicate overly stringent credit terms relative to the competition, which could be detrimental to sales.

Inventory Turnover

We should also examine the liquidity of inventory based on the firm's inventory turnover (i.e., how many times it is sold during a year) and the implied processing time. Inventory turnover can be calculated relative to sales or cost of goods sold. The preferred turnover ratio is relative to cost of goods sold (CGS), which does not include the profit implied in sales.

$$\text{Inventory Turnover} = \frac{\text{CGS}}{\text{Average Inventory}} \qquad \textbf{(38-7)}$$

For Walgreens, the inventory turnover ratios were

$$2004: \quad \frac{27{,}310}{(4{,}739 + 4{,}203)/2} = 6.11 \text{ times}$$

$$2003: \quad \frac{23{,}706}{(4{,}203 + 3{,}645)/2} = 6.04 \text{ times}$$

Given these turnover values, we can compute the average inventory processing time as follows:

$$\text{Average Inventory Processing Period} = \frac{365}{\text{Annual Inventory Turnover}} \qquad \textbf{(38-8)}$$

For Walgreens,

$$2004: \quad \frac{365}{6.11} = 59.8 \text{ days}$$

$$2003: \quad \frac{365}{6.04} = 60.4 \text{ days}$$

Although this seems like a low turnover figure, it is encouraging that the inventory processing period is very stable and has declined over the longer run. Still, it is essential to examine this turnover ratio relative to an industry norm and/or the firm's prime competition. Notably, this ratio will also be affected by the products carried by the chain—for instance, if a drugstore chain adds high-profit margin items, such as cosmetics and liquor, these products may have a lower turnover.

As with receivables, a firm does not want an extremely low inventory turnover value and long processing time, because this implies that capital is being tied up in inventory and could signal obsolete inventory (especially for firms in the technology sector). Alternatively, an abnormally high inventory turnover and a short processing time could mean inadequate inventory that could lead to outages, backorders, and slow delivery to customers, which would eventually have an adverse effect on sales.

Cash Conversion Cycle   A very useful measure of overall internal liquidity is the cash conversion cycle, which combines information from the receivables turnover, the inventory turnover, and the accounts payable turnover. Cash is tied up in assets for a certain number of days. Specifically, cash is committed to receivables for the collection period and in inventory for a number of days—the inventory processing period. At the same time, the firm receives an offset to this capital commitment from its own suppliers who provide interest-free loans to the firm by carrying the firm's payables. Specifically, the payables' payment period is equal to 365 divided by the payables' turnover ratio. In turn, the payables turnover ratio is

$$\text{Payables Turnover Ratio} = \frac{\text{Cost of Goods Sold}}{\text{Average Trade Payables}} \qquad \textbf{(38-9)}$$

For Walgreens, the payables turnover ratios were

$$2004: \quad \frac{27,310}{(2,642 + 2,408)/2} = 10.8 \text{ times}$$

$$2003: \quad \frac{23,706}{(2,408 + 1,836)/2} = 11.2 \text{ times}$$

$$\text{Payables Payment Period} = \frac{365 \text{ days}}{\text{Payable Turnover}} \qquad \textbf{(38-10)}$$

$$2004: \quad \frac{365}{10.8} = 33.8 \text{ days}$$

$$2003: \quad \frac{365}{11.2} = 32.6 \text{ days}$$

Therefore, the cash conversion cycle for Walgreens (with components rounded) equals:

Year	Receivables Collection Days	+	Inventory Processing Days	−	Payables Payment Period	=	Cash Conversion Cycle
2004	11	+	60	−	34	=	37 days
2003	11	+	60	−	33	=	38 days

Walgreens has experienced stability in its receivables days and in its inventory processing days and is taking one day longer to pay its bills. The overall result is a very small decline in its cash conversion cycle. Although the overall cash conversion cycle appears to be quite good (about 37 days), as always we should examine the firm's long-term trend and compare it to other drugstore chains.

EVALUATING OPERATING PERFORMANCE 6

The operating performance ratios can be divided into two subcategories: (1) **operating efficiency ratios** and (2) **operating profitability ratios**. Efficiency ratios examine how the management uses its assets and capital, measured by dollars of sales generated by various asset or capital categories. Profitability ratios analyze the profits as a percentage of sales and as a percentage of the assets and capital employed.

Operating Efficiency Ratios

Total Asset Turnover   The total asset turnover ratio indicates the effectiveness of the firm's use of its total asset base (net assets equals gross assets minus depreciation on fixed assets). It is computed as

$$\text{Total Asset Turnover} = \frac{\text{Net Sales}}{\text{Average Total Net Assets}} \qquad \textbf{(38-11)}$$

Walgreen Co.'s total asset turnover values were

$$2004: \quad \frac{37,508}{(13,342 + 11,658)/2} = 3.00 \text{ times}$$

$$2003: \quad \frac{32,505}{(11,658 + 9,879)/2} = 3.02 \text{ times}$$

This ratio must be compared to that of other firms *within* an industry because it varies substantially between industries. For example, total asset turnover ratios range from less than 1 for large, capital-intensive industries (steel, autos, and heavy manufacturing companies) to over 10 for some retailing or service operations. It also can be affected by the use of leased facilities.

Again, we must consider a *range* of turnover values consistent with the industry. It is poor management to have an exceedingly high asset turnover relative to the industry because this might imply too few assets for the potential business (sales), or it could be due to the use of outdated, fully depreciated assets. It is equally poor management to have an extremely low asset turnover because this implies that the firm is tying up capital in excess assets relative to the needs of the firm and its competitors.

Beyond the analysis of the firm's total asset base, it is insightful to examine the utilization of some specific assets, such as receivables, inventories, and fixed assets. This is especially important if the firm has experienced a major decline in its total asset turnover because we want to know the cause of the decline, that is, which of the component turnovers (receivables, inventory, fixed assets) contributed to the decline. We have already examined the receivables and inventory turnover as part of our liquidity analysis; we now examine the fixed asset turnover ratio.

Net Fixed Asset Turnover   The net fixed asset turnover ratio reflects the firm's utilization of fixed assets. It is computed as

$$\text{Fixed Asset Turnover} = \frac{\text{Net Sales}}{\text{Average Net Fixed Assets}} \qquad \textbf{(38-12)}$$

Walgreen Co.'s fixed asset turnover ratios were

$$2004: \quad \frac{37,508}{(5,446 + 4,940)/2} = 7.22 \text{ times}$$

$$2003: \quad \frac{32,505}{(4,940 + 4,591)/2} = 6.82 \text{ times}$$

These turnover ratios, which indicate a small increase for Walgreens during the last few years, must be compared with industry competitors and should consider the impact of leased assets (this is especially significant for retail firms). Again, an abnormally low turnover implies capital tied up in excessive fixed assets. An abnormally high asset turnover ratio can indicate a lack of productive capacity to meet sales demand, or it might imply the use of old, fully depreciated plant and equipment that may be obsolete.[4]

Equity Turnover   In addition to specific asset turnover ratios, it is useful to examine the turnover for capital components. An important one, equity turnover, is computed as

$$\text{Equity Turnover} = \frac{\text{Net Sales}}{\text{Average Equity}}$$

(38-13)

Equity includes preferred and common stock, paid-in capital, and total retained earnings.[5] This ratio differs from total asset turnover in that it excludes current liabilities and long-term debt. Therefore, when examining this series, it is very important to consider the firm's capital structure ratios, because the firm can increase (or decrease) its equity turnover ratio by increasing (or decreasing) its proportion of debt capital.

Walgreen Co.'s equity turnover ratios were

$$2004: \quad \frac{37,508}{(8,227 + 7,196)/2} = 4.86 \text{ times}$$

$$2003: \quad \frac{32,505}{(7,196 + 6,230)/2} = 4.84 \text{ times}$$

This ratio has not changed during the past several years. In our later analysis of sustainable growth, we examine the variables that affect the equity turnover ratio to understand what variables might cause changes.

Following an analysis of the firm's operating efficiency, the next step is to examine its profitability in relation to its sales and capital.

Operating Profitability Ratios

There are two facets of profitability: (1) the rate of profit on sales (profit margin) and (2) the percentage return on capital employed. The analysis of profitability of sales actually entails several component profit margins that consider various expense categories. These component margins provide important information relative to the final net profit margin. Thus, if we determine that a firm has experienced a significant increase or decrease in its net profit margin, the analysis of the component profit margins will help us to determine the specific causes of the change. Therefore, we will briefly discuss each of the margins but will defer calculations and comments on the trends until we discuss the common size income statement.

Gross Profit Margin   Gross profit equals net sales minus the cost of goods sold. The gross profit margin is computed as

$$\text{Gross Profit Margin} = \frac{\text{Gross Profit}}{\text{Net Sales}}$$

(38-14)

---

[4] The "DuPont System" section of this reading contains an analysis of this total asset turnover ratio over a longer term.

[5] Some investors prefer to consider only *owner's* equity, which would not include preferred stock.

This ratio indicates the basic cost structure of the firm. An analysis of this ratio over time relative to a comparable industry figure shows the firm's relative cost–price position. As always, we must compare these margins to the industry and major competitors. Notably, this margin can also be impacted by a change in the firm's product mix toward higher or lower profit margin items.

Operating Profit Margin   Operating profit is gross profit minus sales, general, and administrative (SG&A) expenses. It is also referred to as EBIT—earnings before interest and taxes.

$$\text{Operating Profit Margin} = \frac{\text{Operating Profit}}{\text{Net Sales}} \qquad \textbf{(38-15)}$$

The variability of the operating profit margin over time is a prime indicator of the **business risk** for a firm. Again, this volatility should be compared to similar ratios for competitors and the industry.

There are two additional deductions from operating profit—interest expense and net foreign exchange loss. After these deductions, we have income before income taxes.

Some investors add back to the operating income value (EBIT) the firm's depreciation expense and compute a profit margin that consists of earnings before interest, taxes, depreciation, and amortization (EBITDA). This alternative operating profit margin has been used by some analysts as a proxy for pretax cash flow. As noted earlier, we do *not* recommend the use of this series because it is a biased cash flow estimate.

Net Profit Margin   This margin relates after-tax net income to sales. In the case of Walgreens, this is the same as operating income after taxes, because the firm does *not* have any significant nonoperating adjustments. This margin is equal to

$$\text{Net Profit Margin} = \frac{\text{Net Income}}{\text{Net Sales}} \qquad \textbf{(38-16)}$$

This ratio should be computed using sales and earnings from *continuing* operations, because our analysis seeks to derive insights about *future* expectations. Therefore, we do not consider earnings from discontinued operations, the gain or loss from the sale of these operations, or any nonrecurring income or expenses.

Common Size Income Statement   As noted earlier, these profit margin ratios are basically included in a common size income statement, which lists all expense and income items as a percentage of sales. This statement provides useful insights regarding the trends in cost figures and profit margins.

Exhibit 38-5 shows a common size statement for Walgreens for 2000–2004. As noted earlier in the reading when Exhibit 38-5 was presented, the most striking characteristic of the various profit margins for Walgreens (gross, operating, and net) is the *significant stability* in those margins over time. This stability is notable for two reasons. First, the firm experienced significant sales growth during this period (about 14 percent a year), and it is generally a challenge to control costs when growing rapidly. Second, this time interval included the economic recession of 2001–2002 (the official recession was during 2001, but it carried over for most corporations into 2002), and the sales and profit margins of most corporations were negatively impacted by this environment. Therefore, the stability of profit margins for Walgreens is an impressive accomplishment by management.

Beyond the analysis of earnings on sales, the ultimate measure of management performance is the profit earned on the assets or the capital committed to the enterprise. Several ratios help us evaluate this important relationship.

Return on Total Invested Capital The return on total invested capital ratio (referred to as ROIC) relates the firm's earnings to all the invested capital involved in the enterprise (debt, preferred stock, and common stock). Therefore, the earnings figure used is the net income from continuing operations (before any dividends) *plus* the interest paid on debt. While there might be a tendency to equate total capital with total assets, most analysts differentiate due to the term *invested capital,* which does *not* include non-interest-bearing liabilities such as trade accounts payable, accrued expenses, income taxes payable, and deferred income taxes. In contrast, short-term debt such as bank borrowings and principal payments due on long-term debt are interest bearing and would be included as invested capital. Therefore, the ratio would be:

$$\text{Return on Total Invested Capital} = \frac{\text{Net Income} + \text{Interest Expense}}{\text{Average Total Invested Capital}^*} \quad \textbf{(38-17)}$$

* Interest bearing debt plus shareholders' equity

Walgreens incurred interest expense for long- and short-term debt. The gross interest expense value used in this ratio differs from the net interest expense item in the income statement, which is measured as gross interest expense minus interest income.[6]

Walgreen Co.'s rates of return on total invested capital (ROIC) were

$$2004: \quad \frac{1,360 + 0.2}{(8,936.6 + 7,757.4)/2} = \frac{1,360.2}{8,347.0} = 16.29\%$$

$$2003: \quad \frac{1,176 + 0.2}{(7,757.4 + 6,747.1)/2} = \frac{1,176.2}{7,252.3} = 16.22\%$$

This ratio indicates the firm's return on all its invested capital. It should be compared with the ratio for other firms in the industry and the economy. For Walgreens, the results are stable, with an increase during the last several years.

Return on Owner's Equity The return on owner's equity (ROE) ratio is extremely important to the owner of the enterprise (the common stockholder) because it indicates the rate of return that management has earned on the capital provided by stockholders after accounting for payments to all other capital suppliers. If we consider all equity (including preferred stock), this return would equal

$$\text{Return on Total Equity} = \frac{\text{Net Income}}{\text{Average Total Equity}} \quad \textbf{(38-18)}$$

If we are concerned only with owner's equity (the common stockholder's equity), the ratio would be[7]

$$\text{Return on Owner's Equity} = \frac{\text{Net Income} - \text{Preferred Dividend}}{\text{Average Common Equity}} \quad \textbf{(38-19)}$$

---

[6] Subsequently, in connection with the analysis of financial risk, we discuss why and how to capitalize the operating lease payments that are reported in footnotes. When we do this, we will add this capitalized value to the balance sheet additional leased assets and also lease obligations along with the implied interest on the leases. At that point, we demonstrate the affect of this on the firm's ROIC and several other financial ratios—mainly financial risk ratios.

[7] In the case of Walgreens, return on total equity and return on owner's equity is the same, since there is no preferred stock outstanding (it is authorized but not issued).

Walgreens generated return on owner's equity of

$$2004: \quad \frac{1,360 - 0}{(8,227 + 7,196)/2} = 17.64\%$$

$$2003: \quad \frac{1,176 - 0}{(7,196 + 6,230)/2} = 17.52\%$$

This ratio reflects the rate of return on the stockholder's capital. It should be consistent with the firm's overall business risk, but it also should reflect the financial risk assumed by the common stockholder because of the prior claims of the firm's bondholders.

The DuPont System   The importance of ROE as an indicator of performance makes it desirable to divide the ratio into several component ratios that provide insights into the causes of a firm's ROE or any changes in it. This breakdown is generally referred to as the **DuPont System**. First, the return on equity (ROE) ratio can be broken down into two ratios that we have discussed—net profit margin and equity turnover.

$$\text{ROE} = \frac{\text{Net Income}}{\text{Common Equity}} = \frac{\text{Net Income}}{\text{Net Sales}} \times \frac{\text{Net Sales}}{\text{Common Equity}} \qquad \textbf{(38-20)}$$

This breakdown is an identity because we have both multiplied and divided by net sales. To maintain the identity, the common equity value used is the year-end figure rather than the average of the beginning and ending value.[8] This identity reveals that ROE equals the net profit margin times the equity turnover, which implies that a firm can improve its return on equity by *either* using its equity more efficiently (increasing its equity turnover) *or* by becoming more profitable (increasing its net profit margin).

As noted previously, a firm's equity turnover is affected by its capital structure. Specifically, a firm can increase its equity turnover by employing a higher proportion of debt capital. We can see this effect by considering the following relationship:

$$\frac{\text{Net Sales}}{\text{Common Equity}} = \frac{\text{Net Sales}}{\text{Total Assets}} \times \frac{\text{Total Assets}}{\text{Common Equity}} \qquad \textbf{(38-21)}$$

Similar to the prior breakdown, this is an identity because we have both multiplied and divided the equity turnover ratio by total assets. This equation indicates that the equity turnover ratio equals the firm's *total asset turnover* (a measure of efficiency) times the ratio of *total assets to equity* (a measure of financial leverage). Specifically, this leverage ratio indicates the proportion of total assets financed with debt. *All assets have to be financed by either equity or some form of debt* (either current liabilities or long-term debt). Therefore, the higher the ratio of assets to equity, the higher the proportion of debt to equity. A total asset–equity ratio of 2, for example, indicates that for every two dollars of assets there is a dollar of equity, which means the firm financed one-half of its assets with equity and the other half with debt. Likewise, a total asset–equity ratio of 3 indicates

---

[8] The effect of using the year-end equity rather than the average for the year will cause a lower ROE since the equity is generally increasing over time. Two points regarding this difference: First, the conservative bias is generally small—for Walgreens (which is growing fast), the average equity result above was 17.64% versus 16.53% using the year-end equity. Second, the important trend results will show, along with the component trends that are very important.

that only one-third of total assets was financed with equity and two-thirds must have been financed with debt. Thus a firm can increase its equity turnover either by increasing its total asset turnover (becoming more efficient) or by increasing its financial leverage ratio (financing assets with a higher proportion of debt capital). This financial leverage ratio is also referred to as the financial leverage multiplier, because the first two ratios (profit margin times total asset turnover) equal return on total assets (ROTA), and ROTA times the financial leverage multiplier equals ROE.

Combining these two breakdowns, we see that a firm's ROE is composed of three ratios, as follows:

$$\frac{\text{Net Income}}{\text{Common Equity}} = \frac{\text{Net Income}}{\text{Net Sales}} \times \frac{\text{Net Sales}}{\text{Total Assets}} \times \frac{\text{Total Assets}}{\text{Common Equity}} \quad \textbf{(38-22)}$$

$$= \frac{\text{Profit}}{\text{Margin}} \times \frac{\text{Total Asset}}{\text{Turnover}} \times \frac{\text{Financial}}{\text{Leverage}}$$

As an example of this important set of relationships, the figures in Exhibit 38-6 indicate what has happened to the ROE for Walgreens and the components of its ROE during the 23-year period from 1982 to 2004. As noted, these ratio values employ year-end balance sheet figures (assets and equity) rather than the average of beginning and ending data, so they will differ from our individual ratio computations.

The DuPont results in Exhibit 38-6 indicate several significant trends:

1. The total asset turnover ratio was relatively stable: a total range of 2.79 to 3.31, with a small decline in the ratio to its level in 2004 of 2.81.

2. The profit margin series experienced a stable increase from 2.75 to almost a peak value of 3.63 in 2004.

3. The product of the total asset turnover and the net profit margin is equal to return on total assets (ROTA), which experienced an overall increase from 9.09 percent to a peak of 10.94 percent in 2000, followed by a small decline to 10.20 percent in 2004.

4. The financial leverage multiplier (total assets/equity) experienced a steady decline from 2.06 to 1.62. Notably, most of this debt is trade credit, which is non-interest-bearing. The fact is, the firm has almost no interest-bearing debt, except for the long-term leases on drugstores that are not on the formal balance sheet but are discussed and analyzed in the subsequent financial risk section.

5. Finally, as a result of the overall increase in ROTA and a clear decline in financial leverage, the firm's ROE has experienced a small decline overall, beginning at 18.73 and ending at 16.52.

An Extended Dupont System   Beyond the original DuPont system, some analysts have suggested using an **extended DuPont system,**[9] which provides additional insights into the effect of financial leverage on the firm and also pinpoints the effect of income taxes on the firm's ROE. Because both financial leverage and tax rates have changed dramatically over the past decade, these additional insights are important. The concept and use of the model is the same as the basic DuPont system except for a further breakdown of components.

---

[9] The original DuPont system was the three-component breakdown discussed in the prior section. Because this extended analysis also involves the components of ROE, some still refer to it as the DuPont system. In our presentation, we refer to it as the extended DuPont system to differentiate it from the original three-component analysis.

EXHIBIT 38-6		Components of Return on Total Equity for Walgreen Co.[a]		
Year	(1) Sales–Total Assets	(2) Net Profit Margin (%)	(3)[b] Return On Total Assets	(4) Total Assets–equity	(5)[c] Return On Equity (%)
1982	3.31	2.75	9.09	2.06	18.73
1983	3.29	2.96	9.72	2.04	19.84
1984	3.26	3.11	10.16	2.03	20.60
1985	3.29	2.98	9.79	2.00	19.58
1986	3.06	2.82	8.62	2.16	18.64
1987	3.14	2.42	7.60	2.19	16.63
1988	3.23	2.64	8.54	2.12	18.12
1989	3.20	2.87	9.18	2.04	18.74
1990	3.16	2.89	9.12	2.02	18.42
1991	3.21	2.90	9.31	1.94	18.04
1992	3.15	2.95	9.30	1.92	17.90
1993	3.27	2.67	8.74	1.84	16.07
1994	3.17	3.05	9.69	1.85	17.91
1995	3.20	3.09	9.86	1.81	17.85
1996	3.24	3.16	10.23	1.78	18.19
1997	3.18	3.26	10.37	1.77	18.35
1998	3.12	3.34	10.42	1.72	17.93
1999	3.02	3.50	10.57	1.70	17.91
2000	2.99	3.66	10.94	1.68	18.35
2001	2.79	3.60	10.03	1.70	17.01
2002	2.90	3.55	10.32	1.59	16.36
2003	2.85	3.62	10.31	1.59	16.34
2004	2.81	3.63	10.20	1.62	16.52

[a] Ratios use year-end data for total assets and common equity rather than averages of the year.

[b] Column (3) is equal to column (1) times column (2).

[c] Column (5) is equal to column (3) times column (4).

Note: When you multiply the three component ratios, this product may not be equal to the ROE based on year-end statements due to the rounding of the three ratios.

In the prior presentation, we started with the ROE and divided it into components. In contrast, we now begin with the operating profit margin (EBIT divided by sales) and introduce additional ratios to derive an ROE value. Combining the operating profit margin and the total asset turnover ratio yields the following:

$$\frac{EBIT}{Net\ Sales} \times \frac{Net\ Sales}{Total\ Assets} = \frac{EBIT}{Total\ Assets}$$

This ratio is the operating profit return on total assets. To consider the negative effects of financial leverage, we examine the effect of interest expense as a percentage of total assets:

$$\frac{EBIT}{Total\ Assets} - \frac{Interest\ Expense}{Total\ Assets} = \frac{Net\ Before\ Tax\ (NBT)}{Total\ Assets}$$

We consider the positive effect of financial leverage with the financial leverage multiplier as follows:

$$\frac{Net\ Before\ Tax\ (NBT)}{Total\ Assets} \times \frac{Total\ Assets}{Common\ Equity} = \frac{Net\ Before\ Tax\ (NBT)}{Common\ Equity}$$

This indicates the pretax return on equity. Finally, to arrive at ROE, we must consider the tax-rate effect. We do this by multiplying the pre-tax ROE by a tax-retention rate as follows:

$$\frac{Net\ Before\ Tax}{Common\ Equity} \times \left(100\% - \frac{Income\ Taxes}{Net\ Before\ Tax}\right) = \frac{Net\ Income}{Common\ Equity}$$

In summary, we have the following five components:

1. $\dfrac{EBIT}{Sales}$ = Operating Profit Margin

2. $\dfrac{Sales}{Total\ Assets}$ = Total Asset Turnover

3. $\dfrac{Interest\ Expense}{Total\ Assets}$ = Interest Expense Rate

4. $\dfrac{Total\ Assets}{Common\ Equity}$ = Financial Leverage Multiplier

5. $\left(100\% - \dfrac{Income\ Taxes}{Net\ Before\ Tax}\right)$ = Tax Retention Rate

To demonstrate the use of this extended DuPont system, Exhibit 38-7 contains the calculations, using the five components for the years 1982 through 2004. The first column indicates that the firm's operating profit margin peaked in 1985, subsequently declined to a low point in 1990, followed by an increase to a new peak of 5.81 percent in 2003. We know from the prior discussion that the firm's total asset turnover (Column 2) experienced an overall decline to around 2.80 in 2003–2004. The resulting operating profit return on assets declined to a low point in 2001 followed by a partial recovery through 2004. As discussed, because of virtually no interest-bearing debt (except off-balance sheet leases), Column 4 shows zero negative impact on leverage.

Column 5 reflects the firm's operating performance before the positive impact of financing (the leverage multiplier) and the impact of taxes. These results are virtually identical to Column 3 due to no debt. Column 6 reflects the steady decline in non-lease financial leverage. As a result of the reduced leverage multiplier, the before-tax ROE in Column 7 has declined since 1984. Column 8 shows the strong positive effect of lower tax rates, which caused a higher tax-retention rate that increased from the mid-50 percent range to the recent 62 percent rate.

| EXHIBIT 38-7 | Extended DuPont System Analysis for Walgreens: 1982–2004[a] |

	1	2	3	4	5	6	7	8	9
Year	EBIT/ Sales (Percent)	Sales/ Total Assets (Times)	EBIT/ Total Assets (Percent)[b]	Interest Expense/ Total Assets (Percent)	Net before Tax/ Total Assets (Percent)[c]	Total Assets/ Common Equity (Times)	Net before Tax/ Common Equity (Percent)[d]	Tax Retention Rate	Return on Equity (Percent)[e]
1982	4.32	3.31	14.30	(0.85)	15.15	2.06	31.20	0.60	18.75
1983	5.16	3.29	17.00	0.25	16.75	2.04	34.20	0.56	19.30
1984	5.57	3.26	18.20	(0.24)	18.44	2.03	37.40	0.55	20.65
1985	5.63	3.29	18.50	0.43	18.07	2.00	36.10	0.54	19.57
1986	5.37	3.06	16.40	0.74	15.66	2.16	33.90	0.55	18.63
1987	4.92	3.14	15.50	1.22	14.28	2.19	31.30	0.53	16.69
1988	4.59	3.23	14.80	1.01	13.79	2.12	29.30	0.62	18.10
1989	4.71	3.20	15.10	0.57	14.53	2.04	29.70	0.63	18.79
1990	4.70	3.16	14.90	0.17	14.73	2.02	29.80	0.62	18.52
1991	4.77	3.21	15.30	0.44	14.86	1.94	28.80	0.63	18.00
1992	4.80	3.15	15.10	0.23	14.87	1.92	28.60	0.62	17.87
1993	4.90	3.31	16.20	0.26	15.94	1.82	29.00	0.61	17.80
1994	4.93	3.21	15.90	(0.10)	16.00	1.83	29.20	0.62	17.96
1995	5.00	3.20	15.99	0.04	15.95	1.81	28.90	0.61	17.70
1996	5.13	3.24	16.62	0.06	16.56	1.78	29.50	0.61	18.07
1997	5.30	3.18	16.85	0.05	16.80	1.77	29.74	0.61	18.14
1998	5.46	3.12	17.04	0.02	17.02	1.72	29.28	0.61	17.93
1999	5.69	3.02	17.19	0.00	17.19	1.70	29.22	0.61	17.83
2000	5.77	2.99	17.25	0.00	17.25	1.68	28.98	0.61	17.78
2001	5.08	2.79	15.84	0.00	16.11	1.70	27.33	0.62	17.07
2002	5.71	2.90	16.57	0.00	16.57	1.62	26.28	0.62	16.36
2003	5.81	2.79	16.20	0.00	16.20	1.62	26.25	0.62	16.34
2004	5.80	2.81	16.31	0.00	16.31	1.62	26.45	0.62	16.53

[a] The percents in this table may not be the same as in Exhibit 38-6 due to rounding.

[b] Column 3 is equal to Column 1 times Column 2.

[c] Column 5 is equal to Column 3 minus Column 4.

[d] Column 7 is equal to Column 5 times Column 6.

[e] Column 9 is equal to Column 7 times Column 8.

In summary, this breakdown helps you to understand *what* happened to a firm's ROE and *why* it happened. The intent is to determine what happened to the firm's internal operating results, what has been the effect of its financial leverage policy, and what was the effect of external government tax policy. Although the two breakdowns should provide the same ending value, they typically differ by small amounts because of the rounding of components.

RISK ANALYSIS

7

Risk analysis examines the uncertainty of income flows for the total firm and for the individual sources of capital (that is, debt, preferred stock, and common stock). The typical approach examines the major factors that cause a firm's income flows to vary. More volatile income flows mean greater risk (uncertainty) facing the investor.

The total risk of the firm has two internal components: business risk and financial risk. We first discuss the concept of business risk: how to measure it, what causes it, and how to measure its individual causes. Then we consider financial risk and the several ratios by which we measure it. Following this analysis of a firm's internal risk factors, we discuss an important external risk factor, external liquidity risk—that is, the ability to buy or sell the firm's stock in the secondary equity market.

Business Risk

Recall that **business risk**[10] is the uncertainty of operating income caused by the firm's industry. In turn, this uncertainty is due to the firm's variability of sales caused by its products, customers, and the way it produces its products. Specifically, a firm's operating earnings vary over time and is measured by the volatility of the firm's operating income over time, which is due to two factors: (1) the volatility of the firm's sales over time, and (2) how the firm produces its products and its mix of fixed and variable costs—that is, its operating leverage. Specifically, a firm's operating earnings vary over time because its sales and production costs vary. As an example, the earnings for a steel firm will probably vary more than those of a grocery chain because (1) over the business cycle, steel sales are more volatile than grocery sales; and (2) the steel firm's large fixed production costs (operating leverage) make its earnings vary more than its sales.

Business risk is generally measured by the variability of the firm's operating income over time. In turn, the earnings variability is measured by the standard deviation of the historical operating earnings series. The standard deviation is influenced by the size of the numbers, so investors standardize this measure of volatility by dividing it by the mean value for the series (i.e., the average operating earnings). The resulting ratio of the standard deviation of operating earnings divided by the average operating earnings is the **coefficient of variation (CV)** of operating earnings:

$$\text{Business Risk} = f(\text{Coefficient of Variation of Operating Earnings})$$

$$= \frac{\text{Standard Deviation of Operating Earnings (OE)}}{\text{Mean Operating Earnings}}$$

$$= \frac{\sqrt{\sum_{i=1}^{n} (OE_i - \overline{OE})^2 / n}}{\sum_{i=1}^{n} OE_i / n}$$

The CV of operating earnings allows comparisons between standardized measures of business risk for firms of different sizes. To compute the CV of operating earnings, you need a minimum of 5 years up to about 10 years. Less than 5 years

---

[10] For further discussion of this topic, see Brigham and Gapenski (2003), Chapters 6 and 10.

is not very meaningful, and data more than 10 years old are typically out of date. Besides measuring overall business risk, it is very insightful to examine the two factors that contribute to the variability of operating earnings: sales variability and operating leverage.

Sales Variability   Sales variability is the prime determinant of operating earnings variability. In turn, the variability of sales is mainly caused by a firm's industry and is largely outside the control of management. For example, sales for a firm in a cyclical industry, such as automobiles or steel, will be quite volatile over the business cycle compared to sales of a firm in a noncyclical industry, such as retail food or hospital supplies. Like operating earnings, the variability of a firm's sales is typically measured by the CV of sales during the most recent 5 to 10 years. The CV of sales equals the standard deviation of sales divided by the mean sales for the period.

$$\text{Sales Volatility} = f(\text{Coefficient of Variation of Sales})$$

$$= \frac{\sqrt{\sum_{i=1}^{n}(S_i - \bar{S})^2/n}}{\sum_{i=1}^{n} S_i/n}$$

Adjusting Volatility Measure for Growth   Besides normalizing the standard deviation for size by computing the CV, it is also important to recognize that the standard deviation is measured relative to the mean value for the series—that is, it computes deviations from "expected value." The problem arises for firms that experience significant growth that will create very large deviations from the mean for the series even if it is *constant* growth. The way to avoid this bias is to measure deviations from the growth path of the series.

Operating Leverage   The variability of a firm's operating earnings also depends on its mixture of production costs. Total production costs of a firm with no *fixed* production costs would vary directly with sales, and operating profits would be a constant proportion of sales. In such an example, the firm's operating profit margin would be constant and its operating profits would have the same relative volatility as its sales. Realistically, firms always have some fixed production costs such as buildings, machinery, or relatively permanent personnel. Fixed production costs cause operating profits to vary more than sales over the business cycle. Specifically, during slow periods, operating profits will decline by a larger percentage than sales, while during an economic expansion, operating profits will increase by a larger percentage than sales.

The employment of fixed production costs is referred to as **operating leverage**. Clearly, greater operating leverage (caused by a higher proportion of fixed production costs) makes the operating earnings series more volatile relative to the sales series (see Lee, Finnerty, and Norton, 2003). This basic relationship between operating profit and sales leads us to measure operating leverage as the percentage change in operating earnings relative to the percentage change in sales during a specified period as follows:

$$\text{Operating Leverage} = \frac{\sum_{i=1}^{n}\left|\dfrac{\%\Delta OE}{\%\Delta S}\right|}{n}$$

We take the absolute value of the percentage changes because the two series can move in opposite directions. The direction of the change is not important, but the relative size of the change is relevant. By implication, the more volatile the operating earnings as compared to the volatility of sales, the greater the firm's operating leverage.

Financial Risk

Financial risk, you will recall, is the additional uncertainty of returns to equity holders due to a firm's use of fixed financial obligation securities. This financial uncertainty is in addition to the firm's business risk. When a firm sells bonds to raise capital, the interest payments on this capital precede the computation of common stock earnings, and these interest payments are fixed contractual obligations. As with operating leverage, during an economic expansion, the net earnings available for common stock after the fixed interest payments will experience a larger percentage increase than operating earnings. In contrast, during a business decline, the earnings available to stockholders will decline by a larger percentage than operating earnings because of these fixed financial costs (i.e., interest payments). Notably, as a firm increases its relative debt financing with fixed contractual obligations, it increases its financial risk and the possibility of default and bankruptcy.

Relationship between Business Risk and Financial Risk   A very important point to remember is that *the acceptable level of financial risk for a firm depends on its business risk.* If the firm has low business risk (i.e., stable operating earnings), investors are willing to accept higher financial risk. For example, retail food companies typically have stable operating earnings over time, which implies *low* business risk, and means that investors and bond-rating firms will allow the firms to have *higher* financial risk. In contrast, if a firm is in an industry that is subject to high business risk (i.e., it experiences high sales volatility and it has high operating leverage), such as steel, auto, and airline companies, an investor would *not* want these firms to also have high financial risk. The two risks would compound and the probability of bankruptcy would be substantial.[11]

In our analysis, we employ three sets of financial ratios to measure financial risk, and *all three* sets should be considered. First, there are balance sheet ratios that indicate the proportion of capital derived from debt securities compared to equity capital. Second are ratios that consider the earnings or cash flows available to pay fixed financial charges. Third are ratios that consider the cash flows available and relate these cash flows to the book value of the outstanding debt. Before we discuss and demonstrate these financial risk ratios, it is necessary to consider the topic of operating lease obligations.

Consideration of Lease Obligations   Many firms lease facilities (buildings) and equipment rather than borrow the funds and purchase the assets—it is basically a lease or borrow decision since the lease contract is like a bond obligation. The accounting for the lease obligation depends on the type of lease. If it is a *capital* lease, the value of the asset and the lease obligation is included on the balance sheet as an asset and liability. If it is an *operating* lease, it is noted in the footnotes but is not specifically included on the balance sheet.[12] Because operating leases are a form of financing used extensively by retailers (such as Walgreens, Sears,

---

[11] Support for this specific relationship is found in a set of tables (see Standard & Poor, 2002, p. 57) that suggest specific required financial risk ratios necessary for a firm to be considered for a specific bond rating. The required ratios differ on the basis of the perceived business risk of the firm.

[12] A discussion of the technical factors that will cause a lease to be capital versus operating is beyond the scope of this book, but it is covered in most intermediate accounting texts.

and McDonald's) and airlines, it is necessary to recognize this obligation, capitalize estimated future lease payments, and include this capitalized lease value on the balance sheet as both an asset and a long-term liability. In the following subsection, we discuss how to do this, and we demonstrate the significant impact this adjustment can have on several financial risk ratios.

Capitalizing Operating Leases   Capitalizing leases basically involves an estimate of the present value of a firm's future required lease payments. Therefore, an analyst must estimate: (1) an appropriate discount rate (typically the firm's long-term debt rate) and (2) the firm's future lease payment obligations as specified in a footnote.

An estimate of the discounted value of the future lease payments can be done one of two ways: (1) a multiple of the forthcoming minimum lease payments or (2) the discounted value of the future lease payments provided in the annual report at the firm's cost of long-term debt. The traditional multiple technique multiplies the minimum lease payment in year $t + 1$ by 8. In the case of Walgreens, the future minimum lease payments in the annual report for the year 2004 are as follows:

Years Relating to Year-End	1	2	3	4	5	Later
Minimum Payments ($ millions)	1,309	1,346	1,309	1,242	1,215	15,455

Given these data, the estimate using the first technique would produce an estimate of $8 \times \$1.309$ million = $10.47 billion. To derive an estimate using the second technique, we need to estimate the firm's cost of long-term debt and consider how to handle the lump-sum later payments. Our debt rate estimate is 7.00 percent, which is consistent with the prevailing rate on 20-year, A-rated corporate bonds, which is conservative for Walgreens (it is probably between AA and A). For the later lump-sum payment, we need to derive a reasonable estimate regarding how many years to assume for this payout. A liberal assumption is that the lump-sum payment is spread evenly over 15 years, based on a typical building lease of 20 years ($15,455/15 = $1.030 million per year). An alternative estimate of the spread period is derived by dividing the lump-sum payment in period $t + 6$ by the $t + 5$ payment, which implies a time estimate ($15,455/1,215 = 12.72$). If we round this up to 13 years, we have an annual payment of $15,455/13 = $1,189 million per year for 13 years.

If we discount at 7.00 percent all the annual flows and the later flows over 15 years, we derive an estimate of the lease debt of $11.97 *billion*. A similar computation using the 13-year spread indicates an estimate of lease debt of $12.37 *billion*. Therefore, we have the following three estimates:[13]

8 times the $t + 1$ lease payment	$10.47 billion
Discounting the lease payments assuming a 15-year spread	$11.97 billion
Discounting the lease payments assuming a 13-year spread	$12.37 billion

We will use the $11.97 billion discounted lease payment estimate since this estimate is midway between the liberal multiple method and the conservative

---

[13] Notably, the "8 times" estimate almost always provides the lowest estimate of debt value, which means that this rule of thumb will tend to underestimate the financial leverage for these firms and the resulting implied interest expense. As noted, we have opted to use the discounted value of future lease payments, assuming a 15-year spread of the later payments.

discounting method that assumes a 13-year spread. If we add this amount (or that estimated by the other methods) to both fixed assets and long-term debt we will have a better measure of the assets utilized by the firm and the complete funding of the assets (recognition of more debt).

Implied Interest for Leased Assets When computing the return on total capital (ROTC) that considers these leased assets, we must also add the implied interest expense for the leases. The interest expense component of a lease is typically estimated by bond-rating agencies and many other analysts as equal to one-third of the lease payment in year $t + 1$ (in our example, $1,309 million/3 = $436 million).

An alternative to this rule of thumb would be to derive a specific estimate based on an estimate of the firm's cost of debt capital (7.00 percent) and the estimate of the present value (PV) of the lease obligation, as follows:

Estimating Technique	PV of Lease Obligation ($ Billion)	Interest Expense at 7.00 Percent ($ Million)
8 times estimate of $t + 1$ payment	10.47	733
PV with 15-year spread	11.97	838
PV with 13-year spread	12.37	866

Notably, all of these estimates of the implied interest expense are substantially higher than the one-third rule-of-thumb estimate of $436 million. Again, the rule of thumb underestimates the financial leverage related to these lease obligations.

To calculate the ROTC for 2003 and 2004, we need to compute the value of the lease obligations and the implied interest expense for the three years (2002, 2003, and 2004) as follows:

Year	Estimate of PV of Lease Obligation ($ Billion)	Estimate of Interest Component of Lease[a] ($ Million)
2004	11.97	838
2003	10.63	744
2002	8.37	586

[a] Equal to 0.07 of the PV of lease obligation.

Adding these values to the prior ratios results in the following lease-adjusted return on total invested capital (ROIC) values

$$2004: \quad \frac{1,360 + 0.2 + 838}{(20,908.7 + 18,390.7)/2} = \frac{2,198.2}{19,649.7} = 11.19\%$$

$$2003: \quad \frac{1,176 + 0.2 + 744}{(18,390.7 + 15,121.5)/2} = \frac{1,920.2}{16,756.1} = 11.46\%$$

As shown, the ROICs that include the leased assets and lease debt are lower (over 11 percent versus over 16 percent), but they are still quite reasonable.

Implied Depreciation on Leased Assets   Another factor is the implied depreciation expense that would be taken if these were not leased assets. One way to calculate this value is to simply use the typical term of the lease or weighted-average term. In the case of Walgreens, this is reasonably clear since almost all leases are 20-year leases on buildings. However, if the value were not clear, a second alternative would be the average percent of depreciation as a percent of beginning-of-year net fixed assets. In the case of Walgreens, for 2004 this would be

Depreciation (2004) $403 million; Net Fixed Assets at End of 2003: $4,940

This implies a percent of 0.0816 (403/4,940), which is clearly higher than the 5 percent on buildings. Obviously, Walgreens has many assets being depreciated over shorter lives. For these calculations related to leases on buildings, we assume the 20-year life as follows:

Year	Estimate of PV of Lease Obligation ($ Billion)	Estimate of Implied Depreciation Expense of Lease* ($ Million)
2004	11.97	599
2003	10.63	532
2002	8.37	419

* Assumes straight-line depreciation over a 20-year life.

These implied depreciation charges should be included in ratios that include depreciation expenses.

Proportion of Debt (Balance Sheet) Ratios

The proportion of debt ratios indicate what proportion of the firm's capital is derived from debt compared to other sources of capital, such as preferred stock, common stock, and retained earnings. A higher proportion of debt capital compared to equity capital makes earnings more volatile (i.e., more financial leverage) and increases the probability that a firm could default on the debt. Therefore, higher proportion of debt ratios indicate greater financial risk. The following are the major proportion of debt ratios used to measure financial risk.

Debt–Equity Ratio   The debt–equity ratio is

$$\text{Debt–Equity Ratio} = \frac{\text{Total Long-Term Debt}}{\text{Total Equity}} \qquad \textbf{(38-23)}$$

The debt figure includes all long-term fixed obligations, including subordinated **convertible bonds**. The equity typically is the **book value of equity** and includes preferred stock, common stock, and retained earnings. Some analysts prefer to exclude preferred stock and consider only common equity. Total equity is preferable if some of the firms being analyzed have preferred stock.

Notably, debt ratios can be computed *with and without deferred taxes*. Most balance sheets include an accumulated deferred tax figure. There is some controversy regarding whether these deferred taxes should be treated as a liability or as part of permanent capital. Some argue that if the deferred tax has accumulated because of the difference in accelerated and straight-line depreciation, this liability may never be paid. That is, as long as the firm continues to grow and add new assets, this total deferred tax account continues to grow. Alternatively, if the deferred tax account is caused by differences in the recognition of income on long-term contracts, there will be a reversal and this liability must eventually be paid. As suggested by White, Sondhi, and Fried (2003), to resolve this question, the analyst must determine the reason for the deferred tax account and examine its long-term trend. Walgreen Co.'s deferred tax account is because of a depreciation difference and it has typically grown over time.

A second consideration when computing debt ratios is the existence of operating leases, as mentioned in a prior section. As noted, given a firm like Walgreens with extensive leased facilities, it is necessary to include an estimate of the present value of the lease payments as long-term debt.

To show the effect of these two significant items on the financial risk of Walgreens, we define the ratios to include both of these factors, but they will be broken out to identify the effect of each of the components of total debt. Thus, the debt–equity ratio is

$$\text{Debt--Equity Ratio} = \frac{\text{Total Long-Term Debt}}{\text{Total Equity}}$$

$$= \frac{\text{Noncurrent Liabilities} + \text{Deferred Taxes} + \text{PV of Lease Obligations}}{\text{Total Equity}}$$

(38-24)

For Walgreens, the debt–equity ratios were

$$2004: \quad \frac{709 + 328 + 11{,}972}{8{,}228} = \frac{13{,}009}{8{,}228} = 158.1\%$$

$$2003: \quad \frac{562 + 228 + 10{,}633}{7{,}196} = \frac{11{,}423}{7{,}196} = 158.7\%$$

$$2002: \quad \frac{517 + 177 + 8{,}374}{6{,}230} = \frac{9{,}068}{6{,}230} = 145.6\%$$

These ratios demonstrate the significant impact of including the present value of the lease payments as part of long-term debt—for example, the debt–equity percent for 2004 went from less than 13 percent without lease obligations to over 158 percent when capitalized leases are included.

Long-Term Debt–Total Capital Ratio The long-term debt-total capital ratio indicates the proportion of long-term capital derived from long–term debt capital. It is computed as

$$\text{Long-Term Debt--Total Capital Ratio} = \frac{\text{Total Long-Term Debt}}{\text{Total Long-Term Capital}} \quad \textbf{(38-25)}$$

The total long-term debt values are the same as above. The total long-term capital would include all long-term debt, any preferred stock, and total equity. The long-term debt–total capital ratios for Walgreens were

Including Deferred Taxes and Lease Obligations as Long-Term Debt

$$2004: \quad \frac{13{,}009}{13{,}009 + 8{,}228} = 61.3\%$$

$$2003: \quad \frac{11{,}423}{11{,}423 + 7{,}196} = 61.4\%$$

$$2002: \quad \frac{9{,}068}{9{,}068 + 6{,}230} = 59.3\%$$

Again, this ratio, which includes the present value of lease obligations, shows that a significant percent of long-term capital is debt obligations, which differs substantially from a ratio without the lease obligations.

Total Debt–Total Capital Ratios   In many cases, it is useful to compare *total* debt to *total* invested capital. Earlier when we computed return on invested capital, we did not consider non-interest-bearing capital such as accounts payable, accrued expenses, income taxes payable, or deferred taxes (caused by depreciation). In such a case, total debt would be long-term debt (without deferred taxes), which would be other noncurrent liabilities plus capitalized leases. Total capital would be this interest-bearing debt plus shareholders' equity, as follows:

$$\text{Total Debt–Total Capital Ratio} = \frac{\text{Total Interest-Bearing Debt}}{\text{Total Invested Capital}}$$

$$= \frac{\text{Capitalized Leases} + \text{Noncurrent Liabilities}}{\text{Total Interest-Bearing Debt} + \text{Shareholders' Equity}}$$

$$2004: \quad \frac{11{,}972 + 709}{11{,}972 + 709 + 8{,}228} = \frac{12{,}681}{20{,}909} = 60.6\%$$

$$2003: \quad \frac{10{,}633 + 562}{10{,}633 + 562 + 7{,}196} = \frac{11.195}{18{,}391} = 60.9\%$$

$$2002: \quad \frac{8{,}374 + 517}{8{,}374 + 517 + 6{,}230} = \frac{8{,}891}{15{,}121} = 58.8\%$$

While these adjustments cause the debt percents to be lower, they are still quite high, which confirms the importance of considering the impact of lease obligations on the financial risk of firms like Walgreens that employ this form of financing.

Earnings and Cash Flow Coverage Ratios

In addition to ratios that indicate the proportion of debt on the balance sheet, investors are very conscious of ratios that relate the *flow* of earnings or cash flows available to meet the required interest and lease payments. A higher ratio of available earnings or cash flow relative to fixed financial charges indicates lower financial risk.

Interest Coverage Ratio   The standard interest coverage ratio is computed as

$$\text{Interest Coverage} = \frac{\text{Income before Interest and Taxes (EBIT)}}{\text{Debt Interest Charges}}$$

$$= \frac{\text{Net Income} + \text{Income Taxes} + \text{Interest Expense}}{\text{Interest Expense}}$$

(38-26)

This ratio indicates how many times the fixed interest charges are earned, based on the earnings available to pay these expenses.[14] Alternatively, one minus the reciprocal of the interest coverage ratio indicates how far earnings could decline before it would be impossible to pay the interest charges from current earnings. For example, a coverage ratio of 5 means that earnings could decline by 80 per-

---

[14] The interest expense for Walgreens other than for leased assets is clearly insignificant (about $200,000), so it is not included in the computations although it is in the formulas to be considered for other firms.

cent (1 minus ⅓), and the firm could still pay its fixed financial charges. Again, for firms like Walgreens that have heavy lease obligations, it is necessary to consider the impact of the lease obligations on this ratio because if we only consider Walgreen Co.'s public interest-bearing debt, the interest cost is about a half-million dollars and the coverage ratio exceeds 3,000 times. In contrast, if we recognize the lease obligations as debt and include the implied interest on the capitalized leases as computed earlier, the coverage ratio would be restated as follows:

$$\frac{\text{Fixed Financial}}{\text{Cost Coverage}} = \frac{\text{Earnings before Interest and Taxes} + \text{Implied Lease Interest}}{\text{Gross Interest Expense} + \text{Implied Lease Interest}} \quad \textbf{(38-27)}$$

Hence, the fixed financial cost coverage ratios for Walgreens were

$$2004: \quad \frac{1{,}360 + 816 + 838}{838} = \frac{3{,}014}{838} = 3.60 \text{ times}$$

$$2003: \quad \frac{1{,}176 + 713 + 744}{744} = \frac{2{,}633}{744} = 3.54 \text{ times}$$

$$2002: \quad \frac{1{,}019 + 618 + 586}{586} = \frac{2{,}233}{586} = 3.79 \text{ times}$$

These fixed financial cost coverage ratios show a substantially different picture than the coverage ratios that do not consider the impact of the lease obligations. Even so, these coverage ratios are not unreasonable for a firm with very low business risk.

The trend of Walgreen Co.'s coverage ratios has been consistent with the overall trend in the proportion of debt ratios. The point is, the proportion of debt ratios and the earnings flow ratios do not always give consistent results because the proportion of debt ratios are not sensitive to changes in earnings or to changes in the interest rates on the debt. For example, if interest rates increase or if the firm replaces old debt with new debt that has a higher interest rate, no change would occur in the proportion of debt ratios, but the interest coverage ratio would decline. Also, the interest coverage ratio is sensitive to an increase or decrease in earnings. Therefore, the results using balance sheet ratios and coverage ratios can differ. Given a difference between the two sets of ratios, we have a strong preference for the coverage ratios that reflect the ability of the firm to meet its financial obligations.

Alternatives to these earnings coverage ratios are several ratios that relate the cash flow available from operations to either interest expense or total fixed charges.

Cash Flow Coverage Ratio   The motivation for this ratio is that a firm's earnings and cash flow typically will differ substantially (these differences have been noted and will be considered in a subsequent section). The cash flow value used is the cash flow from operating activities figure contained in the cash flow statement. As such, it includes depreciation expense, deferred taxes, and the impact of all working capital changes. Again, it is appropriate to specify the ratio in terms of total fixed financial costs including leases, as follows:

Cash Flow Coverage of Fixed Financial Cost

$$\textbf{(38-28)}$$

$$= \frac{\text{Net Cash Flow from Operating Activities} + \text{Interest Expense} + \text{Implied Lease Interest}}{\text{Interest Expense} + \text{Implied Lease Interest}}$$

We use the values given in the cash flow statement, since we are specifically interested in the cash flow effect.

The cash flow coverage ratios for Walgreens were:

$$2004: \quad \frac{1{,}652 + 838}{838} = \frac{2{,}490}{838} = 2.97 \text{ times}$$

$$2003: \quad \frac{1{,}504 + 744}{744} = \frac{2{,}248}{744} = 3.02 \text{ times}$$

$$2002: \quad \frac{1{,}504 + 586}{586} = \frac{2{,}090}{586} = 3.57 \text{ times}$$

While these coverage ratios are not alarming for a firm with very low business risk, it is noteworthy that they have declined steadily over the past three years.

Cash Flow–Long-Term Debt Ratio   Several studies have used a ratio that relates cash flow to a firm's outstanding debt. The cash flow-outstanding debt ratios are unique because they relate the *flow* of earnings plus noncash expenses to the *stock* of outstanding debt. These ratios have been significant variables in numerous studies concerned with predicting bankruptcies and bond ratings. (These studies are listed in the reference section.) The cash flow figure we use is the cash flow from operating activities. Obviously, the higher the percent of cash flow to long-term debt, the stronger the company—i.e., the lower its financial risk. This ratio would be computed as

$$\frac{\text{Cash Flow}}{\text{Long-Term Debt}} \qquad \text{(38-29)}$$
$$= \frac{\text{Cash Flow from Operating Activities}}{\text{Book Value of Long-Term Debt} + \text{Present Value of Lease Obligations}}$$

For Walgreens, the ratios were as follows, assuming that deferred taxes are not included, since they are not interest-bearing. Thus, the long-term debt is noncurrent liabilities and the lease obligations:

$$2004: \quad \frac{1{,}653}{709 + 11{,}972} = \frac{1{,}653}{12{,}681} = 13.0\%$$

$$2003: \quad \frac{1{,}504}{562 + 10{,}633} = \frac{1{,}504}{11{,}195} = 13.4\%$$

$$2002: \quad \frac{1{,}504}{517 + 8{,}374} = \frac{1{,}504}{8{,}891} = 16.9\%$$

The large percent during 2002 was caused by the increase in cash flow due to a smaller increase in inventory during the year (see Exhibit 38.3).

Cash Flow—Total Debt Ratio   Investors also should consider the relationship of cash flow to *total* debt to check that a firm has not had a significant increase in its short-term borrowing.

$$\frac{\text{Cash Flow}}{\text{Total Debt}} = \frac{\text{Cash Flow from Operating Activities}}{\text{Total Long-Term Debt} + \text{Interest-Bearing Current Liabilities}} \qquad \text{(38-30)}$$

For Walgreens, these ratios are the same as with long-term debt because the firm does not have any interest-bearing short-term debt. When firms do have short-term debt, the percents for this ratio will be lower: how much lower will indicate the amount of short-term borrowing by the firm. As before, it is important to compare these flow ratios with similar ratios for other companies in the industry and with the overall economy to gauge the firm's relative performance.

Alternative Measures of Cash Flow   As noted, many past studies that included a cash flow variable used the traditional measure of cash flow. The requirement that companies must prepare and report the statement of cash flows to stockholders has raised interest in other exact measures of cash flow. The first alternative measure is the *cash flow from operations,* which is taken directly from the statement of cash flows and is the one we have used. A second alternative measure is *free cash flow,* which is a modification of the cash flow from operations—that is, capital expenditures (minus the cash flow from the sale of assets) are also deducted and some analysts also subtract dividends. The following table summarizes the values for Walgreens derived earlier in the section entitled "Measures of Cash Flow."

Year	Traditional Cash Flow	Cash Flow from Operations	Net Cap Exp	FREE CASH FLOW Before Div.	Div.	After Div.
2004	1863	1653	933	719	177	542
2003	1581	1492	711	781	152	629
2002	1349	1474	566	908	147	761

As shown, Walgreens has strong and growing cash flow from operations even after considering significant working capital requirements, but the firm experiences positive but declining free cash flow because of substantial net capital expenditures necessitated by the firm's growth.

External Market Liquidity Risk

External Market Liquidity Defined   External market liquidity is the ability to buy or sell an asset quickly with little price change from a prior transaction assuming no new information. GE and Pfizer are examples of liquid common stocks because investors can sell them quickly with little price change from the prior trade. Investors might be able to sell an illiquid stock quickly, but the price would be significantly different from the prior price. Alternatively, the broker might be able to get a specified price, but could take several days doing so.

Determinants of External Market Liquidity   Investors should know the liquidity characteristics of the securities they currently own or may buy because liquidity can be important if they want to change the composition of their portfolios. Although the major determinants of market liquidity are reflected in market trading data, several internal corporate variables are good proxies for these market variables. The most important determinant of external market liquidity is the number of shares or the dollar value of shares traded (the dollar value adjusts for different price levels). More trading activity indicates a greater probability that one can find someone to take the other side of a desired transaction. A very good measure that is usually available is **trading turnover** (the percentage of outstanding shares traded during a period of time), which indicates relative trading activity. During calendar year 2004, about 700 million shares of Walgreens were traded, which indicates annual trading turnover of approximately 68 percent (700 million/1,032 million). This compares with the average turnover for the NYSE of about 90 percent. Another measure of market liquidity is the bid–ask spread, where a smaller spread indicates greater liquidity. In addition, certain corporate variables are correlated with these trading variables:

1. Total market value of outstanding securities (number of common shares outstanding times the market price per share)
2. Number of security owners

Numerous studies have shown that the main determinant of the bid–ask spread (besides price) is the dollar value of trading.[15] In turn, the value of trading correlates highly with the market value of the outstanding securities and the number of security holders because with more shares outstanding, there will be more stockholders to buy or sell at any time for a variety of purposes. Numerous buyers and sellers provide liquidity.

We can estimate the market value of Walgreen Co.'s outstanding stock as the average number of shares outstanding during the year (adjusted for stock splits) times the average market price for the year (equal to the high price plus the low price divided by 2) as follows:[16]

$$2004: \quad 1,032 \times \frac{39 + 32}{2} = \$36.64 \text{ billion}$$

$$2003: \quad 1,032 \times \frac{40 + 31}{2} = \$36.64 \text{ billion}$$

$$2002: \quad 1,032 \times \frac{45 + 31}{2} = \$39.22 \text{ billion}$$

These market values clearly would place Walgreens in the large-cap category, which usually begins at about \$5 billion. Walgreens stockholders number 600,000, including more than 650 institutions that own approximately 56 percent of the outstanding stock. These large values for market value, the number of stockholders, institutional holders, and the high trading turnover indicate a highly liquid market in Walgreens stock, which implies extremely low external **liquidity risk**.

8   ANALYSIS OF GROWTH POTENTIAL

Importance of Growth Analysis

The analysis of **sustainable growth potential** examines ratios that indicate how fast a firm should grow. Analysis of a firm's growth potential is important for both lenders and owners. Owners know that the value of the firm depends on its future growth in earnings, cash flow, and dividends. In Reading 59, we discuss

---

[15] Studies on this topic will be discussed in Reading 55.

[16] These stock prices (which are for the calendar year) are rounded to the nearest whole dollar.

various valuation models that are based on alternative cash flows, the investor's required rate of return for the stock, and the firm's expected growth rate of earnings and cash flows.

Creditors also are interested in a firm's growth potential because the firm's future success is the major determinant of its ability to pay obligations, and the firm's future success is influenced by its growth. Some **credit analysis** ratios measure the book value of a firm's assets relative to its financial obligations, assuming that the firm can sell these assets to pay off the loan in case of default. Selling assets in a forced liquidation will typically yield only about 10 to 15 cents on the dollar. Currently, it is widely recognized that the more relevant analysis is the ability of the firm to pay off its obligations as an ongoing enterprise, which is impacted by its growth potential. This analysis of growth is also relevant to changes of bond ratings.

Determinants of Growth

The growth of business, like the growth on any economic entity, including the aggregate economy, depends on

1. The amount of resources retained and reinvested in the entity

2. The rate of return earned on the reinvested funds

The more a firm reinvests, the greater its potential for growth. Alternatively, for a given level of reinvestment, a firm will grow faster if it earns a higher rate of return on the funds reinvested. Therefore, the growth rate of equity earnings and cash flows is a function of two variables: (1) the percentage of net earnings retained (the firm's retention rate) and (2) the rate of return earned on the firm's equity capital (the firm's ROE), because when earnings are retained they become part of the firm's equity.

$$g = \text{Percentage of Earnings Retained} \times \text{Return on Equity}$$
$$= RR \times ROE$$

(38-31)

where:

g = potential (i.e., sustainable) growth rate
RR = the retention rate of earnings
ROE = the firm's return on equity

The retention rate is a decision by the board of directors based on the investment opportunities available to the firm. Theory suggests that the firm should retain earnings and reinvest them as long as the **expected rate of return** on the investment exceeds the firm's cost of capital.

As discussed earlier regarding the DuPont System, a firm's ROE is a function of three components:

▶ Net profit margin

▶ Total asset turnover

▶ Financial leverage (total assets/equity)

Therefore, a firm can increase its ROE by increasing its profit margin, by becoming more efficient (increasing its total asset turnover), or by increasing its financial leverage (and its financial risk). As discussed, investors should examine and estimate each of the components when estimating the ROE for a firm.

The sustainable growth potential analysis for Walgreens begins with the retention rate (RR):

$$\text{Retention Rate} = 1 - \frac{\text{Dividends Declared}}{\text{Operating Income after Taxes}} \qquad \textbf{(38-32)}$$

Walgreens RR figures were

$$2004: \quad 1 - \frac{0.18}{1.33} = 0.86$$

$$2003: \quad 1 - \frac{0.16}{1.14} = 0.86$$

$$2002: \quad 1 - \frac{0.15}{0.99} = 0.85$$

The historical results in Exhibit 38-7 indicate that the retention rate for Walgreens has been relatively stable during the 22-year period in excess of 70 percent, including recent increases to about 85 percent.

Exhibit 38-6 contains the three components of ROE for the period 1982–2004. Exhibit 38-7 contains the two factors that determine a firm's growth potential and the implied growth rate during the past 23 years. Overall, Walgreens experienced a slight decline in its growth potential during the early 1990s, but since 1995 the firm has experienced a potential growth rate in excess of 14 percent, which is very consistent with its actual performance.

Exhibit 38-8 reinforces our understanding of the importance of the firm's ROE. Walgreen Co.'s retention rate was quite stable throughout the period with an increase during the last five years. Even with this, it has been the firm's ROE that has mainly determined its **sustainable growth rate**. This analysis indicates that the important consideration is *the long-run outlook for the components of sustainable growth*. Investors need to *project* changes in each of the components of ROE and employ these projections to estimate an ROE to use in the growth model along with an estimate of the firm's long-run retention rate. We will come back to these concepts on numerous occasions when discussing stock valuation. This detailed analysis of ROE is extremely important for growth companies where the ROEs are notably above average for the economy and, therefore, vulnerable to competition.

9   COMPARATIVE ANALYSIS OF RATIOS

We have discussed the importance of comparative analysis, but so far we have concentrated on the selection and computation of specific ratios. Exhibit 38-9 contains most of the ratios discussed for Walgreens, the retail drug store industry (as derived from the *S&P Analysts Handbook*), and the S&P Industrials Index. The three-year comparison should provide some insights, although we typically would want to examine data for a 5- to 10-year period. It was necessary to do the comparison for the period 2001–2003 because industry and market data from Standard and Poor's were not available for 2004 at the time of this writing.

Internal Liquidity

The three basic ratios (current ratio, quick ratio, and cash ratio) provided mixed results regarding liquidity for Walgreens relative to the industry and market. The

EXHIBIT 38-8	Walgreen Co. Components of Growth and the Implied Sustainable Growth Rate		
Year	(1) Retention Rate	(2) Return on Equity[a]	(3)[b] Sustainable Growth Rate
1982	0.72	18.73	13.49
1983	0.74	19.84	14.68
1984	0.74	20.60	15.24
1985	0.71	19.58	13.90
1986	0.70	18.64	13.05
1987	0.68	16.63	11.31
1988	0.71	18.12	12.87
1989	0.73	18.74	13.68
1990	0.72	18.42	13.26
1991	0.71	18.04	12.81
1992	0.71	17.90	12.71
1993	0.67	16.07	10.77
1994	0.70	17.91	12.54
1995	0.69	17.85	12.32
1996	0.71	18.19	12.91
1997	0.73	18.35	13.40
1998	0.75	17.93	13.44
1999	0.79	17.91	14.15
2000	0.82	18.35	15.05
2001	0.84	17.01	14.29
2002	0.85	16.36	13.91
2003	0.86	16.34	14.05
2004	0.86	16.52	14.21

[a] From Exhibit 38-6.

[b] Column (3) is equal to column (1) times column (2).

current ratio is about equal to the industry and above the market. The firm's receivables collection period is substantially less than the S&P Industrials and below the retail drugstore industry. Because the collection period has been fairly steady, the difference is due to the firm's basic credit policy.

Overall, the comparisons indicate reasonably strong internal liquidity. An additional positive liquidity factor is the firm's ability to sell high-grade commercial paper and several major bank credit lines.

Operating Performance

This segment of the analysis considers efficiency ratios (turnovers) and profitability ratios. The major comparison is relative to the industry. Walgreen Co.'s turnover ratios were consistently substantially above those of the retail drugstore industry.

EXHIBIT 38-9   Summary of Financial Ratios for Walgreens, S&P Retail Drugstores, S&P Industrials Index, 2001–2003

	2003			2002			2001		
	Walgreens	Drugstores	S&P Industrials	Walgreens	Drugstores	S&P Industrials	Walgreens	Drugstores	S&P Industrials
Internal liquidity									
Current ratio	1.8	1.82	1.43	1.75	1.81	1.36	1.46	1.58	1.29
Quick ratio	0.62	0.56	1.05	0.48	0.47	0.98	0.27	0.32	0.92
Cash ratio	0.35	0.23	0.37	0.15	0.16	0.32	0.01	0.04	0.26
Receivables turnover	32.95	38.30	4.43	32.72	27.54	4.24	34.86	27.03	4.30
Average collection period	11.08	9.53	82.40	11.20	13.30	86.10	10.50	13.50	84.90
Working capital–sales	0.09	0.07	0.16	0.06	0.09	0.11	0.05	0.08	0.09
Operating performance									
Total asset turnover	3.02	4.01	0.79	3.07	2.8	0.76	3.09	2.69	0.79
Inventory turnover (sales)	6.04	10.07	11.43	8.05	6.68	10.89	7.8	6.29	10.94
Working capital turnover	11.06	14.13	6.43	15.96	11.74	8.88	18.73	13.07	11.34
Net fixed asset turnover	6.82	11.81	2.96	6.42	8.11	2.77	6.34	7.71	2.8
Equity turnover	4.84	6.85	2.48	5.02	5.05	2.38	5.22	4.99	2.32
Profitability									
Gross profit margin	27.07	NA*	NA	26.52	NA	NA	26.70	NA	NA
Operating profit margin	5.81	5.29	9.76	5.71	5.41	12.81	5.78	5.38	10.53
Net profit margin	3.62	2.40	6.35	3.55	3.29	7.07	3.60	2.81	4.89
Return on total capital	10.92	9.91	8.72	10.89	9.54	6.85	11.15	9.01	5.41
Return on owners' equity	17.52	16.47	22.90	17.82	16.64	16.80	18.76	15.86	11.33

(Exhibit continued on next page . . . .)

EXHIBIT 38-9   (continued)

	2003			2002			2001		
	Walgreens	Drugstores	S&P Industrials	Walgreens	Drugstores	S&P Industrials	Walgreens	Drugstores	S&P Industrials
Financial risk									
Debt–equity ratio	143.05	16.33	157.03	126.43	17.82	139.93	132.07	16.91	113.6
Long-term debt–long-term capital	58.86	14.09	61.09	55.84	15.12	58.32	56.91	14.46	53.18
Total debt–total capital	66.79	68.55	589.40	63.49	42.17	69.81	65.71	45.7	66.09
Interest coverage	5.77	60.95	6.21	6.45	49.18	6.68	6.47	30.77	5.24
Cash flow–long-term debt	15.33	534.95	40.40	24.09	381.10	36.78	15.37	231.48	37.78
Cash flow–total debt	13.3	22.26	19.20	16.9	26.16	17.11	8.81	25.49	16.92
Growth analysis									
Retention rate	0.86	0.87	0.68	0.85	0.86	0.72	0.84	0.81	0.58
Return on equity	16.34	15.38	13.80	16.36	15.37	17.84	17.01	13.14	11.02
Total asset turnover	2.79	3.78	0.72	2.9	2.69	0.76	2.99	2.59	0.76
Total asset–equity	1.62	1.69	3.02	1.59	1.73	3.3	1.68	1.88	2.96
Net profit margin	3.62	2.40	6.35	3.55	3.29	3.12	3.66	2.81	2.26
Sustainable growth rate	14.05	13.39	9.45	13.96	13.18	12.77	14.24	10.67	6.38

* NA: not available.

The comparison of profitability from sales was mixed. Operating profit margins were about equal to the industry, but net margins beat the industry performance. The strong operating profit margin was in spite of the higher growth rate of new stores relative to the competition, and the fact that new stores require 18 to 24 months to reach the firm's "normal" profit rate.

The profit performance related to invested capital was historically strong. The return on total capital (including capitalized leases) for Walgreens was consistently above both the S&P Industrials and the retail drugstore industry. Walgreens likewise always attained higher ROEs than its industry and the market.

Risk Analysis

Walgreen Co.'s financial risk ratios, measured in terms of proportion of debt, were consistently inferior to those of the industry and the market when both deferred taxes and capitalized leases were included as long-term debt for Walgreens, but it was not possible to do a comparable adjustment for the S&P Industrials or the industry. Such an adjustment would have a significant impact on the industry results. Similarly, the financial risk ratios that use cash flow for Walgreens were below the market and its industry. These comparisons indicate that Walgreens has a reasonable amount of financial risk, but it is not of major concern because the firm has very low business risk based on consistently high growth in sales and operating profit. Notably, there are no specific comparative ratios available for both business and external liquidity risk. Regarding business risk, the analysis of relative sales and EBIT volatility adjusted for growth as demonstrated in the Appendix indicated that this adjusted volatility was very low indicating low business risk. Also, the trading turnover and market value data indicated low external liquidity risk.

Growth Analysis

Walgreens has generally maintained a sustainable growth rate above its industry and the aggregate market, based on both a higher ROE and a consistently higher retention rate. In sum, Walgreens has adequate liquidity; a good operating record, including a very consistent growth record that implies low business risk; reasonable financial risk even when we consider the leases on stores; and clearly above-average growth performance. Your success as an investor depends on how well you use these historical numbers to derive meaningful *estimates* of *future* performance for use in a valuation model. As noted previously, everybody is generally aware of the valuation models, so it is the individual who can provide the best *estimates* of relevant valuation variables who will experience superior risk-adjusted performance.

10   ANALYSIS OF NON-U.S. FINANCIAL STATEMENTS

As we have stressed several times, your portfolio should encompass other economies and markets, numerous global industries, and many foreign firms in these global industries. However, because accounting conventions differ among countries, non-U.S. financial statements will differ from those in this reading and from what you will see in a typical accounting course. While it is beyond the scope of this text to discuss these alternative accounting conventions in detail, we encourage you to examine the source entitled *Analysis of International Financial Statements.*

THE QUALITY OF FINANCIAL STATEMENTS   11

Analysts sometimes speak of the quality of a firm's earnings or the quality of a firm's balance sheet. In general, **quality financial statements** are a good reflection of reality; accounting tricks and one-time changes are not used to make the firm appear stronger than it really is. Some factors that lead to lower-quality financial statements were mentioned previously when we discussed ratio analysis. Other quality influences are discussed here and in Palepu, Healy, and Bernard (2004, Chapter 3).

Balance Sheet

A high-quality balance sheet typically has limited use of debt or leverage. Therefore, the potential of financial distress resulting from excessive debt is quite low. Little use of debt also implies the firm has unused borrowing capacity, which implies that the firm can draw on that unused capacity to make profitable investments.

A quality balance sheet contains assets with market values greater than their book value. The capability of management and the existence of intangible assets—such as goodwill, trademarks, or patents—will make the market value of the firm's assets exceed their book values. In general, as a result of inflation and historical cost accounting, we might expect the market value of assets to exceed their book values. Overpriced assets on the books occur when a firm has outdated, technologically inferior assets; obsolete inventory; and nonperforming assets such as a bank that has not written off nonperforming loans.

The presence of off-balance-sheet liabilities also harms the quality of a balance sheet. Such liabilities may include joint ventures and loan commitments or guarantees to subsidiaries, which are discussed in Stickney, Brown, and Wahlen (2004, Chapter 6).

Income Statement

High-quality earnings are *repeatable* earnings. For example, they arise from sales to customers who are expected to do repeat business with the firm and from costs that are not artificially low as a result of unusual and short-lived input price reductions. One-time and nonrecurring items—such as accounting changes, mergers, and asset sales—should be ignored when examining earnings. Unexpected exchange rate fluctuations that work in the firm's favor to raise revenues or reduce costs should also be viewed as nonrecurring.

High-quality earnings result from the use of conservative accounting principles that do not result in overstated revenues and understated costs. The closer the earnings are to cash, the higher the quality of the income statement. Suppose a firm sells furniture on credit by allowing customers to make monthly payments. A higher-quality income statement will recognize revenue using the "installment" principle; that is, as the cash is collected each month, in turn, annual sales will reflect only the cash collected from sales during the year. A lower-quality income statement will recognize 100 percent of the revenue at the time of sale, even though payments may stretch well into next year. A detailed discussion of income items is in Stickney, Brown, and Wahlen (2004, Chapter 5).

Footnotes

A word to the wise: **read the footnotes**! The purpose of the footnotes (that have come to include three or more pages in most annual reports) is to provide information on how the firm handles balance sheet and income items. While the footnotes may not reveal everything you should know (e.g., Enron), if you do not read them you cannot hope to be informed. The fact is, many analysts recommend that you should read an annual report *backward*, so that you read the footnotes first!

12 THE VALUE OF FINANCIAL STATEMENT ANALYSIS

Financial statements, by their nature, are backward-looking. They report the firm's assets, liabilities, and equity as of a certain (past) date; they report a firm's revenues, expenses, or cash flows over some (past) time period. An **efficient capital market** will have already incorporated this past information into security prices; so it may seem, at first glance, that analysis of a firm's financial statements and ratios is a waste of the analyst's time.

The fact is, the opposite is true. Analysis of financial statements allows the analyst to gain knowledge of a firm's operating and financial strategy and structure. This, in turn, assists the analyst in determining the effects of *future* events on the firm's cash flows. Combining knowledge of the firm's strategy, operating and financial leverage, and possible macro- and microeconomic scenarios is necessary to determine an appropriate market value for the firm's stock. Combining the analysis of historical data with potential future scenarios allows analysts to evaluate the risks facing the firm and then to develop an expected return forecast based on these risks. The final outcome of the process, as future readings will detail, is the determination of the firm's current **intrinsic value** based on expected cash flows, which is compared to its security price. The point is, the detailed analysis of the historical results ensures a better estimation of the expected cash flows and an appropriate discount rate that leads to a superior valuation of the firm.

13 SPECIFIC USES OF FINANCIAL RATIOS

In addition to measuring firm performance and risk, financial ratios have been used in four major areas in investments: (1) stock valuation, (2) the identification of internal corporate variables that affect a stock's systematic risk (beta), (3) assigning credit quality ratings on bonds, and (4) predicting insolvency (bankruptcy) of firms.

Stock Valuation Models

Most valuation models attempt to derive a value based on one of several present value of cash flow models or appropriate relative valuation ratios for a stock. As will be noted, all the valuation models require an estimate of the expected growth rate of earnings, cash flows, or dividends and the required rate of return on the stock. Clearly, financial ratios can help in estimating these critical inputs.

The growth rate estimate for earnings, cash flow, or dividends employs the ratios discussed in the potential growth rate section.

When estimating the required rate of return on an investment (i.e., either the cost of equity, k, or the weighted average cost of capital, WACC), recall that these estimates depend on the risk premium for the security, which is a function of business risk, financial risk, and liquidity risk. Business risk typically is measured in terms of earnings variability; financial risk is identified by either the debt proportion ratios or the earnings or cash flow ratios. Insights regarding a stock's liquidity risk can be obtained from the external liquidity measures we discussed.

The typical empirical valuation model has examined a cross section of companies and used a multiple regression model that relates one of the relative valuations ratios for the sample firms to some of the following corporate variables (the averages generally consider the past 5 or 10 years).

Financial Ratios
1. Average debt–equity
2. Average interest coverage
3. Average dividend payout
4. Average return on equity
5. Average retention rate
6. Average market price to book value
7. Average market price to cash flow
8. Average market price to sales

Variability Measures
1. Coefficient of variation of operating earnings
2. Coefficient of variation of sales
3. Coefficient of variation of net income
4. Systematic risk (beta)

Nonratio Variables
1. Average growth rate of earnings

Estimating Systematic Risk

As we will discuss in Reading 54, the **capital asset pricing model (CAPM)** asserts that the relevant risk variable for an asset should be its systematic risk, which is its beta coefficient related to the market portfolio of all risky assets. In efficient markets, a relationship should be exist between internal corporate risk variables and market-determined risk variables such as beta. Numerous studies have tested the relationship between a stock's systematic risk (beta) and the firm's internal corporate variables intended to reflect business risk and financial risk. The significant variables (usually five-year averages) included were as follows.

Financial Ratios
1. Dividend payout
2. Total debt–total assets
3. Cash flow–total debt
4. Interest coverage

5. Working capital–total assets

6. Current ratio

Variability Measures

1. Coefficient of variation of net earnings

2. Coefficient of variation of operating earnings

3. Coefficient of variation of operating profit margins

4. Operating earnings beta (company earnings related to aggregate earnings)

Nonratio Variables

1. Asset size

2. Market value of stock outstanding

Estimating the Ratings on Bonds

Three financial services assign credit ratings to bonds on the basis of the issuing company's ability to meet all its obligations related to the bond. An AAA or Aaa rating indicates high quality and almost no chance of default, whereas a C rating indicates the bond is already in default. Numerous studies have used financial ratios to predict the rating to be assigned to a bond. The major financial variables considered in these studies were as follows:

Financial Ratios

1. Long-term debt–total assets

2. Total debt–total capital

3. Net income plus depreciation (cash flow)–long-term senior debt

4. Cash flow–total debt

5. Earnings before interest and taxes (EBIT)–interest expense (fixed charge coverage)

6. Cash flow from operations plus interest–interest expense

7. Market value of stock–par value of bonds

8. Net operating profit–sales

9. Net income–owners' equity (ROE)

10. Net income–total assets (ROA)

11. Working capital–sales

12. Sales–net worth (equity turnover)

Variability Measures

1. Coefficient of variation of sales

2. Coefficient of variation of net earnings

3. Coefficient of variation of return on assets

Nonratio Variables

1. Subordination of the issue

2. Size of the firm (total assets)

3. Issue size

4. Par value of all publicly traded bonds of the firm

Predicting Insolvency (Bankruptcy)

Analysts have always been interested in using financial ratios to identify firms that might default on a loan or declare bankruptcy. The typical study examines a sample of firms that have declared bankruptcy against a matched sample of firms in the same industry and of comparable size that have not failed. The analysis involves examining a number of financial ratios expected to reflect declining liquidity for several years prior to the declaration of bankruptcy. The goal is to determine which set of ratios correctly predict that a firm will be in the bankrupt or nonbankrupt group. The better models have typically correctly classified more than 80 percent of the firms one year prior to failure. Some of the financial ratios included in successful models were as follows:

Financial Ratios
1. Cash flow–total debt
2. Cash flow–long-term debt
3. Sales–total assets*
4. Net income–total assets
5. EBIT/total assets*
6. Total debt/total assets
7. Market value of stock–book value of debt*
8. Working capital–total assets*
9. Retained earnings–total assets*
10. Current ratio
11. Working capital–sales

In addition to the several studies that have used financial ratios to predict bond ratings and failures, other studies have also used cash flow variables or a combination of financial ratios and cash flow variables for these predictions, and the results have been quite successful. The five ratios designated by an asterisk (*) are the ratios used in the well-known Altman Z-score model (Altman, 1968).

Limitations of Financial Ratios

We must reinforce an earlier point: you should always consider *relative* financial ratios. In addition, you should be aware of other questions and limitations of financial ratios:

1. Are alternative firms' accounting treatments comparable? As you know from prior accounting courses, there are several generally accepted methods for treating various accounting items, and the alternatives can cause a difference in results for the same event. Therefore, you should check on the accounting treatment of significant items and adjust the values for major differences. Comparability becomes a critical consideration when dealing with non-U.S. firms.

2. How homogeneous is the firm? Many companies have divisions that operate in different industries, which can make it difficult to derive comparable industry ratios.

3. Are the implied results consistent? It is important to develop a total profile of the firm and not depend on only one set of ratios (for example, internal liquidity ratios). As an example, a firm may be having short-term liquidity

problems but be very profitable—the profitability will eventually alleviate the short-run liquidity problems.

4. Is the ratio within a reasonable range for the industry? As noted on several occasions, you typically want to consider a *range* of appropriate values for the ratio because a value that is either too high or too low for the industry can be a problem.

THE INTERNET

Investments Online

Many publicly traded companies have Web sites, which, among other pieces of information, contain financial information. Sometimes complete copies of the firm's annual report and SEC filings are on their home page. Since the focus of this reading has been Walgreen Co.'s financial statements, here are some relevant sites:

www.walgreens.com Walgreen Co.'s home page, with financial information available through links from this page. At least four of Walgreen Co.'s competitors have Web sites featuring financial information. These include:

www.cvs.com The home page for CVS Pharmacy.

www.riteaid.com Rite Aid Corporation's home page.

www.longs.com The Web site for Longs Drug Stores.

www.duanereade.com Duane Reade's home page.

Commercially oriented and government-sponsored databases are also available through the Web.

www.sec.gov The Web home page for the Securities and Exchange Commission allows entrance into the SEC's EDGAR (electronic data gathering, analysis, and retrieval) database. Most firm's SEC filings are accessible through EDGAR, including filings for executive compensation, 10-K, and 10-Q forms.

www.hoovers.com Hoovers Online is a commercial source of company-specific information, including financial statements and stock performance. Some data are free, including a company profile, news, stock prices and a chart of recent stock price performance. It contains links to a number of sources, including the firm's annual report, SEC filings, and earnings per share estimates by First Call.

www.dnb.com Dun & Bradstreet is a well-known gatherer of financial information. Corporations make use of its business credit reporting services. D&B publishes industry average financial ratios which are useful in equity and fixed income analysis.

SUMMARY

- ► The overall purpose of financial statement analysis is to help investors make decisions on investing in a firm's bonds or stock. Financial ratios should be examined relative to the economy, the firm's industry, the firm's main competitors, and the firm's past relative ratios.

- ► The specific ratios can be divided into four categories, depending on the purpose of the analysis: internal liquidity, operating performance, risk analysis, and growth analysis.

- ► When analyzing the financial statements for non-U.S. firms, analysts must consider differences in format and in accounting principles that cause different values for specific ratios.

- ► Four major uses of financial ratios are (1) stock valuation, (2) analysis of variables affecting a stock's systematic risk (beta), (3) assigning credit ratings on bonds, and (4) predicting insolvency (bankruptcy).

A final caveat: you can envision numerous financial ratios to examine almost every possible relationship. The goal is not more ratios, but to limit and group the ratios so you can examine them in a meaningful way. This entails analyzing the ratios over time relative to the economy, the industry, or the past. You should concentrate on deriving better comparisons for a limited number of ratios that provide insights into the questions of interest to you.

QUESTIONS

1. Why do analysts use financial ratios rather than the absolute numbers? Give an example.

2. How might a jewelry store and a grocery store differ in terms of asset turnover and profit margin? Would you expect their return on total assets to differ assuming equal business risk? Discuss.

3. Why is the analysis of growth potential important to the common stockholder? Why is it important to the debt investor?

PROBLEMS FOR READING 38

1. Three companies have the following results during the recent period.

	K	L	M
Net profit margin	0.04	0.06	0.10
Total assets turnover	2.20	2.00	1.40
Total assets/equity	2.40	2.20	1.50

  a. Derive for each its return on equity based on the three DuPont components.

  b. Given the following earnings and dividends, compute the estimated sustainable growth rate for each firm.

	K	L	M
Earnings/share	2.75	3.00	4.50
Dividends/share	1.25	1.00	1.00

2. Given the following balance sheet, fill in the ratio values for 2006 and discuss how these results compare with both the industry average and past performance of Sophie Enterprises.

SOPHIE ENTERPRISES CONSOLIDATED BALANCE SHEET, YEARS ENDED DECEMBER 31, 2006 AND 2007

ASSETS ($ THOUSANDS)	2007	2006
Cash	$ 100	$ 90
Receivables	220	170
Inventories	330	230
Total current assets	650	490
Property, plant, and equipment	1,850	1,650
Depreciation	350	225
Net properties	1,500	1,425
Intangibles	150	150
Total assets	2,300	2,065

(continued)

SOPHIE ENTERPRISES CONSOLIDATED BALANCE SHEET, YEARS ENDED DECEMBER 31, 2006 AND 2007 (continued)

LIABILITIES AND SHAREHOLDERS' EQUITY

	2007	2006
Accounts payable	$ 85	$ 105
Short-term bank notes	125	110
Current portion of long-term debt	75	—
Accruals	65	85
Total current liabilities	350	300
Long-term debt	625	540
Deferred taxes	100	80
Preferred stock (10%, $100 par)	150	150
Common stock ($2 par, 100,000 issued)	200	200
Additional paid-in capital	325	325
Retained earnings	550	470
Common shareholders' equity	1,075	995
Total liabilities and shareholders' equity	2,300	2,065

SOPHIE ENTERPRISES CONSOLIDATED STATEMENT OF INCOME, YEARS ENDED DECEMBER 31, 2006 AND 2007 ($ THOUSANDS)

	2007	2006
Net sales	$3,500	$2,990
Cost of goods sold	2,135	1,823
Selling, general and administrative expenses	1,107	974
Operating profit	258	193
Net interest expense	62	54
Income from operations	195	139
Income taxes	66	47
Net income	129	91
Preferred dividends	15	15
Net income available for common shares	114	76
Dividends declared	40	30

(continued)

SOPHIE ENTERPRISES CONSOLIDATED STATEMENT OF INCOME, YEARS ENDED DECEMBER 31, 2006 AND 2007 ($ THOUSANDS) (continued)			
	Sophie (2007)	**Sophie's Average**	**Industry Average**
Current ratio	—	2.000	2.200
Quick ratio	—	1.000	1.100
Receivables turnover	—	18.000	18.000
Average collection period	—	20.000	20.000
Total asset turnover	—	1.500	1.400
Inventory turnover	—	11.000	12.500
Fixed-asset turnover	—	2.500	2.400
Equity turnover	—	3.200	3.000
Gross profit margin	—	0.400	0.350
Operating profit margin	—	8.000	7.500
Return on capital	—	0.107	0.120
Return on equity	—	0.118	0.126
Return on common equity	—	0.128	0.135
Debt–equity ratio	—	0.600	0.500
Debt–total capital ratio	—	0.400	0.370
Interest coverage	—	4.000	4.500
Fixed charge coverage	—	3.000	4.000
Cash flow–long-term debt	—	0.400	0.450
Cash flow–total debt	—	0.250	0.300
Retention rate	—	0.350	0.400

3. *CFA Examination Level 1 (Adapted)*

(Question 3 is composed of two parts, for a total of 20 minutes.)

The DuPont formula defines the net return on shareholders' equity as a function of the following components:

▶ Operating margin

▶ Asset turnover

▶ Interest burden

▶ Financial leverage

▶ Income tax rate

Using *only* the data in the table shown below:

A. Calculate *each* of the *five* components listed above for 2002 *and* 2006, and calculate the return on equity (ROE) for 2002 *and* 2006, using all of the *five* components. Show calculations. (15 minutes)

B. Briefly discuss the impact of the changes in asset turnover *and* financial leverage on the change in ROE from 2002 to 2006. (5 minutes)

	2002	2006
Income Statement Data		
Revenues	$542	$979
Operating income	38	76
Depreciation and amortization	3	9
Interest expense	3	0
Pretax income	32	67
Income taxes	13	37
Net income after tax	19	30
Balance Sheet Data		
Fixed assets	$ 41	$ 70
Total assets	245	291
Working capital	123	157
Total debt	16	0
Total shareholders' equity	159	220

DILUTIVE SECURITIES AND EARNINGS PER SHARE

by Donald E. Kieso, Jerry J. Weygandt, and Terry D. Warfield

LEARNING OUTCOMES

The candidate should be able to:

a. differentiate between simple and complex capital structures for purposes of calculating earnings per share (EPS), describe the components of EPS, and calculate a company's EPS in a simple capital structure;

b. calculate a company's weighted average number of shares outstanding;

c. determine the effect of stock dividends and stock splits on a company's weighted average number of shares outstanding;

d. distinguish between dilutive and antidilutive securities and calculate a company's basic and diluted EPS in a complex capital structure, and describe and determine the effects of convertible securities, options and warrants on a company's EPS;

e. compare and contrast the requirements for EPS reporting in simple versus complex capital structures.

JUST LIKE CANDY KISSES   1

OPTIONAL SEGMENT BEGINS

What do President George Bush, Federal Reserve Board Chair Alan Greenspan, Senators Joseph Lieberman and John McCain, and the guru of investing Warren Buffet all have in common? Each of them has a strong opinion on whether stock options should be reported as an expense in corporate income statements.

You might wonder why such important individuals are interested in such an arcane dispute about how to account for these options. The reason: CEOs now get over 60 percent of their total pay from stock options—with only minimal performance standards for most. The punishing bear market in which many investors have lost considerable wealth, coupled with the accounting scandals at **Enron, WorldCom, Global Crossing,** and a host of other companies, has transformed once-blessed stock options into potent symbols of executive abuse and a compensation system gone haywire.

As the excesses of the 1990s are laid bare, it's becoming clear that options played a central role at numerous companies. Options were touted as a way to align the interests of corporate managers with those of stockholders. But, option grants that promised to turn caretaker corporate managers into multimillionaires in just a few years encouraged some to ignore the basics of management in favor of pumping up stock prices, exercising options, and cashing out.

As disenchantment with greedy managers has grown, investors, regulators, and politicians believe that more regulation is needed in this area. One area under intense scrutiny is the accounting for stock options. Presently most companies are generally not required to expense options. Although under current acocunting standards, the potential dilution from stock options is reflected in earnings per share, many believe that not recording option grants as an expense gives the impression that options are free. As a result, options tend to be given out like candy kisses. Stay tuned. Worse may be yet to come. Companies are still issuing options at a furious pace. In fact, in recent years 200 of the largest companies have handed out amounts approaching 3 percent of their outstanding shares every year, more than double the pace of a decade ago.[1]

As indicated in the opening story, the widespread use of options and other dilutive securities has led the accounting profession to examine the area closely. Specifically, the profession has directed its attention to accounting for these securities at date of issuance and to the presentation of earnings per share figures that recognize their effect. The first section of this reading discusses convertible securities, warrants, stock options, and contingent shares. These securities are called **dilutive securities** because a reduction—dilution—in earnings per share often results when these securities become common stock. The second section indicates how these securities are used in earnings per share computations. The content and organization of the reading are as follows.

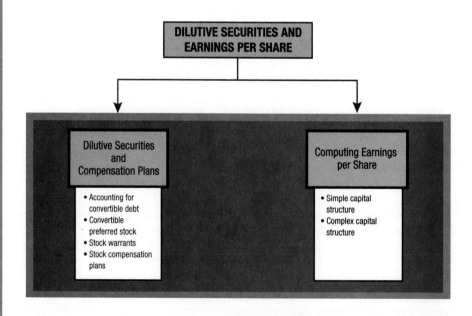

---

[1] Adapted from David Henry, Michelle Conlin, Nanette Byrnes, Michael Mandel, Stanley Holmes, and Stanley Reed, "Too Much of a Good Incentive?" *Business Week Online* (March 4, 2002).

ACCOUNTING FOR CONVERTIBLE DEBT

2

If bonds can be converted into other corporate securities during some specified period of time after issuance, they are called **convertible bonds**. **A convertible bond combines the benefits of a bond with the privilege of exchanging it for stock at the holder's option.** It is purchased by investors who desire the security of a bond holding—guaranteed interest—plus the added option of conversion if the value of the stock appreciates significantly.

Corporations issue convertibles for two main reasons. One is the desire **to raise equity capital** without giving up more ownership control than necessary. To illustrate, assume that a company wants to raise $1,000,000 at a time when its common stock is selling at $45 per share. Such an issue would require sale of 22,222 shares (ignoring issue costs). By selling 1,000 bonds at $1,000 par, each convertible into 20 shares of common stock, the enterprise may raise $1,000,000 by committing only 20,000 shares of its common stock.

A second reason why companies issue convertible securities is **to obtain debt financing at cheaper rates**. Many enterprises could issue debt only at high interest rates unless a convertible covenant were attached. The conversion privilege entices the investor to accept a lower interest rate than would normally be the case on a straight debt issue. For example, **Amazon.com** at one time issued convertible bonds that pay interest at an effective yield of 4.75 percent, a rate much lower than Amazon.com would have had to pay if it had issued straight debt. For this lower interest rate, the investor receives the right to buy Amazon.com's common stock at a fixed price until maturity.[2]

Accounting for convertible debt involves reporting issues at the time of (1) issuance, (2) conversion, and (3) retirement.

At Time of Issuance

The method for recording convertible bonds **at the date of issue follows the method used to record straight debt issues** (with none of the proceeds recorded as equity). Any discount or premium that results from the issuance of convertible bonds is amortized to its maturity date because it is difficult to predict when, if at all, conversion will occur. However, the accounting for convertible debt as a straight debt issue is controversial; we discuss it more fully later in this reading.

At Time of Conversion

If bonds are converted into other securities, the principal accounting problem is to determine the amount at which to record the securities exchanged for the bond. Assume Hilton, Inc. issued at a premium of $60 a $1,000 bond convertible into 10 shares of common stock (par value $10). At the time of conversion the unamortized premium is $50, the market value of the bond is $1,200, and the stock is quoted on the market at $120. **The book value method of recording the conversion of the bonds is the method most commonly used in practice and is**

---

[2] As with any investment, a buyer has to be careful. For example, **Wherehouse Entertainment Inc.** which had 6 ¼ percent convertibles outstanding, was taken private in a leveraged buyout. As a result, the convertible was suddenly as risky as a junk bond of a highly leveraged company with a coupon of only 6 ¼ percent. As one holder of the convertibles noted, "What's even worse is that the company will be so loaded down with debt that it probably won't have enough cash flow to make its interest payments. And the convertible debt we hold is subordinated to the rest of Wherehouse's debt." These types of situations have made convertibles less attractive and have led to the introduction of takeover protection covenants in some convertible bond offerings. Or, sometimes convertibles are permitted to be called at par and therefore the conversion premium may be lost.

considered GAAP. To illustrate the specifics of this approach, the entry for the conversion of the Hilton, Inc. bonds would be:

Bonds Payable	1,000	
Premium on Bonds Payable	50	
Common Stock		100
Paid-in Capital in Excess of Par		950

Support for the book value approach is based on the argument that an agreement was established at the date of the issuance either to pay a stated amount of cash at maturity or to issue a stated number of shares of equity securities. Therefore, when the debt is converted to equity in accordance with the preexisting contract terms, no gain or loss should be recognized upon conversion.

Induced Conversions

Sometimes the issuer wishes to encourage prompt conversion of its convertible debt to equity securities in order to reduce interest costs or to improve its debt to equity ratio. As a result, the issuer may offer some form of additional consideration (such as cash or common stock), called a "sweetener," to **induce conversion**. The sweetener should be reported as an expense of the current period at an amount equal to the fair value of the additional securities or other consideration given.

Assume that Helloid, Inc. has outstanding $1,000,000 par value convertible debentures convertible into 100,000 shares of $1 par value common stock. Helloid wishes to reduce its annual interest cost. To do so, Helloid agrees to pay the holders of its convertible debentures an additional $80,000 if they will convert. Assuming conversion occurs, the following entry is made.

Debt Conversion Expense	80,000	
Bonds Payable	1,000,000	
Common Stock		100,000
Additional Paid-in Capital		900,000
Cash		80,000

The additional $80,000 is recorded as **an expense of the current period** and not as a reduction of equity. Some argue that the cost of a conversion inducement is a cost of obtaining equity capital. As a result, they contend, it should be recognized as a cost of—a reduction of—the equity capital acquired and not as an expense. However, the FASB indicated that when an additional payment is needed to make bondholders convert, the payment is for a service (bondholders converting at a given time) and should be reported as an expense. This expense is not reported as an extraordinary item.[3]

---

[3] "Induced Conversions of Convertible Debt," *Statement of Financial Accounting Standards No. 84* (Stamford, Conn.: FASB, 1985).

Retirement of Convertible Debt

As indicated earlier, the method for recording the **issuance** of convertible bonds follows that used in recording straight debt issues. Specifically this means that no portion of the proceeds should be attributable to the conversion feature and credited to Additional Paid-in Capital. Although theoretical objections to this approach can be raised, to be consistent, a gain or loss on **retiring convertible debt needs to be recognized in the same way as a gain or loss on retiring debt** that is not convertible. For this reason, differences between the cash acquisition price of debt and its carrying amount should be reported **currently in income as a gain or loss.**

CONVERTIBLE PREFERRED STOCK
3

The major difference between accounting for a convertible bond and a **convertible preferred stock** at the date of issue is that convertible bonds are considered liabilities, whereas convertible preferreds (unless mandatory redemption exists) are considered a part of stockholders' equity.

In addition, when convertible preferred stocks are exercised, there is no theoretical justification for recognition of a gain or loss. No gain or loss is recognized when the entity deals with stockholders in their capacity as business owners. The **book value method is employed**: Preferred Stock, along with any related Additional Paid-in Capital, is debited; Common Stock and Additional Paid-in Capital (if an excess exists) are credited.

A different treatment develops when the par value of the common stock issued exceeds the book value of the preferred stock. In that case, Retained Earnings is usually debited for the difference.

Assume Host Enterprises issued 1,000 shares of common stock (par value $2) upon conversion of 1,000 shares of preferred stock (par value $1) that was originally issued for a $200 premium. The entry would be:

Convertible Preferred Stock	1,000	
Paid-in Capital in Excess of Par (Premium on Preferred Stock)	200	
Retained Earnings	800	
Common Stock		2,000

The rationale for the debit to Retained Earnings is that the preferred stockholders are offered an **additional return** to facilitate their conversion to common stock. In this example, the additional return is charged to retained earnings. Many states, however, require that this charge simply reduce additional paid-in capital from other sources.

DESPERATE DEAL

When you're in dire straits, you do what you have to do.

So it is now with **Corning**, the once great company that provided the glass for Edison's first light bulb. It was a steady company until it fell for the great fiber optic bubble. It sold profitable divisions that seemed less exciting and spent billions on overpriced fiber optic acquisitions.

Recently, needing cash to finance operating losses and with the credit rating agencies having determined that its bonds are junk and its commercial paper unsalable, Corning came up with a glorified common stock offering that devastated an already depressed share price, which fell 50 percent in just three days.

Formally, this is a convertible preferred offering. But that is fiction. Of the $500 million put up by investors, $102 million was used to buy Treasury bonds that will pay the promised 7 percent dividends for three years, after which the preferred must be converted into common. If Corning goes bankrupt before then, the preferred holders are supposed to get the dividends immediately.

This is a bear market vehicle. In three years, the preferred shares will be converted into somewhere between 214 million and 312 million common shares. For a company that now has 952 million shares outstanding, that means dilution of at least a quarter, and maybe a third, depending on where the stock is by then.

Why not just issue common now? Why should buyers pay Corning to manage a portfolio of Treasuries? Corning's investment bankers figured they could attract a different class of investors. People now want income, so Wall Street will give it to them, even if in reality it is nothing more than common stock in drag.

Source: Adapted from Floyd Norris, "Corning's Desperate Deal Destroys Value," *New York Times* (August 2, 2002), p. C1. Reprinted with permission.

4   STOCK WARRANTS

Warrants are certificates entitling the holder to acquire shares of stock at a certain price within a stated period. This option is similar to the conversion privilege: Warrants, if exercised, become common stock and usually have a dilutive effect (reduce earnings per share) similar to that of the conversion of convertible securities. However, a substantial difference between convertible securities and stock warrants is that upon exercise of the warrants, the holder has to pay a certain amount of money to obtain the shares.

The issuance of warrants or options to buy additional shares normally arises under three situations:

1. When issuing different types of securities, such as bonds or preferred stock, warrants are often included **to make the security more attractive**—to provide an "equity kicker."

2. Upon the issuance of additional common stock, existing stockholders have a **preemptive right to purchase common stock** first. Warrants may be issued to evidence that right.

3. Warrants, often referred to as stock options, are given as **compensation to executives and employees**.

The problems in accounting for stock warrants are complex and present many difficulties—some of which remain unresolved.

Stock Warrants Issued with Other Securities

Warrants issued with other securities are basically long-term options to buy common stock at a fixed price. Although some perpetual warrants are traded, generally their life is 5 years, occasionally 10.

A warrant works like this: **Tenneco Automotive Inc.** offered a unit comprising one share of stock and one detachable warrant exercisable at $24.25 per share and good for 5 years. The unit sold for $22.75. Since the price of the common the day before the sale was $19.88, the difference suggests a price of $2.87 for the warrants.

In this situation, the warrants had an apparent value of $2.87, even though it would not be profitable at present for the purchaser to exercise the warrant and buy the stock, because the price of the stock is much below the exercise price of $24.25.[4] The investor pays for the warrant in order to receive a possible future call on the stock at a fixed price when the price has risen significantly. For example, if the price of the stock rises to $30, the investor has gained $2.88 ($30 minus $24.25 minus $2.87) on an investment of $2.87, a 100 percent increase! But, if the price never rises, the investor loses the full $2.87.[5]

The proceeds from the sale of debt with **detachable stock warrants** should be allocated between the two securities.[6] The reason: Two separable instruments are involved—that is, (1) a bond and (2) a warrant giving the holder the right to purchase common stock at a certain price. Warrants that are detachable can be traded separately from the debt, and therefore a market value can be determined. The two methods of allocation available are:

1. The proportional method.

2. The incremental method.

Proportional Method

AT&T's offering of detachable 5-year warrants to buy one share of common stock (par value $5) at $25, at a time when a share was selling for approximately $50, enabled it to price its offering of bonds at par with a moderate 8¾ percent yield. To place a value on the two securities, one would determine (1) the value of the bonds without the warrants and (2) the value of the warrants.

For example, assume that AT&T's bonds (par $1,000) sold for 99 without the warrants soon after they were issued. The market value of the warrants at that time was $30. (Prior to sale the warrants will not have a market value.) The allocation is based on an estimate of market value, generally as established by an investment banker, or on the relative market value of the bonds and the warrants soon after they are issued and traded. The price paid for 10,000, $1,000 bonds with the warrants attached was par, or $10,000,000. The allocation between the bonds and warrants is shown in Illustration 39-1.

---

[4] Later in this discussion it will be shown that the value of the warrant is normally determined on the basis of a relative market value approach because of the difficulty of imputing a warrant value in any other manner.

[5] From the illustration, it is apparent that buying warrants can be an "all or nothing" proposition.

[6] A detachable warrant means that the warrant can sell separately from the bond. *APB Opinion No. 14* makes a distinction between detachable and nondetachable warrants because nondetachable warrants must be sold with the security as a complete package; thus, no allocation is permitted.

ILLUSTRATION 39-1 Proportional Allocation of Proceeds between Bonds and Warrants

Fair market value of bonds (without warrants) ($10,000,000 × .99)		$ 9,900,000
Fair market value of warrants (10,000 × $30)		300,000
Aggregate fair market value		$10,200,000
Allocated to bonds:	$\dfrac{\$9,900,000}{\$10,200,000} \times \$10,000,000 =$	$ 9,705,882
Allocated to warrants:	$\dfrac{\$300,000}{\$10,200,000} \times \$10,000,000 =$	294,118
Total allocation		**$10,000,000**

In this situation the bonds sell at a discount and are recorded as follows.

Cash	9,705,882	
Discount on Bonds Payable	294,118	
Bonds Payable		10,000,000

In addition, the company sells warrants that are credited to paid-in capital. The entry is as follows.

Cash	294,118	
Paid-in Capital—Stock Warrants		294,118

The entries may be combined if desired; they are shown separately here to indicate that the purchaser of the bond is buying not only a bond, but also a possible future claim on common stock.

Assuming that all 10,000 warrants are exercised (one warrant per one share of stock), the following entry would be made.

Cash (10,000 × $25)	250,000	
Paid-in Capital—Stock Warrants	294,118	
Common Stock (10,000 × $5)		50,000
Paid-in Capital in Excess of Par		494,118

What if the warrants are not exercised? In that case, Paid-in Capital—Stock Warrants is debited for $294,118, and Paid-in Capital from Expired Warrants is credited for the same amount. The additional paid-in capital reverts to the existing stockholders.

Incremental Method

In instances where the fair value of either the warrants or the bonds is not determinable, the incremental method used in lump-sum security purchases may be used. That is, the security for which the market value is determinable is used, and the remainder of the purchase price is allocated to the security for which the market value is not known.

For example, assume that the market price of the **AT&T** warrants was known to be $300,000, but the market price of the bonds without the warrants could not be determined. In this case, the amount allocated to the warrants and the stock would be as follows.

ILLUSTRATION 39-2   Incremental Allocation of Proceeds between Bonds and Warrants

Lump-sum receipt	$10,000,000
Allocated to the warrants	300,000
Balance allocated to bonds	**$ 9,700,000**

Conceptual Questions

The question arises whether the allocation of value to the warrants is consistent with the handling accorded convertible debt, in which no value is allocated to the conversion privilege. The FASB has concluded that the features of a convertible security are **inseparable** in the sense that choices are mutually exclusive: the holder either converts or redeems the bonds for cash, but cannot do both. No basis, therefore, exists for recognizing the **conversion value** in the accounts. The FASB, however, indicates that the issuance of bonds with **detachable warrants** involves two securities, one a debt security, which will remain outstanding until maturity, and the other a warrant to purchase common stock. At the time of issuance, separable instruments exist, and therefore separate treatment is justified. **Nondetachable warrants**, however, **do not require an allocation of the proceeds between the bonds and the warrants**. The entire proceeds are recorded as debt.

Many argue that the conversion feature is not significantly different in nature from the call represented by a warrant. The question is whether, although the legal forms are different, sufficient similarities of substance exist to support the same accounting treatment. Some contend that inseparability per se is not a sufficient basis for restricting allocation between identifiable components of a transaction. Examples of allocation between assets of value in a single transaction are not uncommon, such as allocation of values in basket purchases and separation of principal and interest in capitalizing long-term leases. Critics of the current accounting for convertibles say that to deny recognition of value to the conversion feature merely looks to the form of the instrument and does not deal with the substance of the transaction.

The authors disagree with the FASB as well. In both situations (convertible debt and debt issued with warrants), the investor has made a payment to the firm for an equity feature—the right to acquire an equity instrument in the future. The only real distinction between them is that the additional payment made when the equity instrument is formally acquired takes different forms.

INTERNATIONAL INSIGHT
International accounting standards require that the issuer of convertible debt record the liability and equity components separately.

The warrant holder pays additional cash to the issuing firm; the convertible debt holder pays for stock by forgoing the receipt of interest from conversion date until maturity date and by forgoing the receipt of the maturity value itself. Thus, it is argued that the difference is one of method or form of payment only, rather than one of substance. **Until the profession officially reverses its stand in regard to accounting for convertible debt, however, only bonds issued with detachable stock warrants will result in accounting recognition of the equity feature.**[7]

Rights to Subscribe to Additional Shares

If the directors of a corporation decide to issue new shares of stock, the old stockholders generally have the right (preemptive privilege) to purchase newly issued shares in proportion to their holdings. The privilege, referred to as a **stock right**, saves existing stockholders from suffering a dilution of voting rights without their consent. Also, it may allow them to purchase stock somewhat below its market value. The warrants issued in these situations are of short duration, unlike the warrants issued with other securities.

The certificate representing the stock right states the number of shares the holder of the right may purchase, as well as the price at which the new shares may be purchased. Each share owned ordinarily gives the owner one stock right. The price is normally less than the current market value of such shares, which gives the rights a value in themselves. From the time they are issued until they expire, stock rights may be purchased and sold like any other security.

No entry is required when rights are issued to existing stockholders. Only a memorandum entry is needed to indicate the number of rights issued to existing stockholders and to ensure that the company has additional unissued stock registered for issuance in case the rights are exercised. No formal entry is made at this time because no stock has been issued and no cash has been received.

If the rights are exercised, usually a cash payment of some type is involved. If the cash received is equal to the par value, an entry crediting Common Stock at par value is made. If it is in excess of par value, a credit to Paid-in Capital in Excess of Par develops. If it is less than par value, a charge to Paid-in Capital is appropriate.

5 STOCK COMPENSATION PLANS

Another form of warrant arises in stock compensation plans used to pay and motivate employees. This warrant is a **stock option**, which gives selected employees the option to purchase common stock at a given price over an extended period of time. As indicated in the opening story, stock options are very popular. For example, the following chart shows stock options as a percentage of total

---

[7] Recent research indicates that estimates of the debt and equity components of convertible bonds are subject to considerable measurement error. See Mary Barth, Wayne Landsman, and Richard Rendleman, Jr., "Option Pricing–Based Bond Value Estimates and a Fundamental Components Approach to Account for Corporate Debt," *The Accounting Review* (January 1998). The FASB is currently working on a standard that will address the accounting for securities with both debt and equity features, such as convertible bonds. In its exposure draft, the Board requires that the issuer classify separately the liability and equity components of a financial instrument. As a result, it now appears likely that financial instruments such as convertible debt will be divided into liability and equity components for accounting and reporting purposes in the near future.

ILLUSTRATION 39-3   Stock Options as a Portion of Total Compensation

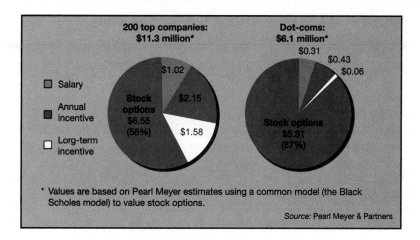

compensation for 1999–2000 given to the top 200 CEOs and to 100 dot-com company CEOs.

These figures show the dramatic change in the way many top executives (and for that matter, regular employees) are compensated.

Effective compensation has been a subject of considerable interest lately. A consensus of opinion is that effective compensation programs are ones that (1) motivate employees to high levels of performance, (2) help retain executives and allow for recruitment of new talent, (3) base compensation on employee and company performance, (4) maximize the employee's after-tax benefit and minimize the employee's after-tax cost, and (5) use performance criteria over which the employee has control. Although straight cash compensation plans (salary and, perhaps, bonus) are an important part of any compensation program, they are oriented to the short run. Many companies recognize that a more long-run compensation plan is often needed in addition to a cash component.

Long-term compensation plans attempt to develop in key employees a strong loyalty toward the company. An effective way to accomplish this goal is to give the employees "a piece of the action"—that is, an equity interest based on changes in long-term measures such as increases in earnings per share, revenues, stock price, or market share. These plans, generally referred to as **stock option plans**, come in many different forms. Essentially, they provide the employee with the opportunity to receive stock or cash in the future if the performance of the company (by whatever measure) is satisfactory.

The Major Reporting Issue

Suppose that you are an employee for Hurdle Inc. and you are granted options to purchase 10,000 shares of the firm's common stock as part of your compensation. The date you receive the options is referred to as the **grant date.** The options are good for 10 years. The market price and the exercise price for the stock are both $20 at the grant date. **What is the value of the compensation you just received?**

Some believe you have not received anything: That is, the difference between the market price and the exercise price is zero, and therefore no compensation results. Others argue these options have value: If the stock price goes above $20 any time over the next 10 years and you exercise these options, substantial compensation results. For example, if at the end of the fourth year, the market price of the stock is $30 and you exercise your options, you will have earned $100,000 [10,000 options × ($30 − $20)], ignoring income taxes.

How should the granting of these options be reported by Hurdle Inc.? In the past, GAAP required that compensation cost be measured by the excess of the market price of the stock over its exercise price at the grant date. This approach is referred to as the **intrinsic value method** because the computation is not dependent on external circumstances: **The compensation cost is the difference between the market price of the stock and the exercise price of the options at the grant date**. Hurdle would therefore not recognize any compensation expense related to your options because at the grant date the market price and exercise price were the same.

The FASB **encourages but does not require recognition of compensation cost for the fair value of stock-based compensation paid to employees for their services**.[8] The FASB position is that the accounting for the cost of employee services should be based on the value of compensation paid, which is presumed to be a measure of the value of the services received. Accordingly, the compensation cost arising from employee stock options should be measured based on the fair value of the stock options granted.[9] To determine this value, acceptable option pricing models are used to value options at the date of grant. This approach is referred to as the **fair value method** because the option value is estimated based on the many factors that determine its underlying value.[10]

The FASB met considerable resistance when it proposed requiring the fair value method for recognizing the costs of stock options in the financial statements. As a result, it was decided that a company **can choose** to use **either** the intrinsic value method **or** the fair value method when accounting for compensation cost on the income statement. However, if a company uses the intrinsic value method to recognize compensation costs for employee stock options, it must provide expanded disclosures on these costs. Specifically, companies that choose the intrinsic value method are required to disclose in a note to the financial statements pro-forma net income and earnings per share (if presented by the company), **as if it had used the fair value method**.

Accounting for Stock Compensation

A company is given a choice in the recognition method for stock compensation. However, **the FASB encourages adoption of the fair value method**. Our discussion in this section illustrates both methods. Stock option plans involve two main accounting issues:

1. How should compensation expense be determined?

2. Over what periods should compensation expense be allocated?

---

[8] "Accounting for Stock-Based Compensation," *Statement of Financial Accounting Standards No. 123* (Norwalk, Conn.: FASB, 1995).

[9] Stock options issued to non-employees in exchange for other goods or services must be recognized according to the fair value method in *SFAS 123*.

[10] These factors include the volatility of the underlying stock, the expected life of the options, the risk-free rate during the option life, and expected dividends during the option life.

Determining Expense

Under the fair value method, total compensation expense is computed based on the fair value of the options expected to vest[11] on the date the options are granted to the employee(s) (i.e., the **grant date**). Fair value for public companies is to be estimated using an option pricing model, with some adjustments for the unique factors of employee stock options. No adjustments are made after the grant date, in response to subsequent changes in the stock price—either up or down.[12]

Under the intrinsic value method, total compensation cost is computed as the excess of the market price of the stock over the option price on the date when both the number of shares to which employees are entitled and the option or purchase price for those shares are known. This date is called the **measurement date**. For many plans, the measurement date is the **grant date**. However, the measurement date may be later for plans with variable terms (either number of shares and/or option price are not known) that depend on events after the date of grant. For such variable plans, compensation expense may have to be estimated on the basis of assumptions as to the final number of shares and the option price (usually at the exercise date).

Allocating Compensation Expense

In general, under both the fair and intrinsic value methods, compensation expense is recognized in the periods in which the employee performs the service—the **service period**. Unless otherwise specified, the service period is the vesting period—the time between the grant date and the vesting date. Thus, total compensation cost is determined at the grant date and allocated to the periods benefited by the employees' services.

Illustration

To illustrate the accounting for a stock option plan, assume that on November 1, 2002, the stockholders of Chen Company approve a plan that grants the company's five executives options to purchase 2,000 shares each of the company's $1 par value common stock. The options are granted on January 1, 2003, and may be exercised at any time within the next 10 years. The option price per share is $60, and the market price of the stock at the date of grant is $70 per share. **Under the intrinsic value method**, the total compensation expense is computed below.

ILLUSTRATION 39-4   Computation of Compensation Expense— Intrinsic Value Method

Market value of 10,000 shares at date of grant ($70 per share)	$700,000
Option price of 10,000 shares at date of grant ($60 per share)	600,000
Total compensation expense (intrinsic value)	$100,000

---

[11] "To vest" means "to earn the rights to." An employee's award becomes vested at the date that the employee's right to receive or retain shares of stock or cash under the award is no longer contingent on remaining in the service of the employer.

[12] Nonpublic companies frequently do not have data with which to estimate the fair-value element. Therefore, nonpublic companies are permitted to use a minimum value method to estimate the value of the options. The minimum value method does not consider the volatility of the stock price when estimating option value.

A LITTLE HONESTY GOES A LONG WAY

You might think investors would punish companies that have decided to expense stock options. After all, most of corporate America has been battling for years to avoid such a fate, worried that accounting for those perks would destroy earnings. And indeed, Merrill Lynch estimates that if all S&P 500 companies were to expense options [in 2002], reported profits would fall 10 percent.

And yet, as a small but growing band of big-name companies makes the switch, investors have for the most part showered them with love. With a few exceptions, the stock prices of the expensers, from **Cinergy** to **Fannie Mae**, have outpaced the market since they announced the change.

The few, the brave

	Estimated 2002 EPS		% change since announcement**
	Without options	**With options expensed***	**Company stock price**
Cinergy	$ 2.80	$ 2.77	22.4%
Washington Post	20.48	20.10	16.4
Computer Associates	−0.46	−0.62	11.1
Fannie Mae	6.15	6.02	6.7
Bank One	2.77	2.61	2.6
General Motors	5.84	5.45	2.6
Procter & Gamble	3.57	3.35	−2.3
Coca-Cola	1.79	1.70	−6.2
General Electric	1.65	1.61	−6.2
Amazon	0.04	−0.99	−11.4

* Assumes options expenses for 2002 are the same as 2001 and that all outstanding grants are counted
** As of 8/6/02.
Data sources: Merrill Lynch; company reports.

Source: David Stires, "A Little Honesty Goes a Long Way," *Fortune* (September 2, 2002), p. 186. Reprinted by permission.

Under the fair value method, total compensation expense is computed by applying an acceptable fair value option pricing model (such as the **Black-Scholes option pricing model**). To keep this illustration simple, we will assume that the fair value option pricing model determines total compensation expense to be $220,000.

Basic Entries. The value of the options under either method is recognized as an expense in the periods in which the employee performs services. In the case of Chen Company, assume that the expected period of benefit is 2 years, starting with the grant date. The journal entries to record the transactions related to this **option contract** using both the intrinsic value and fair value method are shown below.

ILLUSTRATION 39-5   Comparison of Entries for Option Contract
—Intrinsic Value and
Fair Value Methods

Intrinsic Value	Fair Value

At date of grant (January 1, 2003)

No entry	No entry

To record compensation expense for 2003 (December 31, 2003)

Compensation Expense 50,000	Compensation Expense 110,000
Paid-in Capital—Stock Options	Paid-in Capital—Stock Options
($100,000 ÷ 2) 50,000	($220,000 ÷ 2) 110,000

To record compensation expense for 2004 (December 31, 2004)

Compensation Expense 50,000	Compensation Expense 110,000
Paid-in Capital—Stock Options	Paid-in Capital—Stock Options
50,000	110,000

Under both methods, compensation expense is allocated evenly over the 2-year service period. The only difference between the two methods is the amount of compensation recognized.

Exercise. If 20 percent, or 2,000, of the 10,000 options were exercised on June 1, 2006 (3 years and 5 months after date of grant), the following journal entry would be recorded using the **intrinsic value method**.

June 1, 2006

Cash (2,000 × $60)	120,000	
Paid-in Capital—Stock Options (20% × $100,000)	20,000	
Common Stock (2,000 × $1)		2,000
Paid-in Capital in Excess of Par		138,000

Under the **fair value approach**, the entry would be:

June 1, 2006

Cash (2,000 × $60)	120,000	
Paid-in Capital—Stock Options (20% × $220,000)	44,000	
Common Stock (2,000 × $1)		2,000
Paid-in Capital in Excess of Par		162,000

Expiration. If the remaining stock options are not exercised before their expiration date, the balance in the Paid-in Capital—Stock Options account should be transferred to a more properly titled paid-in capital account, such as Paid-in Capital from Expired Stock Options. The entry to record this transaction at the date of expiration would be as follows.

ILLUSTRATION 39-6   Comparison of Entries for Stock Option Expiration—Intrinsic Value and Fair Value Methods

Intrinsic Value		Fair Value	
January 1, 2013 (expiration date)			
Paid-in Capital—Stock Options	80,000	Paid-in Capital—Stock Options	176,000
Paid-in Capital from Expired Stock Options (80% × $100,000)	80,000	Paid-in Capital from Expired Stock Options (80% × $220,000)	176,000

Adjustment. The fact that a stock option is not exercised does not nullify the propriety of recording the costs of services received from executives and attributable to the stock option plan. Under GAAP, compensation expense is, therefore, not adjusted upon expiration of the options.

However, if a stock option is forfeited because **an employee fails to satisfy a service requirement** (e.g., leaves employment), the estimate of compensation expense recorded in the current period should be adjusted (as a change in estimate). This change in estimate would be recorded by debiting Paid-in Capital—Stock Options and crediting Compensation Expense, thereby decreasing compensation expense in the period of forfeiture.

Types of Plans

Many different types of plans are used to compensate key employees. In all these plans the amount of the reward depends upon future events. Consequently, continued employment is a necessary element in almost all types of plans. The popularity of a given plan usually depends on the firm's prospects in the stock market and on tax considerations. For example, if it appears that appreciation will occur in a company's stock, a plan that offers the option to purchase stock is attractive. Conversely, if it appears that price appreciation is unlikely, then compensation might be tied to some performance measure such as an increase in book value or earnings per share.

Three common compensation plans that illustrate different objectives are:

1. Stock option plans (incentive or nonqualified).
2. Stock appreciation rights plans.
3. Performance-type plans.

Most plans follow the general guidelines for reporting established in the previous sections.

Noncompensatory Plans

In some companies, stock purchase plans permit all employees to purchase stock at a discounted price for a short period of time. These plans are usually classified as noncompensatory. Noncompensatory means that the primary purpose of the plan is not to compensate the employees but, rather, to enable the employer to secure equity capital or to induce widespread ownership of an enterprise's common stock among employees. Thus, compensation expense is not reported for these plans. **Noncompensatory plans** have three characteristics:

1. Substantially all full-time employees may participate on an equitable basis.
2. The discount from market price is small. That is, it does not exceed the greater of a per share discount reasonably offered to stockholders or the per share amount of costs avoided by not having to raise cash in a public offering.
3. The plan offers no substantive option feature.

For example, Masthead Company had a stock purchase plan under which employees who meet minimal employment qualifications are entitled to purchase Masthead stock at a 5 percent reduction from market price for a short period of time. The reduction from market price is not considered compensatory because the per share amount of the costs avoided by not having to raise the cash in a public offering is equal to 5 percent. **Plans that do not possess all of the above mentioned three characteristics are classified as compensatory.**

Disclosure of Compensation Plans

To comply with *SFAS No. 123,* companies offering stock-based compensation plans must determine the fair value of the options. Companies must then decide whether to use the fair value method and recognize expense in the income statement, or to use the intrinsic value approach and disclose in the notes the pro forma impact on net income and earnings per share (if presented), as if the fair value method had been used.

Regardless of whether the intrinsic value or fair value method is used, full disclosure should be made about the status of these plans at the end of the periods presented, including the number of shares under option, options exercised and forfeited, the weighted average option prices for these categories, the weighted average fair value of options granted during the year, and the average remaining contractual life of the options outstanding.[13] In addition to information about the status of the stock option plans, companies must also

---

[13] These data should be reported separately for each different type of plan offered to employees.

ILLUSTRATION 39-7   Disclosure of Pro Forma Effect of Stock Option Plans

Gateway, Inc.

Had compensation expense for employee and director stock options been determined based on the fair value of the options on the date of grant, net income (loss) and net income (loss) per share would have resulted in the pro forma amounts indicated below (in thousands, except per share amounts):

	2001	2000	1999
Net income (loss)—as reported	$(1,033,915)	$241,483	$427,944
Net income (loss)—pro forma	(1,106,376)	(53,675)	319,494
Net income (loss) per share—as reported			
Basic	$ (3.20)	$ 0.75	$ 1.36
Diluted	$ (3.20)	$ 0.73	$ 1.32
Net income (loss) per share—pro forma			
Basic	$ (3.42)	$ (0.17)	$ 1.02
Diluted	$ (3.42)	$ (0.17)	$ 0.98

The pro forma effect on net income (loss) for 2001, 2000, and 1999 is not fully representative of the pro forma effect on net income (loss) in future years because it does not take into consideration pro forma compensation expense related to the vesting of grants made prior to 1997.

disclose the method and significant assumptions used to estimate the fair values of the stock options.

If the intrinsic value method is used in the financial statements, companies must still disclose the pro forma net income and pro forma earnings per share (if presented), as if the fair value method had been used to account for the stock-based compensation cost. Illustration 39-7 illustrates this disclosure, as provided by **Gateway, Inc**.

Debate over Stock Option Accounting

In general, use of the fair value approach results in greater compensation costs relative to the intrinsic value model. As indicated in the story on page 273, a study of the companies in the Standard & Poor's 500 stock index documented that, on average, earnings in 2002 could be overstated by 10 percent through the use of the intrinsic value method. Until recently, only two major companies, **Boeing Co**. and **Winn-Dixie Stores**, used the fair value method in recording compensation expense. However, a number of companies, such as **Coca-Cola, General Electric**, **Wachovia, Bank One**, and **The Washington Post**, have decided to use the fair value method. As the CFO of Coke stated, "There is no doubt that stock options are compensation. If they weren't, none of us would want them."

Even given the exemplary behavior of certain companies, many in corporate America are fighting hard not to use the fair value method. Many small high-technology companies are particularly vocal in their opposition, arguing that only through offering stock options can they attract top professional management. They contend that if they are forced to recognize large amounts of compensation expense under these plans, they will be at a competitive disadvantage with larger companies that can withstand higher compensation charges. As one high-tech executive stated, "If your goal is to attack fat-cat executive compensation in multi-billion dollar firms, then please do so! But not at the expense of the people who are 'running lean and mean,' trying to build businesses and creating jobs in the process."

UNDERLYING CONCEPTS
The stock option controversy involves economic consequence issues. The FASB believes the neutrality concept should be followed. Others disagree, noting that factors other than accounting theory should be considered.

The stock option saga is a classic example of the difficulty the FASB faces in issuing an accounting standard. Many powerful interests aligned against the Board; even some who initially appeared to support the Board's actions later reversed themselves. The whole incident is troubling because the debate for the most part is not about the **proper accounting** but more about the **economic consequences** of the standards. If we continue to write standards so that some social, economic, or public policy goal is achieved, financial reporting will lose its credibility.

We are hopeful that many companies will decide to follow the **Coca-Cola** and **General Electric** examples and use the fair value method to record option expense. The fiction that options are free has led to abuse at many companies. Providing a faithful representation of the cost of these options on the income statement will lead to a better understanding of a company's financial performance.[14]

OPTIONAL SEGMENT

ENDS

COMPUTING EARNINGS PER SHARE

6

International Insight
In many nations (e.g., Switzerland, Sweden, Spain, and Mexico) there is no legal requirement to disclose earnings per share.

Earnings per share data are frequently reported in the financial press and are widely used by stockholders and potential investors in evaluating the profitability of a company. **Earnings per share (EPS)** indicates the income earned by each share of common stock. Thus, **earnings per share is reported only for common stock.** For example, if Oscar Co. has net income of $300,000 and a weighted average of 100,000 shares of common stock outstanding for the year, earnings per share is $3 ($300,000 ‖ 100,000).

Because of the importance of earnings per share information, most companies are required to report this information on the face of the income statement.[15] The exception is nonpublic companies: because of cost-benefit considerations they do not have to report this information.[16] Generally, earnings per share information is reported below net income in the income statement. For Oscar Co. the presentation would be as given in Illustration 39-8.

ILLUSTRATION 39-8 Income Statement Presentation of EPS

Net income	$300,000
Earnings per share	$ 3.00

---

[14] Recently, the FASB has indicated that companies that voluntarily switch to the fair value method will be provided one of three transition methods for initial adoption. In addition, the Board has tentatively concluded that all companies will have to disclose the following in their accounting policy note to the financial statements: (1) the method of accounting for stock options, (2) total stock compensation cost recognized in the income statement, (3) total stock compensation that would have been recorded had *FASB 123* been adopted as of its effective date, and (4) pro forma net income and earnings per share that would have been reported had *FASB 123* been adopted as of its effective date.

[15] "Earnings per Share," *Statement of Financial Accounting Standards No. 128* (Norwalk, Conn.: FASB, 1997). For an article on the usefulness of EPS reported data and the application of the qualitative characteristics of accounting information to EPS data, see Lola W. Dudley. "A Critical Look at EPS." *Journal of Accountancy* (August 1985), pp. 102–11.

[16] A nonpublic enterprise is an enterprise (1) whose debt or equity securities are not traded in a public market on a foreign or domestic stock exchange or in the over-the-counter market (including securities quoted locally or regionally) or (2) that is not required to file financial statements with the SEC. An enterprise is no longer considered a nonpublic enterprise when its financial statements are issued in preparation for the sale of any class of securities in a public market.

When the income statement contains intermediate components of income earnings per share should be disclosed for each component. Illustration 39-9 shows the income statement presentation of EPS components.

ILLUSTRATION 39-9   Income Statement Presentation of EPS Components

Earnings per share:

Income from continuing operations	$4.00
Loss from discontinued operations, net of tax	0.60
Income before extraordinary item and cumulative effect of change in accounting principle	3.40
Extraordinary gain, net of tax	1.00
Cumulative effect of change in accounting principle, net of tax	0.50
Net income	$4.90

These disclosures enable the user of the financial statements to recognize the effects of income from continuing operations on EPS, as distinguished from income or loss from irregular items.[17]

7   EARNINGS PER SHARE— SIMPLE CAPITAL STRUCTURE

A corporation's capital structure is considered **simple** if it consists only of common stock or includes no **potential common stock** that upon conversion or exercise could dilute earnings per common share. (A capital structure is considered **complex** if it includes securities that could have a dilutive effect on earnings per common share.) The computation of earnings per share for a simple capital structure involves two items (other than net income)—preferred stock dividends and weighted average number of shares outstanding.

Preferred Stock Dividends

As indicated earlier, earnings per share relates to earnings per common share. When a company has both common and preferred stock outstanding, **the current-year preferred stock dividend is subtracted from net income to arrive at income available to common stockholders**. The formula for computing earnings per share is given in Illustration 39-10.

ILLUSTRATION 39-10   Formula for Computing Earnings per Share

$$\text{Earnings per Share} = \frac{\text{Net Income} - \text{Preferred Dividends}}{\text{Weighted Average Number of Shares Outstanding}}$$

---

[17] Per share amounts for discontinued operations, an extraordinary item, or the cumulative effect of an accounting change in a period should be presented either on the face of the income statement or in the notes to the financial statements.

In reporting earnings per share information, dividends on preferred stock should be subtracted from each of the intermediate components of income (income from continuing operations and income before extraordinary items) and finally from net income to arrive at income available to common stockholders. If dividends on preferred stock are declared and a net loss occurs, **the preferred dividend is added to the loss** in order to compute the loss per share. If the preferred stock is cumulative and the dividend is not declared in the current year, **an amount equal to the dividend that should have been declared for the current year only** should be subtracted from net income or added to the net loss. Dividends in arrears for previous years should have been included in the previous years' computations.

Weighted Average Number of Shares Outstanding

In all computations of earnings per share, the **weighted average number of shares outstanding** during the period constitutes the basis for the per share amounts reported. Shares issued or purchased during the period affect the amount outstanding and must be **weighted by the fraction of the period they are outstanding.** The rationale for this approach is to find the equivalent number of **whole shares** outstanding for the year.

To illustrate, assume that Stallone Inc. has the following changes in its common stock shares outstanding for the period (Illustration 39-11).

ILLUSTRATION 39-11   Shares Outstanding, Ending Balance Stallone Inc.

Date	Share Changes	Shares Outstanding
January 1	Beginning balance	90,000
April 1	Issued 30,000 shares for cash	30,000
		120,000
July 1	Purchased 39,000 shares	39,000
		81,000
November 1	Issued 60,000 shares for cash	60,000
December 31	Ending balance	141,000

To compute the weighted average number of shares outstanding, the following computation is made (Illustration 39-12).

ILLUSTRATION 39-12   Weighted Average Number of Shares Outstanding

Dates Outstanding	(A) Shares Outstanding	(B) Fraction of Year	(C) Weighted Shares (A × B)
Jan. 1–Apr. 1	90,000	3/12	22,500
Apr. 1–July 1	120,000	3/12	30,000
July 1–Nov. 1	81,000	4/12	27,000
Nov. 1–Dec. 31	141,000	2/12	23,500
Weighted average number of shares outstanding			103,000

International Insight
Where EPS disclosure is prevalent, it is usually based on the weighted average of shares outstanding.

As illustrated, 90,000 shares were outstanding for 3 months, which translates to 22,500 whole shares for the entire year. Because additional shares were issued on April 1, the shares outstanding change, and these shares must be weighted for the time outstanding. When 39,000 shares were purchased on July 1, the shares outstanding were reduced, and again a new computation must be made to determine the proper weighted shares outstanding.

Stock Dividends and Stock Splits

When **stock dividends** or **stock splits** occur, computation of the weighted average number of shares requires restatement of the shares outstanding before the stock dividend or split. For example, assume that a corporation had 100,000 shares outstanding on January 1 and issued a 25 percent stock dividend on June 30. For purposes of computing a weighted average for the current year, the additional 25,000 shares outstanding as a result of the stock dividend are assumed to have been **oustanding since the beginning of the year.** Thus the weighted average for the year would be 125,000 shares.

The issuance of a stock dividend or stock split is restated, but the issuance or repurchase of stock for cash is not. Why? The reason is that stock splits and stock dividends do not increase or decrease the net assets of the enterprise; only additional shares of stock are issued, and therefore the weighted average shares must be restated. By restating, valid comparisons of earnings per share can be made between periods before and after the stock split or stock dividend. Conversely, the issuance or purchase of stock for cash changes the amount of net assets. As a result, the company either earns more or less in the future as a result of this change in net assets. Stated another way, **a stock dividend or split does not change the shareholders' total investment**—it only increases (unless it is a reverse stock split) the number of common shares representing this investment.

To illustrate how a stock dividend affects the computation of the weighted average number of shares outstanding, assume that Rambo Company has the following changes in its common stock shares during the year (Illustration 39-13).

**ILLUSTRATION 39-13   Shares Outstanding, Ending Balance
Rambo Company**

Date	Share Changes	Shares Outstanding
January 1	Beginning balance	100,000
March 1	Issued 20,000 shares for cash	20,000
		120,000
June 1	60,000 additional shares (50% stock dividend)	60,000
		180,000
November 1	Issued 30,000 shares for cash	30,000
December 31	Ending balance	210,000

The computation of the weighted average number of shares outstanding would be as follows (Illustration 39-14).

**ILLUSTRATION 39-14   Weighted Average Number of Shares
Outstanding—Stock Issue and Stock Dividend**

Dates Outstanding	(A) Shares Outstanding	(B) Restatement	(C) Fraction of Year	(D) Weighted Shares (A × B × C)
Jan. 1–Mar. 1	100,000	1.50	2/12	25,000
Mar. 1–June 1	120,000	1.50	3/12	45,000
June 1–Nov. 1	180,000		5/12	75,000
Nov. 1–Dec. 31	210,000		2/12	35,000
Weighted average number of shares outstanding				180,000

The shares outstanding prior to the stock dividend must be restated. The shares outstanding from January 1 to June 1 are adjusted for the stock dividend, so that these shares are stated on the same basis as shares issued subsequent to the stock dividend. Shares issued after the stock dividend do not have to be restated because they are on the new basis. The stock dividend simply restates existing shares. **The same type of treatment applies to a stock split.**

If a stock dividend or stock split occurs after the end of the year, but before the financial statements are issued, the weighted average number of shares outstanding for the year (and for any other years presented in comparative form) must be restated. For example, assume that Hendricks Company computes its weighted average number of shares to be 100,000 for the year ended December 31, 2004. On January 15, 2005, before the financial statements are issued, the company splits its stock 3 for 1. In this case, the weighted average number of shares used in computing earnings per share for 2004 would be 300,000 shares. If earnings per share information for 2003 is provided as comparative information, it also must be adjusted for the stock split.

Comprehensive Illustration

Sylvester Corporation has income before extraordinary item of $580,000 and an extraordinary gain, net of tax, of $240,000. In addition, it has declared preferred dividends of $1 per share on 100,000 shares of preferred stock outstanding. Sylvester Corporation also has the following changes in its common stock shares outstanding during 2004 (Illustration 39-15).

ILLUSTRATION 39-15　Shares Outstanding, Ending Balance Sylvester Corp.

Dates	Share Changes	Shares Outstanding
January 1	Beginning balance	180,000
May 1	Purchased 30,000 treasury shares	30,000
		150,000
July 1	300,000 additional shares (3-for-1 **stock split**)	300,000
		450,000
December 31	Issued 50,000 shares for cash	50,000
December 31	Ending balance	500,000

To compute the earnings per share information, the weighted average number of shares outstanding is determined in Illustration 39-16.

ILLUSTRATION 39-16　Weighted Average Number of Shares Outstanding

Dates Outstanding	(A) Shares Outstanding	(B) Restatement	(C) Fraction of Year	(D) Weighted Shares (A × B × C)
Jan. 1–May 1	180,000	3	4/12	180,000
May 1–Dec. 31	150,000	3	8/12	300,000
Weighted average number of shares outstanding				480,000

In computing the weighted average number of shares, the shares sold on December 31, 2004, are ignored because they have not been outstanding during the year. The weighted average number of shares is then divided into income before extraordinary item and net income to determine earnings per share (Illustration 36-10). Sylvester Corporation's preferred dividends of $100,000 are subtracted from income before extraordinary item ($580,000) to arrive at income before extraordinary item available to common stockholders of $480,000 ($580,000 − $100,000).

Deducting the preferred dividends from the income before extraordinary item has the effect of also reducing net income without affecting the amount of the extraordinary item. The final amount is referred to as **income available to common stockholders**.

ILLUSTRATION 39-17   Computation of Income Available to Common Stockholders

	(A) Income Information	(B) Weighted Shares	(C) Earnings per Share (A ÷ B)
Income before extraordinary item available to common stockholders	$480,000*	480,000	$1.00
Extraordinary gain (net of tax)	240,000	480,000	0.50
Income available to common stockholders	$ 720,000	480,000	$1.50

*$580,000 – $100,000

Disclosure of the per share amount for the extraordinary item (net of tax) must be reported either on the face of the income statement or in the notes to the financial statements. Income and per share information reported on the face of the income statement is given in Illustration 39-18.

ILLUSTRATION 39-18   Earnings per Share, with Extraordinary Item

Income before extraordinary item	$580,000
Extraordinary gain, net of tax	240,000
Net income	$820,000
Earnings per share:	
Income before extraordinary item	$1.00
Extraordinary item, net of tax	0.50
Net income	$1.50

EARNINGS PER SHARE—COMPLEX CAPITAL STRUCTURE

8

One problem with a **basic EPS** computation is that it fails to recognize the potentially dilutive impact on outstanding stock when a corporation has dilutive securities in its capital structure. **Dilutive securities** are securities that can be converted to common stock and that upon conversion or exercise reduce—dilute—earnings per share. Dilutive securities present a serious problem because conversion or exercise often has an adverse effect on earnings per share. This adverse effect can be significant and, more important, unexpected, unless financial statements call attention to the potential dilutive effect in some manner.[18]

A complex capital structure exists when a corporation has convertible securities, options, warrants or other rights that upon conversion or exercise could dilute earnings per share. Therefore when a company has a complex

---

[18] Issuance of these types of securities is typical in mergers and compensation plans.

International Insight
The provisions in U.S. GAAP are substantially the same as those in International Accounting Standard No. 33, *Earnings per Share,* issued by the IASB.

capital structure, both a basic and diluted earnings per share are generally reported.

The computation of **diluted EPS** is similar to the computation of basic EPS. The difference is that diluted EPS includes the effect of all dilutive potential common shares that were outstanding during the period. The formula in Illustration 39-19 shows the relationship between basic EPS and diluted EPS.

Note that companies with complex capital structures will not report diluted EPS if the securities in their capital structure are antidilutive. **Antidilutive securities** are securities that upon conversion or exercise increase earnings per share (or reduce the loss per share). The purpose of the dual presentation is to inform financial statement users of situations that will likely occur and to provide "worst case" dilutive situations. If the securities are antidilutive, the likelihood of conversion or exercise is considered remote. Thus, companies that have only antidilutive securities are not permitted to increase earnings per share and are required to report only the basic EPS number.

The computation of basic EPS was illustrated in the prior section. The discussion in the following sections addresses the effects of convertible and other dilutive securities on EPS calculations.

ILLUSTRATION 39-19   Relation between Basic and Diluted EPS

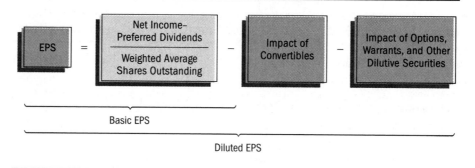

Diluted EPS—Convertible Securities

At conversion, convertible securities are exchanged for common stock. The method used to measure the dilutive effects of potential conversion on EPS is called the **if-converted method**. The if-converted method for a convertible bond assumes the following: (1) the conversion of the convertible securities at the beginning of the period (or at the time of issuance of the security, if issued during the period), and (2) the elimination of related interest, net of tax. Thus the **denominator**—the weighted average number of shares outstanding—is increased by the additional shares assumed issued. The **numerator**—net income—is increased by the amount of interest expense, net of tax associated with those convertible securities.

Comprehensive Illustration—If-Converted Method

As an example, Marshy Field Corporation has net income for the year of $210,000 and a weighted average number of common shares outstanding during the period of 100,000 shares. The **basic earnings per share** is, therefore, $2.10 ($210,000 ÷ 100,000). The company has two convertible debenture bond issues outstanding. One is a 6 percent issue sold at 100 (total $1,000,000) in a prior year and convertible into 20,000 common shares. The other is a 10 percent issue

WHAT DO THE NUMBERS MEAN?

The Source of My Dilution

What is the source of dilutive securities, which give rise to complex capital structures? Merger activity is a major source.

Typical mergers in the 1990s were combinations of information, entertainment, or financial (banking) companies. For example, **Bell Atlantic Corp.** and **Nynex Corp.** combined in a $22.7 billion deal, **Time** acquired **Warner Communications** for $10.1 billion, and **Walt Disney Co.** purchased **Capital Cities/ABC, Inc.** Even larger were the mergers of **Nations Bank** and **BankAmerica** ($62 billion), and **Bell Atlantic** and **GTE** ($71 billion) in 1998.

One consequence of heavy merger activity is an increase in the use of securities such as convertible bonds, convertible preferred stocks, stock warrants, and contin-gent shares to structure these deals. Although not common stock in form, these securities enable their holders to obtain common stock upon exercise or conversion.

Although merger and acquisition activity has declined in the recent bear market, the presence of dilutive securities on corporate balance sheets is still very prevalent. As discussed in the prior section, the use of stock option plans, which also are dilutive in nature, is increasing. In addition, companies that have difficulty selling common stock at a reasonable price often use some form of convertible preferred or bond to help finance their operations.

Source: Farrell Kramer, "Mergers Have Been in Fashion in 1996, With Seven Big Ones," *St. Louis Post-Dispatch* (December 16, 1996), p. A7; and Geoffrey Colvin, "The Year of the Mega Merger," *Fortune* (January 11, 1999), p. 62.

sold at 100 (total $1,000,000) on April 1 of the current year and convertible into 32,000 common shares. The tax rate is 40 percent.

As shown in Illustration 39-20, to determine the numerator, we add back the interest on the if-converted securities, less the related tax effect. Because the if-converted method assumes conversion as of the beginning of the year, no interest on the convertibles is assumed to be paid during the year. The interest on the 6 percent convertibles is $60,000 for the year ($1,000,000 $\times$ 6%). The increased tax expense is $24,000 ($60,000 $\times$ .40), and the interest added back net of taxes is **$36,000** [$60,000 $-$ $24,000 or simply $60,000 $\times$ (1 $-$ .40)].

Because 10 percent convertibles are issued subsequent to the beginning of the year, the shares assumed to have been issued on that date, April 1, are weighted as outstanding from April 1 to the end of the year. In addition, the interest adjustment to the numerator for these bonds would reflect the interest for only 9 months. Thus the interest added back on the 10 percent convertible would be **$45,000** [$1,000,000 $\times$ 10% $\times$ 9/12 year $\times$ (1 $-$ .40)]. The computation of earnings (the numerator) for diluted earnings per share is shown in Illustration 39-20.

Illustration 39-20   Computation of Adjusted Net Income

Net income for the year	$210,000
Add: Adjustment for interest (net of tax)	
6% debentures ($60,000 $\times$ [1 $-$ .40])	36,000
10% debentures ($100,000 $\times$ 9/12 $\times$ [1 $-$ .40])	45,000
Adjusted net income	$291,000

The computation for shares adjusted for dilutive securities (the denominator) for diluted earnings per share is shown in Illustration 39-21.

Illustration 39-21   Computation of Weighted Average Number of Shares

Weighted average number of shares outstanding	100,000
Add: Shares assumed to be issued:	
6% debentures (as of beginning of year)	20,000
10% debentures (as of date of issue, April 1; 9/12 × 32,000)	24,000
Weighted average number of shares adjusted for dilutive securities	144,000

Marshy Field would then report earnings per share based on a dual presentation on the face of the income statement; basic and diluted earnings per share are reported.[19] The presentation is shown in Illustration 39-22.

ILLUSTRATION 39-22   Earnings per Share Disclosure

Net income for the year	$210,000
Earnings per Share (Note X)	
Basic earnings per share ($210,000 ÷ 100,000)	$2.10
Diluted earnings per share ($291,000 ÷ 144,000)	$2.02

Other Factors

The example above assumed that Marshy Field's bonds were sold at the face amount. If the bonds are sold at a premium or discount, interest expense must be adjusted each period to account for this occurrence. Therefore, the amount of interest expense added back, net of tax, to net income is the interest expense reported on the income statement, not the interest paid in cash during the period.

In addition, the conversion rate on a dilutive security may change over the period during which the dilutive security is outstanding. In this situation, for the diluted EPS computation, the **most advantageous conversion rate available to the holder is used**. For example, assume that a convertible bond was issued January 1, 2003, with a conversion rate of 10 common shares for each bond starting January 1, 2005. Beginning January 1, 2008, the conversion rate is 12 common shares for each bond, and beginning January 1, 2012, it is 15 common shares for each bond. In computing diluted EPS in 2003, the conversion rate of 15 shares to one bond is used.

Finally, if the 6 percent convertible debentures were instead 6 percent convertible preferred stock, the convertible preferred would be considered potential common shares and included in shares outstanding in diluted EPS calculations. Preferred dividends are not subtracted from net income in computing the numerator. Why not? Because it is assumed that the convertible preferreds are converted and are outstanding as common stock for purposes of computing EPS. Net income is used as the numerator—**no tax effect** is computed because preferred dividends generally are not deductible for tax purposes.

---

[19] Conversion of bonds is dilutive because EPS with conversion ($2.02) is less than basic EPS ($2.10).

Diluted EPS—Options and Warrants

Stock options and warrants outstanding (whether or not presently exercisable) are included in diluted earnings per share unless they are antidilutive. Options and warrants and their equivalents are included in earnings per share computations through the **treasury stock method.**

The treasury stock method assumes that the options or warrants are exercised at the beginning of the year (or date of issue if later) and that the proceeds from the exercise of options and warrants are used to purchase common stock for the treasury. If the exercise price is lower than the market price of the stock, then the proceeds from exercise are not sufficient to buy back all the shares. The incremental shares remaining are added to the weighted average number of shares outstanding for purposes of computing diluted earnings per share.

For example, if the exercise price of a warrant is $5 and the fair market value of the stock is $15, the treasury stock method would increase the shares outstanding. Exercise of the warrant would result in one additional share outstanding, but the $5 received for the one share issued is not sufficient to purchase one share in the market at $15. Three warrants would have to be exercised (and three additional shares issued) to produce enough money ($15) to acquire one share in the market. Thus, a net increase of two shares outstanding would result.

To see this computation using larger numbers, assume 1,500 options outstanding at an exercise price of $30 for a common share and a common stock market price per share of $50. Through application of the treasury stock method there would be 600 **incremental shares** outstanding, computed in Illustration 39-23.[20]

ILLUSTRATION 39-23   Computation of Incremental Shares

Proceeds from exercise of 1,500 options (1,500 × $30)	$45,000
Shares issued upon exercise of options	1,500
Treasury shares purchasable with proceeds ($45,000 ÷ $50)	900
Incremental shares outstanding (potential common shares)	600

Thus, if the exercise price of the option or warrant is **lower than** the market price of the stock, dilution occurs. If the exercise price of the option or warrant is **higher than** the market price of the stock, common shares are reduced. In this case, the options or warrants are **antidilutive** because their assumed exercise leads to an increase in earnings per share.

For both options and warrants, exercise is not assumed unless the average market price of the stock is above the exercise price during the period being reported.[21] As a practical matter, a simple average of the weekly or monthly prices is adequate, so long as the prices do not fluctuate significantly.

---

[20] The incremental number of shares may be more simply computed:

$$\frac{\text{Market price} - \text{Option price}}{\text{Market price}} \times \text{Number of options} = \text{Number of shares}$$

$$\frac{\$50 - \$30}{\$50} \times 1,500 \text{ options} = 600 \text{ shares}$$

[21] Options and warrants have essentially the same assumptions and computational problems, although the warrants may allow or require the tendering of some other security such as debt, in lieu of cash upon exercise. In such situations, the accounting becomes quite complex. *SFAS No. 128* explains the proper disposition in this situation.

Comprehensive Illustration—Treasury Stock Method

To illustrate application of the treasury stock method, assume that Kubitz Industries, Inc. has net income for the period of $220,000. The average number of shares outstanding for the period was 100,000 shares. Hence, basic EPS—ignoring all dilutive securities—is $2.20. The average number of shares under outstanding options (although not exercisable at this time), at an option price of $20 per share, is 5,000 shares. The average market price of the common stock during the year was $28. The computation is shown in Illustration 39-24.

ILLUSTRATION 39-24   Computation of Earnings per Share—Treasury Stock Method

	Basic Earnings per Share	Diluted Earnings per Share
Average number of shares under option outstanding:		5,000
Option price per share		× $20
Proceeds upon exercise of options		$100,000
Average market price of common stock		$28
Treasury shares that could be repurchased with proceeds ($100,000 ÷ $28)		3,571
Excess of shares under option over the treasury shares that could be repurchased (5,000 − 3,571)—potential common incremental shares		1,429
Average number of common shares outstanding	100,000	100,000
Total average number of common shares outstanding and potential common shares	100,000 (A)	101,429 (C)
Net income for the year	$220,000 (B)	$220,000 (D)
Earnings per share	$2.20 (B ÷ A)	$2.17 (D ÷ C)

Contingent Issue Agreement

In business combinations, the acquirer may promise to issue additional shares—referred to as **contingent shares**—if certain conditions are met. If these shares are issuable upon the **mere passage of time or upon the attainment of a certain earnings or market price level, and this level is met at the end of the year,** the contingent shares should be considered as outstanding for the computation of diluted earnings per share.[22]

For example, assume that Walz Corporation purchased Cardella Company and agreed to give Cardella's stockholders 20,000 additional shares in 2007 if Cardella's net income in 2006 is $90,000. In 2005 Cardella Company's net income is $100,000. Because the 2006 stipulated earnings of $90,000 are already

---

[22]In addition to contingent issuances of stock, other types of situations that might lead to dilution are the issuance of participating securities and two-class common shares. The reporting of these types of securities in EPS computations is beyond the scope of this textbook.

being attained, diluted earnings per share of Walz for 2005 would include the 20,000 contingent shares in the shares outstanding computation.

Antidilution Revisited

In computing diluted EPS, the aggregate of all dilutive securities must be considered. But first we must determine which potentially dilutive securities are in fact individually dilutive and which are antidilutive. **Any security that is antidilutive should be excluded** and cannot be used to offset dilutive securities.

Recall that antidilutive securities are securities whose inclusion in earnings per share computations would increase earnings per share (or reduce net loss per share). Convertible debt is antidilutive if the addition to income of the interest (net of tax) causes a greater percentage increase in income (numerator) than conversion of the bonds causes a percentage increase in common and potentially dilutive shares (denominator). In other words, convertible debt is antidilutive if conversion of the security causes common stock earnings to increase by a greater amount per additional common share than earnings per share was before the conversion.

To illustrate, assume that Kohl Corporation has a 6 percent, $1,000,000 debt issue that is convertible into 10,000 common shares. Net income for the year is $210,000, the weighted average number of common shares outstanding is 100,000 shares, and the tax rate is 40 percent. In this case, assumed conversion of the debt into common stock at the beginning of the year requires the following adjustments of net income and the weighted average number of shares outstanding (Illustration 39-25).

ILLUSTRATION 39-25   Test for Antidilution

Net income for the year	$210,000	Average number of shares outstanding	100,000
Add: Adjustment for interest (net of tax) on 6% debentures $60,000 × (1 − .40)	36,000	Add: Shares issued upon assumed conversion of debt	10,000
Adjusted net income	$246,000	Average number of common and potential common shares	110,000

Basic EPS = $210,000 ÷ 100,000 = $2.10

Diluted EPS = $246,000 ÷ 110,000 = $2.24 = **Antidilutive**

As a shortcut, the convertible debt also can be identified as antidilutive by comparing the EPS resulting from conversion, $3.60 ($36,000 additional earnings ÷ 10,000 additional shares), with EPS before inclusion of the convertible debt, $2.10.

With options or warrants, whenever the exercise price is higher than the market price, the security is antidilutive. **Antidilutive securities should be ignored in all calculations and should not be considered in computing diluted earnings per share.** This approach is reasonable because the profession's intent was to inform the investor of the **possible dilution** that might occur in reported earnings per share. The intent was not to highlight securities that, if converted or exercised, would result in an increase in earnings per share. The appendix to

WHAT DO THE NUMBERS MEAN?

Pro Forma EPS Confusion

Many companies are reporting pro forma EPS numbers along with U.S. GAAP-based EPS numbers in the financial information provided to investors. Pro forma earnings generally exceed GAAP earnings because the pro forma numbers exclude such items as restructuring charges, impairments of assets, R&D expenditures, and stock compensation expense. See some examples that follow.

The SEC has expressed concern that pro forma earnings may be misleading. For example, **Trump Hotels & Casino Resorts Inc.** (DJT) was cited for abuses related to its 1999 third-quarter pro forma EPS release. The SEC noted that the firm misrepresented its operating results by excluding a material, one-time $81.4 million charge in its pro forma EPS statement and including an undisclosed nonrecurring gain of $17.2 million. The gain enabled DJT

to post a profit in the quarter. The SEC emphasized that DJT's pro forma EPS statement deviated from conservative U.S. GAAP reporting. Therefore, it was "fraudulent" because it created a "false and misleading impression" that DJT had actually (1) recorded a profit in the third quarter of 1999 and (2) exceeded consensus earnings expectations by enhancing its operating fundamentals.

The Sarbanes-Oxley Act of 2002 requires the SEC to develop regulations on pro forma reporting. As a consequence, the SEC now requires companies that provide pro forma financial information to make sure that the information is not misleading. In addition, a reconciliation between pro forma and GAAP information is required.

Sources: SEC Accounting and Enforcement Release No. 1499 (January 16, 2002); "SEC Proposes Rules to Implement Sarbanes-Oxley Act Reforms," SEC Press Release 2002-155 (October 30, 2002).

Company	U.S. GAAP EPS	Pro Forma EPS
Adaptec, Inc.	$(0.62)	$ 0.05
Corning Inc.	(0.24)	0.09
General Motors Corp.	(0.41)	0.85
Honeywell International Inc.	(0.38)	0.44
International Paper Co.	(0.57)	0.14
QUALCOMM Inc.	(0.06)	0.20
Broadcom Corp.	(6.36)	(0.13)
Lucent Technologies Inc.	(2.16)	(0.27)

Source: Company press releases.

this reading provides an extended example of how antidilution is considered in a complex situation wth multiple securities.

EPS Presentation and Disclosure

If a company's capital structure is complex, the EPS presentation would be as given in Illustration 39-26.

ILLUSTRATION 39-26   EPS Presentation—Complex Capital Structure

Earnings per common share	
Basic earnings per share	$3.30
Diluted earnings per share	$2.70

When the earnings of a period include irregular items, per share amounts (where applicable) should be shown for income from continuing operations, income before extraordinary items, income before accounting change, and net income. Companies that report a discontinued operation, an extraordinary item, or the cumulative effect of an accounting change should present per share amounts for those line items either on the face of the income statement or in the notes to the financial statements. A presentation reporting extraordinary items only is presented in Illustration 39-27.

ILLUSTRATION 39-27 EPS Presentation, with Extraordinary Item

Basic earnings per share	
Income before extraordinary item	$3.80
Extraordinary item	0.80
Net income	$3.00
Diluted earnings per share	
Income before extraordinary item	$3.35
Extraordinary item	0.65
Net income	$2.70

Earnings per share amounts must be shown for all periods presented. Also, all prior period earnings per share amounts presented should be restated for stock dividends and stock splits. If diluted EPS data are reported for at least one period, they should be reported for all periods presented, even if they are the same as basic EPS. When results of operations of a prior period have been restated as a result of a prior period adjustment, the earnings per share data shown for the prior periods should also be restated. The effect of the restatement should be disclosed in the year of the restatement.

Complex capital structures and dual presentation of earnings per share require the following additional disclosures in note form.

1. Description of pertinent rights and privileges of the various securities outstanding.

2. A reconciliation of the numerators and denominators of the basic and diluted per share computations, including individual income and share amount effects of all securities that affect EPS.

3. The effect given preferred dividends in determining income available to common stockholders in computing basic EPS.

4. Securities that could potentially dilute basic EPS in the future that were not included in the computation because they would be antidilutive.

5. Effect of conversions subsequent to year-end, but before statements have been issued.

Illustration 39-28 presents the reconciliation and the related disclosure that is needed to meet disclosure requirements for EPS.

ILLUSTRATION 39-28   Reconciliation for Basic and Diluted EPS

	For the Year Ended 2005		
	Income (Numerator)	Shares (Denominator)	Per Share Amount
Income before extraordinary item and accounting change	$7,500,000		
Less: Preferred stock dividends	(45,000)		
Basic EPS			
Income available to common stockholders	7,455,000	3,991,666	$1.87
Warrants		30,768	
Convertible preferred stock	45,000	308,333	
4% convertible bonds (net of tax)	60,000	50,000	
Diluted EPS			
Income available to common stockholders + assumed conversions	$7,560,000	$4,380,767	$1.73

Stock options to purchase 1,000,000 shares of common stock at $85 per share were outstanding during the second half of 2005 but were not included in the computation of diluted EPS because the options' exercise price was greater than the average market price of the common shares. The options were still outstanding at the end of year 2005 and expire on June 30, 2015.[23]

---

[23]Note that *Statement No. 123* has specific disclosure requirements as well regarding stock option plans and earnings per share disclosures.

SUMMARY

As you can see, computation of earnings per share is a complex issue. It is a controversial area because many securities, although technically not common stock, have many of its basic characteristics. Some companies have issued these types of securities rather than common stock in order to avoid an adverse dilutive effect on earnings per share.

Illustrations 39-29 and 39-30 show the elementary points of calculating earnings per share in a simple capital structure and in a complex capital structure.

ILLUSTRATION 39-29   Calculating EPS, Simple Capital Structure

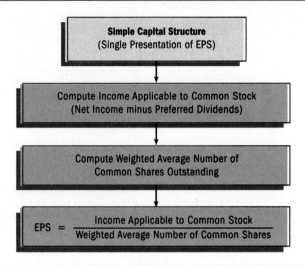

ILLUSTRATION 39-30   Calculating EPS, Complex Capital Structure

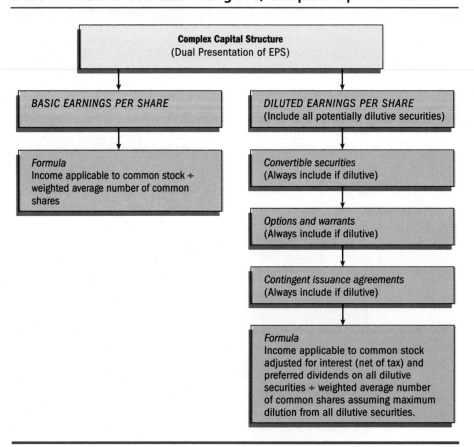

Comprehensive Earnings per Share Illustration

The purpose of this appendix is to illustrate the method of computing dilution when many securities are involved. The following section of the balance sheet of Webster Corporation is presented for analysis (Illustration 39-1). Assumptions related to the capital structure follow the balance sheet.

ILLUSTRATION 39-1   Balance Sheet for Comprehensive Illustration

Webster Corporation
Balance Sheet (Partial)
At December 31, 2004

Long-term debt	
Notes payable, 14%	$ 1,000,000
8% convertible bonds payable	2,500,000
10% convertible bonds payable	2,500,000
Total long-term debt	$6,000,000
Stockholders' equity	
10% cumulative, convertible preferred stock, par value $100; 100,000 shares authorized, 25,000 shares issued and outstanding	$ 2,500,000
Common stock, par value $1,5,000,000 shares authorized, 500,000 shares issued and outstanding	500,000
Additional paid-in capital	2,000,000
Retained earnings	9,000,000
Total stockholders' equity	$14,000,000

Notes and Assumptions
December 31, 2004

1. Options were granted in July 2002 to purchase 50,000 shares of common stock at $20 per share. The average market price of Webster's common stock during 2004 was $30 per share. No options were exercised during 2004.

2. Both the 8 percent and 10 percent convertible bonds were issued in 2003 at face value. Each convertible bond is convertible into 40 shares of common stock. (Each bond has a face value of $1,000.)

3. The 10 percent cumulative, convertible preferred stock was issued at the beginning of 2004 at par. Each share of preferred is convertible into four shares of common stock.

4. The average income tax rate is 40 percent.

5. The 500,000 shares of common stock were outstanding during the entire year.

6. Preferred dividends were not declared in 2004.

7. Net income was $1,750,000 in 2004.

8. No bonds or preferred stock were converted during 2004.

The computation of basic earnings per share for 2004 starts with the amount based upon the weighted average of common shares outstanding, as shown in Illustration 39-2.

ILLUSTRATION 39-2   Computation of Earnings per Share—Simple Capital Structure

Net income	$1,750,000
Less: 10% cumulative, convertible preferred stock dividend requirements	250,000
Income applicable to common stockholders	$1,500,000
Weighted average number of common shares outstanding	500,000
Earnings per common share	$3.00

Note the following points concerning the calculation above.

1. When preferred stock is cumulative, the preferred dividend is subtracted to arrive at income applicable to common stock whether the dividend is declared or not.

2. The earnings per share of $3 must be computed as a starting point, because it is the per share amount that is subject to reduction due to the existence of convertible securities and options.

DILUTED EARNINGS PER SHARE

The steps for computing diluted earnings per share are:

1. Determine, for each dilutive security, the per share effect assuming exercise/conversion.

2. Rank the results from step 1 from smallest to largest earnings effect per share. That is, rank the results from most dilutive to least dilutive.

3. Beginning with the earnings per share based upon the weighted average of common shares outstanding ($3), recalculate earnings per share by adding the smallest per share effects from step 2. If the results from this recalculation are less than $3, proceed to the next smallest per share effect and recalculate earnings per share. Continue this process so long as each recalculated earnings per share is smaller than the previous amount. The process will end either because there are no more securities to test or a particular security maintains or increases earnings per share (is antidilutive).

We'll now apply the three steps to Webster Corporation. (Note that net income and income available to common stockholders are not the same if preferred dividends are declared or cumulative.) Webster Corporation has four securities (options, 8 percent and 10 percent convertible bonds, and the convertible preferred stock) that could reduce EPS.

The first step in the computation of diluted earnings per share is to determine a per share effect for each potentially dilutive security. Illustrations 39-3 through 39-6 illustrate these computations.

ILLUSTRATION 39-3   Per Share Effect of Options (Treasury Stock Method), Diluted Earnings per Share

Number of shares under option	50,000
Option price per share	× $20
Proceeds upon assumed exercise of options	$1,000,000
Average 2004 market price of common	$30
Treasury shares that could be acquired with proceeds ($1,000,000 ÷ $30)	33,333
Excess of shares under option over treasury shares that could be repurchased (50,000 − 33,333)	16,667

Per share effect:

$$\frac{\text{Incremental Numerator Effect}}{\text{Incremental Denominator Effect}} = \frac{\text{None}}{16,667 \text{ shares}} = \$0$$

ILLUSTRATION 39-4   Per Share Effect of 8% Bonds (If-Converted Method), Diluted Earnings per Share

Interest expense for year (8% × $2,500,000)	$200,000
Income tax reduction due to interest (40% × $200,000)	80,000
Interest expense avoided (net of tax)	$120,000
Number of common shares issued assuming conversion of bonds (2,500 bonds × 40 shares)	100,000

Per share effect:

$$\frac{\text{Incremental Numerator Effect}}{\text{Incremental Denominator Effect}} = \frac{\$120,000}{100,000 \text{ shares}} = \underline{\underline{\$1.20}}$$

ILLUSTRATION 39-5   Per Share Effect of 10% Bonds (If-Converted Method), Diluted Earnings per Share

Interest expense for year (10% × $2,500,000)	$250,000
Income tax reduction due to interest (40% × $250,000)	100,000
Interest expense avoided (net of tax)	$150,000
Number of common shares issued assuming conversion of bonds (2,500 bonds × 40 shares)	100,000

Per share effect:

$$\frac{\text{Incremental Numerator Effect}}{\text{Incremental Denominator Effect}} = \frac{\$150,000}{100,000 \text{ shares}} = \underline{\underline{\$1.50}}$$

ILLUSTRATION 39-6   Per Share Effect of 10% Convertible Preferred (If-Converted Method), Diluted Earnings per Share

Dividend requirement on cumulative preferred (25,000 shares × $10)	$250,000
Income tax effect (dividends not a tax deduction)	none
Dividend requirement avoided	$250,000
Number of common shares issued assuming conversion of preferred (4 × 25,000 shares)	100,000

Per share effect:

$$\frac{\text{Incremental Numerator Effect}}{\text{Incremental Denominator Effect}} = \frac{\$250,000}{100,000 \text{ shares}} = \underline{\underline{\$2.50}}$$

Illustration 39-7 shows the ranking of all four potentially dilutive securities.

ILLUSTRATION 39-7   Ranking of per Share Effects (Smallest to Largest), Diluted Earnings per Share

	Effect per Share
1. Options	$ 0
2. 8% convertible bonds	1.20
3. 10% convertible bonds	1.50
4. 10% convertible preferred	2.50

The next step is to determine earnings per share giving effect to the ranking in illustration 39-7. Starting with the earnings per share of $3 computed previously, add the incremental effects of the options to the original calculation, as in Illustration 39-8.

ILLUSTRATION 39-8   Recomputation of EPS Using Incremental Effect of Options

Options

Income applicable to common stockholders	$1,500,000
Add: Incremental numerator effect of options	none
Total	$1,500,000
Weighted average number of common shares outstanding	500,000
Add: Incremental denominator effect of options (Illustration 36-3)	16,667
Total	516,667
Recomputed earnings per share ($1,500,000 ÷ 516,667 shares)	$2.90

Since the recomputed earnings per share is reduced (from $3 to $2.90), the effect of the options is dilutive. Again, this effect could have been anticipated because the average market price ($30) exceeded the option price ($20).

Recomputed earnings per share, assuming the 8 percent bonds are converted, is given in Illustration 39-9.

ILLUSTRATION 39-9   Recomputation of EPS Using Incremental Effect of 8% Convertible Bonds 8%

8% Convertible Bonds

Numerator from previous calculation	$1,500,000
Add: Interest expense avoided (net of tax)	120,000
Total	$1,620,000
Denominator from previous calculation (shares)	516,667
Add: Number of common shares assumed issued upon conversion of bonds	100,000
Total	616,667
Recomputed earnings per share ($1,620,000 ÷ 616,667 shares)	$2.63

Since the recomputed earnings per share is reduced (from $2.90 to $2.63), the effect of the 8 percent bonds is dilutive.

Next, earnings per share is recomputed assuming the conversion of the 10 percent bonds. This is shown in Illustration 39-10.

ILLUSTRATION 39-10   Recomputation of EPS Using Incremental Effect of 10% Convertible Bonds

10% Convertible Bonds

Numerator from previous calculation	$1,620,000
Add: Interest expense avoided (net of tax)	150,000
Total	$1,770,000
Denominator from previous calculation (shares)	616,667
Add: Number of common shares assumed issued upon conversion of bonds	100,000
Total	716,667
Recomputed earnings per share ($1,770,000 ÷ 716,667 shares)	$2.47

Since the recomputed earnings per share is reduced (from $2.63 to $2.47), the effect of the 10 percent convertible bonds is dilutive.

The final step is the recomputation that includes the 10 percent preferred stock. This is shown in Illustration 39-11.

ILLUSTRATION 39-11 Recomputation of EPS Using Incremental Effect of 10% Convertible Preferred

10% Convertible Preferred

Numerator from previous calculation	$1,770,000
Add: Dividend requirement avoided	250,000
Total	$2,020,000
Denominator from previous calculation (shares)	716,667
Add: Number of common shares assumed issued upon conversion of preferred	100,000
Total	816,667
Recomputed earnings per share ($2,020,000 ÷ 816,667 shares)	$2.47

Since the recomputed earnings per share is not reduced, the effect of the 10 percent convertible preferred is not dilutive. Diluted earnings per share is $2.47, and the per share effects of the preferred are not used in the computation.

Finally, the disclosure of earnings per share on the income statement for Webster Corporation is shown in Illustration 39-12.

ILLUSTRATION 39-12 Income Statement Presentation, EPS

Net income	$1,750,000
Basic earnings per common share (Note X)	$3.00
Diluted earnings per common share	$2.47

A company uses **income from continuing operations (adjusted for preferred dividends) to determine whether potential common stock is dilutive or antidilutive**. (Some refer to this measure as the **control number**.) To illustrate, assume that Barton Company provides the following information (Illustration 39-13).

ILLUSTRATION 39-13 Barton Company Data

Income from continuing operations	$2,400,000
Loss from discontinued operations	3,600,000
Net loss	$1,200,000
Weighted average shares of common stock outstanding	1,000,000
Potential common stock	200,000

The computation of basic and dilutive earnings per share is given in Illustration 39-14.

ILLUSTRATION 39-14   Basic and Diluted EPS

Basic earnings per share	
Income from continuing operations	$2.40
Loss from discontinued operations	3.60
Net loss	$1.20
Diluted earnings per share	
Income from continuing operations	$2.00
Loss from discontinued operations	3.00
Net loss	$1.00

As shown in Illustration 39-14, basic earnings per share from continuing operations is higher than the diluted earnings per share from continuing operations. The reason: The diluted earnings per share from continuing operations includes an additional 200,000 shares of potential common stock in its denominator.[1]

Income from continuing operations is used as the control number because many companies will show income from continuing operations (or a similar line item above net income if it appears on the income statement), but report a final net loss due to a loss on discontinued operations. If the final net loss is used as the control number, basic and diluted earnings per share would be the same because the potential common shares are antidilutive.[2]

---

[1] A company that does not report a discontinued operation but reports an extraordinary item or the cumulative effect of a change in accounting principle should use that line item (for example, income before extraordinary items) as the control number.

[2] If a loss from continuing operations is reported, basic and diluted earnings per share will be the same because potential common stock will be antidilutive, even if the company reports final net income. The FASB believes that comparability of EPS information will be improved by using income from continuing operations as the control number.

QUESTIONS

1. Define the following terms.

   A. Basic earnings per share.

   B. Potentially dilutive security.

2. Discuss why options and warrants may be considered potentially dilutive common shares for the computation of diluted earnings per share.

3. Explain how convertible securities are determined to be potentially dilutive common shares and how those convertible securities that are not considered to be potentially dilutive common shares enter into the determination of earnings per share data.

1. **(EPS: Simple Capital Structure)** On January 1, 2005, Wilke Corp. had 480,000 shares of common stock outstanding. During 2005, it had the following transactions that affected the common stock account.

February 1	Issued 120,000 shares
March 1	Issued a 10% stock dividend
May 1	Acquired 100,000 shares of treasury stock
June 1	Issued a 3-for-1 stock split
October 1	Reissued 60,000 shares of treasury stock

Instructions

A. Determine the weighted average number of shares outstanding as of December 31, 2005.

B. Assume that Wilke Corp. earned net income of $3,456,000 during 2005. In addition, it had 100,000 shares of 9%, $100 par nonconvertible, noncumulative preferred stock outstanding for the entire year. Because of liquidity considerations, however, the company did not declare and pay a preferred dividend in 2005. Compute earnings per share for 2005, using the weighted-average number of shares determined in part (a).

C. Assume the same facts as in part (b), except that the preferred stock was cumulative. Compute earnings per share for 2005.

D. Assume the same facts as in part (b), except that net income included an extraordinary gain of $864,000 and a loss from discontinued operations of $432,000. Both items are net of applicable income taxes. Compute earnings per share for 2005.

2. (EPS with Complex Capital Structure) Diane Leto, controller at Dewey Yaeger Pharmaceutical Industries, a public company, is currently preparing the calculation for basic and diluted earnings per share and the related disclosure for Yaeger's external financial statements. Following is selected financial information for the fiscal year ended June 30, 2005.

Dewey Yaeger Pharmaceutical Industries
Selected Statement of
Financial Position Information
June 30, 2005

Long-term debt	
Notes payable, 10%	$ 1,000,000
7% convertible bonds payable	5,000,000
10% bonds payable	6,000,000
Total long-term debt	$12,000,000
Shareholders' equity	
Preferred stock, 8.5% cumulative, $50 par value, 100,000 shares authorized, 25,000 shares issued and outstanding	$ 1,250,000
Common stock, $1 par, 10,000,000 shares authorized, 1,000,000 shares issued and outstanding	1,000,000
Additional paid-in capital	4,000,000
Retained earnings	6,000,000
Total shareholders' equity	$12,250,000

The following transactions have also occurred at Yaeger.

1. Options were granted in 2003 to purchase 100,000 shares at $15 per share. Although no options were exercised during 2005, the average price per common share during fiscal year 2005 was $20 per share.

2. Each bond was issued at face value. The 7% convertible debenture will convert into common stock at 50 shares per $1,000 bond. It is exercisable after 5 years and was issued in 2004.

3. The 8.5% preferred stock was issued in 2003.

4. There are no preferred dividends in arrears; however, preferred dividends were not declared in fiscal year 2005.

5. The 1,000,000 shares of common stock were outstanding for the entire 2005 fiscal year.

6. Net income for fiscal year 2005 was $1,500,000, and the average income tax rate is 40%.

Instructions

For the fiscal year ended June 30, 2005, calculate the following for Dewey Yaeger Pharmaceutical Industries.

    A. Basic earnings per share.

    B. Diluted earnings per share.

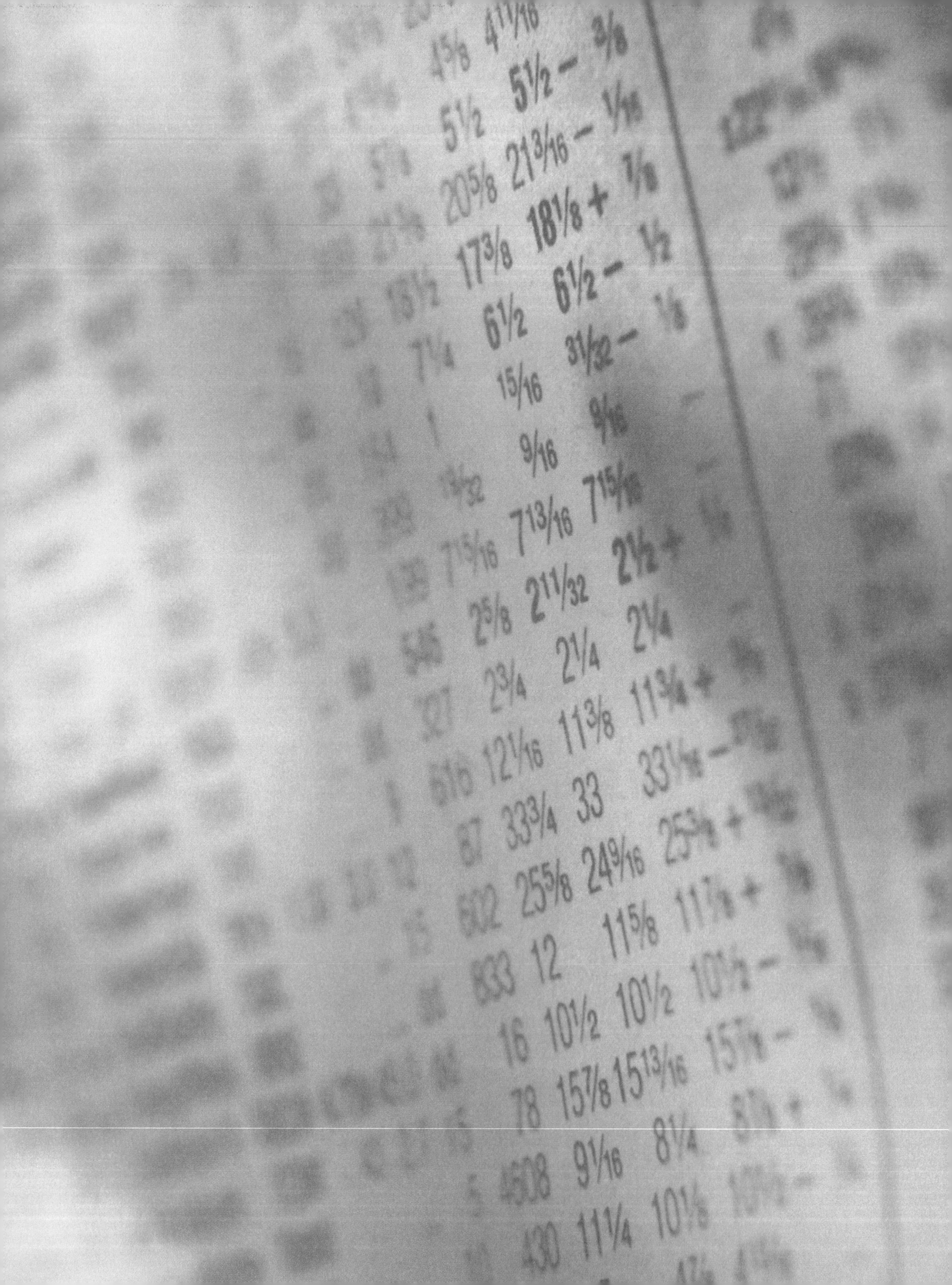

FINANCIAL STATEMENT ANALYSIS:
Inventories, Long-Term Assets and Economic Reality

READING ASSIGNMENTS

Reading 40 Analysis of Inventories
Reading 41 Long-Term Assets
Reading 42 Analysis of Long-Lived Assets: Part I — The Capitalization Decision
Reading 43 Analysis of Long-Lived Assets: Part II — Analysis of Depreciation and Impairment

The readings in this study session discuss and illustrate the comparative financial statement effects from using alternative accounting policies and estimates when determining a company's inventory and long-term operating asset expenses and carrying values. Other classifications of assets (e.g., receivables and prepaid expenses) are generally devoid of any accounting policy alternatives, making them relatively more comparable among companies, i.e., not needing analyst adjustments.

The description and measurement of inventories require careful attention because the investment in inventories is frequently the largest current asset for merchandizing and manufacturing companies. For these companies, the measurement of inventory cost (i.e., cost of goods sold) is a critical factor in determining gross profit and other measures of company profitability. Long-term operating assets are often the largest category of assets on a company's balance sheet. The sheer magnitude of these operational assets and the array of options provided for their cost recognition to the income statement (i.e., depreciation/amortization/depletion expense and impairment loss) by alternative accounting policies and estimates mean the analyst must give them careful scrutiny. The wide range of accounting policies and estimates for operational assets can lead to financial statement manipulation over a long period of time.

LEARNING OUTCOMES

Reading 40: Analysis of Inventories

The candidate should be able to:

a. compute ending inventory balances and cost of goods sold using the LIFO, FIFO, and average cost methods to account for product inventory and explain the relationship among and the usefulness of inventory and cost of goods sold data provided by the LIFO, FIFO, and average cost methods when prices are 1) stable or 2) changing;

b. analyze the financial statements of companies using different inventory accounting methods to compare and describe the effect of the different methods on cost of goods sold and inventory balances, discuss how a company's choice of inventory accounting method affects other financial items such as income, cash flow, and working capital, and compute and describe the effects of the choice of inventory method on profitability, liquidity, activity, and solvency ratios;

c. discuss the reasons that a LIFO reserve might decline during a given period and discuss the implications of such a decline for financial analysis;

d. discuss how inventories are reported in the financial statements and how the lower of cost or market principle is used and applied.

Reading 41: Long-Term Assets

The candidate should be able to:

a. describe the factors that distinguish long-term assets from other assets and identify the common types of long-term assets and how carrying value is determined on the balance sheet;

b. determine the costs that are capitalized to property, plant and equipment and determine which costs are expensed as incurred;

c. explain depreciation accounting (including the reasons for depreciation), calculate depreciation using the straight-line, production (also known as units-of-production), and declining-balance methods, and calculate depreciation after revising the estimated useful life of an asset;

d. describe how to account for the sale, exchange, or disposal of depreciable assets, and determine whether a gain or loss is recorded;

e. identify assets that should be classified as natural resources, determine their carrying values on the balance sheet and calculate depletion;

f. identify the types of intangible assets and describe how the accounting treatment for goodwill under U.S. GAAP differs from the accounting treatment for other intangible assets.

Reading 42: Analysis of Long-Lived Assets: Part I — The Capitalization Decision

The candidate should be able to:

a. compute and describe the effects of capitalizing versus expensing on net income, shareholders' equity, cash flow from operations, and financial ratios including the effect on the interest coverage ratio (times interest earned) of capitalizing interest costs;

b. explain the circumstances in which intangible assets, including software development costs and research and development costs are capitalized;

c. calculate and describe both the initial and long-term effects of asset revaluations on financial ratios.

Reading 43: Analysis of Long-Lived Assets: Part II — Analysis of Depreciation and Impairment

The candidate should be able to:

a. identify the different depreciation methods and discuss how the choice of depreciation method affects a company's financial statements, ratios, and taxes;

b. explain the role of depreciable lives and salvage values in the computation of depreciation expenses, and compute and describe how changing depreciation methods or changing the estimated useful life or salvage value of an asset affects financial statements and ratios;

c. discuss the use of fixed asset disclosures to compare companies' average age of depreciable assets, and calculate, using such disclosures, the average age and average depreciable life of fixed assets;

d. define impairment of long-lived assets and explain what effect such impairment has on a company's financial statements and ratios;

e. discuss the liability for closure, removal, and environmental effects of long-lived operating assets, and discuss the financial statement impact and ratio effects of that liability.

$4\frac{5}{8}$ $4\frac{11}{16}$ $-\frac{3}{8}$

$5\frac{1}{2}$ $5\frac{1}{2}$ $-\frac{3}{8}$

$20\frac{5}{8}$ $21\frac{3}{16}$ $-\frac{1}{16}$

$17\frac{3}{8}$ $18\frac{1}{8}$ $+\frac{7}{8}$

$13\frac{1}{2}$ $6\frac{1}{2}$ $6\frac{1}{2}$ $-\frac{1}{2}$

$7\frac{1}{4}$ $3\frac{1}{32}$ $-\frac{1}{8}$

$\frac{15}{16}$ $\frac{9}{16}$

$\frac{9}{16}$ $\frac{9}{16}$

$\frac{9}{32}$

$7\frac{15}{16}$ $7\frac{13}{16}$ $7\frac{15}{16}$

$2\frac{5}{8}$ $2\frac{11}{32}$ $2\frac{1}{2}$ $+$

$2\frac{3}{4}$ $2\frac{1}{4}$ $2\frac{1}{4}$

$12\frac{1}{16}$ $11\frac{3}{8}$ $11\frac{3}{4}$ $+$

$33\frac{3}{4}$ 33 $33\frac{1}{8}$ $-$

$25\frac{5}{8}$ $24\frac{9}{16}$ $25\frac{3}{8}$ $+$

12 $11\frac{5}{8}$ $11\frac{7}{8}$ $+$

$10\frac{1}{2}$ $10\frac{1}{2}$ $10\frac{1}{8}$ $-$

$15\frac{7}{8}$ $15\frac{13}{16}$ $15\frac{7}{8}$ $-$

$9\frac{1}{16}$ $8\frac{1}{4}$

$11\frac{1}{4}$ $10\frac{1}{8}$

ANALYSIS OF INVENTORIES

by Gerald I. White, Ashwinpaul C. Sondhi, and Dov Fried

LEARNING OUTCOMES

The candidate should be able to:

a. compute ending inventory balances and cost of goods sold using the LIFO, FIFO, and average cost methods to account for product inventory and explain the relationship among and the usefulness of inventory and cost of goods sold data provided by the LIFO, FIFO, and average cost methods when prices are 1) stable or 2) changing;

b. analyze the financial statements of companies using different inventory accounting methods to compare and describe the effect of the different methods on cost of goods sold and inventory balances, discuss how a company's choice of inventory accounting method affects other financial items such as income, cash flow, and working capital, and compute and describe the effects of the choice of inventory method on profitability, liquidity, activity, and solvency ratios;

c. discuss the reasons that a LIFO reserve might decline during a given period and discuss the implications of such a decline for financial analysis;

d. discuss how inventories are reported in the financial statements and how the lower of cost or market principle is used and applied.

INTRODUCTION   1

During 1999, the **spot price** of crude oil[1] rose from less than $10 per barrel to more than $25 per barrel, an increase of more than 150%. Crude oil continued to rise in early 2000, nearing $32 per barrel in March. Simultaneously, the price of gasoline sold at the pump increased dramatically in most countries. Consumers and politicians criticized oil companies for immediately raising the price of gasoline sold at the retail level. They argued that the gasoline being sold had been refined

---

[1] Measured by the Brent Crude "near contract generic future" as reported on Bloomberg.

from oil purchased at a price of $10 per barrel and, hence, raising the price of this "old" gasoline resulted in windfall profits.

The oil companies countered that since the market price of oil had risen, replacing the old oil now cost more and thus raising the price of gasoline was justified by current market conditions.

The accounting choice of last-in, first-out (LIFO) versus first-in, first-out (FIFO) for inventory and cost of goods sold (COGS) mirrors this debate as to the more appropriate measure of income. The choice affects the firm's income statement, balance sheet, and related ratios. Perhaps more important, in contrast to most financial reporting choices, the choice of inventory method has real cash flow effects as it affects income taxes paid by the firm.

2   INVENTORY AND COST OF GOODS SOLD: BASIC RELATIONSHIPS

The inventory account is affected by two events: the purchase (or manufacture) of goods (P) and their subsequent sale (COGS). The relationship between these events and the balance of beginning inventory (BI) and ending inventory (EI) can be expressed as

(1) $EI = BI + P - \text{COGS}$ or
(2) $BI + P = \text{COGS} + EI$

For any period, prior to the preparation of financial statements for the period, the left side of the second equation is known: the beginning inventory plus purchases (cost of goods acquired for sale during the period). Preparation of the income statement and balance sheet for the period requires the allocation of these costs ($BI + P$) between COGS and ending inventory. This process is illustrated under two scenarios:

Beginning inventory: 200 units @ $10/unit = $2,000

Quarter	Purchases Units	Scenario 1: Stable Prices		Scenario 2: Rising Prices	
		Unit Cost	Purchases Dollars	Unit Cost	Purchases Dollars
1	100	$10	$1,000	$11	$1,100
2	150	10	1,500	12	1,800
3	150	10	1,500	13	1,950
4	100	10	1,000	14	1,400
Total	500		$5,000		$6,250
			$BI + P = \$7,000$		$BI + P = \$8,250$

Units sold: 100 units per quarter for a total of 400 units
Ending inventory: 300 units

Scenario 1: Stable Prices

Beginning inventory plus purchases equals $7,000. Since unit costs are constant at $10 per unit and 400 units were sold, the COGS equals $4,000 (400 × $10) and the cost of the 300 units in ending inventory equals $3,000 (300 × $10).

$$BI + P = COGS + EI$$
$$\$2,000 + \$5,000 = \$4,000 + \$3,000$$

However, perfectly stable prices are the exception rather than the norm. In addition to general inflationary pressures, costs and prices for specific goods are constantly changing. Accounting for inventory and COGS in such an environment, as a result, becomes more complex.

Scenario 2: Rising Prices

Beginning inventory plus purchases equals $8,250. Unlike the case of stable prices, the allocation between COGS and the cost of ending inventory requires an assumption as to the flow of costs. Essentially, three alternative assumptions are possible: *FIFO, LIFO,* and *weighted-average cost.*

FIFO accounting assumes that the costs of items *first purchased* are deemed to be the costs of items *first sold* and these costs enter COGS; ending inventory is made up of the cost of the most recent items purchased.

At the opposite extreme is LIFO accounting where items *last purchased* are assumed to be the ones *first sold* and the ending inventory is made up of the earliest costs incurred.

Finally, as its name implies, weighted-average cost accounting uses the (same) average cost for both the items sold and those remaining in closing inventory.

In our example, *the assumptions of rising prices and an increase in the inventory balance generate three alternative allocations of the cost of goods available for sale (BI + P),* on the income statement and balance sheet (the calculations are shown in Exhibit 40-1):

Method	BI	+	P	=	COGS	+	EI
FIFO	$2,000	+	$6,250	=	$4,300	+	$3,950
Weighted-average	2,000	+	6,250	=	4,714	+	3,536
LIFO	2,000	+	6,250	=	5,150	+	3,100

COMPARISON OF INFORMATION PROVIDED BY ALTERNATIVE METHODS

3

This section compares the information provided by the three alternative accounting methods.

Balance Sheet Information: Inventory Account

The ending inventory consists of 300 units. At current replacement cost (i.e., the fourth-quarter unit cost of $14), the inventory would have a carrying value of $4,200. The FIFO inventory of $3,950 comes closest to this amount because FIFO

EXHIBIT 40-1	**Allocation of Costs Under Different Inventory Methods, Scenario 2**

A. FIFO

The 400 units sold (COGS) are assumed to carry the earliest costs incurred and the 300 units left in inventory carry the latest costs:

COGS		Ending Inventory	
200 @ $10 = $2,000		100 @ $14 = $1,400	
100 @ $11 = $1,100		150 @ $13 = $1,950	
100 @ $12 = $1,200		50 @ $12 = $ 600	
400	$4,300	300	$3,950

B. LIFO

The 400 units sold (COGS) are assumed to carry the latest costs incurred and the 300 units left in inventory carry the earliest costs:

COGS		Ending Inventory	
100 @ $14 = $1,400		200 @ $10 = $2,000	
150 @ $13 = $1,950		100 @ $11 = $1,100	
150 @ $12 = $1,800			
400	$5,150	300	$3,100

C. Weighted-Average

The total costs for the 700 units = $8,250. On a per-unit basis, this results in a weighted-average unit cost of:

$$\frac{\$8,250}{700} = \$11.786$$
$$\text{COGS} = 400 \times \$11.786 = \$4,714$$
$$\text{Ending inventory} = 300 \times \$11.786 = \$3,536$$

allocates the earliest costs to COGS, leaving the most recent costs in ending inventory.

Conversely, the LIFO balance of $3,100 is furthest from the current cost as LIFO accounting allocates the earliest (outdated) costs to ending inventory. In fact, the cost of ending inventory for many companies using LIFO may be decades old[2] and virtually useless as an indicator of the current or replacement cost of inventories on hand.

---

[2] For example, Caterpillar has stated that the LIFO method "was first adopted for the major portion of inventories in 1950."

From a balance sheet perspective, therefore, inventories based on FIFO are preferable to those presented under LIFO, as carrying values most closely reflect current cost. In other words, FIFO provides a measure of inventory that is closer to its current (economic) value.

The carrying amount of inventory can also be affected by changes in market value as discussed below.

Inventory Valuation: Lower of Cost or Market

GAAP requires the use of the lower-of-cost-or-market valuation basis (LCM) for inventories, with market value defined as replacement cost.[3] The LCM valuation basis follows the principle of conservatism (on both the balance sheet and income statement) since it recognizes losses or declines in market value as they occur, whereas increases are reported only when inventory is sold. LCM can be used with LIFO for financial statement purposes. However, for tax purposes LIFO cannot be combined with LCM. Firms using LIFO cannot recognize (and obtain tax benefits from) writedowns and declines in market value for tax purposes.[4]

Income Statement Information: Cost of Goods Sold

Consider a situation where an item purchased for $6 is sold for $10 at a time when it costs $7 to replace it. Prior to replacement of the item, reported income is $4 ($10 − $6). However, if income is defined as the amount available for distribution to shareholders without impairing the firm's operations, then it can be argued that income is only $3, as $7 (not the original cost of $6) are needed to replace the item in inventory and continue operations. The $1 difference between the original cost of the item and the cost of replacement is referred to as a holding gain or inventory profit,[5] and it is debatable whether this amount should be considered income.[6]

In our hypothetical case, *only if the item were not replaced* would there be $10 to distribute to shareholders, indicating income of $4. Under a going-concern assumption, however, firms that sell their inventory need to replenish it constantly for sales in the future. Thus, income should be measured after providing for the replacement of inventory. In addition, the increase in inventory costs suggests that income of $3 is a better indicator of expected future income than $4.

In our example, the replacement cost of the items sold (using the unit cost for each quarter) is $5,000[7] [(100 × $11) + (100 × $12) + (100 × $13) + (100 × $14)]. As U.S. GAAP uses a historical cost framework, however, replacement cost accounting is not permitted. LIFO allocates the most recent purchase prices

---

[3] However, replacement cost cannot exceed the net realizable value or be below the net realizable value less the normal profit margin.

[4] Otherwise, the firm could have the best of both worlds and obtain tax savings whether costs were rising or declining.

[5] If we use terminology, economic income equals $4. As the holding gain is $1, sustainable (future) income is $3. Jennings, Simko, and Thompson (1996) confirm that LIFO-based cost of goods sold is a more useful indicator of the firm's future resource outflows than ("as-if") non-LIFO cost of goods sold as LIFO-based income statements explained more of the variation in equity valuations than non-LIFO income statements. However, in contrast to our earlier argument, they did not find ("as-if") non-LIFO balance sheets to be more informative than LIFO-based balance sheets.

[6] The situation is analogous to having purchased a home before a rapid increase in real estate prices and not being able to benefit from your good fortune because any replacement home would cost as much as the home you live in now.

[7] If the computation were done on an annual basis, the replacement cost would be $5,600 (400 × $14) using the most recent purchase price to measure replacement cost.

to COGS. The reported LIFO COGS of $5,150 is, therefore, closest to the replacement cost, with the FIFO COGS of $4,300 furthest from this cost. *During periods of changing prices and stable or growing inventories, LIFO is the most informative accounting method for income statement purposes, in that it provides a better measure of current income and future profitability.* This leaves us in something of a quandary, since FIFO provides the best measure for the balance sheet.[8]

The preceding discussion implied the use of a single method for all inventories of the firm. In practice, firms often use more than one inventory method. They may use different methods for their foreign operations since LIFO is rarely used outside the United States, or they may use different methods for particular business segments. This factor serves to disguise further the impact of reported inventory on the income statement and balance sheet.

Additionally, the LIFO measurements are based on assumptions and estimates that are complex in a multiproduct environment and are affected by management choice.

Finally, the use of FIFO, LIFO, or weighted-average for the allocation of cost of goods available for sale is preceded by the measurement of costs included in inventory. In a manufacturing environment, as Box 40-1 illustrates, such measurement is also affected by management choice.

From an analyst's perspective the use of different methods is not so grim. Information is often available to permit restatement of financial statements from one method to the other. Such restatement is illustrated later in this reading. Our discussion now, however, turns to the financial statement effects of the choice between LIFO and FIFO.

4   LIFO VERSUS FIFO: INCOME, CASH FLOW, AND WORKING CAPITAL EFFECTS

The above example illustrates that, in periods of rising prices and stable or increasing inventory quantities, the use of LIFO results in higher COGS expense and lower reported income. In the absence of income taxes, there would be no difference in cash flow. Cash flow would equal payments made for inventory purchases and be independent of the accounting method used.

When LIFO is a permitted method for income taxes, however, lower income translates into lower taxes and thus higher operating cash flows. In the United States, unlike other accounting policy choices that allow differing methods of accounting for financial statements and tax purposes, *IRS regulations require that the same method of inventory accounting used for tax purposes also be used for financial reporting.* From an economic perspective, given rising prices, LIFO is the better choice, as taxes will be lower and cash flows will be higher despite the lower reported income.[9]

It was noted that working capital is used as a broad liquidity measure because it includes cash and near-cash assets. Inventory accounting can distort the working

---

[8] The weighted-average method falls someplace in between the FIFO and LIFO methods both in terms of the balance sheet and income statement. It is seen by some as a compromise method. Alternatively, we can argue that it is the worst of the three choices: Unlike LIFO and FIFO, which provide good information on one financial statement, the weighted-average method does not do so for either statement. Practically speaking, however, the weighted-average method tends to be closer to FIFO than LIFO, especially with respect to inventory costs on the balance sheet.

[9] The question of why, given the foregoing, all firms do not use LIFO will be considered later in the reading.

BOX 40-1 INVENTORY COSTING IN A MANUFACTURING ENVIRONMENT

Accounting for inventories in a manufacturing environment adds another dimension to the problem of inventory costing. Unlike merchandising operations, which carry only finished goods inventory, manufacturing operations carry three types of inventory: (1) raw material, (2) work in process, and (3) finished goods.

Inventories include raw material costs as well as labor and overhead costs required to transform the raw materials into finished goods. Determining the amount of overhead (indirect) costs poses the most problems. Included in (factory) overhead are items such as: supervisors' salaries, depreciation/rent of factory plant and equipment, utilities, repairs and maintenance, and quality control costs.

Such costs are *joint costs* and, in a multiproduct environment, are difficult to allocate among products. As the inventory carrying amount of any one product line depends on the allocation procedure, that amount can be somewhat arbitrary and capable of manipulation. For example, a manufacturer can increase reported income by choosing an allocation method that charges more of the joint costs to slower moving items. These costs then remain in inventory longer, and products with higher turnover rates appear more profitable.

A second aspect of this problem is the fixed nature (in the short run) of items such as depreciation, rent, or supervisors' salaries. Allocating such costs to products involves an averaging process that is affected by changing levels of production. A simple example in a single-product environment will illustrate this effect.

Assume a company has factory rent of $12,000 and it sells 10,000 units. If it produces 10,000 units, the full $12,000 of factory rent will be expensed through COGS (at a rate of $1.20/unit). If production increases to 12,000 units, then factory rent is allocated to inventory at $1.00/unit. But if only 10,000 units are sold, then only $10,000 is expensed as part of COGS and $2,000 of unallocated (but incurred) rent remains in inventory. Income increases by changing production levels rather than increasing sales.

The income effect of changing production rates can be the result of either intentional management decision (manipulation) or the unintended result of sales levels that differ from expectation. In either case it is imperative for the analyst to recognize:

▶ The accounting policies used by different firms in the same industry

▶ The effects of fluctuations in production on COGS and reported income

Finally, which costs are charged to inventory (and expensed when sold) and which costs are expensed as incurred vary among firms. Schiff (1987) notes that, although it is commonly suggested in accounting textbooks that fixed overhead costs must be allocated to inventory, in practice, many companies* have (historically) charged certain overhead costs (e.g., depreciation, pension costs, and property taxes) directly to expense. For such companies, variations in production and inventory levels will not affect the amount expensed. However, for firms that allocate such costs to inventory, when inventory levels increase, the amount expensed will be less than the amount actually incurred, with the difference remaining in inventory. On the balance sheet, those firms that capitalize more indirect costs in inventory will have higher carrying values of inventory, working capital, and equity balances. Unfortunately, not all companies disclose their practices in this respect. This can make comparisons between companies difficult.†

---

* The steel industry is one example noted by Schiff.

† The matter is further complicated by the increased emphasis in recent years in improvements in manufacturing processes. As a result, many firms have adjusted their method of inventory costing. [Bartley and Chen (1992) also report tax-related motivations for firms to switch from expensing to capitalization of certain items.]

capital measure and lead to erroneous and contradictory conclusions. LIFO accounting results in higher cash flows, but it reports lower working capital because the inventory balances retain earlier (lower) costs and the cash saved is only a percentage (the marginal tax rate) of the difference in inventory values.

In periods of rising prices and stable or increasing inventory quantities, the impact of LIFO and FIFO on the financial statements can be summarized as

	LIFO	FIFO
COGS	Higher	Lower
Income before taxes	Lower	Higher
Income taxes	Lower	Higher
Net Income	Lower	Higher
Cash flow	**Higher**	**Lower**
Inventory balance	Lower	Higher
Working capital	Lower	Higher

Cash flow has been highlighted because it is the only amount with direct economic impact. The others are accounting constructs and their economic significance is indirect and informational.

Continuing with the previous numeric example and assuming that 400 units are sold for $10,000 (average price of $25) with a tax rate of 40%, we can illustrate the above differences as follows. The resulting income statements are

	FIFO	LIFO	LIFO Higher/(Lower) by
Sales	$10,000	$10,000	$ 0
COGS	(4,300)	(5,150)	850
Income before tax	$ 5,700	$ 4,850	$(850)
Income tax @ 40%	(2,280)	(1,940)	(340)
Net income	$ 3,420	$ 2,910	$(510)

If we assume that sales are for cash and payments for purchases and taxes are made immediately, then cash flows are

	FIFO	LIFO	LIFO Higher/(Lower) by
Sales inflows	$10,000	$10,000	$ 0
Purchases	(6,250)	(6,250)	0
Inflows before tax	$ 3,750	$ 3,750	$ 0
Income tax paid	(2,280)	(1,940)	(340)
Operating cash flow	$ 1,470	$ 1,810	$340

Therefore, changes in balance sheet accounts are

Assets

	FIFO	LIFO	LIFO Higher/(Lower) by
Operating cash*	$1,470	$1,810	$340
Inventory†	1,950	1,100	(850)
Working capital	$3,420	$2,910	$(510)

Liabilities and Stockholders' Equity

	FIFO	LIFO	LIFO Higher/(Lower) by
Retained earnings‡	$3,420	$2,910	$(510)

* Net cash flow for period.
† Purchases less COGS.
‡ Net income for period.

The difference in net income of $510 and the difference in cash flows of $340 are related to the difference in COGS (equivalently the difference in inventory balances) of $850 as follows:

$$\text{Income Difference} = (1\text{-Tax Rate}) \times \text{COGS Difference}$$
$$\$510 = 0.6 \times \$850$$
$$\text{Cash Flow Difference} = \text{Tax Rate} \times \text{COGS Difference}$$
$$\$340 = 0.4 \times \$850$$

However, these differences are in *opposite directions*, with higher income for the FIFO firm and higher operating cash flows for the LIFO firm. The difference in working capital is the net of the difference in inventory balance and cash flow:

$$\$510 = \$850 - \$340$$

This results in misleading liquidity measures for the LIFO firm as its working capital is understated.[10] The increase in cash is more than offset by the understatement of inventory.

Our illustration shows that the choice of inventory method can greatly affect reported operating results. Moreover, depending on whether the focus is the balance sheet or income statement, differing methods may be preferred. Thus, the analyst needs to be able to adjust between LIFO and FIFO in order to:

▶ Eliminate differences between firms due to accounting methods so that any remaining differences reflect economic and operating variations.

▶ Obtain the measure(s) most relevant for their analytical purpose.

The next sections describe how such adjustments can be made.

---

[10] Johnson and Dhaliwal (1988) studied firms that abandoned LIFO in favor of FIFO. Their evidence suggests one possible motivation for the abandonment decision was to increase their reported working capital. Compared to firms that retained LIFO, the abandonment firms had tighter working capital constraints under their debt covenants.

5   ADJUSTMENT FROM LIFO TO FIFO

Adjustment of Inventory Balances

LIFO inventory balances generally contain older costs with little or no relationship to current costs. Because of this deficiency, firms are required to disclose the *LIFO reserve*. The LIFO reserve (usually shown in the financial statement footnotes, but sometimes on the face of the balance sheet) is the difference between the inventory balance shown on the balance sheet and the (approximately current or replacement cost) amount that would have been reported had the firm used FIFO.

To adjust inventory balances of firms using LIFO to current or FIFO cost, we must add the LIFO reserve to the LIFO inventory amount. We can express this as

$$\text{LIFO Reserve} = \text{Inventory}_F - \text{Inventory}_L$$

or

$$\text{Inventory}_F = \text{Inventory}_L + \text{LIFO Reserve}$$

(where the subscripts F and L represent the accounting methods FIFO and LIFO, respectively).

Example 40-1

Sunoco

Exhibit 40-2 contains details of inventory and portions of financial statement footnotes from the 1996–1999 annual reports of Sunoco, a large U.S. oil refiner. Sunoco uses the LIFO method to account for virtually all crude oil and refined product inventories.

Exhibit 40-3A shows the adjustment of inventory from LIFO to FIFO, adding the LIFO reserve to the LIFO inventory. Sunoco's LIFO reserve is large, indicating that the balance sheet carrying amount significantly understates inventories. This understatement is typical of firms whose products have risen in price and that have used LIFO for many years. In the case of Sunoco, the LIFO cost of inventories is only 30% of the FIFO cost in 1999. As the price of oil is volatile, the difference between Inventory$_F$ and Inventory$_L$ is highly variable over the period shown in Exhibit 40-3.

Adjustment of Cost of Goods Sold

COGS can be derived using the opening and closing inventory balances and purchases for the period:

$$\text{COGS} = BI + P - EI$$

Thus, to arrive at FIFO cost of goods sold (COGS$_F$), these amounts must be restated from LIFO to FIFO. The adjustment of inventory balances was illustrated earlier. Purchases (which are not a function of the accounting method

EXHIBIT 40-2	Sunoco

Inventory Disclosures

Inventories of crude oil and refined products are valued at the lower of cost or market. The cost of such inventories is determined principally using LIFO.

	Inventories* at December 31 (in $millions)			
	1996	**1997**	**1998**	**1999**
Crude oil	$157	$150	$184	$158
Refined products	252	214	219	163
Inventories valued at LIFO	**$409**	**$364**	**$403**	**$321**

The current replacement cost of all inventories valued at LIFO exceeded their carrying cost by $780, $492, $205, and $763 million at December 31, 1996 through 1999, respectively.

	1996	**1997**	**1998**	**1999**
Cost of goods sold (in $millions)	$8,718	$7,610	$5,646	$7,365

* The above data only include inventories intended for resale. Sunoco also carries materials and supplies on its balance sheet as inventories.

Source: Sunoco, 1996–1999 annual reports.

EXHIBIT 40-3	Sunoco

Adjustment from LIFO to FIFO, 1996–1999

A. Adjusting LIFO Inventory to FIFO (Current Cost)

	1996	**1997**	**1998**	**1999**
Inventories carried at LIFO	$ 409	$364	$403	$ 321
LIFO reserve	780	492	205	763
Inventories adjusted to FIFO	$1,189	$856	$608	$1,084

B. Adjusting LIFO COGS to FIFO COGS

		1996	**1997**	**1998**	**1999**
Cost of goods sold at LIFO ($COGS_L$)			$7,610	$5,646	$7,365
Less: LIFO effect*			(288)	(287)	558
Equals: cost of goods sold at FIFO ($COGS_F$)			$7,898	$5,933	$6,807

*Change in LIFO reserve from previous year-end.

Source: Data from Sunoco, 1996–1999 annual reports.

used) need not be adjusted and can be derived directly from the (opening and closing) inventory balances and COGS reported in the financial statements:

$$P = COGS_L + EI_L - BI_L$$

Example 40-2

Sunoco

Sunoco's purchases for 1999 can be calculated (in $millions) as

$$P = \$7,365 \text{ million} + \$321 \text{ million} - \$403 \text{ million}$$
$$= \$7,283 \text{ million}$$

Using 1999 purchases, just calculated, and the FIFO inventory amounts derived in Exhibit 40-3A yields the 1999 COGS on a FIFO basis for Sunoco:

$$COGS_F = BI_F + P - EI_F$$
$$= \$608 \text{ million} + \$7,283 \text{ million} - \$1,084 \text{ million}$$
$$= \$6,807 \text{ million}$$

Thus COGS on a FIFO basis is lower than on a LIFO basis by $558 million ($7,365 million − $6,807 million). The astute reader will note that this amount equals the increase in the LIFO reserve during the year (from $205 to $763 million). This is no coincidence and the adjustment from LIFO to FIFO COGS can be made directly from the LIFO reserve accounts without going through the intermediate steps of calculating purchases and adjusting inventories. The direct adjustment (shown in Exhibit 40-3B) is[11]

$$COGS_F = COGS_L - \text{Change in LIFO Reserve}$$

or

$$COGS_F = COGS_L - (\text{LIFO Reserve}_E - \text{LIFO Reserve}_B)$$
$$\$6,807 \text{ million} = \$7,365 \text{ million} - (\$763 \text{ million} - \$205 \text{ million})$$

where the subscripts E and B refer to ending (inventory) and beginning (inventory), respectively. The change in LIFO reserve during the year, sometimes called the *LIFO effect* for the year, is thus the difference between the COGS computed under the two methods.

---

[11] For those with a more mathematical bent, this result can be proven as follows:

Purchases ($P = COGS + EI - BI$) are identical for both accounting methods.
Thus $COGS_F + EI_F - BI_F = COGS_L + EI_L - BI_L$.
Rearranging terms yields $COGS_F = COGS_L - [(EI_F - EI_L) - (BI_F - BI_L)]$.
or $COGS_F = COGS_L - [(\text{LIFO Reserve}_E - \text{LIFO Reserve}_B)]$.

Before leaving this discussion, consider two questions. First, why does conversion to FIFO in 1996 to 1998 increase COGS (see Exhibit 40-3B) when we normally expect $COGS_F$ to be lower than $COGS_L$? Second, why did the LIFO reserve decrease in those years?

The answer to both questions is the same: Oil prices decreased. This decline reduced the difference between inventory cost on a LIFO basis and cost on a FIFO basis. The LIFO reserve, which represents this difference, is thus reduced. In both years, use of the LIFO method reduced COGS by almost $290 million, increasing pretax earnings by an equal amount. The lesson here should be clear: *When prices are declining, LIFO produces lower COGS and, therefore, higher earnings.*

In 1999, when prices (and the LIFO reserve) increased, the expected effect was obtained. $COGS_L$ was higher and pretax income was reduced by the amount of increase in the LIFO reserve. In industries such as oil and gas, based on volatile commodity prices, fluctuations in the LIFO reserve due to price changes are common.

ADJUSTMENT OF INCOME TO CURRENT COST INCOME

6

This section discusses the adjustment of FIFO (and weighted-average) COGS to reflect current costs.[12] There are two reasons for making this adjustment. One is to estimate the impact of price changes on a firm's COGS and earnings; we wish to separate price effects from operating effects. The second reason is to compare the firm with other firms in the same industry using LIFO accounting.

Note that *only the adjustment of COGS to LIFO COGS is relevant.* Adjustments of inventory balances to LIFO serve no purpose, as LIFO inventory costs are outdated and almost meaningless.

Unlike the adjustment from LIFO to FIFO discussed in the previous section, information needed to adjust COGS to LIFO is not generally provided in the financial statements of firms using FIFO (or average cost). An approximate adjustment, however, is often possible.[13]

This adjustment requires multiplying the opening inventory by the (specific) inflation rate and adding the result to $COGS_F$ to arrive at $COGS_L$. More formally,

$$COGS_L = COGS_F + (BI_F \times r)$$

---

[12]Although we use the terms LIFO and current cost COGS interchangeably, our objective is to estimate current cost COGS. Generally, as long as the firm does not deplete any of its opening inventory, these two are equivalent. When opening inventory quantities are reduced (known as a LIFO liquidation), LIFO COGS and income are both distorted, as old costs flow into the income statement and COGS no longer reflects the current cost of inventory sold. When a LIFO liquidation occurs, LIFO COGS does not equal current cost COGS; in a subsequent section of the reading we illustrate how to adjust for this distortion.

[13]A more complex adjustment taking into consideration the firm's inventory turnover is possible. Falkenstein and Weil (1977) discuss the use of turnover, but note (p. 51 of their article) that estimates from the more basic procedure (used here) have always approximated the estimates from the more complex methods.

where r is the *specific inflation rate appropriate for the products in which the firm deals*.[14]

To the extent that a firm's inventory purchases are steady throughout the period, the above adjustment will approximate the actual FIFO-to-LIFO (current cost) adjustment.

Weighted-average COGS (with subscript w) can be similarly adjusted to current cost (LIFO); the adjustment to opening inventory can be appoximated[15] by one-half the (specific) inflation rate:

$$COGS_L = COGS_W + (BI_W \times r/2)$$

Obtaining r. The inflation rate needed for the adjustment is not a general producer or consumer price index, but rather should be the specific price index appropriate to the firm in question. (For a multi-industry firm, the calculation should be done on a segmented basis.) Many industry indices are readily available, published by government or private sources. For companies whose inputs are commodities (oil, coffee, steel scrap), the spot price for the commodity may be used.

Alternatively, the specific price level change, r, for a given FIFO (or weighted average) firm can be estimated from data of a competing (LIFO) firm (in the same industry) by making use of the following relationship:[16]

$$r = \frac{\Delta LIFO \text{ reserve}}{BI_F}$$

This procedure provides a reasonable approximation of r as long as the LIFO firm has not had a *significant* reduction of its inventory from year to year. The example that follows illustrates the adjustment procedure to LIFO.

---

[14] The appropriateness of the approximation can be illustrated by the following proof. Assume that a firm carries a *quantity* Q of inventory and this quantity is equal to three months of inventory. The inventory level Q is replenished every three months. Assume further that the inflation rate over the year is equal to r. Finally, let P be the unit cost at which the opening inventory Q_0 was purchased at the end of the previous year. Thus, the unit cost of the inventory at the end of the current year will equal $P(1 + r)$. The following illustrates the actual flow of goods purchased throughout the year:

$$\begin{aligned}
\text{Beginning inventory} &= Q_0 = \text{Sales during 1st Quarter} \\
\text{End of 1st Quarter Purchase} &= Q_1 = \text{Sales during 2nd Quarter} \\
\text{End of 2nd Quarter Purchase} &= Q_2 = \text{Sales during 3rd Quarter} \\
\text{End of 3rd Quarter Purchase} &= Q_3 = \text{Sales during 4th Quarter} \\
\text{End of 4th Quarter Purchase} &= Q_4 = \text{Ending Inventory}
\end{aligned}$$

Under FIFO, the cost of Q_0, Q_1, Q_2, and Q_3 will appear in COGS. Under LIFO, the cost of Q_1, Q_2, Q_3, and Q_4 will appear in COGS. Thus, the difference between the two methods lies in the difference between the cost of the beginning (Q_0) and ending (Q_4) inventory. Hence, the difference between LIFO and FIFO equals

$$Q_4 P(1 + r) - Q_0 P = Q_0 Pr$$

since the inventory quantity purchased each period is the same.

[15] When weighted-average cost is used, the inventory turnover rate affects the adjustment.

[16] This can be proven since

$$COGS_F = COGS_L - \Delta LIFO \text{ reserve}$$
and

$$COGS_L = COGS_F + (r \times BI_F)$$
Therefore

$$(r \times BI_F) = \Delta LIFO \text{ reserve}$$
and

$$r = \frac{\Delta LIFO \text{ reserve}}{BI_F}$$

Example 40-3

Caltex Australia

Exhibit 40-4 part A contains relevant income statement and balance sheet information for Caltex Australia, a major oil producer and refiner in Australia. LIFO is not permitted under Australian GAAP and Caltex Australia uses the weighted-average cost method to account for inventory. Our objective is to demonstrate the adjustment of COGS and earnings to a current cost basis using the methodology described previously.

One advantage of using Caltex Australia as our example is that the company discloses (Exhibit 40-4, part B) the estimated effects of inventory holding gains on its earnings. Thus, we can double-check our estimates with those provided by management. The company states that it provides this information because:

> As a general rule using the historic cost basis of accounting, rising crude prices will result in increased operating profit for Caltex, falling crude oil prices will result in decreased operating profit. This movement in operating profit, often referred to as an inventory gain or loss, can create large variations in Caltex's results as calculated by the historic cost method. *Consequently, in order to provide a better insight into the operating performance of the company, Caltex's Financial reporting now includes earnings on a replacement cost of sales basis.* Replacement cost of sales earnings exclude inventory gains and losses and are calculated by restating cost of sale using the replacement cost of goods sold rather than the historic cost. (Caltex Australia's *1999 Annual Review,* emphasis added.)

The price of crude oil increased dramatically in 1999. In Australia, the price increased from \$10.60/barrel at the beginning of the year to \$23.85/barrel at year-end.[17] This implies a specific price index (r) of 125% for oil products.[18] The adjustment to Caltex Australia's weighted average COGS (the LIFO effect) is

$$(BI_W \times r / 2) = (\$AUS \ 235 \ million \times 1.25/2) = \$AUS \ 147 \ million$$

where the \$AUS 235 million is the inventory balance at the beginning of 1999.

This \$AUS 147 million is the holding gain included in income reported under the weighted-average method. Removing the holding gain from income (adding it to COGS) results in a better measure of reported income ($AUS in millions):

Operating income (reported)	\$AUS 217
Adjustment for holding gain	(147)
Operating income (approximate current cost)	\$AUS 70

---

[17] *Source:* U.S. Energy Information Administration, Department of Energy.

[18] This estimate of r reflects the price increase in U.S. dollars. To more accurately measure the effect on Caltex Australia, the analysis should be done with oil prices expressed in Australian dollars, thereby taking into account exchange rate effects as well. However, as the method demonstrated is only an approximation and the exchange rate effect is relatively small, for ease of exposition we have ignored this technicality. (Exhibit 40-4 indicates that the exchange rate effect was only \$3.2 million of the total \$142 million effect.)

| EXHIBIT 40-4 | Caltex Australia |

Selected Income, Balance Sheet and Replacement Cost Disclosures
(in $AUS millions)

A. Income Statement and Balance Sheet Data

	1998	1999
Net revenue	$2,891	$3,153
Operating costs and expenses	(2,693)	(2,936)
Operating profit (before interest, income tax, and abnormal items)	$ 198	$ 217
Ending inventory	234.8	429.0

Caltex Australia uses the weighted-average method to account for its inventory.

B. Replacement Cost of Sales Basis of Accounting

► To assist in understanding the company's operating performance, the directors have provided additional disclosure of the company's results for the year on a replacement-cost-of-sales basis, which excludes net inventory gains and losses adjusted for foreign exchange.

► Operating profit before interest, income tax, and abnormal items on a replacement-cost-of-sales basis was $75.0 million, a reduction of $221.8 million over 1998.

	1995	1996	1997	1998	1999	Total
Historical cost operating profit before interest, income tax, and abnormal items	$263.7	$272.6	$200.6	$216.7	$198.2	$1,151.8
Add/(deduct) inventory losses/(gains)*	(15.5)	(27.9)	53.4	98.6	(141.7)	(33.1)
Replacement cost operating profit before interest, income tax, and abnormal items	$248.2	$244.7	$254.0	$296.8	$ 75.0	$1,118.7

* Historical cost results includes gross inventory gains or losses from the movement in crude prices, net of the related exchange impact. In 1999, historical cost result includes $141.7 million net inventory gain (1998: $98.6 million net inventory loss) from the increase in crude oil prices, made up of **$144.9** million in inventory gains (1998: $124.7 million in inventory losses) net of an unfavorable exchange impact of $3.2 million (1998: $26.1 million gain).

Source: Caltex Australia, *Annual Review 1999.*

Note that this approximation almost equals the estimated ($AUS 144.9 million) inventory holding gain provided by the firm itself in the footnote to part B of Exhibit 40-4.

An alternative approach to arrive at the specific price index appropriate for the oil refining industry would be to examine the financial statements of a competing firm in that industry using LIFO. The LIFO reserve information presented earlier in Exhibit 40-3 for Sunoco Company can be used to approximate the effect of inflation on Caltex Australia.

The 1999 increase in Sunoco's LIFO reserve of $558 million ($205 to $763 million) represents the increase in current costs during 1999. The specific inflation rate r was, therefore,

$558 million/$608 million $= 92\%$

where $608 million is Sunoco's Inventory$_F$ on December 31, 1998.

This estimated r of 92% is considerably smaller than the estimated r of 125% derived from the spot price of oil. However, from Exhibit 40-3, we see that Sunoco's *physical* inventory must have been reduced by approximately 20%. Inventory$_L$ decreased from $403 million to $321 million. As noted, the estimate of r is biased when inventory is reduced dramatically and the greater the change in the relevant price index, the greater the distortion.

We can eliminate the distortion by estimating r based on only 80% of the opening inventory:

Estimating r from Sunoco Data After Adjusting for Reduction in Inventory

	1999 Opening Inventory	80% of 1999 Opening Inventory	1999 Closing Inventory
Inventory$_L$	$403	$321	$321
LIFO reserve	205	164	763
Inventory$_F$	$608	$485	$1,084

Using the second and third columns, the change in the LIFO Reserve equals $599 ($763 − $164) and BI_F = $485. By using the price change (LIFO effect) only for those inventories that Sunoco retained the whole year, our estimate of r becomes 123.5% ($599/$485). This estimate is virtually identical to the 125% estimate using the alternative methodology and, as we showed earlier, is consistent with Caltex Australia's estimate of 1999 inventory holding gains.

Before proceeding to the next section it is worthwhile to explore further Caltex Australia's estimates of its inventory holding gains/losses for the years 1997–1999.

First, compare the pattern of Caltex Australia's adjustments to replacement cost with the pattern of Sunoco's COGS on a FIFO and LIFO basis (Exhibit 40-3). For both companies, the effect of declining prices in 1997 and 1998 was that replacement cost income exceeded operating income ($COGS_L < COGS_F$); in 1999, when prices rose, the situation reversed.

The data in Exhibit 40-4 speak for themselves. Historical cost profit experienced a sharp decline in 1997–1998 relative to 1995–1996 and then recovered slightly in 1999. When holding gains and losses are excluded, however, a different picture emerges: replacement cost profit rose steadily from 1995–1998 (20% increase) and experienced a dramatic 75% decrease in 1999 as prices rose. *Reported operating earnings over this time period were significantly affected by inventory holding gains or losses virtually every year.*

If we recall our discussion of the meaning of income, it seems clear that replacement cost profit is a better measure of earnings. Holding gains and losses are not predictable. Moreover, holding gains must be reinvested in inventory for the firm to remain in business; they are not available for distribution.

Although Caltex Australia, given wide swings in the price of oil, may be an extreme case, it illustrates the necessity of analyzing the inventory accounting of a firm to understand the impact of changing prices on its earnings and net worth.

7   FINANCIAL RATIOS: LIFO VERSUS FIFO

Exhibit 40-5, based on Dopuch and Pincus (1988), compares selected financial characteristics of FIFO and LIFO firms.[19] The comparison is made first on the basis of amounts reported in financial statements (part A) and again after adjusting to the alternative accounting method (part B).

Using reported financial data, part A shows that, based on median values, LIFO firms have higher turnover ratios, less inventory as a percentage of sales or total assets, and lower variation in inventory levels and pretax income.[20] However, for the most part, these differences are not real operating differences but rather are differences due to the accounting choice. In part B the FIFO firms are adjusted to LIFO and the LIFO firms are adjusted to FIFO. The appropriate comparison can now be made with all firms using the same accounting method; that is, the numbers in part B should be compared with those directly above them in part A.

Once the data are adjusted for accounting methods, the differences tend to disappear. For example, the inventory turnover ratio as reported is 4.97 for LIFO firms and 3.88 for FIFO firms—a difference of 28%. After we adjust to the same method, the turnover ratios are:

▶ With all firms on FIFO, 4.03 for LIFO-reporting firms and 3.88 for FIFO-reporting firms—a difference of only 4%

---

[19] Although the data used in their sample (1963–1981) may be outdated, (the direction and degree of) distortion resulting from inventory accounting differences remains relevant.

[20] The variation in inventory and pretax income is measured by the coefficient of variation—(standard deviation divided by the mean).

► With all firms on a LIFO basis, 4.97 versus 4.72, respectively—a difference of only 5%

Similar patterns exist for the other variables.

With Exhibit 40-5 as a prologue, we now focus on how the FIFO/LIFO choice distorts measures of financial performance.

The FIFO/LIFO choice impacts reported profitability, liquidity, activity, and leverage ratios. For some ratios, LIFO provides a better measure, whereas for others, FIFO does. The LIFO-to-FIFO and FIFO-to-LIFO adjustment procedures discussed earlier, however, allow the analyst to make the appropriate adjustments to arrive at the "correct" ratio regardless of the firm's choice of accounting method. *The general guideline is to use LIFO numbers for ratio components that are income related and FIFO-based data for components that are balance sheet related.*

Profitability: Gross Profit Margin

The argument that LIFO better measures current income can be made with reference to gross profit margins. When input prices increase, firms pass along the added costs to customers. Moreover, they try to mark up not only those items purchased at the higher price but also all goods previously purchased. (This

| EXHIBIT 40-5 | Analysis of FIFO/LIFO Firms Based on Median Data, 1963–1981 |

A. Data as Reported

	LIFO	FIFO
COGS/average Inventory	4.97	3.88
Inventory/sales	0.16	0.20
Inventory/assets	0.21	0.29
C.V. inventory*	0.42	0.63
C.V. pretax income	0.74	0.79

B. FIFO Firms Adjusted to LIFO and LIFO Firms to FIFO

	FIFO to LIFO	LIFO to FIFO
COGS/average inventory	4.72	4.03
Inventory/sales	0.17	0.22
Inventory/assets	0.25	0.24
C.V. inventory	0.52	0.67
C.V. pretax income	0.81	0.77

* C.V. is the coefficient of variation (standard deviation divided by the mean).

Source: Nicholas Dopuch and Morton Pincus, "Evidence of the Choice of Inventory Accounting Methods: LIFO Versus FIFO," *Journal of Accounting Research* (Spring 1988), pp. 28–59, Tables 4 and 5, p. 44 (adapted).

policy is economically defensible using the argument made earlier that the real cost of an item sold is its replacement cost.)

Thus, if the pricing policy of the firm in our opening example is to mark up cost by 100% (implying gross profit margin of 50% of sales), the $10,000 of sales in our example would have been arrived at as follows:

Sales: 100 units per quarter for a total of 400 units
Sales Price: Assume 100% markup over current costs

| | Unit | | Sales | |
Quarter	Cost	Price	Units	Dollars
1	$11	$22	100	$ 2,200
2	12	24	100	2,400
3	13	26	100	2,600
4	14	28	100	2,800
Total			400	$10,000

Gross profit margin under FIFO and LIFO would be

Method	Sales	−	COGS	=	Gross Profit	Percent Margin
FIFO	$10,000	−	$4,300	=	$5,700	$5,700/$10,000 = 57.0%
LIFO	$10,000	−	$5,150	=	$4,850	$4,850/$10,000 = 48.5%

The 48.5% gross profit margin reported when LIFO is used is clearly closer to the profit margin intended by the firm's pricing policy. FIFO accounting, in times of rising (falling) prices, will tend to overstate (understate) reported profit margins.

The gross profit margin, by measuring the profitability of current sales, also provides an indication of the future profitability of a firm. Clearly, FIFO net income (which includes holding gains resulting from rising prices) inflates expectations regarding future profitability as future holding gains may be smaller (or negative) if future price increases are lower (or prices fall). *LIFO gives a more accurate forecast of the firm's prospects by removing the impact of price changes.*

Liquidity: Working Capital

LIFO misstates working-capital-based ratios because, as discussed, the inventory component of working capital reports outdated costs. As the purpose of the current ratio is to compare a firm's cash or near-cash assets and liabilities, use of the current value of inventory (FIFO) results in the better measure.

For Sunoco, working capital and current ratios for 1996 to 1999 based on reported data are:

Sunoco
Current Position Based on Reported LIFO Inventory

	Years Ended December 31 (in $millions)			
	1996	**1997**	**1998**	**1999**
Current assets	$1,535	$1,248	$1,180	$1,456
Current liabilities	(1,817)	(1,464)	(1,384)	(1,766)
Working capital	$ (282)	$ (216)	$ (204)	$ (310)
Current ratio	0.84	0.85	0.85	0.82

Adjusting LIFO inventory (and hence current assets) to current cost (FIFO) by adding the LIFO reserves (see Exhibits 40-2 and 40-3) changes Sunoco's current position to:

Sunoco
Adjusted Current Position Based on Current Cost (FIFO) Inventory

	Years Ended December 31 (in $millions)			
	1996	**1997**	**1998**	**1999**
Current assets	$1,535	$1,248	$1,180	$1,456
LIFO reserve	780	492	205	763
Adjusted current assets	$2,315	$1,740	$1,385	$2,219
Current liabilities	(1,817)	(1,464)	(1,384)	(1,766)
Adjusted working capital	$ 498	$ 276	$ 1	$ 453
Adjusted current ratio	1.27	1.19	1.00	1.26

The adjustments convert negative working capital to a positive measure for each year. Similarly, adjusted current ratios are (approximately 20–50%) higher than the unadjusted measures. The adjusted current ratio is also more volatile than the original ratio, reflecting the volatility of the current cost of oil-based inventories.

Activity: Inventory Turnover

Inventory turnover, defined as COGS/average inventory, is often meaningless for LIFO firms due to the mismatching of costs. The numerator represents current costs, whereas the denominator reports outdated historical costs. Thus, the turnover ratio under LIFO will, when prices increase, trend higher irrespective of the trend of physical turnover.

This point is illustrated in Exhibit 40-6. We assume an actual physical turnover of four times per year; that is, the average inventory is sufficient for one quarter. Further, it is assumed that unit costs increase 10% per quarter.

The FIFO inventory ratio is unaffected by the change in price, and at 3.77 is a rough approximation of the actual physical turnover of 4. The

EXHIBIT 40-6	Illustration of Turnover Ratio Under LIFO and FIFO

Year	Quarter	Purchases = Sales	Cost per Unit	Total		For Entire Year	
Opening inventory		100	$10.00	$1,000			
1	1	100	$11.00	$1,100	FIFO	COGS	$4,641
1	2	100	$12.10	$1,210		Avg. inv.	$1,232
1	3	100	$13.31	$1,331	LIFO	COGS	$5,105
1	4	100	$14.64	$1,464		Avg. inv.	$1,000
2	1	100	$16.11	$1,611	FIFO	COGS	$6,795
2	2	100	$17.72	$1,772		Avg. inv.	$1,804
2	3	100	$19.49	$1,949	LIFO	COGS	$7,474
2	4	100	$21.44	$2,144		Avg. inv.	$1,000

	Turnover Ratios	
	Year 1	Year 2
FIFO	3.77	3.77
LIFO	5.11	7.47
Current cost	4.14	4.14

LIFO-based ratios of 5.11 and 7.47 are, however, far from the actual measure of 4, and the discrepancy grows over time. *Thus, to arrive at a reasonable approximation of the inventory turnover ratio for a LIFO firm, we must first convert stated inventory to FIFO.*

The preferred measure of inventory turnover (labeled "current cost" in Exhibit 40-6), however, is based solely on current cost. It combines the two methods, using LIFO COGS in the numerator and the FIFO inventory balance in the denominator. This approach provides the best matching of costs, as current costs are used in both the numerator and denominator. The current cost ratio (4.14) comes closest to the actual measure (based on physical units) of 4.

Using data for Sunoco (Exhibit 40-3), the computed inventory turnover ratios for 1998 and 1999 are (in $millions)

Method	1998		1999	
	Turnover	#Days	Turnover	#Days
LIFO (reported)	$\dfrac{\$5,646}{(\$364 + \$403)/2} = 14.72$	25	$\dfrac{\$7,365}{(\$403 + \$321)/2} = 20.34$	18
FIFO (adjusted)	$\dfrac{\$5,933}{(\$856 + \$608)/2} = 8.10$	45	$\dfrac{\$6,807}{(\$608 + \$1,084)/2} = 8.04$	45
Current cost	$\dfrac{\$5,646}{(\$856 + \$608)/2} = 7.71$	47	$\dfrac{\$7,365}{(\$608 + \$1,084)/2} = 8.70$	42

Comparing the 1998 and 1999 inventory turnover ratios for Sunoco, we see the importance of making current cost adjustments. Based on reported data, it appears that Sunoco turns its inventory very rapidly and increased its efficiency (turnover ratio) by almost 50% in 1999. After adjustment to current cost, however, a different picture emerges as the adjusted ratios imply a six-week rather than a three-week supply of inventory on hand and a much smaller year-to-year improvement in turnover.

Note also the small differences between the FIFO turnover ratios and the more refined current cost ratios. The ratio levels are similar although the current cost ratio shows higher turnover in 1999 whereas the FIFO ratio does not. The similarity is empirically true in most situations and for all practical purposes these two ratio calculations are equivalent as long as prices are not rising too rapidly (as was the case for 1999 oil prices).

Our example illustrates the usefulness of the LIFO-to-current cost adjustment for the analysis of a given company's turnover ratio. The same methodology can be used to compare two companies in the same industry when one uses FIFO and the other LIFO. The first step would be to adjust the LIFO turnover ratio to current cost. *Having made the ratios comparable (by eliminating the effect of different accounting methods), the analyst can then look for other explanations for any difference in the current cost turnover ratio.*

Inventory Theory and Turnover Ratios

Computing the inventory turnover ratio implies that there is some standard against which to measure or that there is an optimal ratio. As for all turnover ratios, one's first instinct is to believe that higher is better, that more rapid inventory turnover indicates a more efficient use of capital. In practice, however, that assumption may be overly simplistic.

The management science literature has devoted much study to the design of optimal inventory ordering policies. The traditional literature in the United States has focused on the economic order quantity (EOQ). More recently, in line with developments in Japanese management practices, focus has turned to just-in-time inventory policies. It is worthwhile to note the implications of these theories for the interpretation of the turnover ratio.

Economic Order Quantity

The construction and use of ratios for cross-sectional and time-series comparisons implicitly assume that the relationship between the numerator and denominator is linear. Applying this assumption to the inventory turnover ratio implies that, as demand increases, the quantity of inventory held should increase proportionately. The EOQ model, however, argues that the optimal level of inventory is proportionate to the *square root* of demand.

Thus, for example, if demand (COGS) increases by four times, one would expect average inventory to double (2 = the square root of 4). As a result, the turnover ratio would also double. Generally, under the EOQ model, turnover ratios should rise as sales increase and smaller firms should have lower turnover ratios. A high turnover ratio for a small firm might not be a sign of efficiency but, on the contrary, an indication that the firm was not managing its inventories in the most economic fashion.

Just in Time

Japanese management practices strive for the ideal that firms should not hold any inventory but rather should receive and ship orders "just in time" (JIT) as needed. Carried to its ultimate conclusion, this would argue for a turnover ratio approaching infinity with zero inventory held. Hence, we would expect the turnover ratios of Japanese firms to be considerably higher than those of American firms. To the extent that U.S. firms adopt these practices, they can be expected to have higher turnover ratios in the future.

One interesting byproduct of the trend toward JIT inventory is that it renders the LIFO/FIFO choice less meaningful. If a firm has no inventories (or relatively small quantities), then there is no significant difference between FIFO and LIFO.[21]

The FIFO/LIFO Choice and Inventory Holding Policy

Another important consideration is that the LIFO/FIFO choice may be related to a firm's actual inventory holding policy. Biddle (1980) found that LIFO firms tend to maintain higher inventory balances (in units) than comparably sized FIFO firms.[22] This finding is consistent with the following three factors:

1. Firms with higher inventory balances have larger potential tax savings from the use of LIFO. Thus, the higher inventory levels that result from the firm's production and operating environment may explain why the firm chose LIFO in the first place.

2. These higher balances may result from the LIFO choice, as LIFO firms attempt to get the most advantage from it by increasing their inventory levels.

3. To avoid LIFO liquidations and consequent higher income taxes, LIFO firms must buy (produce) at least as many items as they sell each year. For LIFO firms it is costly to reduce inventory levels, even when lower expected levels of demand might dictate lower levels.

Solvency: Debt-to-Equity Ratio

We have argued that, to compute liquidity ratios, understated LIFO inventory balances should be restated to current cost by adding the LIFO reserve. For the same reason, the firm's stockholders' equity should be increased by the same amount.[23] The rationale for this adjustment is that the reported equity of the

---

[21] However, suppliers may hold inventory and if a firm owns or controls its suppliers, it may indirectly bear the residual risk usually borne by the suppliers. To properly include the effect of captive suppliers, turnover ratios and other inventory measures should be based on consolidated financial statements, where consolidation reflects economic rather than legal or regulatory control. Admittedly, such consolidation is not always feasible given the paucity of disclosure regarding such relationships.

[22] Barlev et al. (1984) examined Canadian and Israeli firms that were not permitted to use LIFO but used an alternative method of tax adjustment for inflation. They found that inventory balances were higher for firms with large tax benefits from the inflation adjustment.

[23] Lasman and Weil (1978) suggest that the LIFO reserve should not be adjusted for taxes unless a liquidation of LIFO layers is assumed. Further, as liquidations are reported in reverse LIFO order (latest layers are liquidated first), the largest gains reside in the earliest layers. Thus, there is a low probability that the tax effect of "minor" liquidations will be significant and (if we assume that the firm remains in business) extensive liquidations are unlikely, also arguing against tax adjustment. Note that firms have strong incentives to avoid liquidations that would result in significant tax payments. See, however, the discussion regarding the Dhaliwal, Trezevant and Wilkins (2000) paper.

firm is understated because the firm owns inventory whose current value exceeds its carrying value.[24]

For analytical purposes, the inventory choice should be treated like other accounting choices. The fact that the Internal Revenue Service does not permit any difference between financial reporting and tax accounting methods should not tie the hands of the analyst. The valuation of a LIFO firm should not be penalized because it takes advantage of the tax savings inherent in LIFO.

DECLINES IN LIFO RESERVE

8

LIFO reserves can decline for either of the following reasons:

▶ Liquidation of inventories
▶ Price declines

In either case, COGS will be smaller (and income larger) relative to what it would have been had the reserve not declined. *The response of the analyst should not be the same in both cases, however.* For LIFO liquidations, the analyst should exclude the effects of the LIFO liquidation to arrive at a better measure of the firm's operating performance. In the second case, no adjustment is required, as price decreases are a normal part of the firm's operating results (just as much as price increases).

LIFO Liquidations

The discussion of LIFO in this reading thus far has assumed that inventory quantities are stable or increasing. When more goods are sold than are purchased (or manufactured), goods held in opening inventory are included in COGS. For LIFO companies, this results in the liquidation of LIFO layers established in prior years, and such *LIFO liquidations* can materially distort reported operating results.

The carrying cost of the old (in an accounting sense) inventories (which becomes the cost of goods sold associated with the inventory reduction) may be abnormally low and the gross profit margin abnormally high. Thus, LIFO cost no longer approximates current cost. For companies whose base inventory is very old, the distortion from these "paper profits" can be quite large;[25] for analysis, that distortion needs to be removed.

The higher income resulting from LIFO liquidations translates into increased income taxes and lower operating cash flows as taxes that were postponed through the use of LIFO must now be paid. To postpone taxes indefinitely, purchases (production) must always be greater than or equal to sales.[26]

---

[24] Using FIFO values for equity does not contradict our statement that the optimal choice for income presentation is LIFO. Recalling the example in footnote 6, the fact that your house doubled in value from $100,000 to $200,000 at a time when all houses doubled in value means that you do not benefit from selling the house as you will need the larger amount to buy a replacement house. The value of (your equity in) your house is, nevertheless, $200,000.

[25] Schiff (1983) showed that in the recession of 1980–1981, LIFO layers that were liquidated dated back as far as World War II.

[26] See Biddle (1980) for a discussion of the impact of LIFO/FIFO on inventory purchases and holding policy.

LIFO liquidations may result from inventory reductions because of strikes, recession, or declining demand for a particular product line.[27] The paradoxical result is that companies may report surprisingly high profits during economic downturns, as production cuts result in the liquidation of low-cost LIFO inventories. Given the trend toward lower inventory levels in recent years as companies move toward just-in-time or other means of reducing their investment in inventories, LIFO liquidations have become common. Such liquidations are usually disclosed in the inventory footnote of the financial statements. *As profits from LIFO liquidations are nonoperating in nature, they should be excluded from earnings for purposes of analysis.*

Example 40-4

Oilgear

Exhibit 40-7 presents data from the inventory footnote for Oilgear, a manufacturer and distributor of systems and value-engineered components for a broad range of industrial machinery and industrial processes. The company uses the LIFO method of inventory for more than two-thirds of its inventory and reported inventory declines and LIFO liquidations in each of the years 1995–1999.[28] The motivation for the inventory declines (reported in the company's Management Discussion and Analysis) was to "align inventory levels with current (lower) customer demand."

LIFO liquidations added to Oilgear's reported earnings in each of the years 1995 to 1999. As the effect of LIFO liquidations is completely nonoperating in nature, operating results (COGS) should be adjusted to exclude it. Adjustments for each year follow (data in $000):

	1995	1996	1997	1998	1999
Sales	$82,157	$89,621	$90,904	$96,455	$90,709
COGS	(55,858)	(60,184)	(62,507)	(70,634)	(65,521)
Gross margin (reported)	**$26,299**	**$29,437**	**$28,397**	**$25,821**	**$25,188**
LIFO liquidation	800	1,350	750	740	850
Adjusted gross margin	**$25,499**	**$28,087**	**$27,647**	**$25,081**	**$24,338**
Liquidation effect:					
Gross margin increases	**3%**	**5%**	**3%**	**3%**	**3%**
Pretax income (reported)	**$ 3,070**	**$ 3,620**	**$ 3,363**	**$ 1,284**	**$ 1,864**
LIFO liquidation	800	1,350	750	740	850
Adjusted pretax income	**$ 2,270**	**$ 2,270**	**$ 2,613**	**$ 544**	**$ 1,014**

[27] A LIFO liquidation may not be a one-time, random occurrence but a signal that a company is entering an extended period of decline. Stober (1986) found that over 60% of his sample of firms had liquidations in more than one year and 33% experienced liquidations in three or more years. Similarly, Davis et al. (1984) found that liquidations were industry related, indicating a systematic effect, and Fried et al. (1989) found that writedowns and/or restructurings were often preceded by LIFO liquidations.

[28] Exhibit 40-7, from the *1999 Annual Report*, provides information only about 1997–1999 liquidations. Information as to prior-year liquidations was obtained from prior-year annual reports.

Liquidation effect:

Pretax income increases	**35%**	**59%**	**29%**	**136%**	**84%**

Removing the LIFO liquidation effectively adjusts reported LIFO COGS to a current cost basis. Although the effects on gross margin are relatively small (3% to 5%), the effects on income are significant. As a result of the liquidation, Oilgear's reported (pretax) income was 29% to 136% higher than without the liquidation!

EXHIBIT 40-7   **Oilgear**

LIFO Liquidations

From Notes to Financial Statements

INVENTORIES

Inventories at December 31, 1999 and 1998 consist of the following:

	1998	1999
Raw materials	$ 2,601.718	$ 2,447,402
Work in process	21,773,524	17,634,558
Finished goods	6,281,776	4,777,960
Total	$30,657,018	$24,859,920
LIFO reserve	(1,996,000)	(1,627,000)
Total (net of LIFO reserve)	$28,661,018	$23,232,920

During 1999, 1998, and 1997, LIFO inventory layers were reduced. These reductions resulted in charging lower inventory costs prevailing in previous years to cost of sales, thus reducing cost of sales by approximately $850,000, $740,000, and $750,000 below the amount that would have resulted from liquidating inventory recorded at December 31, 1999, 1998, and 1997 prices, respectively.

From Income Statement (in $millions)

	1997	1998	1999
Sales	$90,904	$96,455	$90,709
COGS	(62,507)	(70,634)	(65,521)
Gross margin	28,397	25,821	25,188
Pretax income	3,363	1,284	1,864

Source: Oilgear, *1999 Annual Report.*

Declining Prices

Our discussion thus far has assumed rising price levels. In the analysis of Sunoco, we saw that the LIFO reserve declines when prices fall. In some industries (notably those that are technology related), input prices decline steadily over time; in others (mainly commodity-based industries such as metals and petroleum), prices may fluctuate cyclically.

Declines in LIFO reserves occur whenever inventory costs fall as the lower-cost current purchases enter reported LIFO COGS, decreasing the cost difference between LIFO and FIFO ending inventories. Such declines are not considered LIFO liquidations, and disclosure of their impact is not required.

The theoretical arguments as to which accounting method provides better information still hold. LIFO provides more recent (or current) cost on the income statement and outdated costs on the balance sheet. The direction of the LIFO versus FIFO differences, however, reverses when prices decline. LIFO closing inventories are overstated, and FIFO COGS tends to be higher. Thus, although the pragmatic incentives to use LIFO for tax purposes are lost in an environment of declining prices[29] (LIFO results in higher taxes and lower cash flow), the nature of the information provided does not change. *The LIFO amounts on the balance sheet are not current and require adjustment, whereas the income statement amounts are current and do not need adjustment.*

Example 40-5

Wyman-Gordon

Exhibit 40-8 presents data from the inventory footnote for Wyman-Gordon,[30] a producer of components for the aerospace industry. Wyman-Gordon used the LIFO method for many years and had a large LIFO reserve on its balance sheet. Weak industry conditions led to inventory declines, resulting in significant LIFO liquidations; declining prices also reduced the LIFO reserve. The exhibit indicates that in 1992 and 1993 the LIFO reserve declined $22.838 and $7.917 million, respectively. Wyman-Gordon separated the effects of liquidations and price declines:

	(in $thousands)	
	1992	**1993**
Effect of LIFO liquidation	$(18,388)	$(5,469)
Effect of lower prices	(4,450)	(2,448)
Total LIFO effect	$(22,838)	$(7,917)

When analyzing Wyman-Gordon, the LIFO liquidation effect and the declining price effect should be treated differently. If the analyst's objec-

---

[29] In addition, companies whose inventories are subject to obsolescence often take advantage of the ability (not available, for tax purposes, under LIFO) to write down inventory to market value.

[30] Wyman-Gordon is no longer a public company.

tive is to obtain a more accurate estimate of current cost income, then (*just*) the LIFO liquidation effect should be removed; the effects of declining prices on current purchases and sales, which are operating in nature, should not be removed. However, *for purposes of comparison with firms using FIFO* (i.e., calculating COGS on a FIFO basis), adjustment should be made for the total LIFO effect (liquidations *and* declining prices).

EXHIBIT 40-8	Wyman-Gordon

Inventories and Declines in LIFO Reserve

	in ($thousands)		
	1991	**1992**	**1993**
Inventory		$ 53,688	$42,388
LIFO reserve	64,203	41,365	33,448
Change in LIFO reserve (LIFO effect)		$(22,838)	$ (7,917)

If all inventories valued at LIFO cost had been valued at FIFO cost or market, which approximates current replacement cost, inventories would have been $41,365,000 and $33,448,000 higher than reported at December 31, 1992 and 1993, respectively.

Inventory quantities were reduced in 1991, 1992, and 1993, resulting in the liquidation of LIFO inventories carried at lower costs prevailing in prior years as compared with the cost of current purchases. The effect of lower quantities decreased 1991 loss from operations by $1,529,000, increased 1992 income from operations by $18,388,000, and decreased 1993 loss from operations by $5,469,000, whereas the effect of deflation had no impact on 1991 loss from operations, increased 1992 income from operations by $4,450,000, and decreased 1993 loss from operations by $2,448,000.

Source: Wyman-Gordon, *1993 Annual Report.*

INITIAL ADOPTION OF LIFO AND CHANGES TO AND FROM LIFO

9

Changes in the inventory accounting method require examination for two reasons:

1. Reporting methods for these changes are not symmetric; changing from FIFO to LIFO is not accorded the same treatment as a LIFO to FIFO switch.

2. The implications and motivation behind the accounting change are equally important; the change itself may convey information about the company's operations.

Initial Adoption of LIFO

In the United States the change to LIFO is made only on a prospective basis: GAAP do not require either retroactive restatement or the disclosure of any cumulative effect of the adoption of LIFO. Records necessary for restatement or *pro forma* disclosures often do not exist. Opening inventory in the year of adoption is the base-period inventory for subsequent LIFO computations.

When LIFO is adopted, required footnote disclosures include the impact of the adoption on the period's income before extraordinary items, net income, and related earnings per share amounts. A brief explanation of the reasons for the change in method must be provided and the absence of any cumulative effect disclosures or retroactive adjustment must be noted.

Exhibit 40-9 provides an example of the required disclosures. Effective January 1, 1999, Amerada Hess adopted the LIFO method for its crude oil and refined petroleum products. As Amerada Hess reported earnings per share of $4.88 for that year, the LIFO adoption reduced reported earnings by 18% from the $5.96 that would have been reported without the change. On the other hand, the change to LIFO resulted in a substantial tax saving as calculated below:

From inventory note: LIFO adjustment (effect)	$149,309,000
From accounting change note: effect on net income	97,051,000
Tax savings	$ 52,258,000

Amerada Hess was the last major U.S. oil refiner to adopt LIFO. In its footnote the company states that it switched to LIFO because the "LIFO method more closely matches current costs and revenues and will improve comparability with other oil companies." That may be so but the $52.3 million tax savings may also have had something to do with the company's decision. Note that the company chose to adopt LIFO in 1999, a year in which oil prices rose significantly, justifying the cost of changing accounting methods.

Indeed, adoptions of LIFO are often made to take advantage of the tax benefits inherent in the LIFO method and the propensity to switch is often a function of inflationary conditions. For example, in the early 1970s, over 400 firms switched to LIFO, reflecting double-digit inflation. Interestingly, the stock market has not always regarded such switches favorably despite their (positive) cash flow implications. The empirical section of the reading examines the reasons for this market reaction more closely.

Change from LIFO Method

Unlike changes to LIFO, changes from LIFO to other methods require retroactive restatement of reported earnings to the new method for prior years. The cumulative effect of adopting the new inventory accounting method is credited to retained earnings at the beginning of the earliest restated year to avoid a misstatement of current period income.

SEC regulations require a preferability letter from the firm's independent auditor stating its concurrence with and the rationale for the change. Additionally, a change from LIFO requires Internal Revenue Service approval.[31] The IRS considers changes from LIFO as a loss of tax deferral privileges, and the previous

---

[31] Firms switching from LIFO to another method also agree not to switch back to LIFO for at least 10 years, except under "extraordinary circumstances."

| EXHIBIT 40-9 | Amerada Hess |

Initial Adoption of LIFO

Accounting Changes

Effective January 1, 1999, the Corporation adopted the last-in, first-out (LIFO) inventory method for valuing its refining and marketing inventories. The corporation believes that the LIFO method more closely matches current costs and revenues and will improve comparability with other oil companies. The change to LIFO decreased net income by $97,051,000 for the year ended December 31, 1999 ($1.08 per share basic and diluted). There is no cumulative effect adjustment as of the beginning of the year for this type of accounting change.

Inventories

Inventories at December 31 are as follows:

	Thousands of Dollars	
	1998	**1999**
Crude oil and other charge stocks	$ 35,818	$ 67,539
Refined and other finished products	386,917	393,064
	$422,735	$460,603
Less: LIFO adjustment		(149,309)
		$311,294
Materials and supplies	59,447	61,419
Total	$482,182	$372,713

Source: Amerada Hess, *Annual Report 1999.*

LIFO reserve becomes immediately taxable. Thus, a change from LIFO may bring significant adverse tax and cash flow consequences and requires evaluation of the impact on operations as well as management incentives for the switch. These motivations are also discussed in the following section.

LIFO: A HISTORICAL AND EMPIRICAL PERSPECTIVE

10

Overview of FIFO/LIFO Choice

Out of 600 (generally very large) firms sampled in *Accounting Trends and Techniques*,[32] about half use LIFO for at least part of their inventories. Few firms use LIFO for all inventories. Use by industry classification varies widely. LIFO is used by all rubber and plastic product firms (in this sample) and virtually all firms in the food and drug store, petroleum refining, furniture, and textile industries. None of the firms in the computer and data services, computer software, semiconductors, or telecommunications sectors do so.

---

[32] American Institute of Certified Public Accountants, 2000 edition.

Given the powerful incentives to use LIFO (tax savings and cash flow), two interrelated[33] questions arise:

1. Why do some firms continue to use FIFO?

2. Are firms that use LIFO perceived as being "better off" by the market despite lower reported earnings?

Many empirical studies have examined these issues; in this section we summarize their findings. Before doing so, we note that empirical research related to inventories is not confined to the FIFO/LIFO choice. Box 40-2 shows how analysts can use trends in inventory balances as an aid in forecasting future sales and profitability.

BOX 40-2 USING INVENTORY BALANCES TO AID IN FORECASTING*

Changes in inventory balances can provide ambiguous signals about a firm's future sales and earnings prospects. An unanticipated (from the analyst's perspective) increase in the inventory balance may signal either:†

1. An unexpected decrease in recent demand, causing an unplanned increase in inventory that signals lower future demand, or‡

2. A (planned) increase in inventory levels by management anticipating higher future demand.

These two arguments are, of course, mutually exclusive. Which condition prevails cannot be determined from changes in the inventory account itself. Rather, the change itself acts as a signal for the analyst to investigate (using other sources of information) which condition is most likely for the company in question.§

The previous dichotomy relates only to changes in finished goods inventory. In a manufacturing environment, changes in work-in-process inventory (and to some degree changes in raw materials inventory) may indicate that management is increasing production to meet an increase in actual or anticipated orders.

Consistent with the above, Bernard and Noel (1991) examined whether changes in inventory could be used to forecast future sales and earnings. They found that the implications of inventory changes are not homogeneous for all firms, but differ between retailers and manufacturers.

For retailers, inventory increases signal higher sales but lower earnings and profit margins. This may seem paradoxical but the explanation is straightforward; a drop in demand results in increased inventory. To eliminate "excess" inventory, retailers reduce prices to stimulate sales ("dumping" inventory). Therefore, sales increase but with lower earnings. These effects generally are short-lived as the effect on sales dissipates over time.

For manufacturers, increases in finished goods inventory again indicate lower future demand; higher sales and lower earnings in the short run follow these increases as manufacturers dump unwanted inventory. However, unlike retailers, in the long run (once the initial increase is worked down) the drop in demand persists and future sales and earnings decrease. For raw materials and work in process, on the other hand, increases in inventory levels are consistent with higher future demand and higher future sales.

(continued)

---

[33] These questions are interrelated because if the market reacts (for whatever reason) negatively to a switch to LIFO, it may explain why some firms choose to remain on FIFO.

BOX 40-2 *(continued)*

The foregoing discussion provides a different analytical application of information contained in financial reports. The lessons of the reading, however, must not be forgotten. Any changes in inventory balances must take into consideration the inventory method used. Thus, for a LIFO company, analysis of changes should be based on current cost inventory amounts. In addition, an effort should be made to ensure that the change in inventory balances is driven by quantity changes, not increased prices for the same inventory quantity.

---

* See Bernard and Noel (1991) for a more elaborate discussion of the issues discussed here.

† Unplanned inventory changes may also have a direct impact on future unit production costs. When excess inventory must be reduced, production levels decline and unit costs increase as fixed overhead is spread over fewer units. Conversely, inventory building reduces unit costs by spreading overhead over increased production.

‡ Throughout this section, a distinction between demand and sales must be kept in mind. Lower current demand can be associated with higher future sales if a company, in response to lower demand, cuts prices, thus stimulating sales.

§ The analyst must also be sure that the change is not (1) a result of a change in accounting method, (2) due to acquisitions of other companies, or (3) management's acquisition of more inventory in an attempt to beat an anticipated price increase.

The large number of studies devoted to the FIFO/LIFO choice is due to its richness as the choice has opposite effects on reported income and cash flow. Moreover, the ability to adjust from one method to the other permits "as-if" comparisons in research design. The main empirical findings are relevant to the analyst as they provide evidence that the implications of the FIFO/LIFO choice (or any other accounting choice) are often complex and go beyond the simple trade-off of lower taxes (higher cash flow) versus higher reported income articulated in research designs. We provide a synopsis of the findings in the next section, using the work of Cushing and LeClere (1992) to motivate the discussion.

Summary of FIFO/LIFO Choice

Cushing and LeClere (1992) asked 32 LIFO firms and 70 FIFO firms to rank their reasons for their choice of inventory method. For LIFO firms, the overwhelming primary reason was the favorable tax effect. This result is consistent with research findings that firms using LIFO are primarily motivated by its favorable tax effects and these firms stand to gain the most from using LIFO.

The market, however, does not always regard a switch to LIFO favorably. By switching to LIFO, the firm may be providing (unfavorable) information about its sensitivity to changing prices (or other firm characteristics). Thus, reaction to a change in accounting method may reflect this other information rather than the tax advantage alone.

Reasons for choosing FIFO are complex. Based on the responses in Cushing and LeClere, no single reason emerges as most important for FIFO firms. Over half suggested economic reasons as their motivation. Twenty of the 70 firms (approximately 30%) indicated that LIFO did not provide them with any tax benefits (e.g., declining prices). Others claimed that the accounting and administrative costs to maintain LIFO records and/or ensure that there are no LIFO liquidations kept them from using LIFO. However, just as many firms stated that they chose FIFO because it was a "better accounting method" as it better reflected the physical flow of goods. Close to 40% indicated, as one of their two primary reasons, their concern about the lower earnings resulting from LIFO.[34]

Consistent with the tax effects argument, Dopuch and Pincus (1988) found that FIFO firms were less likely (relative to LIFO firms) to have significant tax savings from LIFO. With respect to the income-enhancing arguments, Hunt (1985) did find some evidence that supported the bonus plan hypothesis.

Many of the inventory studies found the choice of inventory method closely related to industry and size factors, with larger firms opting for LIFO. The industry factor is a consequence of similar production, operating, and *inflation conditions* faced by firms in the same industry. The size factor has been explained in two ways. As noted, adoption of LIFO increases inventory management and control costs, which mitigate the benefit received from tax savings. For large firms, these costs are more readily absorbed and small relative to the potential tax benefits. Alternatively, the size effect reflects the fact that, for political reasons, larger firms tend to choose accounting methods that lower reported earnings.

Exhibit 40-10, based on Cushing and LeClere (1992), summarizes their findings; the variables and the rationale behind them are indicated in the table. Seven of the eight variables that explain the FIFO/LIFO choice are significant in the predicted direction. The estimated tax savings are significantly greater for

---

EXHIBIT 40-10	Variables Hypothesized to Affect FIFO-LIFO Choice

1. *Estimated tax savings* from use of LIFO expected to be larger for LIFO companies.

2. *Inventory materiality:* The larger a firm's inventory balance, the greater the incentive to use LIFO as the potential tax savings is larger.

3. *Tax loss carryforward:* The larger a firm's tax loss carryforward, the less incentive it has to use LIFO.

4. *Inventory variability:* The more variable a firm's inventory balance, the more likely it is to face inventory liquidations. This would tend to favor choosing FIFO over LIFO.

5. *Inventory obsolescence:* If a firm's inventory tends to become obsolete because of new product innovation, then the replacement of old products by new ones raises a difficult LIFO accounting question for which there is no authoritative answer. Such companies may prefer FIFO.

6. *Size as proxy for bookkeeping costs:* The larger the accounting costs required to use LIFO, the less likely a firm would choose LIFO. Larger firms would be able to absorb these costs more readily.

7. *Leverage:* Under the debt covenant hypothesis, firms with higher leverage would prefer FIFO as it would improve their debt/equity ratios.

8. *Current ratio:* Under the debt covenant hypothesis, firms with low current ratios would prefer FIFO, which improves their current ratio.

Source: Barry E. Cushing and Marc J. LeClere, "Evidence on the Determinants of Inventory Accounting Policy Choice," *Accounting Review* (April 1992), pp. 355–366, Table 4, p. 363.

---

[34] These percentages are considerably higher than those reported by Granof and Short (1984) in an earlier survey.

LIFO firms. Consistent with this, FIFO firms have higher average loss carryforwards. Inventory variability is higher for FIFO firms, increasing the chances of LIFO liquidations. FIFO firms tend to be smaller, more highly leveraged, and less liquid. Similarly, the likelihood of inventory obsolescence is also a significant factor. Only the materiality measure is not statistically significant.

These variables indicate possible motivations to stay on FIFO. For a given firm, the analyst should try to determine which of these motivations apply and, thus, whether the firm is justified in staying on FIFO or management is inefficient (or self-serving) by foregoing tax savings from the use of LIFO. Management that remains on FIFO for motives that are either selfish or based on the belief that the market can be fooled should not inspire confidence.

OPTIONAL SEGMENT ENDS

INTERNATIONAL ACCOUNTING AND REPORTING PRACTICES

11

FIFO and the weighted-average method are the most commonly used methods worldwide. Historically, the use of LIFO was essentially limited to companies in the United States, and the significant tax benefits this method can provide suggest that the method will continue to enjoy widespread acceptance. These benefits have resulted in gradual adoption of LIFO as a permitted alternative in countries such as Germany, Italy, and Japan.[35] In some countries, LIFO is allowed for financial reporting but not income taxes, which may account for its lack of popularity in these countries. In practice, LIFO is rarely used in these countries, perhaps because of the low inflation rates of recent years. Non-U.S. reporting standards do not require disclosure of LIFO reserves, reducing the analyst's ability to make the adjustments discussed in this reading.

In the United Kingdom, Statement of Standard Accounting Practice (SSAP) 9 holds that LIFO may not result in a true and fair valuation and, in addition, the method is not allowed for tax purposes.

Average cost is the most widely used method in Germany, although LIFO has been allowed for tax purposes since 1990, and it may change reporting habits.

IASB Standard 2

In 1993, the IASB issued revised International Accounting Standard (IAS) 2, designating FIFO and weighted-average costs as the benchmark treatments and LIFO as the allowed alternative. Firms using LIFO are required to provide FIFO/weighted-average or current cost disclosures, facilitating the adjustments discussed in this reading.

Inventories are reported at the lower of cost or market value; cost depends on the method used. Market is generally defined as the net realizable value with specific limitations in the United States;[36] any writedown is determined on an item-by-item basis. Revised IAS 2 limits itself to net realizable value (NRV), and it does not specify whether the cost versus NRV comparison should be made on an item-by-item basis or by groups of similar items. This standard is similar to those of most other countries.

---

[35] Financial reporting and tax reporting are identical in these countries.

[36] Generally, these limitations ensure that inventories are written down to approximate current cost.

SUMMARY

The choice of accounting method for inventories is one of the basic decisions made by nearly all companies engaged in the manufacturing and distribution of goods. Ideally, the method chosen should result in the best measure of income and financial condition. However, no single method accomplishes these objectives in most cases and, in an environment of changing prices, assumptions as to the flow of costs affect reported income, balance sheet amounts, and associated ratios.

For companies operating in the United States, under conditions of rising prices, the cash flow advantage of LIFO usually dictates the choice of that method. When LIFO is not chosen, therefore, the first question should be: Why not? As the empirical work indicates, managers offer a number of reasons for not using LIFO, only some of which appear valid. Thus, companies that should use LIFO but do not may appear unattractive to investors.

In many cases, the analytical techniques presented in this reading enable the analyst to approximate the effect of LIFO on a company using FIFO or average cost. Such analysis can provide estimates of both the cash savings foregone (relevant to the discussion in the previous paragraph) and the holding gains included in reported income. Similarly, the reading demonstrates how the analyst can adjust from LIFO to FIFO where appropriate. The reading also explores the effects of liquidations and the incentives for the FIFO/LIFO choice, and concludes with a review of inventory accounting standards applied internationally.

PROBLEMS FOR READING 40

1. [Allocation of purchase costs under different inventory methods; CFA© adapted] Assume the following:

Quarter	Units Purchased	Per Unit Cost	Dollar Purchases	Unit Sales
I	200	$22	$ 4,400	200
II	300	24	7,200	200
III	300	26	7,800	200
IV	200	28	5,600	200
Year	1,000		$25,000	800

Inventory at beginning of Quarter I: 400 units at $20 per unit 5 $ 8,000
Inventory at end of Quarter IV: 600 units

A. Calculate reported inventory at the end of the year under *each* of the following inventory methods:

  i. FIFO

  ii. LIFO

  iii. Average cost

B. Calculate the cost of goods sold for the year under each method listed in part a.

C. Discuss the effect of the differences among the three methods on:

  i. Reported income for the year

  ii. Stockholders' equity at the end of the year

2. [Effect of inventory methods on financial statements; CFA© adapted] Compare the effect of the use of the LIFO inventory method with use of the FIFO method on each of the following, assuming rising prices and stable inventory quantities:

  i. Gross profit margin

  ii. Net income

  iii. Cash from operations

  iv. Inventories

  v. Inventory turnover ratio

  vi. Working capital

  vii. Total assets

  viii. Debt-to-equity ratio

3. [Inventory methods; basic relationships] The M&J Company begins operations on January 1, 20X0 with the following balance sheet:

Cash $10,000   Common stock $10,000

During the year, the company maintains its inventory accounts using the FIFO method. Before a provision for income tax, the balance sheet at December 31, 20X0, is:

Cash	$ 5,000	Common stock	$10,000
Inventory	10,000	Pretax income	5,000
	$15,000		$15,000

M&J has 20X0 sales of $25,000. The company sells half of the *units* purchased during the year. Operating expenses (excluding COGS) are $12,000.

Prior to issuing financial statements, the company considers its choice of inventory method. Assume a tax rate of 40% and a dividend payout ratio of 50%.

A. Using the information provided, complete the following table:

	FIFO	Weighted Average	LIFO
Sales	$25,000	$25,000	$25,000
COGS			
Other expenses	12,000	12,000	12,000
Pretax income			
Income tax expense			
Net income			
Dividends paid			
Retained earnings			
Cash from operations			
Closing cash balance			
Closing inventory			
Inventory purchases			

B. Prepare a balance sheet for M&J at December 31, 20X0, assuming use of the:

   i. LIFO inventory method

   ii. Weighted-average method

   iii. FIFO inventory method

C. Discuss the advantages and disadvantages of each of the three possible choices of inventory method.

Problem 4 is based on the following data, adapted from the actual financial statements of two firms in the automobile replacement parts industry.

Zenab Distributors, Balance Sheets, at December 31

	20X1	20X2
Cash	$ 500	$ 100
Accounts receivable (net)	8,100	8,300
Inventory	24,900	25,200
Current assets	$33,500	$33,600
Current liabilities	11,600	12,700

Zenab Distributors uses the LIFO method of accounting for 70% of its inventories; it uses FIFO for the remainder. If all inventories were carried at FIFO, inventory would be higher by $3,600 and $5,100 in 20X1 and 20X2, respectively.

Faybech Parts, Balance Sheets, at December 31

	20X1	20X2
Cash	$ 1,000	$ 600
Accounts receivable (net)	11,400	13,900
Inventory	22,300	30,300
Current assets	$34,700	$44,800
Current liabilities	10,700	12,200

Faybech Parts uses FIFO accounting for all inventories.

Income Statements, Year Ended December 31, 20X2

	Zenab	Faybech
Sales	$92,700	$77,000
COGS	61,300	52,000
Gross profit	$31,400	$25,000
Selling and general expense	26,400	21,500
Pretax income	$ 5,000	$ 3,500
Income tax expense	2,000	1,400
Net income	$ 3,000	$ 2,100

4. [LIFO versus FIFO; effect on ratios; adjusting ratios]
   A. Using *only reported* financial data, compute each of the following ratios for both Zenab and Faybech:
      i. Current ratio (20X1 and 20X2)
      ii. Inventory turnover (20X2)
      iii. Gross profit margin (20X2)
      iv. Pretax profit margin (EBT to sales) (20X2)
   B. Briefly compare the performance of the two firms in 20X2 based on the ratios computed in part a.
   C. Recalculate each of the ratios in part a with both companies:
      i. On FIFO
      ii. On LIFO
      iii. Using the current cost method
   D. Select the basis of comparison for *each* of the four ratios that you feel is most meaningful. Justify *each* choice.

5. [LIFO versus FIFO; effect on ratios; adjusting ratios; CFA© adapted] The Zeta Corp. uses LIFO inventory accounting. The footnotes to the 20X4 financial statements contain the following data as of December 31:

	20X3	20X4
Raw materials	$392,675	$369,725
Finished products	401,325	377,075
Inventory on FIFO basis	$794,000	$746,800
LIFO reserve	(46,000)	(50,000)
Inventory on LIFO basis	$748,000	$696,800

You are also provided with the following data:

▶ The company has a marginal tax rate of 35%.

▶ COGS for 20X4 is $3,800,000.

▶ Net income for 20X4 is $340,000.

▶ Return on equity for 20X4 is 4.6%.

A. Calculate 20X4 net income for Zeta, assuming that it uses the FIFO inventory method.

B. Calculate the company's inventory turnover ratio on both a FIFO and LIFO basis.

C. Calculate Zeta's return on equity on a FIFO basis. (Remember to adjust both the numerator and denominator.)

D. Discuss the usefulness of the adjustments made in parts a, b, and c to a financial analyst.

E. Describe alternative measures of inventory turnover and return on equity that would be more useful to assess Zeta's operating performance.

6. [Adjusting for alternative accounting methods; effects of liquidation] The Noland Company [NOLD] reported the following operating results:

Years Ended December 31 in ($thousands)			
	1997	**1998**	**1999**
Sales	$464,965	$465,479	$482,830
COGS	328,172	348,587	362,108
Gross margin	$ 93,753	$ 93,446	$ 96,938

In its 1999 annual report, the company states that

> 1999's gross profit margin suffered from the year-end LIFO adjustment which increased cost of goods sold by $1,391,000 compared to $381,000 a year ago.

Information from the company's inventory footnote is presented below:

December 31 (in $thousands)			
	1997	**1998**	**1999**
Inventory, at approximate replacement cost	$98,965	$103,446	$104,106
Reduction to LIFO	32,495	32,876	34,267
LIFO inventory	$66,470	$ 70,570	$ 69,839

Liquidation of certain inventory layers carried at the higher/lower costs that prevailed in prior years as compared with the costs of 1999, 1998, and 1997 purchases had the effect of increasing 1999 and 1997 net income $47 thousand and $393 thousand, respectively, and decreasing 1998 net income $150 thousand.

A. Describe the "year-end LIFO adjustment" and show how the company calculated it for both 1998 and 1999.

B. Compute the company's 1998 and 1999 COGS using the FIFO method.

C. Explain how it is possible for a LIFO liquidation to decrease income as in 1998.

D. Excluding the effects of the LIFO liquidation, compute COGS for 1998 and 1999 using:

    i. The company's current accounting method

    ii. The FIFO method

E. State and justify which of the following measures of COGS is most appropriate to use to measure Noland's profitability:

    i. As reported

    ii. As computed in part b

    iii. As computed in part d

F. Describe how to use the inventory footnote data to adjust Noland's net worth (book value) to a current cost basis for 1998 and 1999.

7. [Decline in LIFO reserve] The following footnote appeared in the annual report of A. T. Cross [ATX], a pen manufacturer:

Note B—Inventories

Domestic writing instrument inventories, approximating $13,404,000 and $5,695,000 at December 30, 2000 and January 1, 2000, respectively, are priced at the lower of LIFO cost or market. The remaining inventories are priced at the lower of FIFO cost or market. If the FIFO method of inventory valuation had been used for those inventories priced using the LIFO method, inventories would have been approximately $9,614,000 and $11,227,000 higher than reported at December 30, 2000 and January 1, 2000, respectively. The Company believes the LIFO method of inventory valuation ordinarily results in a more appropriate matching of its revenues to their related costs, since current costs are included in cost of goods sold, and distortions in reported income due to the effect of changing prices are reduced.

A. Cross did not report any LIFO liquidation for 2000. Explain how its LIOF reserve could decline.

B. State two reasons why Cross might choose to continue to use the LIFO method despite the decline in the LIFO reserve.

8. [Effect of LIFO liquidations on gross margins] The following data were obtained from annual reports of Stride-Rite [SRR], a shoe manufacturer and retailer:

Years Ended December 31 (in $thousands)			
	1997	**1998**	**1999**
Sales	$515,728	$539,413	$572,696
COGS	(328,172)	(348,587)	(362,108)
Gross profit	$187,556	$190,826	$210,588
LIFO liquidation (net of tax)	$ 3,379	$ 1,733	0

A. Compute the gross margin percentage for each year, 1997–1999.

B. Stride-Rite disclosed the effect of LIFO liquidations net of income tax. Assuming a tax rate of 35%, recompute Stride-Rite's gross margin for the years 1997–1999 after removing the effect of LIFO liquidations.

C. Explain why the trend in gross margins shown in part b is a better indictor of Stride-Rite's performance than the reported gross margins.

9. [Effect of inventory methods on contracts] The Sechne Company has entered into a number of agreements in the past year. These agreements contain provisions that depend on the firm's reported financial statements:

    i. *Management compensation plan.* Bonuses are based on a weighted average of reported net income and cash from operations.

    ii. *Bond indenture.* Specifies that the firm must maintain a minimum level of working capital, and dividend payments to shareholders require a minimum level of retained earinings.

    iii. *Labor contract.* Employees have a profit-sharing plan that pays them a share of reported net income in excess of a specified level.

Sechne's corporate controller, who is *both* a manager and a shareholder, must select the accounting methods used for financial reporting. Discuss how these agreements may affect the controller's choice of an inventory accounting method for Sechne.

LONG-TERM ASSETS

by Belverd E. Needles and Marian Powers

LEARNING OUTCOMES

The candidate should be able to:

a. describe the factors that distinguish long-term assets from other assets and identify the common types of long-term assets and how carrying value is determined on the balance sheet;

b. determine the costs that are capitalized to property, plant and equipment and determine which costs are expensed as incurred;

c. explain depreciation accounting (including the reasons for depreciation), calculate depreciation using the straight-line, production (also known as units-of-production), and declining-balance methods, and calculate depreciation after revising the estimated useful life of an asset;

d. describe how to account for the sale, exchange, or disposal of depreciable assets, and determine whether a gain or loss is recorded;

e. identify assets that should be classified as natural resources, determine their carrying values on the balance sheet and calculate depletion;

f. identify the types of intangible assets and describe how the accounting treatment for goodwill under U.S. GAAP differs from the accounting treatment for other intangible assets.

INTRODUCTION   1

Long-term assets include tangible asset, such as land, buildings, and equipment, natural resources, such as timberland and oil fields and intangible assets, such as patents and copyrights. These assets represent a company's strategic commitments well into the future. The judgments related to their acquisition, operation, and disposal and to the allocation of their costs will affect a company's performance for years to come. Investors and creditors rely on accurate and full reporting of the assumptions and judgments that underlie the measurement of long-term assets.

Financial Accounting, Ninth Edition, by Belverd E. Needles and Marian Powers, Copyright © 2004. Reprinted with permission of the Houghton Mifflin Company.

DECISION POINT A USER'S FOCUS

APPLE COMPUTER, INC.

▶ What are Apple's long-term assets?

▶ What are its policies in accounting for long-term assets?

▶ Does the company generate enough cash flow to finance its continued growth?

Long known for its innovative technology and design of computers, **Apple** revolutionized the music industry with its digital iPod music player. The company's success stems from its willingness to invest in research and development and long-term assets to create new products. Each year, it spends almost $500 million on research and development and about $175 million on new long-term assets. Almost 40 percent of its assets are long term. You can get an idea of the extent and importance of Apple's long-term assets by looking at the Financial Highlights from its balance sheet.[1]

APPLE COMPUTER'S FINANCIAL HIGHLIGHTS
(In millions)

	2004	2003
Property, Plant, and Equipment:		
Land and buildings	$ 351	$ 350
Machinery, equipment, and internal-use software	422	393
Office furniture and equipment	79	74
Leasehold improvements	446	357
	1,298	1,174
Less accumulated depreciation and amortization	591	505
Total property, plant, and equipment, net	$ 707	$ 669
Other Noncurrent Assets:		
Goodwill	80	85
Acquired intangible assets	17	24
Other noncurrent assets	191	150
Total other noncurrent assets	$ 288	$ 259

2

MANAGEMENT ISSUES RELATED TO LONG-TERM ASSETS

Study Note
For an asset to be classified as property, plant, and equipment, it must be "put in use," which means it is available for its intended purpose. An emergency generator is "put in use" when it is available for emergencies, even if it is never used.

Long-term assets were once called fixed assets, but this term has fallen out of favor because it implies that the assets last forever, which they do not. Long-term assets have the following characteristics:

▶ *They have a useful life of more than one year.* This distinguishes them from current assets, which a company expects to use up or convert to cash within one year or during its operating cycle, whichever is longer. They also differ from current assets in that they support the operating cycle, rather than being part of it. Although there is no strict rule for defining the useful life of a long-term asset, the most common criterion is that the

[1] Apple Computer, Inc., *Annual Report*, 2004.

asset be capable of repeated use for at least a year. Included in this category is equipment used only in peak or emergency periods, such as electric generators.

▶ *They are used in the operation of a business.* Assets not used in the normal course of business, such as land held for speculative reasons or buildings no longer used in ordinary business operations, should be classified as long-term investments, not as long-term assets.

▶ *They are not intended for resale to customers.* An asset that a company intends to resell to customers should be classified as inventory—not as a long-term asset—no matter how durable it is. For example, a printing press that a manufacturer offers for sale is part of the manufacturer's inventory, but it is a long-term asset for a printing company that buys it to use in its operations.

Figure 41-1 shows the relative importance of long-term assets in various industries. Figure 41-2 shows how long-term assets are classified and defines the methods of accounting for them. Plant assets, which are **tangible assets**, are accounted for through **depreciation**. (Although land is a tangible asset, it is not depreciated because it has an unlimited life.) **Natural resources**, which are also tangible assets, are accounted for through **depletion**. **Intangible assets** are accounted for through **amortization**. (Although goodwill is an intangible asset, it is not expensed; however, it is reviewed for impairment each year.)

Long-term assets are generally reported at carrying value. As shown in Figure 41-3, **carrying value** (also called *book value*) is the unexpired part of an asset's cost. If a long-term asset loses some or all of its potential to generate revenue before the end of its useful life, it is deemed *impaired,* and its carrying value is reduced.

All long-term assets are subject to an annual impairment evaluation. **Asset impairment** occurs when the carrying value of a long-term asset exceeds its fair value.[2] F*air value* is the amount for which the asset could be bought or sold in a

FIGURE 41-1   Long-Term Assets as a Percentage of Total Assets for Selected Industries

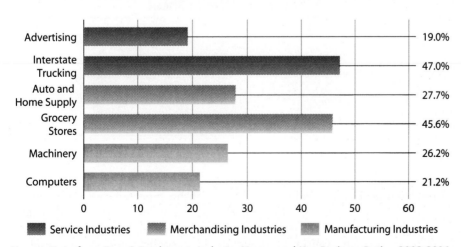

Source: Data from Dun & Bradstreet, *Industry Norms and Key Business Ratios,* 2003-2004

---

[2] *Statement of Financial Accounting Standards* No. 144, "Accounting for the Impairment or Disposal of Long-Lived Assets" (Norwalk, Conn.: Financial Accounting Standards Board, 2001).

FIGURE 41-2   Classification of Long-Term Assets and Methods of Accounting for Them

BALANCE SHEET
Long-Term Assets

INCOME STATEMENT
Expenses

Tangible Assets: long-term assets that have physical substance

Land

Plant, Buildings, Equipment (plant assets)

Land is not expensed because it has an unlimited life.

Depreciation: periodic allocation of the cost of a tangible long-lived asset (other than land and natural resources) over its estimated useful life

Natural Resources: long-term assets purchased for the economic value that can be taken from the land and used up, as with ore, lumber, oil, and gas or other resources contained in the land

Mines

Timberland

Oil and Gas Fields

Depletion: exhaustion of a natural resource through mining, cutting, pumping, or other extraction, and the way in which the cost is allocated

Intangible Assets: long-term assets that have no physical substance but have a value based on rights or advantages accruing to the owner

Patents, Copyrights, Trademarks, Franchises, Leaseholds, Goodwill

Amortization: periodic allocation of the cost of an intangible asset to the periods it benefits

Goodwill is not expensed, but its value is reviewed annually.

FIGURE 41-3   Carrying Value of Long-Term Assets on the Balance Sheet

Plant Assets	Natural Resources	Intangible Assets
Less Accumulated Depreciation	Less Accumulated Depletion	Less Accumulated Amortization
Carrying Value	Carrying Value	Carrying Value

current transaction. For example, if the sum of the expected cash flows from an asset is less than its carrying value, the asset would be impaired. Reducing carrying value to fair value, as measured by the present value of future cash flows, is an application of conservatism. A reduction in carrying value as the result of impairment is recorded as a loss. When the market prices used to establish fair value are not available, the amount of an impairment must be estimated from the best available information.

In 2004, **Apple** recognized losses of $5.5 million in asset impairments. A few years earlier, in the midst of an economic slowdown in the telecommunications industry, **WorldCom** recorded asset impairments that totaled $79.8 billion, the largest impairment write-down in history. Since then, other telecommunications companies, including **AT&T** and **Qwest Communications**, have taken large impairment write-downs. Due to these companies' declining revenues, the carrying value of some of their long-term assets no longer exceeded the cash flows that they were meant to help generate.[3] Because of the write-downs, these companies reported large operating losses.

Taking a large write-down in a bad year is often called "taking a big bath" because it "cleans" future years of the bad year's costs and thus can help a company return to a profitable status. In other words, by taking the largest possible loss on a long-term asset in a bad year, companies hope to reduce the costs of depreciation or amortization on the asset in subsequent years.

In the next few pages, we discuss the management issues related to long-term assets—how management decides whether it will acquire them, how it will finance them, and how it will account for them.

Acquiring Long-Term Assets

The decision to acquire a long-term asset is a complex process. For example, **Apple's** decision to invest capital in establishing its own retail stores throughout the country required very careful analysis. Methods of evaluating data to make rational decisions about acquiring long-term assets are grouped under a topic called capital budgeting, which is usually covered as a managerial accounting topic. However, an awareness of the general nature of the problem is helpful in understanding the management issues related to long-term assets.

To illustrate an acquisition decision, suppose that Apple's management is considering the purchase of a $50,000 customer-relations software package, Management estimates that the new software will save net cash flows of $20,000 per year for four years, the usual life of new software, and that the software will be worth $10,000 at the end of that period. These data are summarized as follows:

	20 × 5	20 × 6	20 × 7	20 × 8
Acquisition cost	($50,000)			
Net annual savings in cash flows	$20,000	$20,000	$20,000	$20,000
Disposal price				10,000
Net cash flows	($30,000)	$20,000	$20,000	$30,000

[3] Sharon Young, "Large Telecom Firms, After WorldCom Moves, Consider Writedowns," *The Wall Street Journal,* March 18, 2003.

To put the cash flows on a comparable basis, it is helpful to use present values tables. If the interest rate set by management as a desirable return is 10 percent compounded annually, the purchase decision would be evaluated as follows:

		Present Value
Acquisition cost	Present value factor = 1.000	
	1.000 × $50,000	($50,000)
Net annual savings in cash flows	Present value factor = 3.170 (Table 4: 4 periods, 10%)	
	3.170 × $20,000	63,400
Disposal price	Present value factor = .683 (Table 3: 4 periods, 10%)	
	.683 × $10,000	6,830
Net present value		$20,230

As long as the net present value is positive, Apple will earn at least 10 percent on the investment. In this case, the return is greater than 10 percent because the net present value is a positive $20,230. Moreover, the net present value is large relative to the investment. Based on this analysis, it appears that Apple's management should make the decision to purchase. However, in making its decision, it should take other important considerations into account, including the costs of training personnel to use the software. It should also allow for the possibility that because of unforeseen circumstances, the savings may not be as great as expected.

Information about acquisitions of long-term assets appears in the investing activities section of the statement of cash flows. In referring to this section of its 2004 annual report, Apple's management makes the following statement:

> The company's total capital expenditures were $176 million during fiscal 2004. . . . The company currently anticipates it will utilize approximately $240 million for capital expenditures during 2005, approximately $125 million of which is expected to be utilized for further expansion of the Company's Retail segment and the remainder utilized to support normal replacement of existing capital assets.

Financing Long-Term Assets

When management decides to acquire a long-term asset, it must also decide how to finance the purchase. Many financing arrangements are based on the life of the asset. For example, an automobile loan generally spans 4 or 5 years, whereas a mortgage on a house may span 30 years. For a major long-term acquisition, a company may issue stock, long-term notes, or bonds. Some companies are profitable enough to pay for long-term assets out of cash flows from operations. A good place to study a company's investing and financing activities is its statement of cash flows, and a good measure of its ability to finance long-term assets is free cash flow.

Free cash flow is the amount of cash that remains after deducting the funds a company must commit to continue operating at its planned level. The commitments to be covered include current or continuing operations, interests, income taxes, dividends, and net capital expenditures (purchases of plant assets minus sales of plant assets). If a company fails to pay for current or continuing operations, interest, and income taxes, its creditors and the government can take legal action. Although the payment of dividends is not strictly required, dividends normally represent a commitment to stockholders. If they are reduced or eliminated, stockholders will be unhappy, and the price of the company's stock will fall. Net capital expenditures represent management's plans for the future.

A positive free cash flow means that a company has met all its cash commitments and has cash available to reduce debt or to expand its operations. A negative free cash flow means that it will have to sell investments, borrow money, or issue stock in the short term to continue at its planned level. If free cash flow remains negative for several years, a company may not be able to raise cash by issuing stock or bonds.

Using data from **Apple's** statement of cash flows in its 2004 annual report, we can compute the company's free cash flow as follows (in millions):

$$
\begin{aligned}
\text{Free Cash Flow} &= \text{Net Cash Flows from Operating Activities} - \text{Dividends} \\
&\quad - (\text{Purchases of Plant Assets} - \text{Sales of Plant Assets}) \\
&= \$934 - \$0 - (\$176 - \$0) \\
&= \$758
\end{aligned}
$$

This analysis confirms Apple's strong financial position. Its cash flow from operating activities far exceeds its net capital expenditures of $176 million. A factor that contributes to its positive free cash flow of $758 million is that the company pays no dividends. The financing activities section of Apple's statement of cash flows also indicates that the company, rather than incurring debt for expansion, actually reduced its long-term debt by $300 million.

> **Study Note**
> The computation of free cash flow uses *net capital expenditures* in place of *(purchases of plant assets— sales of plant assets)* when plant assets are small or immaterial.

Applying the Matching Rule

When a company records an expenditure as a long-term asset, it is deferring an expense until a later period. Thus, the current period's profitability looks better than it would if the expenditure had been expensed immediately. Management has considerable latitude in making the judgments and estimates necessary to account for all types and aspects of long-term assets. Sometimes, this latitude is used unwisely and unethically. For example, in the infamous **WorldCom** accounting fraud, management ordered that certain expenditures that should have been recorded as operating expenses be capitalized as long-term assets and written off over several years. The result was an overstatement of income by about $10 billion, which ultimately led to the largest bankruptcy in the history of U.S. business.

To avoid fraudulent reporting of long-term assets, a company's management must apply the matching rule in resolving two important issues. The first is how much of the total cost of a long-term asset to allocate to expense in the current accounting period. The second is how much to retain on the balance sheet as an asset that will benefit future periods. To resolve these issues, management must answer four important questions about the acquisition, use, and disposal of each long-term asset (see Figure 41-4):

1. How is the cost of the long-term asset determined?

2. How should the expired portion of the cost of the long-term asset be allocated against revenues over time?

3. How should subsequent expenditures, such as repairs and additions, be treated?

4. How should disposal of the long-term asset be recorded?

FIGURE 41-4   Issues in Accounting for Long-Term Assets

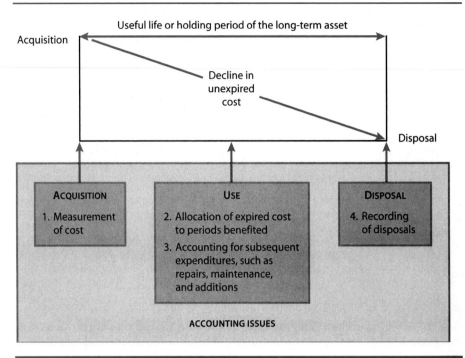

Management's answers to these questions can be found in the company's annual report under management's discussion and analysis and in the notes in the financial statements.

ACQUISITION COST OF PROPERTY, PLANT, AND EQUIPMENT

Expenditure refers to a payment or an obligation to make a future payment for an asset, such as a truck, or for a service, such as a repair. Expenditures are classified as capital expenditures or revenue expenditures.

▶ A **capital expenditure** is an expenditure for the purchase or expansion of a long-term asset. Capital expenditures are recorded in asset accounts because they benefit several future accounting periods.

▶ A **revenue expenditure** is an expenditure made for the ordinary repairs and maintenance needed to keep a long-term asset in good operating condition. For example, trucks, machines, and other equipment require periodic tune-ups and routine repairs. Expenditures of this type are recorded in expense accounts because their benefits are realized in the current period.

Capital expenditures include outlays for plant assets, natural resources, and intangible assets. They also include expenditures for the following:

▶ **Additions**, which are enlargements to the physical layout of a plant asset. For example, if a new wing is added to a building, the benefits from the expenditure will be received over several years, and the amount paid should be debited to an asset account.

▶ **Betterments**, which are improvements to a plant asset but that do not add to the plant's physical layout. Installation of an air-conditioning system is an example. Because betterments provide benefits over a period of years, their costs should be debited to an asset account.

▶ **Extraordinary repairs**, which are repairs that significantly enhance a plant asset's estimated useful life or residual value. For example, a complete overhaul of a building's heating and cooling system may extend the system's useful life by five years. Extraordinary repairs are typically recorded by reducing the Accumulated Depreciation account; the assumption in doing so is that some of the depreciation previously recorded on the asset has now been eliminated. The effect of the reduction is to increase the asset's carrying value by the cost of the extraordinary repair. The new carrying value should be depreciated over the asset's new **estimated useful life**.

The distinction between capital and revenue expenditures is important in applying the matching rule. For example, if the purchase of a machine that will benefit a company for several years is mistakenly recorded as a revenue expenditure, the total cost of the machine becomes an expense on the income statement in the current period. As a result, current net income will be reported at a lower amount (understated), and in future periods, net income will be reported at a higher amount (overstated). If, on the other hand, a revenue expenditure, such as the routine overhaul of a piece of machinery, is charged to an asset account, the expense of the current period will be understated. Current net income will be overstated by the same amount, and the net income of future periods will be understated.

General Approach to Acquisition Costs

The acquisition cost of property, plant, and equipment includes all expenditures reasonable and necessary to get an asset in place and ready for use. For example, the cost of installing and testing a machine is a legitimate cost of acquiring the machine. However, if the machine is damaged during installation, the cost of repairs is an operating expense, not an acquisition cost.

Acquisition cost is easiest to determine when a purchase is made for cash. In that case, the cost of the asset is equal to the cash paid for it plus expenditures for freight, insurance while in transit, installation, and other necessary related costs. Expenditures for freight, insurance while in transit, and installation are included in the cost of the asset because they are necessary if the asset is to function. In accordance with the matching rule, these expenditures are allocated over the asset's useful life rather than charged as expenses in the current period.

Any interest charges incurred in purchasing an asset are not a cost of the asset; they are a cost of borrowing the money to buy the asset and are therefore an operating expense. As exception to this rule is that interest costs incurred during the construction of an asset are properly included as a cost of the asset.[4]

As a matter of practicality, many companies establish policies that define when an expenditure should be recorded as an expense or as an asset. For example,

Study Note
Expenditures necessary to prepare an asset for its intended use are a cost of the asset.

---

[4] *Statement of Financial Accounting Standards* No. 34, "Capitalization of Interest Cost" (Norwalk, Conn.: Financial Accounting Standards Board, 1979), par. 9-11.

small expenditures for items that qualify as long-term assets may be treated as expenses because the amounts involved are not material in relation to net income. Thus, although a wastebasket may last for years, it would be recorded as supplies expense rather than as a depreciable asset.

Specific Applications

In the sections that follow, we discuss some of the problems of determining the cost of long-term plant assets.

Study Note
Many costs may be incurred to prepare land for its intended use and condition. All such costs are a cost of the land.

Land   The purchase price of land should be debited to the Land account. Other expenditures that should be debited to the Land account include commissions to real estate agents; lawyers' fees; accrued taxes paid by the purchaser; costs of preparing the land to build on, such as the costs of tearing down old buildings and grading the land; and assessments for local improvements, such as putting in streets and sewage systems. The cost of landscaping is usually debited to the Land account because such improvements are relatively permanent. Land is not subject to depreciation because it has an unlimited useful life.

Let us assume that a company buys land for a new retail operation. The net purchase price is $170,000. The company also pays brokerage fees of $6,000, legal fees of $2,000, $10,000 to have an old building on the site torn down, and

To make way for its new headquarters in Birmingham, Alabama, Energen Corporation had this ten-story building imploded. Like other costs involved in preparing land for use, the cost of implosion is debited to the Land account. Other expenditures debited to the Land account include the purchase price of the land, brokerage and legal fees involved in the purchase, taxes paid by the purchaser, and landscaping.

Courtesy of AP/Wide World Photos.

$1,000 to have the site graded. It receives $4,000 in salvage from the old building. The cost of the land is $185,000, calculated as follows:

Net purchase price		$170,000
Brokerage fees		6,000
Legal fees		2,000
Tearing down old building	$10,000	
Less salvage	4,000	6,000
Grading		1,000
Total cost		$185,000

Study Note
The costs of tearing down existing buildings can be major. Companies may spend millions of dollars imploding buildings so they can remove them and build new ones.

Land Improvements Some improvements to real estate, such as driveways, parking lots, and fences, have a limited life and thus are subject to depreciation. They should be recorded in an account called Land Improvements rather than in the Land account.

Buildings When a company buys a building, the cost includes the purchase price and all repairs and other expenditures required to put the building in usable condition. When a company uses a contractor to construct a building, the cost includes the net contract price plus other expenditures necessary to put the building in usable condition. When a company constructs its own building, the cost includes all reasonable and necessary expenditures, including the costs of materials, labor, part of the overhead and other indirect costs, architects' fees, insurance during construction, interest on construction loans during the period of construction, lawyers' fees, and building permits. Because buildings have a limited useful life, they are subject to depreciation.

Leasehold Improvements Improvements to leased property that become the property of the lessor (the owner of the property) at the end of the lease are called **leasehold improvements**. For example, a tenant's installation of light fixtures, carpets, or walls would be considered a leasehold improvement. These improvements are usually classified as tangible assets in the property, plant, and equipment section of the balance sheet. Sometimes, they are included in the intangible assets section; the theory in reporting them as intangibles is that because they revert to the lessor at the end of the lease, they are more of a right than a tangible asset. The cost of a leasehold improvement is depreciated or amortized over the remaining term of the lease or the useful life of the improvement, whichever is shorter.

Leasehold improvements are fairly common in large businesses. A study of large companies showed that 19 percent report leasehold improvements. The percentage is likely to be much higher for small businesses because they generally operate in leased premises.[5]

Equipment The cost of equipment includes all expenditures connected with purchasing the equipment and preparing it for use. Among these expenditures are the invoice price less cash discounts; freight, including insurance; excise taxes and tariffs; buying expenses; installation costs; and test runs to ready the equipment for operation. Equipment is subject to depreciation.

Study Note
The wiring and plumbing of a dental chair are included in the cost of the asset because they are a necessary cost of preparing the asset for use.

---

[5] American Institute of Certified Public Accountants, *Accounting Trends & Techniques* (New York: AICPA, 2004).

Group Purchases   Companies sometimes purchase land and other assets for a lump sum. Because land has an unlimited life and is a nondepreciable asset, it must have a separate ledger account, and the lump-sum purchase price must be apportioned between the land and the other assets. For example, suppose a company buys a building and the land on which it is situated for a lump sum of $85,000. The company can apportion the costs by determining what it would have paid for the building and for the land if it had purchased them separately and applying the appropriate percentages to the lump-sum price. Assume that appraisals yield estimates of $10,000 for the land and $90,000 for the building if purchased separately. In that case, 10 percent of the lump-sum price, or $8,500, would be allocated to the land, and 90 percent, or $76,500, would be allocated to the building, as follows:

	Appraisal		*Percentage*	*Apportionment*	
Land	$ 10,000	10%	($10,000 ÷ $100,000)	$ 8,500	($85,000 × 10%)
Building	90,000	90%	($90,000 ÷ $100,000)	76,500	($85,000 × 90%)
Totals	$100,000	100%		$85,000	

4   DEPRECIATION

As we noted earlier, *depreciation* is the periodic allocation of the cost of a tangible asset (other than land and natural resources) over the asset's estimated useful life. In accounting for depreciation, it is important to keep the following points in mind:

> ▶ *All tangible assets except land have a limited useful life, and the costs of these assets must be distributed as expenses over the years they benefit.* Physical deterioration and obsolescence are the major factors in limiting a depreciable asset's useful life.

> > ▶ **Physical deterioration** results from use and from exposure to the elements, such as wind and sun. Periodic repairs and a sound maintenance policy may keep buildings and equipment in good operating order and extract the maximum useful life from them, but every machine or building must at some point be discarded. Repairs do not eliminate the need for depreciation.

> > ▶ **Obsolescence** refers to the process of going out of date. Because of fast changing technology and fast-changing demands, machinery and even buildings often become obsolete before they wear out.

Accountants do not distinguish between physical deterioration and obsolescence because they are interested in the length of an asset's useful life, not in what limits its useful life.

> ▶ *Depreciation refers to the allocation of the cost of a plant asset to the periods that benefit from the asset, not to the asset's physical deterioration or decrease in market value.* The term *depreciation* describes the gradual conversion of the cost of the asset into an expense.

> ▶ *Depreciation is not a process of valuation.* Accounting records are not indicators of changing price levels; they are kept in accordance with the cost principle. Because of an advantageous purchase price and market conditions, the

Study Note
A computer may be functioning as well as it did on the day it was purchased four years ago, but because much faster, more efficient computers have become available, the old computer is now obsolete.

Study Note
Depreciation is the allocation of the acquisition cost of a plant asset, and any similarity between undepreciated cost and current market value is pure coincidence.

How Long is the Useful Life of an Airplane?

Most airlines depreciate their planes over an estimated useful life of 10 to 20 years. But how long will a properly maintained plane really last? Western Airlines paid $3.3 million for a new Boeing 737 in July 1968. More than 78,000 flights and 30 years later, this aircraft was still flying for Vanguard Airlines, a no-frills airline. Among the other airlines that have owned this plane are Piedmont, **Delta,** and **US Airways.** Virtually every part of the plane has been replaced over the years. **Boeing** believes the plane could theoretically make double the number of flights before it is retired.

The useful lives of many types of assets can be extended indefinitely if the assets are correctly maintained, but proper accounting in accordance with the matching rule requires depreciation over a "reasonable" useful life. Each airline that owned the plane would have accounted for the plane in this way.

value of a building may increase. Nevertheless, because depreciation is a process of allocation, not valuation, depreciation on the building must continue to be recorded. Eventually, the building will wear out or become obsolete regardless of interim fluctuations in market value.

Factors in Computing Depreciation

Four factors affect the computation of depreciation:

1. *Cost.* As explained earlier, cost is the net purchase price of an asset plus all reasonable and necessary expenditures to get it in place and ready for use.

2. *Residual value.* **Residual value** is an asset's estimated scrap, salvage, or trade-in value on the estimated date of its disposal. Other terms used to describe residual value are *salvage value* and *disposal value.*

3. *Depreciable cost.* **Depreciable cost** is an asset's cost less its residual value. For example, a truck that cost $12,000 and that has a residual value of $3,000 would have a depreciable cost of $9,000. Depreciable cost must be allocated over the useful life of the asset.

4. *Estimated useful life.* **Estimated useful life** is the total number of service units expected from a long-term asset. Service units may be measured in terms of the years an asset is expected to be used, the units it is expected to produce, the miles it is expected to be driven, or similar measures. In computing an asset's estimated useful life, an accountant should consider all relevant information, including past experience with similar assets, the asset's present condition, the company's repair and maintenance policy, and current technological and industry trends.

> **Study Note**
> Residual value is the portion of an asset's acquisition cost that a company expects to recover when it disposes of the asset.

> **Study Note**
> It is depreciable cost, not acquisition cost, that is allocated over a plant asset's useful life.

Depreciation is recorded at the end of an accounting period with an adjusting entry that takes the following form:

Depreciation Expense, Asset Name	XXX	
Accumulated Depreciation, Asset Name		XXX
To record depreciation for the period		

A	= L +	SE
−XXX		−XXX

Methods of Computing Depreciation

Many methods are used to allocate the cost of plant assets to accounting periods through depreciation. Each is appropriate in certain circumstances. The most common methods are the straight-line method, the production method, and an accelerated method known as the declining-balance method.

Straight-Line Method   When the **straight-line method** is used to calculate depreciation, the asset's depreciable cost is spread evenly over the estimated useful life of the asset. The straight-line method is based on the assumption that depreciation depends only on the passage of time. The depreciation expense for each period is computed by dividing the depreciable cost (cost of the depreciating asset less its estimated residual value) by the number of accounting periods in the asset's estimated useful life. The rate of depreciation is the same in each year.

Suppose, for example, that a delivery truck cost $10,000 and has an estimated residual value of $1,000 at the end of its estimated useful life of five years. Under the straight-line method, the annual depreciation would be $1,800, calculated as follows:

Study Note
Residual value and useful life are, at best, educated guesses.

$$\frac{\text{Cost} - \text{Residual Value}}{\text{Estimated Useful Life}} = \frac{\$10,000 - \$1,000}{5 \text{ years}} = \$1,800 \text{ per year}$$

The depreciation schedule for the five years would be as follows:

Depreciation Schedule, Straight-Line Method

	Cost	Annual Depreciation	Accumulated Depreciation	Carrying Value
Date of purchase	$10,000	—	—	$10,000
End of first year	10,000	$1,800	$1,800	8,200
End of second year	10,000	1,800	3,600	6,400
End of third year	10,000	1,800	5,400	4,600
End of fourth year	10,000	1,800	7,200	2,800
End of fifth year	10,000	1,800	9,000	1,000

Note that in addition to annual depreciation's being the same each year, the accumulated depreciation increases uniformly, and the carrying value decreases uniformly until it reaches the estimated residual value.

Production Method   The **production method** is based on the assumption that depreciation is solely the result of use and that the passage of time plays no role in the process. If we assume that the delivery truck in the previous example has an estimated useful life of 90,000 miles, the depreciation cost per mile would be determined as follows:

Study Note
The production method is appropriate when a company has widely fluctuating rates of production. For example, carpet mills often close during the first two weeks in July but may run double shifts in September. With the production method, depreciation would be in direct relation to a mill's units of output.

$$\frac{\text{Cost} - \text{Residual Value}}{\text{Estimated Units of Useful Life}} = \frac{\$10,000 - \$1,000}{90,000 \text{ miles}} = \$0.10 \text{ per mile}$$

If the truck was driven 20,000 miles in the first year, 30,000 miles in the second, 10,000 miles in the third, 20,000 miles in the fourth, and 10,000 miles in the fifth, the depreciation schedule for the truck would be as follows:

Depreciation Schedule, Production Method

	Cost	Miles	Annual Depreciation	Accumulated Depreciation	Carrying Value
Date of purchase	$10,000	—	—	—	$10,000
End of first year	10,000	20,000	$2,000	$2,000	8,000
End of second year	10,000	30,000	3,000	5,000	5,000
End of third year	10,000	10,000	1,000	6,000	4,000
End of fourth year	10,000	20,000	2,000	8,000	2,000
End of fifth year	10,000	10,000	1,000	9,000	1,000

As you can see, the amount of depreciation each year is directly related to the units of use. The accumulated depreciation increases annually in direct relation to these units, and the carrying value decreases each year until it reaches the estimated residual value.

The production method should be used only when the output of an asset over its useful life can be estimated with reasonable accuracy. In addition, the unit used to measure the estimated useful life of an asset should be appropriate for the asset. For example, the number of items produced may be an appropriate measure for one machine, but the number of hours of use may be a better measure for another.

Declining-Balance Method An **accelerated method** of depreciation results in relatively large amounts of depreciation in the early years of an asset's life and smaller amounts in later years. This type of method, which is based on the passage of time, assumes that many plant assets are most efficient when new and so provide the greatest benefits in their first years. It is consistent with the matching rule to allocate more depreciation to an asset in its earlier years than to later ones if the benefits it provides in its early years are greater than those it provides later on.

Fast changing technologies often cause equipment to become obsolescent and lose service value rapidly. In such cases, using an accelerated method is appropriate because it allocates more depreciation to earlier years than to later ones. Another argument in favor of using an accelerated method is that repair expense is likely to increase as an asset ages. Thus, the total of repair and depreciation expense will remain fairly constant over the years. This result naturally assumes that the services received from the asset are roughly equal from year to year.

The **declining-balance method** is the most common accelerated method of depreciation. With this method, depreciation is computed by applying a fixed rate to the carrying value (the declining balance) of a tangible long-term asset. It therefore results in higher depreciation charges in the early years of the asset's life. Though any fixed rate can be used, the most common rate is a percentage equal to twice the straight-line depreciation percentage. When twice the straight-line rate is used, the method is usually called the **double-declining-balance method**.

In our example of the straight-line method, the delivery truck had an estimated useful life of five years, and the annual depreciation rate for the truck was therefore 20 percent (100 percent ÷ 5 years). Under the double-declining-balance method, the fixed rate would be 40 percent (2 × 20 percent). This fixed rate is applied to the carrying value that remains at the end of each year. With this method, the depreciation schedule would be as follows:

Depreciation Schedule, Double-Declining-Balance Method

	Cost	Annual Depreciation		Accumulated Depreciation	Carrying Value
Date of purchase	$10,000		—	—	$10,000
End of first year	10,000	(40% × $10,000)	$4,000	$4,000	6,000
End of second year	10,000	(40% × $6,000)	2,400	6,400	3,600
End of third year	10,000	(40% × $3,600)	1,440	7,840	2,160
End of fourth year	10,000	(40% × $2,160)	864	8,704	1,296
End of fifth year	10,000		296*	9,000	1,000

Note that the fixed rate is always applied to the carrying value at the end of the previous year. Depreciation is greatest in the first year and declines each year after that. The depreciation in the last year is limited to the amount necessary to reduce carrying value to residual value.

Comparison of the Three Methods

Figure 41-5 compares yearly depreciation and carrying value under the three methods. The graph on the left shows yearly depreciation. As you can see, straight-line depreciation is uniform at $1,800 per year over the five-year period. The double-declining balance method begins at $4,000 and decreases each year to amounts that are less than straight-line (ultimately, $296). The production method does not generate a regular pattern because of the random fluctuation of the depreciation from year to year.

FIGURE 41-5   Graphic Comparison of Three Methods of Determining Depreciation

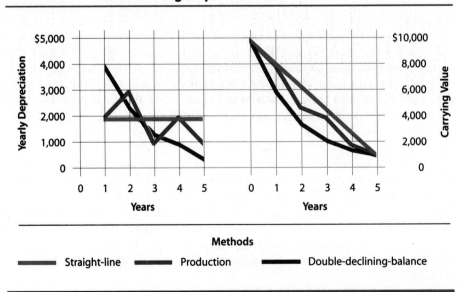

* Depreciation is limited to the amount necessary to reduce carrying value to residual value: $296 = $1,296 (previous carrying value) − $1,000 (residual value).

FOCUS ON BUSINESS PRACTICE

Accelerated Methods Save Money!

As shown in Figure 41-6, an AICPA study of 600 large companies found that the overwhelming majority used the straight-line method of depreciation for financial reporting. Only about 11 percent used some type of accelerated method, and 5 percent used the production method. These figures tend to be misleading about the importance of accelerated depreciation methods, however, especially when it comes to income taxes. Federal income tax laws allow either the straight-line method or an accelerated method, and for tax purposes, about 75 percent of the 600 companies studied preferred an accelerated method. Companies use different methods of depreciation for good reason. The straight-line method can be advantageous for financial reporting because it can produce the highest net income, and an accelerated method can be beneficial for tax purposes because it can result in lower income taxes.

The graph on the right shows the carrying value under the three methods. Each method starts in the same place (cost of $10,000) and ends at the same place (residual value of $1,000). However, the patterns of carrying value during the asset's useful life differ. For instance, the carrying value under the straight line method is always greater than under the double-declining-balance method, except at the beginning and end of the asset's useful life.

Special Issues in Depreciation

Other issues in depreciating assets include group depreciation, depreciation for partial years, revision of depreciation rates, and accelerated cost recovery for tax purposes.

Group Depreciation   The estimated useful life of an asset is the average length of time assets of the same type are expected to last. For example, the average useful life of a particular type of machine may be six years, but some machines in this category may last only two or three years, while others may last eight or nine years or longer. For this reason, and for convenience, large companies group similar assets, such as machines, trucks, and pieces of office equipment, to

FIGURE 41-6   Depreciation Methods Used by 600 Large Companies for Financial Reporting

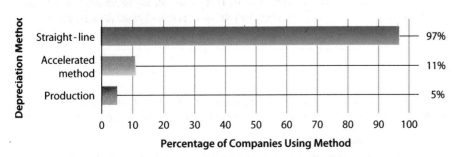

Total percentage exceeds 100 because some companies used different methods for different types of depreciable assets.

©2004 by the American Institute of Certified Public Accountants, Inc. (AICPA). Reproduced with permission.

calculate depreciation. This method, called **group depreciation**, is widely used in all fields of industry and business. A survey of large businesses indicated that 65 percent used group depreciation for all or part of their plant assets.[6]

Depreciation for Partial Years　To simplify our examples of depreciation, we have assumed that plant assets were purchased at the beginning or end of an accounting period. Usually, however, businesses buy assets when they are needed and sell or discard them when they are no longer needed or useful. The time of year is normally not a factor in the decision. Thus, it is often necessary to calculate depreciation for partial years. Some companies compute depreciation to the nearest month. Others use the half-year convention, in which one-half year of depreciation is taken in the year the asset is purchased and one-half year is taken in the year the asset is sold.

Revision of Depreciation Rates　Because a depreciation rate is based on an estimate of an asset's useful life, the periodic depreciation charge is seldom precise. It is sometimes very inadequate or excessive. Such a situation may result from an underestimate or overestimate of the asset's useful life or from a wrong estimate of its residual value. What should a company do when it discovers that a piece of equipment that it has used for several years will last a shorter—or longer—time than originally estimated? Sometimes, it is necessary to revise the estimate of useful life so that the periodic depreciation expense increases or decreases. Then, to reflect the revised situation, the remaining depreciable cost of the asset is spread over the remaining years of useful life.

With this technique, the annual depreciation expense is increased or decreased to reduce the asset's carrying value to its residual value at the end of its remaining useful life. For example, suppose a delivery truck cost $7,000 and has a residual value of $1,000. At the time of the purchase, the truck was expected to last six years, and it was depreciated on the straight-line basis. However, after two years of intensive use, it is determined that the truck will last only two more years, but its residual value at the end of the two years will still be $1,000. In other words, at the end of the second year, the truck's estimated useful life is reduced from six years to four years. At that time, the asset account and its related accumulated depreciation account would be as follows:

DELIVERY TRUCK	ACCUMULATED DEPRECIATION, DELIVERY TRUCK	
Cost　7,000	Depreciation, Year 1	1,000
	Depreciation, Year 2	1,000

The remaining depreciable cost is computed as follows:

Cost	−	**Depreciation Already Taken**	−	**Residual Value**	
$7,000	−	$2,000	−	$1,000	= $4,000

The new annual periodic depreciation charge is computed by dividing the remaining depreciable cost of $4,000 by the remaining useful life of two years.

---

[6] Ibid.

Therefore, the new periodic depreciation charge is $2,000. This method of revising depreciation is used widely in industry. It is also supported by *Opinion No. 9* and *Opinion No. 20* of the Accounting Principles Board of the AICPA.

Accelerated Cost Recovery for Tax Purposes   Over the years, to encourage businesses to invest in new plant and equipment, Congress has revised the federal income tax law to allow rapid write-offs of plant assets. Depreciation allowed for tax purposes differs considerably from depreciation calculated for financial statements. Tax methods of depreciation are usually not acceptable for financial reporting because the periods over which deductions may be taken are often shorter than the assets' estimated useful lives.

Recent changes in the federal income tax law allow a small company to expense the first $100,000 of equipment expenditures rather than recording them as assets. The law also allows an accelerated method of writing off expenditures that are recorded as assets. This method discards the concepts of estimated useful life and residual value. For most property other than real estate, it uses a 200 percent declining balance with a half-year convention (only one half-year's depreciation is allowed in the year of purchase, and one half-year's depreciation is taken in the last year). This method enables businesses to recover most of the cost of their investments early in the depreciation process.

Study Note
For financial reporting purposes, the objective is to measure performance accurately. For tax purposes, the objective is to minimize tax liability.

DISPOSAL OF DEPRECIABLE ASSETS

When plant assets are no longer useful because they have physically deteriorated or become obsolete, a company can dispose of them by discarding them, selling them for cash, or trading them in on the purchase of a new asset. Regardless of how a company disposes of a plant asset, it must record depreciation expense for the partial year up to the date of disposal. This step is required because the company used the asset until that date and, under the matching rule, the accounting period should receive the proper allocation of depreciation expense.

In the next sections, we show how a company records each type of disposal. As our example, we assume that MGC Company purchased a machine on January 2, 20X2, for $6,500 and planned to depreciate it on a straight-line basis over an estimated useful life of eight years. The machine's residual value at the end of eight years was estimated to be $300. On December 31, 20X7, the balances of the relevant accounts were as follows:

MACHINERY	ACCUMULATED DEPRECIATION, MACHINERY
6,500	4,650

On January 2, 20X8, management disposed of the asset.

Discarded Plant Assets

A plant asset rarely lasts exactly as long as its estimated life. If it lasts longer than its estimated life, it is not depreciated past the point at which its carrying value equals its residual value. The purpose of depreciation is to spread the depreciable cost of an asset over its estimated life. Thus, the total accumulated depreciation should never exceed the total depreciable cost. If an asset remains in use

Study Note
When it disposes of an asset, a company must bring the depreciation up to date and remove all evidence of ownership of the asset, including the contra account Accumulated Depreciation.

beyond the end of its estimated life, its cost and accumulated depreciation remain in the ledger accounts. Proper records will thus be available for maintaining control over plant assets. If the residual value is zero, the carrying value of a fully depreciated asset is zero until the asset is disposed of. If such an asset is discarded, no gain or loss results.

In our example, however, the discarded equipment has a carrying value of $1,850 at the time of its disposal. The carrying value is computed from the T accounts above as machinery of $6,500 less accumulated depreciation of $4,650. A loss equal to the carrying value should be recorded when the machine is discarded, as follows:

A	= L +	SE
+ 4,650		
− 6,500		− 1,850

20X8			
Jan. 2	Accumulated Depreciation, Machinery	4,650	
	Loss on Disposal of Machinery	1,850	
	Machinery		6,500
	Discarded machine no longer used in the business		

Gains and losses on disposals of plant assets are classified as other revenues and expenses on the income statement.

Plant Assets Sold For Cash

The entry to record a plant asset sold for cash is similar to the one just illustrated, except that the receipt of cash should also be recorded. The following entries show how to record the sale of a machine under three assumptions about the selling price. In the first case, the $1,850 cash received is exactly equal to the $1,850 carrying value of the machine; therefore, no gain or loss occurs:

Study Note
When an asset is discarded or sold for cash, the gain or loss equals cash received minus carrying the value.

A	= L + SE
+ 1,850	
+ 4,650	
− 6,500	

20X8			
Jan. 2	Cash	1,850	
	Accumulated Depreciation, Machinery	4,650	
	Machinery		6,500
	Sale of machine for carrying value; no gain or loss		

In the second case, the $1,000 cash received is less than the carrying value of $1,850, so a loss of $850 is recorded:

A	= L +	SE
+ 1,000		− 850
+ 4,650		
− 6,500		

20X8			
Jan. 2	Cash	1,000	
	Accumulated Depreciation, Machinery	4,650	
	Loss on Sale of Machinery	850	
	Machinery		6,500
	Sale of machine at less than carrying value; loss of $850 ($1,850 − $1,000) recorded		

In the third case, the $2,000 cash received exceeds the carrying value of $1,850 so a gain of $150 is recorded:

20X8			
Jan. 2	Cash	2,000	
	Accumulated Depreciation, Machinery	4,650	
	Gain on Sale of Machinery		150
	Machinery		6,500
	Sale of machine at more than the carrying value; gain of $150 ($2,000 − $1,850) recorded		

A	= L +	SE
+ 2,000		+ 150
+ 4,650		
+ 6,500		

Exchanges of Plant Assets

As we have noted, businesses can dispose of plant assets by trading them in on the purchase of other plant assets. Exchanges may involve similar assets, such as an old machine traded in on a newer model, or dissimilar assets, such as a cement mixer traded in on a truck. In either case, the purchase price is reduced by the amount of the trade-in allowance.

Basically, accounting for exchanges of plant assets is similar to accounting for sales of plant assets for cash. If the trade-in allowance is greater than the asset's carrying value, the company realizes a gain. If the allowance is less, it suffers a loss.

NATURAL RESOURCES

6

Natural resources are long-term assets that appear on a balance sheet with descriptive titles like Timberlands, Oil and Gas Reserves, and Mineral Deposits. The distinguishing characteristic of these assets is that they are converted to inventory by cutting, pumping, mining, or other extraction methods. They are recorded at acquisition cost, which may include some costs of development. As a natural resource is extracted and converted to inventory, its asset account must be proportionally reduced. For example, the carrying value of oil reserves on the balance sheet is reduced by the proportional cost of the barrels pumped during the period. As a result, the original cost of the oil reserves is gradually reduced, and depletion is recognized in the amount of the decrease.

Study Note
Natural resources are not intangible assets. They are correctly classified as components of property, plant, and equipment.

Depletion

Depletion refers not only to the exhaustion of a natural resource, but also to the proportional allocation of the cost of a natural resource to the units extracted. The way in which the cost of a natural resource is allocated closely resembles the production method of calculating depreciation. When a natural resource is purchased or developed, the total units that will be available, such as barrels of oil, tons of coal, or board-feet of lumber, must be estimated. The depletion

When you season your food with salt, you probably don't think of it as using a natural resource, but that is what salt is. Table salt is produced by evaporation methods; rock salt, which is used for highway maintenance, is mined. Natural resources are considered components of property, plant, and equipment. These long-term assets are recorded at acquisition cost, which may include some costs of development.

Courtesy of AP/Wide World Photos.

cost per unit is determined by dividing the cost of the natural resource (less residual value, if any) by the estimated number of units available. The amount of the depletion cost for each accounting period is then computed by multiplying the depletion cost per unit by the number of units extracted and sold.

For example, suppose a mine was purchased for $1,800,000 and that it has an estimated residual value of $300,000 and contains an estimated 1,500,000 tons of coal. The depletion charge per ton of coal is $1, calculated as follows:

$$\frac{\$1,800,000 - \$300,000}{1,500,000 \text{ tons}} = \$1 \text{ per ton}$$

Thus, if 115,000 tons of coal are mined and sold during the first year, the depletion charge for the year is $115,000. This charge would be recorded as follows:

A	= L +	SE
− 115,000		−115,000

Dec. 31	Depletion Expense, Coal Deposits	115,000	
	Accumulated Depletion, Coal Deposits		115,000
	To record depletion of coal mine: $1 per ton for 115,000 tons mined and sold		

On the balance sheet, data for the mine would be presented as follows:

Coal deposits	$1,800,000	
Less accumulated depletion	115,000	$1,685,000

Sometimes, a natural resource is not sold in the year it is extracted. It is important to note that it would then be recorded as a depletion *expense* in the year it is *sold*. The part not sold is considered inventory.

Depreciation of Related Plant Assets

The extraction of natural resources generally requires special on-site buildings and equipment (e.g., conveyors, drills, and pumps). The useful life of these plant assets may be longer than the estimated time it will take to deplete the resources. However, a company may plan to abandon these assets after all the resources have been extracted because they no longer serve a useful purpose. In this case, they should be depreciated on the same basis as the depletion.

For example, if machinery with a useful life of ten years is installed on an oil field that is expected to be depleted in eight years, the machinery should be depreciated over the eight-year period, using the production method. That way, each year's depreciation will be proportional to the year's depletion. If one-sixth of the oil field's total reserves is pumped in one year, then the depreciation should be one-sixth of the machinery's cost minus the residual value.

If the useful life of a long-term plant asset is less than the expected life of the resource, the shorter life should be used to compute depreciation. In such cases, or when an asset will not be abandoned after all reserves have been depleted, other depreciation methods, such as straight-line or declining-balance, are appropriate.

> **Study Note**
> A company may abandon equipment that is still in good working condition because of the expense involved in dismantling the equipment and moving it to another site.

Development and Exploration Costs in the Oil and Gas Industry

The costs of exploring and developing oil and gas resources can be accounted for under one of two methods. Under **successful efforts accounting**, the cost of successful exploration—for example, producing an oil well—is a cost of the resource. It should be recorded as an asset and depleted over the estimated life of the resource. The cost of an unsuccessful exploration—such as the cost of a dry well—is written off immediately as a loss. Because of these immediate write-offs, **successful efforts accounting** is considered the more conservative method and is used by most large oil companies.

On the other hand, smaller, independent oil companies argue that the cost of dry wells is part of the overall cost of the systematic development of an oil field and is thus a part of the cost of producing wells. Under the **full-costing method**, all costs, including the cost of dry wells, are recorded as assets and depleted over the estimated life of the producing resources. This method tends to improve a company's earnings performance in its early years.

The Financial Accounting Standards Board permits the use of either method.[7]

---

[7] *Statement of Financial Accounting Standards* No. 25, "Suspension of Certain Accounting Requirements for Oil and Gas Producing Companies" (Norwalk, Conn.: Financial Accounting Standards Board, 1979).

How Do You Measure What's Underground? With a Good Guess.

Accounting standards require publicly traded energy companies to disclose in their annual reports their production activities, estimates of their proven oil and gas reserves, and estimates of the present value of the future cash flows those reserves are expected to generate. The figures are not easy to estimate. After all, the reserves are often miles underground or beneath deep water. As a result, these figures are considered "supplementary" and not reliable enough to be audited independently. Nevertheless, it appears that some companies, including **Royal Dutch/Shell Group,** have overestimated their reserves and thus overestimated their future prospects. Apparently, some managers at Royal Dutch/Shell Group receive bonuses based on the amount of new reserves added to the annual report. When the company recently announced that it was reducing its reported reserves by 20 percent, the price of its stock dropped.[8]

7   INTANGIBLE ASSETS

An intangible asset is both long term and nonphysical. Its value come from the long-term rights or advantages it affords its owner. Table 41-1 describes the most common types of intangible assets—goodwill, trademarks and brand names, copyrights, patents, franchises and licenses, lease holds, software, noncompete covenants, and customer lists—and their accounting treatment. Like intangible assets, some current assets—for example, accounts receivable and certain prepaid expenses—have no physical substance, but because current assets are short term, they are not classified as intangible assets.

Figure 41-7 shows the percentage of companies that report the various types of intangible assets. For some companies, intangible assets make up a substantial portion of total assets. As noted in this reading's Decision Point, **Apple Computer's** goodwill and other acquired intangible assets amounted to $97 million in 2004. How these assets are accounted for has a substantial effect on Apple's performance.

Who's Number One in Brands?

Brands are intangible assets that often do not appear on a company's balance sheet because rather than purchasing them, the company has developed them over time. A recent report attempted to value brands by the discounted present value of future cash flows.[9] According to the report, the ten most valuable brands in the world were as follows:

Coca-Cola	**Nokia**
Microsoft	**Disney**
IBM	**McDonald's**
GE	**Marlboro**
Intel	**Mercedes**

Coca-Cola's brand was valued at almost $70 billion, whereas the Mercedes brand was valued at $21 billion. Where did **Apple** stand? It was number 50 at $5.3 billion, but this analysis was made before taking into account. Apple's successful iPod, which has certainly increased its brand power.

---

[8]Jonathan Weil, "Oil Reserves Can Sure Be Slick," *The Wall Street Journal,* March 11, 2004.

[9]"The Top 100 Brands," *BusinessWeek,* August 5, 2002.

TABLE 41-1   Accounting for Intangible Assets

Type	Description	Accounting Treatment
Goodwill	The excess of the amount paid for a business over the fair market value of the business's net assets.	Debit Goodwill for the acquisition cost, and review impairment annually.
Trademark, brand name	A registered symbol or name that can be used only by its owner to identify a product or service.	Debit Trademark or Brand Name for the acquisition cost, and amortize it over a reasonable life.
Copyright	An exclusive right granted by the federal government to reproduce and sell literary, musical, and other artistic materials and computer programs for a period of the author's life plus 70 years.	Record at acquisition cost, and amortize over the asset's useful life, which is often much shorter than its legal life. For example, the cost of paperback rights to a popular novel would typically be amortized over a useful life of two to four years.
Patent	An exclusive right granted by the federal government for a period of 20 years to make a particular product or use a specific process. A design may be granted a patent for 14 years.	The cost of successfully defending a patent in a patent infringement suit is added to the acquisition cost of the patent. Amortize over the asset's useful life, which may be less than its legal life.
Franchise, license	A right to an exclusive territory or market, or the right to use a formula, technique, process, or design.	Debit Franchise or License for the acquisition cost, and amortize it over a reasonable life, not to exceed 40 years.
Leasehold	A right to occupy land or buildings under a long-term rental contract. For example, if Company A sells or subleases its right to use a retail location to Company B for ten years in return for one or more rental payments, Company B has purchased a leasehold.	The lessor (Company A) debits Leasehold for the amount of the rental payment and amortizes it over the remaining life of the lease. The lessee (Company B) debits payments to Lease Expense.
Software	Capitalized costs of computer programs developed for sale, lease, or internal use.	Record the amount of capitalizable production costs, and amortize over the estimated economic life of the product.
Noncompete covenant	A contract limiting the rights of others to compete in a specific industry or line of business for a specified period.	Record at acquisition cost, and amortize over the contract period.
Customer list	A list of customers or subscribers.	Debit Customer Lists for amount paid, and amortize over the asset's expected life.

FOCUS ON BUSINESS PRACTICE

What is the Useful Life of a Customer List?

One of the most valuable intangible assets some companies have is a list of customers. For example, the **Newark Morning Ledger Company**, a newspaper chain, purchased a chain of Michigan newspapers whose list of 460,000 subscribers was valued at $68 million. The U.S. Supreme Court upheld the company's right to amortize the value of the subscriber list because the company showed that the list had a limited useful life. The Internal Revenue Service had argued that the list had an indefinite life and therefore could not provide tax deductions through amortization. This ruling has benefited other types of businesses that purchase everything from bank deposits to pharmacy prescription files.[10]

---

[10] "What's in a Name?" *Time,* May 3, 1993.

FIGURE 41-7   Intangible Assets Reported by 600 Large Companies

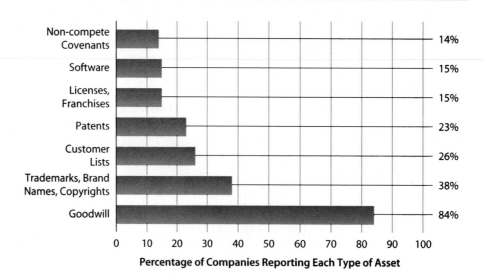

Percentage of Companies Reporting Each Type of Asset

Source: Data from American Institute of Certified Public Accountants, *Accounting Trends & Techniques* (New York: AICPA, 2004).

The purchase of an intangible asset is a special kind of capital expenditure. Such assets are accounted for at acquisition cost—that is, the amount that a company paid for them. Some intangible assets, such as goodwill and trademarks, may be acquired at little or no cost. Even though these assets may have great value and be needed for profitable operations, a company should include them on its balance sheet only if it purchased them from another party at a price established in the marketplace. When a company develops its own intangible assets, it should record the costs of development as expenses. An exception is the cost of internally developed computer software after a working prototype of the software has been developed.

The issues in accounting for intangible assets, other than goodwill, are the same as those in accounting for other long-term assets. In its *Opinion* No. 17, the Accounting Principles Board lists them as follows:

1. Determining an initial carrying amount
2. Accounting for that amount after acquisition under normal business conditions—that is, through periodic write-off or amortization—in a manner similar to depreciation
3. Accounting for the amount if the asset's value declines substantially and permanently[11]

An intangible asset that has a determinable useful life, such as a patent, copyright, or leasehold, should be written off through periodic amortization over the asset's useful life in much the same way that a plant asset is depreciated. Some intangible assets, such as brand names and trademarks, have no measurable limit on their lives, but they should still be amortized over a reasonable length of time.

Study Note
The cost of mailing lists may be recorded as an asset because the mailing lists will be used over and over and will benefit future accounting periods.

---

[11] Adapted from Accounting Principles Board, *Opinion* No. 17, "*Intangible* Assets" (New York: AICPA, 1970), par. 2.

To illustrate these procedures, suppose Soda Bottling Company purchases a patent on a unique bottle cap for $18,000. The purchase would be recorded with an entry of $18,000 in the asset account Patents. (Note that if the company developed the bottle cap internally instead of purchasing the patent, the costs of developing the cap—such as researchers' salaries and the costs of supplies and equipment used in testing—would be expensed as incurred.) Although the patent for the bottle cap will last for 20 years, Soda determines that it will sell the product that uses the cap for only six years.

The entry to record the annual amortization expense would be for $3,000 ($18,000 ÷ 6 years). The Patents account is reduced directly by the amount of the amortization expense. This is in contrast to the treatment of other longterm asset accounts, for which depreciation or depletion is accumulated in separate contra accounts.

If the patent becomes worthless before it is fully amortized, the remaining carrying value is written off as a loss by removing it from the Patents account.

Research and Development Costs

Most successful companies carry out research and development (R&D) activities, often within a separate department. Among these activities are development of new products, testing of existing and proposed products, and pure research. The costs of these activities are substantial for many companies. In a recent year, **General Motors** spent $5.7 billion, or about 3 percent of its revenues, on R&D.[12] R&D costs can be even greater in high-tech fields like pharmaceuticals. For example, **Abbott Laboratories** recently spent $1.7 billion, or 8.6 percent of its revenues, on R&D.[13]

The Financial Accounting Standards Board requires that all R&D costs be treated as revenue expenditures and charged to expense in the period in which they are incurred.[14] The reasoning behind this requirement is that it is too hard to trace specific costs to specific profitable developments. Also, the costs of research and development are continuous and necessary for the success of a business and so should be treated as current expenses. To support this conclusion, the FASB cited studies showing that 30 to 90 percent of all new products fail and that 75 percent of new-product expenses go to unsuccessful products. Thus, their costs do not represent future benefits.

Computer Software Costs

The costs that companies incur in developing computer software for sale or lease or for their own internal use are considered research and development costs until the product has proved technologically feasible. Thus, costs incurred before that point should be charged to expense as they are incurred. A product is deemed technologically feasible when a detailed working program has been designed. Once that occurs, all software production costs are recorded as assets and are amortized over the software's estimated economic life

---

[12] General Motors Corporation, *Annual Report*, 2003.

[13] Abbott Laboratories, *Annual Report*, 2004.

[14] *Statement of Financial Accounting Standards* No. 2, "Accounting for Research and Development Costs" (Norwalk, Conn.: Financial Accounting Standards Board, 1974), par. 12.

using the straight-line method. If at any time the company cannot expect to realize from the software the amount of the unamortized costs on the balance sheet, the asset should be written down to the amount expected to be realized.[15]

Goodwill

Goodwill means different things to different people. Generally, it refers to a company's good reputation. From an accounting standpoint, goodwill exists when a purchaser pays more for a business than the fair market value of the business's net assets. In other words, the purchaser would pay less if it bought the assets separately. Most businesses are worth more as going concerns than as collections of assets.

When the purchase price of a business is more than the fair market value of its physical assets, the business must have intangible assets. If it does not have patents, copyrights, trademarks, or other identifiable intangible assets of value, the excess payment is assumed to be for goodwill. Goodwill reflects all the factors that allow a company to earn a higher-than-market rate of return on its assets, including customer satisfaction, good management, manufacturing efficiency, the advantages of having a monopoly, good locations, and good employee relations. The payment above and beyond the fair market value of the tangible assets and other specific intangible assets is properly recorded in the Goodwill account.

The FASB requires that purchased goodwill be reported as a separate line item on the balance sheet and that it be reviewed annually for impairment. If the fair value of goodwill is less than its carrying value on the balance sheet, goodwill is considered impaired. In that case, it is reduced to its fair value, and the impairment charge is reported on the income statement. A company can perform the fair value measurement for each reporting unit at any time as long as the measurement date is consistent from year to year.

A company should record goodwill only when it acquires a controlling interest in another business. The amount to be recorded as goodwill can be determined by writing the identifiable net assets up to their fair market values at the

FOCUS ON BUSINESS PRACTICE

Wake up, Goodwill Is Growing!

As Figure 41-7 shows, 84 percent of 600 large companies separately report goodwill as an asset. Because much of the growth of these companies has come through purchasing other companies, goodwill as a percentage of total assets has also grown. As the table at the right shows, the amount of goodwill can be material.[16]

	Goodwill (in billions)	Percentage of Total Assets
General Mills	$6,684	36
Heinz	$1,956	20
Tribune Company	$5,467	38

---

[15] *Statement of Financial Accounting Standards* No. 86, "Accounting for the Costs of Computer Software to Be Sold, Leased, or Otherwise Marketed" (Norwalk, Conn.: Financial Accounting Standards Board, 1985).

[16] General Mills, Inc., *Annual Report,* 2004; H.J. Heinz Company, *Annual Report,* 2004; Tribune Company, *Annual Report,* 2004.

time of purchase and subtracting the total from the purchase price. For example, suppose a company pays $11,400,000 to purchase another business. If the net assets of the business (total assets − total liabilities) are fairly valued at $10,000,000, then the amount of the goodwill is $1,400,000 ($11,400,000 − $10,000,000). If the fair market value of the net assets is more or less than $10,000,000, an entry is made in the accounting records to adjust the assets to the fair market value. The goodwill would then represent the difference between the adjusted net assets and the purchase price of $11,400,000.

A LOOK BACK AT APPLE COMPUTER, INC.

We began the reading by emphasizing that **Apple's** success as an innovator and marketer comes from wise and steady investments in long-term assets and related expenditures like research and development. In evaluating Apple's performance, investors and creditors look for answers to the following questions:

▶ **What are Apple's long-term assets?**

▶ **What are its policies in accounting for long-term assets?**

▶ **Does the company generate enough cash flow to finance its continued growth?**

Apple's tangible long-term assets include land, manufacturing facilities, office buildings, machinery, equipment, and leasehold improvements to its retail stores. Its balance sheet also includes goodwill and intangible assets that it acquired through acquisitions. Because internally developed intangible assets are not recorded as assets, the value of Apple's own brand name is not reflected on the balance sheet. Clearly, however, it far exceeds the value of the intangible assets that are listed.

In accordance with GAAP, Apple's accounting policies include using the straightline depreciation method for tangible assets, amortizing intangible assets over a reasonable useful life, and expensing research and development costs. In addition, it evaluates its long-term assets for impairment each year to ensure that it is not carrying assets on its balance sheet at amounts that exceed their value.

A good measure of the funds that Apple has available for growth is its free cash flow:

Free Cash Flow = Net Cash Flows from Operating Activities − Dividends − (Purchases of Plant Assets − Sales of Plant Assets)

	2004	2003
Free Cash Flow =	$934 − $0 − ($176 − $0)	$289 − $0 − ($164 − $0)
=	$758	= $125

This two-year view of Apple's free cash flow shows great improvement in 2004. The company obviously generated enough cash to finance its continued growth. Its policy of not paying dividends contributes to the amount of cash it has available for this purpose. Although Apple may have sold some plant assets, the amounts were sufficiently immaterial that it did not report them separately.

SUMMARY

Long-term assets have a useful life of more than one year, are used in the operation of a business, and are not intended for resale. They can be tangible or intangible. In the former category are land, plant assets, and natural resources. In the latter are patents, trademarks, franchises, and other rights, as well as goodwill. The management issues related to long-term assets include decisions about whether to acquire the assets, how to finance them, and how to account for them.

Capital expenditures are recorded as assets, whereas revenue expenditures are recorded as expenses of the current period. Capital expenditures include not only outlays for plant assets, natural resources, and intangible assets, but also expenditures for additions, betterments, and extraordinary repairs that increase an asset's residual value or extend its useful life. Revenue expenditures are made for ordinary repairs and maintenance. The error of classifying a capital expenditure as a revenue expenditure, or vice versa, has an important effect on net income.

The acquisition cost of property, plant, and equipment includes all expenditures reasonable and necessary to get the asset in place and ready for use. Among these expenditures are purchase price, installation cost, freight charges, and insurance during transit. The acquisition cost of a plant asset is allocated over the asset's useful life.

Depreciation—the periodic allocation of the cost of a plant asset over its estimated useful life—is commonly computed by using the straight-line method, the production method, or an accelerated method. The straight-line method is related directly to the passage of time, whereas the production method is related directly to use or output. An accelerated method, which results in relatively large amounts of depreciation in earlier years and reduced amounts in later years, is based on the assumption that plant assets provide greater economic benefits in their earlier years than in later ones. The most common accelerated method is the declining-balance method.

A company can dispose of a long-term plant asset by discarding or selling it or exchanging it for another asset. Regardless of the way in which a company disposes of such an asset, it must record depreciation up to the date of disposal. To do so, it must remove the carrying value from the asset account and the depreciation to date from the accumulated depreciation account. When a company sells a depreciable long-term asset at a price that differs from its carrying value, it should report the gain or loss on its income statement. In recording exchanges of similar plant assets, a gain or loss may arise.

Natural resources are depletable assets that are converted to inventory by cutting, pumping, mining, or other forms of extraction. They are recorded at cost as long-term assets. As natural resources are sold, their costs are allocated as expenses through depletion charges. The depletion charge is based on the ratio of the resource extracted to the total estimated resource. A major issue related to this subject is accounting for oil and gas reserves.

The purchase of an intangible asset should be treated as a capital expenditure and recorded at acquisition cost, which in turn should be amortized over the useful life of the asset. The FASB requires that research and development costs be treated as revenue expenditures and charged as expenses in the periods of expenditure. Software costs are treated as research and development costs and expensed until a feasible working program is developed, after which time the costs may be capitalized and amortized over a reasonable estimated life. Goodwill is the excess of the amount paid for a business over the fair market value of the net assets and is usually related to the business's superior earning potential. It should be recorded only when a company purchases an entire business, and it should be reviewed annually for possible impairment.

PROBLEMS FOR READING 41

Comparison of Depreciation Methods

Norton Construction Company purchased a cement mixer on January 2, 20x5, for $14,500. The mixer was expected to have a useful life of five years and a residual value of $1,000. The company's engineers estimated that the mixer would have a useful life of 7,500 hours. It was used for 1,500 hours in 20x5, 2,625 hours in 20x6, 2,250 hours in 20x7, 750 hours in 20x8, and 375 hours in 20x9. The company's fiscal year ends on December 31.

1. Compute the depreciation expense and carrying value for 20x5 to 20x9, using the following methods: (a) straight-line, (b) production, and (c) double-declining-balance.

2. Show the balance sheet presentation for the cement mixer on December 31, 20x5. Assume the straight-line method.

3. What conclusions can you draw from the patterns of yearly depreciation?

$4\frac{5}{8}$ $4\frac{11}{16}$ $\frac{3}{8}$

$5\frac{1}{2}$ $5\frac{1}{2}$ $-$ $\frac{3}{8}$

$5\frac{1}{2}$ $21\frac{13}{16}$ $-$ $\frac{1}{16}$

$20\frac{5}{8}$ $18\frac{1}{8}$ $+$ $\frac{7}{8}$

$17\frac{3}{8}$ $18\frac{1}{8}$ $+$

$19\frac{1}{2}$ $6\frac{1}{2}$ $-$ $\frac{1}{2}$

$6\frac{1}{2}$ $6\frac{1}{2}$ $-$

$7\frac{1}{4}$ $31\frac{1}{32}$ $-$ $\frac{1}{8}$

$15\frac{1}{16}$

$\frac{9}{16}$

$9\frac{1}{16}$

$\frac{9}{32}$ $7\frac{15}{16}$

$7\frac{13}{16}$ $7\frac{15}{16}$

$7\frac{15}{16}$

$2\frac{5}{8}$ $2\frac{11}{32}$ $2\frac{1}{2}$ $+$

546 $2\frac{1}{4}$ $2\frac{1}{4}$

827 $2\frac{3}{4}$ $2\frac{1}{4}$

$5\frac{1}{2}$ $12\frac{1}{16}$ $11\frac{3}{8}$ $11\frac{3}{4}$ $+$

87 $33\frac{3}{4}$ 33 $33\frac{1}{16}$ $-$

802 $25\frac{5}{8}$ $24\frac{9}{16}$ $25\frac{3}{8}$ $+$

833 12 $11\frac{5}{8}$ $11\frac{7}{8}$ $+$

16 $10\frac{1}{2}$ $10\frac{1}{2}$ $10\frac{1}{2}$ $-$

78 $15\frac{1}{8}$ $15\frac{13}{16}$ $15\frac{7}{8}$ $-$

608 $9\frac{1}{16}$ $8\frac{1}{4}$ $8\frac{1}{4}$ $+$

430 $11\frac{1}{4}$ $10\frac{1}{8}$

ANALYSIS OF LONG-LIVED ASSETS: PART I — THE CAPITALIZATION DECISION

by Gerald I. White, Ashwinpaul C. Sondhi, and Dov Fried

LEARNING OUTCOMES

The candidate should be able to:

a. compute and describe the effects of capitalizing versus expensing on net income, shareholders' equity, cash flow from operations, and financial ratios including the effect on the interest coverage ratio (times interest earned) of capitalizing interest costs;

b. explain the circumstances in which intangible assets (including software development costs and research and development costs) are capitalized;

c. calculate and describe both the initial and long-term effects of asset revaluations on financial ratios.

INTRODUCTION   1

The long-lived operating assets of a firm, unlike inventory, are not held for resale but are used in the firm's manufacturing, sales, and administrative operations. Such assets include tangible fixed assets (plant, machinery, and office facilities) as well as intangible assets such as computer software, patents, and trademarks.

This reading examines financial reporting and analysis issues when these assets are originally acquired, with emphasis on:

► Which costs are included in the carrying amount of fixed assets

► The financial statement effects of capitalization versus expensing

► The capitalization of interest

▶ The circumstances under which research and development, computer software, and other intangible costs can be capitalized

▶ Analytical adjustments required to compare companies with different capitalization policies

▶ The analysis of fixed asset disclosures

Reading 43 discusses the accounting for and analysis of the use, impairment, and disposal of these long-lived assets.

2   ACQUIRING THE ASSET: THE CAPITALIZATION DECISION

The costs of acquiring resources that provide services over more than one operating cycle are capitalized and carried as assets on the balance sheet. All costs incurred until the asset is ready for use must be capitalized, including the invoice price, applicable sales tax, freight and insurance costs incurred delivering the equipment, and any installation costs.[1]

However, considerable debate surrounds the application of these principles and significant differences remain (across countries and firms) with respect to three major issues:

1. Should some components of acquisition cost be included in the capitalized cost (e.g., interest during construction)?

2. Do some types of costs merit capitalization (e.g., software development and research and development costs)?

3. What accounting method should be used to determine the amount of costs capitalized (e.g., oil and gas properties)?

These choices affect the balance sheet, income and cash flow statements, and ratios both in the year the choice is made and over the life of the asset. Management discretion can result in smoothing or manipulation of reported income, cash flows, and other measures of financial performance. Moreover, unlike some accounting choices whose effects reverse over time, some effects of the decision to capitalize or expense may never reverse.

This reading is devoted to the controversial issue of capitalization versus expensing of expenditures for long-lived assets. We start with an overview of the conceptual issues and a review of the implications of capitalization for financial statement analysis. The remaining sections then examine the specific components and categories of cost where capitalization practices vary.

---

[1] In June 2001, the Accounting Standards Executive Committee (AcSEC) of the AICPA issued an exposure draft of a proposed Statement of Position: Accounting for Certain Costs and Activities Related to Property, Plant, and Equipment. The SOP would require that:

▶ Costs incurred prior to asset acquisition must be expensed, with the exception of option payments and other costs directly related to specific PPE assets.

▶ All repair and maintenance costs during the life of PPE assets must be expensed.

▶ Overhead costs (including general and administrative and other support costs) must be expensed.

CAPITALIZATION VERSUS EXPENSING: CONCEPTUAL ISSUES

3

The Financial Accounting Standards Board (FASB), in its Statement of Financial Accounting Concepts (SFAC) 6, defines accounting assets as probable future economic benefits. Analytically, the concept of long-lived assets can also serve as:

1. An index of initial investment outlays, used as a base for measuring profitability (return on assets)

2. A measure of the firm's wealth, used for valuation and to measure solvency

3. Inputs in the firm's production function, used to measure capital intensity, leverage, and operating efficiency

Different analytical objectives require distinct definitions of what constitutes an asset. Although returns on research and development should be evaluated in the same way as returns on a purchased factory, measurement problems may preclude recognition of such expenditures as assets for assessment of shareholder wealth or collateral for bondholders.

For this reason, traditional, historical cost-based accounting rules cannot satisfy all contexts; analysts must evaluate asset definitions used for financial reporting and make necessary adjustments. The appropriate adjustment may require the capitalization of previously expensed costs, or the reverse. In some cases, particularly for intangible assets, there is no one "correct" choice that serves all analytical needs.

Financial Statement Effects of Capitalization

Box 42-1 (Figures 42-1 to 42-5) uses a simple illustration to demonstrate the financial statement effects of the capitalize-versus-expense choice on growing firms. That choice will have significant effects on reported cash flows, as well as on the balance sheet and income statement.

Income Variability

Firms that capitalize costs and depreciate them (systematically allocate them to income) over time show smoother patterns of reported income (Figure 42-2). Firms that expense costs as incurred have greater variance in reported income, as the variance in spending is transmitted directly to income. That variance declines as the firm matures and is lower for larger firms (or those with other sources of income).

Profitability

In the early years, expensing lowers profitability, both in absolute terms (as the cost of new assets exceeds depreciation of previously capitalized expenditures) and relative to assets, sales, etc. *Profitability remains lower for expensing firms as long*

BOX 42-1 COMPARISON OF FINANCIAL STATEMENT EFFECTS: CAPITALIZATION VERSUS EXPENSING

For our illustration we consider two hypothetical firms, each with an asset base of $1,000 on which it earns $150, which begin to grow. Growth requires the acquisition of an "asset," which has a three-year life. Each asset costs $100 and generates cash flows of $50 per year. The pattern of growth* (the number of assets acquired each year and the replacement of old assets) is illustrated in Figure 42-1.

Growth is assumed to continue for 15 years after which maturity is reached, and all subsequent acquisitions are for replacement only. We further assume that the asset cost may be capitalized or expensed at the discretion of management under the provisions of generally accepted accounting principles (GAAP). One firm capitalizes the acquisition cost; the other expenses it. The firms are otherwise operationally identical. Their reported income, cash flow from operations, and related ratios, however, will differ markedly.

Figure 42-2 compares the pattern of reported income. The "expensing" firm exhibits a fluctuating pattern of income growth through maturity. The "capitalizing" firm, on the other hand, exhibits a smooth pattern of income growth. For firms that are initially larger,† the fluctuations are not as great throughout the growth and maturity cycle because of the larger base.

Figure 42-3 compares the return on assets (ROA) ratio for the two firms. The choice of accounting method affects both the numerator and denominator of the ROA. The expensing firm, having fewer recorded assets, will have a smaller denominator, increasing its reported ROA. The numerator (earnings) is volatile, so that sometimes ROA increases but at other times decreases. At the early stage of growth, the

Figure 42-1

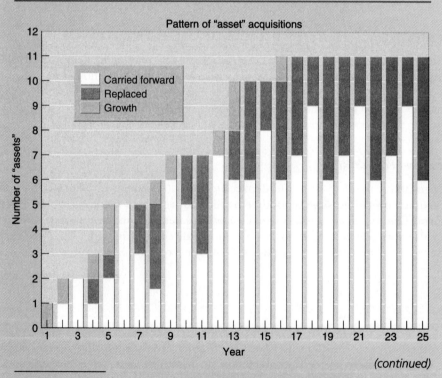

Pattern of "asset" acquisitions

(continued)

---

*A variable growth rate is used in the illustration because it is more descriptive of reality (it has greater external validity). Any growth rate, other than a perfectly constant one, will create a similar pattern of differences between a capitalizing and expensing firm. At maturity or steady state, a constant growth rate generates identical (and constant) total expense for both firms. (ROA and cash flow from operations would still differ.)
† The term "larger" does not necessarily relate only to absolute size. It can also denote that the firm engages in other activities that offset the variability of the costs that are expensed.

BOX 42-1 *(continued)*

expensing firm's ROA gyrates about that of the capitalizing firm but will initially tend to be lower. As the expensing firm grows larger, the fluctuations persist, but its ROA is higher because the effect of lower reported assets on the denominator dominates.

Figure 42-4 compares reported cash from operations for the capitalizing and expensing firms. The capitalizing firm always shows higher cash from operations; the difference increases and does not reverse over the life of the asset (see Figure 42-5).

Figure 42-2

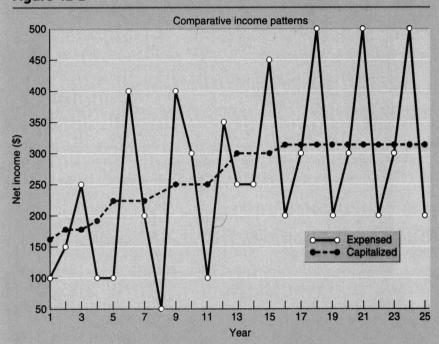

Figure 42-3

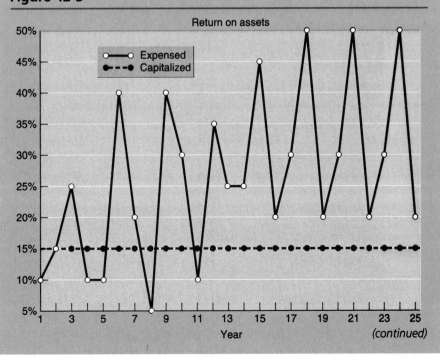

(continued)

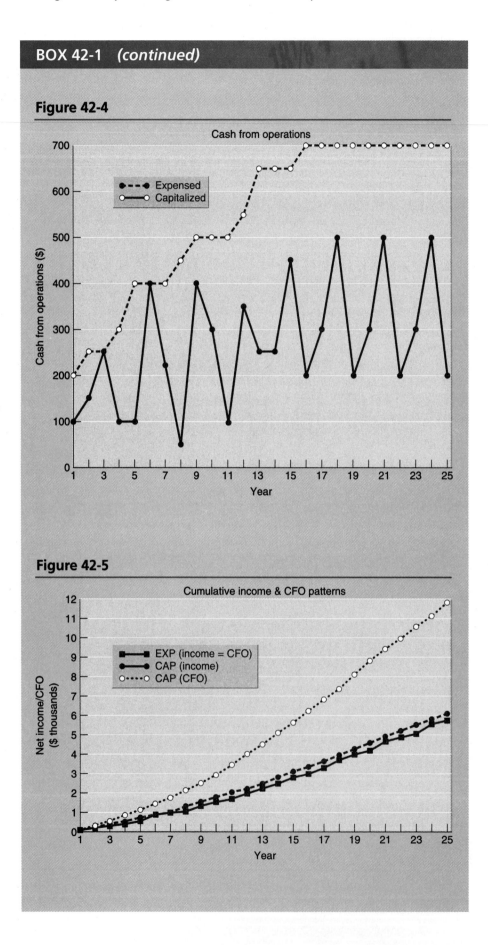

BOX 42-1 *(continued)*

Figure 42-4

Figure 42-5

as the level of expenditures is increasing (positive growth). However, because they report lower assets (and equity), their ROA/ROE measures can be higher than those of firms that capitalize costs (Figure 42-3). In general, whether ROA and ROE will be higher depends on the relationship between profitability and growth.[2]

Cash Flow from Operations

Reported *net cash flow*, unlike net income, is immune to accounting alternatives.[3] However, the capitalization decision has a significant impact on the components of cash flow, with a trade-off between *cash from operations (CFO) and cash from investment (CFI)*. As discussed in Reading 33, cash expenditures for capitalized assets are included in investing cash flow and *never* flow through CFO. Firms that expense these outlays, however, include these expenditures in CFO. Thus, CFO will always be higher for the capitalizing firm (Figure 42-4),[4] and the cumulative difference (rather than reversing) increases over time (Figure 42-5). *Thus, the capitalization of long-lived assets results in a permanent shift of expenditures from CFO to CFI.*

Leverage Ratios

Expensing firms report lower assets and equity balances.[5] As a result, debt-to-equity and debt-to-assets solvency ratios will appear worse for expensing firms as compared with firms that capitalize the same costs.

Given management discretion as to capitalization, a great deal of care must be exercised when assessing financial performance. The remainder of this reading considers particular areas where this problem occurs. Some issues are pervasive and cut across all industries; others are industry specific.

CAPITALIZATION VERSUS EXPENSING: GENERAL ISSUES

Capitalization of Interest Costs

Companies often construct long-lived assets, such as new operating facilities, for their own use and capitalize costs incurred during construction until the assets are ready to be placed in service. How should the firm measure the cost of these self-constructed assets? Should the interest cost on funds used for

---

[2] Sarath, Lev, and Sougiannis (2000) show that for a firm whose relevant expenditures are growing at a rate g, ROE on an expensing basis will be higher if that $ROE > g/(1 + g/2)$. For growth rates (in the relevant range) below 30%, that relationship is equivalent to comparing ROE and g. As long as they are close, there is little difference between ROE on an expense basis and ROE on a capitalized basis. The greater the difference between ROE and g, the greater the difference between ROE on an expense basis and ROE on a capitalized basis. (A similar relationship holds for pretax ROA.)

For (after-tax) ROA, ROA will be higher for the expensing firm if its
$ROA > (1 - \text{tax rate}) g/(1 + g/2)$.

[3] Ignoring any income tax effects.

[4] This affects the cash from operations/capital expenditures ratio that measures the degree to which the firm's internally generated funds finance the replacement and expansion of productive capacity.

[5] These effects are not directly shown in Box 42-1. However, they can be deduced from the discussion of the return-on-investment (ROA/ROE) measures.

construction be capitalized or expensed? Should interest capitalization require specific borrowing to finance construction? Should the firm capitalize a return on equity when there is no debt or the firm has borrowed less than the total construction cost? The answers to these questions vary from country to country.

In the United States, SFAS 34 (1979) requires the capitalization of interest costs incurred during the construction period. When a specific borrowing is associated with the construction, the interest cost incurred on that borrowing is capitalized. If no specific borrowing is identifiable, the weighted-average interest rate on outstanding debt (up to the amount invested in the project) is capitalized. When the firm has no interest expense, no borrowing costs may be capitalized. Capitalization of the cost of equity is not permitted under any circumstances. SFAS 34 requires the disclosure of the amount of interest capitalized.

The argument for interest capitalization is that the cost of a self-constructed asset should equal the cost of one purchased after completion. In the latter case, the purchase price would presumably include the cost of capital of the seller. Capitalization of interest for self-constructed assets, it is argued, replicates this process. This argument should apply even when the firm has no debt; in that case, return on equity capital used for construction should be capitalized.

On the other hand, there are strong arguments against the capitalization of interest in general and SFAS 34 in particular. On a conceptual level, interest, as a financing cost, is different from the other costs of acquiring and getting the asset ready for service. It results from a financing decision rather than an operating decision.

Under SFAS 34, interest is capitalized only if the firm is leveraged. It seems illogical that two identical assets should be carried at different costs, depending on the firm's financing decisions. Further, the capitalization of interest creates differences between reported earnings and cash flow. Given these arguments, we believe that expensing of all interest is the preferable treatment.

For purposes of analysis, therefore, the income statement capitalization of interest should be reversed, resulting in the following effects:

1. *Capitalized interest should be added back to interest expense.* The adjusted interest expense provides a better representation of the level and trend of a firm's financing costs.

2. *Adding capitalized interest back to interest expense reduces net income.* Unfortunately, although the amount of interest capitalized in the current year must be disclosed, disclosure of the amortization of previously capitalized interest (included in the fixed asset account) is not required and is rarely provided.[6] This amortization must be deducted from depreciation expense to accurately determine the net effect of interest capitalization on net income. *However, if the amount of interest capitalization in previous years is not large and asset lives are long, the amortization (over the asset life) is likely to be immaterial and can be ignored.* If interest capitalization has been large, the analyst must estimate the amortization.[7]

---

[6] See Problem 42-1, based on Chevron, which does disclose the amortization of previously capitalized interest.

[7] The amortization of capitalized interest is included in depreciation expense. Thus, one can use the historical ratio of interest capitalized to total capital expenditures to estimate the portion of depreciation applicable to capitalized interest expense.

3. *The capitalization of interest also distorts the classification of cash flows. Interest capitalized as part of the cost of fixed assets will never be reported as CFO, but as an investment outflow. To restore comparability with firms that do not capitalize interest, the amount of interest capitalized should be added back to cash for investment and subtracted from CFO.* The cash flows for capitalized interest are then included with other interest payments.[8]

4. *The interest coverage ratio should be calculated with interest expense adjusted to add back capitalized interest.* Otherwise, it is overstated.[9]

These adjustments tend to be small relative to cash flows but may be significant for interest expense and net income. The following example illustrates how adding back capitalized interest affects profitability and the interest coverage ratio.

Example 42-1

Westvaco

Note F in Westvaco's fiscal 1999 financial statements reports capitalized interest, which can be used to adjust the interest coverage ratio:[10]

Westvaco, Years Ended October 31 (in $thousands)

	1997	1998	1999	% Change 1997–1999
As reported:				
EBIT	$339,872	$314,575	$271,514	(20%)
Interest expense	93,272	110,162	123,538	32%
Pretax income	$246,600	$204,413	$147,976	(40%)
Interest coverage	3.64X	2.86X	2.20X	(39%)
Interest capitalized	$ 25,962	$ 20,752	$ 8,890	(66%)
After adjustment:				
EBIT (unchanged)	$339,872	$314,575	$271,514	(20%)
Interest expense	119,234	130,914	132,428	11%
Pretax income	$220,638	$183,661	$139,086	(37%)
Interest coverage	2.85X	2.40X	2.05X	(28%)

---

[8] These interest payments would be deducted from cash from operations, as required by SFAS 95. Alternatively, as we argue in Reading 36, interest payments should be considered financing cash flows and thus excluded from both CFO and cash for investment regardless of capitalization.

[9] The SFAS 95 requirement for the disclosure of interest paid makes it possible to make this adjustment and compute interest coverage accurately on a cash flow basis. On an accrual basis, the numerator, EBIT (and hence the coverage ratio), will be underestimated if the amortization of previous years' capitalized interest is not removed. However, as noted, this effect is relatively insignificant.

[10] Due to lack of disclosure, no adjustment has been made for the amortization of previously capitalized interest.

Based on Westvaco's reported data, the interest coverage ratio fell 39% due to declining earnings before interest and taxes (EBIT) and rising interest expense. While adding back capitalized interest does not radically change the data, it does show that:

▶ Adjusted interest coverage, based on interest incurred before capitalization, is, as expected, below the (reported) ratio based on interest expense after capitalization.

▶ Interest expense over the period rose only 11% rather than 32% as reported.

▶ Interest coverage fell 28% based on interest incurred, a smaller decline than the 39% decline based on reported data.

▶ While pretax income is lower each year, the two-year decline in pretax income was slightly lower after adjustment.

Capitalization of interest provides additional information. Despite rising interest costs, capitalized interest declined 66%, apparently due to a lower level of qualifying assets. *A significant change in capitalized interest may signal a shift in the amount or nature of capital spending, and should be investigated by the analyst.*

Interest Capitalization Outside the United States

IAS 23, Borrowing Costs (revised 1993), makes expensing all borrowing costs the benchmark treatment. Alternatively, borrowing costs that are directly attributable to the acquisition, construction, or production of qualifying assets may be capitalized. Interest capitalization is also permitted in many jurisdictions worldwide. When comparing firms that capitalize interest with those do not, adjustment is required to achieve a base for proper valuation.

Intangible Assets

Growth of the computer, Internet, telecommunications, and service industries has led to significantly increased investment in and use of intangible assets. Licenses, computer software, patents, leasehold rights, brand names, and copyrights are among the more familiar examples of assets without tangible, physical substance. As a result of their increased use, the financial reporting and analysis of such intangible assets have gained importance; for some firms they are important on- or off-balance-sheet revenue-producing assets that account for a substantial portion of the value of a firm.

Intangible assets are identifiable, nonmonetary resources controlled by firms.[11] When acquired in an arm's-length transaction, recognition and measurement rules are similar to those for tangible assets. However, practice is diverse with respect to the recognition and measurement of such assets when they are internally developed. In addition, practices differ with respect to the revaluation, amortization, and impairment of intangible assets, regardless of their origin.

---

[11] Goodwill is an intangible asset although it is not identifiable.

The decision whether to capitalize or expense the cost of asset acquisition is especially difficult when applied to intangible resources. The variations in legal protection available for intellectual property and other intangible assets in many countries also make the assessment of value more difficult than for tangible assets. We begin, therefore, with a review of the recognition and measurement issues associated with intangible assets.

Recognition and Measurement Issues

The cost of acquiring intangible assets from unrelated entities is capitalized at acquisition, measured by the amount paid to acquire them. Given an arm's-length transaction, the acquisition price is assumed to equal the market value of the assets acquired.

Intangible assets may also be received through government grants or generated internally by the firm. Few, if any, costs may be incurred in obtaining assets through government grants. Financial statement recognition of such assets would be informative, but in the absence of secondary markets it is difficult to defend any measurement basis other than cost. When active secondary markets do exist (such as for broadcast properties and cellular licenses), then market price can be a reliable measure of the value of these assets.

Internally generated intangible assets are the most troublesome category because:

▶ The costs incurred in developing these assets may not be easily separable.

▶ It is difficult to measure the amount and duration of benefits from such expenditures as advertising when they are made, or even later.

▶ There may be little relationship between the costs incurred and the value of the asset created.

For many internally generated intangible assets, discounted cash flow analysis may be the only way to measure their fair value. However, such measurement is subject to accurate forecasting of the amount and timing of cash flows and the choice of discount rates.

To illustrate these issues, we turn to a discussion of capitalization issues for specific intangible assets.

Research and Development

Companies invest in research and development (R&D) because they expect the investment to produce profitable future products. However, absent a resultant commercial product, these expenditures may have no value to the firm. Further, the value of the resulting product may be unrelated to the amount spent on R&D. Due to such valuation uncertainties, R&D is generally unacceptable to creditors as security for loans.

SFAS 2, Accounting for Research and Development Costs. SFAS 2 (1974) requires that virtually all R&D costs be expensed[12] in the period incurred and the amount disclosed. In effect, assets with uncertain future economic benefits are barred from the balance sheet. The impact of SFAS 2 on the financial

---

[12] The main exception is contract R&D performed for unrelated entities. In this case, R&D is carried as an asset (similar to inventory) until completion of the contract.

statements of firms with significant R&D is substantial, and there is some evidence of a decrease in R&D expenditures when SFAS 2 was adopted. Accounting aside, R&D expenditures are clearly investments in the economic sense, albeit risky ones. Further, empirical evidence[13] suggests that benefits from R&D expenditures last, on average, seven to nine years (depending on the industry), supporting the argument that R&D is an economic asset. Pfizer, for example, spent nearly $2.8 billion (17.1% of revenue) on R&D in 1999.

Accounting for Research and Development Costs Outside the United States. IAS 9 (1993) requires the expensing of research costs but requires capitalization of development costs[14] when all of the following criteria are met:

1. The product (process) is clearly defined.

2. Costs can be clearly identified.

3. Technical feasibility has been established.

4. The firm intends to produce the product (use the process).

5. The market has been clearly defined.

6. The firm has sufficient resources to complete the project.

Capitalized costs must be reviewed periodically to ensure that these conditions are still operable and that capitalized costs do not exceed net realizable value.[15] The standard also requires disclosure of the accounting methods followed, amortization methods and lives, and a reconciliation of the carrying amount.

Example 42-2

Nokia

Nokia, an international telecommunications manufacturer, follows IASB GAAP and capitalized R&D costs in its 1998 and 1999 financial statements.

As expensing research and development costs is the dominant accounting method worldwide, financial statements of companies such as Nokia that capitalize R&D must be restated (by expensing all such expenditures) to make them comparable with similar companies that expense these costs. Alternatively (or for other analytical purposes), it may be desirable to restate another firm's financial statements by capitalizing previously expensed R&D costs. Box 2 describes the procedures required to make the adjustments in both directions. Next we illustrate the capitalization-to-expense adjustment, using Nokia as an example. Later (see Microsoft example) we adjust from expense to capitalization.

---

[13] Research in this area can be found in both the accounting and economics literature. Lev and Sougiannis (1996) provide a brief review of the literature in this area. See also the discussion of valuation in Box 42-3.

[14] IAS 9 defines development costs as expenditures incurred to translate research output into the production of materials, devices, products, processes, systems, and services.

[15] See Reading 43 for a discussion of impairment.

Nokia: Capitalized R&D Costs

	Years Ended December 31 (millions of euros)		
	1997	**1998**	**1999**
Opening balance	€426	€469	€650
Additions	156	182	271
Disposals	(113)	(1)	(110)
Closing balance	€469	€650	€811
Accumulated depreciation (year-end)*	(242)	(361)	(398)
Closing balance (net)	€227	€289	€413
Depreciation expense		119	110

*Note that the 1998 depreciation expense equals the change in accumulated depreciation; in 1999 accumulated depreciation has been reduced by the amount allocated to the disposal of R&D. We can deduce that reduction to equal €73 (361 + 110 − 398).

We can use these disclosures to compute the effect of capitalization compared to expense.

Adjustment to Pretax Income: Subtract the difference between R&D expenditure (additions) and depreciation/writedowns from reported income. This adjustment essentially amounts to subtracting the change in net (unamortized) closing balance from reported income:

(Millions of Euros)	1998	1999
Pretax income (reported)	€2,456	€3,845
Less: change in net (unamortized) closing balance	62	124
Pretax income (adjusted)	€2,394	€3,721
% reduction	2.5%	3.2%

We can also adjust reported cash flows:

Adjustment to Cash Flows: Subtract R&D expenditure (additions) from CFO and add back to CFI:

(Millions of Euros)	1998	1999
Cash from operations	€1,687	€3,102
Cash flow from investing	(780)	(1,341)
Additions (R&D expenditures)	182	271
After adjustment		
Cash from operations	1,505	2,831
% reduction	10.8%	8.7%
Cash flow from investing	€(598)	€(1,070)

Finally, to make Nokia comparable to companies that expense all R&D, we must reduce equity[16] by the closing balance of unamortized R&D expense, net of tax effect:

(Millions of Euros)	1998	1999
Shareholders' equity (as reported)	€5,109	€7,378
Closing R&D balance (net of depreciation)	289	413
Less tax @ 28% (rate in Finland)	(81)	(116)
Net reduction in equity	€208	€297
Shareholders' equity (adjusted)	4,901	7,081
% reduction	4.1%	4.0%

These adjustments vary from 2% to 10% depending on the item being adjusted. Nokia is a very large company (1999 sales were nearly €20 billion). Depending on the size of the firm and the variability in expenditures, the effect on other firms may be more significant.[17]

One additional benefit of this analysis is that it highlights the actual expenditures on R&D activities. Changes in amount or trend (note the large 1999 increase for Nokia) should be examined for implications regarding the company's future sales and earnings.

BOX 42-2 ADJUSTING FINANCING STATEMENTS FOR CAPITALIZATION VERSUS EXPENSING

The capitalization-versus-expense decision has pervasive effects on firms' financial statements and ratios. In this box, we illustrate the adjustments from one method to the other. For convenience we use research and development (R&D) as the expenditure that can either be capitalized or expensed.

Adjusting from Capitalization to Expense

Income Statement:

Pretax Income: Deduct difference between R&D additions (expenditures) and amount amortized (or written off). This adjustment is equivalent to the *change in the net (unamortized) R&D asset.*

Net Income: Deduct (1 − tax rate) × (change in the net (unamortized) R&D asset).

(continued)

---

[16] To adjust assets, we would deduct the closing balance of unamortized R&D expense.

[17] Nokia's 20-F report, in the required reconciliation between IASB and U.S. GAAP, shows somewhat different amounts for the income statement and balance sheet adjustments. These differences reflect the fact that, even under U.S. GAAP, Nokia could have capitalized a portion of these expenditures (computer software). The adjustments shown here eliminate the entire capitalized amount, facilitating comparison with firms that expense all R&D.

BOX 42-2   *(continued)*

Balance Sheet:

Assets:	Deduct net (unamortized) R&D asset from assets.
Liabilities:	Deduct (tax rate) × (decrease in assets) from deferred tax liability.*
Equity:	Deduct (1 − tax rate) × (decrease in assets) from equity.
Cash Flow Statement:	Deduct R&D expenditures from CFO and add same amount to CFI

Adjusting from Expense to Capitalization

To capitalize expenditures, we need an assumption as to the period of amortization. This illustration assumes amortization over three years beginning in the year of the expenditure (year t).

Income Statement:

Pretax Income:[†]	In year t, increase pretax income by $R\&D_t − 1/3(R\&D_t + R\&D_{t−1} + R\&D_{t−2})$.
Net Income:	Add (1 − tax rate) × (pretax income adjustment).

Balance Sheet:[‡]

Assets:	Increase by $[2/3\ R\&D_t + 1/3\ R\&D_{t−1}]$.
Liabilities:	Add (tax rate) × (increase in assets) to deferred tax liability.[§]
Equity:	Increase by (1 − tax rate) × (increase in assets).
Cash Flow Statement:	Add $R\&D_t$ to CFO and deduct same amount from CFI.

---

* Assumes that R&D was expensed for tax purposes, creating a deferred tax liability (see Reading 42).

[†] General case, for amortization over n years: Increase pretax income by $[R\&D_t − 1/n\ (R\&D_t + R\&D_{t−1} + \ldots\ R\&D_{t−(n−1)})]$.

[‡] Increase assets by $[(n − 1)/n\ R\&D_t + (n − 2)/n\ R\&D_{t−1} + \ldots\ 1/n\ R\&D_{t−(n−2)}]$.

[§] Assumes that R&D is expensed for tax purposes, so that capitalization results in a deferred tax liability (see Reading 44).

OPTIONAL SEGMENT ENDS

Research and Development Affiliates.   Although SFAS 2 does not permit the capitalization of R&D costs, companies have found ways to defer the recognition of such costs. One method is the R&D partnership. Another involves the issuance of "callable common" shares to the public.

Patents and Copyrights

All costs incurred in developing patents and copyrights are expensed in conformity with the treatment of R&D costs.[18] Only the legal fees incurred in registering internally developed patents and copyrights can be capitalized. However, the full acquisition cost is capitalized when such assets are purchased from other entities.

---

[18] However, publishers and motion picture producers capitalize all costs of creating their inventory.

Patents have a legal life of 17 years under U.S. patent law; copyrights have a legal life of 50 years beyond the creator's life. However, these periods should be viewed as upper limits. Successful patented products invite competition and the development of comparable or improved products that can diminish the value of the patent or make it obsolete. In addition, there is often a gap between the time that a patent is registered and the time the product comes to market.

In the pharmaceutical industry, for example, even after a patent is registered, the product cannot be marketed in most countries until it obtains regulatory approval, which can take a number of years. The analysis of companies that are heavily dependent on patented or proprietary products must consider the remaining legal life of patents on existing products and the number of patents in the pipeline.

Franchises and Licenses

Companies may sell the right to use their name, products, processes, or management expertise to others for some negotiated time period or market. The franchisee or licensee capitalizes the cost of purchasing these rights.

Brands and Trademarks

The cost of acquiring brands and trademarks in arm's-length transactions is capitalized. However, as in the case of other intangibles, U.S. GAAP prohibit recognition of the value of *internally created* brands or trademarks. IAS 38 also prohibits recognition of internally generated brands, mastheads, publishing titles, customer lists, and similar items. Some national accounting standards do permit recognition of such assets.

Advertising Costs

Successful advertising campaigns can contribute to generating a customer base and establishing brand or firm loyalty for many years. However, as with R&D, these benefits are uncertain and difficult to measure, and hence advertising costs are expensed as incurred. Even though there may be economic benefits, no asset is recorded because of measurement problems.

In December 1994, the Accounting Standards Executive Committee (AcSEC) of the AICPA issued Practice Bulletin 13,[19] Direct-Response Advertising and Probable Future Benefits, requiring capitalization of the costs of direct-response advertising that result in probable future benefits.[20] These costs are amortized over the estimated life of the future benefits. Capitalization is not allowed when the advertising produces leads that require additional marketing efforts to convert into sales.[21]

Goodwill

The difference between the cost of an acquired firm and the fair market value of its net assets is accounted for as an intangible asset, goodwill. It represents the

---

[19] This bulletin provides an interpretation of AICPA SOP 93-7, Reporting on Advertising Costs.

[20] An example would be advertising that results in a telephone response with an order.

[21] America On Line (AOL) capitalized marketing costs prior to 1996 as "deferred subscriber acquisition costs." After pressure from the SEC and analysts, AOL took a $385 million write-off in 1997 to eliminate these assets from its financial statements. In March 2000, AOL paid a $3.5 million fine to the SEC to settle charges that it had inflated profits in the years prior to 1997.

amount paid for the acquired firm's ability to earn excess profits, or value that cannot be assigned to tangible assets like property. The United States and most other GAAP limit the recognition of goodwill to cases where it is acquired in purchase method transactions.

Asset Revaluation

The balance sheet is more informative when assets and liabilities are stated at market value rather than historical cost. Although the recognition of changes in fixed asset value is not permitted under U.S. GAAP, IASB standards do permit such revaluations.

IAS 16 (revised 1998), Property, Plant, and Equipment, allows firms to report fixed assets at fair value less accumulated depreciation.[22] Revaluations must be made with sufficient regularity to keep them current. All items in an asset class must be revalued if any are. Revaluation decreases that place the asset value below historical cost must be included in reported earnings. Revaluations are credited directly to equity except when they reverse writedowns that were included in reported income. IAS 16 has extensive disclosure provisions regarding revaluations and requires a full reconciliation of fixed assets. Footnote 12 to the Roche 2000 financial statements is a typical reconciliation.

IAS 41 (2000), Agriculture, requires that agricultural produce (e.g. cotton, milk, and logs) and biological assets (plants and animals) be measured at fair value for financial reporting. This standard becomes effective in 2003.

Revaluation is permitted under some non-U.S. GAAP as well.[23] Unfortunately, revaluation is applied inconsistently as standards in most countries do not specify either the method(s) to be used for revaluations or the intervals at which they must be made. The resulting balance sheet accounts are not comparable and, in some cases, may be misleading.

Example 42-3

Holmen

Footnote 10 to Holmen's 1999 financial statements reports total revaluation surplus of SKr 4,372, almost all of which reflects the revaluation of forest land. No other data are provided although this item exceeds 27% of equity.

The revaluation of forest land has the following effects on Holmen compared with firms that do not revalue:

▶ Lower asset turnover due to the higher asset value for land

▶ Lower return on assets (ROA) due to higher assets

▶ Higher reported book value per share

▶ Lower return on equity (ROE) due to higher equity

▶ Lower debt ratios due to higher equity

---

[22] Although historical cost is the benchmark treatment, revaluation is an allowed alternative.

[23] Australian GAAP, for example, permits revaluations. Barth and Clinch (1998) examined a sample of revaluations in Australia and found that both tangible and intangible revaluations tended to be value relevant.

As forestland is not depreciated, there is no effect on reported income. For assets that are depreciated, revaluation has the following additional effects:

▶ Lower earnings due to higher depreciation expense
▶ Lower interest coverage due to reduced EBIT

The earnings reduction further reduces ROA and ROE and dilutes the positive impact of the revaluation on book value per share.

5 CAPITALIZATION VERSUS EXPENSING: INDUSTRY ISSUES

Regulated Utilities

Even prior to the issuance of SFAS 34, almost all U.S. regulated utilities capitalized interest on construction work in progress. In addition, utilities capitalize many cash outflows that unregulated companies cannot. The reason is that accounting rules have direct economic impact for utilities. Rates charged to customers are largely a function of accounting-generated numbers.[24]

Regulators allow utilities to earn profits equal to a specified allowable rate of return on assets (rate base). Adding expenses to this allowable profit yields the rates they can charge their customers. Revenues are derived as follows:

Revenues = Expenses + (Rate of Return × Rate Base)

Using interest for a self-constructed asset as an example, expensing increases revenue immediately as the interest expense is recovered in the year incurred. Capitalizing results in recovery of the expense over time as depreciation of the additional fixed asset. However, the total allowable profit is increased due to the fact that the asset base has been increased. Hence, although revenues are deferred, the total amount collected over the life of the asset is greater. As the average life of utility fixed assets (mainly generating plants) is quite long, the incentive to capitalize costs in fixed assets (increasing the rate base) is powerful.

Fairness to customers is often one argument for capitalization; as current customers do not (yet) benefit from investments in capacity growth, they should not bear the cost. Thus, the cost of financing new capacity is capitalized and spread over time, matching the costs with the benefits (service to ratepayers). This logic is also appealing to regulators who prefer (for political reasons) to defer rate increases to future time periods. Logic and fairness aside, utilities have a direct economic incentive to capitalize.[25]

---

[24] For this reason, virtually all regulators that set prices also mandate the accounting principles followed by the companies that they regulate. This has given rise to so-called RAP (regulatory accounting principles), which may differ materially from GAAP.

[25] This discussion assumes that the capitalized interest will, in fact, be recovered from future revenues. In practice, "regulatory lag" often results in actual rates of return below the "allowable" rate of return. In addition, by capitalizing interest, the recovery of that interest is delayed to a later period and thus current period cash flow is reduced. For these reasons, some utilities have successfully petitioned regulators to allow some portion of the interest on construction work in progress (CWIP) to be recovered currently (expensed) rather than capitalized.

Regulatory accounting results in the creation of *regulatory assets* and *regulatory liabilities*. Regulatory assets are expenditures that regulators will permit the utility to recover in future periods, even though these expenditures do not qualify as assets for unregulated companies under GAAP. Examples include:

▶ Capitalization (as part of fixed assets) of return on equity as well as interest. These are called the allowance for funds used during construction (AFUDC).

▶ Capitalization (as part of fixed assets) of employee costs and other overhead.

▶ Demand-side management costs (expenditures to reduce demand).

▶ Costs to buy out coal or gas purchase contracts.

Under SFAS 71, such expenditures can be recorded as regulatory assets (regulatory liabilities) as long as recovery (settlement) is expected. If an adverse regulatory ruling is made, such assets must be written off.

When deregulation occurs, the company must reassess the carrying value of its assets and liabilities under these new circumstances. In the United States, deregulation of the telephone industry resulted in significant write-offs by companies in that industry as they:

▶ Wrote down fixed assets to reflect shorter economic lives

▶ Wrote off regulatory assets that were no longer recoverable

The use of shorter asset lives as a result of the accounting change increases depreciation expense, somewhat offset by the elimination of depreciation on older assets that were fully written off as part of the change. The change also sharply reduces reported stockholders' equity, increasing the reported debt-to-equity ratio.

The deregulation of the electric utility industry in the United States is in its early stages. Such deregulation is likely to result in similar write-offs of regulatory assets and the use of shorter lives for fixed assets.[26]

Computer Software Development Costs

The growing importance of computer software led the FASB to issue SFAS 86 (1985), which applies to software intended for sale or lease to others. SFAS 86 requires that all costs incurred to establish the technological and/or economic feasibility of software be viewed as R&D costs and expensed as incurred. Once economic feasibility has been established, subsequent costs can be capitalized as part of product inventory and amortized based on product revenues or on a straight-line basis.

Although this provision allows software firms to increase reported assets and income, some software firms[27] (most notably, Microsoft[28]) have not taken advantage

---

[26] Deregulation also eliminates the incentives for investments in generating plants by eliminating the guaranteed recovery of the investment and a return on investment. Shortages of generating capacity started to appear in 1999.

[27] In 1996, the Software Publishers Association (SPA) petitioned the FASB to abolish SFAS 86 and make expensing the required method of accounting. The SPA argued that the uncertainty surrounding eventual product sales made capitalization both inappropriate and not beneficial to investors. As noted in Box 42-3, Aboody and Lev (1998) found, on the contrary, that software capitalization was indeed value relevant to investors. Aboody and Lev suggested (using recent trends in software development costs) that perhaps the SPA was motivated by the fact that software development expenditures had declined to a low level and that expensing would now show higher income than capitalization. By eliminating the previous years' capitalization overhang with a onetime accounting charge, software developers could (under the SPA's proposal) get the best of both worlds, using capitalization when costs were growing and expensing when costs declined.

[28] Microsoft's fiscal 2000 annual report states that it adopted SOP 98-1 (discussed shortly) in 2000 but provides no disclosure of the effects. On page 22 it states that SFAS 86 "does not materially affect the Company."

of the provisions of SFAS 86. Disparate accounting for software hinders the comparison of computer software firms, requiring restatement to the same accounting method. SFAS 86 disclosures are sufficient to evaluate (and eliminate) the impact of capitalization. For some firms, the effect may be significant, as illustrated by the following example.

Example 42-4

Lucent

The following data were obtained from Lucent's annual report for fiscal 1999:

Capitalized Software		
(in $millions)	1998	1999
Opening balance	$293	$298
Closing balance	298	470
Amortization	234	249

where the balances were obtained from Lucent's balance sheet and the amortization amount from the statement of cash flows. By adding the year-to-year increase in the balance to the amortization, we can deduce the amount invested during the year (which is included in capital expenditures under investing activities):

(in $millions)	1998	1999
New investment	$239	$421

If Lucent expensed this amount each year (as does Microsoft), its income would have been reduced by:

	(in $millions)	1998	1999
Income adjustment	Investment less amortization	$ 5	$ 172
	Tax offset (35%)	(2)	(60)
	Net adjustment	$ 3	$ 112
Net Income	Reported	$1,035	$3,458
	Adjusted	1,032	3,346
	% reduction	−0.3%	−3.2%

Note that the 1999 effect is much greater than the 1998 effect, reflecting the substantial increase in expenditures. Capitalization and amortization smoothes the effect of spending changes on reported income. It also obscures the large increase, which may suggest that Lucent hopes to expand its software sales.

Perhaps more important, however, is that amounts capitalized are included in cash for investing activities rather than cash from operations. By subtracting the new investment amount, we can adjust cash from operations:

Cash from Operations

(in $millions)	1998	1999
Reported	$1,860	$(276)
Adjusted	1,621	(697)
% reduction	−12.8%	−152.5%

While reported CFO turned negative in 1999, the effect is even greater when software expenditures are reclassified from investing to operating activities.

SOP 98-1 governs accounting for the cost of developing computer software for internal use (rather than sale or lease).[29] This standard requires the capitalization and subsequent amortization of the cost of developing internal-use software once technical feasibility has been established. EITF Issue 00-2[30] extends SOP 98-1 to website development costs, allowing capitalization of costs to develop or add applications for websites. IBM, for example, capitalized $81 million of website development costs in 2000.

Example 42-5

Lucent

The 10-Q report filed by Lucent for the first quarter of fiscal 2000 (ending December 31, 1999) states:

> Effective October 1, 1999, Lucent adopted Statement of Position 98-1, "Accounting for the Costs of Computer Software Developed or Obtained for Internal Use" ("SOP 98-1"). As a result, certain costs of computer software developed or obtained for internal use have been capitalized and will be amortized over a three-year period. The impact of adopting SOP 98-1 was a reduction of costs and operating expenses of $80 million during the three months ended December 31, 1999.

---

[29] Issued by the Accounting Standards Executive Committee of the American Institute of Certified Public Accountants. For full discussion of SOP 98-1, see Daniel Noll, "Accounting for Internal Use Software," *Journal of Accountancy* (September 1998), pp. 95–98.

[30] Accounting for Web Site Development Costs, issued by the Emerging Issues Task Force based on discussions in January and March 2000. EITF 00-2 was effective for costs incurred after June 30, 2000.

The impact of the new standard increased pretax income by $80 million, equal to nearly 5% of pretax income excluding "one-time items." If not for the accounting change, that adjusted pretax income would have declined by more than 28% instead of the reported decline of 25%. The effect of the accounting change was not reported in the January 20, 2000 press release announcing Lucent's first quarter earnings, providing an illustration of the importance of reviewing SEC filings.

Accounting for Oil and Gas Exploration

Oil and gas exploration results in drilling both productive wells and dry holes.[31] As failure is an integral part of successful exploration, the cost of dry holes can be considered part of the cost of drilling productive ones. As in the case of R&D, the value of an oil discovery is frequently unrelated to the cost of drilling.

The FASB, in SFAS 19 (1977), required all firms to use the successful efforts (SE) accounting method that expenses all dry hole costs. Like the FASB's R&D reporting standard, this rule was conservative and eliminated assets with uncertain future benefits from the balance sheet. The Securities and Exchange Commission (SEC), fearing that the adoption of this rule would result in the curtailment of oil exploration (especially by smaller companies), forced the FASB to suspend SFAS 19 (SFAS 25, 1979). The SEC (ASR 253, 1978) permits public companies to use either SE or full cost (FC) methods of accounting. The latter permits the capitalization of dry hole costs.

Under current accounting practice, therefore, firms have the option of capitalizing the cost of dry holes (FC method) or expensing them as they occur (SE method). The choice between these two methods has a significant impact on the financial statements of oil and gas exploration companies and on many ratios as well. Exhibit 42-1 illustrates the difference between the SE and FC methods of accounting for oil and gas exploration costs. The balance sheet carrying amount of reserves, $4,000, is higher under the FC method because of the inclusion of the cost of dry holes ($3,000). The SE firm carries its reserves at only $1,000.[32]

The reported profitability (both levels and trends over time) of production is also affected. The SE firm reports a net loss of $250 in year 1 but net income of $2,750 per year for years 2 through 4, for a total net income of $8,000. The FC firm shows constant net income of $2,000 per year, again for a total of $8,000 over the four years. The effect of the FC method is to defer (capitalize) exploration costs and, therefore, accelerate the recognition of profit.

CFO may also differ. As previously discussed, although the income difference reverses over time, the difference in CFO does not. The cumulative CFO over the life of the well is higher for the FC firm by the cost of the capitalized dry holes ($12,000 − $9,000 = $3,000).

---

[31] Dry holes are wells drilled that do not find commercial quantities of oil or gas.

[32] Using a sample of oil and gas companies, Harris and Ohlson (1987) found that the market distinguished between SE and FC companies in a rational fashion. Book values of full cost companies were given less weight than those of SE companies. Additionally, they found that FC book values had less explanatory power than those of SE companies. This finding is consistent with a survey that indicated analysts prefer SE.

The differences between the methods cause SE firms to report:

► Lower carrying costs of oil and gas reserves than FC firms
► Lower stockholders' equity due to lower asset values
► Lower earnings than FC firms when exploration efforts are rising
► Lower cash from operations than FC firms

EXHIBIT 42-1	COMPARISON OF SUCCESSFUL EFFORTS AND FULL COST IMPACT ON NET INCOME AND CASH FROM OPERATIONS

Assumptions:
1. $1,000 cost of drilling well (dry or productive).
2. Four wells are drilled: One is productive, the other three are dry.
3. The productive well has a four-year life, with revenues (net of cost of production) of $3,000 per year.

Successful Efforts Method

The $3,000 cost of dry holes is expensed immediately. Only the $1,000 cost of the productive well is capitalized and amortized over its four-year life.

Year	1	2	3	4	Total
Net revenues	$ 3,000	$3,000	$3,000	$3,000	$12,000
Dry hole expense	(3,000)	0	0	0	(3,000)
Amortization	(250)	(250)	(250)	(250)	(1,000)
Net income	$ (250)	$2,750	$2,750	$2,750	$ 8,000
Cash Flows					
Operations*	$ 0	$3,000	$3,000	$3,000	$ 9,000
Investment	(1,000)	0	0	0	(1,000)
Total	$(1,000)	$3,000	$3,000	$3,000	$ 8,000

* Net revenues less dry hole expense.

Full Cost Method

The entire $4,000 drilling cost ($3,000 for dry holes and $1,000 for the productive well) is capitalized and amortized over the four-year life of the productive well.

Year	1	2	3	4	Total
Net revenues	$ 3,000	$3,000	$3,000	$3,000	$12,000
Amortization	(1,000)	(1,000)	(1,000)	(1,000)	(4,000)
Net income	$ 2,000	$2,000	$2,000	$2,000	$ 8,000
Cash Flows					
Operations*	$ 3,000	$3,000	$3,000	$3,000	$12,000
Investment	(4,000)	0	0	0	(4,000)
Total	$(1,000)	$3,000	$3,000	$3,000	$ 8,000

* Net revenues.

In practice, however, oil and gas firms using the SE method adjust their reported cash flow statements for this difference. They add exploration costs expensed back to net income (assuming use of the indirect method) and include those costs in capital expenditures. For example, Texaco's 1999 annual report states:

> We present cash flows from operating activities using the indirect method. We exclude exploratory expenses from cash flows of operating activities and apply them to cash flows of investing activities. On this basis, we reflect all capital and exploratory expenditures as investing activities.

However, Repsol, the large Spanish oil company, does not appear to make this adjustment. As a result, its reported cash flow components are not comparable with those of companies that make the adjustment.

6 ANALYTICAL ADJUSTMENTS FOR CAPITALIZATION AND EXPENSING

Need for Analytical Adjustments

Because the choices between capitalization and expensing discussed in this chapter affect reported corporate performance, analysts must sometimes adjust reported data to facilitate analysis and comparisons.

Software companies, as noted earlier, are allowed to capitalize software costs, and most do so. A notable exception is Microsoft. Comparisons with other (software) companies can be facilitated and insight as to Microsoft's motivations can be gained by comparing Microsoft's reported income with income had it capitalized R&D. In our analysis, we assume a three-year amortization period.

(in $millions)

	1996	1997	1998	1999	2000
Net income as reported			$4,490	$7,785	$9,421
Adjustment					
R&D as reported	$1,432	$1,925	2,601	2,970	3,775
Amortization of R&D*			(1,986)	(2,499)	(3,115)
Pretax adjustment			$ 615	$ 471	$ 660
After-tax @ 35% tax rate			400	306	429
Adjusted income			4,890	8,091	9,850
% increase in income			8.9%	3.9%	4.6%

* For example, for 2000: ($2,601 + $2,970 + $3,775)/3 = $3,115.

Note that, as Microsoft's R&D is increasing, expensing R&D reduces reported income by 4% to 9%. Although one cannot be sure, it is possible that Microsoft opted not to capitalize costs in order to lessen pressure from antitrust authorities by reporting lower income.

In Microsoft's case, the adjustments to R&D do not significantly affect ROE and ROA.[33] However, that is a function of Microsoft's profitability and pattern of R&D expenditures. For other industries, the effects on ROE and ROA can be considerable.

The pharmaceutical industry, for example, reports ROE that is among the highest of all U.S. industries. Some suggest that this reflects a higher return for the risks inherent in R&D. Others contend that the industry simply earns excess profits, and drug prices have periodically become a political issue. To some extent, however, high drug-industry returns reflect the accounting method used for R&D. Expensing these costs understates equity, the denominator of the ROE ratio. Capitalizing R&D costs (treating them as an investment) would give a more accurate measure of ROE.

Figure 42-6 illustrates this point. Sougiannis (1994) and Lev and Sougiannis (1996) examined the effect on return on equity (ROE) of recalculating the financial results of Merck as if the company capitalized R&D expense and amortized the capitalized amounts over seven years.[34] Using the implied amortization schedule for Merck,[35] Figure 42-6 shows the effects of their conversion process graphically for the period 1982 to 1991. Adjusted ROE is significantly lower for all years, although the trend is unchanged.[36]

From the analyst's perspective, the problem is that accounting does not (and probably cannot) accurately measure the value of expenditures on research and development.[37] Thus the analyst must perform two tasks:

1. Adjust financial data to reflect differences in capitalization policy among firms.

2. Evaluate the flow of new products resulting from R&D expenditures.

The Merck example shows the effects of restating by capitalizing an expense. At times, it may be more appropriate to restate capitalized expenditures to expenses. Westvaco (capitalized interest) and Nokia (capitalized development costs) are examples of such restatements. The second task, far more difficult, is beyond the scope of financial statement analysis.

Similar adjustments are required for firms that differ in the extent to which they buy operating assets or lease them. Airlines, for example, may buy or lease airplanes. Similarly, retail store chains may own or lease stores. This choice has financial statement effects similar to those stemming from capitalizing or expensing. Reported ROA may be misleading; adjustments are required for comparability. Reading 46 discusses leasing and other off-balance-sheet financing techniques in detail.

---

[33] In 2000, average equity was $34,903 million, yielding ROE of 27.0%. Capitalizing R&D would increase equity for

$$1999\left[.65x\left(\left(\frac{2}{3}\right)2{,}970 + \left(\frac{1}{3}\right)2{,}601\right)\right] = 1{,}851 \text{ and for } 2000\left[.65x\left(\left(\frac{2}{3}\right)3{,}775 + \left(\frac{1}{3}\right)2{,}970\right)\right] = 2{,}280$$

Average equity would increase by [.5 × ($1,851 + $2,280) = $2,065] to $36,968 and adjusted ROE would be ($9,850/$36,968=) 26.6%. The reason for the small adjustment is related to the discussion in footnote 3. Note the growth rate in Microsoft's R&D expenditures for 2000 is 27.1%. As that growth rate is almost identical to the ROE of 27.0%, the differences in reported and adjusted ROE (ROA) will be negligible.

[34] Their analysis suggests that R&D has (on average) a seven-year duration for the pharmaceutical industry.

[35] The amortization schedule is neither straight-line nor declining balance. Rather, it amortizes capitalized R&D in proportion to the benefits received. As there is a lag between the time of the expenditure and benefits received, amortization increases over the first three years and declines thereafter.

[36] In this case, Merck's profitability as measured by ROE was in the 40% range whereas growth in R&D expenditures was considerably smaller at 15%.

[37] It is precisely this difficulty that prompted the FASB to require the expensing of R&D expenditures.

FIGURE 42-6   Recalculation of Profitability Ratios Assuming Capitalization of R&D Expenditures

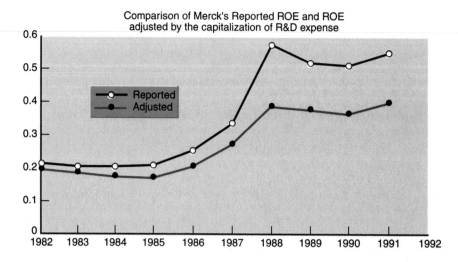

Comparison of Merck's Reported ROE and ROE adjusted by the capitalization of R&D expense

Source: "The Capitalization, Amortization, and Value-Relevance of R&D," *Journal of Accounting and Economics,* Baruch Lev and Theodore Sougiannis, Table 6 (Feb. 1996), pp. 107–138.

Valuation Implications

Expenditures for R&D and advertising are generally expensed because it is difficult, if not impossible, to reliably estimate their future benefits. That does not mean that these expenditures do not affect firm valuation. An outflow that is truly an expense reduces stockholder wealth; an outflow that generates future cash flows may actually increase it.

There are two types of valuation models: earnings based and asset based. Box 42-3 discusses how the capitalization decision affects these valuation models and presents empirical evidence that the market recognizes the asset characteristics of outflows in categories such as R&D, advertising, and oil and gas wells. These results suggest that the analyst cannot apply either capitalization or expensing mechanically, but must try to forecast the future benefits of these expenditures.

Other Economic Consequences

Although differences in accounting methods are cosmetic, they can have real consequences, as suggested by positive theory.

First, a firm's borrowing ability may be limited by unfavorable profitability or leverage ratios resulting from, for example, expensing R&D expenditures. Second, because of these unfavorable ratios, a firm may curtail these expenditures, effectively scaling back operations. Finally, whether or not managers actually reduce R&D, the fact that the market perceives such a possibility can cause negative market reaction.

Mandated accounting changes is one area where such effects can be examined, as they provide a laboratory environment permitting before-and-after comparisons. Box 42-4 reviews empirical evidence regarding mandated accounting changes for R&D and oil and gas accounting.

BOX 42-3   CAPTALIZATION AND VALUATION

Consider the following simplified valuation model:

$$\text{Value} = p \times \text{Net Inflows}$$

The model can be used to represent a (constant) discounted earnings model, where net inflows represent revenue and expense flows and the coefficient p is simply the **price/earnings (P/E)** ratio. Disaggregating the net inflows into inflows and outflows yields

$$\text{Value} = p \times \text{Inflows} - p \times$$
$$\text{Expense Outflows} + b \times \text{Asset Outflows}$$

where asset outflows represent expenditures for such categories as R&D. If these outflows are actually expenses, then $b = -p$.

From a valuation perspective, the difference between asset and expense outflows should be whether the associated outflow has expected future benefits. The level and sign of the coefficient b measure whether the outflow should be considered an expense. An expense benefits only the period of occurrence, and the outlay reduces value by $-p$ times the outflow.* An asset outflow benefits future periods and, therefore, the coefficient b should be positive.†

Bublitz and Ettredge (1989) compared the market valuation of unexpected changes in advertising, R&D, and other expenses. Advertising was included because, like R&D, it is expected to provide benefits for more than one period, albeit for a shorter term than R&D. They expected the coefficient for R&D to be larger (more positive) than the coefficient for advertising, and both larger than the coefficient for other expenses. The results were mixed, but on balance they were consistent with a market assessment of advertising as short-lived and R&D as long-lived.‡

Their valuation model used a discounted earnings-based perspective. Shevlin (1991) used an asset-based valuation model for R&D partnerships. In such a model, the value of the firm is defined as

$$\text{Value} = \text{Assets} - \text{Liabilities}$$

Shevlin§ found that when R&D expenditures were considered assets, they contributed to firm value. Moreover, the market weighting given these expenditures was larger than for other assets, indicating that the expected benefit from these expenditures exceeds their book value.

Lev and Sougiannis (1996) and Sougiannis (1994) estimated stock prices and returns as functions of *both* earnings and book values. They also found that the capitalized components of R&D have value relevance** and are associated with current-period stock returns. More important, Lev and Sougiannis found a significant association between capitalized R&D and *subsequent* stock returns. This implied either a (systematic) mispricing by the market of R&D-intensive companies or compensation for (extra-market) risk associated with R&D.

Aboody and Lev (1998) compared companies that capitalized software development costs with those that chose not to. They found software capitalization (as well as the subsequent amortization) to be value relevant. Amounts capitalized were strongly associated with (contemporaneous) market prices and returns and were also positively associated with subsequent earnings changes. Moreover, consistent with the reasoning underlying SFAS 86,

> the coefficient of capitalized software . . . is larger than the coefficient of the
> development costs expensed by "expensers" . . . which in turn is larger than

(continued)

BOX 42-3 *(continued)*

the coefficient of the development costs expensed by "capitalizers". . . . *This order of coefficient sizes is consistent with the reasoning of SFAS No. 86 that capitalized software reflects the costs of projects close to fruition and should be strongly associated with near-term earnings, whereas the development costs of "expensers" reflect the costs of both feasible and prefeasibility projects, which should not be as strongly associated with near-term earnings. The development costs expensed by "capitalizers" reflect both prefeasibility costs and costs of failed projects, consistent with little or no association with subsequent earnings.*[tt]

Lev, in a series of publications,[‡‡] attempts to arrive at capitalization values in an indirect manner. Rather than capitalizing intangible expenditures, he capitalizes *intangible-driven earnings*. More specifically, Lev argues that a firm's earnings are a function of its physical, financial, and intangible assets; i.e.,

$$\text{Earnings} = f\,(\text{Physical Assets, Financial Assets, Intangible Assets})$$

Using a combination of past and forecasted earnings as well as "normal" returns on (known) physical and financial assets, he imputes *intangible-driven earnings* (i.e., earnings above those normally generated by a firm's physical and financial assets). Forecasted values of these intangible-driven earnings are then discounted to arrive at a capitalized value of intangible assets.

Such assets, known alternatively as "knowledge," "intellectual," or "intangible" capital, are not confined to technology companies. Lev shows that in addition to industries such as aerospace, telecommunications, computer hardware/software, and pharmaceuticals, the home products and food and beverage industries are also rich in intangible capital. This intangible capital he attributes to strong brand recognition.

Gu and Lev (2001) also test the valuation relevance of intangibles-driven earnings. They argue that their findings indicate that intangibles-driven earnings provide more relevant information to investors than conventional earnings and cash flows.

---

* The current benefits are reflected in the inflows.

[†] The asset outflows representing future benefits can be thought of as a growth component. For a firm with growth, its value can be expressed as

$$\text{Value} = \frac{E}{r} + \left[\frac{1}{r}\left(\frac{r^{*} - r}{r - ar^{*}} \right) \right] aE$$

where E is earnings, r the appropriate discount rate, r^{*} the amount the firm earns on its investment, and aE the amount the firm reinvests. In our example, $p = 1/r$ and b is the coefficient of the asset investment aE. That is, b is equal to the term in brackets. On the margin, it may be zero (if $r^{*} = r$) as the firm undertakes zero or break-even net present value investments.

[‡] Their R&D results are consistent with those of Hirschey and Weygandt (1985), who found that the market valuation of R&D implies it is an asset outflow. Hirschey and Weygandt also found that advertising had characteristics similar to a long-lived asset.

[§] Shevlin applied option-pricing models to the valuation of R&D partnerships.

** Sougiannis, for example, shows that (on average) a one-dollar increase in R&D expenditures produces a five-dollar increase in market value.

[tt] David Aboody and Baruch Lev, "The Value Relevance of Intangibles: The Case of Software Capitalization, *Journal of Accounting Research* (Supplement 1998), p. 178, emphasis added.

[‡‡] See, for example, Lev (2001), Gu and Lev (2001), and articles published in *Fortune* ("Accounting Gets Radical," by Thomas A. Stewart, April 16, 2001) and *CFO* ("Knowledge Capital Scorecard: Treasures Revealed," by Andrew Osterland, April 2001) for a general description of the methodology and results. The exact methodology is proprietary.

The research confirms that, even if an accounting change has no direct economic impact, the effects of the change on reported income can have real indirect consequences, such as the curtailment of expenditures and negative market reaction. Indirect effects may also result from debt covenant constraints or the influence of management compensation contracts. Accounting choices may also be motivated by firm characteristics.

Additional Analysis of Fixed Asset Data

Changes in the balance sheet cost of fixed assets result from four types of events:

1. Capital spending (acquisition of fixed assets)

2. Sale, impairment, or retirement (no longer in use) of fixed assets

3. Increases (decreases) in fixed assets due to acquisitions (disposals)

4. Changes due to the effects of foreign currency translation

The following sections discuss capital expenditures and the sale/retirement of assets.

Capital Expenditures

The capital expenditure decision provides information to the investor as to a firm's future profitability and growth prospects. Management often announces major capital expenditure plans separately. McConnell and Muscarella (1986) and Kerstein and Kim (1995) provide evidence that there is positive (negative) market reaction to unexpected increases (decreases) in capital expenditures. Similarly, Lev and Thiagarajan (1993) show that firms with higher (lower) changes in capital expenditures than their industry average experience positive (negative) market reaction. Thus, it is important to monitor (changes in) the level of a firm's capital expenditures.

In doing so, note that capital expenditures tend to be seasonal, with the majority of such expenditures being carried out in the fourth quarter. Different

---

BOX 42-4   MANDATED ACCOUNTING CHANGES: ECONOMIC CONSEQUENCES AND MARKET REACTION

The capitalization-versus-expense issue has proved a fruitful area of empirical research. The issues examined provide interesting parallels between R&D (SFAS 2) and oil and gas accounting (SFAS 19). In both cases, mandated accounting changes favored expensing over capitalization (albeit in the case of SFAS 19, the standard was suspended).

Economic Consequences

Proponents of capitalization argued that the accounting change would lead to a reduction of risk-taking activities such as expenditures for R&D and exploration activities, as the cost of risk taking would increase. These fears were generally expressed for smaller companies* who feared that markets (at least private lenders) would focus on the effects on reported income (both amounts and variability). The change would thus impair their ability to raise capital.

As SFAS 19 was never implemented, the validity of these claims could not be verified. However, for SFAS 2, a number of studies attempted to verify whether the new standard curtailed R&D.

(continued)

BOX 42-4   *(continued)*

Horwitz and Kolodny (1980) reported that a majority of firms (58% to 67%) believed that small firms reduced planned R&D expenditures as a consequence of SFAS 2. Using a sample of small high-technology firms, they found evidence that the actual levels of R&D expenditures dropped following the introduction of SFAS 2.

In contrast, Dukes et al. (1980) found no evidence of curtailment of R&D subsequent to the adoption of SFAS 2. Their sample, however, consisted of larger companies, and in a subsequent study Elliott et al. (1984) confirmed the finding that small companies that had previously capitalized R&D curtailed R&D expenditures after the issuance of SFAS 2. However, they noted that the downward trend in R&D expenditures for these companies had already begun years prior to the issuance of SFAS 2. Comparing the operating performance of the "capitalizers" with a control sample of firms that had always expensed R&D, they found that the operating performance of the capitalizers was worse. They conjectured that financial difficulties, rather than the accounting change, may have caused the curtailment of R&D. In fact, it could be argued that the original decision to capitalize R&D by these firms may have been motivated by an effort to improve reported financial performance in the face of financial stress.

Selto and Clouse (1985) argued that firms would be likely to anticipate the effects of an accounting change such as SFAS 2 and adapt to it. Thus, if divisional managers would be motivated to reduce R&D expenditures because of the effect on their compensation (through earnings-based compensation plans), firms would adjust their compensation plans accordingly or, alternatively, take steps to centralize the R&D decision-making process. They found that although not all firms made such changes, those that did were the ones most likely to be affected by the provisions of SFAS 2. Thus, to the extent accounting changes have economic consequences, they may be manifested internally rather than externally.

Market Reaction

Vigeland (1981) found no market reaction to the mandated accounting change for R&D expenditures. There is little controversy with respect to this mandated accounting change. This is not true with respect to the mandated change(s) affecting accounting for oil and gas exploration. This issue spawned a cottage industry of research with studies examining the reaction to the announcement of (the exposure draft of) SFAS 19 and Accounting Series Release (ASR) 253, issued by the SEC, that suspended SFAS 19.

The research examined whether firms using the full cost method (FC) had negative (positive) returns when SFAS 19 (ASR 253) was announced. Generally negative reaction was found around the time of the announcement of the SFAS 19 exposure draft. Not everyone, however, agreed with its significance† and the results were found to be sensitive to the time period examined and (at the time of the exposure draft announcement) "confounding" news affecting the oil industry. Thus, even though negative market reaction was found, its cause was not clear.

With respect to the ASR 253 announcement, Collins et al. (1982) compared the market reaction at the time the SFAS 19 exposure draft was announced with the reaction experienced when ASR 253 was announced. They found that there was a significant negative correlation for the FC firms; that is, negative reaction to the first announcement was followed by positive reaction to the subsequent (suspension) announcement.

These studies tested market reaction without considering any factors that might cause differential market reactions across firms due to differential impacts on income and equity. Such factors might include firm size, the relative importance of exploration, firm leverage, and the existence of debt covenants and accounting-based management compensation schemes. Collins et al. (1981) and Lys (1984) tested for such factors with some success, finding, for example, that the degree of market reaction was related to (1) the size of the reduction in owner's equity that would result

(continued)

from SFAS 19, (2) the existence of debt covenants, and (3) management compensation schemes based on reported income.

---

*The standards primarily affected smaller firms, as for both R&D and exploration costs, larger firms generally used the expensing method. See Box 40-1 for further discussion of the differential impact of the capitalize-versus-expense decision on larger and small firms.

† Collins and Dent (1979) and Lev (1979) claimed that the results were statistically significant, whereas Dyckman and Smith (1979) argued that the market reaction was not statistically different from that experienced by firms using successful efforts (SE).

theories exist as to whether this phenomenon is tied to a firm's budgetary cycle [Callen et al. (1996)] or the timing is tax related [Kinney and Trezevant (1993)].

Sale, Impairment, or Retirement of Assets

The sale or retirement of fixed assets removes these assets from the balance sheet. For most firms, sale or retirement also generates gains or losses, included in reported income.

In the case of Westvaco, gains on asset sales are included in other income (see financial statement Note B). In 1999, such gains accounted for 12% of pre-tax income. Some companies report gains or losses on a separate line in the income statement, whereas others include them elsewhere.[38] The analyst should examine such gains or losses for several reasons.

First, gains and losses resulting from asset sales are considered nonrecurring and the inclusion of such gains in reported income lowers the quality of earnings. However, if such gains or losses occur in most years, it is difficult to consider them "nonrecurring." As asset sales are to a great extent subject to management discretion, their timing and variation from year to year must be closely monitored as they can be used to distort operating trends. Bartov (1993) reported that firms use gains or losses from asset sales to smooth reported income.[39] Additionally, highly leveraged firms sell more long-lived assets than less leveraged firms in an effort to improve their reported debt-to-equity ratios.

A second reason for looking at asset sales is more fundamental. Sale of a significant portion of fixed assets is an indicator of change—in product line or production location. The examination of trends in capital spending and fixed asset sales can help the analyst ask perceptive questions regarding changes in future operations.

Finally, a pattern of gains suggests that the company's depreciation method is conservative, understating reported income and the net carrying amounts of fixed assets. A pattern of losses suggests that depreciation expense is understated (income is overstated) and fixed assets are overvalued on the balance sheet. In extreme cases, such losses are recognized as "impairments." Issues relating to depreciation and impairments are discussed in Reading 43.

---

[38] Undisclosed gains and losses can sometimes be deduced from the statement of cash flows. Gains and losses from asset sales are non-operating in nature, and must be subtracted from cash from operations. The proceeds from asset sales must be reported in cash from investment.

[39] Whether this constitutes "good" or "bad" behavior depends on whether one views income smoothing (see Reading 35) as "variance reducing" (providing information to investors as to a firm's expected performance) or manipulative behavior that hides a firm's actual performance.

SUMMARY

This reading considers the financial statement effects of the capitalize-versus-expense decision for long-lived assets. This decision is significant not only for firms with large investments in buildings and machinery, but also for those who have large expenditures on research, development, and computer software. The reading reviews the analytical techniques that can be used to restore comparability despite the use of differing accounting methods for similar transactions.

Once the capitalized amount is determined, the firm must choose an appropriate pattern of depreciation or amortization. Analysts must also contend with financial reporting for impairments and disposal of these assets. We discuss these issues in the next reading.

PROBLEMS FOR READING 42

1. [Capitalization of interest] The following data were obtained from the annual reports of Chevron, a multinational oil company (all data in $millions):

	1995	1996	1997	1998	1999
Interest expense	$ 401	$ 364	$ 312	$ 405	$ 472
Pretax income	1,789	4,740	5,502	1,834	3,648
Net income	930	2,607	3,256	1,339	2,070
Capitalized interest	141	108	82	39	59
Amortization of capitalized interest	47	24	28	35	9

A. Using reported interest expense, compute the earnings coverage ratio (times interest earned) for each year, 1995 to 1999.

B. Assuming that Chevron had always expensed interest as incurred:

  i. Recompute the earnings coverage ratio for each year.

  ii. Compare the two ratios (based on reported versus restated data).

  iii. Recompute income (assume a 35% tax rate each year).

  iv. Discuss the effect on net income of restatement to expense all interest.

C. Discuss the effect of restatement on the five-year trend of Chevron's:

  i. Interest expense

  ii. Interest coverage ratio

  iii. Pretax and net income

D. State which calculation of the interest coverage ratio is better for financial analysis and justify your choice.

2. [Capitalization of computer software expenditure] Ericsson [ERICA], a multinational producer of wireless telephone equipment, produces its financial statements in accordance with Swedish GAAP but reconciles net income and shareholders' equity to U.S. GAAP. Swedish GAAP does not permit the capitalization of the cost of software development cost for either:

▶ Software to be sold externally

▶ Software developed for internal use

Ericsson's 1999 reconciliation, however, shows the effect of applying SFAS 86 (capitalization of software to be sold) for all years and SOP 98-1 (capitalization of software for internal use) starting in 1999 as shown in the following data.

Ericsson: 1999 Financial Data (SEK millions)

Under U.S. GAAP	1997	1998	1999
Development costs for software to be sold:			
Opening balance	6,100	7,398	10,744
Capitalization	5,232	7,170	7,898
Amortization	(3.934)	(3,824)	(4,460)
Writedown			(989)
Year-end balance	7,398	10,744	13,193
Development costs for software for internal use:			
Opening balance			
Capitalization			1,463
Amortization			(152)
Year-end balance			1,311
Under Swedish GAAP:			
Net sales	167,740	184,438	215,403
Pretax income	17,218	18,210	16,386
Total assets	147,440	167,456	202,628
Stockholders' equity	52,624	63,112	69,176

A. Compute each of the following ratios under Swedish GAAP for 1998 and 1999:

   i. Asset turnover (on average assets)

   ii. Pretax return on average equity

B. Using the data provided, adjust the 1997-1999 Swedish GAAP amounts assuming the capitalization of software development costs to be sold and for internal use. Using the adjusted data, compute the percentage change form the amounts originally reported for:

   i. Pretax income

   ii. Total assets

   iii. Shareholders' equity
   (Assume a 35% tax rate.)

C. Recompute each of the followint ratios using the adjusted data for 1998 and 1999:

   i. Asset turnover (on average assets)

   ii. Pretax return on average equity

D. Discuss the implications of your analysis for the comparison of firms that capitalize software development costs with those that do not.

E. Discuss whether the capitalization and amortizaiton of software development costs under U.S. GAAP has any usefulness for investment analysis.

3. [Capitalization versus expensing] American Woodmark [AMWD] is a manufacturer of kitchen cabinets and similar items. Its fiscal year 2000 annual report contains the following footnote under Significant Accounting Policies:

Promotisonal Displays: The Company's investment in promotional displays is carried at cost less applicable amortization. Amortizaiton is provided by the straight-line method on an individual display basis over the estimated period of benefit (approximately 30 months).

Financial data at April 30 (in $thousands)

	1999	2000
Promotional displays	$ 8,451	$ 10,099
Total assets	140,609	166,656
Shareholders' equity	78,337	92,612
Sales	327,013	387,301
Net income	17,509	14,467

A. Explain why American Woodmark may have chosen to capitalize the cost of promotional displays rather than expense them.

B. Calculate the effect of that accounting choice on the following reported amounts for fiscal year 2000:

   i. Net income

   ii. Shareholders' equity

   iii. Return on assets

(Assume a 35% tax rate.)

$4\frac{5}{8}$ $4\frac{11}{16}$ $-\frac{3}{8}$

$5\frac{1}{2}$ $5\frac{1}{2}$ $-\frac{3}{8}$

$20\frac{5}{8}$ $21\frac{3}{16}$ $-\frac{1}{16}$

$17\frac{3}{8}$ $18\frac{1}{8}$ $+\frac{7}{8}$

$15\frac{1}{2}$ $6\frac{1}{2}$ $6\frac{1}{2}$ $-\frac{1}{2}$

$7\frac{1}{4}$ $31\frac{31}{32}$ $-\frac{1}{8}$

$\frac{15}{16}$ $\frac{9}{16}$

$\frac{9}{16}$

$\frac{15}{32}$ $7\frac{13}{16}$ $7\frac{15}{16}$

$7\frac{15}{16}$ $7\frac{13}{16}$ $2\frac{1}{2}$ $+$

$2\frac{5}{8}$ $2\frac{11}{32}$ $2\frac{1}{4}$

327 $2\frac{3}{4}$ $2\frac{1}{4}$

$5\frac{1}{6}$ $12\frac{1}{16}$ $11\frac{3}{8}$ $11\frac{3}{4}$ $+$

87 $33\frac{3}{4}$ 33 $33\frac{1}{8}$ $-$

602 $25\frac{5}{8}$ $24\frac{9}{16}$ $25\frac{1}{8}$ $+$

833 12 $11\frac{5}{8}$ $11\frac{1}{8}$ $+$

16 $10\frac{1}{2}$ $10\frac{1}{2}$ $10\frac{1}{2}$ $-$

78 $15\frac{7}{8}$ $15\frac{13}{16}$ $15\frac{7}{8}$ $-$

5 4508 $9\frac{1}{16}$ $8\frac{1}{4}$ $8\frac{1}{8}$ $+$

430 $11\frac{1}{4}$ $10\frac{7}{8}$

ANALYSIS OF LONG-LIVED ASSETS: PART II — ANALYSIS OF DEPRECIATION AND IMPAIRMENT

by Gerald I. White, Ashwinpaul C. Sondhi, and Dov Fried

LEARNING OUTCOMES

The candidate should be able to:

a. identify the different depreciation methods and discuss how the choice of depreciation method affects a company's financial statements, ratios, and taxes;

b. explain the role of depreciable lives and salvage values in the computation of depreciation expenses, and compute and describe how changing depreciation methods or changing the estimated useful life or salvage value of an asset affects financial statements and ratios;

c. discuss the use of fixed asset disclosures to compare companies' average age of depreciable assets, and calculate, using such disclosures, the average age and average depreciable life of fixed assets;

d. define impairment of long-lived assets and explain what effect such impairment has on a company's financial statements and ratios;

e. discuss the liability for closure, removal, and environmental effects of long-lived operating assets, and discuss the financial statement impact and ratio effects of that liability.

INTRODUCTION 1

This reading continues the analysis of long-lived assets begun in the previous reading where we examined financial reporting and analysis issues arising at acquisition. We now consider the reporting and analysis of long-lived assets:

1. Over their useful lives, with emphasis on

  ▶ Depreciation methods

  ▶ Depreciable lives and salvage values

  ▶ Impact of choices on financial statements

2. When they are disposed of, or written off when impaired, or at the end of their useful lives, with particular attention to the effects of impairment write-downs on financial statements and ratios

Amortization, depletion, and depreciation are all terms used for the systematic allocation of the capitalized cost of an asset to income over its useful life. Depreciation, the most frequently used of these terms, is often used generically in discussions of the concept. Strictly speaking, *depreciation* represents the allocation of the cost of tangible fixed assets, *amortization* refers to the cost of intangible assets, and *depletion* applies to natural resource assets.

2 THE DEPRECIATION CONCEPT

For accountants, depreciation is an allocation process, not a valuation process. It is important, therefore, for analysts to differentiate between accounting depreciation and economic depreciation. Although the accounting process may be purely allocative, the concept of depreciation also has economic meaning.

In Reading 34, income was defined as the amount that can be distributed during the period without impairing the productive capacity of the firm. The cash flows generated by an asset over its life, therefore, cannot be considered income until a provision is made for its replacement. These cash flows must be reduced by the amount required to replace the asset to determine the earnings generated by that asset.

This is the underlying principle of economic depreciation; profits are overstated if no allowance is made for the replacement of the asset. The periodic depreciation expense, therefore, segregates a portion of cash flows for reinvestment, preserving that sum from distribution as dividends and taxes.[1]

Continuing this conceptual argument, suppose an asset costs $240 and is expected to generate net cash flows of $100 per year over its three-year life. Over the life of the asset, income equals $60 ($300 − $240) as $240 is required to replace the asset (if we assume that the asset is worthless at the end of the three-year period and price levels do not change). As financial statements report income annually, it is necessary to determine how much income (how much depreciation) to report each year. This requires the allocation of a portion of the multiperiod return to each period.

The next section describes the depreciation methods used in financial reporting, followed by a discussion of the impact of depreciation methods on financial statements. A separate analysis of accelerated depreciation methods used for income taxes is followed by a discussion of the interaction of inflation and depreciation methods. Analysis of financial statement depreciation disclosures, changes in depreciation methods, and a comprehensive examination of fixed asset disclosures round out the discussion.

Depreciation Methods

Annuity or Sinking Fund Depreciation

From an economic perspective, the income reported each year should reflect the rate of return earned by the asset. For example, the asset just described generates

---

[1] This does not mean that cash equal to depreciation expense is set aside for reinvestment but, rather, that the definition of income requires a subtraction for asset replacement.

EXHIBIT 43-1	Sinking Fund Depreciation				
Year	(1) Opening Balance Asset	(2) Cash Flow	(3) Depreciation Expense	(4) = (2) − (3) Net Income	(5) = (4)/(1) Rate of Return
1	$240	$100	$ 71	$29	12%
2	169	100	80	20	12
3	89	100	89	11	12
Totals		$300	$240	$60	

a return of 12% over its three-year life.[2] To report a 12% return for each year requires the pattern of depreciation shown in Exhibit 43-1.

This pattern, with the amount of depreciation increasing every year, is known as *annuity or sinking fund depreciation*. U.S. GAAP, however, do not permit this form of depreciation. In Canada, increasing charge methods are used for income-producing properties in the real estate industry and by a few utilities, but they are not generally acceptable depreciation methods.

Straight-line and accelerated depreciation (discussed shortly) can also produce a constant rate of return when cash flows generated by the asset decline over time. Exhibit 43-2 illustrates this case; the rate of return is constant and reflects the true return earned by the asset.

Instead of depreciation patterns that generate a constant rate of return, accountants generally use depreciation patterns that result in constant or declining expense. These patterns are sometimes justified by the matching principle. Generally, however, they are arbitrary, their sole purpose being a systematic allocation of the asset cost over time.

Straight-Line Depreciation

Given the same asset and the pattern of constant cash flows shown in Exhibit 43-1, accountants (using the matching principle) argue that since the revenues (cash

EXHIBIT 43-2	Straight-Line Depreciation with Declining Cash Flows				
Year	(1) Opening Balance Asset	(2) Cash Flow	(3) Depreciation Expense	(4) = (2) − (3) Net Income	(5) = (4)/(1) Rate of Return
1	$240	$109	$ 80	$29	12%
2	160	99	80	19	12
3	80	90	80	10	12
Totals		$298	$240	$58	

[2] The present value of a three-year annuity of $100 per year discounted at 12% is (approximately) equal to $240.

flows of $100) generated by the asset are the same each year, the income shown each year should also be the same. The result of this line of reasoning is the *straight-line method*, the pattern of depreciation expense exhibited in Exhibit 43-3. *Straight-line depreciation is the dominant method in the United States and most countries worldwide.* Westvaco, for example, states in the summary of significant accounting policies in its fiscal 1999 annual report:

> The cost of plant and equipment is depreciated, generally by the straight-line method, over the estimated useful lives of the respective assets. . . .

Note that the use of this method results in an *increasing* rate of return rather than the actual rate of return earned over the life of the asset.

Accelerated Depreciation Methods

The matching principle can also justify accelerated depreciation patterns, with higher depreciation charges in early years and smaller amounts in later years. There are two arguments:

1. Benefits (revenues) from an asset may be higher in early years, declining in later years as efficiency falls (the asset wears out). The matching process suggests that depreciation should decline with benefits.

2. Even if revenues are constant over time, an asset requires maintenance and repairs over time, costs that tend to increase as the asset ages. Accelerated depreciation methods compensate for the rising trend of maintenance and repair costs so that total asset costs are level over the asset's life.

However, both the efficiency and maintenance of an asset are difficult to forecast, and, in any case, accelerated depreciation methods are (like straight-line) arbitrary procedures designed to yield the desired pattern of higher depreciation amounts in earlier years. Accelerated methods have historically been used for tax reporting, where they are justified by the desire to promote capital investment, rather than accounting theory.

The two most common accelerated methods are the *sum-of-years' digits* (SYD) method and the family of *declining-balance* methods. A comparison of these methods (using the double-declining-balance method) with straight-line (SL) depreciation

EXHIBIT 43-3	Straight-Line Depreciation with Constant Cash Flows				
Year	(1) Opening Balance Asset	(2) Cash Flow	(3) Depreciation Expense	(4) = (2) − (3) Net Income	(5) = (4)/(1) Rate of Return
1	$240	$100	$ 80	$20	8.3%
2	160	100	80	20	12.5
3	80	100	80	20	25.0
Totals		$300	$240	$60	

is presented in Exhibit 43-4. In the example used, the concept of *salvage value*, the estimated amount for which the asset can be sold at the end of its useful life, is introduced into the calculations.

While U.S. firms rarely use accelerated methods, they are more widely used outside of the United States. Takeda, for example, states in its summary of significant accounting policies (Note 2 in fiscal 1999 annual report) that:

Depreciation is primarily computed by the declining balance method. . . .

EXHIBIT 43-4	Comparison of Straight-Line and Accelerated Depreciation Methods

Original Cost = \$18,000

Salvage Value = \$3,000

Depreciable Life $n = 5$

A. Straight-Line Depreciation

Depreciation in Year $i = \dfrac{1}{n} \times$ (Original Cost − Salvage Value)

Depreciation expense is constant each year; at the end of the five-year period, the net book value of the asset equals its salvage value of \$3,000.

Year	Rate	(Original Cost— Salvage Value)	Depreciation Expense	Accumulated Depreciation	Net Book Value
0					\$18,000
1	1/5	\$15,000	\$ 3,000	\$ 3,000	15,000
2	1/5	15,000	3,000	6,000	12,000
3	1/5	15,000	3,000	9,000	9,000
4	1/5	15,000	3,000	12,000	6,000
5	1/5	15,000	3,000	15,000	3,000
Total			\$15,000		

B and C. Accelerated Depreciation Methods
B. Sum-of-Years' Digits (SYD) Method

Depreciation in Year $i = \dfrac{(n - i + 1)}{SYD} \times$ (Original Cost − Salvage Value)

where SYD = $1 + 2 + 3 + \ldots + n$ the summation over the depreciable life of n years or simply SYD = $n(n + 1)/2$. For our example, $n = 5$.

SYD = $1 + 2 + 3 + 4 + 5 = 15$

or, alternatively, SYD = $\dfrac{(5)(5 + 1)}{2} = 15$

The rate of depreciation thus varies from year to year (as i varies) in reverse counting order of the years; that is, the pattern is 5/15, 4/15, 3/15, 2/15, and 1/15 and is depicted as follows:

(Exhibit continued on next page ...)

EXHIBIT 43-4 **(continued)**

Year	Rate	(Original Cost— Salvage Value)	Depreciation Expense	Accumulated Depreciation	Net Book Value
0					$18,000
1	5/15	$15,000	$ 5,000	$5,000	13,000
2	4/15	15,000	4,000	9,000	9,000
3	3/15	15,000	3,000	12,000	6,000
4	2/15	15,000	2,000	14,000	4,000
5	1/15	15,000	1,000	15,000	3,000
Total			$15,000		

C. Double-Declining-Balance

$$\text{Depreciation in Year } i = \frac{2}{n} \times (\text{Original Cost} - \text{Accumulated Depreciation})$$

or

$$\frac{2}{n} \times (\text{Net Book Value})$$

The rate of $(2/n)$ is what gives the double-declining-balance (DDB) method its name. The depreciation rate is double* the straight-line rate. The declining pattern occurs because the fixed rate is applied to an ever-decreasing asset balance (net book value),[†] and in our example it is calculated as follows:

Year	Rate	Net Book Value	Depreciation Expense	Accumulated Depreciation	Net Book Value
0					$18,000
1	2/5	$18,000	$ 7,200	$ 7,200	10,800
2	2/5	10,800	4,320	11,520	6,480
3	2/5	6,480	2,592	14,112	3,888
4	NA	NA	888	15,000	3,000
5	NA	NA	0	15,000	3,000
Total			$15,000		

NA = not applicable.
* The DDB method is actually only one case of the family of declining-balance methods. The same principle can be applied to other multiples of the straight-line rate (e.g., 150% declining balance). Higher multiples result in more accelerated patterns of depreciation expense.

† Note that salvage value is not used to calculate depreciation under declining-balance methods but acts as a floor for net book value.

Note that in year 4 the DDB procedure is discontinued. This is because depreciation can be taken only until the salvage value is reached. Following DDB in year 4 and beyond would have reduced net book value below salvage. When the DDB method is applied to longer-lived assets, a switch to the straight-line method often occurs in later years, when the latter method results in higher depreciation expense.

Units-of-Production and Service Hours Method

These methods depreciate assets in proportion to their actual use rather than as a function of the passage of time. Thus, more depreciation is recognized in years of higher production. Measurement requires an initial estimate of the total number of units of output or service hours expected over the life of the machine. The methods differ in whether asset usage is measured by output or hours used.

Assume that the asset described in Exhibit 43-4 is expected to produce 60,000 units of output over its life and have a service life of 150,000 hours. The actual hours of service and output, and the resultant depreciation schedules, are presented in Exhibit 43-5.

These methods make depreciation expense a variable rather than a fixed cost, decreasing the volatility of reported earnings as compared to straight-line or accelerated methods. Some companies use a mix of depreciation methods.

International Paper, for example, reports on its depreciation methods as follows:

Plants, Properties and Equipment

Plants, properties and equipment are stated at cost, less accumulated depreciation. For financial reporting purposes, we use the units-of-production method of depreciation for our major pulp and paper mills and certain wood products facilities and the straight-line method for other plants and equipment.[3]

EXHIBIT 43-5	**Service Hours and Units-of-Production Methods**

Original Cost = $18,000

Salvage Value = $3,000

	Service Hours Method Expected Service Hours = 150,000 Cost/Service Hour = $0.10*			**Units-of-Production Method** Expected Output = 60,000 Cost/Unit of Output = $0.25†		
Year	**Hours Worked**	**Depreciation**	**Net Book Value**	**Units of Output**	**Depreciation**	**Net Book Value**
0			$18,000			$18,000
1	40,000	$ 4,000	14,000	15,000	$ 3,750	14,250
2	35,000	3,500	10,500	16,000	4,000	10,250
3	45,000	4,500	6,000	20,000	5,000	5,250
4	20,000	2,000	4,000	10,000	2,250‡	3,000
5	40,000	1,000‡	3,000	12,500	0‡	3,000
Total		$15,000			$15,000	

* ($18,000 − $3,000)/150,000.

† ($18,000 − $3,000)/60,000.

‡ Note that in both cases, the asset is never depreciated below the salvage value even when actual use exceeds estimated use.

---

[3] *Source:* International Paper, 10-K report, year ended December 31, 1999.

A significant drawback of these two methods occurs when the firm's productive capacity becomes obsolete as it loses business to more efficient competitors. The units-of-production and service hours methods decrease depreciation expense during periods of low production. The result is to overstate reported income and asset values at the same time as the asset's economic value declines. This danger is particularly acute for mature industries facing increased competition from new entrants or imports. Competition frequently increases the rate of economic depreciation of fixed assets. However, the corporate response is often to relieve the pressure on earnings by decreasing depreciation expense by changing to a method such as units-of-production. Alternatively, firms may get the same effect by lengthening lives.

Sooner or later, however, the firm will recognize the impairment (see the discussion later in this reading) of its productive capacity. Once impairment exists, companies report "restructuring" or similar charges to correct the overvaluation of fixed assets. Analysts often exclude such "nonrecurring" charges when evaluating corporate earnings. But to the extent that these charges represent an adjustment for past underdepreciation of assets, they correct a systematic overstatement of past earnings. As past earnings are used to forecast the future, this issue should not be ignored.

The following footnote from the 1992 financial statements of Brown & Sharpe, a machine tool manufacturer, illustrates this phenomenon:

> In 1992, the Company extended the estimated useful lives of machinery and equipment at its Swiss subsidiary, based upon the current low rate of utilization. The effect of this change was to reduce 1992 depreciation expense and net loss by $921,000 or $.19 per share.

Total depreciation expense for Brown & Sharpe fell from $8 million in 1992 to $6.8 million in 1993; the change in accounting estimate was apparently the major factor in that decline. In 1994, however, Brown & Sharpe reported restructuring charges that included: "costs . . . for . . . property, plant, and equipment . . . writeoffs . . . due to a plant closing in Switzerland."

Although the corporate temptation to change accounting methods when business is weak is understandable, that change can mislead investors. Furthermore, on occasion, a company recognizes the impairment of fixed assets gradually, by accelerating depreciation on a group of assets in danger of becoming obsolete. From an analytical point of view, it is preferable to recognize the impairment immediately. Because accounting depreciation is a systematic allocation of cost, its acceleration when the asset is impaired (and its use has declined or it has been temporarily idled) fails to match costs and revenues and misstates the earning power of the company.

Group and Composite Depreciation Methods

Depreciation methods described in the preceding sections apply to single assets; they may be impractical when firms use large numbers of similar assets in their operations. Group (composite) depreciation methods allocate the costs of similar (dissimilar) assets using depreciation rates based on a weighted average of the service lives of the assets.

Gains or losses on the disposal of assets depreciated using group or composite methods are either:

▶ Recognized in reported income, or
▶ Reported instead as a component of accumulated depreciation[4]

Example. Texaco uses group methods for most assets (see the Description of Significant Accounting Policies). Gains and losses are recognized only when a complete unit is disposed of.

Depletion

Financial reporting requirements for natural resources are similar to those for tangible assets. The carrying costs of natural resources include the costs of acquiring the land or mines and the costs of exploration and development of the resources. These costs may be capitalized or expensed as a function of the firm's accounting policies (such as successful efforts or full cost for oil and gas exploration).

The carrying costs of natural resources (excluding costs of machinery and equipment used in extraction or production) are allocated to accounting periods using the units-of-production method. This method requires an initial estimate of the units (of oil, coal, gold, or timber) in the resource base to compute a unit cost, which is then applied to the actual units produced, extracted, or harvested.

Amortization

Amortization of intangible assets may be based on useful lives as defined by law (e.g., patents) or regulation, or such assets may be depreciated over the period during which the firm expects to receive benefits from them (computer software). Companies use either straight-line or units-of-production methods. Goodwill and indefinite-term franchises and licenses may be amortized over periods not exceeding 40 years. Note that SFAS 142 (2001) eliminated the amortization of goodwill and certain intangible assets.

Example. In Reading 42 we examined Lucent's capitalization of software development costs; now we discuss amortization. The accounting policies footnote is vague about amortization periods.

Lucent's financial statements show the following (in $millions):

Years Ended September 30

	1997	1998	1999
Capitalized software costs (net)	293	298	470
Amortization	380	234	249

[4] At the time of the sale, the proceeds are added to cash, the original asset cost is removed from gross PPE, and the accumulated depreciation for the asset is removed from that account. The difference between the cash proceeds and the net book value of the assets sold is then credited-debited to the accumulated depreciation account; no gain or loss is recorded.

Amortization of capitalized software declined sharply in fiscal 1998. Amortization rose only slightly in fiscal 1999 despite the large increase in capitalized cost. There is no discussion of amortization in Lucent's Management Discussion and Analysis.

Depreciation Method Disclosures

As we have shown, the choice of the depreciation method can greatly affect the pattern of reported income. Disclosure of the depreciation method used is required and can usually be found in the footnote listing accounting policies. Most (more than 90%) American firms use straight-line depreciation, but accelerated methods are more widely used in other countries. The use of accelerated methods in the United States has declined in recent years as firms have changed to straight-line depreciation.

Depreciation Lives and Salvage Values

Even when the same depreciation method is used, comparability for a firm over time and among companies at a given point in time may be lacking. The *useful life* (the period over which the asset is depreciated) can vary from firm to firm, and excessively long lives understate reported depreciation expense. Although companies are required to disclose depreciation lives, in practice such disclosures are often vague, providing ranges rather than precise data. In such cases, the analyst must use available data to compute approximate depreciation lives (see the analysis of fixed asset disclosures later in the reading).

Example 43-1

Westvaco

Westvaco's summary of significant accounting policies states that:

> The cost of plant and equipment is depreciated . . . over the estimated useful lives . . . which range from 20 to 40 years for buildings and 5 to 30 years for machinery and equipment.

Although usually a less significant factor, *salvage values* also affect comparisons; they (like asset lives) are also management estimates. High estimates reduce the depreciation base (cost less salvage value) and, therefore, reduce depreciation expense. (Note that salvage values are not employed in declining-balance depreciation methods.) In practice, companies rarely disclose data regarding salvage values, except when estimates are changed.[5]

---

[5] Changes in accounting estimates receive less disclosure than changes in method. APB 20 (para. 33) requires disclosure of the effect of a change that affects future periods, such as changes in depreciable lives.

Impact of Depreciation Methods on Financial Statements

The choice of depreciation method impacts both the income statement and balance sheet; for capital-intensive companies, the impact can be significant. As depreciation is an allocation of past cash flows, the method chosen for financial reporting purposes has no impact on the statement of cash flows.[6]

Accelerated depreciation methods, with higher depreciation expense in the early years of asset life, tend to depress both net income and stockholders' equity when compared with the straight-line method. As the percentage effect on net income is usually greater than the effect on net assets, return ratios tend to be lower when accelerated depreciation methods are used. Consequently, these methods are considered more conservative.

Toward the end of an asset's life, however, the effect on net income reverses. In Exhibit 43-4, depreciation expense in years 4 and 5 is lower using accelerated methods than under the straight-line method. This is true for individual assets. However, for companies with stable or rising capital expenditures, the early-year impact of new assets acquired dominates, and depreciation expense on a total firm basis is higher under an accelerated method. When capital expenditures decline, however, accelerated depreciation decreases depreciation expense as the later-year effect on older assets dominates.

Depreciable lives and salvage values impact both depreciation expense and stated asset values. Shorter lives and lower salvage values are considered conservative in that they lead to higher depreciation expense. These factors interact with the depreciation method to determine the expense; for example, use of the straight-line method with short depreciation lives may result in depreciation expense similar to that obtained from the use of an accelerated method with longer lives. Conservative depreciation practices also increase asset turnover ratios by decreasing the denominator of that ratio. Fixed-asset turnover ratios should be computed using gross fixed-asset investment in the denominator, although that is not done in practice.

Accelerated Depreciation and Taxes

Notwithstanding the theoretical arguments and the financial statement effects discussed, the primary reason for accelerated depreciation methods is their beneficial effect on the firm's tax burden. At the onset of an asset's life, the total amount of depreciable cost available is fixed. Depreciation acts as a tax shield by reducing the amount of taxes paid in any given year. Given a positive interest rate, firms are better off using accelerated depreciation methods to obtain the benefit of increased cash flows (from reduced taxes) in the earlier years.

Governments have long used the tax code to encourage investment, and this was the intent of the U.S. government when it first allowed accelerated depreciation methods for tax purposes in 1954. Many foreign governments also permit the use of accelerated depreciation methods. Since 1954, the U.S. government has frequently changed tax depreciation regulations to increase or decrease investment incentives in certain types of fixed assets or simply to raise revenues. The present system is known as MACRS—modified accelerated cost recovery system—which consists of specified depreciation patterns and depreciable lives (generally shorter than actual useful service lives) for different property classes.

---

[6] This assumes that the method chosen for tax purposes is independent of the method chosen for financial statement purposes.

MACRS uses the double-declining-balance and 150% declining-balance methods, which few companies use for financial reporting purposes. Thus, in the United States the depreciation method and lives used for financial statements almost always differ from those used for tax purposes. The implications of these differences are discussed in Reading 44, which also illustrates the use of tax disclosures to obtain insights into the depreciation practices used for financial reporting.

Impact of Inflation on Depreciation

Historical cost-based depreciation expense may be used to define income as long as the total expense over the asset's life is enough to replace the asset after it has been fully utilized. If, however, the replacement cost of the asset increases, then depreciation expense based on the original cost will be insufficient.

Returning to the example in Exhibit 43-1, assume that after three years the firm requires $300 to replace the asset. Now the total economic income earned by the firm is $0, as total cash flows equal the cost to replace. If we use the historical cost basis, however, total depreciation is limited to the original $240 cost, and reported income is overstated. In addition, because firms are only allowed to use historical cost basis depreciation for tax reporting, the resultant taxes are too high. Income taxes become, in effect, a tax on capital rather than a tax on income. Box 43-1 illustrates the resulting disincentives for investment in the context of a simple capital budgeting model.

Accelerated depreciation methods partially compensate for this inflation effect by shortening the (tax) recovery period. Depreciating the asset over a shorter life serves a similar purpose. A number of studies have examined whether accelerated methods compensate for inflation and/or reflect economic depreciation (variously defined).

Kim and Moore (1988), for example, report that, for the Canadian trucking industry, tax depreciation exceeded economic depreciation, resulting in a tax subsidy. Most (1984), focusing on reported income, found that in the United States the useful life (used for financial reporting) is generally longer than the economic life of the asset, understating reported depreciation and overstating reported income. Skinner (1982), on the other hand, reported the opposite phenomenon in the United Kingdom.

Beaver and Dukes (1973) examined firm price/earnings ratios and found that market prices, on average

assign a more accelerated form of depreciation than is implied by reported earnings.[7]

They did not attempt to discern the reasons for this result but recognized that it was consistent with either a constant rate of return depreciation model (with declining cash flows) or depreciation based on current costs rather than a historical cost system.

Generalizing these results to other time periods, particularly for studies that examined whether depreciation practices (whether for tax or book purposes) compensated for the actual economic or physical depreciation of assets, requires a great deal of caution, given changing economic environments. These comparisons are a function of the provisions of the tax code, the inflation rate, and varying degrees of technological obsolescence across industries during the comparison

---

[7] William H. Beaver and Roland E. Dukes, "Interperiod Tax Allocation and δ-Depreciation Methods: Some Empirical Results," *Accounting Review* (July 1973), pp. 549–559.

BOX 43-1 DISINCENTIVES FOR INVESTMENT ARISING FROM HISTORICAL COST DEPRECIATION

We begin by assuming that the inflation rate p is equal to zero. A project is profitable if the net present value (NPV) of the cash flows of the investment:

$$\mathbf{NPV}_{(p=0)} = -I + (1 - t) \sum \frac{C_i}{(1 + r)^i} + t \sum \frac{d_i I}{(1 + r)^i}$$

is greater than zero (i.e., NPV > 0), where C_i is the pretax (real) cash flow in period i, t is the marginal tax rate, d_i is the rate of depreciation in period i, I is the cost of the original investment, and r is the appropriate real discount rate.* The summation on the right reflects the depreciation tax shelter, and the NPV can be disaggregated into

$$\mathbf{NPV} = -\mathbf{investment} + \mathbf{present\ value\ (after\text{-}tax\ cash\ flows)}$$
$$+ \mathbf{present\ value\ (depreciation\ tax\ shelter)}$$

If we introduce an annual inflation rate of $p > 0$, then the expected (nominal) cash flows in any period will increase. In addition, the discount rate will change to reflect inflation. The depreciation deduction based on historical costs will not change. The expression for net present value now becomes

$$\mathbf{NPV}_{(p>0)} = -I + (1 - t) \sum \frac{(1 + p)^i C_i}{(1 + p)^i (1 + r)^i} + t \sum \frac{d_i I}{(1 + p)^i (1 + r)^i}$$

As the $(1 + p)^i$ terms in the first summation cancel, inflation (when it is expected) will not affect the after-tax cash flows. However, the depreciation tax shelter will now be worth less as

$$t \sum \frac{d_i I}{(1 + r)^i} > t \sum \frac{d_i I}{(1 + p)^i (1 + r)^i}$$

The decline in the depreciation tax shelter will reduce the profitability of the project:

$$\mathbf{NPV}_{(p>0)} < \mathbf{NPV}_{(p=0)}$$

and *ceteris paribus*, there is less likelihood that the project will be undertaken.

---

* Generally, the depreciation tax shelter would be discounted at a rate lower than the cash flows themselves as the tax deduction is "riskless." We do not make the distinction here for the sake of simplification. Alternatively, one can view this problem in the context of certainty, and r is the risk-free rate.

period. During the 1980s, the depreciation provisions of the U.S. tax code were changed three times, inflation declined to approximately 4% from double-digit rates, and technological change was rapid in many industries. International differences are an additional difficulty.

The benchmark issue emerging from these studies is: How does one determine the "correct" useful life and economic depreciation rate? This is an important question for analytical purposes. Estimates of economic lives on an aggregate industry basis can be derived from Department of Commerce data.

In 1982, the FASB issued SFAS 33 (Changing Prices), which required very large firms[8] to disclose supplementary, unaudited data on the effects of changing prices. Among the required disclosures were:

▶ The current cost of fixed assets

▶ Depreciation expense on a current cost basis

These disclosures were intended to help financial statement users adjust for the shortcomings of historical cost depreciation discussed earlier. However, studies that examined the informational content of the replacement cost data found that, although historical cost earnings had informational content above and beyond that of current cost data provided by SFAS 33, the reverse did not hold.[9] Inflation-adjusted data did not appear to have any marginal information content above that provided by historical cost data. The reasons offered for this surprising result were that the data were:

▶ Too difficult to comprehend, and the market had not yet learned how to use them

▶ Not new, as the market knew how to adjust historical costs for inflation without SFAS 33 disclosures[10]

▶ Irrelevant, either from a conceptual point of view or in the manner in which they were prepared and reported

Whatever the reason, in practice the data were difficult to prepare and use. Facing intense complaints regarding the cost of the disclosures and empirical research that seemed to belie the usefulness of the data, the FASB subsequently made the disclosures voluntary.

Changes in Depreciation Method

Companies may change the reported depreciation of fixed assets in different ways:

▶ Change in method applicable only to newly acquired assets

▶ Change in method applicable to all assets

▶ Changes in asset lives or salvage value

Change in Method Applicable Only to Newly Acquired Assets. A company can change its depreciation method only for newly acquired assets and continue to depreciate previously acquired similar assets using the same method(s) as in the past. The impact of the new method will be gradual, increasing as fixed assets acquired after the change grow in relative importance.

---

[8] SFAS 33 applied to firms with inventories and gross (before deducting depreciation) property exceeding $125 million (in the aggregate) or with total assets exceeding $1 billion.

[9] Some studies [e.g., Beaver et al. (1980, 1982)] found little information content, focusing on ASR 190 disclosures. Others [Beaver and Landsman (1983)] examined the SFAS 33 data with similar results. Although the consensus was that these data did not have information content, the conclusions were by no means unanimous [see, e.g., Easman et al. (1979) and Murdoch (1986)].

[10] One example is the work of Angela Falkenstein and Roman L. Weil, "Replacement Cost Accounting: What Will Income Statements Based on the SEC Disclosures Show?—Part I," *Financial Analysts Journal* (January–February 1977), pp. 46–57 and "Replacement Cost Accounting: What Will Income Statements Based on the SEC Disclosures Show?—Part II," *Financial Analysts Journal* (March—April 1977), pp. 48–57.

DuPont, for example, changed from the sum-of-the-years' digits method (for nonpetroleum properties) to the straight-line method for properties placed in service in 1995, with the following footnote disclosure:

> Property, plant and equipment (PP&E) is carried at cost and, except for petroleum PP&E, PP&E placed in service prior to 1995 is depreciated under the sum-of-the-years' digits method and other substantially similar methods. PP&E placed in service after 1994 is depreciated using the straight-line method. This change in accounting was made to reflect management's belief that the productivity of such PP&E will not appreciably diminish in the early years of its useful life, and it will not be subject to significant additional maintenance in the later years of its useful life. In these circumstances, straight-line depreciation is preferable in that it provides a better matching of costs with revenues. Additionally, the change to the straight-line method conforms to predominant industry practice. The effect of this change on net income will be dependent on the level of future capital spending; it did not have a material effect in 1995.[11]

This is a common method of changing accounting principles, as it does not require the restatement of past earnings.

The company made the uninformative statement that "the change is not expected to have a material effect on 1995 results." Nonetheless, *the change increased subsequent reported income* as depreciation charges for new PPE were lower (depreciation charges on old PPE continued to be computed using the SYD method).

Exhibit 43-6 contains an extract from DuPont's segment disclosures for the years 1994 to 1996. As petroleum assets are depreciated by the units of production method, we must remove the capital spending and depreciation for that segment:

	1994	1995	1996
Capital spending	$3,151	$3,394	$3,317
Petroleum segment	(1,635)	(1,714)	(1,616)
All nonpetroleum	$1,516	$1,680	$1,701
% change		10.8%	1.3%
Total depreciation	$3,106	$2,823	$2,719
Petroleum segment	(1,266)	(1,111)	(1,128)
All nonpetroleum	$1,840	$1,712	$1,591
% change		−7.0%	−7.1%

Although nonpetroleum capital spending rose in both 1995 and 1996, depreciation expense fell 7% in both years. The decline is clearly due to the combined effect of straight-line (lower than SYD) depreciation expense relating to new assets and declining SYD depreciation on old assets.

Change in Method Applicable to All Assets. Instead of being implemented prospectively, the new method can be applied retroactively so that all fixed assets are depreciated using the new method. In this case, the effect is greater and can be significant in the year of the switch as well as in future years. For a sample of

---

[11] *Source:* DuPont 10-K report, 1995.

EXHIBIT 43-6	DuPont Segment Disclosures ($millions)

	Chemicals	Fibers	Polymers	Petroleum	Life Sciences	Diversified Businesses	Consolidated
1996:							
Depreciation, etc.	$330	$609	$350	$1,128	$70	$232	$2,719
Capital expenditures	338	611	446	1,616	93	213	3,317
1995:							
Depreciation, etc.	352	626	362	1,111	78	294	2,823
Capital expenditures	417	593	399	1,714	73	198	3,394
1994:							
Depreciation, etc.	405	686	386	1,266	79	284	3,106
Capital expenditures	258	640	356	1,635	47	215	3,151

Source: DuPont 10-K report, December 31, 1996.

38 companies that switched to straight-line depreciation, Healy et al. (1987) estimated that the median increase in income was 8% to 10% in the 10-year period following the change. In addition to the effect on current and future depreciation expense (and net income), there is a cumulative effect, given the retroactive nature of the change: the cumulative difference between originally reported depreciation and the restated depreciation for all past periods. When the new method is applied retroactively, companies must also disclose the pro forma impact of the new method on prior periods.

A change in depreciation method for all assets is considered a change in accounting principle under APB 20, Accounting Changes. *The cumulative effect of the change must be reported separately and net of taxes.*

Changes in Asset Lives or Salvage Value.   *Changes in asset lives and salvage values are changes in accounting estimates and are not considered changes in accounting principle.* Their impact is only prospective, and no retroactive or cumulative effects are recognized. Estimate changes attract much less notice than do changes in depreciation methods (see footnote 5). They are not, for example, referred to in the auditor's opinion. Thus, it is important to read financial statement footnotes carefully to be sure that no changes in accounting estimates have been made.

Example 43-2

AMR

Exhibit 43-7 contains extracts from the *1999 Annual Report* of AMR, the parent of American Airlines, which changed the estimated useful lives *and* the salvage values used to compute depreciation on its flight equipment, effective January 1, 1999. Given the asset intensity of airlines, this change had a significant impact on reported earnings, as shown in the following table:

AMR (in $millions)

| | Years Ended December 31 | | |
	1997	1998	1999
As Reported (with Depreciation Changes)			
Depreciation expense	$1,040	$1,040	$1,092
% Change from previous year		0.0%	5.0%
Operating income	$1,595	$1,988	$1,156
% Change from previous year		24.6%	−41.9%
After Adjustment for Depreciation Change			
Depreciation expense	$1,040	$1,040	$1,250
% Change from previous year		0.0%	20.2%
Operating income	$1,595	$1,988	$ 998
% Change from previous year		24.6%	−49.8%

Despite the accounting change, depreciation expense rose 5% in 1991 due to new equipment. If not for the change, depreciation expense would have been more than 20% higher. Without the accounting change, the 1999 decline in operating income would have been steeper, 50% instead of 42%. This may have been the motivation for the change. *When analyzing firms that change depreciation methods or assumptions, it is important to remember that the effect of such changes persists, as depreciation on both old and new fixed assets is stretched out, increasing reported income.*

Increases in asset lives have been common in recent years. The effect of such increases is, of course, to increase reported earnings. Such changes are often made by more than one firm in an industry, as firms compete to show higher reported earnings and ROE. For example, in the airline industry, Delta Airlines changed both the estimated lives and the salvage values used to compute depreciation on flight equipment in 1993. Both Southwest Airlines and UAL (United Airlines) extended aircraft depreciable lives in 1999.

Box 43-2 examines the motivation for and reaction to depreciation changes. Whenever a change in depreciation method or lives is reported, the effect of the change on current year reported earnings should be removed to evaluate operating performance on a comparable basis. The change should also be factored into estimates of future reported income.

ANALYSIS OF FIXED ASSET DISCLOSURES   3

In practice, firms use varying accounting methods, lives, and residual value assumptions for fixed assets, hampering comparisons between firms. To improve comparability, the analyst must use financial statement disclosures to gain insight into a company's depreciation accounting. Unfortunately, in 1994 the SEC

EXHIBIT 43-7	AMR Corporation Change in Depreciation Lives of Flight Equipment

A. Extract from Depreciation Footnote

Effective January 1, 1999, in order to more accurately reflect the expected useful life of its aircraft, the Company changed its estimate of the depreciable lives of certain aircraft types from 20 to 25 years and increased the residual value from five to 10 percent. It also established a 30-year life for its new Boeing 777 aircraft, first delivered in the first quarter of 1999. As a result of this change, depreciation and amortization expense was reduced by approximately $158 million and net earnings were increased by approximately $99 million, or $0.63 per common share diluted, for the year ended December 31, 1999.

B. Extract from Income Statement

Years Ended December 31 (in $millions)

	1999	1998	1997
Revenues	$17,730	$17,516	$16,957
Expenses:			
Depreciation and amortization	1,092	1,040	1,040
Total operating expenses	16,574	15,528	15,362
Operating Income	1,156	1,988	1,595

C. Extract from Management Discussion and Analysis

Depreciation and amortization expense increased $52 million, or 5.0 percent, due primarily to the addition of new aircraft, partially offset by the change in depreciable lives and residual values for certain types of aircraft in 1999 (see Note 1 to the consolidated financial statements).

Source: AMR Corp. 10-K Report, December 31, 1999.

deleted the requirement for firms to disclose details of their property accounts.[12] However, the Commission has proposed restoring the requirement following complaints from financial analysts regarding the loss of these useful data. As a result, for American firms, only a broad analysis is possible except when detailed data are made available by the company. However, IAS 16 and many foreign GAAP require detailed disclosures about fixed assets, permitting detailed analysis as shown later in this reading.

---

[12] Financial Reporting Release (FRR) 44 (December 13, 1994) amended Rule 5-04 of Regulation S-X to eliminate Schedule V, Property, Plant and Equipment, and Schedule VI, Accumulated Depreciation, Depletion and Amortization of Property, Plant and Equipment. See FRR 44 for a listing of other schedules eliminated.

BOX 43-2 CHANGES IN DEPRECIATION METHODS: MOTIVATION AND REACTION

When the Internal Revenue Code of 1954 permitted the use of accelerated depreciation for tax purposes, many firms also adopted these methods for financial statement purposes. Subsequently, many of these firms "switched back" to straight-line depreciation for financial reporting purposes. The effect of the switch-back was to increase the firm's reported net income, (tangible) assets, and retained earnings.

Unlike the FIFO-LIFO switch discussed in Reading 40, the depreciation switch-back was a "pure accounting" change without any direct cash flow consequences as accelerated depreciation was retained for tax purposes. The phenomenon was originally studied by Archibald (1972) and Kaplan and Roll (1972) as a test of whether the efficient market hypothesis (EMH) or the functional fixation hypothesis prevailed with respect to financial statements; that is, was the market "fooled" by the numbers, or did it see through the accounting change, realizing that it had no economic consequence? The results of these studies (using weekly and monthly data) were consistent with the EMH, finding no market reaction to the switch.

With the advent of positive accounting research, the assumption of no economic consequences to a "pure accounting" change was reexamined. Management compensation contracts as well as debt covenants based on accounting numbers are affected by accounting changes. Holthausen (1981) examined the accounting switch-backs in this framework. He argued that an accounting change that increases reported income, given earnings-based management contracts, should result in negative market reaction, as there would be a wealth transfer from the owners of the firm to the managers. Conversely, the presence of debt covenants should result in a positive market reaction, as the increase in reported earnings and assets would generally increase the slack associated with any leverage constraints. Empirical results did not confirm these hypotheses.

Studies of market reaction to voluntary accounting changes have generally not found results consistent with the positive accounting framework, as (it is argued that) by the time the change is made, it has been generally anticipated that the firm (or its managers) will make the change to improve reported performance. Thus, although the motivation for the change (compensation, debt covenants) is as specified, the market has already taken it into account.

Evidence consistent with the compensation motivation for depreciation switch-backs is reported by Dhaliwal et al. (1982), who found that management-controlled firms are more likely to adopt straight-line depreciation methods. Furthermore, Healy et al. (1987) found that when firms changed reporting methods to straight-line depreciation,

> the CEO's bonus and salary awards are based on reported earnings both before and after the accounting changes. We find no evidence that subsequent to either the inventory change or the depreciation change, reported earnings are transformed to earnings under the original accounting method for computing compensation awards.*

Generally, however, they note that the percentage of the CEO's compensation attributable to the accounting change is small relative to their overall compensation package. On average, these results do not find a debt covenant or (significant) management compensation motivation for the change in depreciation method. For a given company, however, an analyst would be wise to check these factors whenever an income-increasing accounting change is implemented.

---

* Paul H. Healy, Sok-Hyon Kang, and Krishna Palepu, "The Effect of Accounting Procedure Changes on CEO's Cash Salary and Bonus Compensation," *Journal of Accounting and Economics* (1987), pp. 7–34.

Estimating Relative Age and Useful Lives

Fixed-asset data can be used to estimate the relative age of companies' property, plant, and equipment. The relative age as a percentage of depreciable ("useful") life is calculated as

Relative Age (%) = Accumulated Depreciation/Ending Gross Investment

As long as straight-line depreciation is used,[13] this is an accurate estimate of asset age as a percentage of depreciable life. Neither changes in asset mix (additions with longer or shorter lives than existing assets) nor the timing of purchases affect the calculation. The relative age is a useful measure of whether the firm's fixed-asset base is old or new. Newer assets are likely to be more efficient; when relative age is high, the firm has not been adding to (or modernizing) its capital stock and may find it difficult to compete with firms that have more modern facilities. Remember, however, that this calculation is affected by the firm's accounting methods in the following areas:

▶ Depreciation lives[14]
▶ Salvage values

Another useful calculation is the average depreciable life of fixed assets:

Average Depreciable Life = Ending Gross Investment/Depreciation Expense

This calculation is only a rough approximation as it can be affected by changes in asset mix. During periods of rapid growth in fixed assets, the time (within the year) when assets are placed into service can also affect the ratio. Over longer time periods, however, this ratio is a useful measure of a firm's depreciation policy and can be used for comparisons with competitors.

Estimating the Age of Assets

We can also calculate the approximate age (in years) of a firm's fixed assets by comparing accumulated depreciation with depreciation expense:[15]

Average Age = Accumulated Depreciation/Depreciation Expense

As in the case of depreciable life, average age calculations may be distorted by changes in asset mix and by acquisitions. Nonetheless, these data are useful for comparison purposes and can suggest a useful line of questioning when meeting with management.

Average age data, either as a percentage of gross cost or in absolute terms, are useful for two reasons. First, older assets tend to be less efficient; inefficient or obsolete fixed assets may make the firm uncompetitive. Second, knowing past

---

[13] The use of accelerated depreciation methods invalidates this analysis. However, since more than 90% of companies use straight-line depreciation, the method has general application.

[14] As noted earlier, depreciable lives and economic lives for reporting purposes are not equivalent. See the earlier reference to Most (1984).

[15] Average age can also be computed as relative age multiplied by average depreciable life.

patterns of capital replacement helps the analyst estimate when major capital expenditures will be required. The financing implications of capital expenditure requirements may be significant. Furthermore, when forecasting capital expenditures, the data should be compared with benchmark data on the useful (economic) life of fixed assets for that industry.

Example 43-3

Forest Products Industry Comparison

Exhibit 43-8 contains average age and average depreciable life statistics for four Scandinavian companies in the forest products industry for 1999. Statistics for buildings and for machinery and equipment are shown separately, as required by Swedish GAAP.[16]

The statistics show significant differences among these four companies:

▶ SCA's fixed assets appear youngest and Assidoman's appear oldest.

▶ Holmen appears to use the shortest depreciable lives, followed by SCA.

These statistics are, however, only the starting point for analysis. They assume that all four firms have comparable assets when in fact they may have differing mixes of assets with different depreciable lives. Differences in product mix (requiring different fixed-asset mixes) and acquisitions and divestitures also affect the comparison. These statistics should be used to ask questions of management rather than to make decisions.

Several of these firms had major acquisitions or divestitures over the 1997–1999 period, making three-year comparisons meaningless. However data for SCA follow:

SCA: Analysis of Fixed Asset Disclosures by Property Class (SEK millions)

	1997	1998	1999
Buildings et al.			
Gross investment	12,566	13,986	12,513
Accumulated depreciation	(3,299)	(3,909)	(3,680)
Net investment	9,267	10,077	8,833
Depreciation expense	519	515	513
Average age %	26.3%	27.9%	29.4%
Average depreciable life years	24.2	27.2	24.4
Average age years	6.4	7.6	7.2

---

[16] IAS 16 requirements are similar.

Machinery and Equipment

Gross investment	42,404	47,256	47,487
Accumulated depreciation	(17,488)	(20,729)	(20,289)
Net investment	24,916	26,527	27,198
Depreciation expense	3,117	2,912	3,117
Average age %	41.2%	43.9%	42.7%
Average depreciable life years	13.6	16.2	15.2
Average age years	5.6	7.1	6.5

Even within one company, the fixed asset statistics can show significant change over short periods. The apparent increase in average depreciable life in 1998 and the 1999 decline may be due to significant asset acquisitions and dispositions in those years (note the changes in gross investment and accumulated depreciation). As in the case of comparisons with other companies, these statistics are a means rather than an end.

EXHIBIT 43-8	Analysis of Fixed Assets for Scandinavian Forest Products Industry

1999	Assidoman	Holmen	SCA	Stora Enso
Buildings				
Average age %	41.6	49.1	29.4	35.1
Average depreciable life years	27.3	21.0	24.4	27.6
Average age years	11.3	10.3	7.2	9.7
Machinery and Equipment				
Average age %	55.7	50.0	42.7	48.3
Average depreciable life years	16.3	13.4	15.2	17.4
Average age years	9.1	6.7	6.5	8.4

Source: Data from 1999 annual reports.

4   IMPAIRMENT OF LONG-LIVED ASSETS

Fixed assets used in continuing operations are carried at acquisition cost less accumulated depreciation. The carrying amount of fixed assets may also be affected by changes in market conditions and technology. These changes may increase or decrease the fair value of fixed assets. Unlike some foreign countries (and the IASB), U.S. GAAP do not allow firms to recognize increases in value.

This section is concerned with the recognition, measurement, and disclosure problems associated with decreases in fair value, often called impairment, of long-lived assets. Impairment means that some or all of the carrying cost cannot be recovered from expected levels of operations. Due to unfavorable economic conditions, technological developments, or declines in market demand, firms may temporarily idle, continue to operate at a significantly reduced level, sell, or abandon impaired assets. These economic conditions may also call for fewer employees or those with different skills.

Financial Reporting of Impaired Assets

Impairments are sometimes reported as part of "restructuring" provisions. Such provisions (see Reading 34 for further discussion) contain elements that fall into two general categories. Some elements, including impairment writedowns, write off past cash flows.[17] Others reflect a major restructuring of the firm and may result in current and expected future cash outflows for such items as employee severance and lease payments. Restructuring provisions must, therefore, be separated into impairment (noncash writedowns of past cash outflows) and those with cash flow implications.

In October 2001, the FASB issued SFAS 144, Accounting for the Impairment or Disposal of Long-Lived Assets. The new standard superseded SFAS 121 (Accounting for Impairment) and APB 30,[18] and also nullified most of the guidance (EITF 94-3) on obligations associated with disposal activities.

SFAS 144 broadened the application of "discontinued operation" accounting[19] and changed the treatment of assets intended for disposal. SFAS 121 (1995) had distinguished between assets held for sale and those remaining in use.

Impairment of Assets Held for Sale

The new standard requires that long-lived assets held for sale:

▶ Be written down to fair value less cost to sell when lower than the carrying amount. In most cases estimated fair value would be the present value of expected cash flows, discounted at the credit-adjusted risk-free rate.[20] Costs to sell exclude costs associated with the ongoing operations of assets held for sale.

▶ Cease to be depreciated after reclassification as held for sale.

Subsequent increases in fair value less cost to sell would be recognized as gains only to the extent of previously recognized writedowns.

Impairment of Assets Remaining in Use

The standard requires the recognition of impairment when there is evidence that the carrying amount of an asset or a group of assets still in use can no longer be recovered. One or more of the following indicators may signal lack of recoverability:

---

[17] However, they may signal departure from a business segment or the need for significant capital expenditures for investments in new and improved technologies.

[18] APB 30 deals with disposal of a segment and the classification of items as extraordinary.

[19] See Reading 34 for discussion of discontinued operations accounting.

[20] See discussion of SFAC 7 in Box 33-1.

> ▶ A significant decrease in the market value, physical change, or use of the assets
> ▶ Adverse changes in the legal or business climate
> ▶ Significant cost overruns
> ▶ Current period operating or cash flow losses combined with a history of operating or cash flow losses and a forecast of a significant decline in the long-term profitability of the asset

SFAS 144 provides a two-step process. First is the recoverability test: Impairment must be recognized when the carrying value of the assets exceeds the *undiscounted* expected future cash flows from their use and disposal. The second stage is loss measurement: the excess of the carrying amount over the fair value of the assets. When fair value cannot be determined, the *discounted* present value of future cash flows (discounted at the firm's incremental borrowing rate) must be used.[21]

For assets to be held and used, the new standard permits either a probability-weighted or a best-estimate approach when applying the undiscounted cash flows recoverability test. Estimates of future cash flows used in these tests would be based on the remaining useful life of the primary asset of the group, which may be recognized identifiable intangible assets that are being amortized. The standard includes guidance on the present value methods described in SFAC 7.

The recoverability test and loss measurement are based on assets grouped at the lowest level for which cash flows can be identified independently of cash flows of other asset groups. The impairment loss is reported pretax as a component of income from continuing operations.

The standard prohibits restoration of previous impairments. It requires disclosure of the amount of the loss, segments affected, events and circumstances surrounding the impairment, and how fair value was determined.

SFAS 144 does not require firms to disclose cash flows and discount rates used to measure impairment. Firms do not have to disclose impaired assets (even though one or more impairment indicators are present) as long as their gross *undiscounted* cash flows exceed their carrying amount (even when the discounted cash flows are below the carrying amount). Thus, there is no disclosure of early-warning signals.

SFAS 144 was effective in fiscal years beginning after December 15, 2001. The new standard applied prospectively to new disposal activities. Retroactive application was prohibited except for restatement for comparative purposes.

Analysts must develop supplementary techniques to counter inadequate disclosure requirements and the absence of early-warning signals. Significant declines in market value, abnormal technological changes, and overcapacity are good indicators of possible asset impairments. Research indicates that managers are slow to report impairments.

The telecommunications industry provides a good example; the three indicators mentioned earlier in the preceding paragraph were present during 2001. A June 25, 2001 article in the *Wall Street Journal* asked whether companies had delayed impairment announcements because asset writedowns would violate bond covenants based on minimum levels of fixed assets relative to debt. Impairment recognition would have reduced access to capital markets and risked technical insolvency.

---

[21] When the recoverability test is applied to assets acquired in purchase method business combinations, the standard requires the elimination of goodwill before recording writedowns of related impaired tangible and identifiable intangible assets. When only some of the acquired assets are subject to the recoverability test, goodwill must be allocated to the affected assets on a pro-rata basis using the relative fair values of all assets acquired. SFAS 142 (2001) made significant changes in accounting for the impairment of goodwill.

The need to evaluate recoverability periodically may result in the review of depreciation methods, lives, and salvage values. Changes in depreciation may precede or accompany a firm's reporting of asset impairment.

Example 43-4

Texaco

Note 6 of Texaco's 1999 financial statements provides an example of impairment recognition and disclosure. Texaco, a multinational oil company, reported asset impairments (included in unusual items) in 1997, 1998, and 1999. While the impairment amounts are small compared to Texaco's net income, the disclosures illustrate the poor quality of disclosures in this area. Texaco's disclosures are very broad and uninformative. The statement that "fair value was determined by discounting expected future cash flows" provides no detail regarding the assumptions used.

Financial Statement Impact of Impairments

Impairment writedowns of long-lived assets have pervasive and significant effects on financial statements and financial ratios.

The principal balance sheet impacts of the writedowns are reductions in the:

▶ Carrying value of plant, equipment, and other production assets

▶ Deferred tax liabilities

▶ Stockholders' equity

The lower level of fixed assets is a direct consequence of the impairment writedown. As a result, the firm's fixed-asset and total-asset turnover increases, affecting any comparison with firms that have not recognized impairments.

The reduction in deferred tax liabilities reflects the fact that the impairment loss is not recognized for tax purposes until the property is disposed of. However, because virtually all firms depreciate fixed assets more quickly for tax purposes than for financial reporting, the impairment has the effect of reducing the difference between the tax basis and reporting basis of these assets. Thus, previously established deferred tax liabilities are reduced (see Reading 44 for further discussion of deferred taxes).

The reduction in equity is the net effect of the impairment provision. This reduction increases the firm's debt-to-equity ratio and decreases reported book value per share. The price-to-book value ratio is increased.

Future financial statements are also affected by the writedown. Depreciation expense declines as a direct result of the reduction in the carrying value of fixed assets; reported earnings are higher than if no impairment were recognized. With higher earnings and lower assets and equity, return ratios (ROA and ROE) also increase.

The ratios used to evaluate fixed assets and depreciation policy earlier in this reading are also distorted by the impairment writedown. For example, the apparent average age of fixed assets increases, and fixed assets appear older than they really are.

Effect of SFAS 121 on Analysis of Impairment

The lack of reporting guidelines for impairments prior to SFAS 121 resulted in widely divergent timing, measurement, and reporting practices. Fried, Schiff, and Sondhi (FSS) (1989) and two Financial Executives Institute surveys[22] found that a majority of companies used net realizable values (NRV) to measure impairments. However, NRV meant different things to different firms, and the definition used was rarely disclosed.[23] The use of undiscounted cash flows under SFAS 121 reduces the probability of recognition of impairments and overstates asset values because of the failure to recognize the time value of money.

It is difficult to forecast impairment writedowns because managements have so much discretion as to timing. Substandard profitability, especially when persistent, is probably the surest sign of impaired assets. LIFO liquidations and changes in depreciation methods, estimated useful lives, and salvage values provide useful but very imprecise signals. Segment data can help the analyst spot underperforming operations.

The cash flow and tax implications of write-offs are also unclear in some cases. Generally, impairments recognized for financial reporting are not deductible for tax purposes until the affected assets are disposed of. Recognition of the impairment, therefore, leads to a deferred tax asset (a probable future tax benefit), not a current refund. Beneficial cash flow impacts may occur only in the future, when tax deductions are realized. Close attention to the income tax footnote should be helpful, but a complete understanding may require posing questions to management.

Timely recognition of impairments may correct understated past depreciation or permit recognition of the effect of changes in markets or technology on operating assets. Higher frequency of impairment announcements and the absence of reporting guidelines resulted in diverse accounting practices that were not comparable across companies and inconsistently applied within firms over time. The FASB recognized this problem when it placed asset impairment on its agenda. SFAS 144, and SEC efforts to improve disclosures regarding "restructuring" provisions have improved disclosure.

Empirical Findings

The frequency and dollar amount of writedowns have increased considerably in the last 25 years.[24] Elliott and Hanna (1996) report that fewer than 200 (5%) firms in the Compustat database reported write-offs in 1975, almost 800 (14%) did so in 1985, and over 1,200 (21%) in 1993. Moreover, in a phenomenon dubbed by Bleakley (1995) as a "recurring nonrecurring item," firms that report write-offs in one year tend to report write-offs again in subsequent years.[25]

---

[22] Financial Executives Institute, Committee on Corporate Reporting, "Survey on Unusual Charges," 1986 and 1991.

[23] The problem is compounded by SFAC 5, in which NRV is defined as a short-term, gross, undiscounted cash flow.

[24] The majority of write-offs (55%–60%) are taken in the fourth quarter. Given the detailed review (both by management and auditors) during preparation of the annual report, it is likely that the fourth quarter will always contain the largest number of write-offs.

[25] Elliott and Hanna found that 27% of the companies that take a write-off report a subsequent one the next year and approximately 60% do so within three years. Fried et al. (1990) also document multiple write-offs. Their probabilities, however, are higher (45% within one year and approximately 70% within three years).

The analysis of write-offs has been confounded by the existence of conflicting beliefs as to the nature and motivations behind such actions. Some view managers as manipulating earnings[26] by recognizing impairments only when it is to their benefit rather than as they occur. Others view impairment announcements as information provided by managers as to declines in asset values due to poor performance, technological shifts, and/or changes in the firm's objectives.

Articles in the financial and popular press as well as in academic journals often talk about the "big bath"—a tendency to take large write-offs during adverse times—and about "house cleaning"—large write-offs assumed to accompany changes in senior management. Consequently, write-off announcements often are viewed as a signal of improvement in future reported performance. However, debate lingers as to whether the subsequent improvement (should it materialize) is evidence that the upturn is real or merely a consequence of earnings management.

A number of studies have examined the write-off phenomenon. These studies document a number of recurring characteristics of write-offs.

1. *Poor financial as well as stock market performance usually precede write-offs.*

Francis, Hanna, and Vincent (1996), Rees, Gill, and Gore (1996), and Elliott and Shaw (1988) all report poor stock market performance of write-off firms from three to five years prior to the write-off. Consistent with the foregoing, within their respective industries, firms with write-offs had lower operating performance as measured by ROA (Rees et al.), earnings, and ROE (Elliott and Shaw). These results hold for the year of the write-off[27] as well as the three-year period preceding the write-off.[28] Francis et al. showed similar results (with respect to ROA) but only for firms classifying their write-offs as restructurings.

2. *Overall, negative returns occur around the time of the write-off and for up to 18 months following the write-off. These results, however, depend on the nature of the write-off.*

Elliott and Shaw reported that the negative return experienced around the time of the write-off was directly related to the size of the write-off; the larger the write-off, the more negative the reaction. On the other hand, Francis et al., as well as Lindhal and Ricks (1990), indicate that although, in general, market reaction to write-offs was negative, the results depend on whether the event is

a. A *writedown* comprising purely accounting decisions to reduce the carrying value of assets with no (apparent) change in operations; or

b. A *restructuring* that consists of decisions to modify operations (e.g., asset sales, employee layoffs, plant closings)

For the latter type of event, they report positive market reaction. Francis et al. argue that restructurings are associated with positive returns because they indicate decisions taken to modify and improve future operations and corporate strategy.[29]

---

[26] Earnings management can operate in both directions. Zucca and Campbell (1992) argue that firms may engage in big-bath behavior, taking write-offs when earnings are severely depressed, as well as smoothing behavior by taking write-offs when earnings are "too high."

[27] These conditions hold even without taking the write-off into consideration.

[28] FSS (1989), using a control group of firms matched by industry and size, found similar results. Strong and Meyer (1987), however, reported that although the write-off firms were not the best performers in their industry, they were not the worst either, but tended to cluster in the middle quintiles.

[29] Bartov, Lindhal, and Ricks (1996) similarly partitioned their write-off sample into a *writedown category* and an *operating decision category*. Although they found negative returns for both categories, the stock performance of the writedown category was much worse than that of the operating decision category.

3. *Problems leading to write-offs are rarely short-lived and generally persist after the write-off.*

This persistence is especially true for firms taking multiple write-offs. Rees et al. show that such firms had market-adjusted returns that were significantly negative for up to two years after the initial write-off. Furthermore, (industry-adjusted) ROA for these firms did not recover after the write-off. These results are consistent with Elliott and Hanna, who found that bond ratings were lower and default probability higher for firms with sequential write-offs.

Taken together, the evidence seems to indicate that firms write down assets during periods of poor performance. However, the assumption of big-bath behavior may not be well founded. The writedown may also be a response to the (negative) change in the firm's economic situation. The prevalence of multiple write-offs and their increasing size is inconsistent with big-bath behavior, usually associated with a once-and-for-all write-off.[30] Similarly, the persistent negative financial performance and market returns following writedowns are consistent not with an expected reversal following a big-bath but rather with a permanent deterioration in the firm's prospects. Furthermore, positive returns following write-offs are generally confined to those situations where the firm has made explicit operating decisions (restructurings) to modify operations.

Given the significance and frequency of impairments, it is unfortunate that indicators of initial write-offs other than poor financial condition are hard to find.[31] Better disclosure in financial statements (or the Management Discussion and Analysis) of problems with particular segments would make it easier to predict write-offs. However, the evidence indicates that care must be taken to distinguish whether the write-off is purely an accounting decision or is coupled with corrective operating decisions.

5
LIABILITIES FOR ASSET RETIREMENT OBLIGATIONS

Governments often require that owners of operating assets remedy the environmental damage caused by operating those assets or restore land to its preexisting condition. Common examples include:

▶ Restoration of **strip** mines after mining is completed

▶ Dismantlement of an offshore oil platform after the end of its useful life

▶ Removal of toxic wastes caused by production

▶ Decontamination of site when a nuclear power plant is decommissioned

Prior to SFAS 143, current period costs of these activities were often expensed except for capital expenditures that were capitalized.[32] As no standards have

---

[30] In effect, if anything, firms seem to warehouse bad news and report it through multiple write-offs.

[31] FSS (1989) do report that LIFO liquidations are leading indicators of writedowns.

[32] SFAS 19 required the accrual of an asset retirement obligation in some cases. Under SFAS 19, ARO was recognized over the life of the asset and measured using a cost-accumulation approach; it was not discounted, and was often recorded as a contra asset with no recognition of a separate liability. In addition, many electricity producers accrued for the decontamination of nuclear facilities.

existed for the accrual of future expenditures, practice has been inconsistent with respect to:

▶ Whether (or when) accrual takes place

▶ Whether accruals increase the carrying amount of the related asset (and whether they must be depreciated)

▶ Whether accruals are included in depreciation expense

▶ Measurement of the liability (whether or not discounted, and at what rate)

▶ Disclosure

Because of inconsistent accounting practice, the FASB issued SFAS 143, Accounting for Asset Retirement Obligations (AROs), in June 2001.

Provisions of SFAS 143

The requirements of SFAS 143 become effective for fiscal years starting after June 15, 2002 (calendar 2003 for most companies). However some companies will apply the standard earlier.

This standard changes accounting standards for ARO in the following ways:

▶ It applies to all entities[33] and to all legal obligations (including contractual obligations[34]) connected with the retirement of tangible fixed assets.

▶ Affected firms must recognize the fair value of an ARO liability in the period in which it is incurred (normally at acquisition).

▶ Absent a market value, fair value is the present value of the expected cash flows required to extinguish the liability.[35]

▶ As the liability is carried at its present value, the firm must recognize accretion expense in its income statement each period.

▶ An amount equal to the initial liability must be added to the carrying value of the asset, and depreciated over its useful life.

▶ Changes in the estimated liability are accounted for prospectively; prior period amounts are not restated.

▶ Required disclosures include:
  ▶ Description of the ARO and associated asset
  ▶ Reconciliation of the ARO liability, showing the effect of:
    ▶ New liabilities incurred
    ▶ Liabilities extinguished
    ▶ Accretion expense
    ▶ Revisions of the estimated AROs
  ▶ Fair value of any restricted assets (such as funds) set aside for ARO obligations.

Further detail regarding SFAS 143 is contained in Box 43-3.

---

[33] Paragraph 17 of SFAS 143 governs its application to leased assets.

[34] The standard also applies to legally enforceable contracts arising from promises made. One example would be a company's publicly stated promise to restore a site it is not required to restore by existing laws.

[35] See Box 43-3 for details.

BOX 43-3 SFAS 143 (2001): ACCOUNTING FOR ASSET RETIREMENT OBLIGATIONS

Explanation of Accounting Method

Initial Recognition and Measurement

SFAS 143 requires the recognition of the fair value of the ARO liability in the period it is incurred if a reasonable estimate of fair value can be made. The fair value of the liability is defined as the amount at which the liability can be settled in a current transaction between willing parties. Quoted market prices are presumed to be the best evidence of fair value. In their absence, firms must estimate fair value using the best available information on prices of similar liabilities and present value (or other valuation) methods.

For present value techniques, SFAS 143 applies the provisions of SFAC 7 (see Box 33-1) to the measurement of ARO liabilities:

A. Estimate the expected (gross) cash flows required to extinguish the obligation, assuming an outside contractor is hired. Given uncertainty regarding future costs, the firm uses the expected value. Other assumptions (such as inflation rates) may be required.

B. The present value of the expected cash flows is computed using an interest rate based on the risk-free rate, but increased to reflect the **credit risk** of the firm (credit-adjusted risk-free rate).

C. The resulting measure of the ARO is recognized on the balance sheet, with periodic accretion (using the interest method) so that the liability equals the expected gross cash flows at the expected payment date. Use of the interest method means that accretion increases each year.

D. An equal amount is added to the carrying basis of the related asset and depreciated over that asset's useful life, using the same method used to depreciate the cost of the asset.

Subsequent Recognition and Measurement

E. If the timing or the amount of estimated gross cash flows change after the initial recognition, the ARO (and the related asset) is increased or decreased accordingly. Any increase is discounted using interest rates at the date of change; any decrease is discounted at the original interest rate. Accretion and depreciation charges change prospectively; there is no restatement of prior periods.

F. When the liability is extinguished (the cash flows occur), any difference between the amount paid and the carrying amount of the ARO liability is recognized as a gain or loss in the income statement.

Transition Method

The provisions of SFAS 143 were effective in fiscal years beginning after June 15, 2001, with earlier application encouraged. The new standard required use of the cumulative change method to recognize existing AROs. Such recognition was accomplished as follows:

1. Estimate gross obligation based on information available at the (current) transition date.

2. Discount to present value using current interest rates.

3. Replace any previous accrual with the following:

    a. Asset equal to ARO at date of asset acquisition

(continued)

> ### BOX 43-3 *(continued)*
>
> **b.** Accumulated depreciation to transition date, assuming SFAS 143 implemented at asset acquisition date
>
> **c.** ARO liability at transition date
>
> **4.** Record the difference between any previous accruals and those listed in the previous paragraph as the *cumulative effect* of implementing the new standard, shown in the income statement on a separate line.
>
> **5.** Provide pro forma disclosure of the ARO liability for each year presented in the financial statement.

OPTIONAL SEGMENT ENDS

Effects of SFAS 143

Implementation of the new standard will result in the following financial statement effects for most firms:[36]

► Increase in the carrying value of fixed assets.

► Increase in liabilities due to recognition of the ARO.

► Lower net income due to recognition of additional depreciation (higher fixed assets) and accretion expense (on the ARO). Due to the nature of the accretion process, this expense will increase every year.

The following ratio effects will also occur:

► Lower asset turnover (higher asset levels)

► Higher debt-to-equity ratio as equity is depressed by lower net income[37]

► Lower return on assets (lower income, higher assets)

► Lower interest coverage (lower income due to higher depreciation, higher interest expense)

Bond covenants that rely on these ratios will also be affected, unless rewritten to ignore the accounting change. Disclosures will be improved in almost all cases. Cash flows will be unaffected.

IAS 16 (1998) requires firms that recognize the liability for remediation costs to include such cost in the carrying amount of fixed assets and depreciate it. The liability recognition is governed by IAS 37 (1998), which (similar to SFAS 143) requires that companies recognize the present value of asset retirement obligations.

---

[36] For firms that have already recognized ARO liabilities (based on expected gross cash outflows), it is possible that the ARO liability will decrease under SFAS 143 because that standard measures the ARO at its present value.

[37] The debt-to-equity ratio is also affected by whether AROs are considered debt or operating liabilities.

Example 43-5

Texaco

In the Management Discussion and Analysis section of its 1999 annual report, Texaco reports (p. 29):

Restoration and Abandonment Costs and Liabilities

> Expenditures in 1999 for restoration and abandonment of our oil and gas producing properties amounted to $26 million. At year-end 1999, accruals to cover the cost of restoration and abandonment were $911 million.

Further, in its accounting policy section (p. 30), Texaco states that:

> We include estimated future restoration and abandonment costs in determining amortization and depreciation rates of productive properties.

These minimal disclosures are representative of practice prior to SFAS 143. The December 31, 1999 total accrual equals 7.6% of stockholders' equity. Note that the accrual is undiscounted and may be offset by expected recoveries from state funds. While it appears that accruals are made through depreciation charges, Texaco does not write up fixed assets. The accounting effect of the proposed accounting standard cannot be estimated due to the complexity of the transition requirements.

SUMMARY

The capitalization decision is only the start of the accounting cycle for long-lived assets. Depreciation expense depends on the choice of accounting method and asset life and salvage value assumptions. Thus, the same asset can produce different amounts of depreciation expense, limiting the comparability of reported income. Economic depreciation may be entirely different from accounting depreciation.

Economic changes often result in asset lives that differ from those anticipated by accounting conventions. In such cases, asset impairment may require accounting recognition. Although SFAS 144 provides standards for impairment writedowns in the United States, management retains considerable discretion over their timing and amounts. The accrual (if any) for future environmental costs related to long-lived assets is another area where practice is highly inconsistent.

PROBLEMS FOR READING 43

1. [Depreciation methods; CFA© adapted] An analyst gathered the following information about a fixed asset purchased by a company:

   ▶ Purchase price: $12,000,000

   ▶ Estimated useful life: 5 years

   ▶ Estimated salvage value: $2,000,000

   Compute the depreciation expense for this asset over its useful life using *each* of the following methods:

   i. Straight-line

   ii. Sum-of-years' digits (SYD)

   iii. Double-declining balance

2. [Effect of depreciation methods; CFA© adapted] Compare the straight-line method of depreciation with accelerated methods with respect to their impact on:

   i. Trend of depreciation expense

   ii. Trend of net income

   iii. Reported return on equity

   iv. Reported return on assets

   v. Reported cash from operations

   vi. Asset turnover

3. [Depreciation methods and cash flows, courtesy of Professor Stephen Ryan] The Capital Company considers investing in either of two assets. Cash flows of these assets are:

Year	Asset A	Asset B
1	$36	$26
2	23	24
3	11	22

   A. At an interest rate of 10%, how much should Capital be willing to pay for each asset?

   B. Assuming that the amount calculated in part a is paid for each asset, calculate the depreciation schedule for each asset that results in a constant rate of return.

   C. What type of historical cost depreciation is equal to present value depreciation for Asset A? Asset B?

4. [Effects of accelerated depreciation] Exhibit 43P-1 contains data from the 1999 annual report of Boeing [BA], a leading manufacturer of aviation equipment.

   A. Despite more than $5 billion of capital expenditures over the four years 1996–1999, Boeing's net plant and equipment rose by barely 4%. One explanation is the sale of fixed assets in 1999 (proceeds $359 million). Discuss *two* other reasons for the slow growth in net plant and equipment.

EXHIBIT 43P-1	BOEING
	Extracts from 1999 Financial Statements ($millions)

Note 1. Summary of Significant Accounting Policies

Property, plant and equipment

Property, plant and equipment are recorded at cost, including applicable construction-period interest, and depreciated principally over the following estimated useful lives: new buildings and land improvements, form 20 to 45 years; and machinery and equipment, from 3 to 13 years. The principal methods of depreciation are as follows: buildings and land improvements, 150% declining balance; and machinery and equipment, sum-of-the-years' digits. The Company periodically evaluates the appropriateness of remaining depreciable lives assigned to long-lived assets subject to management's plan for use and disposition.

Note 11. Property, Plant and Equipment

Property, plant and equipment at December 31 consisted of the following:

	1999	1998
Land	$ 430	$ 499
Buildings	8,148	8,244
Machinery and equipment	10,411	10,521
Construction in progress	1,130	977
	$20,119	$20,241
Less accumulated depreciation	(11,874)	(11,652)
	$ 8,245	$ 8,589

Balances are net of impairment asset valuation reserve adjustments for real property available for sale of $76 and $64 for December 31, 1999 and 1998.

Depreciation expense was $1,330, $1,386 and $1,266 for 1999, 1998 and 1997, respectively. Interest capitalized as construction-period property, plant and equipment costs amounted to $64, $45 and $28 in 1999, 1998 and 1997, respectively.

Five-Year Summary

	1999	1998	1997	1996	1995
Total sales	$57,993	$56,154	$45,800	$35,453	$32,960
Net earnings (loss)	2,309	1,120	(178)	1,818	(36)
Additions to plant and equipment, net	1,236	1,665	1,391	971	747
Depreciation of plant and equipment	1,330	1,386	1,266	1,132	1,172
NEt plant and equipment at year-end	8,245	8,589	8,391	8,266	7,927

Source: Boeing, 10-K report, December 31, 1999.

B. Boeing reported gains on the disposition of fixed assets of $100 million over the 1998–99 period. Discuss how that gain was affected by Boeing's depreciation method.

C. Assume that in 1999 Boeing adopted the straight-line depreciation method retroactively, with no change in depreciable lives. Describe the expected effect of that change on Boeing's:

    i. Net income for 1998 and 1999. (*Hint:* Consider the trend of capital expenditures for those two years.)

    ii. Stockholders' equity at December 31, 1999.

    iii. Cash from operations for 1998 and 1999.

    iv. Fixed-asset turnover for 1999.

D. Assume that Boeing adopted the straight-line depreciation method prospectively as of January 1, 2000, with no change in depreciable lives. Describe the expected effect of that change on Boeing's:

    i. Net income for 2000 compared with net income assuming no accounting change

    ii. Trend of depreciation expense over the 1999 to 2004 period

E. As a financial analyst, what conclusions might you draw form either change (part c or d)?

5. [Change in depreciation lives] On March 6, 2000, Pepsi Bottling Group [PBG] issued a press release containing the following:

> In recognition of its long-standing success in preventive maintenance programs, The Pepsi Bottling Group, Inc. (NYSE: PBG) today announced a change in the depreciation lives of certain categories of assets. This change will result in a reduction of about $58 million in depreciation expense, an increase in earnings per share of $0.22 and an increase in return on invested capital of 0.6% in the year 2000.

Exhibit 43P-2 contains extracts form the first-quarter 10-Q issued by PBG.

A. Compute each of the following ratios for the first quarter of 1999 and 2000, using reported data:

    i. Gross profit margin

    ii. Operating margin

B. Compute each of the following ratios for the first quarter of 1999 and 2000, after adjusting reported data for the depreciation change:

    i. Gross profit margin

    ii. Operating margin

C. Compute how much of the apparent improvement of each of these two ratios was due to the depreciation change.

D. Discuss the effect of the depreciation change on PBG's:

    i. Fixed-asset turnover ratio

    ii. Trend of reported earnings, 1999–2004

    iii. Quality of earnings

    iv. Cash from operations

The March 6 press release also contained the following statement:

> "We maintain that cash profits remain the best method of tracking our perform-ance. However, since some investors look at us and other bottlers in terms of reported earnings, we thought it was important to reflect our depreciation

EXHIBIT 43P-2	PEPSI BOTTLING GROUP

The Pepsi Bottling Group, Inc.
Condensed Consolidated Statements of Operations
(in millions, unaudited)

| | 12 Weeks Ended | |
	March 20, 1999	March 18, 2000
Net revenues	$1,452	$1,545
Cost of sales	(835)	(845)
Gross profit	$ 617	$ 700
Selling, delivery and administrative expenses	(575)	(625)
Operating income	$ 42	$ 75

Note 6. Comparability of Results

Asset Lives

At the beginning of fiscal year 2000, we changed the estimated useful lives of certain categories of assets to reflect the success of our preventive maintenance programs in extending the useful lives of these assets. The changes, which are detailed in the table below, lowered total depreciation cost for the quarter by $14 million ($8 million after tax and minority interest, or $0.05 per share) reducing cost of sales by $8 million and selling, delivery and administrative expenses by $6 million.

Estimated Useful Lives

	1999	2000
Manufacturing equipment	10	15
Heavy fleet	8	10
Fountain dispensing equipment	5	7
Small specialty coolers and marketing equipment	5 to 7	3

Source: Pepsi Bottling Group, 10-Q Report, March 18, 2000.

expenses and reported profit more accurately," said John Cahill, Executive Vice President and Chief Financial Officer for PBG. "Even with these changes, the new policies still present our financial results conservatively."

E. Evaluate the benefits to PBG of making the depreciation change.

6. [Analysis of fixed assets] Roche's summary of significant accounting policies states:

Property, plant and equipment are initially recorded at cost of purchase or construction and are depreciated on a straight-line basis, except for land, which is not depreciated. Estimated useful lives of major classes of depreciable assets are as follows:

Buildings and land improvements	40 years
Machinery and equipment	5–15 years
Office equipment	3 years
Motor vehicles	5 years

The following data were obtained from Roche's annual reports (the 1999 data are located in Note 12 of its 2000 annual report):

Property, plant, and equipment (CHF millions)			
	1997	**1998**	**1999**
Buildings and land improvements:			
Gross investment	$ 7,576	$ 7,947	$ 8,578
Accumulated depreciation	(2,580)	(2,695)	(2,944)
Net investment	$ 4,996	$ 5,252	$ 5,634
Depreciation expense	233	195	210
Machinery and equipment:			
Gross investment	$10,529	$11,350	$13,174
Accumulated depreciation	(5,755)	(6,079)	(7,015)
Net investment	$ 4,774	$ 5,271	$ 6,159
Depreciation expense	692	948	1,036

A. Using the above data, compute each of the following ratios for all three years:

  i. Average depreciable life (years)

  ii. Average age (years)

  iii. Average age (%)

B. Compare the result of part a (i) with the accounting policy statement above.

C. Discuss the three-year trend of the three ratios in part a for both fixed-asset classes.

D. State the questions you would ask management after reviewing parts a through c above.

7. [Impairment] Roche, in its report for the half-year ended June 30, 2000, adopted IAS 36 (Impairment), with the following disclosure:

'Impairment of assets'. When the recoverable amount of an asset, being the higher of its net selling price and its value in use, is less than its carrying amount, then the carrying amount is reduced to its recoverable value. This reduction is reported as an impairment loss. Value in use is calculated using estimated cash flows, generally over a five-year period, with extrapolating projections for subsequent years. These are discounted using an appropriate long-term interest rate. Previously the permitted alternative method for calculating value in use was applied, whereby it was calculated using cash flow projections on an undiscounted basis.

As a result, the Group recognized impairment charges of 1,161 million Swiss francs relating to acquired intangible assets. A reduction in deferred tax liabilities of 348 million Swiss francs was also recorded, giving a net charge of 813 million Swiss francs in the consolidated results. Also included within this is a minor amount relating to impairment on a small number of products acquired in an earlier acquisition as a consequence of reduced market expectations. Under the Group's previous accounting policy, no impairment would have arisen. As a result of the impairment, the net book value of intangible assets was reduced by the amount of the impairment charge, and consequently amortization in the first half of 2000 was 64 million Swiss francs lower than it would have been under the previous policy.

A. Describe the effect of the accounting change on the year 2000:

    i. Income before the effect of accounting changes

    ii. Net income

    iii. Stockholders' equity

    iv. Cash from operations

B. Describe the effect of the accounting change on the year 2001:

    i. Net income

    ii. Return on equity

    iii. Cash from operations

$4\frac{5}{8}$ $4\frac{11}{16}$ $-\frac{3}{8}$

$5\frac{1}{2}$ $5\frac{1}{2}$ $-$

$20\frac{5}{8}$ $21\frac{3}{16}$ $-\frac{1}{16}$

$17\frac{3}{8}$ $18\frac{1}{8}$ $+\frac{7}{8}$

$6\frac{1}{2}$ $6\frac{1}{2}$ $-\frac{1}{2}$

$7\frac{1}{4}$ $31\frac{1}{32}$ $-\frac{3}{8}$

$15\frac{1}{16}$

1 $9\frac{9}{16}$ $9\frac{7}{8}$

$1\frac{3}{32}$

$7\frac{15}{16}$ $7\frac{13}{16}$ $7\frac{15}{16}$

$2\frac{5}{8}$ $2\frac{11}{32}$ $2\frac{1}{2}$ $+$

$2\frac{3}{4}$ $2\frac{1}{4}$ $2\frac{1}{4}$

$6\frac{1}{8}$ $12\frac{1}{16}$ $11\frac{3}{8}$ $11\frac{3}{4}$ $+$

87 $33\frac{3}{4}$ 33 $33\frac{1}{8}$ $-$

602 $25\frac{5}{8}$ $24\frac{9}{16}$ $25\frac{3}{8}$ $+$

833 12 $11\frac{5}{8}$ $11\frac{7}{8}$ $+$

16 $10\frac{1}{2}$ $10\frac{1}{2}$ $10\frac{1}{2}$ $-$

78 $15\frac{7}{8}$ $15\frac{13}{16}$ $15\frac{7}{8}$ $-$

4508 $9\frac{1}{16}$ $8\frac{1}{4}$ $8\frac{1}{4}$ $+$

430 $11\frac{1}{4}$ $10\frac{5}{8}$

STUDY SESSION 10
FINANCIAL STATEMENT ANALYSIS:
Deferred Taxes, On- and Off-Balance-Sheet Debt and Economic Reality

READING ASSIGNMENTS

Reading 44 Analysis of Income Taxes
Reading 45 Analysis of Financing Liabilities
Reading 46 Leases and Off-Balance-Sheet Debt

The readings in this study session discuss and illustrate the financial statement effects of differences between the objectives of tax and financial reporting and the analyst's economic assessment of recorded financing liabilities and other off-balance-sheet debt and obligations.

Deferred taxes are applicable globally with respect to consolidated financial statements and, therefore, are the focus of the learning outcomes for this study session. The financial statement differences between tax reporting and financial reporting are primarily attributable to the timing differences that occur when recognizing revenue and expense items in the measurement of tax and financial income (loss). These differences create deferred tax assets or deferred tax liabilities that are often difficult to assess because they may not be viable indicators of future cash flow or true economic value.

Evaluating both on- and off-balance-sheet debt to assess a company's liquidity and solvency positions is important because both are crucial for a company's long-term growth and viability. In this process, careful attention must be given to the notes of the financial statements to ensure that all potential liabilities (e.g., leasing arrangements and other contractual commitments) are appropriately evaluated for their economic reality. Adjustments are then made to achieve company comparability for improved credit and investment decision processes.

LEARNING OUTCOMES

Reading 44: Analysis of Income Taxes
The candidate should be able to:

a. discuss the key terms (e.g., deferred tax asset, valuation allowance, deferred tax liability, taxes payable, income tax expense, temporary difference, permanent difference, etc.) used in income tax accounting, explain why and how deferred tax liabilities and assets are created, and describe the liability method of accounting for deferred taxes;

b. discuss the implications of a valuation allowance for deferred tax assets (i.e., when it is required, what impact it has on the financial statements, and how it might affect an analyst's view of a company);

c. explain the factors that determine whether a company's deferred tax liabilities should be treated as a liability or as equity for purposes of financial analysis;

d. distinguish between temporary and permanent items in pretax financial income and taxable income;

e. determine income tax expense, income taxes payable, deferred tax assets, and deferred tax liabilities, and calculate and interpret the adjustment to the financial statements related to a change in the tax rate;

f. analyze disclosures relating to deferred tax items and the effective tax rate reconciliation and discuss how information included in these disclosures affects a company's financial statements and financial ratios;

g. compare and contrast a company's deferred tax items and effective tax rate reconciliation between reporting periods and/or to other companies.

Reading 45: Analysis of Financing Liabilities
The candidate should be able to:

a. compute the effects of debt issuance and amortization of bond discounts and premiums on the financial statements and ratios, and discuss the effect on the financial statements from issuing zero-coupon debt;

b. determine the appropriate classification for debt with equity features and calculate the effect of issuance of such instruments on the debt to total capital ratio;

c. describe the disclosures relating to financing liabilities, and discuss the advantages/disadvantages to the company of selecting a given instrument and the effect of the selection on a company's financial statements and ratios;

d. determine the effects of changing interest rates on the market value of debt and on financial statements and ratios;

e. explain the role of debt covenants in protecting creditors by limiting a company's freedom to invest, pay dividends, or make other operating and strategic decisions.

Reading 46: Leases and Off-Balance-Sheet Debt

The candidate should be able to:

a. discuss the motivations for leasing assets instead of purchasing them and the incentives for reporting the leases as operating leases rather than capital leases;

b. determine the effects of capital and operating leases on the financial statements and ratios of the lessees and lessors;

c. describe the types and economic consequences of off-balance-sheet financing and determine how take-or-pay contracts, throughput arrangements, and the sale of receivables affect selected financial ratios;

d. distinguish between a sales-type lease and a direct financing lease and determine the effects on the financial statements and ratios of the lessors.

$4\frac{5}{8}$ $4^{11}/_{16}$

$5\frac{1}{2}$ $5\frac{1}{2}$ — $\frac{3}{8}$

$5\frac{1}{2}$ $21^{13}/_{16}$ — $\frac{1}{16}$

$20\frac{5}{8}$ $21^{13}/_{16}$ — $\frac{7}{8}$

$17\frac{3}{8}$ **$18\frac{1}{8}$ +**

$6\frac{1}{2}$ $6\frac{1}{2}$ — $\frac{1}{2}$

$7\frac{1}{4}$ $6\frac{1}{2}$ $3^{1}/_{32}$ — $\frac{1}{8}$

$15/_{16}$

$\frac{9}{16}$

$9/_{16}$

$1^{1}/_{32}$ $7^{13}/_{16}$ $7^{15}/_{16}$

$7^{15}/_{16}$ $7^{13}/_{16}$ $7^{15}/_{16}$

$2\frac{5}{8}$ $2^{11}/_{32}$ $2\frac{1}{2}$ +

$2\frac{3}{4}$ $2\frac{1}{4}$ $2\frac{1}{4}$

$12^{1}/_{16}$ $11\frac{3}{8}$ $11\frac{3}{4}$ +

87 $33\frac{3}{4}$ 33 $33\frac{1}{8}$ —

602 $25\frac{5}{8}$ $24^{9}/_{16}$ $25\frac{3}{8}$ +

833 12 $11\frac{5}{8}$ $11\frac{7}{8}$ +

16 $10\frac{1}{2}$ $10\frac{1}{2}$ $10\frac{1}{2}$ —

78 $15\frac{7}{8}$ $15^{13}/_{16}$ $15\frac{7}{8}$ —

608 $9^{1}/_{16}$ $8\frac{1}{4}$ $8\frac{1}{4}$ +

430 $11\frac{1}{4}$ $10\frac{1}{8}$

ANALYSIS OF INCOME TAXES

by Gerald I. White, Ashwinpaul C. Sondhi, and Dov Fried

LEARNING OUTCOMES

The candidate should be able to:

a. discuss the key terms (e.g., deferred tax asset, valuation allowance, deferred tax liability, taxes payable, income tax expense, temporary difference, permanent difference, etc.) used in income tax accounting, explain why and how deferred tax liabilities and assets are created, and describe the liability method of accounting for deferred taxes;

b. discuss the implications of a valuation allowance for deferred tax assets (i.e., when it is required, what impact it has on the financial statements, and how it might affect an analyst's view of a company);

c. explain the factors that determine whether a company's deferred tax liabilities should be treated as a liability or as equity for purposes of financial analysis;

d. distinguish between temporary and permanent items in pretax financial income and taxable income;

e. determine income tax expense, income taxes payable, deferred tax assets, and deferred tax liabilities, and calculate and interpret the adjustment to the financial statements related to a change in the tax rate;

f. analyze disclosures relating to deferred tax items and the effective tax rate reconciliation and discuss how information included in these disclosures affects a company's financial statements and financial ratios;

g. compare and contrast a company's deferred tax items and effective tax rate reconciliation between reporting periods and/or to other companies.

INTRODUCTION 1

Differences in the objectives of financial and tax reporting make income taxes a troublesome issue in financial reporting. The objective of financial reporting is to provide users with information needed to evaluate a firm's financial position, performance, and cash flows. The accrual basis of financial reporting allows management to select revenue and expense recognition methods that best reflect performance and smooth or otherwise manage (maximize or minimize) reported net income. As discussed throughout the text, management incentives to manage reported income result from management compensation contracts, bond covenants, political considerations, and the (presumed) effect of those factors on financial markets.

Tax reporting, in contrast, is the product of political and social objectives. Current-period *taxable income* is measured using the modified cash basis; revenue and expense recognition methods used in tax reporting often differ from those used for financial reporting as the firm has strong incentives to select methods allowing it to minimize taxable income and, therefore, taxes paid, maximizing cash from operations.[1]

Thus, differences between *taxes payable* for the period and reported *income tax expense* result from:

▶ The difference between accrual and modified cash bases of accounting

▶ Differences in reporting methods and estimates

These differences create *deferred tax liabilities* (credits) and prepaid taxes or *deferred tax assets* (debits) that are difficult to interpret. There are disagreements as to (1) whether they are true assets or liabilities and (2) their usefulness as indicators of future cash flows. When these deferrals become very large, their interpretation can have a significant effect on the financial analysis of a firm or group of firms.

Note: Terminology related to income tax accounting can be confusing because two terms that seem similar can have very different meanings. A glossary of terms used in this reading is therefore provided in Box 44-1. Each term in the glossary is shown in italics when first used in the reading.

2   BASIC INCOME TAX ACCOUNTING ISSUES

Basic accounting issues are discussed in Box 44-2. There we provide a discussion and an illustration of how temporary differences between tax and financial reporting affect the balance sheet and the income statement. The box also contains a review of the impact of tax law and rate changes on deferred tax assets and liabilities. This permits us to focus on analytical issues in the reading.

---

[1] In countries such as Japan, Germany, and Switzerland, statutory financial reporting is required to conform to tax reporting. In these countries, the problems discussed in this reading do not occur for statutory (usually, parent company only) statements. However, consolidated financial statements, for example, those prepared under IAS GAAP, do not conform to tax reporting and deferred tax issues must be dealt with. See the discussion of financial reporting practices outside the United States later in this reading.

BOX 44-1 GLOSSARY: INCOME TAX ACCOUNTING

Amounts in Tax Return:

Taxable income	Income subject to tax.
Taxes payable (current tax expense)	Tax return liability resulting from current period taxable income. SFAS 109 calls this "current tax expense or benefit"
Income tax paid	Actual cash outflow for income taxes, including payments (refunds) for other years.
Tax loss carryforward	Tax return loss that can be used to reduce taxable income in future years.

Amounts in Financial Statements:

Pretax income	Income before income tax expense.
Income tax expense	Expense based on current period pre-tax income; includes taxes payable and deferred income tax expense.
Deferred income tax expense	Accrued income tax expense expected to be paid (or recovered) in future years; difference between taxes payable and income tax expense. Under SFAS 109, the amount depends on changes in deferred tax assets and liabilities.
Deferred tax asset (debit)	Balance sheet amounts; expected to be recovered from future operations.
Deferred tax liability (credit)	Balance sheet amounts; expected to result in future cash outflows.
Valuation allowance	Reserve against deferred tax assets (debits) based on likelihood that those assets will not be realized.
Timing difference	The difference between tax return and financial statement treatment (timing or amount) of a transaction.
Temporary difference	Difference between tax and financial statement reporting, which will affect taxable income when those differences reverse; similar to but broader than timing differences.

Note: SFAS 109 contains a more technical glossary of terms used in that standard.

BOX 44-2 BASIC INCOME TAX ACCOUNTING ISSUES

We use a simple example to illustrate the issues faced when tax accounting differs from accounting for financial statements. We begin this example assuming that depreciation is the only item of expense. Part A of Exhibit 44-B1 depicts income tax reporting where the company depreciates a $6,000 asset over two years, giving rise to *taxes payable* of $800, $800, and $2,000 over the three-year period.

For financial reporting (Part B of Exhibit 44-B1), the firm depreciates the asset over three years. *Pretax income* exceeds taxable income in the first two years; taxable income is higher in year 3.* What *tax expense* should the company report in its financial statements?

Part B1 of Exhibit 44-B1 displays one approach (not permitted under U.S. GAAP) where the tax expense equals taxes payable. Pretax income is the same for all three years, but tax expense differs as the tax deferred in earlier years is paid in year 3. As a result, tax expense, as a percentage of pretax income, does not reflect the prevailing statutory tax rate, 40%. The reported tax rate is 26.7% for the first two years and 66.7% for year 3.

Timing Differences: Deferred Tax Liabilities

Part B2 of Exhibit 44-B1 illustrates the U.S. GAAP treatment, SFAS 109, which requires the recognition of deferred tax liabilities when future taxable income is expected to exceed pretax income. IAS 12 has the same requirement. In our example, pretax income exceeds taxable income in years 1 and 2, but year 3 taxable income is expected to exceed pretax income by $2,000. At the end of years 1 and 2, a deferred tax liability of $400 (timing difference of $1,000 × 40% tax rate) is recognized to reflect the tax on the $1,000 *timing difference* that will be paid in year 3. This liability is reported each year as a portion of that year's tax expense. Thus, income tax expense is $1,200 in both years 1 and 2: tax payable or current tax expense ($800) plus *deferred income tax expense* ($400). The matching principle is satisfied as the relationship between revenues and expenses (40% tax rate) is maintained. At the end of year 2, the cumulative timing difference is $2,000 and the aggregate deferred tax liability is $800.

No tax depreciation remains to be recorded in year 3, but book depreciation expense equals $2,000. At the end of year 3, the machine has been fully depreciated for both tax and financial reporting purposes. The effect of the year 1 and 2 timing differences must be reversed; year 3 income tax expense equals $1,200 or taxes payable ($2,000) *less* the reversal of the deferred tax liability of $800 accumulated over the first two years.

Timing Differences: Deferred Tax Assets

Differences between financial accounting and tax accounting can also give rise to *deferred tax assets* (debits) when future pretax income is expected to exceed taxable income. Part B3 of Exhibit 44-B1 introduces another timing difference, warranty expense, which gives rise to a deferred tax asset in years 1 and 2. As warranty payments are tax-deductible when paid rather than when accrued, larger amounts are charged to warranty expense earlier for financial statement purposes; tax deductions occur in later periods when the repairs or replacement services are provided.

As shown in part B3,† the firm recognizes a warranty expense of $500 in each of years 1 and 2, but receives no tax deduction because no expenditures are incurred in those years. The higher taxable income results in a prepayment of taxes; tax expense in the financial statements reflects lower pretax income. The difference of $500 in each of the first two years generates a deferred tax debit of $200 ($500 × 0.40) each year and decreases tax expense by that amount each year. At the end of year 2, there is a deferred tax asset of $400.

In year 3, tax-deductible expenditures of $1,500 are incurred for repairs, reducing taxable income and tax payments. These expenditures exceed the $500 of financial statement warranty expense of year 3 by $1,000; equal to the total additional expense accrued in the first two years. The temporary difference reverses, deferred income tax expense is reduced by $400 ($1,000 × 0.40), and the deferred tax debit generated during the first two years is eliminated.

Comprehensive Example: Deferred Tax Liabilities and Deferred Tax Assets

Exhibit 44-B1 separately illustrates the treatment of timing differences that gave rise to a deferred tax liability and a deferred tax asset. In practice, firms report both deferred tax assets and liabilities, resulting from multiple timing differences. Exhibit 44-B2 shows the accounting when a firm has both types of timing differences.

---

* Of the $3,000 pretax income reported in years 1 and 2, $1,000 (the excess tax depreciation) is not subject to taxes in those years. The $2,000 (2 × $1,000) deferred in the first two years is subject to taxation in the third as taxable income ($5,000) exceeds pretax income ($3,000) by $2,000.

† In part B3, we ignore depreciation expense to illustrate the accounting treatment of timing differences that generate deferred tax assets.

‡ In these examples, income tax expense could also have been computed by applying the income tax rate of 40% directly to pretax income in each year. However, in more complex situations, discussed later, this approach would produce a different result.

(continued)

BOX 44-2 *(continued)*

Taxes payable equal the tax rate multiplied by taxable income and reflect the effects of tax depreciation and allowable warranty deductions on the tax return. Income tax expense is based on pretax income, which reflects financial statement depreciation and estimated warranty expense for products sold. Over the three-year period, total revenues are $15,000, total depreciation expense is $6,000, and total warranty expense is $1,500 for both financial and tax reporting. The timing of expense recognition differs, but the total amount is the same.§

| EXHIBIT 44-B1 | Alternative Approaches to Reported Income Tax Expense |

Assumptions:

▶ The firm purchases a machine costing $6,000 with a three-year estimated service life and no salvage value.

▶ For financial reporting purposes, the firm uses straight-line depreciation over the three-year life.

▶ For income tax reporting, the machine is depreciated over two years using the straight-line depreciation method.

▶ Products manufactured using the machine generate annual revenues of $5,000 for three years.

▶ The statutory tax rate is 40% in all three years.

Part A. Income Tax Reporting: Straight-line Depreciation over Two Years

	Year 1	Year 2	Year 3	Total
Revenues	$5,000	$5,000	$5,000	$15,000
Depreciation expense	(3,000)	(3,000)	0	(6,000)
Taxable income	$2,000	$2,000	$5,000	$ 9,000
Taxes payable @ 40%	(800)	(800)	(2,000)	(3,600)
Net income	$1,200	$1,200	$3,000	$ 5,400

Part B. Financial Statements: Straight-line Depreciation over Three Years

B1: Flow-Through Method—Not Permitted by GAAP

▶ No recognition of deferred taxes.

▶ Tax expense defined as taxes payable.

	Year 1	Year 2	Year 3	Total
Revenues	$5,000	$5,000	$5,000	$15,000
Depreciation expense	(2,000)	(2,000)	(2,000)	(6,000)
Pretax income	$3,000	$3,000	$3,000	$ 9,000
Tax expense = taxes payable .	(800)	(800)	(2,000)	(3,600)
Net income	$2,200	$2,200	$1,000	$ 5,400

(Exhibit 44-B1 continued on next page ...)

---

§ Warranty expense and actual repair costs are assumed to be identical for illustration only; it is difficult to predict the frequency and level of repair costs perfectly. Bad debt expenses and litigation losses are other examples of timing differences where predictions are uncertain.

(continued)

BOX 44-2 *(continued)*

EXHIBIT 44-B1   (continued)

B2: SFAS 109 and IAS 12—Deferred Tax Liabilities
- ▶ Recognition of deferred taxes.
- ▶ Tax expense differs from taxes payable.

	Year 1	Year 2	Year 3	Total
Revenues	$5,000	$5,000	$5,000	$15,000
Depreciation expense	(2,000)	(2,000)	(2,000)	(6,000)
Pretax income	$3,000	$3,000	$3,000	$ 9,000
Tax expense @ 40%	(1,200)	(1,200)	(1,200)	(3,600)
Net income	$1,800	$1,800	$1,800	$ 5,400
Taxes payable (from part A)	800	800	2,000	3,600
Deferred tax expense	400	400	(800)	0
Balance sheet deferred tax liability	400	800	0	N. A.

Journal Entries

Years 1 and 2: Origination of the deferred tax liability

Tax expense	$1,200	
Deferred tax liability		$ 400
Taxes payable		800

Year 3: Reversal of the deferred tax liability

Tax expense	$1,200	
Deferred tax liability	800	
Taxes payable		$2,000

B3: SFAS 109 and IAS 12—Deferred Tax Assets

Assumption: Warranty expenses estimated at 10% of revenues each year; all repairs provided in year 3

Income Tax Reporting	Year 1	Year 2	Year 3	Total
Revenues	$5,000	$5,000	$5,000	$15,000
Warranty expense	0	0	(1,500)	(1,500)
Taxable income	$5,000	$5,000	$3,500	$13,500
Tax payable @ 40%	(2,000)	(2,000)	(1,400)	(5,400)
Net income	$3,000	$3,000	$2,100	$ 8,100

(Exhibit 44-B1 continued on next page ...)

(continued)

BOX 44-2 *(continued)*

EXHIBIT 44-B1   (continued)

Financial Statements

Revenues	$5,000	$5,000	$5,000	$15,000
Warranty expense	(500)	(500)	(500)	(1,500)
Pretax income	$4,500	$4,500	$4,500	$13,500
Tax expense @ 40%	(1,800)	(1,800)	(1,800)	(5,400)
Net income	$2,700	$2,700	$2,700	$ 8,100
Prepaid (deferred) tax	200	200	(400)	0
Balance sheet deferred tax asset	200	400	(400)	N. A.

Journal Entries

Years 1 and 2: Origination of deferred tax assets

Tax expense	$1,800	
Deferred tax asset	200	
Taxes payable		$2,000

Year 3: Reversal of deferred tax asset

Tax expense	$1,800	
Deferred tax asset		$ 400
Taxes payable		1,400

Do the deferred tax liabilities at the end of years 1 and 2 actually represent a liability for tax payments due in year 3? Similarly, does the deferred tax asset qualify as an asset? In this simple case, they do, as the forecast reversals occurred as expected and the firm did not engage in any other transactions with timing differences. In the real world, the answer is not so clear; these are important issues from an analytical perspective and the reading provides a comprehensive discussion of those issues.

Effect of Tax Rate and Tax Law Changes

The balance sheet orientation of SFAS 109 requires adjustments to deferred tax assets and liabilities to reflect the impact of a change in tax rates or tax laws. Using the example in Exhibit 44-B2, Exhibit 44-B3 depicts the impact of a tax rate decrease from 40% to 35% at the beginning of year 2. In panel A, we assume that the future tax decrease *was enacted before* the year 1 financial statements were prepared. Panel B illustrates the accounting under the assumption that the year 2 tax decrease *was enacted after* year 1 financial statements were prepared.

(continued)

BOX 44-2 *(continued)*

Panel A: Future Tax Rate Change Enacted in Current Year.

Taxes payable for year 1 are based on the current tax rate of 40%, and the deferred tax assets and liabilities are based on the tax rate expected to be in effect when the differences reverse, 35%.

Note that year 1 tax expense as a percentage of pretax income (the effective tax rate) is 39% ($975/$2,500): a weighted average of the current tax rate of 40% and the 35% rate that will be in effect when the timing differences that gave rise to the deferred taxes reverse. There is no attempt to match income tax expense directly with pretax income, and one cannot calculate tax expense directly by multiplying pretax income by the current tax rate. For years 2 and 3, the calculations are similar to those in Exhibit 44-B2 except that the new tax rate of 35% (rather than 40%) is used for all calculations.

EXHIBIT 44-B2   Financial Reporting Under SFAS 109

Income Tax Reporting	Year 1	Year 2	Year 3	Total
Revenues	$5,000	$5,000	$5,000	$15,000
Depreciation expense	(3,000)	(3,000)	0	(6,000)
Warranty expense	0	0	(1,500)	(1,500)
Taxable income	$2,000	$2,000	$3,500	$ 7,500
Tax payable @ 40%	(800)	(800)	(1,400)	(3,000)
Net Income	$1,200	$1,200	$2,100	$ 4,500

Financial Statements				
Revenues	$5,000	$5,000	$5,000	$15,000
Depreciation expense	(2,000)	(2,000)	(2,000)	(6,000)
Warranty expense	(500)	(500)	(500)	(1,500)
Pretax income	$2,500	$2,500	$2,500	$ 7,500
Tax expense @ 40%	(1,000)	(1,000)	(1,000)	(3,000)
Net Income	$1,500	$1,500	$1,500	$ 4,500
Deferred tax expense	400	400	(800)	0
Balance sheet deferred tax liability	400	800	0	N. A.
Prepaid tax	200	200	(400)	0
Balance sheet deferred tax asset	200	400	0	N. A.

(Exhibit 44-B2 continued on next page ...)

(continued)

BOX 44-2 *(continued)*

EXHIBIT 44-B2   (continued)

Journal Entries

Years 1 and 2: Origination of deferred tax liabilities and deferred tax assets

Tax expense	$1,000	
Deferred tax asset	200	
Deferred tax liability		$ 400
Taxes payable		800

Year 3: Reversal of deferred tax liabilities and deferred tax assets

Tax expense	$1,000	
Deferred tax liability	800	
Deferred tax asset		$ 400
Taxes payable		1,400

EXHIBIT 44-B3   Impact of Tax Rate Change: The Liability Method

Assumptions

Identical to Exhibit 44-B2

▶ A firm purchases a machine costing $6,000 with a three-year estimated service life and no salvage value.

▶ For financial reporting purposes, the firm uses straight-line depreciation with a three-year life.

▶ For income tax reporting, the machine is depreciated straight-line over two years.

▶ The machine is used to manufacture a product that will generate annual revenue of $5,000 for three years.

▶ Warranty expenses are estimated at 10% of revenues each year; all repairs are provided in year 3.

A. Year 2 Tax Rate Change Enacted in Year 1

Year 1: Tax Rate = 40%

Year 2 Tax Rate Will Be 35%

Selected T-Accounts

			Deferred Tax Asset		Deferred Tax Liability	
Income tax expense	975					
Deferred tax asset	175					
Deferred tax liability		350	$175			$350
Taxes payable		800	$175			$350

Year 2: Tax Rate = 35%

(Exhibit 44-B3 continued on next page ...)

(continued)

BOX 44-2 *(continued)*

EXHIBIT 44-B3   *(continued)*

Income tax expense	875
Deferred tax asset	175
Deferred tax liability	350
Taxes payable	700

Deferred Tax Asset

$175	
175	
$350	

Deferred Tax Liability

	$350
	350
	$700

Year 3: Tax Rate = 35%

Income tax expense	875
Deferred tax liability	700
Deferred tax asset	350
Taxes payable	1,225

Deferred Tax Asset

$350	
	350
$ 0	

Deferred Tax Liability

	$700
700	
$ 0	

Calculations

Temporary Differences

	Depreciation (Liability)	Warranty (Asset)	Taxes Payable	Income Tax Expense
Year 1	35% × $1,000	35% × $(500)	40% × $2,000	$350 − $175 + $ 800
Year 2	35% × 1,000	35% × (500)	35% × 2,000	350 − 175 + 700
Year 3	35% × (2,000)	35% × 1,000	35% × 3,500	− 700 + 350 + 1,225

B. Year 2 Tax Rate Change Enacted in Year 2

Year 1: Tax Rate = 40%

Selected T-Accounts

Income tax expense	1,000
Deferred tax asset	200
Deferred tax liability	400
Taxes payable	800

Deferred Tax Asset

$200	
$200	

Deferred Tax Liability

	$400
	$400

Year 2: Tax Rate Reduced to 35%

(i) Adjustment of Prior-Year Deferrals

Deferred tax liability	50
Deferred tax asset	25
Income tax expense	25

Deferred Tax Asset

$200	
	25
$175	

Deferred Tax Liability

	$400
50	
	$350

(Exhibit 44-B3 continued on next page ...)

(continued)

BOX 44-2 *(continued)*

EXHIBIT 44-B3 (continued)

(ii) *Current Year Operations*

			Deferred Tax Asset		Deferred Tax Liability
Income tax expense	875		$175		$350
Deferred tax asset	175		175		
Deferred tax liability		350			350
Taxes payable		700	$350		$700

Year 3: Tax Rate = 35%

			Deferred Tax Asset		Deferred Tax Liability
Income tax expense	875		$350		$700
Deferred tax liability	700				700
Deferred tax asset		350		350	
Taxes payable		1,225	$ 0		$ 0

Calculations

Temporary Differences

	Depreciation (Liability)	Warranty (Asset)	Taxes Payable	Income Tax Expense
Year 1	40% × $1,000	40% × $(500)	40% × $2,000	$400 − $200 + $ 800
Year 2	(5%) × 1,000	(5%) × (500)		−50 + 25
	35% × 1,000	35% × (500)	35% × 2,000	350 − 175 + 700
Year 3	35% × (2,000)	35% × 1,000	35% × 3,500	−700 + 350 + 1,225

Panel B: Future Tax Rate Change Enacted after Year 1 Statements Have Been Prepared.

Calculations for year 1 tax expense, taxes payable, and deferred taxes are based on the year 1 tax rate of 40% and are identical to those in Exhibit 44-B2. A deferred tax asset of $200 and a deferred tax liability of $400 are created.

In year 2, when the rate decrease is effective, two steps are necessary to calculate the current year's tax expense:

1. Exhibit 44-B3 illustrates the restatement of end of year 1 deferred tax asset and liability balances to the new (lower) tax rate of 35% (assumed to be in effect when the deferred taxes will be paid). Year 2 tax expense is reduced (income is increased) since the lower rate reduces the expected tax payment when the depreciation difference reverses, partially offset by a lower expected tax benefit when the warranty expense difference reverses. The adjustment results in a deferred tax asset of $175 and liability of $350.**

2. The taxes payable and deferred taxes arising from current year operations are calculated using the new rate of 35%.

** These balances are now identical to those shown in panel A of the exhibit when the tax law change was known prior to the issuance of the year 1 financial statements. The only difference between the two panels is the timing of the restatement at the lower rate.

(continued)

BOX 44-2 *(continued)*

Tax expense for year 2 is calculated as follows:

Adjustment of Year 1 Balances to New Rate:

Deferred tax asset of $200 restated to $175	$ 25
Deferred tax liability of $400 restated to $350	(50)

Year 2 Taxes Payable and New Temporary Differences:

Taxes payable = $2,000 taxable income × 35%	700
Deferred tax asset = $500 temporary difference × 35%	(175)
Deferred tax liability = $1,000 temporary difference × 35%	350
Income tax expense	$850

Note that, as in panel A, the income tax expense of $850 is affected by changes in the deferred tax liability and asset accounts and there is no attempt to directly match the relationship of tax expense to pretax income.

---

3   THE LIABILITY METHOD: SFAS 109 AND IAS 12

The central accounting issue is whether the tax effects of transactions for which GAAP-based and tax-based accounting rules differ should be recognized in the period(s) in which they affect taxable income (in which case no deferred taxes would be recognized) or in the period(s) in which they are recognized in the financial statements (giving rise to deferred taxes). These alternatives produce different measures of operating and financial performance, affecting the evaluation of a firm's operating performance and earning power. Cash flows for taxes are not affected by financial reporting choices except when conformity between tax and financial reporting is required.

Both U.S. and IAS standards are based on the liability method, which is consistent with the second alternative.[2] This method measures the balance sheet deferred tax assets and liabilities first, under the assumption that temporary differences will reverse. Income tax expense reflects both the effect of any current period pretax income and future changes in the tax rate used to measure the tax effect of tax expense resulting from those reversals.

Accounting for taxes in the United States is based on SFAS 109 (1992), whose two objectives are to recognize:

1. Taxes payable or refundable for the current year
2. The deferred tax liabilities and assets (adjusted for recoverability) measured as the future tax consequences of events that have been recognized in financial statements or tax returns

---

[2] The deferral method (also consistent with the second alternative) measures income tax expense first. Changes in deferred tax assets and liabilities result *only* from current year deferred tax expense. These assets and liabilities are based on tax rates when they originated; the effect of tax rate changes is recognized only when timing differences actually reverse.

SFAS 109 recognizes the deferred tax consequences of *temporary differences*.[3] Deferred tax assets (adjusted for recoverability) and liabilities are calculated directly and reported on the balance sheet; *deferred income tax expense* used to determine reported income is a consequence of the resulting balance sheet amounts.

IAS 12 (2000) is also based on the liability method, with minor differences. Those differences are explained in the "Financial Reporting Outside the United States" section of this reading.

Deferred Tax Liabilities

SFAS 109 emphasizes tax liabilities, focusing on the balance sheet. *The standard mandates the recognition of deferred tax liabilities for all temporary differences expected to generate net taxable amounts in future years.*

The FASB argued that deferred tax consequences of temporary differences that will result in net taxable amounts in future years meet the SFAC 6 definition of liabilities.[4] The board contended that deferred taxes are legal obligations imposed by tax laws and temporary differences will affect taxable income in future years as they reverse.

Treatment of Operating Losses

Operating losses are due to an excess of tax deductions over taxable revenues. Tax losses can be carried back to prior years to obtain refunds of taxes paid; the impact of the carryback on income tax expense is recognized in the loss period because it can be measured and is recoverable.

Tax losses may also be carried forward to future periods if insufficient taxes were paid during the carryback period or the firm would lose valuable tax credits if losses were carried back to that period. Because the realization of *tax loss carryforwards* depends on future taxable income, the expected benefits are recognized as deferred tax assets. Under SFAS 109, such assets are recognized in full but a *valuation allowance* may be required if recoverability is unlikely.

Deferred Tax Assets and the Valuation Allowance

SFAS 109 is permissive regarding the recognition of deferred tax assets whenever deductible temporary differences generate an operating loss or tax credit carryforward. However, management (and its auditors) must defend recognition of

---

[3] This concept extends beyond chronological (timing) differences (e.g., earlier recognition of revenues and expenses on either the financial statements or tax returns), and also includes certain other events that result in differences between the tax bases of assets and liabilities and their carrying amounts in financial statements. Such differences arise when

1. The tax basis of an asset is reduced by tax credits.
2. Investment tax credits are deferred and amortized.
3. The tax basis of a foreign subsidiary's assets is increased as a result of indexing.
4. The carrying amounts and tax bases of assets differ in purchase method acquisitions.

[4] A common temporary difference is a firm's use of longer depreciation lives for financial reporting than for tax return reporting, creating a difference between the carrying amount of the asset and its tax basis. Use of the asset in operations results in taxable income in the year(s) no depreciation can be recorded on the tax return. The board acknowledged that other events may offset the net taxable amounts that would be generated when temporary differences reverse, but because those events have not yet occurred, and they are not assumed in the financial statements, their tax consequences should not be recognized. See SFAS 109 (paras. 75–79) for more discussion of this issue.

all deferred tax assets. A valuation allowance reducing the deferred tax asset is required if an analysis of the sources of future taxable income suggests that it is more likely than not that some portion or all of the deferred tax asset will not be realized.[5]

Example 44-1

Bethlehem Steel [BS] reported a net deferred tax asset at December 31, 2000 of about $985 million ($1,325 million less a valuation allowance of $340 million). This asset equaled 88% of stockholders' equity on that date. The company provided a valuation allowance equal to 50% of the deferred tax asset related to operating loss carryforwards and some temporary differences. BS stated,

> Based on our current outlook for 2001 and beyond, we believe that our net deferred tax asset will be realized by future operating results, asset sales, and tax planning opportunities.[6]

In the quarter ended June 30, 2001, however, BS recognized a 100% valuation allowance for its deferred tax assets, increasing income tax expense and net loss for the quarter by $1,009 million ($7.77 per diluted share) and for the first half of 2001 by $984 million ($7.58 per diluted share). Mainly due to the increased valuation allowance, Bethlehem's equity at June 30, 2001 became negative. The company stated that it now expected a financial accounting and tax loss in 2001 and that the outlook for the balance of 2001 was worse than earlier anticipated. Given its record of cumulative financial accounting losses, excluding unusual items, SFAS 109 required the increased valuation allowance. This is an excellent example of how management discretion with respect to the amount and timing of recognition of the valuation allowance affords management significant opportunity to manage earnings.

Tax-planning strategies can be used to reduce required valuation allowances, but they must be disclosed. SFAS 109 provides examples of positive and negative evidence that must be weighed to determine the need for a valuation allowance and to measure the amount of the allowance.[7] *Changes in the valuation allowance are included in income from continuing operations except when they are generated by unrecognized changes in the carrying amount of assets or liabilities.*[8]

Bethlehem reported that it expected to realize the deferred tax assets from future operating results and tax planning opportunities. The

---

[5] Sources of future taxable income include existing taxable temporary differences, future taxable income net of reversing temporary differences, taxable income recognized during qualifying carry-back periods, and applicable tax-planning strategies.

[6] *Source:* Note D to 2000 financial statements.

[7] Existing contracts or backlogs expected to be profitable, appreciated assets, earnings over the past few years, and the nature (nonrecurring) of the loss would suggest that a valuation allowance is not needed. Examples of negative evidence include cumulative losses in recent years and the past inability to use loss or tax credit carryforwards.

[8] The most common example is the deferred tax assets that arise when the market value of "available-for-sale" securities is less than cost; the unrealized loss is included in equity, under SFAS 115, net of the related deferred income tax assets.

company included choices of depreciation methods and lives, sales of assets, and the timing of contributions to the pension trust fund as examples of tax-planning opportunities.

When there are significant deferred tax assets, the analyst should review the company's financial performance and its accounting choices to assess the likelihood of realization of those assets.

Financial Statement Presentation and Disclosure Requirements

Large multinational companies operate in dozens of tax jurisdictions and their financial reports must summarize their tax position for all consolidated entities. Such firms often generate deferred tax assets and liabilities in different tax jurisdictions. *SFAS 109 permits offsets of deferred tax effects only within each tax-paying component and tax jurisdiction of the firm.*

Example 44-2

Texaco reported (Note 8) a valuation allowance of $800 million at December 31, 1999, mostly related to foreign tax loss carryforwards and related book versus tax asset differences stemming from operations in Denmark. The company notes that the valuation allowance was required because these loss carryforwards are based on individual (oil and gas) fields and cannot be netted against taxable income from other fields.

Deferred tax assets and liabilities must be separated into current and noncurrent components based on the types of the assets and liabilities generating the deferral. However, deferred tax assets due to carryforwards are classified by reference to expected reversal dates. SFAS 109 specifically requires:

1. Separate disclosure of all deferred tax assets and liabilities, any valuation allowance, and the net change in that allowance for each reporting period.

2. Disclosure of any unrecognized deferred tax liability for the undistributed earnings of domestic or foreign subsidiaries and joint ventures. These disclosures should facilitate the comparison of the operating results of firms that have different policies with respect to deferred tax recognition or the remission of income from such affiliates.

3. Disclosure of the current-year tax effect of each type of temporary difference.

4. Disclosure of the components of income tax expense.

5. Reconciliation of reported income tax expense with the amount based on the statutory income tax rate (the reconciliation can use either amounts or percentages of pre-tax income).

6. Disclosure of tax loss carryforwards and credits.

These six requirements determine income tax disclosures in financial statements, the raw material for the analysis provided later in this reading.

4   DEFERRED TAXES: ANALYTICAL ISSUES

Estimates of the firm's future cash flows and earning power and the analysis of financial leverage must consider changes in deferred tax assets and liabilities, deferred tax expense, and any changes in the valuation allowance. *The key analytic issue is whether the deferred tax assets and liabilities will reverse in the future. If they will not, then it is highly debatable whether deferred taxes are assets or liabilities (that is, have cash flow consequences); it may be more appropriate to consider them as decreases or increases to equity.*

To resolve that issue, we need to understand the factors that determine the level of and trends in reported deferred taxes, to decide whether they are assets (or liabilities) and to evaluate their expected cash consequences.

Factors Influencing the Level and Trend of Deferred Taxes

In general, temporary differences originated by individual transactions will reverse and offset future taxable income and tax payments. However, *these reversals may be offset by other transactions, for example, newly originating temporary differences.* The cash consequences of deferred tax debits and credits depend on the following factors:

► Future tax rates and tax laws
► Changes in accounting methods
► The firm's growth rate (real or nominal)
► Nonrecurring items and equity adjustments

We discuss these factors next.

Effects of Changes in Tax Laws and Accounting Methods

Management incentives for choosing revenue and expense recognition methods on the tax return and financial statements differ, as mentioned previously. Choices (and subsequent changes) of tax and/or accounting methods determine taxes payable, income tax expense, and both the amounts and rate of change of reported deferred tax balances.

Under the liability method,[9] when a new tax law is enacted its effects must be recognized immediately. Thus, lower tax rates will reduce deferred tax liabilities and assets, and the adjustment is included in current-period income tax expense. Assuming a net deferred tax liability, equity will increase. The larger the net deferred tax liability, the greater the impact of the tax cut, as previous-year deferrals are adjusted to the lower rate. For analytical purposes, one need not wait for the actual tax change to be enacted; estimates can be made when legislation is proposed.

Changes in GAAP can also significantly impact deferred taxes. For example, in 1992, many companies adopted SFAS 106, Accounting for Postretirement Benefits Other Than Pensions. That standard required accrual accounting for postretirement costs (mainly medical benefits for current employees after retire-

---

[9] See the illustration in Exhibit 44-B3 of Box 44-2.

ment) rather than cash-basis accounting. As cash-basis accounting was used for income tax purposes, there was no temporary difference associated with these benefits prior to the adoption of SFAS 106.

Example 44-3

Upon adoption of SFAS 106 in 1992, DuPont recognized a postretirement benefit liability of $5.9 billion and deferred tax asset of $2.1 billion. Was this $2.1 billion an asset? Would it reduce future taxes? The answers depend on the $5.9 billion liability associated with it. Eight years later, at December 31, 2000, DuPont's postretirement benefit liability was $5.76 billion. Benefits paid exceeded cost recognized in both 1999 and 2000, reducing the liability. Assuming this trend continues, DuPont will realize the deferred tax asset, but over a very long time period. A fair-value balance sheet should recognize the discounted present value of the deferred tax asset rather than its gross amount.

Thus, *realization of a deferred tax asset or liability depends on the realization of the temporary difference that created it.*

Effect of the Growth Rate of the Firm

For most firms, the deferred tax liability grows over time; temporary differences do not reverse on balance.[10] For growing firms, increased or higher-cost investments in fixed assets result in ever-increasing deferred tax liabilities due to the use of accelerated depreciation methods for tax reporting.

Exhibit 44-1 illustrates this effect by focusing on the deferred tax consequences of depreciation differences. Assume that a firm purchases one machine each year for $6,000 and uses the straight-line depreciation method over two years on its tax return and over three years in its financial statements. If we assume a 40% tax rate and zero residual value on both the tax return and the financial statements, the depreciation differences will produce a deferred tax expense (a deferred tax liability) of $400 in each year during the first two years of each machine's operation, with a reversal of $800 in its third year to eliminate the deferred tax liability generated over the first two years.

The acquisition of a second machine in year 2 generates another difference of $400; the deferred tax liability increases to $1,200 at the end of year 2. In year 3, the firm acquires and uses the third machine, originating its first-year temporary difference, and the asset acquired in year 2 originates its second-year difference. However, these originating differences are offset by the reversal of the

---

[10] This statement may not apply to deferred tax assets. Deferred tax assets (more precisely, prepaid taxes) stem from both recurring transactions (such as deferred revenues, warranty expenses, management compensation, employee benefits, and bad-debt reserves), and from more irregular events (such as restructuring costs, impairments, environmental remediation obligations, and provisions for litigation losses) that are accrued on the financial statements prior to their deduction on the tax return.

Management often has substantial discretion over the amount and timing of the origination of these debit balances as it controls the recognition of these expenses. However, the amount and timing of their reversal may not be as discretionary or predictable as the temporary differences (such as depreciation differences) that generate deferred tax liabilities.

EXHIBIT 44-1	Impact of Growth on Deferred Tax Liability

Assumptions

A firm purchases one machine during each year of operation. All other assumptions are identical to those used in Exhibit 44-B1. Most important, temporary differences are originated and reversed as in Exhibit 44-B1 and at the same tax rate, which is assumed to remain constant over time.

Deferred Tax Liability

Year 1	$ 400	Machine 1 (origination)
Year 2	400	Beginning balance
	400	Machine 1 (origination)
	400	Machine 2 (origination)
Year 3	$1,200	Beginning balance
	(800)	Machine 1 (reversal)
	400	Machine 2 (origination)
	400	Machine 3 (origination)
Year 4	$1,200	Beginning balance
	(800)	Machine 2 (reversal)
	400	Machine 3 (origination)
	400	Machine 4 (origination)
Year 5	$1,200	Beginning balance

Note: The balance stabilizes at $1,200 in this example at the end of year 3, with the originations exactly offset by the reversals. This result assumes constant levels of asset acquisitions, price levels, tax rates, and regulations. Increases in either price levels or acquisitions would result in rising balances of deferred tax liabilities.

accumulated temporary differences on the machine acquired in year 1 as it is depreciated in the financial statements, but no depreciation remains to be recorded for the asset on the tax return.

The deferred tax liability remains $1,200 and *stabilizes at that level* if asset acquisitions, depreciation methods, and tax rates and tax laws remain unchanged. Increased asset purchases above present levels (either in physical quantity or due to higher prices) would result in a growing deferred tax liability as originations exceeded reversals. Thus, as a result of growth, either in real or nominal terms, the net deferred tax liability will increase over time; *in effect, it will never be paid.*

If the firm reduces its acquisition of fixed assets and reversals exceed originations, the related deferred tax liability will decline. The cash consequences of this scenario, however, are uncertain. If the decrease in asset acquisitions results from declining product demand, then lower asset acquisitions may be accompanied by poor profitability. Without taxable income, the deferred taxes will never be paid. Alternatively, the firm may originate other temporary differences that offset depreciation reversals; in the aggregate, deferred tax liabilities may not decline.

The cash consequences of reversing temporary differences, therefore, depend on both future profitability and other activities of the firm that affect future taxable income.

Effects of Nonrecurring Items and Equity Adjustments

The following may also affect income tax expense, taxes paid, and deferred tax assets and liabilities:

▶ Nonrecurring items

▶ Extraordinary items

▶ Accounting changes

▶ Equity adjustments

Nonrecurring items (such as restructuring charges) may have future as well as current-period tax consequences, and complicate the analysis of the firm's tax position. Texaco, for example, reported restructuring changes in 1999, as detailed throughout its MD&A. These charges generated deferred tax assets.

Extraordinary items, such as a loss from the early retirement of debt, are reported after tax; the tax effect is often shown separately in the tax footnote. Transition effects of accounting changes often generate deferred tax effects, especially when the new method is not a permitted method of tax reporting. The large deferred tax asset resulting from the adoption of SFAS 106 (as discussed using DuPont) is a typical example.

Finally, equity adjustments that bypass the income statement may have current and deferred tax consequences. Common examples include:

▶ Unrealized gains or losses on marketable securities

▶ Currency translation adjustments

The items discussed previously may obscure the cash and deferred tax effects of continuing operations. Although firms generally disclose their associated tax effect, discerning their cash and deferred tax impact may require careful reading of the tax footnote supplemented by discussions with management.

Liability or Equity?

How should analysts treat deferred tax liabilities in the analysis of a firm's solvency?

As indicated previously, changes in a firm's operations or tax laws may result in deferred taxes that are never paid (or recovered). Moreover, a firm's growth may continually generate deferred tax liabilities. Even if temporary differences do reverse, future losses may forestall tax payments. These factors suggest that, in many cases, deferred taxes are unlikely to be paid.

Even if deferred taxes are eventually paid, the present value of those payments is considerably lower than the stated amounts. Thus, the deferred tax liability should be discounted at an appropriate interest rate.[11]

These arguments suggest that the components of the deferred tax liability should be analyzed to evaluate the likelihood of reversal or continued growth. Only those components that are likely to reverse should be considered a liability.[12] In addition, the liability should be discounted to its present value based on

---

[11] Discounting of deferred taxes is not allowed under either U.S. or IAS GAAP and is rare elsewhere. It is currently allowed in the Netherlands; however, few firms discount. The UK accounting standard FRS 19, Deferred Tax, permits but does not require discounting of deferred tax liabilities (only for the time value of money) that are not expected to settle for some time.

[12] Prior to the issuance of FRS 19, Deferred Tax, the United Kingdom allowed partial allocation and deferred taxes were recognized only when reversal was expected within the foreseeable future.

an estimate of the year(s) of reversal. If the temporary differences giving rise to deferred tax liabilities are not expected to reverse, those amounts should not be considered liabilities.

SFAS 109 requires disclosure of the components of the deferred tax liability at each year-end. These components should be examined over time to see which tend to reverse and which do not. For example, the effect of using accelerated depreciation methods for tax reporting tends not to reverse.[13] If reversal is expected, as capital expenditures decline, the liability should be discounted to present value. Similar analysis can be applied to other major differences, keeping in mind any expected tax law changes.

To the extent that deferred taxes are not a liability, then they are stockholders' equity. Had they not been recorded, prior-period tax expense would have been lower and both net income and equity higher. This adjustment reduces the debt-to-equity ratio, in some cases considerably.[14]

In some cases, however, deferred taxes are neither liability nor equity. For example, if tax depreciation is a better measure of economic depreciation than financial statement depreciation, adding the deferred tax liability to equity overstates the value of the firm. However, if the deferred tax liability is unlikely to result in a cash outflow, it is not a liability either. Ultimately, the financial analyst must decide on the appropriate treatment of deferred taxes on a case-by-case basis.

In practice, the analytical treatment of deferred tax liabilities varies. Some creditors, notably banks, do not consider them to be liabilities (but neither do they include them as part of equity). In calculating solvency and other ratios, many analysts ignore deferred taxes altogether.

Standard and Poor's, a major U.S. rating agency, includes noncurrent deferred taxes in permanent capital for its computation of pretax return on permanent capital. However, it does not consider deferred tax liabilities as debt.[15].

Box 44-3 discusses evidence provided by market research regarding the relevance of deferred taxes to securities valuation. The evidence indicates that the market incorporates the growth rate of an entity, the probability of reversal of deferred taxes, and the time value of money in its assessment of deferred taxes as liability or equity.

Analysis of Deferred Tax Assets and the Valuation Allowance

Deferred tax assets may be indicators of future cash flow, reported income, or both. Therefore, as with liabilities, one should examine the source of those assets and evaluate the likelihood and timing of reversal. Any valuation allowance should also be reviewed. To the extent that deferred tax assets have been offset by a valuation

---

[13] However, the recognition of fixed asset impairment (see the discussion in Reading 43) may instantaneously offset many years of accelerated depreciation. Such writedowns do not affect tax reporting unless the affected assets are sold. As a result, previously established deferred tax liabilities relating to these assets reverse. If the carrying value of the impaired assets is reduced below their tax basis, deferred tax assets must be established. But this reversal has no effect on taxable income or, therefore, taxes payable. This is another case where the reversal of temporary differences may not generate income tax cash outflows.

[14] Some creditors treat deferred tax liabilities as debt. In this case, there is a double effect; debt is decreased and equity increased by the same amount, with an even greater decrease in the debt-to-equity ratio.

[15] See Standard and Poor's "Formulas for Key Ratios," *Corporate Ratings Criteria* (New York: McGraw-Hill, 2000), p. 55.

BOX 44-3   VALUATION OF DEFERRED TAXES

Surprisingly, not many empirical studies have examined whether the market as a whole treats deferred taxes as debt. However, the results of those few studies that examined this issue are consistent with our view that the extent to which deferred tax liabilities should be treated as debt is a function of the probability that the deferrals will be reversed and the debt (if considered) should be discounted to its present value.

Amir, Kirschenheiter, and Willard (1997) found that, overall, deferred taxes are value relevant in explaining the cross-sectional variation in market values of equity. However, the degree of value relevance was related to the probability of future reversal. For example, the valuation coefficient on deferred tax liabilities arising from depreciation was close to zero, reflecting investors' expectations that firms would continue to invest in depreciable assets, increasing the likelihood that tax deferrals would not reverse in the future. On the other hand, deferred tax components related to restructurings had the highest valuation coefficients, consistent with an expectation that they would reverse in the short run (as written-down plants are sold at a loss and/or severance payments are made to employees).

Givoly and Hayn (1992) examined these issues in the context of the Tax Reform Act (TRA) of 1986. The TRA cut the statutory tax rate for U.S. corporations from 46% to 34%. This rate reduction reduced both the current tax obligation and the amount that would have to be repaid if and when future reversals of temporary differences occurred.

The TRA was debated for over two years in Congress. Givoly and Hayn examined the effects on stock prices of events that increased (decreased) the chance of the measure passing. After controlling for the effects on current tax payments, they argued that if the market treated the deferred tax liability as debt, then:

1. The larger the deferred tax liability, the more positive the impact of the TRA on the firm's market price.

2. If temporary differences will not be reversed, or future tax losses will result in nonpayment of the tax at reversal, the effects of the TRA should be minimal regardless of the liability amount. Thus, they argued that the larger the growth rate in the deferred tax account and the greater the probability of tax losses; the less likely there would be a positive impact on stock prices.

If the market ignored the deferred tax liability, none of these factors would have any impact. Overall, their results confirmed that the market incorporated the deferred tax liability into valuation.

When chances of the TRA adoption increased (decreased), then:

1. The larger the deferred tax liability, the more positive (negative) the market reaction.

2. A high liability growth rate and increased probability of losses decreased (increased) the abnormal return.

Givoly and Hayn also found that the market incorporated a discount factor in valuing the deferred tax liability. The deferred tax accounts of high-risk* firms tended to affect market valuation less than low-risk firms. This result is consistent with a higher discount rate being applied to the higher-risk firms.

Sansing (1998), and Guenther and Sansing (2000), however, using a theoretical model, demonstrate analytically that deferred taxes should have value-relevance[†] *irrespective of the probability of eventual reversal.* However, the valuation coefficient on

(continued)

BOX 44-3   *(continued)*

deferred taxes (which in their model is a function of the tax depreciation rate and the (market) rate of interest) is *considerably less than one*. Thus, they argue that the findings of Amir et al. and Givoly and Hayn should not be interpreted as reflecting the effects of the expected timing of the reversal of deferred taxes.

The above studies took a balance sheet perspective and found that deferred taxes are incorporated in valuation. Beaver and Dukes (1972), with an income statement perspective, had also found that market prices reflect the deferral method. They found that market reaction was more closely associated with income that incorporated deferred income taxes than with current tax expense.[‡] Rayburn (1986), however, found that the association between deferred tax accruals and security returns was dependent on the expectations model assumed.

---

* Based on the firm's market beta.

† Their reasoning is that, according to their model, the market (resale) value of the asset includes the tax basis of the asset. Deferred taxes reflect this factor, although not on a dollar-for-dollar basis.

‡ The authors found this result surprising as they expected the measure closer to cash flow (earnings without deferral) to be more closely associated with security prices. In a subsequent paper (Beaver and Dukes, 1973) the authors offered a different explanation. They demonstrated (see the discussion in Reading 43) that the market generally imputes accelerated depreciation rather than straight-line depreciation. As deferred taxes increase total expense for firms using straight-line depreciation, they argued that the observed results may be due to deferred taxes masking as a form of accelerated depreciation.

OPTIONAL SEGMENT ENDS

allowance, realization of those assets will increase reported income (and stockholders' equity) as well as generate cash flow. If no valuation allowance has been provided, then realization will have no effect on reported income or equity, although cash flow will still benefit.

Conversely, when deferred tax assets are no longer realizable, if no valuation allowance had been provided, then the establishment of such an allowance reduces reported income and equity (see the Bethlehem Steel example earlier in the reading).

Given management discretion, the valuation allowance has become another factor used to evaluate the quality of earnings. Some firms are conservative, offsetting most or all deferred tax assets with valuation allowances. Other firms are more optimistic and assume that no valuation allowance is necessary.

The important point is that changes in the valuation allowance often affect reported earnings and can be used to manage them.

Example 44-4

Apple Computer had recorded a significant valuation allowance against its deferred tax assets due to losses in the mid-1990s. With its return to profitability, it realized its loss carryforwards, reducing both deferred tax assets and the valuation allowance. The result was to lower the effective tax rate, as seen on the following page:

Apple Computer	Years Ended September 30			Percent Change	
Amounts in $millions	**1998**	**1999**	**2000**	**1999**	**2000**
As reported:					
Pretax income	$329	$ 676	$1,092	105%	62%
Income tax expense	(20)	(75)	(306)		
Net income	$309	$ 601	$ 786	94%	31%
Tax rate	6.1%	11.1%	28.0%		
Change in valuation allowance	$(97)	$(153)	$ (27)		
Excluding valuation allowance:					
Pretax income	$329	$ 676	$1,092	105%	62%
Income tax expense	(117)	(228)	(333)		
Net income	$212	$ 448	$ 759	111%	69%
Tax rate	35.6%	33.7%	30.5%		

Apple's pretax income increased by 105% in 1999 and 62% in 2000. The growth rate of net income was lower due to the diminishing effect of the valuation allowance. However, net income was inflated by the valuation allowance reductions. To eliminate these distortions, analysis should be based on net income excluding changes in the valuation allowance.

Effective Tax Rates

Valuation models that forecast future income or cash flows use the firm's effective tax rate as one input. Moreover, trends in effective tax rates over time for a firm and the relative effective tax rates for comparable firms within an industry can help assess operating performance and the income available for stockholders. Several alternative measures can be used to assess the firm's effective tax rate. The *reported* effective tax rate is measured as:

$$\frac{\text{Income tax expense}}{\text{Pretax income}}$$

However, both reported tax expense and pretax income are affected by management choices of revenue and expense recognition methods. Although pretax income is a key indicator of financial performance and is an appropriate denominator, other numerators generate tax rates that provide additional information.[16]

---

[16] Some empirical evidence (see Zimmerman, 1983) indicates that effective tax rates calculated using income tax paid and/or current tax expense tend to be higher for large firms. This is cited as evidence of the political cost hypothesis as large firms, being more politically sensitive, are required to make (relatively) larger wealth transfers than smaller firms. As the research results are largely due to the oil and gas industry, it is difficult to tell whether political costs result from size or industrial classification. Wang (1991) notes that because smaller firms are more likely to have operating losses than larger firms, their effective tax rate is more likely to be zero. Ignoring these losses may bias Zimmerman's research results.

The first alternative tax rate uses taxes payable (current tax expense) for the period, based on the revenue and the expense recognition methods used on the tax return:

$$\frac{\text{Taxes payable}}{\text{Pretax income}}$$

This ratio may also be used with cash taxes paid instead of taxes payable. The resulting ratio focuses more on cash flows:

$$\frac{\text{Income tax paid}}{\text{Pretax income}}$$

The amount of cash taxes paid can be easily obtained as both SFAS 95 (Statement of Cash Flows) and IAS 7 (Cash Flow Statements) require separate disclosure of this amount. Due to interim tax payments and refunds, cash taxes paid may be quite different from taxes payable.

Exhibit 44-2 calculates these differing measures of the effective tax rate for Pfizer.

Pfizer's reported effective tax rate (income tax expense/pretax income) rose from 27.0% in 1997 to 28% in 1999; the three-year average rate is 26.9%. All these rates are below the U.S. statutory rate for the period.[17]

Two questions are suggested by these data:

1. Why is Pfizer's effective tax rate below the statutory rate?

2. What is Pfizer's effective tax rate likely to be in the future?

We seek answers to these questions shortly.

EXHIBIT 44-2	Pfizer			

Effective Tax Rates

	1997	1998	1999	Total
Taxes payable	$ 815	$ 918	$1,265	$2,998
Deferred tax expense	(40)	(276)	(21)	(337)
Income tax expense	$ 775	$ 642	$1,244	$2,661
Income taxes paid	809	1,073	1,293	3,175
Pretax income	2,867	2,594	4,448	9,909
Statutory tax rate	35.0%	35.0%	35.0%	35.0%
Income tax expense/pretax income	27.0%	24.7%	28.0%	26.9%
Taxes payable/pretax income	28.4%	35.4%	28.4%	30.3%
Taxes paid/pretax income	28.2%	41.4%	29.1%	32.0%

Source: Data from Pfizer annual reports.

---

[17] The average statutory rate for a multiyear period should be a weighted average, with pretax income providing the weights.

The second effective tax rate (taxes payable/pretax income) calculated in Exhibit 44-2 was 35.4% in 1998 and 28.4% in both 1997 and 1999. The average rate is 30.3% over the three-year period, above the first effective rate and below the statutory rate. Again, we will try to understand the factors causing these differences and the likelihood that they will persist in the future.

The third measure of the effective tax rate, which compares income tax paid with pretax income, is also variable over the three-year period. The average rate of 32.0% is close to the average rate for taxes payable. This congruence should be expected as the timing of taxes paid is affected by technical payment requirements and by errors in management's forecast of tax liability in each jurisdiction. Over time, these factors should cancel out.

We return to the analysis of Pfizer's income tax position shortly. To provide additional background for that analysis, we must first discuss the effect of temporary versus permanent differences on effective tax rates and other specialized issues that highlight differences between tax and financial reporting.

ACCOUNTING FOR TAXES: SPECIALIZED ISSUES   5

Temporary versus Permanent Differences

The different objectives of financial and tax reporting generate temporary differences between pretax financial income and taxable income. In addition, *permanent differences* result from revenues and expenses that are reportable either on tax returns or in financial statements but not both. In the United States, for example, interest income on tax-exempt bonds, premiums paid on officers' life insurance, and amortization of goodwill (in some cases) are included in financial statements but are never reported on the tax return. Similarly, certain dividends are not fully taxed, and tax or statutory depletion may exceed cost-based depletion reported in the financial statements.

Tax credits are another type of permanent difference. Such credits directly reduce taxes payable and are different from tax deductions that reduce taxable income. The Puerto Rico operations credit reported by Pfizer is one example. It partially exempts Pfizer from income, property, and municipal taxes.

No deferred tax consequences are recognized for permanent differences; however, they result in a difference between the effective tax rate and the statutory tax rate that should be considered in the analysis of effective tax rates.

Indefinite Reversals

The amount and timing of the reversal of some temporary differences are subject to management influence or control. Some differences may never reverse. The accounting for these differences is especially troublesome. The uncertainty as to the amount and timing of their cash consequences affects the estimation of cash flows and firm valuation.

The undistributed earnings of unconsolidated subsidiaries and joint ventures are the most common example of this problem. The U.S. tax code requires 80% ownership to consolidate for tax purposes, excluding joint ventures and many subsidiaries that are consolidated for accounting purposes. In addition, foreign subsidiaries are not consolidated in the U.S. tax return.[18]

---

[18] In some cases, even wholly owned U.S. subsidiaries may not be consolidated for tax purposes. Insurance subsidiaries, which are governed by special tax regulations, are one example.

As a result, the income of these affiliates is taxable on the parent's (U.S.) tax return only when dividends are received or the affiliate is sold, not when earnings are recognized. There is a difference between (tax return) taxable income and (financial reporting) pretax income. If the affiliate earnings are permanently reinvested, then affiliate earnings may never be taxable on the parent company's tax return.

SFAS 109 requires the recognition of deferred tax liabilities for temporary differences due to the undistributed earnings of essentially permanent domestic subsidiaries and joint ventures for fiscal years beginning on or after December 15, 1992.[19] SFAS 109 does not, however, require deferred tax provisions in the following cases:

▶ Undistributed earnings of a foreign subsidiary or joint venture that are considered to be permanently reinvested.

▶ Undistributed earnings of a domestic subsidiary or joint venture for fiscal years prior to December 15, 1992.

In its income tax note (Note 9), Pfizer reports that the firm has not recorded a U.S. tax provision of $1.9 billion on $8.2 billion of undistributed earnings of foreign affiliates at December 31, 1999. If the indefinite reversal assumption had not been applicable, the firm would have reported $1.9 billion of additional deferred tax liabilities, reducing equity by 21%. Earnings would also have been reduced in the years during which those provisions were not made.

Accounting for Acquisitions

SFAS 109 requires separate recognition of the deferred tax effects of any differences between the financial statement carrying amounts and tax bases of assets and liabilities recognized in purchase method acquisitions.

In some cases, a valuation allowance must be recorded for deferred tax assets due to the acquired firm's temporary differences or its operating loss or tax credit carryforwards. The tax benefits of subsequent reversals of the valuation allowance must be used, first, to reduce all related goodwill, second, to eliminate all other related noncurrent intangible assets, and third, to reduce reported income tax expense.

6   ANALYSIS OF INCOME TAX DISCLOSURES: PFIZER

Accounting for income taxes is complex; a large company may have many permanent and temporary differences between financial statement income and taxable income. A large multinational pays taxes in a number of jurisdictions, further complicating the process. From an analyst's perspective, unraveling these layers can seem daunting indeed.

Some analysts respond to this complexity by ignoring the issues. They analyze corporate performance on a pretax basis and simply accept that variations in the reported tax rate occur. We agree that analysis on a pretax basis is sound, but also believe that a firm's income tax accounting is too important to ignore.

---

[19] But if the parent has the statutory ability to realize those earnings tax free, no deferred tax provision is required (para. 33, SFAS 109).

The goals of income tax analysis are to:

1. Understand why the firm's effective tax rate differs (or does not differ) from the statutory rate in its home country.
2. Forecast changes in the effective tax rate, improving forecasts of earnings.
3. Review the historical differences between income tax expense and income taxes paid.
4. Forecast the future relationship between income tax expense and income tax payments.
5. Examine deferred tax liabilities and assets, including any valuation allowance, for

   ▶ Possible effects on future earnings and cash flows

   ▶ Their relevance to firm valuation

   ▶ Their relevance in assessing a firm's capital structure

We pursue these five goals, using Pfizer as an example, and illustrate the insights regarding a firm that can be derived from its income tax disclosures.

Analysis of the Effective Tax Rate

The first step is an examination of the firm's tax rate, the trend in that rate, and the rate relative to similar companies. Variations are generally the consequence of:

▶ Different statutory tax rates in different jurisdictions; analysis can offer important clues as to the sources of income.

▶ Tax holidays that some countries offer; earnings from such operations usually cannot be remitted without payment of tax. Be alert to possible changes in the operations in such countries or the need to remit the accumulated earnings.

▶ Permanent differences between financial and taxable income: tax-exempt income, tax credits, and nondeductible expenses.

▶ The effect of tax rate and other tax law changes which, under SFAS 109, are included in income tax expense (a separate disclosure of this effect is required).

▶ Deferred taxes provided on the reinvested earnings of foreign affiliates and unconsolidated domestic affiliates.

As noted earlier, Pfizer's effective tax rate averaged 26.9% over the 1997 to 1999 period. Pfizer's tax footnote provides the required reconciliation between its statutory rate and effective rate for each year.[20] Because of the significance of some of these differences and variation in pretax income over the period, the rate-based disclosures are difficult to analyze. For that reason, Exhibit 44-3 converts them to dollar-based disclosures.

Starting with the three-year totals, the lower tax rate on non-U.S. earnings is the largest single factor in Pfizer's low effective tax rate, deducting nearly $500 million or 5 percentage points over the three-year period. Pfizer's international

---

[20] The reconciliation can be done in either percentages (relative to the statutory tax rate) or monetary amounts (relative to "statutory" income tax expense equal to pretax income multiplied by the statutory rate).

EXHIBIT 44-3	Pfizer

Reconciliation of Effective and Statutory Tax Rates

	1997	1998	1999	1997 to 1999	
				Total	**Rate**
Pretax income	$2,867	$2,594	$4,448	$9,909	
Statutory rate	35.0%	35.0%	35.0%		35.0%
Variations from Statutory Rate (in percent)					
Partially tax-exempt operations in Puerto Rico	−1.8%	−2.2%	−1.5%		
International operations	−5.0%	−5.5%	−4.8%		
Other-net	−1.2%	−2.5%	−0.7%		
Net difference	−8.0%	−10.2%	−7.0%		
Effective tax rate (Income tax expense/ pretax income)	27.0%	24.7%	28.0%		
Tax in millions of dollars = Rate × Pretax Income					
At statutory rate	$1,003.5	$ 907.9	$1,556.8	$3,468.1	
Effect of					
Partially tax-exempt operations in Puerto Rico	$ (51.6)	$ (57.1)	$ (66.7)	$ (175.4)	−1.8%
International operations	(143.4)	(142.7)	(213.5)	(499.5)	−5.0%
Other-net	(34.4)	(64.9)	(31.1)	(130.4)	−1.3%
Net effect	$ (229.4)	$(264.6)	$ (311.4)	$ (805.3)	−8.1%
Income tax expense	$ 774.1	$ 643.3	$1,245.4	$2,662.8	26.9%

Source: Adapted from Pfizer, Note 9, 1999 annual report.

operations accounted for 39% of revenues and 42.5% of income from continuing operations in 1999, as shown in Pfizer's segment data. Thus, Pfizer's low effective tax rate is largely a function of its non-U.S. operations. Forecasting future effective tax rates, therefore, requires explicit forecasts of the earnings of these operations.

Pfizer's effective tax rate also benefits from lower tax rates paid by partially tax-exempt operations in Puerto Rico. This factor reduced the composite three-year tax rate by nearly two percentage points, adding $175 million to net income. Pfizer provides additional data regarding these operations, permitting a determination of the remaining benefits. Unexplained "other" benefits averaging 1.5 percentage points per year (but with considerable variability) further reduce the effective tax rate. Discussion with management should result in a better understanding of the source and likelihood of continuation of these benefits.

The Belgian tax assessment[21] and the limited term of the Puerto Rican tax exemption suggest that significant contributors to Pfizer's lower effective tax rate may not be available in the future.

Now that we understand the reasons for Pfizer's low effective tax rate in the past, we turn to the future. A forecast of future income tax expense should start with estimated pretax income and apply the statutory rate of 35%. The analyst should then adjust for:

▶ Effects of the lower tax rate on foreign income

▶ Effects of the lower tax rate on U.S. possession operations

▶ "Other" effects

These adjustments may require input from Pfizer management or trade publications. Some firms provide periodic forecasts of their tax rate because of the difficulty of making such forecasts externally.

Analysis of Deferred Income Tax Expense

We now examine the effects of temporary differences on income tax expense. Companies are required to provide details of these differences, although formats vary. Pfizer's disclosure is typical, showing a breakdown in dollars for each year.

Temporary differences are generally the result of the use of different accounting policies or estimates for tax purposes than for financial reporting differences. Some of these differences are systematic; others are transaction specific. Frequent examples include:

▶ *Depreciation.* Different methods and/or lives result in different measures of depreciation expense.

▶ *Impairment.* Financial reporting writedowns do not generate tax deductions unless assets are sold.

▶ *Restructuring costs.* Usually tax-deductible when paid rather than when accrued.

▶ *Inventories.* Companies using last-in, first-out (LIFO) accounting for tax purposes in the United States must also use LIFO for reporting purposes; but when other methods are used, differences may occur.

▶ *Postemployment benefits.* The accruals required by SFAS 87 (pensions), SFAS 106 (other retiree benefits), and SFAS 112 (other post-employment benefits) are discussed elsewhere. Tax treatment of these costs is generally cash based, generating deferred tax effects.

▶ *Deferred compensation.* Tax-deductible only when payments are made.

On a cumulative basis, Pfizer generated negative deferred tax expense (taxes payable > income tax expense) over the 1997 to 1999 period.[22] Depreciation generated positive deferred tax expense over this period, reflected in a rising level of deferred tax liabilities for property, plant, and equipment (PP&E). Pfizer used accelerated depreciation methods for most property on its tax return and the straight-line method on its financial statements.

---

[21] However, Pfizer may have benefited from the allocation and transfers of property to selected foreign operations. In 1994, Belgian tax authorities assessed additional taxes ($432 million) and interest ($97 million), claiming jurisdiction on certain income related to property transferred from non-Belgian subsidiaries to Pfizer's operations in Ireland.

[22] See Note 9 in Pfizer's financial statements and data in Exhibit 44-2.

Pfizer also reports deferred tax debits from PP&E, likely due to its asset impairments in both 1997 and 1998. Pfizer reports that, in 1999, it had substantially completed the restructuring announced in 1998; the deferred tax debits due to restructuring and PP&E declined in 1999 after increasing in 1998. *When a restructuring charge is taken, the tax effects generally occur as expenditures are made, with significant effects on deferred tax expense both in the year of the charge and the year(s) of payment.*

Pfizer's Note 9 also shows numerous other sources of deferred tax assets and liabilities, some of them poorly explained. Significant year-to-changes in deferred tax balances reflect differences between the tax and financial reporting treatment of transactions, and should be examined for their implications for cash flow and quality of earnings. The most significant deferred tax assets relate to inventories and employee benefits. There is a significant deferred tax liability for "unremitted earnings." These items are discussed in the next section as part of the analysis of deferred tax assets and liabilities.

Because Pfizer's deferred tax expense was negative over the 1997 to 1999 period, taxes payable (and income tax paid) exceeded income tax expense. Given increasing deferred tax debits for inventories, employee benefits, foreign tax credit, and other carryforwards, deferred tax expense may remain negative in the future.

Using Deferred Taxes to Estimate Taxable Income

Deferred tax expense reflects the difference between taxable income reported to tax authorities and pretax income reported to shareholders. This relationship can be used to estimate components of taxable income. The difference between taxable income and pretax income equals

$$\frac{\text{Deferred tax expense}}{\text{Statutory tax rate}}$$

For example, Pfizer's 1999 financial statement depreciation expense was $499 million (depreciation and amortization expense of $542 reported in the statement of cash flows less amortization of $43 million for goodwill and other intangibles in Note 8). The deferred tax liability related to depreciation was $514 million in 1999, an increase of $81 million over the amount reported in 1998 (Note 9). Using that amount and the statutory tax rate of 35%, we estimate that the additional depreciation expense under tax reporting was $231 million ($81 million divided by 0.35) and tax basis depreciation was $730 million ($499 + $231).

These calculations should be viewed as estimates. They are most reliable when they relate to a single tax jurisdiction as the appropriate tax rate and the difference between tax and financial reporting rules are clear. Although this method can, in theory, be used to calculate taxable income for the entire firm, such calculations for large multinationals are less reliable.

Similar calculations can be made for the cumulative financial reporting-tax differences using deferred tax asset and liability data. The calculation for Pfizer's fixed assets is shown in the next section of this reading.

Deferred tax disclosures can also be used, in some cases, to estimate the taxes paid associated with components of income and expense.

Analysis of Deferred Tax Assets and Liabilities

Our final step is an examination of the balance sheet consequences of Pfizer's income tax accounting. As required by SFAS 109, Note 9 contains a table of significant deferred tax assets and liabilities, as well as the valuation allowance, at each balance sheet date.

The most significant deferred tax asset relates to accrued employee benefits. Financial reporting rules for pension and postretirement benefits often result in large deferred tax assets. The second-largest deferred tax asset is associated with inventories, probably due to the 1999 Trovan write-off. Other contributors include prepaid/deferred items, restructuring charges, and various carryforwards. Pfizer reports a valuation allowance of $27 million at December 31, 1999 ($30 million at December 31, 1998). Note 9 says that tax credit carryforwards are the source of that allowance.

Pfizer's largest single source of deferred tax liabilities, as for most firms, is depreciation. If we assume a 35% tax rate for all depreciation-related deferred tax credits, the reporting difference can be estimated as $1.47 billion ($514/0.35) or 55% of accumulated depreciation of $2.7 billion. This is due to Pfizer's use of accelerated depreciation for tax purposes compared with straight-line for financial reporting.

Another source of large deferred tax credits is unremitted earnings of subsidiaries and joint venture affiliates that are included in financial statement income; the tax return only reflects dividends received.

Pfizer's net balance sheet debit (asset) for income tax is:

Deferred tax debits	$2,109
Less: valuation allowance	(27)
Less: deferred tax credits	(1,456)
Net debits	$ 626

Where do these debits and credits appear on Pfizer's balance sheet? The answer is: *in several places.* As required by SFAS 109, Note 9 discloses their location (in $millions):

Assets		Liabilities	
Prepaid expenses and taxes	$744		
Other assets, deferred taxes, and deferred charges	183	Deferred taxes on income	$301
Totals	$927		$301
		Net debit	$626

Is this $626 million a real asset? Or, to rephrase the question, What are the likely future cash flow effects of Pfizer's deferred tax assets and liabilities?

We begin with the largest deferred tax liability associated with accumulated depreciation. Capital expenditures have been rising (79% since 1997); unless there are decreases in capital spending, it seems unlikely that the deferred tax liability from depreciation will decline over the next few years. The trend in capital spending must, however, be monitored. Based on data available in the annual report, deferred tax credits due to unremitted earnings and other sources seem unlikely to reverse.

Pfizer's largest deferred tax asset, related to accrued employee benefits, might start to reverse at some point if employee levels stabilize or decrease. As retiree benefit payments increase, they may exceed the accrual for additional benefits earned (as in the case of DuPont, discussed earlier). The deferred tax debit from restructuring charges will reduce tax payments as severance payments are made and impaired PP&E is sold.

In total, therefore, it appears unlikely that Pfizer's deferred tax accruals will generate any significant cash flows over the next few years. In addition, given the unlikelihood of near-term reversal, the deferred tax credit should be discounted for the time value of money. The combination of these factors suggests that neither an asset nor a liability should be recognized for valuation purposes.

Other Issues in Income Tax Analysis

The following issues, although not relevant to an analysis of Pfizer, occur frequently enough to warrant brief mention:

▶ Watch for companies that report substantial income for financial reporting purposes but little or no taxes payable (implying little or no taxable income). Such differences often reflect aggressive revenue and expense recognition methods used for financial reporting, and low quality of earnings. In such cases, caution is indicated as the methods used for financial reporting purposes may be based on optimistic assumptions.[23]

▶ Look for current or pending reversals of past temporary differences. For example, a decline in capital spending may result in a greater proportion of depreciation coming from old assets that have already been heavily depreciated for tax purposes. Thus, financial reporting depreciation may exceed tax depreciation, generating a tax liability.

▶ Remember that deferred tax assets and liabilities may point to near-term cash consequences. Restructuring provisions often generate little cash or tax effect in the year they occur, but substantial effects in following years.

▶ Tax law changes may also result in the reversal of past temporary differences. In the United States, tax law changes in recent years have curtailed the use of the completed contract and installment methods for tax purposes, generating substantial tax liabilities for affected companies.

7

FINANCIAL REPORTING OUTSIDE THE UNITED STATES

As already noted, many foreign jurisdictions require conformity between financial reporting and tax reporting in separate (parent company) financial statements. In such cases, the issues discussed in this reading do not occur. That statement is no longer true, however, once consolidated statements include subsidiaries that are not consolidated for tax purposes. Given the worldwide tendency toward consolidated reporting, even firms in tax-conformity countries must grapple with the question of deferred tax accounting.

IASB Standards

IAS 12 (revised 2000) requires use of the liability method but *permits* companies to use "indefinite reversal" criteria to avoid recognizing deferred taxes on the reinvested earnings of subsidiaries, associates, and joint ventures, when both of the following conditions are met:

---

[23] Empirical evidence also suggests that firms cannot costlessly increase financial reporting income and at the same time keep taxable income very low. Mills (1998) shows that IRS audit adjustments increase as book—tax differences increase; that is, "The more book income (or tax expense) exceeds taxable income (or tax payable), the greater the proposed IRS audit adjustments."

1. The parent, investor, or venturer can control the manner and timing of the reversal of the temporary difference.

2. It is probable that the temporary difference will not reverse in the foreseeable future.

As a result, there are significant differences in the recognition of deferred tax liabilities among firms using IAS and U.S. GAAP; the latter group must record deferred taxes for the reinvested earnings of domestic affiliates. In addition, deferred taxes are based on enacted laws and rates whereas IAS 12 uses substantially enacted rates (tax rate changes that have been announced by the government but not yet enacted).

Other National Standards

Virtually all countries require the recognition of deferred taxes on temporary differences. Germany and the United Kingdom use the liability method, whereas France and Japan allow either the deferral (see footnote 2) or liability method. Most countries limit the recognition of deferred tax liabilities and few address the issue of deferred tax assets. In Switzerland, deferred taxes not expected to reverse need not be recognized and the recognition of certain deferred tax assets is discretionary.

German GAAP permits the recognition of deferred tax assets for the elimination of intercompany profits. In general, deferred taxes are computed under the liability method, but the amounts recognized are limited to the excess of consolidated deferred tax liabilities over consolidated deferred tax assets.

The accounting differences among U.S., IAS, and foreign GAAP affect reported net income and stockholders' equity (lower when deferred tax assets are unrecognized or offset by a valuation allowance). Another difficulty when comparing firms using different GAAP is the paucity of disclosure requirements in many cases. Both SFAS 109 and IAS 12 have substantial disclosure requirements; similar information is rarely available in the financial statements of most foreign countries.

Form 20-F reconciliations of reported net income and stockholders' equity show the adjustments due to differences in deferred tax accounting. These differences can be used to restore comparability between U.S. firms and foreign firms that file Form 20-F. In some cases, these adjustments can be used to approximate adjustments for firms not providing Form 20-F reconciliations, when they are similar to firms that do provide them.

Exhibit 44-4 contains disclosures provided by Cadbury Schweppes in its 2000 Form 20-F. Applying UK GAAP, the company calculated deferred tax liabilities of £105 million (1999: £93) using the partial allocation method.[24] Had it used comprehensive allocation (U.S. GAAP), it would have recorded an additional deferred tax liability of £58 million in 2000 (1999: £62 million); most of the difference is attributed to the accelerated depreciation method. No deferred tax is recorded for the effect of accelerated depreciation because it is not expected to reverse.

Although we have recommended this approach in the section "Liability or Equity" and agree that partial allocation is a logical alternative to the comprehensive allocation method, it presents two analytical problems. First, it makes Cadbury's

---

[24] The partial allocation method in UK GAAP limits the recognition of net deferred tax assets to amounts expected to be recovered without the assumption of future taxable income. The standard is permissive regarding deferred tax consequences of pension and postretirement benefits; firms may use either comprehensive or partial allocation with disclosure of the method selected.

EXHIBIT 44-4	Cadbury Schweppes

Panel A—Deferred Taxes: Partial Allocation

The analysis of the deferred tax liabilities/(assets) included in the financial statements at the end of the year is as follows:

in £millions	1999	2000
Accelerated capital allowances	£ 2	£ 3
Other timing differences	91	102
Deferred taxation liability	£93	£105

The deferred taxation liability is included in provisions for liabilities and charges. Gross deferred tax assets at year-end are £15 million (1999: £18 million). The potential liability for deferred taxation not provided comprised:

in £millions	1999	2000
UK accelerated capital allowances	£48	£77
UK property values	5	5
Other timing differences	9	(30)
	£62	£52

To the extent that dividends from overseas undertakings are expected to result in additional taxes, appropriate amounts have been provided. No taxes have been provided for other unremitted earnings since these amounts are considered permanently reinvested by subsidiary undertakings and in the case of associated undertakings the taxes would not be material. Distributable earnings retained by overseas subsidiary undertakings and the principal associated undertakings totaled approximately £846 million at 31 December 2000. The remittance of these amounts would incur tax at varying rates depending on available foreign tax credits.

Tax losses carried forward as at 31 December 2000 for offset against future earnings of overseas companies were approximately £103 million (1999: £103 million). The utilization of losses is dependent upon the level of future earnings and other limiting factors within the countries concerned. Tax losses totaling £22 million have expiration periods in 2001 and 2002, tax losses of £25 million expire in 2003 to 2012 and tax losses totaling £56 million have no **expiry** date.

(Exhibit continued on next page ...)

EXHIBIT 44-4 (continued)

Panel B—US GAAP

The US GAAP analysis of deferred tax liability is as follows:

in £millions	1999	2000
Liabilities		
Fixed asset timing differences	£ 84	£ 84
Other timing differences	71	79
	£155	£163
Assets		
Operating loss carryforwards	(37)	(37)
Less: Valuation allowance	37	37
Net deferred tax liability	£155	£163

Source: Cadbury *20-F*, December 31, 2000

financial statements not comparable to its U.S. competitors, Coca-Cola and PepsiCo, who use comprehensive allocation. Comparability can be restored either by adjusting Cadbury's income statement provision, its deferred taxes (and equity), or by converting its competitors' financial statements to the partial allocation method.

The second problem with partial allocation is management discretion that can be used to manage earnings. This discretion is comparable to that available in the application of valuation allowances under SFAS 109 and IAS 12.

In December 2000, the UK Accounting Standards Board issued FRS 19, Deferred Tax, requiring comprehensive allocation. Cadbury will most likely adopt this standard in 2002 and the resulting financial statements will be more comparable to its U.S. competitors. The UK—U.S. GAAP reconciliation in the form 20-F as it relates to deferred taxes is reproduced in Panel B of Exhibit 44-4. On December 31, 2000, the U.S. GAAP—based deferred tax liability is £163 million (1999: £152 million). This information can be used to make Cadbury's financial statements comparable to those of its U.S. competitors.

OPTIONAL SEGMENT

ENDS

SUMMARY

In this reading, we have seen how income tax expense and deferred tax assets and liabilities are affected by the accounting method used and by management choices and assumptions. As all business enterprises are subject to income tax, no financial analysis is complete until the issues raised in this reading have been examined. Analysts must examine, in particular, the effective tax rate, the cash flow effects of deferred tax accruals, and the relevance of such accruals for valuation.

PROBLEMS FOR READING 44

1. [Deferred tax classification; CFA© adapted] Explain in which of the following categories deferred taxes can be found. Provide an example for each category in your answer.

    i. Current liabilities

    ii. Long-term liabilities

    iii. Stockholders' equity

    iv. Current assets

    v. Long-term assets

2. [Deferred taxes; CFA© adapted] State which of the following statements are correct under SFAS 109. Explain why.

    i. The deferred tax liability account must be adjusted for the effect of enacted changes in tax laws or rates in the period of enactment.

    ii. The deferred tax asset account must be adjusted for the effect of enacted changes in tax laws or rates in the period of enactment

    iii. The tax consequences of an event must not be recognized until that event is recognized in the financial statements.

    iv. Both deferred tax liabilities and deferred tax assets must be accounted for based on the tax laws and rates in effect at their origin.

    v. Changes in deferred tax assets and liabilities are classified as extraordinary items in the income statement.

3. [Permanent versus temporary differences; CFA© adapted]

    A. Define *permanent differences* and describe two events or transactions that generate such differences.

    B. Describe the impact of permanent differences on a firm's effective tax rate.

4. [Treatment of deferred tax liability; CFA© adapted]

    A. When computing a firm's debt-to-equity ratio, describe the conditions for treating the deferred tax liability:

    i. As equity

    ii. As debt

    B. Provide arguments for excluding deferred tax liabilities from both the numerator and the denominator of the debt-to-equity ratio.

    C. Describe the arguments for including a portion of the deferred taxes as equity and a portion as debt.

5. [Depreciation methods and deferred taxes] The Incurious George Company acquires assets K, L, and M at the beginning of year 1. Each asset has the same cost, a five-year life, and an expected salvage value of $3,000. For financial reporting, the firm uses the straight-line, sum-of-the-years' digits, and double-declining-balance depreciation methods for assets K, L, and M, respectively. It uses the double-declining-balance method for all assets on its tax return; its tax rate is 34%. Depreciation expense of $12,000 was reported for asset L for financial reporting purposes in year 2. Using this information:

    A. Calculate the tax return depreciation expense for each asset in year 2.

    B. Calculate the financial statement depreciation expense for assets K and M in year 2.

C. Calculate the deferred tax credit (liability) or debit (asset) for each asset at the end of:

    i. Year 2

    ii. Year 5

6. [Analysis of deferred tax; CFA© adapted] On December 29, 2000, Mother Prewitt's Handmade Cookies Corp. acquires a numerically controlled chocolate chip milling machine. Due to differences in tax and financial accounting, depreciation for tax purposes is $150,000 more than depreciation in the financial statements, adding $52,500 to deferred taxes. At the same time, Mother Prewitt's sells $200,000 worth of cookies on an installment contract, recognizing the $100,000 profit immediately. For tax purposes, however, $80,000 of the profit will be recognized in 2001, requiring $27,200 of deferred taxes.

A. Compare the expected cash consequences of the two deferred tax items just described.

B. Explain your treatment of deferred taxes when calculating Mother Prewitt's solvency and leverage ratios.

C. In 2001, Mother Prewitt's tax rate will be 40%. Discuss the adjustments to *each* of the two deferred tax items in 2001 because of the change in the tax rate, assuming the use of SFAS 109.

D. Discuss the conditions under which Mother Prewitt would need to recognize a valuation allowance for any deferred tax assets.

7. [Tax effect of restructuring] Silicon Graphics [SGI] made the following announcements:

▶ 1998: restructuring charges of $144 million, including a $47 million write-down of operating assets; additional $47 million impairment of long-lived assets.

▶ 1999: $4.2 million of operating asset write-downs and a $16 million write-down of capitalized internal use software.

▶ 2000: Operating asset write-downs of $26.6 million.

The company reported the following deferred tax assets ($ thousands):

Years ended June 30	1997	1998	1999	2000
Depreciation	$57,675	$40,435	$49,226	$37,659

A. Using the U.S. statutory tax rates of 34% for 1998 and 35% for 1999 and 2000, estimate the changes in 1998, 1999, and 2000 deferred tax asset balances resulting from the write-downs of operating assets.

B. Explain why your answer to part a differs from the actual changes in the deferred tax asset during those three years.

8. [Analysis of income tax footnote data] Exhibit 44P-1 contains the income tax footnote from the *2001 Annual Report* of Honda [7267], a multinational automobile manufacturer based in Japan. *Note that these data are prepared under U.S. GAAP.*

A. Calculate the differences (in yen) between Honda's income tax expense and that expense based on the statutory rate.

B. Using your answer to part a, compute the impact on Honda's income tax expense over the 1999 to 2001 period of:

i. Changes in the valuation allowance

ii. Tax law changes

iii. Undistributed earnings of subsidiaries

C. Lower non-Japanese tax rates reduced Honda's tax expense in each year, 1999 to 2001.

    i. Discuss the trend in that reduction.

    ii. Discuss the likely explanation for that trend.

D. Discuss the factors that an analyst must consider when forecasting Honda's effective tax rate for 2002.

9. [Deferred taxes and interim reports] State Auto Financial [STFC] reported the following operating results for the first three quarters of 1991 and 1992 ($ in thousands):

	1991		
	Q1	**Q2**	**Q3**
Pretax income	$4,797	$2,600	$3,244
Income tax expense	(1,224)	(624)	(848)
Net income	$3,573	$1,976	$2,396

	1992		
	Q1	**Q2**	**Q3**
Pretax income	$1,123	$3,723	$ 98
Income tax expense	(232)	(934)	583
Net income	$ 891	$2,789	$681

State Auto's 1992 third-quarter 10-Q reported that

the estimated annual effective tax rate was revised during the third quarter of 1992 form 25% to 17% to reflect the estimated tax impact of a decrease in taxable earnings, as prescribed by generally accepted accounting principles. The effect of this adjustment in the current quarter was a benefit of approximately $600,000.

A. Compute the tax rate used to compute net income for each quarter.

B. Using the data given, show how the change in the estimated tax rate increased third-quarter 1992 income by approximately $600,000.

C. Describe how the changed tax rate assumption distorted the comparison of third-quarter net income for 1991 and 1992.

D. Suggest two ways by which analysis can offset the distortion discussed in part c.

E. Assume that State Auto had estimated a tax rate of 17% for the first two quarters of 1992.

    i. Compute the effect of that assumption on reported net income for those quarters.

    ii. Discuss how that assumption would have affected the year-to-year comparison of operating results for the first two quarters.

EXHIBIT 44P-1	Honda Motor

Income Tax Disclosures

The income before income taxes and equity in income of affiliates ("Income before income taxes") and income tax expense (benefit) for each of the years in the three-year period ended March 31, 2001 consist of the following

	Yen (millions)			
		Income taxes		
	Income before income taxes	Current	Deferred	Total
1999:				
Japanese	¥199,848	¥125,423	¥ 15,144	¥140,567
Foreign (a)	320,663	107,875	(18,818)	89,057
	¥520,511	¥233,298	¥ (3,674)	¥229,624
2000:				
Japanese	¥127,562	¥ 76,015	¥(22,160)	¥ 53,855
Foreign (a)	288,501	136,963	(20,384)	116,579
	¥416,063	¥212,978	¥(42,544)	¥170,434
2001:				
Japanese	¥133,166	¥ 65,444	¥ (4,697)	¥ 60,747
Foreign (a)	251,810	131,419	(13,727)	117,692
	¥384,976	¥196,863	¥(18,424)	¥178,439

(a) Foreign includes income taxes provided on undistributed earnings of foreign subsidiaries and affiliates.

The effective tax rate of Honda for each of the years in the three-year period ended March 31, 2001 differs form the normal Japanese income tax rate for the following reasons.

	1999	2000	2001
Normal income tax rate	48.0%	41.0%	**41.0%**
Valuation allowance provided for current year operating losses of subsidiaries	1.2	2.8	**5.2**
Difference in normal tax rates of foreign subsidiaries	(3.0)	(1.3)	**(1.0)**
Adjustments to deferred tax assets and liabilities for enacted changes in tax laws and rates	(4.2)	—	—
Reversal of valuation allowance due to utilization of operating loss carryforwards	(0.1)	(0.1)	**(0.1)**
Other	2.2	(1.4)	**1.3**
Effective tax rate	44.1%	41.0%	**46.4%**

EXHIBIT 44P-1   (continued)

At March 31, 2001, certain of the company's subsidiaries have operating loss carryforwards for income tax purposes of approximately ¥112,857 million ($910,872 thousand), which are available to offset future taxable income, if any. Periods available to offset future taxable income vary in each tax jurisdiction and range from one year to an indefinite period as follows

	Yen (millions)
Within 1 year	¥ 510
1 to 5 years	11,528
5 to 15 years	4,147
Indefinite periods	96,672
	¥112,857

At March 31, 2000 and 2001, Honda did not recognize deferred tax liabilities of ¥5,131 million and ¥5,987 million ($48,321 thousand) respectively, for certain portions of the undistributed earnings of the company's subsidiaries because such portions were reinvested or were determined to be reinvested. At March 31, 2000 and 2001, the undistributed earnings not subject to deferred tax liabilities were ¥649,929 million and ¥663,540 million ($5,355,448 thousand), respectively. Honda has recognized deferred tax liabilities for undistributed earnings for which decisions of reinvestment have not been made.

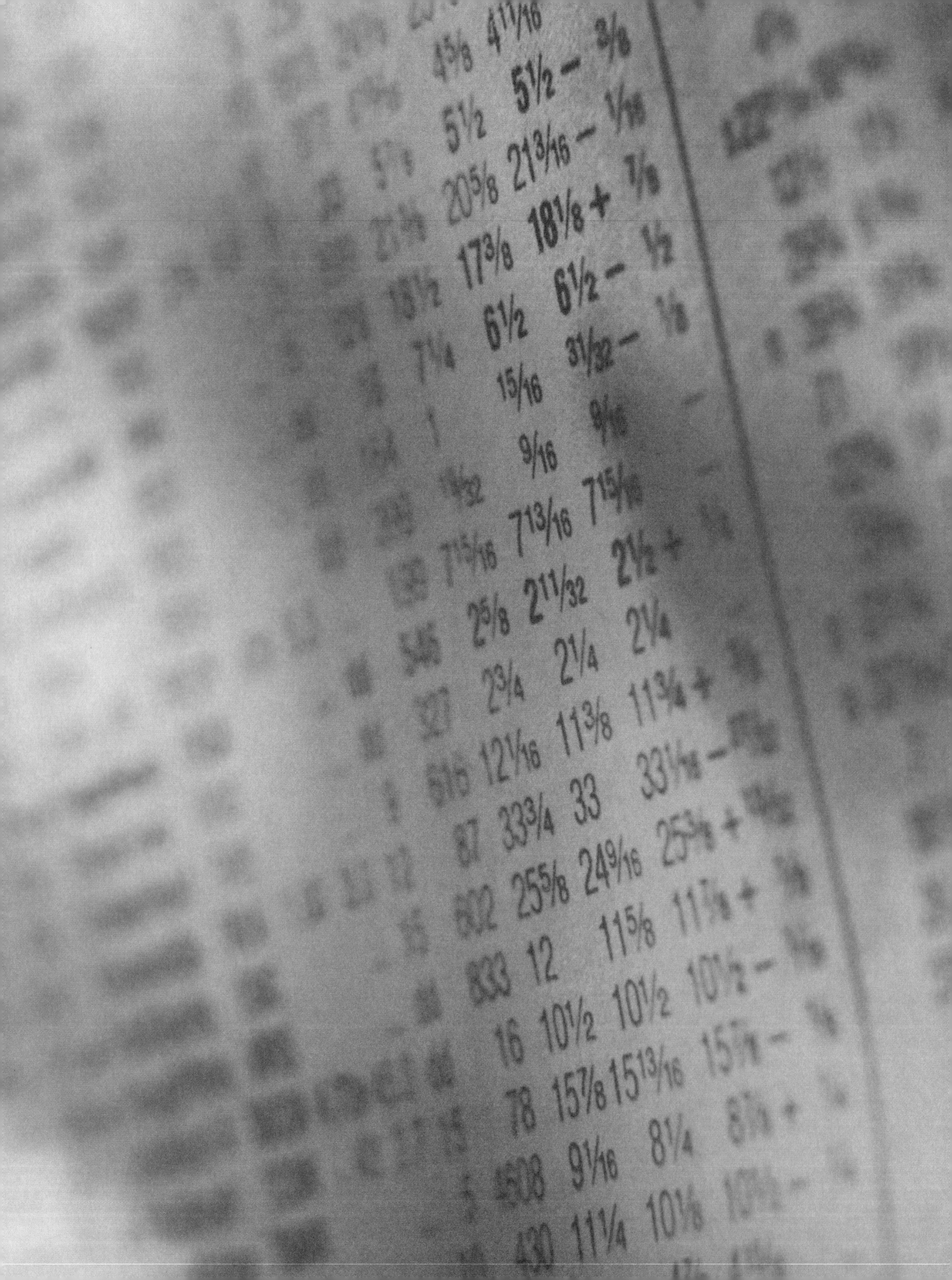
4 5/8 4 11/16
5 1/2 5 1/2 – 3/8
20 5/8 21 3/16 – 1/16
17 3/8 18 1/8 + 7/8
6 1/2 6 1/2 – 1/2
15/16 31/32 – 1/8
9/16 9/16
7 15/16 7 13/16 7 15/16
2 5/8 2 11/32 2 1/2 +
2 3/4 2 1/4 2 1/4
12 1/16 11 3/8 11 3/4 +
87 33 3/4 33 33 1/16 –
602 25 5/8 24 9/16
833 12 11 5/8
16 10 1/2 10 1/2
78 15 7/8 15 13/16
9 1/16 8 1/4
430 11 1/4 10 1/8

ANALYSIS OF FINANCING LIABILITIES

by Gerald I. White, Ashwinpaul C. Sondhi, and Dov Fried

LEARNING OUTCOMES

The candidate should be able to:

a. compute the effects of debt issuance and amortization of bond discounts and premiums on the financial statements and ratios, and discuss the effect on the financial statements from issuing zero-coupon debt;

b. determine the appropriate classification for debt with equity features and calculate the effect of issuance of such instruments on the debt to total capital ratio;

c. describe the disclosures relating to financing liabilities, and discuss the advantages/disadvantages to the company of selecting a given instrument and the effect of the selection on a company's financial statements and ratios;

d. determine the effects of changing interest rates on the market value of debt and on financial statements and ratios;

e. explain the role of debt covenants in protecting creditors by limiting a company's freedom to invest, pay dividends, or make other operating and strategic decisions.

INTRODUCTION 1

The assessment of a firm's liabilities is crucial to the analysis of its long-run viability and growth. A firm can incur obligations in myriad ways; some are a consequence of the firm's operating activities, whereas others result from its financing decisions. The former are characterized by exchanges of goods and services for the later payment of cash (or vice versa), whereas debt arising from financing decisions generally involves current receipts of cash in exchange for later payments of cash. Both forms of debt are generally reported "on balance sheet," and our focus in this reading is on their measurement, interpretation, and analysis.

More complex arrangements, often based on contracts rather than immediate cash exchanges, involve promises to purchase (or use) products, services, or distribution systems in return for specified future payments of cash or equivalent resources. Such contractual arrangements are usually not recorded on the firm's balance sheet but may receive footnote disclosure. A thorough analysis of the firm's financial structure requires recognition of these liabilities as well. Such "off-balance-sheet" debt must first be identified, then measured, interpreted, and analyzed.

The analysis of a firm's short-term liquidity and long-term solvency position requires evaluation of both on- and off-balance-sheet debt. Debt-to-equity and interest coverage ratios based on reported financial data, for example, are affected by the form of transactions (rather than their substance), which determines whether they are recognized and how they are accounted for. This analysis must also consider incentives for management decisions regarding the proportion of on- versus off-balance-sheet debt.

An additional focus of analysis is debt covenants, used by creditors to protect themselves. These restrictions limit the firm's operations, its distributions to shareholders, and the amount of additional debt or leverage the firm can assume. Firms may alter their operating and financing activities and change accounting policies in an effort to operate within the confines of these covenants.

2   BALANCE SHEET DEBT

The liability amount reported on the balance sheet does not equal the total cash outflow required to satisfy the debt. Only the principal portion, that is, the present value of the future cash flow, is recorded. For example, if a firm borrows $100 at an interest rate of 10%, the actual amount payable at year-end is $110. The balance sheet liability equals the present value of the future payment or $100.

Current Liabilities

Current liabilities are defined as those due within one year or one operating cycle; they result from both operating and financing activities. Analysis must distinguish among different types of current operating and financing liabilities:

Consequences of Operating Activities

1. *Operating and trade liabilities*, the most frequent type, are the result of credit granted to the company by its suppliers and employees.
2. *Advances from customers* arise when customers pay in advance for services to be rendered by the company. The firm is obligated to render the service and/or deliver a product to the customer in the near future.

Consequences of Financing Activities

3. *Short-term debt* represents amounts borrowed from banks or the credit markets that are expected to be repaid within one year or less.

4. *Current portion of long-term debt* identifies the portion of long-term debt that is payable within the next year; it is excluded from the long-term liability section of the balance sheet.

Operating and trade debt is reported at the expected (undiscounted) cash flow and is an important exception to the rule that liabilities are recorded at present value. A purchase of goods for $100 on credit, to be paid for within the normal operating cycle of the firm, is recorded at $100 even though its present value is lower. This treatment is justified by the short period between the incurrence of the debt and its payment, rendering the adjustment to present value immaterial.

When analyzing a firm's liquidity, advances from customers should be distinguished from other payables. Payables require a future outlay of cash. Advances from customers, on the other hand, are satisfied by delivery of goods or services,[1] requiring a cash outlay lower[2] than the advances recorded; otherwise, the firm would be selling below cost. Increases in advances should be viewed favorably as *advances are a prediction of future revenues rather than of cash outflows.*

Short-term debt and the current portion of long-term debt are the result of prior financing cash inflows. They indicate the firm's need for either cash or a means of refinancing the debt. The inability to repay short-term credit is a sign of financial distress.

It is important to monitor the relative levels of debt from operating as compared to financing activities. The former arise from the normal course of business activities and represent the required operating capital for a given level of production and sales: *A shift from operating to financing liabilities may signal the beginning of a liquidity crisis, as reduced access to trade credit results in increased reliance on borrowings.*

Example 45-1

Warnaco

The following data for Warnaco Group, a major clothing manufacturer, illustrates this point:

Warnaco Group
Amounts in $000

	1/1/00	12/30/00	Change
Accounts payable	$ 599,768	$ 413,786	$(185,982)
Total debt	1,332,755	1,493,483	160,728

Over one year Warnaco's trade credit fell 31%, requiring borrowing that increased the company's already-large debt burden. The company filed for bankruptcy on June 11, 2001.

---

[1] The firm will have a cash obligation only if the goods and services are not delivered. Thus, the primary liability does not require cash.

[2] This is especially true in industries with high fixed/low variable cost structures (e.g., airlines). The marginal cost for any individual customer is low relative to the selling cost.

Long-Term Debt

Firms obtain long-term debt financing from public issuance; from private placements with insurance companies, pension plans, and other institutional investors; or from long-term bank credit agreements. Creditors may receive a claim on specific assets pledged as security for the debt (e.g., mortgages), or they may have only general claims on the assets of the firm. Some debt, known as *project financing*, is repaid solely from the operations of a particular activity (e.g., a coal mine or office building). Some creditor claims are *subordinated*, in that they rank below those of *senior* creditors, whose claims have priority.

Long-term liabilities are interest-bearing in nature, but the structure of interest and principal payments varies widely. The different payment terms are, however, conceptually identical. As the subtleties of the financing equation(s) can be overwhelming and obscure the sight of the forest for the trees, *we suggest that the reader keep two basic principles in mind:*

1. Debt equals the present value of the remaining future stream of (interest and principal) payments. The book value reported in the financial statements uses the discount rate (market interest rate) in effect when the debt was incurred. Market value measurements use the current market interest rate.

2. Interest expense is the amount paid by the debtor to the creditor in excess of the amount borrowed. Even when the *total* amount of interest paid over time is known, its allocation to individual time periods (both cash outflows and accrual of expense in periodic income statements) may vary with the form of the debt.

These points seem simplistic but reference to them from time to time may help focus the discussions that follow.

Although bonds are only part of the debt universe, they are used for convenience to illustrate the accounting and analysis issues.

A bond is a "contract" or written agreement that obligates the borrower (bond issuer) to make certain payments to the lender (bondholder) over the life of the bond. A typical bond promises two types of payments: periodic interest payments (usually semiannual in the United States but annual in other countries) and a lump-sum payment when the bond matures.

The *face value* of the bond is the lump-sum payment due at maturity. The *coupon rate* is the stated cash interest rate (but not necessarily the actual rate of return).

Periodic Payment = "Coupon Rate" × Face Value

The coupon rate is in quotation marks because it is stated on an annual basis, whereas payments are made semiannually. The coupon rate (CR) used for the payment calculation is therefore equal to one-half the stated coupon rate.

The example in Exhibit 45-1 is based on a three-year bond[3] with the following terms:

Face Value (FV):	$100,000
Coupon:	10%
Interest Payment:	Semiannual

---

[3] Bonds issued for periods of 10 years or less are usually called notes. There is no analytical distinction, and we call all debt issues bonds for convenience.

EXHIBIT 45-1	Comparison of Bond Issued at Par, Premium, and Discount

Face Value (FV) of bond = $100,000
Coupon (CR) = 5% (semiannual payment; 10% annual rate)
Maturity = 3 years
Semiannual payments of $5,000 (0.5 × 10% × $100,000)

A. Bond Issued at Par: Market Rate = 10% (MR = 5%)

Period Ending	(1) Liability Opening	(2) (1) × MR Interest Expense	(3) FV × CR Coupon Payment	(4) (2) − (3) Change in Liability	(5) (1) + (4) Liability Closing	(6) FV Face Value of Bond
01/01/01	Proceeds (see below)				$100,000	$100,000
06/30/01	$100,000	$ 5,000	$ 5,000	$0	100,000	100,000
12/31/01	100,000	5,000	5,000	0	100,000	100,000
06/30/02	100,000	5,000	5,000	0	100,000	100,000
12/31/02	100,000	5,000	5,000	0	100,000	100,000
06/30/03	100,000	5,000	5,000	0	100,000	100,000
12/31/03	100,000	5,000	5,000	0	100,000	100,000
Totals		$30,000	$30,000			

Calculation of Proceeds

Present value of annuity of $5,000 for 6 periods, discounted at 5%:
  $5,000 × 5.0756 = $ 25,378

Present value of $100,000 in 6 periods, discounted at 5%:
  $100,000 × 0.74622 = 74,622

Total $100,000

B. Bond Issued at Premium: Market Rate = 8% (MR = 4%)

Period Ending	(1) Liability Opening	(2) (1) × MR Interest Expense	(3) FV × CR Coupon Payment	(4) (2) − (3) Change in Liability	(5) (1) + (4) Liability Closing	(6) FV Face Value of Bond	(7) (5) − (6) Closing Premium
01/01/01	Proceeds (see below)				$105,242	$100,000	$5,242
06/30/01	$105,242	$ 4,210	$ 5,000	$ (790)	104,452	100,000	4,452
12/31/01	104,452	4,178	5,000	(822)	103,630	100,000	3,630
06/30/02	103,630	4,145	5,000	(855)	102,775	100,000	2,775
12/31/02	102,775	4,111	5,000	(889)	101,886	100,000	1,886
06/30/03	101,886	4,075	5,000	(925)	100,961	100,000	961
12/31/03	100,961	4,039	5,000	(961)	100,000	100,000	0
Totals		$24,758	$30,000	$(5,242)			

(Exhibit continued on next page ...)

EXHIBIT 45-1 (continued)

Calculation of Proceeds

Present value of annuity of $5,000 for 6 periods, discounted at 4%:
$5,000 × 5.2421 = $ 26,211
Present value of $100,000 in 6 periods, discounted at 4%:
$100,000 × 0.79031 =   79,031
Total $105,242

C. Bond Issued at Discount: Market Rate = 12% (MR = 6%)

Period Ending	(1) Liability Opening	(2) (1) × MR Interest Expense	(3) FV × CR Coupon Payment	(4) (2) − (3) Change in Liability	(5) (1) + (4) Liability Closing	(6) FV Face Value of Bond	(7) (5) − (6) Discount
01/01/01	Proceeds (see below)				$95,083	$100,000	$(4,917)
06/30/01	$95,083	$ 5,705	$ 5,000	$ 705	95,788	100,000	(4,212)
12/31/01	95,788	5,747	5,000	747	96,535	100,000	(3,465)
06/30/02	96,535	5,792	5,000	792	97,327	100,000	(2,673)
12/31/02	97,327	5,840	5,000	840	98,167	100,000	(1,833)
06/30/03	98,167	5,890	5,000	890	99,057	100,000	(943)
12/31/03	99,057	5,943	5,000	943	100,000	100,000	0
Totals		$34,917	$30,000	$4,917			

Calculation of Proceeds

Present value of annuity of $5,000 for 6 periods, discounted at 6%:
$5,000 × 4.9173 = $24,587
Present value of $100,000 in 6 periods, discounted at 6%:
$100,000 × 0.70496 =   70,496
Total $95,083

The purchaser of the bond expects six payments of interest (each payment is $5,000) and a final principal payment of $100,000 for a total of $130,000. Note that this stream of payments does not uniquely determine the principal amount borrowed by the bond issuer. *The amount borrowed (the proceeds received on issuance) depends on the market rate of interest for bonds of a similar maturity and risk as well as the payment stream.*

The market rate may be less than, equal to, or greater than the coupon rate. *It is the current market interest rate that allocates payments between interest and principal.*

Exhibit 45-1, parts A through C, shows how the economics of the bond and the accounting treatment of the payments are affected by the relationship between the market and coupon rates. The following points should be noted:

1. The initial liability is the amount paid to the issuer by the creditor (present value of the stream of payments discounted at the market rate), not necessarily the face value of the debt.

2. The *effective interest rate* on the bond is the market (not the coupon) rate at the time of issuance, and interest expense is that market rate times the bond liability.

3. The coupon rate and face value determine the actual cash flows (stream of payments from the issuer).

4. Total interest expense is equal to the payments by the issuer to the creditor in excess of the amount received. (Thus, total interest expense = $130,000 − initial liability.)

5. The balance sheet liability over time is a function of (a) the initial liability and the relationship of (b) periodic interest expense to (c) the actual cash payments.

6. The balance sheet liability at any point in time is equal to the present value of the remaining payments, discounted at the market rate in effect at the time of the issuance of the bonds.

Exhibit 45-1A: Market Rate = Coupon Rate.   When the market rate equals the coupon rate of 10% (compounded semiannually), the bond is issued at par; that is, the proceeds equal the face value.[4] The creditor is willing to pay $100,000, the present value of the stream of payments and the face value of the bond. In this case, the initial liability equals the face value.

Since the debt has been issued at a market rate of 10% (equal to the coupon rate), periodic interest expense (Exhibit 45-1A, column 2) equals the periodic cash payments (column 3). The liability remains $100,000 (column 5) throughout the life of the bond.

Exhibit 45-1B: Market Rate < Coupon Rate.   When the market rate is less than the coupon rate, the creditor is willing to pay (and the bond issuer will demand) a premium above the face value of $100,000.[5] If we assume a market rate of 8%, the proceeds and initial liability (Exhibit 45-1B) equal $105,242 (face value of $100,000 plus premium of $5,242).

After six months, the bondholder earns interest of $4,210 (4% × $105,242) but receives a payment of $5,000 (coupon rate times face value). This $5,000 payment includes interest expense of $4,210 and a $790 principal payment, reducing the liability to $104,452. For the second period, interest expense is $4,178 (4% × $104,452), lower than the first period expense since the liability has been reduced. After the second payment of $5,000, the liability is further reduced. This process is continued until the bond matures. At that time, as shown in Exhibit 45-1B, the liability is reduced to $100,000, the face value of the bond, which is repaid at maturity.

The process by which a bond premium (or discount) is amortized over the life of the bond is known as the *effective interest method.* This process, which results in a constant rate of interest over the life of the obligation, is widely used in financial reporting.

---

[4] We ignore, for simplicity, the underwriting costs and expenses associated with the bond issuance. These costs are generally capitalized and amortized over the life of the bond issue.

[5] Assuming a market interest rate of 8%, the bond issuer could find an investor willing to lend $100,000 in exchange for a semiannual annuity stream of $4,000 (4% × $100,000) in addition to the lump-sum payment at maturity. For the borrower to obligate itself to pay the higher annuity of $5,000 requires additional proceeds above the face value.

Exhibit 45-1C: Market Rate > Coupon Rate.   When the market rate exceeds the coupon rate, the bond buyer is unwilling to pay the full face value of the bond.[6] At a market rate of 12%, the bond would be issued at a discount of $4,917, and the proceeds and initial liability equal $95,083.

Interest expense for the first six months is $5,705 (6% × $95,083), but cash interest paid is only $5,000; the shortfall of $705 is added to the balance sheet liability. As a result, a higher liability is used to calculate interest expense for the second period, increasing interest expense, increasing the shortfall, and further increasing the liability. This cycle is repeated for all remaining periods until the bond matures. At that point, the initial principal of $95,083 plus the accumulated (unpaid) interest of $4,917 equals $100,000, the face value payment that retires the debt. The zero-coupon bond, discussed shortly, is the extreme case; all interest is unpaid until the bond matures.

Financial Statement Effects

Interest expense reported in the income statement (column 2 of Exhibit 45-1) is the effective interest on the loan based on the market rate in effect at issuance times the balance sheet liability at the beginning of the period. The actual cash payments (column 3) may not equal interest expense, but do equal the reduction in cash from operations (CFO). The balance sheet liability is shown in column 5. The initial cash received and the final face value payment of $100,000 are both treated as cash from financing (CFF). The financial statement effects on an annual basis (if we assume a December fiscal year-end) are summarized in Exhibit 45-2. Note that for bonds issued at a premium (discount), the interest expense decreases (increases) over time. This is a direct function of the declining (rising) balance sheet liability; for each period, interest expense is the product of the beginning liability and the effective interest rate. At any point in time, the balance sheet liability equals the present value of the remaining payments discounted at the effective interest rate at the issuance date.[7,8]

The reported cash flows for each period over the life of the bond (Exhibit 45-2) are identical across all three scenarios; the $100,000 face value payment is treated as cash from financing, and the periodic cash payments of $5,000 are reported as reductions in CFO.[9] For bonds issued at a premium or discount, however, these cash flows *incorrectly* describe the economics of the bond transaction.

The misclassification of cash flows results from reporting the coupon payments rather than interest expense as CFO. For bonds sold at a premium, part of the coupon payment is a reduction of principal and should be treated as a

---

[6] The bondholder can purchase a 12% bond and receive periodic payments of $6,000. The periodic payments from this bond are only $5,000. Thus, an investor would only purchase this bond at a *discount.*

[7] To illustrate this property, compute the balance sheet liability of $96,535 at December 31, 2001, for the bond issued at a discount. The present value of the remaining four periodic payments and lump-sum payment equals:

Present value of annuity of $5,000 for 4 periods discounted
  at 6%: $5,000 × 3.46511 = $17,326
Present value of $100,000 for 4 periods discounted at 6%: $100,000 × 0.79209 =   79,209
                                                                             $96,535

[8] The *market* value of the debt, however, is equal to the present value of all remaining payments discounted at the *current market* interest rate.

[9] Under the indirect method, net income is adjusted by the change in bond discount/premium (the periodic amortization of the bond/discount premium) to derive CFO. Thus for the first year, the cash flow statement will show an addback of $1,612 in the premium case and a deduction of $1,452 in the discount case.

EXHIBIT 45-2	Comparison of Financial Statement Effects of Bonds Issued at Par, Premium, and Discount

Bond Face Value = $100,000
Maturity = 3 years
Coupon Rate = 10% (semiannual payments)

Premium Case: Market Rate = 8%
Discount Case: Market Rate = 12%

	Interest Expense Bond Issued at			Balance Sheet Liability Bond Issued at			Cash Flow from	
							Operations	Financing
Year	Par	Premium	Discount	Par	Premium	Discount	(for all cases)	
2001	$10,000	$ 8,388	$11,452	$100,000	$103,630	$ 96,535	$10,000	
2002*	10,000	8,256	11,632	100,000	101,886	98,167	10,000	
2003*	10,000	8,114	11,833	100,000	100,000	100,000	10,000	$100,000
Totals	$30,000	$24,758	$34,917				$30,000	$100,000

*Interest expense and cash flow total of June 30 and December 31 amounts for each year. All data from Exhibit 45-1.

financing cash (out)flow. CFO is understated and financing cash flow is over-stated by an equal amount. Similarly, when bonds are issued at a discount, part of the discount amortization represents additional interest expense. Consequently, CFO is overstated and financing cash flow is understated by that amount.

In summary, the cash flow classification of the debt payments depends on the coupon rates, not the effective interest rate. When these differ, CFO is misstated.

Exhibit 45-3 presents two cash flow reclassifications. The first correctly allocates cash outflows based on interest expense. After reallocation, the cash flows reflect the economics of the debt rather than the coupon payments alone.

The second reclassification, however, goes much further. We argue that all debt-related cash flows should be separated from operating cash flows. The "functional" reclassification in Exhibit 45-3 makes that separation so CFO is unaffected by borrowing. All debt-related cash flows are included in financing cash flow regardless of the coupon or effective interest rates.

Most debt is issued at or close to par (face value), making the distortion from bond premium or discount immaterial. However, when the discount is large, for example, with zero-coupon bonds, the difference between coupon and effective interest rates leads to the significant distortion of reported cash flows.

Zero-Coupon Debt

A zero-coupon bond has no periodic payments (coupon = 0).[10] For that reason, it must be issued at a deep discount to face value. The lump-sum payment at maturity includes all unpaid interest (equal to the face value minus the proceeds) from the time of issuance.

---

[10] The following discussion also applies to bonds sold at deep discounts, that is, with coupons that are far below market interest rates, and to bonds issued with attached warrants that generate debt discount (discussed later in the reading).

| EXHIBIT 45-3 | Reclassification of Cash Flows for Bonds in Exhibits 45-1 and 45-2 |

| | | SFAS 95 Cash Flow for All Bonds | | Reclassification Based on Interest Expense | | | | Functional Reclassification For All Bonds | |
| | Actual Cash Flow | | | Premium Bond | | Discount Bond | | | |
Year		Operations	Financing	Operations	Financing	Operations	Financing	Operations	Financing
2001	$ 10,000	$10,000	0	$ 8,388	$ 1,612	$11,452	$(1,452)	0	$ 10,000
2002	10,000	10,000	0	8,256	1,744	11,632	(1,632)	0	10,000
2003	110,000	10,000	100,000	8,114	101,886	11,833	98,167	0	110,000
Totals	$130,000	$30,000	$100,000	$24,758	$105,242	$34,917	$95,083	0	$130,000

SFAS 95 requires that cash flows be allocated between operations and financing based on the coupon interest rate.

The first reclassification allocates cash outflows based on interest expense. In 2001, for the premium case, $8,388 is shown as operating cash flow and the balance of $1,612 ($10,000 − $8,388) as financing. The interest expense reported for the discount issue, $11,452, is shown as operating cash flow and the excess over interest paid $1,452 ($11,452 − $10,000) is reported as a financing cash inflow. The 2003 financing cash flow for the discount issue, therefore, equals the outflow of $100,000 to repay the debt less $1,833 (interest expense in excess of interest paid).

The second reclassification is based on the authors' view that financing cash flow should include both principal and interest paid. Regardless of whether debt is issued at par, premium, or discount, financing cash flow reflects all payments made in the year of the actual payments.

The proceeds at issuance equal the present value of the face amount, discounted at the market interest rate. Thus, at a market rate of 10%, a $100,000 face value zero-coupon bond payable in three years will be issued at $74,622.

Exhibit 45-4 shows the income statement, cash flow, and balance sheet effects for this bond. Note that the repayment of $100,000 includes $25,378 of interest that is *never* reported as CFO; the full $100,000 payment is treated as cash from financing. The contrast with the bond issued at par (Exhibit 45-1A) is striking.

The interest on a zero-coupon bond never reduces operating cash flow. This surprising result has important analytic consequences. *One is that reported CFO is systematically overstated when a zero-coupon (or deep discount) bond is issued.* Furthermore, solvency ratios, such as cash-basis interest coverage, are improved relative to the issuance of par bonds. Finally, the cash eventually required to repay the obligation may become a significant burden.[11]

EQK Realty Investors (EQK), a real estate investment trust, illustrates this phenomenon. The company issued zero-coupon mortgage notes in 1985 and 1988. Adjustment of reported cash flow for the effect of interest on these zero-coupon bonds results in a quite different CFO trend.

[11] In fact, interest expense increases cash flow by generating income tax deductions. (Zero-coupon bond interest expense is tax-deductible even though it is not paid.) This result can have real-world consequences. When valuing a company for leveraged buyout (LBO) purposes, the use of zero-coupon or low-coupon debt (issued at a discount) can result in the following anomaly: The higher the interest rate, the higher the cash flow, mistakenly resulting in a higher price for the company. An investment banker commented to one of the authors that this factor contributed to overbidding in the late 1980s. Of course, when the zero-coupon bond comes due, the cash must be found to repay the (much higher) face amount.

EXHIBIT 45-4	Zero-Coupon Bond Analysis

Bond: Face Value (FV) = $100,000 Coupon 0%
Maturity = 3 years
Market Rate = 10% (MR = 5%)

	(1) Liability Opening	(2) (1) × MR Interest Expense	(3) FV × CR Coupon Payment	(4) (2) − (3) Change in Liability	(5) (1) + (4) Liability Closing	(6) FV Face Value of Bond	(7) (5) − (6) Discount
01/01/01	Proceeds (see below)				$ 74,622	$100,000	$(25,378)
06/30/01	$74,622	$ 3,731	$0	$ 3,731	78,353	100,000	(21,647)
12/31/01	78,353	3,917	0	3,917	82,270	100,000	(17,730)
06/30/02	82,270	4,114	0	4,114	86,384	100,000	(13,616)
12/31/02	86,384	4,319	0	4,319	90,703	100,000	(9,297)
06/30/03	90,703	4,535	0	4,535	95,238	100,000	(4,762)
12/31/03	95,238	4,762	0	4,762	100,000	100,000	(0)
Totals		$25,378	$0	$25,378			

Calculation of Proceeds

Present value of $100,000 in 6 periods, discounted at 5%: $100,000 × 0.74622 = $74,622

Cash flow from operations: Zero in all periods

Cash flow from financing: $74,622 inflow at 1/1/01; $100,000 outflow at 12/31/03

Exhibit 45-5 presents excerpts from EQK's 1992 Balance Sheet, Cash Flow Statement, and Financial Statement Notes. The zero-coupon notes were retired in December 1992, using cash and a new (conventional) mortgage bond.

Given the opening (January 1, 1992) balance of $89,410 on the zero-coupon bond and the issuance of a mortgage bond having a face value of $75,716 ($75,324 + $392 debt discount), the cash required to retire the bond should have been $13,694 ($89,410 − $75,716). Why then did EQK report a cash payment of $23,038, an excess of $9,344, as cash from financing?

The answer can be found in the cash flows from operating activities section of the statement of cash flows. "Amortization of discount on zero-coupon mortgage notes" of $9,344 appears as an addback to net income, thereby *removing it from CFO;* $9,344 is the amount of interest that accrued on the zero-coupon bond from January 1992 through its retirement in December 1992. This interest, paid in 1992, was treated as a financing rather than an operating cash outflow. The impact of this misclassification on CFO is significant. Reclassifying the interest expense as CFO turns a positive cash flow of over $8 million into a negative $1.276 million:

Reported CFO	$8,068
Reclassify 1992 interest portion	(9,344)
Adjusted CFO	($1,276)

EXHIBIT 45-5	EQK Realty Zero Coupon Financing, Financial Statement Excerpts

Balance Sheet

Year Ended December 31	1991	1992
Liabilities		
Mortgage note payable, net of debt discount of $392	—	$75,324
Zero-coupon mortgage notes, net of unamortized discount of $9,574	$89,410	—

Statement of Cash Flows

Year Ended December 31	1992
Cash flows from operating activities	
Net loss	$ (8,850)
Adjustments to reconcile net loss to net cash provided by operating activities	
Amortization of discount on zero-coupon mortgage notes	9,344
Other adjustments	7,574
Net cash provided by operating activities	$ 8,068
Cash flows from financing activities	
Prepayment of zero-coupon note	$(23,038)
Other adjustments	1,572
Net cash provided by (used in) financing activities	$(21,466)

Note 2: Debt Restructuring

In December 1992, the Company refinanced $75,689,000 representing the balance of its zero-coupon mortgage note that remained after reducing this indebtedness with the proceeds from the sale of properties. . . . The new financing, which is collateralized by first mortgage liens . . . matures in December 1995.

Source: EQK Realty Investors, *1992 Annual Report.*

Similar reclassification can be extended to previous years, when the company accrued (but did not pay) interest cost (amortization of discount) on these notes. Reported CFO obscured the fact that at some point the accrued interest must be repaid. As the maturity of the debt approached, the company faced a liquidity crisis.[12]

The following table presents reported and adjusted CFO for the period 1989 to 1994. The treatment of the interest on the zero-coupon bond causes significant distortions both prior to and following the 1992 refinancing.[13]

---

[12] In 1991 EQK's auditors issued a "going concern qualification" due to the impending maturity of the zero-coupon bond.

[13] The adjustment ignores small amounts of amortization of other discount notes.

EQK Realty Investors Adjustment of Operating Cash Flow (CFO), Years Ending December 31, 1989 to 1994 (in $thousands)

	1989	1990	1991	1992	1993	1994
Reported CFO	$10,458	$9,795	$ 5,728	$ 8,068	$4,087	$2,184
Less: zero-coupon interest	7,486	8,318	9,229	9,344	0	0
Adjusted CFO	$ 2,972	$1,477	$(3,501)	$(1,276)	$4,087	$2,184

After adjustment, the 1989 to 1991 deterioration in CFO is even more striking as 1991 CFO is negative.[14] The 1992 recovery is less impressive as adjusted CFO remains negative. In 1993, CFO rises despite the burden of full-coupon debt; the unadjusted data obscure this improvement. The adjusted CFO data provide better information regarding the operating cash flow trend.

Variable-Rate Debt

Some debt issues do not have a fixed coupon payment; the periodic interest payment varies with the level of interest rates. Such debt instruments are generally designed to trade at their face value. To achieve this objective, the interest rate "floats" above the rate on a specified-maturity U.S. Treasury obligation or some other benchmark rate such as the prime rate or LIBOR (London InterBank Offered Rate). The "spread" above the benchmark depends on the credit rating of the issuer.

Fixed- versus Variable-Rate Debt and Interest Rate Swaps

Borrowers can issue fixed-rate or variable-rate debt directly; alternatively, they can enter into **interest rate swap** agreements that convert a fixed-rate obligation to a floating-rate obligation or vice versa.

Whether a firm prefers to incur fixed-rate or variable-rate debt depends on a number of factors. Variable-rate debt exposes the firm's interest expense, cash flows, and related ratios to higher volatility due to interest rate changes.[15] On the other hand, when the firm's operating cash flows are correlated with movements in interest rates, variable-rate debt minimizes risk. The common notion that fixed rates minimize risk by reducing the volatility of a firm's income and cash flows is, thus, only a half-truth.[16]

Financial intermediaries (banks, finance companies) generally issue a high proportion of variable-rate debt, as their assets tend to be variable-rate in nature. Thus, they match the variability of their assets and liabilities.

---

[14] Note the increasing trend of interest expense on the zero-coupon debt, similar to the trend in Exhibit 45-4.

[15] The impact of interest rate changes can, of course, be either positive or negative.

[16] The investor point of view, however, is different. Variable-rate debt has low price risk; interest rate changes should have minimal impact on its market price. Significant market fluctuation should result only from perceived changes in credit quality. However, the variability of income is higher than for fixed-rate debt.

However, a nonfinancial firm may also view variable-rate debt as hedging variable operating cash flows. For example, the 1996 financial statements of AMR (American Airlines) state:

> Because American's operating results tend to be better in economic cycles with relatively high interest rates and its capital instruments tend to be financed with long-term fixed-rate instruments, interest rate swaps in which American pays the floating rate and receives the fixed rate are used to reduce the impact of economic cycles on American's net income.[17]

Alternatively, a firm may prefer to issue variable-rate debt because management believes that interest rates will fall or short-term rates (the usual basis for variable debt) will remain below long-term rates charged on fixed-rate loans. The analysis of a firm's debt should include a consideration of whether management's choice of financing alternatives is based on the inherent economics of the business or management speculation on future interest rate changes.

Debtors use interest rate swaps to manage the fixed- and variable-rate mix of total borrowings. Box 45-1 presents the mechanics of interest rate swaps.

Example 45-2

Nash-Finch

Nash-Finch [NAFC] is a food wholesaler with annual sales exceeding $4 billion. The company's debt at December 31, 1998 and 1999 was $300 million and $315 million, respectively. For both years, the variable-rate debt was approximately 42% of the total debt ($128 million in 1998 and $132 million in 1999).

The company engaged in interest rate swaps, converting variable-rate to fixed-rate debt. The company disclosed the following information regarding interest rate swaps outstanding at the 1998 and 1999 year-ends (amounts in $thousands):

	Years Ended December 31	
	1998	**1999**
Receive variable/pay fixed	$90,000	$30,000
Average receive rate	5.5%	5.3%
Average pay rate	6.5%	6.5%

Note that Nash remains liable for the original principal and interest payments on the fixed-rate debt (see Box 45-1). *At the inception of the swap, no accounting recognition is required although Nash has altered its debt obligation.* Presumably at that time, the swap was "fair," that is, the net present value of the swap payments was zero. The transaction is an *off-balance-sheet contract.*

---

[17] AMR Corporation, 1996 Financial Statements, Note 6.

The effect of the swap was to reduce the sensitivity of Nash to changes in interest rates:

Effect of Swap on Debt Structure (amounts in $thousands)

	1998		1999	
	Before Swap	After Swap	Before Swap	After Swap
Fixed	$172,125	$262,125	$183,609	$213,609
Variable	127,665	37,665	131,990	101,990
Total	$299,790	$299,790	$315,599	$315,599
% Variable	42.6%	12.6%	41.8%	32.3%

The swap has also affected Nash's interest expense as the required payments (fixed) exceeded the amounts received (based on variable rates):

	Years Ended December 31	
	1998	1999
Swap	$90,000	$30,000
Interest received	4,950	1,590
Interest paid	(5,850)	(1,950)
Net payment	$ (900)	$ (360)
Interest expense:		
Reported	$29,034	$31,213
Ex-swap	28,134	30,853
Increase due to swap	3.2%	1.2%

What conclusions can we draw from these data?

1. Nash entered into the swaps to reduce its vulnerability to higher interest rates. It did not replace swaps expiring in 1999, thus increasing its exposure. Yet total debt (and variable debt) increased from 1998 to 1999.

2. The swaps increased Nash's interest expense as the fixed-rate payments exceeded the variable rate payments. The net payments can be viewed as the cost of insurance against the effect of higher interest rates.

3. While the fair value of the swaps at inception (net present value) can be assumed to be zero, the fair value will fluctuate over the swap term. If the changes are favorable, Nash-Finch will have an unrealized gain; if unfavorable there will be an unrealized loss.

4. Nash also assumed *counterparty risk*, the risk that the other party will default. When Nash must make net payments (as in 1998 and 1999) there is no risk. If variable rates rose sharply, resulting in payments to

Nash, then default risk would be present.[18] *When a company enters into swaps that are material to its financial position, the analyst should ensure that the counterparties are sufficiently strong so that the likelihood of default is insignificant.*[19]

These conclusions result in questions that the analyst may want to pursue by discussing them with management. Especially in the first case, the answer might yield useful insights regarding management's strategy regarding interest rate risk.

BOX 45-1 INTEREST RATE SWAPS

Firms use interest rate swaps* to exchange variable- (floating-) rate debt for obligations with fixed interest rates or, alternatively, to exchange fixed-rate debt for obligations with variable rates.

Swaps are contractual obligations that supplement existing debt agreements. Each firm remains liable for its original debt, makes all payments on that debt, and carries that debt on its books. The firm with variable-rate debt agrees to pay, at specified intervals, amounts equal to a fixed rate times the *notional principal amount*. In return, the counterparty pays variable amounts equal to the variable interest rate (pegged to a specified rate or index) times that same notional principal amount.

Because firms wish to minimize credit risk, they do not engage in swaps with other industrial firms, even when a swap would meet the objectives of both parties. The **counterparty** is normally a bank or other financial institution with a high credit rating. Money center banks, as a result, have large portfolios of swaps.

Given that some firms prefer variable-rate debt and others fixed-rate debt, why do they not arrange their preferred form of financing directly with their creditors? Why incur the additional costs and/or risks of swaps? Frictions in the credit markets and/or the institutional setting of the firm may result in differential borrowing costs that make it cheaper to borrow in the non-preferred mode and swap into the preferred mode of borrowing rather than borrowing directly in the preferred mode. For example, some "household name" American firms can borrow at very low rates in certain foreign markets. A second factor leading to swaps is that preferences change over time. This is especially true of firms that use swaps to "match" assets and liabilities.

Illustration

The Triple A and Triple B companies each want to borrow $100 million. Assume that the Triple A company prefers variable-rate debt, whereas the Triple B company prefers fixed-rate debt. The companies' respective borrowing rates and preferences are:

(continued)

---

* For a further elaboration of these issues, see James Bicksler and Andrew Chen, "An Economic Analysis of Interest Rate Swaps," *Journal of Finance*, July 1986 and John Hull, *Introduction to Futures and Options Markets* (Englewood Cliffs, NJ: Prentice-Hall, 1995), Chapter 6.

---

[18] When the fair value of the swap changes so that Nash-Finch has an unrealized gain, realization of that gain depends on the creditworthiness of the counterparty.

[19] If we assume that the counterparty is a highly rated financial institution, it would not provide collateral to protect Nash against default.

BOX 45-1 *(continued)*

Company	Fixed-Rate	Variable-Rate	Preferred Mode
Triple A	8%	Prime	Variable
Triple B	10%	Prime + 1%	Fixed

The Triple-A company is considered to be more creditworthy than the Triple B company and, hence, is offered more favorable borrowing terms. Note that the rate differential on fixed-rate debt (2%) is greater than the differential (1%) on floating-rate debt. This discrepancy makes it profitable for firms to enter into swaps.

Based on these rates, we demonstrate that the combined borrowing cost for the two firms is 1% lower when each company *borrows in its nonpreferred mode*. This 1% difference is independent of changes in the prime rate.

Company	Borrow Preferred Mode	Borrow Nonpreferred Mode
Triple A	Prime	8%
Triple B	10%	Prime + 1%
Total cost	Prime + 10%	Prime + 9%

The two firms are both better off borrowing in their nonpreferred mode, "swapping" the debt and splitting the 1% savings. The swap agreement requires the following payments:

▶ The Triple A company pays the Triple B company the prime rate (times the notional amount of $100 million).

▶ The Triple B company pays the Triple A company 8.5% (times the notional amount of $100 million).

The cost of the original borrowing and the swap for each company is

Company	Original Loan	To Swap +Counterparty	From Swap -Counterparty	=	Net Cost
Triple A	8%	Prime	(8.5%)		Prime − 0.5%
Triple B	Prime + 1%	8.5%	(Prime)		9.5%

Each company has obtained debt in its preferred mode at a rate one-half percent below the rate available on its preferred mode of borrowing.

(continued)

BOX 45-1 *(continued)*

Economic Effects of the Swap

Assume that the swap illustrated has a five-year term, the prime rate is 6% at inception, payments are made semiannually, and adjustments for changes in the prime rate are also semiannual. The first semiannual assessment results in a net payment of $1.25 million [0.5 × (8.5% − 6%) × $100 million] from Triple B to Triple A. If, for the second semiannual period, the prime rate increases to 7%, then the second scheduled payment will be $0.75 million [0.5 × (8.5% − 7%) × $100 million]. *Although Triple B has borrowed at a variable rate, increases in that rate are passed on to Triple A as Triple B's payments decline. Thus, Triple B's economic cost is the fixed rate of 9.5%. Conversely, Triple A is exposed to rising interest rates although it has incurred only fixed-rate debt. The swap has changed the economic position of both firms.*

Economic Effects of Termination

Now assume that Triple A, expecting increases in interest rates, wishes to terminate the swap agreement after the first payment. How much should Triple A pay to do so? The required payment should equal the fair value of the swap agreement, calculated as follows.‡

Triple B is liable for 9 semiannual payments of $4.25 million (0.5 × 8.5% × $100 million). If Triple B enters into another swap agreement, it would be based on current interest rates. If the fixed rate has increased by 0.5% (while the prime rate has increased by 1%), Triple B would have to make 9 payments of $4.5 million (0.5 × 9% × $100 million), an increase of $250 thousand. The present value of the increase discounted at the *new* rate of 9% is equal to approximately $1.8 million. Thus, to terminate the swap, Triple A must pay Triple B that amount.

---

‡ In our simplified example, we assume that the swap is terminated at the same time when the floating rate is reset. Were this not the case, then a similar calculation would have to be made for the variable-rate bond to compensate for the fact that if Triple B entered into a new swap agreement, while it is true that it would pay a higher fixed rate, it would receive immediately floating-rate payments based on the higher floating rate and not have to wait for the next adjustment date. This calculation, however, is usually not very material; it is for only one payment and the discounting period is less than six months (from the termination date to the interest rate adjustment date).

Debt Denominated in a Foreign Currency

Companies sometimes issue debt for which all interest and principal payments are made in a foreign currency. There are three motivations for such issuance:

1. More favorable terms in foreign markets than domestic ones.[20]

2. Assets denominated in the foreign currency and debt denominated in that currency can hedge[21] against exchange rate movements.

3. Need for foreign currency for a particular investment or other transaction.

The carrying value of foreign currency debt is adjusted for changes in exchange rates.

For example, Note 24 of the 2000 financial statements of Roche reports debt in Japanese yen and U.S. dollars as well as Roche's parent currency of

---

[20] For example, in July 1998, Pepsico issued one-year notes in Japan (to retail investors) and swapped the fixed-rate obligation for floating rate U.S. dollar payments. The company stated that its net borrowing cost was *comfortably below one-month LIBOR.*

[21] If the parent currency strengthens relative to the foreign currency, then the carrying amount of assets denominated in foreign currencies decreases. This decrease is offset by the decrease (in the parent currency) of the debt to be repaid.

Swiss francs. Note that the carrying amounts for the yen and U.S. dollar bonds[22] rose in 2000 due to appreciation of those currencies against the Swiss franc.[23]

This adjustment for exchange rate changes is distinct from any adjustment to current market value. Market value adjustments are based on changes in interest rates.[24] The market value of this debt in local currencies may have increased if interest rates declined since the debt was issued; this change is *not* reflected on the balance sheet. *Thus, the balance sheet liability has been adjusted for exchange rate changes but not interest rate changes.*

Project Debt

Some debt is issued to finance a single project, such as a factory, pipeline, or real estate. In these cases, the debt terms are tailored to the expected cash flows generated by the project. Project debt may be *nonrecourse*, meaning that the lender will be paid only from project cash flows and cannot demand payment from the debtor if the project is unsuccessful. Mortgages on real estate are the major example of nonrecourse debt. Even though such debt is shown on the debtor's balance sheet, the debt is a claim only against the project cash flows and assets. Some project debt is incurred by joint ventures, discussed in Reading 46.

Example 45-3

Forest City Enterprises

Forest City [FCE], a U.S. developer of commercial and residential real estate, finances most of its projects with nonrecourse mortgage debt. The company's capital structure at January 31, 2000 was (in $millions):

Mortgage debt, nonrecourse	$2,382.4	74.5%
Recourse debt	429.9	13.4%
Shareholders' equity	386.5	12.1%
Total capital	$3,198.8	100.0%

The large proportion of nonrecourse debt protects the company from adversity. The effects of one poorly performing project cannot jeopardize others, as the company cannot lose more than its total investment in that project.

---

[22] The rise in the carrying amount of the zero coupon U.S. dollar obligations is due to accretion of discount as well as the appreciation of the U.S. dollar.

[23] See the financial review (p. 51 of the Roche annual report) for foreign currency data.

[24] In theory, exchange rates are also affected by interest rates. However, that influence is based on the *difference* in interest rate levels between the two countries, *not the level* of interest rates.

OPTIONAL SEGMENT
ENDS

Debt with Equity Features

Convertible Bonds and Warrants

To reduce borrowing costs, many companies issue debt convertible into their common shares or issue a combination of bonds and warrants to purchase common shares. Although conceptually these two types of "equity-linked" debt are identical, their accounting consequences may differ.[25]

Convertible Bonds.   Under APB 14 (1969), the conversion feature of a bond is completely ignored when the bond is issued. Thus, the entire proceeds of the bond are recorded as a liability, and interest expense is recorded as if the bond were nonconvertible. However, the conversion feature lowers interest expense. When the bondholder converts the convertible bond into common stock, the entire proceeds are reclassified from debt to equity. As discussed in Box 45-2, however, the FASB issued an exposure draft that would change the accounting for convertible debt.

From an analytic perspective, however, recognition should be given to the equity feature prior to the conversion. When the stock price is (significantly) greater than the conversion price, it is likely that the debt will not have to be repaid, and the convertible bond should be treated as equity rather than debt when calculating solvency ratios such as debt-to-equity. When the stock price is significantly below the conversion price, the bond should be treated as debt. At levels close to the conversion price, the instrument has both debt and equity features, and its treatment becomes a more difficult issue.

One possibility is to separate the debt and equity values of the convertible bond, using option pricing models. This analysis is complex, however, and beyond the scope of this book. IAS 32 (2000) requires issuers to split compound instruments into their component parts. The FASB ED would require such separation. Alternatively, the analyst can examine the sensitivity of key ratios to bond classification, first treating the bond as debt and then as equity to see whether the differences are significant. If they are, then the question of whether the debt will be ultimately converted becomes a key issue, which may depend on the purpose of the analysis.[26]

Example 45-4

Holmen

Note 18 of Holmen's annual report shows that in 1998, the company issued debt of SKr 361 million, convertible into class B common shares in 2004 at a price of SKr 148.10. As the market price of Holmen's class B

---

[25] A convertible bond can be disaggregated into a bond plus an option to convert the bond into common shares. An important difference between a convertible and a debt-plus-warrant issue is that, in the former case, the bond must be surrendered to exercise the option, whereas in the latter case, the bond and warrant are not linked. Thus, the issuer can use the proceeds of exercised warrants for purposes other than the retirement of the associated debt. Another difference is their impact on earnings-per-share calculations. The interest expense on the convertible issue is eliminated when diluted earnings per share are computed, whereas the interest on the debt component of the bond-plus-option alternative will never affect earnings-per-share calculations (however, there is an adjustment for the exercise of dilutive warrants).

[26] For example, in takeover analysis, the intended purchase price will determine whether convertible bonds will be converted to common or remain outstanding debt.

shares was SKr 307 at December 31, 1999, these bonds should be considered equity. The reclassification decreases the debt/total capital ratio:

Holmen Capital Structure
December 31, 1999

	Reported	Reclassification	Adjusted
SKr millions			
Financial liabilities	6,845	(361)	6,484
Equity	15,883	361	16,244
Total capital	22,728		22,728
Financial liabilities	30.1%		28.5%
Equity	69.9%		71.5%

Exchangeable Bonds. Some bond issues are convertible into shares of another firm rather than those of the issuing firm. The analysis of such issues is more complex than the analysis of convertible debt. Exercise of the conversion privilege results in:

▶ Extinguishment of the debt

▶ Elimination of the investment in the underlying shares

▶ Recognition of gain or loss from the "sale" (via debt conversion) of the underlying shares

The motivation for such debt issues may include:

1. The desire to obtain cash while retaining the underlying shares for strategic reasons.

2. Minimizing the market effect of sales; the underlying shares are sold over time as bonds are exchanged.

3. Financial benefits: The interest rate on the exchangeable bonds will be lower (because of the exchange feature) than on straight debt, and the exercise price will contain a premium over the current market price.

4. Delayed recognition of a large unrealized gain; recognition is postponed until the exchange privilege is exercised. This delays the income tax recognition of the gain and may permit management some control over the timing of the gain (it can call the bonds, forcing exchange, when it wishes to report the gain).

5. Hedging the investment. SFAS 133 changed the accounting for such hedges.

BOX 45-2　FASB EXPOSURE DRAFT: ACCOUNTING FOR FINANCIAL INSTRUMENTS WITH CHARACTERISTICS OF LIABILITIES, EQUITY, OR BOTH

On October 27, 2000, the Board issued an exposure draft (ED) that would change the accounting for:

▶ Convertible debt

▶ Redeemable preferred shares

In general, the ED would classify as equity all financial instruments components that establish an ownership relationship with the issuer. A component establishes an ownership relationship if it

1. Is an outstanding equity share not subject to redemption, or

2. Is an obligation that can or must be settled by the issuance of equity shares, and all changes in the monetary value of the obligation are attributable to, equal to, and in the same direction as the change in the fair value of the issuer's equity shares.

The new standard would require that proceeds of issuance of securities with both liability and equity components be allocated between the value of the liability component and that of the equity component. The most important example is the issuance of convertible debt, which would be accounted for as if the company sold a combination of debt and warrants.

When a company issued convertible debt, it would be required to allocate the proceeds (net of underwriting fees and other direct costs of issuance) between the debt (liability) component and the warrant (equity) component using their relative fair values. If the warrant could not be valued, the issuer would estimate the fair value of the debt component, and allocate the remaining proceeds to the equity component.*

Further, if the debt is repurchased or converted, the issuer must recognize gain or loss† equal to the difference between the fair value of the debt component and the carrying amount of the liability.

There would also be a gain or loss on the equity component at the date of repurchase or conversion. This gain or loss would be excluded from income but would affect stockholders' equity.

The accounting change would have the following effects:

1. The difference between the fair value of the debt component and its face value would be amortized over the life of the debt, using the effective interest method. This would result in higher interest expense and lower income than under current accounting.

2. Only the debt component would be shown as a liability; the equity component would be recorded in stockholders' equity. As a result, the debt-to-equity ratio would be lower than under the current accounting method.

3. At redemption or conversion, the company would recognize a gain or loss on the liability component. In general, companies would recognize a loss when interest rates were lower at the time of repurchase or conversion than when the debt was issued. In the case of conversion, the fair value of the liability component would be added to equity, rather than the carrying amount under current accounting.

4. At redemption or conversion, stockholders' equity would reflect the change in value of the equity component. When the underlying shares have risen in value,

(continued)

BOX 45-2 *(continued)*

equity would rise, reducing the debt-to-equity ratio. Under current accounting, the market value at redemption or conversion date has no effect on the balance sheet.

The ED would also change the classification of redeemable preferred shares (and similar instruments such as Trust Preferreds) by requiring that they be recorded as debt in the issuer's balance sheet. Similarly, the "dividends" paid on such shares would be included in interest expense.

The effect of this change would be to increase the reported debt-equity ratio and reduce the interest coverage ratio of affected firms.

A final standard was expected to be issued prior to the end of 2002. It is likely that affected companies would be required to restate their financial statements for the accounting change.

----

* This method is styled the "with-and-without method" in the ED.
† Under SFAS 145 (2002), gains and losses from the extinguishment of debt are treated as extraordinary items only when they meet the APB 30 criteria for classification as an extraordinary item (see Reading 34).

Example 45-5

Times Mirror

In March 1996, Times Mirror [TMC] sold 1.3 million shares of Premium Equity Participating Securities (PEPS) redeemable for shares of Netscape. TMC had purchased Netscape shares less than one year earlier, before Netscape's initial public offering, at a price of $2.25 per share. TMC's Netscape shares were restricted from public sale. The PEPS were sold at a price of $39.25 with a 4.25% coupon and a March 15, 2001 maturity. At that date, each PEPS was redeemable for the cash equivalent of:

▶ One Netscape share if that share's price was below $39.25

▶ .87 Netscape share if its price was $45.15 or higher

▶ $39.25 cash if Netscape's share price was between $45.15 and $39.25

The advantages to TMC of offering PEPS were that TMC:

1. Received the fair market value of its Netscape shares, at a low interest rate of 4.25%, despite the fact that the shares could not be legally sold.

2. Hedged its investment; if Netscape shares declined, the PEPS holders would receive smaller payments at maturity.

3. Maintained part of the upside potential given the reduced conversion rate if Netscape shares exceeded $45.15 in price at maturity.

4. Postponed capital gains tax until the actual sale of Netscape shares was effected through conversion of the PEPS.

5. Enabled TMC to control the timing of its realization of the large gain on the Netscape investment.

> The last two advantages are illustrated by events in 1998 and 1999:
>
> ► In 1998, TMC sold part of its Netscape holding, redeemed a corresponding portion of the PEPS, and realized a pretax gain of $16 million.[27]
>
> ► In 1999, TMC sold shares of AOL (which had acquired Netscape) and redeemed additional PEPS, reporting a pretax gain of nearly $17 million.

Bonds with Warrants. When warrants and bonds are issued together, the accounting treatment differs from that of convertible bonds. The proceeds must be allocated between the two financial instruments.[28] The fair value of the bond portion is the recorded liability. As a result, the bond is issued at a discount, and interest expense includes amortization of that discount. The fair value of the warrants is included in equity and has no income statement impact. When warrants are exercised, the additional cash increases equity capital.

Roche has made extensive use of bonds with equity features (see Note 24 and pages 99–101 of the Roche annual report).

Comparison of Convertible Bonds and Bonds with Warrants. As bonds with warrants are accounted for as if they were issued at a discount, the reported liability is lower (but increases as the discount is amortized) as compared to that of a convertible bond. However, reported interest expense is higher.[29] As discussed earlier in this reading, reported cash flow from operations is the same, equal to the coupon interest.

These differences are summarized in the list below, which also includes a comparison with a conventional bond. Note that issuing debt with equity features:

► Lowers interest expense
► Increases operating cash flows
► Results in a balance sheet liability equal to or below that of a conventional bond

In all respects, such debt appears less costly.

Interest Expense	Balance Sheet Liability	Operating Cash Flow
Conventional bond	Conventional bond	Conventional bond
greater than	*equal to*	*less than*
Bond with warrants	Convertible bond	Convertible bond
greater than	*greater than*	*equal to*
Convertible bond	Bond with warrants	Bond with warrants

---

[27] This gain was previously reflected in equity as TMC carried its investment in Netscape at market value.

[28] As discussed in Box 45-2, the FASB has proposed extending this accounting treatment to convertible bonds as well.

[29] Because of the accounting difference, American companies rarely issue debt/warrant combinations. However, such issues are common outside of the United States.

However, the financial statement effects are misleading as the cost of the equity feature is ignored. When convertible debt is issued, there is a systematic understatement of interest expense.[30]

Commodity Bonds

The interest and principal payments on bond issues are sometimes tied to the price of a commodity, such as gold, silver, or oil. Firms producing the commodity, as part of a hedge strategy, may issue such bonds. A higher commodity price increases the payments to bondholders but is offset by higher operating profitability. These bonds, therefore, convert interest from a fixed to a variable cost. Such bonds were issued during time periods when commodity prices were rising, making the bonds attractive to purchasers. A recent variation on this theme is the issuance of bonds whose payoff depends on losses due to insurance losses resulting from natural catastrophes.

Perpetual Debt

Some debt issues have no stated maturity. When debt does not have a maturity date, it may be considered preferred equity rather than a liability for analytic purposes. An exception would be cases where debt covenants are likely to force repayment or refinancing of the debt.

Example 45-6

SAS

In 1986, SAS (Scandinavian Airlines) issued a perpetual 200 million Swiss franc–denominated subordinated loan, with the interest rate fixed for 10 years and reset every 10 years. While there is no set maturity date, SAS has the exclusive right to terminate the loan once every five years.

In 1994, SAS repurchased SFR 55.35 million at a price of 72. This repurchase shows that perpetual notes are not the same as equity, as changes in market conditions may lead the issuer to refinance them. However, given management control over the refinancing decision, treatment as preferred equity is appropriate absent evidence of refinancing intent.

When long-term interest rates were at low levels, some firms issued debt with a maturity of 100 years. Although such issues are technically debt, their long maturity suggests that, for all practical purposes, they represent permanent capital and should be treated as equity when computing the debt-to-equity ratio. For example, Walt Disney issued 100-year bonds in 1993.[31]

---

[30] Moreover, the impact of equity-linked bonds on earnings per share must always be taken into consideration.

[31] These bonds have a fixed interest rate of 7.55%, protecting Disney against future interest rate increases. As the bonds are not callable until 2023, the buyers were protected against lower interest rates for 30 years.

Preferred Stock

Many companies issue more than one class of shares. Preferred (or preference) shares have priority over common shares with respect to dividends and entitlement to the proceeds of sale or liquidation. In exchange for this privileged position, preferred shareholders usually give up their right to participate fully in the success of the company.

Preferred shares generally have a fixed dividend payment and a fixed preference on liquidation. Dividend payments are almost always *cumulative;* if not paid when due, they remain a liability (but one that is not recorded). Dividend arrears must be paid before any dividend can be paid to common shareholders. When calculating the net worth of a company with preferred shares outstanding, the analyst should:

1. Subtract the liquidating value of the preferred, not the par or stated value, which may be lower.

2. Subtract any cumulative dividends that are in arrears.

Some preferred shares have a variable interest rate. "Auction rate" preferred shares have interest rates that change frequently, making them attractive to buyers seeking "money-market"-type investments.[32] From an analytical perspective, these preferred shares function as short-term liabilities and should be treated as such. They are often called when market conditions change, making them a less permanent source of funds.

Preferred shares are almost always callable by the issuer. Many issues are, however, redeemable by the preferred shareholder, often over a period of years.[33] Because of these "sinking fund" provisions, redeemable preferreds should be treated as debt for analysis; they should be included as debt in solvency ratios, and dividend payments should be treated as interest. The FASB has issued an exposure draft (see Box 45-2) that would require redeemable preferred shares to be reported as debt, and the "dividends" on such shares included in interest expense, as required by IAS 32 (2000).

Consistent with this view, the SEC requires that redeemable preferred shares be excluded from stockholders' equity. However, at the same time, the SEC does not require their classification as debt. The argument against debt classification is that, ultimately, *firms cannot be forced to pay the dividends or redeem the preferred shares. Unlike creditors, preferred shareholders do not have the power to force the firm into bankruptcy for noncompliance* with the terms of the agreement.[34] Often, when dividends are in arrears, they do gain representation on the board of directors.

The ambiguity as to whether these shares are debt or equity was shown in two studies by Kimmel and Warfield (1993, 1995). They found that only 60% of redeemable preferred shares are actually redeemed; the other 40% are eventually converted to common shares, arguing against treating these hybrids as debt. Furthermore, as a firm's systematic risk (its beta) is related to a firm's debt-to-equity ratio, they tested whether the relationship had a better "fit" with the redeemables treated as debt or equity. They found that they *did not fit into either category unless the redeemables had voting rights and were convertible.* Only when these

---

[32] For U.S. corporate buyers, preferred dividends are 70% tax-free when ownership is below 20%, making these issues more attractive on an after-tax basis than many other short-term investments. The exclusion is 80% for ownership of 20% but below 80%.

[33] These provisions provide preferred shareholders with a guaranteed future value for the shares.

[34] In many states, a firm cannot pay dividends or redeem shares if such payments will jeopardize the company's survival.

attributes were present did the securities exhibit equitylike qualities. Thus, on average, one cannot generalize as to the nature of these hybrid securities.

The line between debt and equity has become increasingly blurred in recent years. Companies prefer to issue securities that minimize the after-tax cost of financing yet provide maximum flexibility.[35] Some issues are designated preferreds but are really debt; others are called debt but are functionally equity. Although help from accounting standards setters is on the way, analysts must evaluate such instruments on a case-by-case basis and decide whether to treat them as debt or equity.

Effects of Changes in Interest Rates

Debt reported on the balance sheet is equal to the present value of future cash payments discounted at the *market rate on the date of issuance.* Increases (decreases) in the *current market rate* decrease (increase) the *market value* of the debt. A company that issues fixed-rate debt prior to an increase (decrease) in market rates experiences an economic gain (loss) as a result of the rate change. This economic gain or loss is not reflected in either the income statement or balance sheet.

For some analytical purposes, however, the market value of a company's debt may be more relevant than its book value. It better reflects the firm's economic position and is as important as the current market values of a firm's assets. Analysis of a firm's absolute and relative level of debt and borrowing capacity should be based on current market conditions. Consider two firms reporting the same book value of debt. One firm issued the debt when interest rates were low; the other at higher current interest rates. Debt-to-equity ratios based on book values may be the same. However, the firm that issued the bonds at the lower interest rate has higher borrowing capacity as the economic value of its debt is lower.[36] Ratios calculated using the market value of debt would reflect the stronger solvency position.

Furthermore, in valuation models that deduct the value of debt from the value of the firm (or of its assets), that debt should be measured at market value rather than book value.[37] Firms that issued debt at lower rates are relatively better off when interest rates increase, and this advantage should increase the equity value of the firm.

In the United States, SFAS 107, Disclosures about Fair Value of Financial Instruments, requires that firms report the fair value of outstanding debt. IAS 32 (1998) has similar requirements. Box 45-3 restates the debt of Westvaco from book to market value. This exercise is useful for several reasons.

First, financial statement disclosures are based on year-end (or quarter) prices. When interest rates have changed significantly since the last report date, the analyst may need to recalculate the market value of the firm's debt. Second, most non-U.S. firms, and firms in the United States that are not subject to FASB disclosure requirements, do not provide market value disclosures; analysts must know how to estimate the market value of debt for such firms. Finally, market valuation requires assumptions and (especially for firms with complex financial

---

[35] Trust Preferred Securities (TPS) are an example of such securities. For tax purposes, they are treated as debt. While they cannot be classified as equity, they are not reported as debt but rather as preferred shares or minority interest. Similarly, "dividend" payments are reported as preferred dividends or minority interest. Frischmann, Kimmel, and Warfield (1999) refer to TPSs as the "Holy Grail" of financial instruments and report that, since their introduction in 1993, they have become the primary mode of new issues of preferred shares.

[36] Theoretically, it could refinance its current debt at the same interest rate as the other firm, lowering the book value of debt.

[37] Similarly, in discounted cash flow valuation analysis, the calculation of a firm's (weighted-average) cost of capital is based on market rather than book values of debt (and equity).

instruments) often there are competing valuation methods. In some cases, analysts may want to perform their own market value calculations. To do so, they must disaggregate management's aggregate fair value disclosure; this requires an understanding of how market values are estimated.

Example 45-7

Westvaco

The book value of Westvaco's long-term debt was $1,477 million at October 31, 1999; its market value was $1,494 million, or 1% higher. The October 31, 1998 book value was $1,557 million; its market value was $1,636 million, or 5% higher. Thus, during the 1999 fiscal year, market value relative to book value declined 4%. This decline reflected the rise in interest rates (see Box 45-3), which reduced the fair value. The decline reflects the structure of Westvaco's debt, which is mostly fixed-rate debt with long maturities.

The Westvaco example above is not unique. The market value of the long-term debt of Mead [MEA] was 6.6% higher than book value at December 31, 1998 (Mead was on a calendar year). One year later, the market value was 2.9% below the book value; during calendar 1999, therefore, market value relative to book value declined by 9.5% as interest rates rose. Mead, which merged with Westvaco early in 2002, had a similar debt structure, mostly fixed rate debt with long maturities.

BOX 45-3   ESTIMATING THE MARKET VALUE OF DEBT

In many cases, the replacement of book value with market value is simple. For publicly traded debt, market values are readily available.* If the debt is not publicly traded, its present value can be calculated by applying the current market rate to the original debt terms. The maturity, coupon rate, and other terms of long-term debt are generally disclosed for each debt security issued.

The appropriate current market rate can be obtained from:

1. Other publicly traded debt of the company having approximately the same maturity; estimate the rate used by the market to discount that debt.

2. Publicly traded debt of equivalent companies in the same industry; estimate the rate used to discount that debt.

3. Estimating the risk premium over the rate on government debt of the same maturity. The risk premium depends on the bond-rating "risk" class of the company's bonds.

Calculating the Market Value of Debt

Footnote J in Westvaco's financial statements shows notes payable and long-term obligations at October 31, 1999. The company reports the fair value as required by SFAS 107.† The book and fair values for the three years ended October 31, 2000 are (in $thousands):

(continued)

---

* Sources include rating service publications (such as Standard & Poor's *Bond Guide*), newspapers, and electronic quotation services.

† The book value does not match the total of current and noncurrent obligations in footnote J. The company has apparently excluded some long-term obligations that it considers not to be financial instruments.

BOX 45-3   (continued)

October 31	1998	1999	2000
Book value	$1,557,477	$1,477,162	$2,716,772
Fair value	1,636,093	1,494,290	2,627,696
Difference	$ 78,616	$ 17,128	$ (89,076)

Source: Westvaco *Annual Reports, 1999 and 2000.*

The maturities, coupon rates, and carrying amounts for most obligations are listed in footnote J. Some obligations are publicly traded while others are not.

As Westvaco discloses the fair (market) value of its debt, we forgo the laborious task of calculating the estimated market value for each issue. The following comments are intended as a guide for use when such calculations are required.

Most of Westvaco's debt at October 31, 1999 consists of fixed-rate long-term debentures, some of which have **sinking funds**. Because the rate is fixed and the duration is long, the fair value of these bonds fluctuates with interest rates.

Example:

In 1990 Westvaco, which was A rated, issued $100 million of 9.75% bonds due June 15, 2020. At the issue date, the yield[‡] was 130 basis points (1.3%) above the yield on the U.S. Treasury 8.75% bonds due in May, 2020. The price and yield to maturity of the U.S. Treasury 8.75% issue at October 31, 1998–2001 was reported by Bloomberg as follows:

October 31	1998	1999	2000	2001
Price	142-11*	124-30	131-4	145-11
Yield-to-maturity	5.40%	6.53%	6.02%	4.98%

* US government securities with maturities longer than one year are quoted as a % of face value in 32nds. Thus 142-11 means 142 11/32% of face value or $1,423.44 per $1,000 bond.

Source: Price and yield data from Bloomberg.

Estimation of the fair value of the Westvaco 9¾% bonds requires an estimate of the spread over the U.S. Treasury bond. That spread is a function of the rating of the corporate issuer (Westvaco) and the spread between bonds of different ratings classes. Bond quality spreads are variable over time, tending to compress when the economy is strong (and concerns about credit quality are low) and to widen when economic conditions weaken.

Westvaco was A rated by Standard & Poor's at October 31, 1997 and A rated at October 31, 1998. Standard & Poor's data show little change in quality spreads in 1998 and 1999. Thus, our calculations assume that the Westvaco bonds had a yield to maturity of 130 basis points for both years.

(continued)

‡ Throughout this box, yield means yield-to-maturity.

BOX 45-3   *(continued)*

Extending this analysis to 2000 and 2001, we find two changes:

1. Westvaco's S&P rating was reduced from A– to BBB+ in May 2000 and further reduced to BBB in June 2001. These rating reductions reflected Westvaco's higher leverage.

2. Quality spreads started to widen in 2000 and 2001 as concerns grew about the economic outlook and the possible effect of recession on corporate credit quality. The September 11, 2001 terrorist attacks accelerated this trend.

Thus our estimated **yield spread** for the Westvaco bonds is 180 basis points at October 31, 2000 and 220 basis points at October 31, 2001.

The following table shows the results of these assumptions and the calculated fair value of the Westvaco bonds. These fair value estimates differ from the actual market value reported in Bloomberg by less than 2% each year.

October 31	1998	1999	2000	2001
Yield on U.S. 8.75% bond	5.40%	6.53%	6.02%	4.98%
Assumed spread	1.30%	1.30%	1.80%	2.20%
Assumed yield on Westvaco 9.75% bond	6.70%	7.83%	7.82%	7.18%
Calculated value of Westvaco bond	$1,344.85	$1,194.43	$1,191.50	$1,260.88
Bloomberg value of Westvaco bond	1,369.80	1,217.40	1,169.30	1,245.60
Difference	–1.8%	–1.9%	1.9%	1.2%

Source: Price and yield data from Bloomberg.

Complexities in Market Value Estimation

Because of the conventional nature of Westvaco's debt, the calculation of its market value is straightforward. Westvaco's debt is virtually all fixed rate and dollar denominated. Simple debt structures, however, are becoming the exception rather than the rule for large companies, given globalization and the increased sophistication of financial markets.

Some complexities make the calculation of market values almost impossible as the requisite information is lacking. A few of the complexities summarized below have been discussed earlier, others will be addressed in later sections of the text, and some remain beyond the scope of our book.

Convertible Bonds

Market prices are readily available for most convertible debt issues. However, these prices incorporate both the debt and equity features of the security. Only the debt component of the market value should be included as part of debt.

(continued)

BOX 45-3 *(continued)*

Variable-Rate Debt

Variable-rate debt usually requires no market value adjustment. Because of the continuous adjustment of the interest rate on the debt, market value approximates book value.**

Debt Denominated in a Foreign Currency

For debt denominated in a foreign currency, the present value calculations should be based on current interest rates for the currency in which the debt is denominated.

Hedges and Derivatives

Firms can protect themselves against changes in interest rates and/or currency exchange rates using instruments such as options or forward contracts (including swap agreements). In this reading we confine ourselves to a discussion of *interest rate swaps*.

As previously discussed, *the original debt instrument with its original parameters remains in effect and is reported in the firm's financial statements; if publicly traded, market prices are available.* However, the estimated market value of the underlying debt instrument must reflect any interest rate swap.

When fixed-rate debt has been converted to floating-rate debt with an interest rate swap covering its full term, no adjustment to market value is required. If a swap does not cover the full term of fixed-rate debt, changes in interest rates after the end of the swap term will affect market values. Thus, it is important to discern the terms of any swaps by careful reading of footnotes.

When a swap converts floating-rate debt to fixed-rate debt, however, the market value is exposed to changes in interest rates. Even though the market value of the original obligation does not change, the fair value of the effective (because of the swap) obligation does and should be calculated.

** This is not precisely accurate. The variable-rate adjustment may lag the interest rate change. Nevertheless, given the short period until adjustment, the effect of any lag on present value is usually immaterial. Because of this, SFAS 107 states that, for variable-rate debt, the book value can be used to approximate the market or fair value.

These factors (confirmed by empirical results discussed in Box 45-4) suggest the conditions to be considered before deciding whether the restatement of debt to market value is a useful exercise. All of the following factors should be considered.

Debt: Market or Book Value?

Given the effort and assumptions required to estimate market values when they are not provided, we now turn to a discussion of the factors that determine whether the adjustment from book value to market value is a useful exercise. Empirical results with respect to these factors are discussed in Box 45-4.

Debt Maturities.   The effect of interest rate changes on the market value of debt increases with the maturity of the debt. If a firm's debt is mostly short-term, changes in interest rates will not appreciably affect its market value.[38]

---

[38] Thus, even if its long-term debt is adjusted by 10%, total debt will only be affected by 10% times the percentage of long-term debt. The lower the percentage of long-term debt, the smaller the overall adjustment.

Interest Rates on Debt.   For adjustable-rate debt, whose interest rate varies with the market rate of interest, book value approximates market value and no adjustment is required. On the other hand, the market value of fixed-rate debt issues does change with interest rates. This is especially true of zero-coupon and other discount debt, due to their longer duration relative to debt of the same maturity issued at par.

When a firm has swapped its fixed debt for floating-rate debt, there should be no adjustment, as the value of that debt is no longer exposed to interest rate changes. Conversely, when a firm swaps variable rates for fixed rates, the market value of that portion of its debt will vary with interest rates and adjustment is required.

Changes in Market Interest Rates.   The adjustment to market value depends on changes in the market rate of interest. As long as there is no long-term trend, fluctuations in market value tend to offset, leaving the difference between book and market values small. However, when rates rise or fall greatly over several years, the differences between book and market value can be significant.

Embedded Interest Rate.   Westvaco issued debt at various times and its (weighted) average outstanding coupon rate (*embedded rate*) was approximately 8.39%,[39] within the range of interest rates over the late 1990s. The adjustment from book value does not depend on the change in interest rates itself, but rate changes relative to the imbedded rate. As interest rates were below the embedded rate for both 1998 and 1999, the fair value exceeds book value.

Unless there are limits on the firm's ability to refinance (noncallable debt or deterioration in credit quality), the embedded rate should decline (with some lag) as interest rates fall. The reverse is not true; firms with long-term fixed-rate debt can enjoy low interest costs for many years even though interest rates in general have risen.

BOX 45-4   MARKET OR BOOK VALUES: EMPIRICAL EVIDENCE

Bowman (1980) examined the relationship between firms' market betas and the debt-to-equity ratio. Finance theory predicts that the higher a firm's debt-to-equity ratio (using market values), the higher the firm's beta.

Letting the superscripts M and B refer to the market and book value, respectively, Bowman examined which of the following four measures of the debt-to-equity ratio, D^M/E^M, D^M/E^B, D^B/E^M, and D^B/E^M, were more closely associated with the firm's beta.

Bowman obtained the best results when he used the market value of equity in the denominator. Whether debt was measured on a market basis or book basis made little difference as the ratios D^B/E^M and D^M/E^M yielded similar results. The pure book value ratio D^B/E^B did not perform as well; the measure of the market value of the debt-to-book value of equity (D^M/E^B) performed the poorest.

These results can be partly attributable to the fact that for close to 60% of the debt in Bowman's sample, book value and market value were equivalent. Furthermore, the correlation between the market value of debt and the book value of debt

(continued)

---

[39] Calculated as interest incurred (from Westvaco footnote F) divided by the average debt level. For 1999, the calculation is

$$\frac{\$132,428}{(\$1,552,377 + \$1,605,415)/2} = 8.39\%$$

BOX 45-4 *(continued)*

was close to 100%. As the study ranked debtors by relative rather than absolute levels of debt, changes in the market rates of interest shifted debt valuations without changing ranks.

Mulford (1986) replicated Bowman's study by using a later time period. Bowman's analysis was based on 1973 data, predating the dramatic rise in market interest rates of the late 1970s. Mulford, referring to Bowman's study, noted:

> His failure to find evidence of superior performance for a debt-to-equity ratio based on market values of debt may have been due to small differences between the book and market values of debt which accompanied the general level of interest rates at that time.*

To remedy this deficiency, Mulford focused on 1980, when market rates of interest were historically high. In addition, to alleviate potential measurement problems arising from the conversion of book to market values, he examined the performance of portfolios of firms in addition to individual firms. Mulford's results were more in line with theory, but only on a portfolio basis. No matter which variation was used to measure the relationship between beta and debt-to-equity, the market-based debt-to-equity ratio was always the most closely associated with beta on a portfolio basis. On an individual basis, D^M/E^M did not always perform as well, but the differences between it and the best performing ratio were minimal.

These results suggest, not surprisingly, that the market value of debt is not superior to book value when the difference between the stated and market rates of interest is small; the additional cost of obtaining market values is not worthwhile.† Adjustment is necessary only when the gap between the historic and market rates of interest is large. Even then, potential measurement problems‡ in estimating market values may offset any benefits from the adjustment process.

---

* Charles W. Mulford, "The Importance of a Market Value Measurement of Debt in Leverage Ratios: Replications and Extensions," *Journal of Accounting Research*, Autumn 1984, pp. 897–906.

† Given the high correlation between market and book values of debt, this is especially true for analyses that focus on relative rather than absolute debt burdens.

‡ The issue of a measurement problem also calls into question the results of both Bowman and Mulford from a different perspective. They adjusted only on-balance-sheet debt, ignoring any "off-balance-sheet" debt. As Reading 46 will make clear, the latter can be significant.

Debt of Firms in Distress

When the credit quality of a firm changes significantly (in either direction), the market price of debt will follow, independent of interest rate trends. When credit quality and the market value of debt decline, there appears to be a gain to the firm, yet it is difficult to argue that shareholders are better off. This apparent paradox reflects simultaneous changes in the value of assets as credit quality changes. It is reasonable to assume that some assets of such troubled companies are impaired (see the discussion in Reading 43).

Accounting for Restructured and Impaired Debt

When a debtor is in financial difficulty, creditors may agree to accept assets in payment of the debt or to "restructure" the obligation by modifying its terms (e.g., reducing the interest rate or deferring principal payments). When debt is extinguished, both the debtor and creditor will recognize gain or loss measured as the difference between the fair value of the assets (cash or other assets) used to repay the debt and its carrying amount. This accounting treatment raises neither accounting nor analysis issues.

When the obligation is restructured, however, different accounting rules apply to creditors and debtors. Creditors adhere to SFAS 114 (1993), as amended by SFAS 118 (1994), whereas debtors use SFAS 15 (1977) to account for these transactions.

Under SFAS 114, the creditor must recognize a loss equal to the difference between the carrying value of the loan and the present value of the restructured payment stream *discounted at the original discount rate* (effective interest rate). Thus, if a 12% coupon loan with a face value of $100,000 and three years remaining to maturity is restructured by reducing the interest rate to 8%, the creditor recognizes a loss of $9,610 as the new carrying value of the loan is $90,390.[40] The loan impairment may also be measured using the observable market price of the loan or the fair value of collateral when the loan is collateral dependent.[41]

The FASB was reluctant, however, to allow debtors to record gains resulting from financial distress. SFAS 15 provides that the debtor's carrying amount of the debt be compared with the *undiscounted gross cash flows* (principal and interest) due after restructuring. As long as the gross cash flows exceed the carrying amount, the debtor recognizes no gain. In our example, the future payments are ($100,000 + 3 × $8,000) = $124,000. No gain is recognized.[42]

However, the present value of the cash flows has been reduced; in economic terms, the debtor has gained at the expense of the creditor. The accounting mandated by SFAS 15 recognizes this transfer only over the life of the loan as payments are made; the debtor will show lower interest expense as the loan is amortized at the implicit interest rate of the loan. In our example, interest expense is now calculated at an interest rate of 8% rather than 12%.

A similar approach is mandated by the FASB for loans considered to be "impaired." Creditors are required to recognize the probable loss, but recognition of gains by debtors is not allowed. Under SFAS 114, creditors are required to carry impaired loans at the present value of cash flows expected after modification of the loan terms, *discounted at the original effective interest rate*. For the debtor, however, no gain recognition is permitted.

For purposes of analysis, however, both impaired and restructured debt should be restated to fair market value using a *current market interest rate* to discount the cash flows required by the (actual or expected) restructured obligation. However, as noted earlier, debtor "gains" should be viewed warily; gains resulting from an inability to repay loans are almost certainly offset by asset impairment.

Retirement of Debt Prior to Maturity

Firms generally choose the initial debt maturity of their obligations based on such considerations as cost and investment horizon (when projects funded with debt are expected to generate cash flows). Subsequently, conditions may change and a firm may wish to refinance or retire debt prior to the original maturity. Examples include:

---

[40] If we assume annual payments, the present value of a three-year annuity of $8,000 discounted at 12% + present value of $100,000 in three years discounted at 12% equals $90,390.

[41] SFAS 118 amended SFAS 114 to allow creditors to continue income-recognition methods for impaired loans that had been used prior to the adoption of SFAS 114. For example, cost-recovery or cash-basis methods report investments in impaired loans at less than the present value of expected future cash flows. In these cases, no additional impairment needs to be recognized under SFAS 118. SFAS 114 was also amended to require additional disclosures regarding the investment in certain impaired loans and the recognition of interest income on those loans.

[42] If the payments do not exceed the carrying value, then the gain is limited to the difference between those amounts; the debt is discounted at an implicit interest rate of zero.

▶ Declining interest rates permit the reduction of interest cost.

▶ Increasing cash from operations permits debt retirement earlier than expected.

▶ Sale of assets or additional equity generates funds and the firm decides to reduce financial leverage.

In such cases, the firm can reduce bank debt, commercial paper, and other short-term debt quickly and at small expense. For longer-maturity debt, the firm may exercise **call provisions**, tender offers, or in-substance defeasance. We examine the economic and accounting effects of these choices shortly.

Accounting for Debt Retirement

When firms retire debt prior to maturity, the gain or loss (difference between the book value of the liability and the amount paid at retirement) is treated as a component of continuing operations.[43]

Using the par bond example in Exhibit 45-1A, assume that on December 31, 2001, the market interest rate for the firm is 12%. As a result, the market price of the bonds should be $96,535.[44] If the firm paid $96,535 to retire the bond, the resulting gain on the bond retirement is $3,465 since the book value is $100,000.[45] While this gain must be included in income from continuing operations, there are two reasons why an analyst should consider treating it as a non-operating item:

▶ In reality, the firm is no better off as a result of the refinancing. To finance the retirement of the bond, it must issue new debt[46] bearing at least the same effective interest rate (and must incur transaction costs). Effectively, over the remaining life of the original bond, the net borrowing cost would be identical; the company has simply replaced 10% coupon debt with 12% coupon debt. In economic terms, the gain took place as interest rates rose, not when the refinancing took place. Because of the use of historical cost as a measure of the bond liability, however, only refinancing results in a recognized gain.[47]

▶ The decision to refinance is a function of the change in market interest rates. The analyst should evaluate the transaction to determine whether the gain or loss should be considered as part of normal operations or treated analytically as an extraordinary item.

In the early 1970s, interest rates rose sharply at the same time the U.S. economy entered recession. Firms found their outstanding low-coupon bonds selling at deep discounts. Many of these firms had poor operating profitability, but were

---

[43] SFAS 145 (2002) rescinded both SFAS 4 (1975), which mandated extraordinary item treatment for these gains and losses, and SFAS 64 (1982), which provided an exemption from extraordinary item reporting for gains and losses on normal sinking fund repurchases. Under SFAS 145, gains and losses on retirement of debt are reported as extraordinary items only if they meet APB 30 criteria (see page 54 of text).

[44] This can be seen from Exhibit 45-1C as the carrying amount of the discount bond is the present value at the (original) 12% interest rate.

[45] We have ignored unamortized debt issuance costs. When bonds are retired, the firm must write off these costs that were capitalized when the bonds were issued. This write-off becomes a component of the gain or loss on retirement.

[46] Even if it did not issue new debt to retire the bond but rather used internal funds, the firm would experience an opportunity cost equal to the forgone interest revenue.

[47] If the gain or loss is recognized at all, it should be in the period in which interest rates change, not in the year in which the refinancing takes place. In our example, the year is the same, but that coincidence is rare in practice.

able to increase reported income by retiring bonds. The issuance of SFAS 4 in 1975 was partially a response to this income manipulation activity.

In the late 1990s, lower interest rates resulted in the refinancing of higher coupon debt, resulting in a recognized loss. That loss should be viewed, however, as a signal of lower future interest expense, as high-coupon debt is replaced by lower-coupon debt (also see the following discussion of callable bonds).

Example 45-8

DaimlerChrysler

In 1990, predecessor Chrysler had issued $1.1 billion of 12% debt, due in 2020. The high interest rate was due to the higher level of interest rates and Chrysler's poor debt rating. As a result of lower interest rates and improved financial condition, the bonds sold at a large premium in the late 1990s. Late in 1996, Chrysler repurchased half of the issue, recording an extraordinary pretax loss of $309 million. In 1998, DaimlerChrysler repurchased an additional $300 million of the bonds, recording an extraordinary pretax loss of $230 million (€203 million). The company replaced this high-cost debt with lower coupon debt, reducing interest expense significantly. The combined effect of the extraordinary loss from debt retirement (decreasing equity) and reduced future interest expense (increasing earnings) is a higher reported future return on equity.

Our discussion of discretionary debt retirements indicates that the amounts and timing of the accounting gain and the economic gain from debt retirement are quite different. This especially applies to callable bonds, whose retirement may give rise to economic profit but may generate a loss for accounting purposes.

Callable Bonds

When a bond is callable, the issuer has the option to buy back (call) the bond from bondholders at predetermined dates and prices. This differs from the case in which the issuer retires the old bond at a market price equal to the present value of the future payment stream. The call price is usually set at a premium over the face value of the bond, but is independent of the present value of the payment stream at the time the call is made. However, the actual exercise does depend on the relationship of the call price to that present value.

Exhibit 45-6 contains an analysis of a callable bond. The decline in interest rates constitutes an economic loss at the time of the rate change, as the market value of the bond rises. In the absence of the call provision, a decision to refinance would not impact Cole, which would incur new debt equal to $106,624 to refinance the debt at market rates. However, the call provision permits the firm to retire the bonds for only $102,000; the economic gain is the difference.[48]

---

[48] When bonds are issued, the call provisions are often an important ingredient in the market reception. As call provisions benefit only the issuer, bond buyers will bargain against them. Option-adjusted bond analysis is now routine. See, for example, Frank J. Fabozzi, *Fixed Income Analysis for the Chartered Financial Analyst Program*, New Hope, Pennsylvania; Frank J. Fabozzi Associates, 2000 (pp. 347ff). Many shorter-term issues are noncallable.

| EXHIBIT 45-6 | Analysis of Callable Bond |

On January 1, 2001, Cole issues the following bond:

Face value:	$100,000
Coupon:	10% (annual payments assumed for simplicity
Maturity:	5 years
Call provision:	Callable at any time after one year at 102

If the market interest rate applicable to Cole is 10%, then the bonds will be issued at par.

Reported Liability = $100,000
Annual Interest Expense = $10,000 (10% × $100,000)

Assume that, on December 31, 2001, the market rate applicable to Cole has declined to 8%. The rate change has no accounting impact on the company. However, the present value of the cash flows associated with the debt rises to $106,624 (discounted at 8%). Absent the call provision, the expected market price of the bonds is 106.624.

By calling the bonds at a price of 102, Cole realizes an economic gain of $4,624 [(106.624 − 102) × ($100,000)].

However, the call results in an accounting loss of $2,000 [(100 − 102) × ($100,000)].

Economically, it is beneficial to refinance the debt, but the income statement reports a loss. One can only speculate as to how many firms have not refinanced under such conditions because of the financial statement impact. This is yet another reason why analysts should ignore gains and losses from the retirement of debt.

Defeasance

In some cases, the firm wishes to retire debt but is unable to do so because the debt is non-callable. *In-substance defeasance* involves setting aside riskless securities sufficient to pay all remaining installments of principal and interest. The cash flow characteristics of the securities used must match those of the debt being defeased and must be placed in a trust fund restricted for that purpose.

Although the original debt remained outstanding, U.S. GAAP permitted debtor firms to derecognize the defeased obligations through December 31, 1996.[49] However, SFAS 125 (1996)[50] disallows in-substance defeasance and debt may be extinguished only on repayment or when the debtor is legally released from being the primary obligor. IAS 32 (2000) disallowed defeasance for firms following IAS GAAP.

---

[49] See SFAS 76 (1983) and FASB Technical Bulletin 84-4 for accounting and disclosure requirements related to defeasance.

[50] See SFAS 125, Accounting for the Transfers and Servicing of Financial Assets and Extinguishments of Liabilities.

3

BOND COVENANTS

Creditors use debt covenants in lending agreements to protect their interests by restricting activities of the debtor that could jeopardize the creditor's position. Auditors and management must certify that the firm has not violated the covenants. If any covenant is violated, the firm is in *technical default* of its lending agreement, and the creditor can demand repayment of the debt after the stated grace period. Generally, however, as we shall see, the terms are renegotiated but at a cost to the debtor as the lender demands concessions. The analysis of a firm's debt position must therefore take into consideration the nature of these covenants and the risk that the firm may violate them.

Information on debt covenants is important both to evaluate the firm's credit risk as well as to understand the implications of such restrictions for the firm's dividend and growth (investment) prospects. In addition, to the extent these covenants are accounting-based, they may affect the choice of accounting policies.

Nature of Covenants

Smith and Warner (1979) characterize debt covenants as placing limits on one or more of the following activities:

1. Payment of dividends (includes share repurchases)
2. Production and investment (includes mergers and acquisitions, sale and leaseback, or outright disposal of certain assets)
3. Issuance of new debt (or incurrence of other liabilities)
4. Payoff patterns (includes sinking fund requirements and the priorities of claims on assets)

In addition to direct restrictions on activities, covenants may require maintenance of certain levels of such accounting-based financial variables as stockholders' equity (or retained earnings), working capital, interest coverage, and debt-to-equity ratios. These levels are often related to the four types of activities listed above by restricting a certain activity if the accounting variable violates the specified target level. In some cases, the violation itself may signal a breach of the covenant even without any subsequent firm activity.

Bond covenants may also require that interest rates depend on certain financial ratios.

Example 45-9

Luby's

Based in Texas, Luby's [LUB] operates cafeterias. It entered into a credit agreement with a group of banks early in 1996. That agreement was subsequently amended four times:

1. January 24, 1997
2. July 3, 1997
3. October 27, 2000
4. June 29, 2001

The second and third amendments are of particular interest. The second amendment increased the credit line from $100 million to $125 million but added the following provision with respect to the spread over the LIBOR rate ("applicable margin"):

Applicable margin means the following per-annum percentages, applicable in the following situations:

Applicability If the leverage is:	LIBOR Basis for Advances of One, Two, Three, or Six Months	LIBOR Basis for Advances of Seven to Fourteen Days
not less than 2 to 1	0.225	0.325
less than 2 to 1	0.200	0.300
Difference	0.025	0.025

This provision gives the lender an additional margin over LIBOR of 2.5 basis points (.025%) if the leverage ratio (debt-to-equity ratio as defined in the original credit agreement) exceeds 2.0. This additional margin was presumably intended to compensate the lender for the additional risk.

The third amendment, adopted when Luby's earnings had fallen sharply, changed the *applicable margin* as follows:

Applicability If the Leverage Is:	LIBOR Basis for Advances of One, Two, Three, or Six Months	LIBOR Basis for Advances of Seven to Fourteen Days
greater than or equal to 2.75 to 1	0.500	2.500
greater than or equal to 2.50 to 1 but less than 2.75 to 1	0.375	2.125
greater than or equal to 2.25 to 1 but less than 2.50 to 1	0.000	1.750
less than 2.25 to 1	0.000	1.250

This amendment increased the lending spread to reflect the higher leverage ratio, and provided a sliding scale under which the spread increases and decreases with the leverage ratio (a measure of risk).

Additionally, as detailed in Exhibit 45-7, the third amendment introduced a covenant based on the fixed-charge coverage ratio as well as imposing restrictions on net worth (stockholders' equity) and the leverage ratio. Note the extent to which the ratios as well as their components are defined by the agreement.

These provisions had several effects:

1. To restrict the ability of Luby's to incur additional debt that would dilute the interest of the creditors.

2. To require Luby's to maintain stockholders' equity, limiting its ability to pay dividends (it eliminated its dividend in October 2000) or buy back stock, either of which would reduce cash and the equity cushion.

3. To reward creditors for the level of risk by increasing the interest rate margin as the leverage ratio increases.

Luby's provides an example of bond covenants. Additional discussion regarding the nature of accounting-based debt covenants can be found in Box 45-5.

EXHIBIT 45-7   Excerpts from Luby's Bond Covenants

Fixed Charge Coverage Provision

"Earnings Available for Fixed Charges" means, for any period, calculated for the Borrower and its Subsidiaries on a consolidated basis in accordance with GAAP, the sum of (a) EBITDA, plus (b) all lease and rental expense pursuant to Operating Leases, minus (c) cash taxes paid, minus (d) Capital Expenditures.

"Fixed Charges" means, for any period, calculated for the Borrower and its Subsidiaries on a consolidated basis in accordance with GAAP, the sum of (a) all interest, premium payments, fees, charges and related expenses (including, but not limited to, interest expense pursuant to Capitalized Lease Obligations) in connection with borrowed money or in connection with the deferred purchase price of assets, in each case to the extent treated as interest in accordance with GAAP, (b) all dividends and distributions paid in respect of Capital Stock and (c) all lease and rental expenses pursuant to Operating Leases.

"Fixed Charges Coverage Ratio" means, for any date of determination, the ratio of (a) Earnings Available for Fixed Charges for the period of four consecutive fiscal quarters ending on such date to (b) Fixed Charges for the period of four consecutive fiscal quarters ending on such date.

The Borrower covenants and agrees that it will not allow the Fixed Charges Coverage Ratio to be less than 1.20 to 1 at the fiscal quarter ending November 30, 2000 or at the end of any fiscal quarter thereafter.

Net Worth Provision

The Borrower covenants and agrees that it will not allow its Net Worth at any time to be less than the sum of (i) $190,000,000 plus (ii) 50% of Consolidated Net Income (excluding Consolidated Net Income for any fiscal quarter in which Consolidated Net Income was a negative number) earned on or after September 1, 2000, plus (iii) 75% of the Net Cash Proceeds of any equity issues of the Borrower's Capital Stock in an underwritten public offering pursuant to an effective registration statement under the Securities Act of 1933, as amended, after September 1, 2000.

Leverage Ratio Provision

The Borrower covenants and agrees that it will not allow the Leverage Ratio to be greater than (a) 3.00 to 1 at the fiscal quarters ending November 30, 2000, February 28, 2001 and May 31, 2001, (b) 2.60 to 1 at the fiscal quarter ending August 31, 2001 and (c) 2.50 to 1 at the fiscal quarter ending November 30, 2001 and each fiscal quarter thereafter.

Source: Third Amendment to Credit Agreement, dated October 27, 2000, Exhibit 4(j) to Luby's Form 10-K for year ended August 31, 2000.

BOX 45-5   ACCOUNTING-BASED DEBT CONVENANTS

Exhibit 45-8 contains a summary of the nature of accounting-based debt covenant restrictions, adapted from Duke and Hunt (1990). *Restricted retained earnings* as a constraint on dividend payments, one of the most common forms used, is outlined in Exhibit 45-9. The Luby's covenants discussed in the text are examples of these restrictions.

Information regarding these covenants was obtained by Smith and Warner (1979) and Duke and Hunt (1990) from the American Bar Foundation's *Commentaries on Debentures*, which summarizes typical covenants found in lending agreements. A cursory examination of these restrictions makes it clear that creditors seek to limit the firm's level of risk (investment and debt restrictions) and preserve the assets of the firm to ensure that debts are repaid (payment restrictions). Thus, covenants attempt to limit shareholders' ability to transfer assets to themselves (dividend restrictions), new shareholders (merger and acquisition restrictions), or new creditors (debt restrictions).

The best source of information on specific covenants (and other terms of the bond issue) for publicly issued bonds is the bond indenture, the legal document created when the bond is issued and filed with the registration statement filed with the SEC. The trustee (normally a bank) will have a copy of the indenture and is responsible for the enforcement of its terms. The bond prospectus should contain a good summary of these terms. Bank credit agreements entered into by public companies are filed with SEC annual (10-K) or quarterly (10-Q) reports.

For all debt issues, summarized data can be found in:

▶ Services such as Moody's Industrial Manual

▶ Annual reports

▶ SEC filings by debtors

Press and Weintrop (1990 and 1991) contend that information obtained from annual reports and Moody's is not comprehensive, especially with respect to covenants relating to privately placed debt, and that in these cases, it is necessary to access the original SEC filings.

Calculation of Accounting-Based Constraints

Each type of constraint is defined in the covenants. In addition, the covenants specify:

▶ Whether GAAP definitions are to be used or GAAP is to be modified. Leftwich (1983) noted that such modifications are most often associated with private rather than public debt indentures.

▶ Whether GAAP in effect at the time of the debt issuance are maintained throughout the life of the bond ("frozen" GAAP), or calculations in subsequent years are to be based on GAAP in effect at the date of the calculation ("rolling" GAAP). This is important when important new accounting standards are adopted.

Mohrman (1996) examined a sample of 174 lending agreements that contained covenants based on financial statement information. She found that over half (90) the covenants were based on *fixed* GAAP specified in the agreements. That is, the covenants were not affected by voluntary or FASB-mandated accounting changes, nor were they originally designed to mimic GAAP in effect at the time the contract was signed. Additionally, she found that contracts that contained more accounting-based covenants were more likely to specify fixed GAAP provisions and the use of such provisions in contracts was increasing over time.

(continued)

BOX 45-5   *(continued)*

EXHIBIT 45-8	Common Accounting-Based Debt Covenant Restrictions

Attribute:	Retained earnings
Measured as:	Restricted retained earnings
Limits:	Payments of dividends or stock repurchase below minimum level of restricted retained earnings
Attribute:	Net assets
Measured as:	Net tangible assets or net assets
Limits:	Investments, dividend payments, and new debt issues if net assets fall below a certain level
Attribute:	Working capital
Measured as:	Minimum working capital or current ratio
Limits:	Mergers and acquisitions, dividend payments, and new debt issues if the working capital or the current ratio fall below a certain level
Attribute:	Debt-to-equity
Measured as:	Debt divided by net tangible assets or debt divided by net assets
Limits:	Issuance of additional debt

Source: Joanne C. Duke and Herbert G. Hunt III, "An Empirical Examination of Debt Covenant Restrictions and Accounting-Related Debt Proxies," *Journal of Accounting and Economics,* Jan. 1990, adapted from Table 1, p. 52.

EXHIBIT 45-9	Unrestricted Retained Earnings: Inventory of Payable Funds

The most frequent accounting-based restriction specified is the dividend constraint. Dividends cannot be paid out of restricted retained earnings. Only unrestricted retained earnings, often referred to as the inventory of payable funds (IPF), are available for dividends. The general formulation of IPF is defined (see Smith and Warner, 1979) as the sum of:

1. A specified percentage k of earnings E from the date of the debt issuance to the present period, plus
2. Proceeds from the sale of common shares CS from the date of the debt issuance to the present period, plus
3. A prespecified constant F, less
4. The sum of dividends DV and stock repurchases from the date of the debt issuance to the present period

(Exhibit continued on next page ...)

BOX 45-5   *(continued)*

EXHIBIT 45-9   (continued)

Algebraically, this is equal to

$$\text{IPF}_t = k \sum_{i=0}^{t} E_i + \sum_{i=0}^{t} CS_i + F - \sum_{i=0}^{t} DV_i$$

where period 0 represents the date of the debt issuance and period *t* refers to the current date. The prespecified constant *F* is usually set at approximately one year's earnings.* This builds some slack into the system in the event the firm has a loss.

---

*See Smith and Warner (1979), Note 36.

Costs and Effects of Covenant Violations

Although creditors have a right to demand immediate payment when an accounting-based debt covenant is violated, they do not usually do so. This does not mean that violating such covenants is costless. Waivers of such violations often come with strings attached. Creditors may renegotiate the terms of the debt to demand:

▶ Accelerated principal payments

▶ An increased interest rate

▶ Liens on assets (such as accounts receivable)

▶ New covenants increasing restrictions on the firm's investing, borrowing, and dividend-paying ability

Chen and Wei (1993) examined a sample of 128 companies that disclosed violations of their accounting-based debt covenants. For 71 of these firms, the creditors did not waive the violation but demanded accelerated payments or higher interest rates. Beneish and Press (1993) found the median interest rate increase to be 80 basis points; they estimated that the overall cost of such renegotiations averaged from 1 to 2% of the market value of the firm's equity or 4 to 7% of the balance on the loan.

When waivers were granted, not surprisingly, they were more often granted for secured debt and for smaller-size loans. Similarly, waivers were more likely to be granted to "healthier" firms considered less likely to become bankrupt. When waivers were granted, they were often (24 of the 57 companies) given only for limited time periods.

Successful renegotiation of the debt terms or receipt of a waiver may not be the last word. Chen and Wei found that by the following year creditors demanded payment of the debt for 39 companies (30% of the sample), forcing 13 companies into bankruptcy.

Beneish and Press found that accounting-based covenants were often relaxed as a result of renegotiation. However, they were supplanted with more direct covenants restricting capital expenditures, mergers, assets sales, stock repurchases, and future borrowings.

These results indicate the importance of monitoring debt covenants to ensure that the firm is not close to violating them. Such violations can expose the firm to direct out-of-pocket costs in the form of higher borrowing costs and/or limit the scope of a firm's investing and financing choices.*

---

* Given these costs, one can understand why DeFond and Jiambalvo (1994) reported that managements engage in (accounting) manipulations in an effort to satisfy the covenants.

SUMMARY

In this reading, we have examined the different forms that debt financing can take. The choice of debt issue can have significant effects on the pattern of reported income, cash flows, and financial position. In addition, different debt instruments respond differently to changes in interest rates. The reader should now have an understanding of the following issues:

1. The effects of zero-coupon or low-coupon debt, variable rate debt, and foreign currency debt on the firm's financial statements.

2. The economic and financial statement effects of interest rate swaps.

3. The implications for financial analysis of variable-rate debt versus fixed-rate debt.

4. The economic and accounting effects of debt with equity features.

5. The analyst's need to classify between debt and equity based on the essence of the financial instrument rather than its form.

6. The effect of changes in interest rates on the market value of debt and when the market value should be used instead of carrying value.

7. The accounting effects of debt retirement and analytical adjustments required.

8. The importance of debt covenants to the analysis of the firm.

Debt can also take forms that do not require recognition on the balance sheet. Such off-balance-sheet debt is the subject of the next reading.

PROBLEMS FOR READING 45

1. [Zero-coupon debt; CFA© adapted] Compare the effect of issuing zero-coupon debt with that of issuing full-coupon debt with the same effective interest rate on a company's:

   A. Cash flow from operations over the life of the debt

   B. Cash flow from financing in the year of issuance, the year of maturity, and over the life of the debt.

   C. Cash flow from investing over the life of the debt

   D. Trend of net income over the life of the debt

2. [Zero-coupon bonds] The Null Company issued a zero-coupon bond on January 1, 2000, due December 31, 2004. The face value of the bond was $100,000. The bond was issued at an effective rate of 12% (compounded annually).

   A. Calculate the cash proceeds of the bond issue.

   B. Complete the following table on a *pretax* basis, assuming that all interest is paid in the year it is due:

	2000	2001	2002	2003	2004
Earnings before interest and taxes	$50,000	$50,000	$50,000	$50,000	$50,000
Cash flow from operations before interest and taxes	60,000	60,000	60,000	60,000	60,000
Cash flow from operations					
Times interest earned					
Times interest earned (cash basis)					

C. Assume that Null had raised the same cash proceeds with a conventional bond issued at par, paying interest annually and the principal at maturity. Complete the following table, under the assumptions in part b:

	2000	2001	2002	2003	2004
Earnings before interest and taxes	$50,000	$50,000	$50,000	$50,000	$50,000
Cash flow from operations before interest and taxes	60,000	60,000	60,000	60,000	60,000
Cash flow from operations					
Times interest earned					
Times interest earned (cash basis)					

D. Using the results of parts b and c, discuss the impact on reported cash flow from operations and interest coverage of Null's choice of bond.

E. Explain how consideration of income taxes would change your answers to parts b through d.

3. [Zero-coupon bond; foreign currency debt] Roche has outstanding zero-coupon U.S. dollar notes, with a $2.15 billion face value due 2010, that were issued with a 7% yield to maturity. They are carried at the following amounts:

	12-31-98	12-31-99
Carrying amount (CHF millions)	1,282	1,618
Exchange rate (CHF/dollar)	1.37	1.60

A. Compute the carrying amount of the bonds in $U.S. at December 31, 1998.

B. Explain the difference between your answer to part a and the $2.15 billion face amounts of the notes.

C. Estimate the interest expense (in CHF) for those notes for 1999.

D. Using your answer for part c and the December 31, 1998 carrying value, estimate the carrying amount of the notes (in CHF) at December 31, 1999.

E. Provide two possible explanations for the difference between your answer to part d and the actual carrying amount in Swiss francs at December 31, 1999.

F. Describe the effect of issuing these notes, instead of full coupon notes, on Roche's:

  i. Cash from operations

  ii. Trend of interest expense

G. Describe the effect of the change in the value of the dollar during 1999 on Roche's interest expense on these notes.

4. [Understanding bond relationships; coupon versus effective interest] The Walk & Field Co. has outstanding bonds originally issued at a discount. During 2000, the unamortized bond discount decreased from $8,652 to $7,290. Annual interest paid was $7,200. The market rate of interest was 12% when the bond was issued.

Using the data provided, calculate:

    i. Interest expense for 2000

   ii. The face value of the bond

  iii. The coupon rate of the bond

Note: You do not need present value calculations or tables to solve this problem.)

5. [Foreign currency debt] Bristol-Myers [BMY] reported the following components of its long-term debt (in $millions):

December 31	1998	1999
2.14% yen notes, due 2005	$55	$62
1.73% yen notes, due 2003	54	62

The $U.S. equaled 113.60 Japanese yen at December 31, 1998 and 102.51 at December 31, 1999.

A. Compute the outstanding debt in Japanese yen at December 31, 1998 and 1999 for both issues.

B. Compute the percentage change in the outstanding debt in yen during 1999 for both issues.

C. Assuming that no new bonds were issued, state one conclusion that can be drawn from your answers to parts a and b.

D. State two possible motivations for Bristol-Myers, an American company, to issue debt in Japanese yen.

6. [Convertible debt] Note 5 of Takeda's annual report states that the company had convertible bonds outstanding at March 31, 1998 but none outstanding at March 31, 1999. From the statement of stockholders' equity and cash flow statement we can deduce that most of the bonds (more than 22 billion yen) were converted into approximately 11 million shares, implying a conversion price of approximately 2,000 yen per share. The market price of Takeda shares exceeded 3,000 yen during all of calendar 1998.

Years Ended March 31	1998	1999
As reported in millions yen		
Bank loans	9,509	9,361
Current debt	24,077	2,119
Long-term debt	10,896	9,858
Total debt	44,482	21,338
Equity	829,381	907,373
Total capital	873,863	928,711

A. Describe the advantages to Takeda of having issued these convertible notes rather than nonconvertible notes. State one disadvantage.

B. Compute Takeda's debt-to-total capital ratio at March 31, 1998 and March 31, 1999. State the factor that accounted for most of the change in that ratio.

C. State the appropriate classification for the convertible notes at March 31, 1998 (debt or equity) and justify your choice.

7. [Market value of debt versus book value; interest rate sensitivity] AMR [AMR] is the parent company of American Airlines. Exhibit 45P-1 contains extracts from Note 6 of AMR's 1999 annual report.

A. Based on the fair value data, state whether the long-term rates used to determine fair value rose or fell in 1999. Justify your choice.

B. State whether the interest rate used to determine the fair value of the $437 million "9.0%–10.20% debentures" (due through 2021) at December 31, 1999 was

i. Below 10.20%

ii. Above 10.20%

Justify your choice.

C. Explain why the fair value of the $86 million variable-rate indebtedness equals the carrying value for both years.

EXHIBIT 45P-1   AMR CORP.

Amounts in $millions

---

6. Financial Instruments and Risk Management Fair Values of Financial Instruments

The fair values of the Company's long-term debt were estimated using quoted market prices where available. For long-term debt not actively traded, fair values were estimated using discounted cash flow analyses, based on the Company's current incremental borrowing rates for similar types of borrowing arrangements. The carrying amounts and estimated fair values of the Company's long-term debt, including current maturities, were (in millions):

| | December 31, | | | |
| | 1999 | | 1998 | |
	Carrying Value	Fair Value	Carrying Value	Fair Value
Secured variable and fixed-rate indebtedness	$2,651	$2,613	$890	$1,013
7.875% – 10.62% notes	1,014	1,024	875	973
9.0% – 10.20% debentures	437	469	437	531
6.0% – 7.10% bonds	176	174	176	189
Variable rate indebtedness	86	86	86	86
Other	16	16	20	20
	$4,380	$4,382	$2,484	$2,812

(Exhibit continued on next page ...)

EXHIBIT 45P-1   (continued)

Interest Rate Risk Management

American enters into interest rate swap contracts to effectively convert a portion of its fixed-rate obligations to floating-rate obligations. These agreements involve the exchange of amounts based on a floating interest rate for amounts based on fixed interest rates over the life of the agreement without an exchange of the notional amount upon which the payments are based. The differential to be paid or received as interest rates change is accrued and recognized as an adjustment of interest expense related to the obligation. The related amount payable to or receivable from counterparties is included in current liabilities or assets. The fair values of the swap agreements are not recognized in the financial statements. Gains and losses on terminations of interest rate swap agreements are deferred as an adjustment to the carrying amount of the outstanding obligation and amortized as an adjustment to interest expense related to the obligation over the remaining term of the original contract life of the terminated swap agreement. In the event of the early extinguishment of a designated obligation, any realized or unrealized gain or loss from the swap would be recognized in income coincident with the extinguishment.

The following table indicates the notional amounts and fair values of the Company's interest rate swap agreements (in millions):

| | December 31, | | | |
| | 1999 | | 1998 | |
	Notional Amount	Fair Value	Notional Amount	Fair Value
Interest rate swap agreements	$696	$(9)	$1,054	$38

The fair values represent the amount the Company would pay or receive if the agreements were terminated at December 31, 1999 and 1998, respectively.

At December 31, 1999, the weighted-average remaining life of the interest rate swap agreements in effect was 5.1 years. The weighted-average floating rates and fixed rates on the contracts outstanding were:

| | December 31, | |
	1999	1998
Average floating rate	5.855%	5.599%
Average fixed rate	6.593%	6.277%

Floating rates are based primarily on LIBOR and may change significantly, affecting future cash flows.

Source: AMR 10-K Report, December 31, 1999.

8. [Debt refinancing] On July 14, 2000, the *Wall Street Journal* reported on the earnings report by Fannie Mae [FNM], the largest mortgage lender in the United States. Fannie Mae has substantial outstanding debt and uses hedging techniques to manage its exposure to changing interest rates. Excerpts form that article follow:

Fannie Mae Posts 15% Earnings Gain for the Quarter
By Patrick Barta

Fannie Mae overcame a cooling housing market to report double-digit earnings growth for the second quarter. . . .

However, some pointed out that the company's results included a one-time after-tax gain of $32.7 million from the retirement of debt that helped compensate for a one-time trading loss. Typically, such gains are omitted when a company calculates its earnings-per-share results.

"In our mind, [the gain] should be excluded," says Charles L. Hill, First Call's director of research.

Fannie Mae says the company has long included retirement of debt in its earnings-per-share calculations, because it considers retirement of debt to be part of its continuing operations. The company notes that it reported gains and losses from debt retirement in its earnings-per-share calculations in 27 of the last 40 quarters. "It's something we do on a regular basis," says Mary Lou Christy, vice-president of investor relations.

At the heart of the debate was a one-time loss of about $60 million, attributed to a hedging strategy that lost money after interest rates for Fannie Mae debt rose unexpectedly.

The company was able to offset much of the loss by repurchasing debt at favorable rates, which produced the $32.7 million gain.[51]

A. Present one reason why the gain from debt retirement should be considered part of Fannie Mae's operating earnings and one reason why it should not.

B. Present one reason why the loss from the hedging strategy should be considered part of Fannie Mae's operating earnings and one reason why it should not.

C. Recommend the proper treatment for both items, from an analyst viewpoint, and justify your recommendation.

9. [Debt covenants] Exhibit 45P-2 contains information from NorAm Energy's 1994 Annual Report regarding debt covenants imposed by its creditors. The covenants restrict new borrowings and dividend payments. The exhibit states that as of December 31, 1994 the company has dividend capacity equal to $43.3 million. This amount was computed after reflecting the annual dividend of $42 million declared in 1994.

---

[51] *Wall Street Journal,* July 14, 2000, p. A2.

EXHIBIT 45P-2	NorAm Energy Corp.

Stockholders' Equity and Debt Convenants

Condensed Shareholders' Equity

	1994	**1993**
Capital Stock		
Preferred	$130,000	$130,000
Common stock including paid-in capital	944,870	944,118
	$1,074,870	$1,074,118
Retained Deficit		
Balance at beginning of year	(366,080)	(360,121)
Net income (loss)	48,066	36,087
Cash dividends		
Preferred stock, $3.00 per share	(7,800)	(7,800)
Common stock, $0.28 per share in 1994 and $0.28 per share in 1993	(34,265)	(34,246)
Balance at end of year	$(360,079)	$(366,080)
Unrealized gain on Itron investment, net of tax	2,586	
Total stockholders' equity	$717,377	$708,037

Note 5: Restrictions on Stockholders' Equity and Debt

Stockholders' Equity and Debt Covenants

Under the provisions of the Company's revolving credit facility as described in Note 3, and under similar provisions in certain of the Company's other financial arrangements, the Company's total debt capacity is limited and it is required to maintain a minimum level of stockholders' equity. The required minimum level of stockholders' equity was initially set at $650 million at December 31, 1993, increasing annually thereafter by (1) 50% of positive consolidated net income and (2) 50% of the proceeds (in excess of the first $50 million) of any incremental equity offering made after June 30, 1994. The Company's total debt is limited to $2.055 million. Based on these restrictions, the Company had incremental debt issuance and dividend capacity of $321.2 million and $43.3 million, respectively, at December 31, 1994. The Company's revolving credit facility also contains a provision which limits the Company's ability to reacquire, retire or otherwise prepay its long-term debt prior to its maturity to a total of $100 million.

Source: NorAm Energy, *1994 Annual Report.*

A. Show how the dividend capacity of $43.3 million as of December 31, 1994 was computed.

B. State whether the debt covenants restrict NorAm's ability to maintain its annual dividend through 1998. Justify your answer by preparing a schedule for the years 1995–1998 showing NorAm's expected and minimum shareholders' equity given current income and dividend levels.

C. Compute the level of income that would be required to maintain current dividend levels through 1998.

D. In 1995, NorAm approached its shareholders with a proposal to issue new shares. Suggest why the company was motivated to make this proposal and whether you, as a shareholder, would have supported the proposal.

LEASES AND OFF-BALANCE-SHEET DEBT

by Gerald I. White, Ashwinpaul C. Sondhi, and Dov Fried

LEARNING OUTCOMES

The candidate should be able to:

a. discuss the motivations for leasing assets instead of purchasing them and the incentives for reporting the leases as operating leases rather than capital leases;

b. determine the effects of capital and operating leases on the financial statements and ratios of the lessees and lessors;

c. describe the types and economic consequences of off-balance-sheet financing and determine how take-or-pay contracts, throughput arrangements, and the sale of receivables affect selected financial ratios;

d. distinguish between a sales-type lease and a direct financing lease and determine the effects on the financial statements and ratios of the lessors.

INTRODUCTION   1

Rapid changes in manufacturing and information technology and expanding international trade and capital markets have resulted in the growth of multinational corporations that must cope with increasingly mobile capital, labor, and product markets. Volatile commodity and other factor price levels, fluctuating interest and foreign currency exchange rates, and continuous tax and regulatory changes have accompanied these changes. In addition, general inflation and industry-specific price changes have raised many asset prices and have increased the risks of operations and investments.

This economic climate has required increasing amounts of capital as firms acquire operating capacity (both for expansion and replacement purposes) at ever-higher prices. Because of the volatility of prices and cash flows, the risks of owning operating assets have also increased. These trends have driven firms to seek methods of:

1. Acquiring the rights to assets through methods other than traditional direct purchases (financed by debt)

2. Controlling the risks of operation through derivative and hedging transactions

Executory contracts are the primary alternative form of transactions used by firms to acquire operating capacity, supplies of raw materials, and other inputs. Such contracts or arrangements are the subject of this reading.

The increased use of these financing techniques and hedging transactions has been encouraged by drawbacks in the historical cost-based financial reporting system, in which recognition and measurement depend primarily on actual transactions. As contracts are considered legal promises, and neither cash nor goods may be exchanged at the inception of these contracts, accounting recognition is not required in many cases. The emphasis on accounting assets and liabilities rather than the recognition of economic resources and obligations further encourages firms to keep resources and obligations off the balance sheet.

Firms may engage in these transactions to avoid reporting high debt levels and leverage ratios and to reduce the probability of technical default under restrictive covenants in debt indentures. Off-balance-sheet transactions may also keep assets and potential gains out of the financial statements but under the control of management, which can orchestrate the timing of gain recognition to offset periods of poor operating performance.

Footnote disclosures constitute the best source of information about off-balance-sheet activities. Additional information may be available from disclosures in 10-K filings and from other company publications. In some cases, the economic meaning behind the disclosures requires explanation from management. Thus, a complete analysis of the firm must include a review of all financial statement disclosures to obtain data on off-balance-sheet activities. In many cases, straightforward adjustments can be used to reflect off-balance-sheet assets and liabilities on the balance sheet. Such adjustments result in a balance sheet that presents a more complete portrait of the firm's resources and obligations and financial ratios that are more comparable to those of competitors whose use of off-balance-sheet techniques is different.

The reading begins with a discussion of leases, the most common form of executory contract entered into by firms. The methods used to analyze and adjust for leases serve as a model for the analysis of other off-balance-sheet activities that comprise the second part of the reading.

LEASES   2

Accounting policy makers have grappled with leases for years to develop reporting requirements that emphasize the economic substance rather than the legal form of the leasing transaction. We begin our discussion of leases with a review of incentives for leases. A discussion of reporting requirements and the analysis of leases complete this section of the reading.

Incentives for Leasing

Firms generally acquire rights to use property, plant, and equipment by outright purchase, partially or fully funded by internal resources or externally borrowed funds. In a purchase transaction, the buyer acquires (and the seller surrenders) ownership, which includes all the benefits and risks embodied in the asset. Alternatively, firms may also acquire the use of property, including some or all of the benefits and risks of ownership, for specific periods of time and stipulated rental payments through contractual arrangements called *leases*.

Short-term, or *operating*, leases allow the lessee to use leased property for only a portion of its economic life. The lessee accounts for such leases as contracts, reporting (as rental expense) only the required rental payments as they are made. Because the lessor retains substantially all the risks of ownership of leased property, the leased assets remain on its balance sheet and are depreciated over their estimated economic lives; rental payments are recognized as revenues over time according to the terms of the lease.

However, longer-term leases may effectively transfer all (or substantially all) the risks and rewards of the leased property to the lessee. Such leases are the economic equivalent of sales with financing arrangements designed to effect the purchase (by the lessee) and sale (by the lessor) of the leased property. *Such leases, referred to as finance or capital leases, are treated for accounting purposes as sales.* The asset and associated debt are carried on the books of the lessee, and the lessor records a gain on "sale" at the inception of the lease. The lessee depreciates the asset over its life, and treats lease payments as payments of principal and interest.[1] The lessor records a financing profit over the lease term. The financial reporting differences between accounting for a lease as an operating or capital lease are far-reaching and affect the balance sheet, income statement, cash flow statement, and associated ratios.

One motivation for leasing rather than borrowing and buying an asset is to avoid recognition of the debt and asset on the lessee's financial statements.[2] Lease capitalization eliminates this advantage. Whether a lease is reported as operating or capitalized depends, as we shall see, on the terms of the lease and their relationship to criteria specified by SFAS 13 and IAS 17.

Notwithstanding these financial reporting requirements, leases may be structured to qualify as operating leases to achieve desired financial reporting effects and capital structure benefits. Operating leases allow lessees to avoid recognition of the asset and report higher profitability ratios and indicators of operating efficiency. Reported leverage is also lower because the related liability for contractual payments is not recognized.

---

[1] The lease payments made by the lessee to the lessor are recorded by the latter as receipts of principal and interest.

[2] Firms may believe that investors, lenders, and rating services do not adjust for leases. However, debt covenants sometimes explicitly include operating leases. Ratings services also incorporate leases when setting debt ratings (see, for example, Moody's Investors Service, *Off-Balance-Sheet Leases: Capitalization and Ratings Implications*, October 1999).

Extensive use of operating leases needs careful evaluation and the analyst must adjust financial statements (to reflect unrecognized assets and liabilities) and the leverage, coverage, and profitability ratios for the effects of operating leases.

Box 46-1 reviews the finance literature on the competing incentives of the lease-versus-purchase decision. The impact of the financial reporting alternatives (operating vs. capitalization) on this decision is also discussed.

Lease Classification: Lessees

The preceding discussion suggests that lessees prefer to structure and report leases as operating leases. Their counterparts, lessors, however, prefer to structure leases as capital leases. This allows earlier recognition of revenue and income by reporting transactions that are in substance installment sales or financing arrangements as completed sales. The resulting higher profitability and turnover ratios are powerful incentives for lessors. The final section of the reading is devoted to a discussion of lease accounting from the perspective of the lessor. The discussion that follows retains the lessee perspective.

Lease classifications are not intended to be alternative reporting methods. However, management actively negotiates the provisions of lease agreements and the preferred accounting treatment is an important element of these contractual negotiations.

SFAS 13 (1976) and IAS 17 (revised 1997) attempt to promulgate "objective" and "reliable" criteria to facilitate the evaluation of the economic substance of lease agreements. One goal was to discourage off-balance-sheet financing by lessees and front-end loading of income by lessors. The criteria are designed to ensure that either the lessee or lessor recognize the leased assets on their books.

Capital Leases

A lease that, in economic substance, transfers to the lessee substantially all the risks and rewards inherent in the leased property is a financing or capital lease and should be capitalized. Under U.S. GAAP, the lessee must classify a lease meeting any one of the following SFAS 13 criteria at the inception of the lease as a capital lease:

1. The lease transfers ownership of the property to the lessee at the end of the lease term.

2. The lease contains a bargain purchase option.

3. The lease term is equal to 75% or more of the estimated economic life of the leased property (not applicable to land or when the lease term begins within the final 25% of the economic life of the asset).

4. The present value[3] of the minimum lease payments[4] (MLPs) equals or exceeds 90% of the fair value of leased property to the lessor.

The ownership and bargain purchase criteria imply a transfer of all the risks and benefits of the leased property to the lessee; in economic substance, such leases are financing arrangements. Lease terms extending to at least 75% of the

---

[3] The discount rate used to compute the present values should be the lessee's incremental borrowing rate or the implicit interest rate of the lessor, whichever is *lower*. The use of the lower rate generates the higher of two present values, increasing the probability that this criterion will be met and the lease capitalized. Under IAS 17, there is a similar (but less precise) requirement.

[4] MLPs include residual values when they are guaranteed by lessees since the guarantee results in a contractually fixed residual value and effectively transfers the risk of changes in residual values to the lessee.

BOX 46-1   INCENTIVES FOR LEASING AND THEIR EFFECT ON THE CAPITAL VERSUS OPERATING LEASE CHOICE

Management may have a number of reasons to prefer leasing compared to outright asset purchases. The choice may be a function of strategic investment and capital structure objectives, the comparative costs* of leasing versus equity or debt financing, the availability of tax benefits, and perceived financial reporting advantages. Some of these factors influence whether the lease will be treated as an operating or capital lease; others are unrelated to reporting methods.

Tax Incentives

The tax benefits of owning assets are exploited best by transferring them to the party in the higher marginal tax bracket. Firms with low effective tax rates more readily engage in leasing than firms in high tax brackets as the tax benefits can be passed on to the lessor. El-Gazzar et al. (1986) found that, consistent with this hypothesis, firms with lower effective tax rates had a higher proportion of lease debt to total assets than did firms with higher effective tax rates. Moreover, lessees with high effective tax rates tended to capitalize their leases for financial statement purposes. El-Gazzar et al. argue that tax effects also influence the choice of accounting method as the lessee attempts to influence the tax interpretation (by the IRS) of lease contracts. That is, it is more difficult to argue for capital lease treatment for tax purposes if the lease is treated as an operating lease for book purposes.

Nontax Incentives

Smith and Wakeman (1985) analyzed nontax incentives related to the lease-versus-purchase decision. Their list of eight nontax factors that make leasing more likely than purchasing is presented here. Some of these factors are not directly related to the lessee's choice, but are motivated by the manufacturer or lessor and/or the type of asset involved. We have sorted these conditions by their potential impact on the operating-versus-capitalization accounting choice.

Nontax Incentives for Leasing versus Purchase: Incentives Classified by Potential Impact on Operating versus Capital Lease Choice

Favors Operating Lease per SFAS 13

1. Period of use is short relative to the overall life of the asset.

2. Lessor has comparative advantage in reselling the asset.

Favors Structuring Lease as Operating Lease

3. Corporate bond covenants contain specific covenants relating to financial policies that the firm must follow.

4. Management compensation contracts contain provisions expressing compensation as a function of returns on invested capital.

Not Relevant to Operating versus Capital Lease Decision

5. Lessee ownership is closely held so that risk reduction is important.

6. Lessor (manufacturer) has market power and can thus generate higher profits by leasing the asset (and controlling the terms of the lease) rather than selling it.

(continued)

> **BOX 46-1** *(continued)*
>
> **7.** Asset is not specialized to the firm.
>
> **8.** Asset's value is not sensitive to use or abuse (owner takes better care of asset than lessee).
>
> Short periods of use and the resale factor favor the use of operating leases, and under GAAP, these conditions would lead to lease agreements consistent with operating leases. The bond covenant and management compensation incentives also favor the negotiated structuring of the agreement as an operating lease.
>
> Consistent with the foregoing, both Abdel-Khalik (1981) and Nakayama et al. (1981) note that the expected covenant violations resulting from SFAS 13 influenced firms to lobby against its adoption. Furthermore, Abdel-Khalik notes that firms renegotiated the terms of their leases during SFAS 13's transition period to make them eligible for treatment as operating leases. Imhoff and Thomas (1988) found that subsequent to SFAS 13, there was a general decline in leases as a form of financing.[†] Taken together, these results confirm that debt covenant and compensation factors affect both the choice of leasing as a form of financing as well as the choice of accounting treatment of the lease.
>
> _____
>
> Based on Smith and Wakeman (1985).
>
> * Related to these costs are the risks related to residual values and obsolescence.
>
> [†] Further evidence is provided by El-Gazzar et al., who note that in the pre-SFAS 13 period, firms that had high debt-to-equity ratios and/or had incentive-based contracts based on income after interest expense were more likely to have leases classified as operating leases.

economic life of the leased asset are also considered to achieve such a transfer; there is an implicit assumption that most of the value of an asset accrues to the user within that period. Finally, a lease must be capitalized when the present value of the minimum lease payments is equal to or exceeds 90% of the fair value of the leased property at the inception of the lease. In effect, the lessee has contractually agreed to payments ensuring that the lessor will recover its investment along with a reasonable return. The transaction is, therefore, an installment purchase for the lessee financed by the lessor, and capitalization reflects this economic interpretation of the leasing transaction.[5]

The provisions of IAS 17 are less precise. That standard defines a finance lease (the IAS term for a capital lease) as one:

> that transfers substantially all of the risks and rewards incident to ownership of an asset. Title may or may not eventually be transferred.[6]

As IAS 17 lacks the quantitative criteria of SFAS 13, it is easier for a lease to be classified as an operating lease under IAS standards than under U.S. GAAP.

Operating Leases

Under U.S. GAAP, leases not meeting any of the four SFAS 13 criteria listed above are not capitalized and no asset or obligation is reported in the financial

_____

[5] Leases are classified at the inception of the lease; the classification is not changed when the lessee or lessor is acquired unless the provisions of the lease agreement are changed. See FASB Interpretation 21 (1978).

[6] IAS 17, para. 3. An operating lease is defined as a "lease other than a finance lease."

statements of the lessee since no purchase is deemed to have occurred. Such leases are classified as operating leases, and payments are reported as rental expense. SFAS 13 mandates the use of the straight-line method of recognizing periodic rental payments unless another, systematic basis provides a better representation of the use of leased property. As a result, for leases with rising rental payments, lease expense and cash flow will not be identical.

Financial Reporting by Lessees: Capital versus Operating Leases

Financial reporting by lessees will be illustrated using a noncancellable lease beginning December 31, 2000, with annual MLPs of $10,000 made at the end of each year for four years. Ten percent is assumed to be the appropriate discount rate.

Operating Lease.   If the lease does not meet any criteria requiring capitalization:

▶ No entry is made at the inception of the lease.

▶ Over the life of the lease, only the annual rental expense of $10,000 will be charged to income and CFO.

Capital Lease.   If the lease meets any one of the four criteria of a capital lease:

▶ At the inception of the lease, an asset (leasehold asset) and liability (leasehold liability) equal to the present value of the lease payments, $31,700, is recognized.

▶ Over the life of the lease:

1. The annual rental expense of $10,000 will be allocated between interest and principal payments on the $31,700 leasehold liability according to the following amortization schedule:

Allocation of Payment of $10,000

Year	Opening Liability	Interest*	Principal	Closing Liability†
2000				$31,700
2001	$31,700	$3,170	$6,830	24,870
2002	24,870	2,487	7,513	17,357
2003	17,357	1,735	8,265	9,092
2004	9,092	909	9,092	0

*10% of the opening liability.

†Equals the opening liability less the periodic amortization of the lease obligation. Also equals the present value of the remaining MLPs discounted at the interest rate in effect at the inception of the lease.

2. The cost of the leasehold asset of $31,700 is charged to operations (annual depreciation is $7,925) using the straight-line method over the term of the lease.[7]

---

[7] Generally, depreciation methods used for similar purchased property are applied to leased assets over their estimated economic lives when one of the transfer of ownership criteria (1 or 2) is met and over the lease term when one of the other capitalization criteria (3 or 4) is satisfied.

Comparative Analysis of Capitalized and Operating Leases

Balance Sheet Effects.   No assets or liabilities are recognized if the lease is treated as an operating lease. When leases are capitalized, there is a major impact on a firm's balance sheet at inception and throughout the life of the lease. At the inception of the lease, an asset and a liability equal to the present value of the lease payments are recognized.

Balance Sheet Effects of Lease Capitalization

	2000	2001	2002	2003	2004
Assets					
Leased assets	$31,700	$31,700	$31,700	$31,700	$31,700
Accumulated depreciation	0	7,925	15,850	23,775	31,700
Leased assets, net	$31,700	$23,775	$15,850	$ 7,925	$ 0
Liabilities					
Current portion of lease obligation	6,830	7,513	8,265	9,092	0
Long-term debt: lease obligation	24,870	17,357	9,092	0	0
	$31,700	$24,870	$17,357	$ 9,092	$ 0

The gross and net (of accumulated depreciation) amounts are reported at each balance sheet date. The current and noncurrent components of the lease obligation are reported as liabilities under capitalization. The current component is the principal portion of the lease payment to be made in the following year. Note that, at the inception of the lease, the leased asset and liability are equal at $31,700. Since the asset and liability are amortized using different methods, this equality is not again observed until the end of the lease term when both asset and liability are equal to zero.

Effect on Financial Ratios.   Lease capitalization increases asset balances, resulting in lower asset turnover and return on asset ratios, as compared with the operating lease method, which does not record leased assets.

The most important effect of lease capitalization, however, is its impact on leverage ratios. As lease obligations are not recognized for operating leases, leverage ratios are understated. Lease capitalization adds both current and noncurrent liabilities to debt, resulting in a corresponding decrease in working capital and increases in the debt-to-equity and other leverage ratios.

Income Statement Effects.   The income statement effects of lease reporting are also significant and impact operating income as well as net income. The operating lease method charges the periodic rental payments to expense as accrued, whereas capitalization recognizes depreciation and interest expense over the lease term.

	Operating Lease	Capital Lease		
	Operating = Total Expense	Operating Expense	Nonoperating Expense	
Year	Rent	Depreciation	Interest	Total Expense
2001	$10,000	$ 7,925	$3,170	$11,095
2002	10,000	7,925	2,487	10,412
2003	10,000	7,925	1,735	9,660
2004	10,000	7,925	909	8,834
Totals	$40,000	$31,700	$8,300	$40,000

Income Effects of Lease Classification

Operating Income. Capitalization results in higher operating income (earnings before interest and taxes, or EBIT) since the annual straight-line depreciation expense of $7,925 is lower than the annual rental expense of $10,000 reported under the operating lease method. For an individual lease, this difference is never reversed and remains constant over the lease term given use of the straight-line depreciation method. Accelerated depreciation methods would generate smaller differences in early years, with an increasing difference as depreciation declines, increasing both the level and trend of EBIT.

Total Expense and Net Income. Under capitalization, lease expense includes interest expense and depreciation of the leased asset. Initially, total expense for a capital lease exceeds rental expense reported for an operating lease, but declines over the lease term as interest expense falls.[8] In later years, total lease expense will be less than rental expense reported for an operating lease.

Note that total expense (interest plus depreciation) for a capital lease must equal total rental expense for an operating lease over the life of the lease.[9] Consequently, although total net income over the lease term is not affected by capitalization, the timing of income recognition is changed; lower net income is reported in the early years, followed by higher income in later years. This relationship holds for individual leases, but the effect on a firm depends on any additional leases entered into in subsequent periods. When asset prices (and lease rentals) are rising, the impact of old leases nearing expiration may be swamped by the impact of new leases. If a firm enters into new leases at the same or increasing rate over time, reported net income will remain lower under capitalization.

Effect on Financial Ratios. In general, firms with operating leases report higher profitability, interest coverage (as interest expense is lower), return on equity, and return on assets ratios. The higher ROE ratios are due to the higher profitability (numerator effect), whereas the higher ROA is due primarily to the lower assets (denominator effect).

---

[8] If the company uses accelerated depreciation, then the difference in earlier years will be greater but the subsequent decline will also be rapid.

[9] This equality does not hold when the residual value is not zero.

Cash Flow Effects of Lease Classification.   Lease classification provides another example where accounting methods affect the classification of cash flows.[10] Under the operating lease method, all cash flows are operating and there is an operating cash outflow of $10,000 per year. However, lease capitalization results in both operating and financing cash flows as the rental payments of $10,000 are allocated between interest expense (treated as CFO) and amortization of the lease obligation (reported as cash from financing).

Cash Flow Effects of Lease Classification

	Operating Lease	Capital Lease	
Year	Operations	Operations	Financing
2001	$10,000	$3,170	$6,830
2002	10,000	2,487	7,513
2003	10,000	1,735	8,265
2004	10,000	909	9,091

In 2001, for example, CFO differs between the two methods by $6,830, the amortization of the lease obligation. Because interest expense declines over the lease term and an increasing proportion of the annual payment is allocated to the lease obligation, the difference in CFO increases over the lease term. Thus, lease capitalization systematically decreases the operating cash outflow while increasing the financing cash outflow.

Therefore, although the capital lease method adversely affects some financial statement ratios, it allows firms to report higher operating cash flows compared to those reported using the operating lease method.

Before proceeding, it is important to point out that *at the inception of the lease (year 2000), no cash flows are reported.* This is true even though a capital lease implies the purchase of an asset (cash outflow for investment) financed by the issuance of new debt (cash inflow from financing). Disclosure of the event is reported as part of the "significant noncash financing and investing activities." Analysts attempting to estimate a firm's cash flow requirements for operating capacity should, however, include the present value of such leases as a cash requirement. *Moreover, free cash flow calculations for valuation purposes should incorporate the present value of leases as a cash outflow for investment at the inception of the lease.*

Analysis of Lease Disclosures

A noncancellable lease, whether reported as a capital or operating lease, in effect, constitutes debt and the right to use an asset. If the lease is reported as a capital lease, this information is on-balance-sheet. If it is reported as an operating lease, then the debt and asset are off-balance-sheet and the analyst must adjust accordingly.

---

[10] We discuss only the classification of cash flows. After-tax cash flows are not affected by lease classification as *generally* firms that use the capital lease method for financial reporting purposes use the operating lease method for tax purposes. Tax payments and actual cash flows are therefore identical. Under the capital lease method, the lease expense under financial reporting exceeds the lease expense reported for tax purposes, resulting in a deferred tax asset.

This is especially true in industries such as airlines and retailers where some firms own operating assets (i.e., airplanes or stores), other firms lease them and report the leases as capital leases, and still other lessees account for them as operating leases. Given the same conditions, the firms using operating leases may report the "best" results as they will show minimal debt and their higher profits will appear to be generated by a relatively smaller investment in assets.

However, the disclosure requirements of firms with leases, capital or operating, are sufficiently detailed to provide the information required for adjustments.

Lease Disclosure Requirements

SFAS 13 requires the disclosure of gross amounts of capitalized lease assets as of each balance sheet date, by major classes or grouped by their nature or function; they may be combined with owned assets.

Lessees must also disclose future MLPs for each of the five succeeding fiscal years and the aggregate thereafter as well as the net present value of the capitalized leases.

Lessees reporting operating leases must also disclose future MLPs for each of the five succeeding fiscal years and in the aggregate thereafter (see Exhibit 46-1 for an example). The present value of the MLPs is not required but is occasionally provided. The rental expense under operating leases (classified as to minimum, contingent, and sublease rentals) for each period for which an income statement is presented must be disclosed as of the balance sheet date.

For both operating and capital leases, lessees must also disclose aggregate minimum rentals receivable under noncancellable subleases. Information regarding renewal terms, purchase options, contingent rentals, any escalation clauses, and restrictions on dividends, additional debt, and leasing is also required. However, rather than being informative, such disclosure is usually vague and general in nature.

IAS 17 disclosure requirements are far less extensive:

▶ MLPs due within one year
▶ MLPs due in more than one but less than five years
▶ MLPs due after five years

This abbreviated disclosure (for an example, see Note 12 of the Roche 2000 annual report) makes the analysis that follows less precise, but does permit approximations.

Financial Reporting by Lessees: An Example

Exhibit 46-1 contains balance sheet information and the lease footnote of AMR Corp. [AMR], the parent of American Airlines. From the balance sheet alone, it would seem that AMR primarily purchases rather than leases its equipment. The carrying value of purchased equipment is over seven times that of leased equipment.

The footnote paints an entirely different picture. AMR has substantial leases that are mostly structured as operating leases. As required by GAAP, capital lease obligations and operating leases are shown separately. Future MLPs for the next five years, and the aggregate thereafter, are disclosed for both capital and operating leases. For capital leases, interest has been deducted to report their present value of $1,847 million ($236 million is reported as current and $1,611 million as long-term debt).

EXHIBIT 46-1	AMR Excerpts from Balance Sheet and Lease Footnote, December 31, 1999 (in $millions)

Assets

Equipment and property (net of accumulated depreciation of 7,403)		$14,338
Equipment and property under capital leases (net of accumulated amortization of 1,347)		1,949
Total assets		24,374

Liabilities

Long-term debt		
Current maturity	$ 302	
Noncurrent	4,078	4,380
Capital lease obligations		
Current	$ 236	
Noncurrent	1,611	1,847
Total long-term debt and capital lease obligations		$ 6,227
Shareholders' equity		6,858

Leases

AMR's subsidiaries lease various types of equipment and property, including aircraft and airport and off-airport facilities. The future minimum lease payments required under capital leases, together with the present value of net minimum lease payments, and future minimum lease payments required under operating leases that have initial or remaining noncancellable lease terms in excess of one year as of December 31, 1999, were (in millions):

Years Ending December 31	Capital Leases	Operating Leases
2000	$ 347	$ 1,015
2001	329	1,006
2002	280	952
2003	198	965
2004	249	954
2005 and subsequent	1,081	12,169
	$2,484	$17,061
Less amount representing interest	(637)	
Present value of net minimum lease payments	$1,847	

At December 31, 1999, the Company had 205 jet aircraft and 71 turboprop aircraft under operating leases, and 79 jet aircraft and 61 turboprop aircraft under capital leases.

Source: AMR, *1999 Annual Report.*

Note that the (aggregate) operating lease payments of $17,061 million are almost seven times the capital lease payments ($2,484 million). Moreover, the data suggest that the operating leases are of longer term than the capital leases!

Aggregate MLPs of the capital leases for the next five years are about 56% of total future MLPs, or $1,403 million. Total MLPs for the remaining years are $1,081 million, or 44% of the total MLPs of $2,484 million over the lease terms. The average lease term of the capitalized leases can be estimated by computing the number of payments included in the "later years" amount of $1,081 million; that is, ($1,081 million/$249 million) if we assume that annual payments remain at the 2004 level. This suggests a lease term of approximately 9 (initial five plus the estimated remaining four) years.

For operating leases, the proportion of payments after the first five years is ($12,169/ $17,061) 71% of total payments. This suggests a longer term than for the capital leases. Dividing the remaining payments of $12,169 by the 2004 payment of $954 yields 13, suggesting a lease term of 18 years (5 plus 13) or *twice as long as the term of the capital leases.*

The note indicates that 205 jet aircraft and 71 turboprops are under operating leases. *Neither these assets nor the debt associated with them appear on the balance sheet.*

Investors and analysts can use the lease disclosures to adjust the balance sheet appropriately. The present value of the operating leases can be estimated by discounting the future minimum lease payments. This estimate requires assumptions about the pattern of MLPs after the first five years and the discount rate. The estimation procedure (described below) is "robust," with the calculated present value relatively invariant to the assumptions.

Assumed Pattern of MLPs.   Footnote disclosures reflect the payments to be made over each of the next five years and the total payments thereafter. The present value computation requires an estimate of the number of payments implicit in the latter lump sum. Either the rate of decline suggested by the cash outflows for the next five years or a constant amount over the remaining term may be used to derive the present value of the operating lease payments.

Discount Rate.   The discount rate should reflect the risk class of the leased assets as well as the company being analyzed. The interest rate implicit in the reported capital leases is a good approximation of that rate.[11]

Box 46-2 uses AMR to illustrate the estimation method(s). The procedure yields a rate of between 6.0% and 6.5% depending on the assumptions made; we use 6.4%. The two assumptions regarding pattern of cash flows over the lease term generate present value estimates of $10.1 and $9.9 billion, a difference of only 2%.

Impact of Operating Lease Adjustments

Liabilities.   The impact of the adjustment is highly significant. AMR's reported long-term debt and capital leases total $6.2 billion. Adding approximately $10 billion for off-balance-sheet operating leases increases debt by more than 160% to approximately $16.2 billion. *AMR has more debt off the balance sheet than on the balance sheet.* With equity of $6.9 billion, the debt-to-equity ratio of 0.9 mushrooms to 2.3.

---

[11] Because the implicit rate is an average rate based on terms at inception, it may be significantly different from either the reported or marginal long-term borrowing rate the company faces in the capital markets. The analyst may use a long-term borrowing rate estimated from the debt footnote or based on current market conditions.

BOX 46-2   ESTIMATION OF THE PRESENT VALUE OF OPERATING LEASES

A. The Implicit Discount Rate of a Firm's Capital Leases

Two approaches may be employed to estimate the average discount rate used to capitalize a firm's capital leases. The first uses only the next period's MLP; the second incorporates all future MLPs in the estimation procedure.

1. Using Next Period's MLP

The 2000 MLP for AMR's capital leases is $347 million. That payment includes interest and principal. The principal portion is shown in AMR's current liabilities section as $236 million. The difference, $111 million, represents the interest component of the MLP. As the present value of AMR's capital leases equals $1,847, the interest rate on the capitalized leases can be estimated as ($111/$1,847) 6.01%.

    This calculation assumes that the principal payment of $236 million will be made at the end of the year. If it is made early in the year, then the interest expense is based on the principal outstanding after payment of the current portion. The results can be biased if the current portion is a significant portion of the overall liability. An alternative estimate of the implicit interest rate may be derived using the average liability balance; that is, $111/[0.5 \times (\$1,847 + \$1,611)] = 6.42\%$.

2. Using All Future MLPs

The interest rate can also be estimated by solving for the implicit interest rate (internal rate of return) that equates the MLPs and their present value. This calculation requires an assumption about the pattern of MLPs after the first five years as the MLPs for the first five years (2000 to 2004) are given. From 2004 and on, two assumptions are possible:

1. Constant rate, or
2. Declining rate

Constant Rate

Under the simpler constant rate assumption, it is assumed that the payment level ($249 million) in the fifth year (2004) continues into the future, implying the following payment stream:

Year	2000	2001	2002	2003	2004	2005
MLP	$347	$329	$280	$198	$249	$249

Year	2006	2007	2008	2009[r]	Total	
MLP	$249	$249	$249	$85	$2,484	

[r] Residual.

The internal rate of return that equates this stream to the present value of $1,847 is 6.55%.

Declining Rate

Alternatively, and more realistically, one would expect the payments to decline over time. The rate of decline implicit in the MLPs reported individually for the first five years may be used to estimate the payment pattern after the initial five years. In

(continued)

BOX 46-2 *(continued)*

AMR's case, payments decrease initially and then jump in 2004. On average, the payments are approximately 94% of the previous year.* Using this rate we obtain the following pattern of payments:

Year	2000	2001	2002	2003	2004	2005
MLP	$347	$329	$280	$198	$249	$234

Year	2006	2007	2008	2009	2010[r]	Total
MLP	$220	$207	$194	$183	$43	$2,484

[r] Residual.

The internal rate of return that equates this stream to the present value of $1,847 is 6.40%; a rate close to the 6.55% based on the constant rate assumption. Generally, the differences are not significant and unless the rate of decline is very steep, the constant rate assumption simplifies the computation. The first procedure yields an estimate of 6.0 to 6.4%; the second yields estimates of 6.40 to 6.55%. Based on these estimates, we use 6.4% for our analysis of AMR's operating leases.

B. Finding the Present Value of the Operating Leases

For operating leases the MLPs for the first five years (2000 to 2004) are given. Again we can make two assumptions as to the pattern of payments for 2005 and on.

Under the constant rate assumption, it is assumed that MLPs from the year 2005 and on equal the 2004 payment of $954. Alternatively, based on the payment pattern of the operating lease MLPs over the first five years, one would expect the payments to decline at a rate of 1.5% a year. The assumed patterns and the resultant present values using the discount rate of 6.4% are presented below.

Constant Rate

Year	2000	2001	2002	2003	2004
MLP	$1,015	$1,006	$952	$965	$954

Year	2005–2016	2017[r]	Total	Present Value
MLP	$954	$721	$17,061	$10,060

[r] Residual.

Declining Rate

Year	2000	2001	2002	2003	2004	2005
MLP	$1,015	$1,006	$952	$965	$954	$940

Year	2006 ...	2018	2019[r]	Total	Present Value
MLP	$926 ...	$772	$221	$17,061	$9,911

[r] Residual.

Note that the two present value estimates of $10.1 and $9.9 billion are within 2% of each other.

(continued)

> ## BOX 46-2   *(continued)*
>
> ### C. Executory Costs
>
> Reported MLPs at times include such executory costs as maintenance, taxes, and insurance on the leased assets. These costs are not financing costs and should be excluded from the calculation of the lease present value. However, because footnote disclosures generally do not reduce MLPs by executory costs, the present value calculation described previously is biased.
>
> In most cases that bias is small and can be ignored. However, the estimation method can be modified to adjust for this bias. When the firm discloses the total of the executory costs, we can assume that the pattern of the executory costs follows that of the MLPs. If we define p as the proportion of total executory costs to total MLPs,
>
> $$p = \frac{\text{Total executory costs}}{\text{Total MLPs}}$$
>
> then the procedures described above can be applied† to a pattern of *adjusted MLPs*, where the
>
> $$\text{Adjusted MLP (for any year)} = (1 - p) \times \text{unadjusted MLP (for that year)}$$
>
> ---
>
> * We have used the arithmetic mean. The geometric mean is 92%.
>
> † Alternatively, one can use the unadjusted MLPs and make the following two adjustments:
>
> 1. In calculating the implicit interest rate of the capital leases, gross up the present value of the capital leases by *dividing* by $(1 - p)$.
>
> 2. Using the interest rate calculated in step 1, find the present value of the unadjusted MLPs. *Multiply* that present value by $(1 - p)$.

OPTIONAL SEGMENT ENDS

AMR: Effects of Operating Lease Adjustments (in $billions)

	Reported	+	Operating Leases	=	Adjusted
Debt	$ 6.2		$10.0		$16.2
Equity	6.9				6.9
Debt/equity ratio	0.9X				2.3X
Assets	$24.4		$10.0		$34.4

Assets.   Exhibit 46-1 reports total assets of $24.4 billion. Capitalization of the operating leases increases total assets by $10 billion. AMR is operating 41% more assets than reported on its balance sheet. *Efficiency measures such as turnover or ROA use total assets in the denominator and are highly overstated; adjusted ratios more accurately portray AMR's asset efficiency.*

Income and Cash Flow Effects.   Adjustments for operating leases also affect the income and cash flow statements (as well as related ratios). These effects can be illustrated using the 2000 MLP of $1,015 million as an example. Under the operating lease method, both rent expense and the CFO outflow equal $1,015 million. Capitalization results in allocation of that $1,015 million between interest expense and principal payments; in addition, the leased asset must be depreciated. These changes reduce reported income but increase CFO.

AMR: Effects of Operating Lease Adjustment, 2000 (in $millions)

	As Reported	Adjusted
Income Statement		
Rent expense	$1,015	
Interest expense		$ 640*
Amortization expense		555†
Total expense	$1,015	$1,195
Cash Flow Statement		
If interest payments are treated as CFO (per SFAS 95)		
CFO outflow	$1,015	$ 640
CFF outflow	0	$ 375
If interest payments are treated as CFF (per Reading 33)		
CFO outflow	$1,015	0
CFF outflow	0	$1,015

* Interest expense = interest rate × PV of leases = 0.064 × $10 billion = $640 million.

† Amortization expense = PV of leases divided by lease term = $10 billion/18 = $555 million.

Other Lease-Related Issues

While lease classification affects how leases are reported in financial statements, it is not the only issue that affects financial analysis. The following may also be significant for some companies:

1. *Lease impairment.* Because of changes in market conditions, leased assets can become uneconomic to the firm. In such cases, the firm may recognize an impairment charge similar to the impairment charges for fixed assets. For example, OMI [OMM], an operator of oil tankers, recorded a loss of $6.3 million in June 1999 when it "determined that its current lease obligations for vessels exceeded its undiscounted forecasted future net cash flows."

2. *Sale and leaseback of assets.* Such sales can be a cost-effective source of funds, especially for firms with low credit ratings. Because the assets sold secure the obligation, lenders charge a lower interest rate than for unsecured borrowings. Both SFAS 13 and IAS 17 require the lessee to defer any gain on the asset sale, and recognize it over the lease term, when the lease is a capital (finance) lease. Amortization over the lease term is also required for sale/leasebacks classified as operating leases under SFAS 13. However, under IAS 17, gains on sale/leasebacks classified as operating leases are recognized immediately.[12]

---

[12] The accounting for sale/leasebacks can be quite complex, with numerous variations and exceptions under both U.S. and IAS GAAP. See Box 46-4 for further discussion.

3. *Lease guarantees.* Firms may guarantee leases for affiliates (see discussion of Texaco later in the reading). Companies may also remain obligated for leases when operating units are sold. For example, Kmart [KM] sold its Builders Square subsidiary in 1997 to Hechinger, another chain of home improvement stores. When Hechinger filed for bankruptcy in June 1999, Kmart recognized a pretax charge of $350 million for its guarantees of long-term leases with a net present value of $711 million.

4. *Straight-line recognition.* Both SFAS 13 and IAS 17 require both lessors and lessees to recognize operating lease payments over the life of the lease on a straight-line basis (equal amounts in each year). However, the lease payments may take a different form, resulting in either prepaid rent or rent receivable.

   For example, in the first quarter of 2001, Cisco [CSCO] paid Catellus [CDX] $68 million in connection with a California ground lease. Catellus reported that this sum would be amortized over the 34-year lease term.

5. *Synthetic leases.* Such leases use a special purpose entity to finance an asset purchase. The asset is then leased to the user. While the user receives the tax benefits of ownership, the transaction is accounted for as an operating lease, keeping it off-balance-sheet.

   For example, AOL Time Warner [AOL] used a synthetic lease to finance the construction of its New York headquarters, keeping a reported one billion dollars of debt off its balance sheet.

3   OFF-BALANCE-SHEET FINANCING ACTIVITIES

Leases are but one example of contractual arrangements that give rise to off-balance-sheet debt. In this section, we discuss other such arrangements and show how financial statements should be adjusted to reflect the underlying economic consequences. Like leases, some of these off-balance-sheet activities are commonplace and can be found in many firms and industries. Others tend to be industry specific or are the product of specific market conditions.

Take-or-Pay and Throughput Arrangements

Firms use take-or-pay contracts to ensure the long-term availability of raw materials and other inputs necessary for operations.[13] These agreements are common in the energy, chemical, paper, and metal industries. Under these arrangements, the purchasing firm commits to buy a minimum quantity of an input over a specified time period. Input prices may be fixed by contract or may be related to market prices. Energy companies use throughput arrangements with pipelines or processors (such as refiners) to ensure future distribution or processing requirements.

These contracts are often used as collateral for bank or other financing by unrelated suppliers or by investors in joint ventures. The contract serves as an

---

[13] Inventories can also be financed through product financing arrangements under which inventories are sold and later repurchased. SFAS 49 (1981) requires that such arrangements that do not effectively transfer the risk of ownership to the buyer must be accounted for as debt financing rather than sale of inventory. In such cases, the cost of holding inventories (storage and insurance) and interest cost on the imputed debt must be recognized as incurred. Prior to SFAS 49, companies sometimes used these arrangements to defer these costs and accelerate the recognition of profit. Product financing arrangements may still be accounted for as sales outside of the United States.

indirect guarantee of the related debt. However, neither the assets nor the debt incurred to obtain (or guarantee availability of) operating capacity are reflected on the balance sheet of the purchaser. SFAS 47 (1981) requires that, when a long-term commitment is used to obtain financing, the purchaser must disclose the nature of the commitment and the minimum required payments in its financial statement footnotes.

As take-or-pay contracts and throughput agreements effectively keep some operating assets and liabilities off the balance sheet, the analyst should add the present value of minimum future commitments to both property and debt.

Exhibit 46-2 contains the commitments and contingencies footnote from the 1999 annual report of Alcoa [AA], disclosing a take-or-pay obligation of Alcoa of Australia, a consolidated subsidiary. Note that the disclosure is similar to that required for (capital and operating) leases. We can apply the method used earlier to compute the present value of the debt. The calculation is shown in panel B of the exhibit.

The take-or-pay contracts reported by Alcoa represent $1,780 million of off-balance-sheet assets and debt. The impact of this adjustment on the leverage ratio is as follows:

Alcoa Balance Sheet, at December 31, 1999 (in $millions)

	Reported	Adjusted	Increase
Total debt	$3,067	$4,847	58%
Stockholders' equity	6,318	6,318	None
Debt-to-equity ratio	0.49X	0.77X	58%

Sale of Receivables

Receivables are sometimes financed by their sale (or securitization) to unrelated parties. That is, the firm sells the receivables to a buyer (normally a financial institution or investor group). Depending on the interest (if any) paid by customers and the effective interest rate on the sale transaction, the seller may recognize a gain or loss on the receivables sold. The seller uses the proceeds from the sale for operations or to reduce existing or planned debt. The firm continues to service the original receivables; customer payments are transferred to the new owner of the receivables. Some arrangements are revolving in nature as collected receivables are periodically replaced by new ones.

Such transactions are recorded as sales under SFAS 140, Accounting for Transfers and Servicing of Financial Assets and Extinguishments of Liabilities (2000), as long as there has been a *legal* transfer of ownership from the seller to the buyer.[14] To effect such transactions, firms often set up distinct (nonconsolidated) trusts or subsidiaries (often referred to as a *qualifying special-purpose entity, QSPE*) that the firm's creditors cannot access in the event of bankruptcy.[15] By

---

[14] SFAS 140 states that the transferor (seller) accounts for the transfer as a sale when it surrenders effective control over those assets (see SFAS 140 for details).

[15] LTV, a steel company, filed for bankruptcy late in 2000. LTV argued that the transfer of receivables (and a similar transfer of inventories) to a QSPE was a "disguised finance transaction" and that it still had an interest in the transferred assets. However, the bankruptcy court ruled against the company in March 2001.

| EXHIBIT 46-2 | Alcoa Analysis of Take-or-Pay Contracts |

A: Footnote: Contingent Liabilities

Alcoa of Australia (AofA) is party to a number of natural gas and electricity contracts that expire between 2001 and 2022. Under these take-or-pay contracts, AofA is obligated to pay for a minimum amount of natural gas or electricity even if these commodities are not required for operations. Commitments related to these contracts total $190 in 2000, $182 in 2001, $179 in 2002, $176 in 2003, $176 in 2004, and $2,222 thereafter.

Source: Alcoa, *1999 Annual Report.*

B. Analysis: Take-or-pay Contracts, 2000 to 2004 and Beyond (in $millions)

Year	Take-or-Pay Obligation
2000	$ 190
2001	182
2002	179
2003	176
2004	176
Thereafter	2,222

Using the technique for capitalizing operating leases discussed earlier in the chapter, the above payment stream can be discounted to its present value. Estimated payments continue after 2004 (using, for simplifying purposes, the constant rate assumption) for

$$\frac{\$2,222 \text{ million}}{\$176 \text{ million}} = 12.63 \text{ years}$$

Given this payment stream, the present value can be arrived at using an estimated cost of debt (based on capitalized lease disclosures or other long-term debt). For Alcoa, we estimate an interest rate of 7%. When applied to the minimum payments shown above, the resulting present value equals $1,780 million for take-or-pay obligations. Thus approximately $1.8 billion should be added as an adjustment to Alcoa's consolidated property and total debt.

selling the receivables through such entities, the firm has adhered to the strict legal definition of ownership transfer. Exhibit 46-3 provides examples of such arrangements from the financial statements of Lucent Technologies [LU]. Note that in 2000, Lucent's receivables and loans were sold through a "bankruptcy-remote subsidiary," as required by GAAP for sale recognition.

By reporting such transactions as sales, the company decreases accounts receivable and increases cash from operations in the period of sale. However, most such receivable sales and/or securitizations provide that the seller retains the effective credit risk by either:

EXHIBIT 46-3	Lucent Technologies Receivable Securitization Activities (years ended September 30)

1999

▶ Subsidiary of Lucent sold approximately $625 million of accounts receivable to a nonconsolidated qualified special-purpose entity (QSPE).

▶ The QSPE resold the receivables to an unaffiliated financial institution.

▶ Lucent transferred $700 million of other receivables to the QSPE as collateral.

2000

▶ Lucent and a third-party financial institution arranged for the creation of a nonconsolidated Special Purpose Trust.

▶ Trust purchases, from a wholly owned (bankruptcy-remote) subsidiary of Lucent, customer finance loans, and receivables on a limited-recourse basis.

▶ Balance of receivables sold but uncollected was $1,329 million.

Source: Information from Lucent Technologies, *2000 Annual Report.*

▶ Retaining a portion of the receivables and receiving payment only after the securitized amount has been repaid. If the retained percentage exceeds the historic loss ratio, the seller has retained the effective risk.

▶ Providing other collateral, or agreeing to replace delinquent receivables with current receivables.

As shown in Exhibit 46-3, Lucent provided the second form of implicit guarantee. *When the seller retains the entire expected loss experience, these transactions are effectively collateralized borrowings with the receivables serving as collateral.* Sales of receivables are another form of off-balance-sheet financing and should be adjusted as follows:

1. *Balance Sheet.* Both accounts receivable and current liabilities should be increased by the amount of receivables sold that have not yet been collected.

2. *Cash Flow Statement.* CFO must be adjusted; the change in the uncollected amount should be classified as cash from financing rather than CFO.

These two adjustments usually capture the analytical effects of receivable sales. However, as sales/securitizations of receivables transactions can be quite complex, other aspects of the financial statements may also be affected. Moreover, to the extent amounts received from receivable sales are not equal to the "face value" of receivables sold, the (cash flow) adjustment is only an approximation, albeit a reasonably accurate one.

Box 46-3 illustrates the effects of sales/securitizations on the income statement. Treating the transaction as a sale results in earlier income recognition as compared to treating it as a collateralized borrowing.

BOX 46-3   INCOME STATEMENT EFFECTS OF RECEIVABLE SALES AND SECURIZATIONS

Our illustration assumes that the company is selling (credit) receivables that it carries on its books at $1,000,000. Depending on the interest rate structure of the credit receivables and the risk, the buyer may pay more or less than $1,000,000.

Buyer Pays Less: $900,000

Transaction qualifies as a sale: The seller will *immediately* recognize a $100,000 loss on the sale.*

Transaction does not qualify as a sale and is treated as a financing: The $100,000 is treated as a "discount" on the loan payable taken by the seller.[†] The income statement is not affected at the time of the sale. Over time (as the receivables are collected) the discount is amortized as additional interest expense.[‡]

Buyer Pays More: $1,100,000

Transaction qualifies as a sale: The mirror image of the previous transaction occurs (i.e., the seller will *immediately* recognize a $100,000 gain on the sale).

Transaction does not qualify as a sale and is treated as a financing: The $100,000 is treated as a "premium" on the loan payable taken by the seller.[§] The income statement is not affected at the time of the sale. Over time (as the receivables are collected) the premium is amortized and interest expense is reduced.[**]

Analytical procedures: From an analytical perspective, the two approaches result in different timing of income or loss recognition. Thus, if a company recognized a securitization as a sale and the analyst felt that it would be more appropriate to view the transaction as a financing event, then the financial statement adjustments would be as follows:

▶ Remove gain/loss from current period income.

▶ Add the securitized receivables to the balance sheet amount.

▶ Classify the securitization proceeds as debt.

---

* The entry would be

Cash	$900,000	
Loss on sale	100,000	
Accounts receivable		$1,000,000

[†] The entry would be

Cash	$900,000	
Loan payable (net of discount)		$900,000

[‡] For example, when $200,000 of the receivables are collected, the entry for the "passthrough" would be

Amortization of discount	$ 20,000	
Loan payable	180,000	
Cash		200,000

Note, if the transaction were treated as a sale, there would be no entry at the time of collection.

[§] The entry would be

Cash	$1,100,000	
Loan payable (includes premium)		$1,100,000

[**] For example, when $200,000 of the receivables are collected, the entry would be

Loan payable	220,000	
Amortization of premium		20,000
Cash		200,000

Note, if the transaction were treated as a sale, there would be no entry at the time of collection.

Example 46-1

Lucent Technologies

Exhibit 46-4 continues with our Lucent example. Panel A summarizes data from the financial statements. As indicated in Exhibit 46-3, Lucent engaged in receivables securitization and reported balances of $625 and $1,329 million of outstanding uncollected receivables in 1999 and 2000, respectively. In both years, the receivables were sold through an entity established specifically for this purpose.

Balance Sheet. Lucent recorded the securitizations as sales as they were structured to satisfy the (legalistic) requirements of SFAS 125 and 140. Lucent, however, transferred other (not sold) receivables to the subsidiary as collateral for the receivables sold and therefore ultimately bears the credit risk.

The sale proceeds should therefore not be viewed as a reduction of accounts receivable, but rather as an increase in (short-term) borrowing. As panel B of Exhibit 46-4 indicates, Lucent's 1999 (2000) accounts receivable, current assets, and current liabilities should be increased by $625 ($1,329) million.[16]

Cash Flow Classification. Accounting for these transactions as sales distorts the amount and timing of CFO as the firm received cash earlier than if the receivables had been collected in the normal course of business. An adjustment is required to reclassify *the change in the uncollected receivables sold*[17] from CFO to cash from financing.

Since 1999 was the first year Lucent engaged in sales securitization, the full $625 million should be deducted from CFO (and classified as CFF). For 2000, the adjustment should be the change in sold but uncollected receivables; that is, ($1,329 − $625 =) $704 million. These adjustments are made in Exhibit 46-4, panel B.

Effects of Adjustments. The effects of these adjustments are also demonstrated in Exhibit 46-4. Relative to 1998, sales in 1999 and 2000 increased 26% and 39%, respectively. *Reported* accounts receivable, however, increased only 16% and 26% over that same period; an apparent improvement in receivables management. This improvement is reflected in the receivable turnover with days receivables outstanding improving by 14 days from 117 to 103 days over the 1998–2000 period.

However, after adjustment for receivables sold, the improvement disappears. Restoring the $625 million of receivables sold in 1999 results in an (adjusted) increase of 24% in receivables relative to 1998, similar to the 26% sales increase over the same period. For 2000, we find that, after adjustment, receivables increased 46%, greater than the 39%

---

[16] The manner in which Lucent set up its QSPE in 1999 results in another, more subtle "off-balance-sheet activity." (See subsequent section entitled "Joint Ventures, Finance Subsidiaries, and Investment in Affiliates.") By transferring $700 million of its receivables to the subsidiary as collateral, Lucent effectively removed this amount from its receivables balances (where they belong) and buried it within the investment in subsidiary accounts. Total assets are not affected but the composition of those assets is. To keep the exposition for sale of receivables straightforward, we have ignored this factor in our presentation.

[17] In Reading 36, it was shown that the change in accounts receivable is an adjustment to net income when deriving CFO. Because the uncollected balance of the receivables sold must be added to the reported balance of accounts receivable, calculation of the adjusted CFO requires exclusion of any change in the balance of uncollected receivables sold.

EXHIBIT 46-4	Lucent Technologies Analysis of Receivables Securization				

	A. Reported Data			B. Adjusted Data	
	1998	**1999**	**2000**	**1999**	**2000**
From Footnotes					
Balance of uncollected receivables	$ 0	$ 625	$ 1,329		
From Balance Sheet				*Adjustment:* Add $625	Add $1,329
Accounts receivable	7,821	9,097	10,059	9,722	11,388
Current assets		19,240	21,490	19,865	22,819
Current liabilities		9,150	10,877	9,775	12,206
From Cash Flow Statement				*Adjustment:* Deduct $625	Deduct $704
CFO	1,452	(962)	304	(1,587)	(400)
From Income Statement					
Sales	24,367	30,617	33,813		
Selected Trends and Ratios					
% Change in sales from 1998		26%	39%	26%	39%
% Change in A/R from 1998		16%	26%	24%	46%
# of days A/R outstanding	117	101	103	105	114
Current ratio	1.45	2.10	1.98	2.03	1.87
CFO/Current liabilities	0.13	(0.11)	0.03	(0.16)	(0.03)

Source: Data from Lucent Technologies, *1998–2000 Annual Reports.*

increase in sales. After adjustment, the number of days of outstanding receivables, which declined on a reported basis, rose to 114 in 2000, similar to the 1998 level.[18]

Moving to Lucent's liquidity ratios, we note that both the adjusted current ratio and the CFO/current liabilities ratio are below the reported amounts. For these ratios, there is an adjustment to both the numerator and denominator. For the current ratio, the same amount is added to both; the numerator adjustment improves the ratio whereas the denominator adjustment reduces the ratio. It is only because the (reported) ratio is greater than 1 that the net effect is a lower ratio. Were the ratio less than 1 to begin with, the effect of the adjustment would be to improve the ratio. Both adjustments to the CFO/current liabilities ratio, on the other hand, reduce the ratio as CFO is decreased and current liabilities are increased.

[18] As discussed in Reading 34 (using Lucent as an example), sales of receivables should be added back when assessing the provision for bad debts.

> Turning to CFO, we find that the receivables sales masked the deterioration of the company's operating cash flow: 1998 CFO was $1,452 million; 1999 reported CFO plunged to ($962) million, recovering to $304 million in 2000.
>
> After adjustment for receivables sold, CFO was considerably below the amounts reported. For 1999, adjusted CFO was ($1,587) million, an outflow two-thirds greater than the reported amount of ($962) million. Although 2000 CFO improved, on an adjusted basis it remained negative at ($400) million.
>
> The cash flow trend may have been the motivation for Lucent beginning a program of receivable securitization in 1999; as CFO deteriorated, the company needed another source of cash.

Other Securitizations

While the securitization of accounts receivable remains a major source of financing, other forms of securitization have emerged. A few examples follow:

1. PolyGram, the Dutch film producer, issued bonds in 1998 backed by expected revenues from films.
2. Marne et Champagne issued bonds in 2000 backed by its champagne inventories.
3. Toys "R" Us [TOY] issued bonds in 2000 secured by license-fee income from its Japanese affiliate.
4. Yasuda Fire & Marine Insurance [8755] used auto and mortgage loans and leasing credits to back bonds issued in 2000.

Such issues are a growing form of off-balance-sheet financing, used worldwide, with significant implications for current and future period cash flows. The financial analyst must be alert to such transactions and make the appropriate analytical adjustments.[19]

Joint Ventures, Finance Subsidiaries, and Investment in Affiliates

Firms may acquire manufacturing and distribution capacity through investments in affiliated firms, including suppliers and end users. Joint ventures with other firms may offer economies of scale and provide opportunities to share operating, technological, and financial risks. To obtain financing, the venture may enter into take-or-pay or throughput contracts with minimum payments designed to meet the venture's debt service requirements. Direct or indirect guarantees of the joint venture debt may also be present. Generally, firms account for their investments in joint ventures and affiliates (where they have 20 to 50% ownership) using the equity method whereby the balance sheet reports the firm's *net investment* in the affiliate. The net investment reflects the parent's proportionate share of the assets minus the liabilities of the subsidiary (*i.e., the parent's financial statements do not report its share of the debt of these affiliates*).

---

[19] Bond ratings services recognize the effect of securitizations on a company's debt structure. For example, Moody's March 2000 analysis of Federal-Mogul [FMO] included $450 million of securitized receivables in its calculation of Federal Mogul's total debt.

For example, Micron [MU] stated in its August 31, 2000 10-K report that it participated in two joint ventures (in Singapore and Japan). Micron entered into take-or-pay contracts requiring it to purchase all of the output of the joint ventures and to provide technology, systems support, and other services. These joint ventures are not consolidated although they are clearly part of Micron operationally. They supplied more than one-third of all memory produced by Micron in fiscal 2001 and Micron reported all transactions with the venture as part of cost of goods sold.

Similarly, many firms have long used legally separate finance subsidiaries to borrow funds to finance parent-company receivables. Such debt is often lower-cost than general-purpose borrowings because of the well-defined collateral. Finance subsidiaries enable the parent to generate sales by granting credit to dealers and customers for purchases of its goods and services. Until 1987, most firms used the equity method to account for finance subsidiaries.[20] The FASB eliminated the nonconsolidation option (SFAS 94) and firms must now consolidate the assets and liabilities of controlled financial subsidiaries. As a result, some parent firms reduced their ownership of finance subsidiaries below 50% to gain the benefit of "debt suppression" afforded by the equity method.

From an overall economic entity (parent firm plus share in the affiliate) perspective, however, affiliate debt should be considered explicitly because it is clearly required to maintain the parent's operations. Additionally, the parent firm generally supports affiliate borrowings through extensive income maintenance agreements and direct or indirect guarantees of debt.

The information required for these adjustments to debt and related interest coverage and leverage ratios can be obtained from the footnotes, which may

---

EXHIBIT 46-5   **Georgia-Pacific Joint Venture Financing**

Note 13: Related Party Transactions

The Corporation is a 50% partner in a joint venture (GA-MET) with Metropolitan Life Insurance Company (Metropolitan). GA-MET owns and operates the Corporation's main office building in Atlanta, Georgia. The Corporation accounts for its investment in GA-MET under the equity method.

At January 1, 2000, GA-MET had an outstanding mortgage loan payable to Metropolitan in the amount of $144 million. The note bears interest at 9½%, requires monthly payments of principal and interest through 2011, and is secured by the land and building owned by the joint venture. In the event of foreclosure, each partner has severally guaranteed payment of one-half of any shortfall of collateral value to the outstanding secured indebtedness. Based on the present market conditions and building occupancy, the likelihood of any obligation to the Corporation with respect to this guarantee is considered remote.

Source: Georgia-Pacific, *1999 Annual Report.*

---

[20] Livnat and Sondhi (1986) showed that the exclusion of finance subsidiary debt allowed firms to report higher coverage and lower leverage ratios, stabilized reported debt ratios over time, and reduced the probability of a technical violation of bond covenants. Heian and Thies (1989) identified 182 companies (in 35 industry groups) reporting unconsolidated finance subsidiaries in 1985. Supplementary disclosures provided by 140 of these companies indicated a total of $205 billion in subsidiary debt that had not been reported on the parent's balance sheet. The authors also computed debt-to-capital ratios on the basis of pro forma consolidation and compared them to the pre-consolidation ratios; the average increase in the ratio for the sample was 34%, but nearly 90% for the firms with the 21 largest finance units.

disclose the assets, liabilities, and results of operations of finance subsidiaries in a summarized format.[21]

Exhibit 46-5 contains an excerpt from the footnote on commitments and contingencies in the *1999 Annual Report* issued by Georgia Pacific [GP]. It discloses a joint venture with Metropolitan Life [MET]. GP is clearly liable for one-half of this off-balance-sheet debt, and $72 million should be added to GP's (property and) debt. In the GP example, the parent explicitly guaranteed the debt of the affiliate. Even in the absence of such guarantees, the proportionate share of the affiliate's debt should be added to the reported debt of the investor and the financial statements should be adjusted accordingly. These adjustments will be illustrated shortly in the analysis of Texaco and Exhibits 46-6 and 46-7.

ANALYSIS OF OBS ACTIVITIES: TEXACO

4

Texaco is a major worldwide refiner, marketer, and distributor of oil products. Exhibit 46-6 contains excerpts from footnotes to Texaco's 1999 financial statements relating to its unconsolidated subsidiaries, leases, and commitments and contingencies. *A complete assessment of a company's off-balance-sheet activities requires a review of all financial statement disclosures.*

EXHIBIT 46-6	Texaco Off-Balance-Sheet Activities

Excerpts from 1999 Notes to Financial Statements
Note 5: Investments and Advances

We account for our investments in affiliates, including corporate joint ventures and partnerships owned 50% or less, on the equity method. . . . The following table provides summarized financial information on a 100% basis for the Caltex Group, Equilon, Motiva, Star and all other affiliates that we account for on the equity method, as well as Texaco's total share of the information.

As of December 31, 1999
(Millions of dollars)

	Equilon	Motiva	Caltex Group	Other Affiliates	Texaco's Total Share
Current assets	$ 4,209	$ 1,271	$ 2,705	$ 801	$ 3,796
Noncurrent assets	7,208	5,307	7,604	2,230	9,321
Current liabilities	(5,636)	(1,278)	(3,395)	(736)	(4,916)
Noncurrent liabilities	(735)	(2,095)	(2,639)	(792)	(2,638)
Net equity	$ 5,046	$ 3,205	$ 4,275	$1,503	$ 5,563

(Exhibit continued on next page ...)

---

[21] When the subsidiary or joint venture issues publicly traded debt, then full financial statements are available and can be used for more accurate adjustments.

EXHIBIT 46-6	(continued)

Note 10: Lease Commitments and Rental Expense

We have leasing arrangements involving service stations, tanker charters, crude oil production and processing equipment and other facilities. We reflect amounts due under capital leases in our balance sheet as obligations, while we reflect our interest in the related assets as properties, plant and equipment. The remaining lease commitments are operating leases, and we record payments on such leases as rental expense.

As of December 31, 1999, we had estimated minimum commitments for payment of rentals (net of noncancelable sublease rentals) under leases which, at inception, had a noncancellable term of more than one year, as follows:

(millions of dollars)

	Operating Leases	Capital Leases
2000	$ 134	$ 9
2001	93	9
2002	416	8
2003	50	7
2004	54	7
After 2004	315	14
Total lease commitments	$1,062	$54
Less interest		(8)
Present value of total capital lease obligations		$46

Note 15: Other Financial Information, Commitments and Contingencies

Preferred Shares of Subsidiaries

Minority holders own $602 million of preferred shares of our subsidiary companies, which is reflected as minority interest in subsidiary companies in the Consolidated Balance Sheet.

The above preferred stock issues currently require annual dividend payments of approximately $34 million. We are required to redeem $75 million of this preferred stock in 2003, $65 million (plus accreted dividends of $59 million) in 2005, $112 million in 2024 and $350 million in 2043. We have the ability to extend the required redemption dates for the $112 million and $350 million of preferred stock beyond 2024 and 2043.

Financial Guarantees

We have guaranteed the payment of certain debt, lease commitments and other obligations of third parties and affiliate companies. These guarantees totaled $716 million and $797 million at December 31, 1999 and 1998. The year-end 1999 and 1998 amounts include $336 million and $387 million of operating lease commitments of Equilon, our affiliate.

(Exhibit continued on next page ...)

EXHIBIT 46-6 (continued)

Throughput Agreements

Texaco Inc. and certain of its subsidiary companies previously entered into certain long-term agreements wherein we committed to ship through affiliated pipeline companies and an offshore oil port sufficient volume of crude oil or petroleum products to enable these affiliated companies to meet a specified portion of their individual debt obligations, or, in lieu thereof, to advance sufficient funds to enable these affiliated companies to meet these obligations. In 1998, we assigned the shipping obligations to Equilon, our affiliate, but Texaco remains responsible for deficiency payments on virtually all of these agreements. Additionally, Texaco has entered into long-term purchase commitments with third parties for take or pay gas transportation. At December 31, 1999 and 1998, our maximum exposure to loss was estimated to be $445 million and $500 million.

However, based on our right of counterclaim against Equilon and unaffiliated third parties in the event of non-performance, our net exposure was estimated to be $173 million and $195 million at December 31, 1999 and 1998.

No significant losses are anticipated as a result of these obligations.

Litigation

Texaco and approximately 50 other oil companies are defendants in 17 purported class actions. The actions are pending in Texas, New Mexico, Oklahoma, Louisiana, Utah, Mississippi, and Alabama. . . . Plaintiffs seek to recover royalty underpayments and interest. In some cases plaintiffs also seek to recover severance taxes and treble and punitive damages. Texaco and 24 other defendants have executed a settlement agreement with most of the plaintiffs that will resolve many of these disputes. The federal court in Texas gave final approval to the settlement in April 1999 and the matter is now pending before the U.S. Fifth Circuit Court of Appeal.

Texaco has reached an agreement with the federal government to resolve similar claims. The claims of various state governments remain unresolved.

It is impossible for us to ascertain the ultimate legal and financial liability with respect to contingencies and commitments. However, we do not anticipate that the aggregate amount of such liability in excess of accrued liabilities will be materially important in relation to our consolidated financial position or results of operations.

Source: Texaco, *1999 Annual Report.*

Exhibit 46-7 illustrates the adjustments for off-balance-sheet financing activities discussed in this reading. Panel A presents Texaco's reported and adjusted debt, total liabilities, and equity. Panel B shows each adjustment to the reported amounts, based on the information provided in Exhibit 46-6. The result is a more comprehensive measure of the firm's leverage.

EXHIBIT 46-7	Texaco Adjusted Long-Term Debt, Liabilities, and Solvency Analysis (amounts in $millions)

A. Reported and Adjusted Debt, Liabilities, and Capitalization Ratios

	Reported	Adjustments (Panel B below)	Adjusted	% Increase
Debt	$ 7,647	$4,613	$12,260	60%
Total liabilities	16,930	8,927	25,857	53%
Shareholders' equity	12,042		12,042	
Capitalization Ratios				
Debt to equity	0.64		1.02	60%
Total liabilities to equity	1.41		2.15	53%

B. Adjustments for Off-Balance-Sheet Data

	Debt	Liabilities
Share of affiliate debt	$2,638	$7,554
Capitalization of operating leases	864	864
Redeemable preferred shares	602	—
Guarantees	336	336
Throughput agreements	173	173
Total Adjustments to Debt and Liabilities	**$4,613**	**$8,927**

Adjustments to 1999 Debt

Share of Affiliate Debt. Texaco has entered into a number of joint ventures with other major oil companies. The three primary ones are:

Joint Venture	Partners	Texaco's Share
Equilon	Shell Oil	44.0%
Motiva	Shell Oil, Saudi Refining	32.5%
Caltex	Chevron	50.0%

As Texaco is not the majority owner of any of these ventures, their financial results are not consolidated with Texaco's financial statements and (Texaco's portion of) the debt and liabilities of these joint ventures remains off-balance-sheet. Texaco, however, reports its proportionate share of its joint ventures' assets and liabilities in the final column of Note 5. The adjustment to debt equals Texaco's share in the noncurrent[22] liabilities of its joint ventures; Texaco's liabilities are increased by its share of total (current plus noncurrent) liabilities of its joint ventures.

---

[22] Current liabilities may include financing obligations, but they are excluded in calculating the debt adjustment as no disclosures were provided. This "undercounting" may be partially offset by the "overcount" implied in including all noncurrent liabilities as certain noncurrent liabilities (e.g., deferred taxes) may not constitute debt.

Capitalization of Operating Leases. Note 10 (in Exhibit 46-6) provides information on Texaco's operating and capital leases. The interest rate implicit in the 1999 capital leases is 4.5%, relatively low even considering the low interest rate levels prevalent in the late 1990s. Texaco's long-term debt footnote (not shown) indicated a cost of debt of about 5.5% for new 10-year debt issued in 1999. We used a discount rate of 5% (and a straight-line assumption for payments after 2004), resulting in a present value adjustment of $864 million.

Redeemable Preferred Shares. Redeemable preferred shares should be treated as debt. Note 15 (in Exhibit 46-6) states that Texaco includes $602 million of such preferred shares as part of minority interest. As minority interest is included in total liabilities, no adjustment is required there. However, debt must be increased by $602 million.

Financial Guarantees. As a portion of the $716 million of guarantees relates to affiliate debt, including it would result in double counting as we have already adjusted for Texaco's share of affiliate debt. Thus, we adjust only for $336 million of guarantees of Equilon's operating leases, as that amount is off-balance-sheet for Equilon as well. Note that Texaco's guarantee includes a guarantee of lease residual values.

Throughput Agreements. We have used the net exposure of $173 million, although a conservative approach would use the gross exposure of $445 million.

Litigation. We note only that potential liabilities related to litigation exist. However, a numeric adjustment is not possible based on the information provided.

The effect of these adjustments is summarized in Exhibit 46-7, panel A. Adjusted debt is 60% higher than reported debt in 1999 and total liabilities increase by 53%. The adjusted debt-to-equity and liabilities-to-equity ratios are significantly higher than the reported ratios.

FINANCIAL REPORTING BY LESSORS
5

Many manufacturers and dealers offer customers leases to market their products. Such *sales-type leases* include both a manufacturing or merchandising profit (the difference between the fair value at the inception of the lease and the cost or carrying value of the leased property) and interest income due to the financing nature of the transaction. Financial institutions and leasing intermediaries offer direct financing leases that generate interest income only. Either class of lessors may create operating leases.

The remainder of the reading discusses the accounting by lessors for sales-type and direct financing leases. Leveraged leases are beyond the scope of this text and sales with leasebacks are discussed in Box 46-4.

Lessor financial reporting is illustrated using the lessee example of the beginning of the chapter with the additional assumptions that the leased equipment cost $20,000 to manufacture and the expected residual value (not guaranteed by the lessee) is $2,500 after four years.

Lease Classification: Lessors

Lease capitalization by lessors is required when the lease meets *any one* of the four criteria specified for capitalization by lessees and *both* of the following revenue-recognition criteria:

BOX 46-4   FINANCIAL REPORTING FOR SALES WITH LEASEBACKS

Sale leaseback transactions are sales of property by the owner who then leases it back from the buyer-lessor. Financial reporting for these transactions is governed by SFAS 28, Accounting for Sales with Leasebacks (1979), as amended by SFAS 66, Accounting for Sales of Real Estate (1982).

The amount and timing of profit (or loss) recognized on a sale leaseback transaction are determined by the proportion of the rights to use the leased property retained by the owner-lessee after the sale. If all or substantially all the use rights are retained by the owner-lessee, it is a financing transaction, and no profit or loss on the transaction should be recognized.

The extent of continuing use is determined by the proportion of the present value of reasonable rentals relative to the fair value of assets sold and leased back. This proportion is used to assign sale leaseback transactions to the following financial reporting categories.

Minor Leasebacks. Present value of reasonable rentals is less than 10% of the fair value of the leased property; the buyer-lessor obtains substantially all the rights to use the leased property. Any gain (or loss) on the transaction is recognized in full at the inception of the lease.

More than Minor but Less than "Substantially All" Leasebacks. Present value of reasonable rentals exceeds 10% but is less than 90% of the fair value of the asset sold; depending on specific criteria, some or all of the gain or loss must be deferred and amortized over the lease term.

Substantially All Leasebacks. Present value of MLPs equals or exceeds 90% of the fair value of property sold; the total gain (loss) must be deferred and amortized over the lease term. The leaseback is a financing transaction, and the gain (loss) is recognized as the leased property is used.

Example

OMI [OMM], an oil tanker operator, sold a vessel in May 1997 for $39.9 million and leased it back for five years. The $15.7 million gain was deferred and recognized as an adjustment to lease expense over the five-year lease term. Had the gain been recognized immediately, 1997 pretax income would have been more than twice the reported level.

IAS Standards for Sales with Leasebacks

IAS 17, the accounting standard for these transactions, is significantly different from U.S. GAAP as it requires that:

▶ When a sale/leaseback results in a finance lease, any profit on the sale must be deferred and recognized over the lease term.

▶ When a sale/leaseback results in an operating lease, and the sales price equals the asset's fair value, the seller recognizes any gain or loss.

▶ When a sale/leaseback results in an operating lease, and the sales price is below fair value, the seller recognizes any gain or loss. The exception is that any loss is deferred and amortized when the lease provides for payments that are below market.

▶ When a sale/leaseback results in an operating lease, and the sales price exceeds fair value, the seller defers any gain and amortizes it over the lease term.

1. Collectibility of the MLPs is reasonably predictable.

2. There are no significant uncertainties regarding the amount of unreimbursable costs yet to be incurred by the lessor under the provisions of the lease agreement.

Leases not meeting these criteria must be reported as operating leases since either the risks and benefits of leased assets have not been transferred, or the earnings process is not complete.

Sales-Type Leases

Exhibit 46-8 presents financial reporting by a lessor for a sales-type lease using the lessee example. Part A illustrates the accounting recognition at inception and the determination of gross and net investment in the lease; part B provides the lessor's amortization schedule for the sales-type lease.

The lessor recognizes sales revenue of $31,700, the present value of the MLPs. The cost of goods sold is the carrying amount of the leased property. The present value of the unguaranteed residual value of the leased property constitutes continuing investment by the lessor and is not included in costs charged against income; that is, it is deducted from cost to manufacture.

The lessor's gross investment in the lease is $42,500, the sum of the MLPs and the unguaranteed residual value. Net investment in the lease is $33,407, determined by discounting the MLPs and the unguaranteed residual value at the interest rate implicit in the lease (10%), as shown in part A.

EXHIBIT 46-8	Lessor Financial Reporting

A. Sales-Type Lease

Lessor's **Gross Investment** *in Leased Equipment*	
MLPs: $10,000 × 4	$40,000
Unguaranteed residual value	2,500
	$42,500
Lessor's Net Investment in Leased Equipment	
Present value at 10% of an annuity of 4 payments of $10,000	$31,700
Present value at 10% of $2,500, 4 periods hence	1,707
	$33,407
Unearned Income	
Gross investment in lease	$42,500
Less: Net investment	33,407
	$ 9,093

Accounting Recognition at Lease Inception		
Sales revenue*	$ 31,700	
Cost of goods sold†	(18,293)	
Gross profit on sale		$13,407
Gross investment in lease	$ 42,500	
Unearned income	(9,093)	
Net investment in lease		$33,407

* Present value of lease payments, excluding residual value.
† Cost to manufacture (assumed to be $20,000) less PV of residual value.

(Exhibit continued on next page ...)

EXHIBIT 46-8   (continued)

B. Lessor Amortization Schedule: Sales-Type Lease

Year	Annual Payment Received (A)	Interest Income (B)	Reduction in Investment (C) = (A) − (B)	Net Investment (D)
2000				$33,407
2001	$10,000	$3,340	$ 6,660	26,747
2002	10,000	2,675	7,325	19,422
2003	10,000	1,942	8,058	11,364
2004	10,000	1,136	8,864	2,500
Totals	$40,000	$9,093	$30,907	

C. Balance Sheet Effects

	Capital (Sales-Type) Lease			Operating Lease		
	Net Investment in Leases			Assets Under	Accumulated	
Year	Current	Long-Term	Total	Lease	Depreciation	Net
2000	$6,660	$26,747	$33,407	$20,000	$ 0	$20,000
2001	7,325	19,422	26,747	20,000	4,375	15,625
2002	8,058	11,364	19,422	20,000	8,750	11,250
2003	8,864	2,500	11,364	20,000	13,125	6,875
2004	2,500	0	2,500	20,000	17,500	2,500

D. Income Statement Effects

	Capital (Sales-Type) Lease		Operating Lease		
Year		Income	Rental Revenue	Depreciation	Income
2000	Gain on Sale	$13,407			
2001	Interest	3,340	$10,000	$ 4,375	$ 5,625
2002	Interest	2,675	10,000	4,375	5,625
2003	Interest	1,942	10,000	4,375	5,625
2004	Interest	1,136	10,000	4,375	5,625
Totals		$22,500	$40,000	$17,500	$22,500

(Exhibit continued on next page ...)

The difference between the gross and net investment represents unearned income, the interest component of the transaction. Unearned income is systematically amortized to income over the lease term, using the interest method that reports a constant rate of return of 10% on the net investment in the lease. The lessor reports its net investment in the lease on the balance sheet (see the next section). Contingent rentals, if any, are reported as they are earned. SFAS 13

EXHIBIT 46-8 (continued)

E. Cash Flow Statement Effects

Year	Capital (Sales-Type) Lease			Operating Lease
	CFO	Cash from Investment	Total	CFO
2000	$13,407	$(13,407)	$ 0	$ 0
2001	3,340	6,660	10,000	10,000
2002	2,675	7,325	10,000	10,000
2003	1,942	8,058	10,000	10,000
2004	1,136	8,864	10,000	10,000
Totals	$22,500	$ 17,500	$40,000	$40,000

requires an annual review of the estimated residual value. Nontemporary declines must be recognized; however, increases in value or subsequent reversals of declines cannot be reported.

Balance Sheet Effects (Exhibit 46-8C).   The lessor reports the current and non-current components of its net investment in sales-type leases. Lessors using the operating lease method do not report any investment in leases, but they continue to report the assets on the balance sheet as long-term assets, net of accumulated depreciation. These amounts assume straight-line depreciation over four years of the original cost of the asset less estimated residual value ($20,000 − $2,500). Note that the operating lease method reports lower net assets each year and, ignoring income effects, tends to increase return on assets relative to the sales-type lease method.

Income Statement Effects (Exhibit 46-8D).   For the sales-type lease, the lessor records profit at inception of $13,407. The annual rental of $10,000 is allocated to interest income and return of principal. Reported interest income reflects a constant 10% return on the declining net investment in the lease. The balance of the rental payment is applied to amortize (reduce principal) the net investment systematically over the lease term.

The operating lease method reports constant income over the lease term as straight-line depreciation is charged against the constant annual rental. The use of accelerated depreciation would result in a pattern of increasing income over the lease term as depreciation declines.

The sales-type lease reports substantially higher income in the first year of the lease due to recognition of manufacturing profit at the inception of the lease. However, reported income declines thereafter due to declining interest income over the remainder of the lease term, relative to constant or increasing income under the operating lease method. In our example, reported net income is higher under the operating lease method after the initial year. *Over the lease term, the total net income is the same under both methods.*

Cash Flow Effects (Exhibit 46-8E).   At the inception of the lease, no cash changes hands. The operating lease method reports no cash flow effects on the statement of cash flows. In contrast, the sales-type lease method reports 2000 operating cash flow of $13,407, equal to the sales profit at the inception of the lease. This cash inflow is offset by a net cash outflow for investment equal to

$13,407 (the investment of $33,407 less the $20,000 prior carrying amount of the leased property). Net cash flow remains zero.

In subsequent years, under the operating lease method, CFO is equal to the rental payment of $10,000/year. Under the sale-type lease method, the $10,000 payment is allocated between CFO and cash from investment; CFO is equal to interest income and cash from investment is equal to the reduction in the net investment. Thus, after inception, the operating lease method reports higher CFO and, since interest income declines over the lease term, this difference in CFO increases. Simultaneously, a correspondingly larger reduction in net investment is reported in investment cash flow.

Note that total cash flow (operating plus investing) is unaffected by the method of lease accounting. The actual cash flow in each year is $10,000, the lease payment received. Only under the operating lease method does CFO equal the cash flows associated with the lease. Capitalization of the lease by the lessor reclassifies reported cash flows between operating and investing activities.

The use of sales-type lease accounting allows firms to recognize income earlier than the operating lease method. Lease capitalization also allows firms to report higher CFO at the inception of the lease. This aggressive recognition of income and cash flows ("front-end loading") improves financial ratios; it accurately reflects the firm's operations only if the risks and benefits of leased property have been fully transferred to the lessee and the lessor has no further performance obligation.

Footnote Disclosures.   Footnote disclosure for lessors under U.S. GAAP is similar to that of lessees. The sales-type lease method requires the disclosure of gross MLPs receivable, unearned income, and the current and noncurrent components of the net investment in leases. Lessors must also provide information on lease terms, future MLPs receivable over the next five years, and the aggregate thereafter. Disclosure for operating leases is limited to MLPs receivable over the next five years and the aggregate thereafter.

Direct Financing Leases

In a direct financing lease, the lessor's original cost or carrying value (prior to the lease) of the asset approximates the market value of the leased asset (the present value of the MLPs). Such leases are pure financing transactions and financial reporting for direct financing leases reflects this fact. *No sale is recognized at the inception of the lease, and there is no manufacturing or dealer profit. Only financing income is reported.*

Unearned income is the difference between the gross investment in the lease and the cost or carrying amount of the leased property. It is amortized to report a constant periodic return (effective interest method) on the net investment in the lease (gross investment plus initial direct costs less unearned income). Thus, in our example, the lessor would report (interest) income and cash flows similar to those reported for the sales-type lease over the period 2001–2004. There are no income or cash flow consequences at the inception of the lease in 2000.

Disclosure requirements for financing leases are similar to those for sales-type leases. Lessors must disclose MLPs receivable over the next five fiscal years and the aggregate thereafter. Any allowance for uncollectibles, executory costs, unguaranteed residual value, and unearned income must also be reported.

The income reported on financing leases depends on assumptions made, particularly those regarding uncollectible payments and residual values. When uncollectibles are underestimated, or residual values overestimated, income is overstated. For example, the *New York Times* reported[23] that automobile lessors would lose more than $10 billion in 2000 because they overestimated the residual values of cars and trucks that they had leased to customers.

Financial Reporting by Lessors: An Example

Exhibit 46-9 contains IBM Credit Corp.'s footnote on its activities as lessor. The company finances customer purchases of information-handling equipment through direct financing leases; shorter-term leases of such equipment are treated as operating leases.

IBM discloses aggregate MLPs receivable and reports the periodic payments in each of the next five years and in the aggregate thereafter as a percentage of this total. The terms of both the direct financing leases and operating leases range from two to three years.[24] However, the operating leases generally have shorter terms: 57% of the operating leases are due within one year, higher than the 50% of direct financing leases due within 12 months of the financial statement date.

EXHIBIT 46-9	IBM Credit Corp. Net Investment in Capital Leases

The Company's capital lease portfolio includes direct financing and leveraged leases. The Company originates financing for customers in a variety of industries and throughout the United States. The Company has a diversified portfolio of capital equipment financing for end users.

Direct financing leases consist principally of IBM advanced information processing products with terms generally from two to three years. The components of the net investment in direct financing leases at December 31, 1999 and 1998 are as follows:

(dollars in thousands)

	1999	1998
Gross lease payments receivable	$5,335,352	$5,278,060
Estimated unguaranteed residual values	442,288	397,529
Deferred initial direct costs	18,339	30,634
Unearned income	(604,035)	(571,168)
Allowance for receivable losses	(47,220)	(65,644)
Total	$5,144,724	$5,069,411

(Exhibit continued on next page ...)

---

[23] December 15, 2000, p. F1.

[24] In its 1994 annual report, IBM Credit reported financing lease terms ranging three to five years and operating leases that spanned two to four years. The shortening of lease terms is consistent with the rapid technological changes in the computer industry.

EXHIBIT 46-9   **(continued)**

The scheduled maturities of minimum lease payments outstanding at December 31, 1999, expressed as a percentage of the total, are due approximately as follows:

Within 12 months	50%
13 to 24 months	33
25 to 36 months	13
37 to 48 months	3
After 48 months	1
	100%

Included in the net investment in capital leases is $17.7 million of seller interest at December 31, 1998, relating to the securitization of such leases. These securitizations were terminated and settled in 1999.

Refer to the note, Allowance for Receivable Losses, for a reconciliation of the direct financing leases and leveraged leases allowances for receivable losses.

Equipment on Operating Leases:

Operating leases consist principally of IBM advanced information processing products with terms generally from two to three years. The components of equipment on operating leases at December 31, 1999 and 1998 are as follows:

(dollars in thousands)

	1999	1998
Cost	$ 7,166,892	$ 7,046,757
Accumulated depreciation	(3,780,206)	(3,427,172)
Total	$ 3,386,686	$ 3,619,585

Minimum future rentals were approximately $3,094.2 million at December 31, 1999. The scheduled maturities of the minimum future rentals at December 31, 1999, expressed as a percentage of the total, are due approximately as follows:

Within 12 months	57%
13 to 24 months	30
25 to 36 months	10
37 to 48 months	2
After 48 months	1
	100%

Source: IBM Credit Corp., *1999 Annual Report.*

Additional disclosures are required for the capitalized direct financing leases: current and noncurrent components, allowance for uncollectibles, estimated unguaranteed residual values, and unearned interest. IBM Credit provides most applicable disclosures. No contingent rentals are reported; they may not be significant. However, the current and noncurrent components have not been reported separately. Computation of the implicit interest rate requires additional assumptions.

The footnote disclosure includes the securitization of direct financing lease receivables and reference to a reconciliation of the allowance for losses.

Going beyond the financial effects of IBM's lessor activities, the footnote data indicate that the company is experiencing minimal lease growth. Direct financing leases increased by 1% (using MLPs) during 1999 while operating leases grew at a rate less than 2%. These patterns may represent stable volume and prices, or higher volume offset by lower lease prices, or a shift from leases to sales (reflecting changes in relative prices or customer preferences). This is another example of how attention to footnote detail can suggest worthwhile questions about changes in operations to ask management.

IAS Standards for Lessors

IAS 17 provides accounting standards for lessors that are broadly similar to those of U.S. GAAP. The most significant differences are:

- Lease classification as a finance lease depends on broad principles (see discussion for lessees earlier in the reading) rather than the SFAS 13 rules.
- Disclosure requirements are the same as for lessees, with MLPs disclosed for amounts due
  1. Within one year
  2. One to five years
  3. In more than five years

SUMMARY

Financial liabilities can take many forms, from simple, full-coupon debt to leasing and other more esoteric forms of off-balance-sheet activities. This reading and the previous one illustrated the far-reaching effects of such transactions on a firm's income, cash flow, and capital structure. The principal points made in this reading are:

1. Operating leases are the most common form of off-balance-sheet financing. Such leases should be capitalized and adjustments made to reported financial data.

2. In addition to leases, there are other means of acquiring the use of assets without reflecting them on the balance sheet, such as

▶ Joint ventures

▶ Take-or-pay and throughput agreements

▶ Sales of receivables

The reading illustrates techniques that can be used to adjust financial statements for these activities as well.

The discussion and analysis of OBS activities is not yet complete.

PROBLEMS FOR READING 46

1. [Lease classification and financial statement effects; CFA© adapted] On January 1, 2001, a company entered into a capital lease, recording a balance sheet obligation of $10,000, using an interest rate of 12%. The lease payment for 2001 was $1,300. Compute each of the following:

    i. Interest expense for 2001.

    ii. The lease obligation at the end of 2001

    iii. The effect of the lease payments on each of the three components of cash flow for 2001

    iv. Each of items (i) through (iii) if the lease had been recorded as an operating lease

2. [Analysis of lessee] The Tolrem Company has decided to lease an airplane on January 1, 2002. The firm and its lessor have not yet decided the terms of the lease. Assume that the terms can be adjusted to permit Tolrem to either capitalize the lease or record it as an operating lease.

  A. State the effect (higher, lower, or equal) of the choice of capitalizing the lease on the following for 2002 (the initial year of the lease):

    i. Cash flow from operations

    ii. Financing cash flow

    iii. Investing cash flow

    iv. Net cash flow

    v. Debt-to-equity ratio

    vi. Interest coverage ratio

    vii. Operating income

    viii. Net income

    ix. Deferred tax asset or liability

    x. Taxes paid

    xi. Pre- and posttax return on assets

    xii. Pre- and posttax return on equity

  B. Recall that the difference between net income under the two methods changes direction at some point during the lease term. State which answers to part a will change in the year after the switch occurs and describe the change.

  C. Assume that Tolrem enters into new aircraft leases at a constant annual rate. Describe the effect of the choice of accounting method on the items in part a.

3. [Lease capitalization] In 1999, Liberty Bancorp [LIBB] leased new property and accounted for the lease as a capital lease. Until 1999, it had reported all of its leased assets as operating leases. The following information with respect to the capital lease was obtained form the company's 1999 annual report:

Capital lease assets (net of amortization)	$2,479,570
Capitalized lease obligations	2,596,031
Interest on capitalized leases	223,733
Repayment of capital lease obligations	3,969

Minimum lease payments over the next five years and thereafter (in $thousands):

	2000	2001	2002	2003
Capital Lease MLPs	$272	$280	$288	$297

	2004	Thereafter	Total
Capital Lease MLPs	$305	$4,596	$6,038

A. Determine the amount of the capital lease at its inception.

B. The company states that it amortizes its capital leases over the term of the lease. Determine the amortization expense for 1999 and the term of the lease. Compute the total expense for 1999 as a result of the capital lease.

C. Explain how the capital lease affected the 1999 cash flow statement.

D. Describe the adjustment to the company's 1999 free cash flows that should be made for the capital lease.

E. Assuming that the lease was reported as an operating lease, determine:

    i. Lease expense for 1999

    ii. The effect on the cash flow statement

F. Estimate the interest rate that Liberty used for its capital lease using both methods described in the chapter. Compare your results. (*Note:* Your estimate using the MLPs should use the lease term calculated in part b.)

4. [Effect of lease capitalization on ratios] Exhibit 46P-1 presents selected 1999 financial data provided by The Limited [LTD]. (*Note:* Use 6% as the appropriate interest rate for present-value calculations.)

A. In its 10-K filing, The Limited provides an adjusted "earnings to fixed charge coverage" ratio.

    i. Calculate the ratio without the adjustment.

    ii. Explain why the adjusted ratio is a better measure of the company's interest coverage.

B. Compute the debt-to-equity ratio for The Limited based on reported data.

C. IN its MD&A, the company provides a summary of its working capital position and capitalization. Adjust each of the following for the effect of (capitalization of) the firm's operating leases:

    i. Working capital

    ii. Long-term debt

    iii. Debt-to-equity ratio

5. [Sale of receivables; ratio and cash flow effects] Foster Wheeler [FWC] entered into arrangements to sell receivables in 1998 and 1999. The accounts receivable footnote in the firm's *1999 Annual Report* noted that

EXHIBIT 46P-1	The Limited Inc.

Selected Financial Data

Liquidity and Capital Resources (MD&A)

A summary of the Company's working capital position and capitalization follows (in $thousands):

Year Ended January 30, 1999

Cash provided by operating activities	$ 571,014
Working capital	1,070,249
Capitalization:	
Long-term debt	550,000
Shareholders' equity	2,233,303
Total capitalization	$2,783,303

Leased Facilities and Commitments (Notes to Financial Statements)

Minimum Rent Commitments Under Noncancellable Operating Leases

Year	2000	2001	2002	2003	2004	Thereafter
MLP	$643,828	$632,785	$602,868	$563,468	$502,880	$1,427,862

Ratio of Earnings to Fixed Charges (10-K)

Year Ended January 30, 1999

Adjusted Earnings		
Pretax earnings		$2,363,646
Fixed Charges		
Portion of minimum rent of $689,240 representative of interest	$229,747	
Interest on indebtedness	68, 528	298,275
Minority interest		64,564
Total earnings as adjusted		$2,726,485
Ratio of earnings to fixed charges	9.1X	

Source: The Limited, *1999 Annual Report* and 10-K.

As of December 31, 1999 and December 25, 1998, $50 million and $38.4 million, respectively, in receivables were sold under the agreement and are therefore not reflected in the accounts receivable-trade balance in the Consolidated Balance Sheet.

Selected reported financial data for the company follow:

Years Ended December (in $millions)			
	1997	**1998**	**1999**
Sales	$4,060	$4,537	$3,867
Trade accounts receivable	664	720	739
Current assets		1,673	1,615
Current liabilities		1,492	1,472
Total short- and long-term debt		963	961
Stockholders' equity		572	376
Cash flow from operations	(113)	(59)	(6)

A. Compute the impact of the sale of receivables on FWC's receivable turnover ratio and cash cycle for 1998 and 1999.

B. Compute the reported and adjusted (for the sale of receivables) current and debt-to-equity ratios for 1998 and 1999.

C. Discuss the impact of the sale on (the trend of) the firm's cash flow from operations over the period 1997 to 1999.

6. [Off-balance-sheet obligations; CFA© adapted] Extracts form The Bowie Company's December 31, 2001, balance sheet and income statement are presented in the following schedule, along with its interest coverage ratio:

Debt	$12 million
Equity	20
Interest expense	1
Times interest earned	5.0X

The Bowie Corporation's financial statement footnotes include the following:

i. At the beginning of 2001, Bowie entered into an operating lease with future payments of $40 million ($5 million/year) with a discounted present value of $20 million.

ii. Bowie has guaranteed a $5 million, 10% bond issue, due in 2007, issued by Crockett, a nonconsolidated 30%-owned affiliate.

iii. Bowie has committed itself (starting in 2002) to purchase a total of $12 million of phosphorus from PEPE, Inc., its major supplier, over the next five years. The estimated present value of these payments is $7 million.

A. Adjust Bowie's debt and equity and recompute the debt-to-equity ratio, using the information in footnotes (i) to (iii).

B. Adjust the times-interest-earned ratio for 2001 for these commitments.

C. Discuss the reasons (both financial and operating) why Bowie may have entered into these arrangements.

D. Describe the additional information required to fully evaluate the impact of these commitments on Bowie's current financial condition and future operating trends.

7. [Analysis of lessor] Carignane Corp., a manufacturer/lessor, enters into a sales-type lease agreement with Mourvedre, Inc., as lessee. The lessor capitalizes the lease rather than reporting it as an operating lease.

Describe the effect (lower, higher, or none) of this choice on the following accounts and ratios of Carignane (the lessor) in the first and ninth years of a 10-year lease:

  i. Total assets

  ii. Revenues

  iii. Expenses

  iv. Asset turnover ratio

  v. Interest income

  vi. Cost of goods sold

  vii. Net income

  viii. Retained earnings

  ix. Income taxes paid

  x. Posttax return on assets

  xi. Cash flow form operations

  xii. Investment cash flow

8. [Analysis of lessor and lessee] On January 1, 2001, the Malbec Company leases a Willmess winepress to the Baldes Group under the following conditions:

  i. Annual lease payments are $20,000 for 20 years.

  ii. At the end of the lease term, the press is expected to have a value of $5,500.

  iii. The fair market value of the press is $185,250.

  iv. The estimated economic life of the press is 30 years.

  v. Malbec's implicit interest rate is 12%; Baldes' incremental borrowing rate is 10%.

  vi. Malbec reports similar presses at $150,000 in finished-goods inventory.

A. Based on the data given, state whether Baldes should treat this lease as an operating or a capital lease. Justify your answer. What additional information would help to answer the question?

B. Assume that Baldes capitalizes the lease. List the financial statement accounts affected (at January 1, 2001) by that decision and calculate each effect.

C. Assume that Baldes uses straight-line depreciation for financial reporting purposes. Compute the income statement, balance sheet, and statement of cash flows effects of the lease for 2001 and 2002 under each lease accounting method.

D. Based on the data given, state whether Malbec should treat this lease as an operating or a sales-type lease. Justify your answer. What additional information would help to answer the question?

E. Assume that Malbec treats the lease as an operating lease. List the financial statement accounts affected (at January 1, 2001) by that decision and calculate each effect.

F. Assume that Malbec treats the lease as a sales-type lease and the lessee does not guarantee the residual value of the winepress. List the financial statement accounts affected (at January 1, 2001) by that decision and calculate each effect.

G. Assume that Malbec uses straight-line depreciation for financial reporting purposes. Compute the income statement, balance sheet, and statement of cash flows effects of the lease for 2001 and 2002 under each lease accounting method.

APPENDIX

Appendix A Solutions to End-of-Reading Problems and Questions

SOLUTIONS FOR READING 34

1. {S} a. When the product is a commodity with a known price and liquid market.

   b. When collection is assured because the risk of nonpayment can be estimated.

   c. When collection is uncertain because the risk of nonpayment cannot be estimated.

2. {S} a. (All data in $ millions)

Under the completed contract method, neither revenue nor pretax income would be reported until the project is completed. When the project has been completed, at the end of 2002, LASI Construction would report revenues of $3.0 and pretax income of $0.6 (revenues of $3.0 minus costs of $2.4).

Under the percentage-of-completion method, revenues and pretax income must be reported each year as follows:

Year	Cumulative % Completion	Cumulative Revenue	Current Period Revenue	Current Period Expense	Pretax Income
2000	0.9/2.4 = 37.5%	$1.125	$1.125	$0.900	$0.225
2001	1.7/2.4 = 70.8%	2.125	1.000	0.800	0.200
2002	2.4/2.4 = 100.0%	3.000	0.875	0.700	0.175
Total			$3.000	$2.400	$0.600

b. Computation of construction in progress and advance billings (in $ millions)

	Percentage-of-Completion	Completed Contract
Costs incurred	$ 0.900	$ 0.900
Profit recognized	0.225	0.000
Construction in progress	$ 1.125	$ 0.900
Advance billings	(1.000)	(1.000)
Net asset (liability)	$ 0.125	$(0.100)

Balance Sheet on December 31, 2000 (in $ millions)

	Percentage-of-Completion	Completed Contract
Assets		
Cash	$0.100	$0.100
Construction in progress (net)	0.125	0.000
Total assets	$0.225	$0.100
Liabilities and equity		
Advance billings (net)	$0.000	$0.100
Retained earnings	0.225	0.000
Total liabilities and equity	$0.225	$0.100

    c. The effect on 2001 revenue and pretax income of a change in estimated costs to complete is as follows:

        There is no change in 2001 revenues and pretax income (both are $0.000) under the completed contract method because no revenue or income can be recognized prior to completion.

        Under the percentage-of-completion method, both revenue and pretax income change and are computed as follows:

Year	Cumulative % Completion	Cumulative Revenue	Current Period Revenue	Current Period Expense	Pretax Income
2001	1.7/2.5 = 68.0%	$2.040	$0.915	$0.800	$0.115

Note: All changes are in bold. The change in estimated costs to complete raises the total expected costs to complete to $2.500 from the previous estimate of $2.400. Costs incurred at the end of Year 2001 are $1.700 ($0.900 in 2000 and $0.800 in 2001) because we have assumed that the incremental costs ($0.100) will be incurred in Year 2002. Cumulative revenue of $2.040 must be recognized at the end of 2001; since we recognized $1.125 in revenue in 2000, the difference ($2.040 − $1.125) or $0.915 must be recognized in 2001. The effect of the change is recognized in Year 2001 and Year 2000 results are not changed.

3. {S}

Account	Part a	Part b
Contracts in process	This account reflects the costs actually incurred and the proportionate share of profits on those contracts for which the amount of revenue recognized exceeds payments received from customers.	The account is similar to accounts receivable that also reflects the excess of revenue recognized over cash payments received.
Advance billings	This account reflects those contracts for which payments received exceed revenue recognized.	The account is similar to advances from customers.

c. The company most likely uses the percentage-of-completion method. Under that method, the *contracts in process* account includes estimated earnings on uncompleted contracts, making it larger than under the completed contract method. As a result, it is more likely that some or all contracts will have an excess of contracts in process over advance billings, as illustrated in Exhibit 34-1B on page 59.

4. {M} Required calculations are shown in the table below.

($millions)	1997	1998	1999	2000
Allowance for doubtful accounts				
Opening balance	$ 14.6	$ 18.0	$ 16.3	$ 21.1
Charged to earnings	4.2	(1.4)	5.3	
Writeoffs (net of recoveries)	(0.8)	(0.3)	(0.5)	
Closing balance	$ 18.0	$ 16.3	$ 21.1	$ 27.6
Accounts receivable (net)	386.4	299.2	393.8	350.2
Sales	4,184.5	4,151.2	4,009.3	4,586.1
Pretax income	460.2	415.3	379.2	478.3
Gross receivables*	404.4	315.5	414.9	377.8
a. (i) Closing balance of reserves to gross receivables (%)	**4.45%**	**5.17%**	**5.09%**	**7.31**
(ii) Writeoffs (net of recoveries) to revenues (%)	**0.02%**	**0.01%**	**0.01%**	
b. Adjusted pretax income^	**$ 463.6**	**$ 416.4**	**$ 384.0**	**$ 478.3**
c. Adjusted pretax income^^	**460.2**	**417.6**	**379.6**	**478.3**

* Net receivables plus amounts charged to earnings.

^ Reported pretax income plus amounts charged to earnings minus writeoffs (net of recoveries). (No adjustment made for 2000)

^^ See calculations below.

The following calculation is based on the assumption that Nucor maintained its closing balance of bad debt reserves at the 1997 ratio of 4.45% of gross receivables. Annual amounts charged to earnings are determined after calculation of required closing balance of bad debt reserve at 4.45% of gross receivables.

($millions)	1997	1998	1999	2000
Allowance for doubtful accounts				
Opening balance	$ 14.6	$ 18.0	$ 14.0	$ 18.5
Charged to earnings (plug)	4.2	(3.7)	4.9	
Writeoffs (net of recoveries)	(0.8)	(0.3)	(0.5)	
Closing balance at 4.45% of gross receivables	$ 18.0	$ 14.0	$ 18.5	$ 16.8
Difference between plug and actual charge	0.0	(2.3)	(0.4)	0.0
Adjusted pretax income	460.2	417.6	379.6	478.3

d. One factor should be the actual loss experience (writeoffs). Yet the accrual varied despite continuing low losses. A second factor should be the reserve level relative to receivables. This percentage may reflect economic conditions and should rise when the risk of customer financial distress increases. Nucor's reserve as a percent of gross receivables rose significantly from 1997 to 2000.

e. The actual writeoffs (through 1999) were immaterial, supporting the CFO's statement. However, as the table above shows, Nucor's accruals do not seem to reflect either the actual loss experience or maintaining a reserve that is a fixed percentage of gross receivables.

f. A CFO would prefer not to disclose the actual charge as it preserves management's ability to make accounting decisions without the risk of misinterpretation by analysts. For managements that use this reserve to manage earnings (see reading discussion) nondisclosure hides such activity from investors and analysts.

g. From the analyst perspective, disclosure permits the analyst to see the effect of management decisions regarding the appropriate reserve level. It also allows the analyst to see the actual loss experience. Finally, disclosure permits the analyst to decide whether management is using the reserve to manage reported earnings.

SOLUTIONS FOR READING 36

1. {S} a. Palomba Pizza Stores
Statement of Cash Flows
Year Ended December 31, 2000

Cash Flows from Operating Activities:

Cash Collections from Customers	$250,000	
Cash Payments to Suppliers	(85,000)	
Cash Payments for Salaries	(45,000)	
Cash Payments for Interest	(10,000)	
Net Cash from Operating Activities		$110,000

Cash Flows from Investing Activities:

Sales of Equipment	38,000	
Purchase of Equipment	(30,000)	
Purchase of Land	(14,000)	
Net Cash for Investing Activities		(6,000)

Cash Flows from Financing Activities:

Retirement of Common Stock	(25,000)	
Payment of Dividends	(35,000)	
Net Cash for Financing Activities		(60,000)
Net Increase in Cash		$ 44,000
Cash at Beginning of Year		50,000
Cash at End of Year		$ 94,000

b. Cash Flow from Operations (CFO) measures the cash generating ability of operations, in addition to profitability. If used as a measure of performance, CFO is less subject to distortion than net income. Analysts use the CFO as a check on the quality of reported earnings, although it is not a substitute for net income. Companies with high net income and low CFO may be using overly aggressive income recognition techniques. The ability of a firm to generate cash from operations on a consistent basis is one indication of the financial health of the firm. Analysts search for trends in CFO to indicate future cash conditions and potential liquidity or solvency problems.

Cash Flow from Investing Activities (CFI) reports how the firm is investing its excess cash. The analyst must consider the ability of the firm to continue to grow and CFI is a good indication of the attitude of management in this area. This component of total cash flow includes the capital expenditures made by management to maintain and expand productive capacity. Decreasing CFI may be a forecast of slower future growth.

Cash Flow from Financing (CFF) indicates the sources of financing for the firm. For firms that require external sources of financing (either borrowing or equity financing) it communicates management's preferences regarding financial leverage. Debt financing indicates future cash requirements for principal and interest payments. Equity financing will cause future earnings per share dilution.

For firms whose operating cash flow exceeds investment needs, CFF indicates whether that excess is used to repay debt, pay (or increase) cash dividends, or repurchase outstanding shares.

c. Cash payments for interest should be classified as CFF for purposes of analysis. This classification separates the effect of financial leverage decisions from operating results. It also facilitates the comparison of Palomba with other firms whose financial leverage differs.

d. The change in cash has no analytic significance. The change in cash (and hence, the cash balance at the end of the year) is a product of management decisions regarding financing. For example, the firm can show a large cash balance by drawing on bank lines just prior to year end.

e. and f. There are a number of definitions of free cash flows. In the text, free cash flow is defined as cash from operations less the amount of capital expenditures required to maintain the firm's current productive capacity. This definition requires the exclusion of costs of growth and acquisitions. However, few firms provide separate disclosures of expenditures incurred to maintain productive capacity. Capital costs of acquisitions may be obtained from proxy statements and other disclosures of acquisitions.

In the finance literature, free cash flows available to equity holders are often measured as cash from operations less capital expenditures. Interest paid is a deduction when computing cash from operations as it is paid to creditors. Palomba's free cash flow available to equity holders is calculated as follows:

Net cash flow from operating activities less net cash for investing activities:

$$\$110,000 - \$6,000 = \textbf{\$104,000}$$

The investment activities disclosed in the problem do not indicate any acquisitions.

Another definition of free cash flows, which focuses on free cash flow available to all providers of capital, would exclude payments for interest ($10,000 in this case) and debt. Thus, Palomba's free cash flow available to all providers of capital would be $114,000.

2. {M} a.

	1996	1997	1998	1999	2000	2001
Sales	$ —	$140	$150	$165	$175	$195
Bad debt expense	—	7	7	8	10	10
Net receivables	30	40	50	60	75	95
Cash collections[1]	$ —	**$123**	**$133**	**$147**	**$150**	**$165**

[1] Sales − bad debt expense − increase in net receivables

b.

	1997	1998	1999	2000	2001
Bad debt expense/sales	5.0%	4.7%	4.9%	5.7%	5.1%
Net receivables/sales	28.6	33.3	36.4	42.8	48.7
Cash collections/sales	87.9	88.7	89.1	85.7	84.6

c. The bad debt provision does not seem to be adequate. From 1997–2001 sales increased by approximately 40%, while net receivables more than doubled, indicating that collections have been lagging. The ratios calculated in part b also indicate the problem. While bad debt expense has remained fairly constant at 5% of sales over the 5-year period, net receivables as a percentage of sales have increased from 29% to 49%; cash collections relative to sales have declined. Other possible explanations for these data are that stated payment terms have lengthened or that Stengel has allowed customers to delay payment for competitive reasons.

3. {S} Niagara Company
Statement of Cash Flows 2001

Cash collections	$ 980	[Sales − Δ Accounts Receivable]
Cash inputs	(670)	[COGS + Δ Inventory]
Cash expenses	(75)	[Selling & General Expense − Δ Accounts Payable[1]]
Cash interest paid	(40)	[Interest Expense − Δ Interest Payable]
Income taxes paid	(30)	[Income Tax Expense − Δ Deferred Tax]
Cash from Operations	$ 165	
Purchase of fixed assets	(150)	
Cash used for Investing	(150)	[Depreciation Expense + Δ Fixed Assets (net)]
Increase in LT debt	50	
Decrease in notes payable	(25)	
Dividends paid	(30)	[Net Income − Δ Retained earnings]
Cash Used for Financing	(5)	
Net Change in Cash	$ 10	
Cash Balance 12/31/00	50	
Cash Balance 12/31/01	$ 60	

[1] Can also be used to calculate cash inputs, decreasing that outflow to $645 while increasing cash expenses to $100.

4. {L} a. (i) Statement of Cash Flows—Indirect Method

Cash from operations:		
Net income		$1,080
Add noncash expense: depreciation		600
Add/Subtract changes in working capital:		
Accounts receivable	(150)	
Inventory	(200)	
Accruals	80	
Accounts payable	120	(150)
		$1,530
Cash from investing:		
Capital expenditures		1,150
Cash from financing:		
Short-term borrowing		550
Long-term repayment		(398)
Dividends		(432)
		$ (280)
Net change in cash		$ 100

Worksheet for (Indirect Method) Cash Flow Statement

	Income Statement	Balance Sheet 12/31/00	12/31/01	Change	Cash Effect
Net income	$1,080				$ 1,080
Depreciation	600				600
Accounts receivable		$1,500	$1,650	$150	(150)
Inventory		2,000	2,200	200	(200)
Accruals		800	880	80	80
Accounts payable		1,200	1,320	120	120
Depreciation	(600)				(600)
Net fixed assets		6,500	7,050	550	(550)
Capital expenditures					*$(1,150)*
Note payable		5,500	6,050	550	550
Short-term borrowing					*$ 550*
Long-term debt		2,000	1,602	(398)	(398)
Long-term debt repayment					*$ (398)*
Net income	(1,080)				(1,080)
Retained earnings		500	1,148	648	648
Dividends paid					*$ (432)*
	0				$ 100

The worksheet to create the cash flow statement is presented above. Each balance sheet change (other than cash) is accounted for and matched with its corresponding activity. As a last check, the net income and the add-backs of non-cash items are balanced and "closed" to their respective accounts (PP&E and retained earnings), providing the amounts of capital expenditures and dividends.

a. (ii)　Statement of Cash Flows—Direct Method

Cash from Operations:	
Cash collections	$9,850
Cash payments for merchandise	(6,080)
Cash paid for SG&A	(920)
Cash paid for interest	(600)
Cash paid for taxes	(720)
	$1,530
Cash for Investing Activities:	
Capital expenditures	**(1,150)**
Cash for Financing Activities:	
Short-term borrowing	550
Long-term debt repayment	(398)
Dividends	(432)
	$ (280)
Net Change in Cash	**$ 100**

b. The worksheet to create the cash flow statement is presented on the following page. Each balance sheet change (other than cash) is accounted for and matched with its corresponding activity. Furthermore the operating account changes are matched to their corresponding income statement item. As a last check, the net income is balanced and "closed" to retained earnings providing the amount of dividends.

Note that there is no difference between the indirect and direct methods in the cash flow statement and in the worksheet for cash for investing and financing activities.

Worksheet for (Direct Method) Cash Flow Statement

	Income Statement	Balance Sheet 12/31/00	Balance Sheet 12/31/01	Change	Cash Effect
Sales	$10,000				$10,000
Accounts receivable		$1,500	$1,650	$ 150	(150)
Cash Collections					*$ 9,850*
COGS	(6,000)				(6,000)
Inventory		2,000	2,200	200	(200)
Accounts payable		1,200	1,320	120	120
Cash Paid for Merchandise					*$ (6,080)*
SG&A expense	(1,000)				(1,000)
Accruals		800	880	80	80
Cash Paid for SG&A					*$ (920)*
Interest expense	(600)				(600)
Cash Paid for Interest					*$ (600)*
Taxes	(720)				(720)
Cash Paid for Taxes					*$ (720)*
Depreciation	(600)				(600)
Net fixed assets		6,500	7,050	550	(550)
Capital Expenditures					*$ (1,150)*
Note payable		5,500	6,050	550	550
Short-term Borrowing					*$ 550*
Long-term debt		2,000	1,602	(398)	(398)
Long-term Debt Repaid					*$ (398)*
Net income	(1,080)				(1,080)
Retained earnings		500	1,148	648	648
Dividends					*$ (432)*
	$ 0				$ 100

SOLUTIONS FOR READING 38

Solutions for Questions

1. Analysts employ financial ratios simply because numbers in isolation are typically of little value. For example, a net income of $100,000 has little meaning unless analysts know the sales figure that generated the income and the assets or capital employed in generating these sales or this income. Therefore, ratios are used to provide meaningful relationships between individual values in the financial statements. Ratios also allow analysts to compare firms of different sizes.

2. In general, jewelry stores have very high profit margins but low asset turnover. It could take them months to sell a 1-carat diamond ring, but once it is sold, the profit could be tremendous. On the other hand, grocery stores usually have very low profit margins but very high asset turnover. Assuming the business risk of the firms are equal, the ROA's should likewise be equal.

3. Growth analysis is important to common stockholders because the future value of the firm is heavily dependent on future growth in earnings and dividends. The present value of a firm with perpetual dividends payment is:

$$V = \frac{\text{Dividend Next Period}}{\text{Required Rate of Return} - \text{Growth Rate}}$$

Therefore, an estimation of expected growth of earnings and dividends on the basis of the variables that influence growth is obviously crucial. Growth analysis is also important to debt-investors because the major determinant of the firm's ability to pay an obligation is the firm's future success which, in turn, is influenced by its growth.

SOLUTIONS FOR READING 38

Solutions for Problems

1. A. ROE = Net profit margin × Total asset turnover × Total assets/equity

Company K: ROE = 0.04 × 2.2 × 2.4 = .2112

Company L: ROE = 0.06 × 2.0 × 2.2 = .2640

Company M: ROE = 0.10 × 1.4 × 1.5 = .2100

B. Growth Rate = Retention Rate × ROE
= (1 − Payout Rate) × ROE

Company K: Growth Rate = 1 − (1.25/2.75) × .2112
= .545 × .2112 = .1145

Company L: Growth Rate = 1 − (1.00/3.00) × .2640
= .67 × .2640 = .1769

Company M: Growth Rate = 1 − (1.00/4.50) × .2100
= .778 × .21 = .1634

2. Current ratio = 650/350 = 1.857

Quick ratio = 320/350 = 0.914

Receivables turnover = 3500/195 = 17.95x

Average collection period = 365/17.95 = 20.33 days

Total asset turnover = 3500/2182.5 = 1.60x

Inventory turnover = 2135/280 = 7.625x

Fixed asset turnover = 3500/1462.5 = 2.39x

Equity turnover = 3500/1035 = 3.382x

Gross profit margin = (3500 − 2135)/3500 = .39

Operating profit margin = 258/3500 = .074

Return on capital (130 + 62)/2182.5 = .088

Return on equity = 130/1185 = .110

Return on common equity = 115/1035 = .111

Debt/equity ratio = 625/1225 = .51

Debt/total capital ratio = 625/1850 = .338

Interest coverage = 258/62 = 4.16x

Fixed charge coverage = 258/[62 + (15/.66)] = 3.045x (preferred stock dividends are computed on a before-tax basis)

Cash flow/long-term debt = (130 + 125 − 100)/625 = .248 = Net Income + non-cash charges + change in net working capital (excl. cash)

Cash flow/total debt = (130 + 125 − 100)/975 = .159

Retention rate = 1 − (40/115) = .65

Sophie's current performance appears in line with its historical performance and the industry average except in the areas of profitability (measured by return on capital and return on common equity) and leverage (cash flow to long-term debt and cash flow to total debt ratios). Its retention rate has increased markedly, too.

3. CFA Examination I

A. To clarify a point of possible confusion: operating income in this CFA exam problem excludes depreciation; we need to subtract it from operating income to obtain the appropriate ROE (NI/Equity = 19/159 = 11.93% for 2002, 30/220 = 13.6% for 2006).

2002	**2006**

Operating Margin = (Operating Income − Deprecation)/Sales
= (38 − 3)/542 = 6.46%   = (76 − 9)/979 = 6.84%

Asset Turnover = Sales/Total Assets
= 542/245 = 2.21x   = 979/291 = 3.36x

Interest Burden = Interest Expense/Total Assets
= 3/245 = 1.22%   = 0/291 = 0%

Financial Leverage = Total Assets/Common Shareholders Equity
= 245/159 = 1.54x   = 291/220 = 1.32x

Tax Rate = Income Taxes/Pre-tax Income
= 13/32 = 40.63%   = 37/65 = 55.22%

The recommended formula is:

Return on (ROE) = [(Op. Margin × Asset Turnover) − Int. Burden] × Equity Financial Leverage × (100% − Income Tax Rate)

2002 = [(6.46% × 2.21x) − 1.22%] × 1.54 × (100% − 40.63%)
     = 13.05 × 1.54 × .5937 = 11.93%

2006 = [(6.84% × 3.36x) − 0%] × 1.32 × (100% − 55.22%)
     = 22.98 × 1.32 × .4478 = 13.58%

Two alternative approaches are also correct.

ROE = [(Op. Margin − (Int. Burden/Asset Turnover)] × Financial Leverage × Asset Turnover × (100% − Income Tax Rate)

ROE = [(Financial Leverage × Asset Turnover × Operating Margin) − (Financial Leverage × Interest Burden)] × (100% − Income Tax Rate)

B. Asset turnover measures the ability of a company to minimize the level of assets (current and fixed) to support its level of sales. The asset turnover increased substantially over the period thus contributing to an increase in the ROE.

Financial leverage measures the amount of financing outside of equity including short and long-term debt. Financial leverage declined over the period thus adversely affected the ROE. Since asset turnover rose substantially more than financial leverage declined, the net effect was an increase in ROE.

SOLUTIONS FOR READING 39

Solutions for Questions

1. a. Basic earnings per share is the amount of earnings for the period available to each share of common stock outstanding during the reporting period.

  b. A potentially dilutive security is a security which can be exchanged for or converted into common stock and therefore upon conversion or exercise could dilute (or decrease) earnings per share. Included in this category are convertible securities, options, warrants, and other rights.

2. The concept that a security may be the equivalent of common stock has evolved to meet the reporting needs of investors in corporations that have issued certain types of convertible securities, options, and warrants. A potentially dilutive security is a security which is not, in form, common stock but which enables its holder to obtain common stock upon exercise or conversion. The holders of these securities can expect to participate in the appreciation of the value of the common stock resulting principally from the earnings and earnings potential of the issuing corporation. This participation is essentially the same as that of a common stockholder except that the security may carry a specified dividend yielding a return different from that received by a common stockholder. The attractiveness to investors of this type of security is often based principally upon this potential right to share in increases in the earnings potential of the issuing corporation rather than upon its fixed return or upon other senior security characteristics. In addition, the call characteristic of the stock options and warrants gives the investor potential control over a far greater number of shares per dollar of investment than if the investor owned the shares outright.

3. Convertible securities are considered to be potentially dilutive securities whenever their conversion causes a greater percentage increase in the EPS numerator than in the EPS denominator. If this situation does not result, conversion is not assumed and only basic EPS is reported.

SOLUTIONS FOR READING 39

Solutions for Problems

1. a.

Event	Dates Outstanding	Shares Outstanding	Restatement	Fraction of Year	Weighted Shares
Beginning balance	Jan. 1–Feb. 1	480,000	1.1 × 3.0	1/12	132,000
Issued shares	Feb. 1–Mar. 1	600,000	1.1 × 3.0	1/12	165,000
Stock dividend	Mar. 1–May 1	660,000	3.0	2/12	330,000
Reacquired shares	May 1–June 1	560,000	3.0	1/12	140,000
Stock split	June 1–Oct. 1	1,680,000		4/12	560,000
Reissued shares	Oct. 1–Dec. 31	1,740,000		3/12	435,000
Weighted average number of shares outstanding					1,762,000

b. $\text{Earnings Per Share} = \dfrac{\$3,456,000 \ (\text{Net Income})}{1,762,000 \ (\text{Weighted Average Shares})} = \$1.96$

c. $\text{Earnings Per Share} = \dfrac{\$3,456,000 - \$900,000}{1,762,000} = \$1.45$

d.

Income from continuing operations[a]	$1.72
Loss from discontinued operations[b]	(.25)
Income before extraordinary item	1.47
Extraordinary gain[c]	.49
Net income	$1.96
[a]Net income	$3,456,000
Deduct extraordinary gain	(864,000)
Add loss from discontinued operations	432,000
Income from continuing operations	$3,024,000

[a] $\dfrac{\$3,024,000}{1,762,000} = \$1.72$

[b] $\dfrac{\$(432,000)}{1,762,000} = \$(.25)$

[c] $\dfrac{\$864,000}{1,762,000} = \$.49$

2. The computation of Dewey Yaeger Pharmaceutical Industries' basic earnings per share and the diluted earnings per share for the fiscal year ended June 30, 2005, are shown below.

a. $\text{Basic earnings per share} = \dfrac{\text{Net income} - \text{Preferred dividends}}{\text{Average common shares outstanding}}$

$= \dfrac{\$1,500,000 - \$106,250^{1}}{1,000,000}$

$= \dfrac{\$1,393,750}{1,000,000}$

$= \underline{\$1.3937}$ or $\underline{\$1.39}$ per share

[1] Preferred dividend $= .085 \times \$1,250,000$

$= \$106,250$

b. Diluted earnings per share $= \dfrac{\text{Net income} - \text{Preferred dividends} + \text{Interest (net of tax)}}{\text{Average common shares} + \text{Potentially dilutive common shares}}$

$$= \frac{\$1{,}500{,}000 - \$106{,}250 + \$210{,}000^2}{1{,}000{,}000 + 250{,}000^3 + 25{,}000^4}$$

$$= \frac{\$1{,}603{,}750}{1{,}275{,}000}$$

$$= \underline{\$1.2578} \text{ or } \underline{\$1.26} \text{ per share}$$

[2] Use "if converted" method for 7% bonds

Adjustment for interest expense (net of tax) ($5,000,000 × .07 × .6)	$210,000

[3] Shares assumed to be issued if converted

$5,000,000 ÷ $1,000/bond × 50 shares	250,000

[4] Use treasury stock method to determine incremental shares outstanding

Proceeds from exercise of options (100,000 × $15)	$1,500,000
Shares issued upon exercise of options	100,000
Shares purchasable with proceeds	
(Proceeds ÷ Average market price) ($1,500,000 ÷ $20)	75,000
Incremental shares outstanding	25,000

SOLUTIONS FOR READING 40

1. {S} A. Start with the basic inventory relationship

$$BI + P = COGS + EI$$

Opening inventory	400 units @ $20	$ 8,000
Purchases	1,000	25,000
Total	1,400 units	$33,000

i. Under FIFO, ending inventory consists of 600 units:

100 purchased in second quarter at $24	$ 2,400
300 purchased in third quarter at $26	7,800
200 purchased in fourth quarter at $28	5,600
600 units total	$15,800

ii. Under LIFO, ending inventory consists of 600 units:

400 inventory at January 1 at $20	$ 8,000
200 purchased in first quarter at $22	4,400
600 units total	$12,400

iii. Under average cost, ending inventory consists of 600 units with an average cost of $33,000/1,400 = $23.5714 per unit or $14,142.84 total.

B. COGS for the year equals the $33,000 total of opening inventory plus purchases, less closing inventory under the method chosen:

i. FIFO: $33,000 less $15,800 = $17,200

ii. LIFO: $33,000 less $12,400 = $20,600

iii. Average cost: $33,000 less $14,142.84 = $18,857.16

C.   i. Reported income is highest under FIFO (lowest COGS) and lowest under LIFO (highest COGS). Average cost is in between FIFO and LIFO.

ii. Stockholders' equity is highest under FIFO (highest inventory and retained earnings) and lowest under LIFO (lowest inventory and retained earnings), with average cost in between.

2. {S} Using FIFO instead of LIFO when prices are rising and inventory quantities are stable has the following effects:

i. Gross profit margins are higher under FIFO than under LIFO because revenues at higher current prices are matched with cost-of-goods-sold measured using older (lower) prices.

ii. Net income is lower under LIFO than under FIFO because cost-of-goods-sold is higher.

iii. Cash from operations is higher under LIFO than under FIFO because income tax paid is lower.

iv. Inventory balances are lower under LIFO than under FIFO because cost-of-goods-sold is higher and lower prices remain in inventory.

v. Inventory turnover is lower under FIFO than under LIFO because cost-of-goods-sold is lower and inventory balances higher. Both factors decrease the inventory turnover ratio.

vi. Working capital is lower under LIFO than under FIFO because inventory balances are lower, despite partial offset from higher cash balances (because of lower tax payments).

vii. Total assets are higher under FIFO because FIFO inventory balances are higher.

viii. The debt-to-equity ratio is lower under FIFO than under LIFO because equity is higher, reflecting higher retained earnings.

3. {L} A. The first step is to obtain FIFO cost-of-goods-sold:

Pretax income = sales − COGS − other expenses

$5,000 = $25,000 − COGS − $12,000

Solving: COGS = $8,000

Purchases are equal to COGS + Closing Inventory = $8,000 + $10,000 = $18,000.

The key to this problem is to distinguish between the flow of units and the flow of costs. Purchases are independent of the accounting method used.

Since half the units were sold, half remain in inventory. Under LIFO, therefore, the cost allocations to inventory and COGS are the reverse of those allocated under FIFO. That is, under LIFO, COGS = $10,000 and Closing Inventory = $8,000.

Under the weighted average method, as total purchases equal $18,000, the allocation between COGS and closing inventory will be equal: COGS = Closing Inventory = $9,000.

Recalling that pretax CFO depends on purchases, not COGS, we can now fill in the rest of the table.

	FIFO	Weighted Average	LIFO
Sales	$25,000	$25,000	$25,000
Cost of goods sold	8,000	9,000	10,000
Other expenses	12,000	12,000	12,000
Pretax income	5,000	4,000	3,000
Tax expense	2,000	1,600	1,200
Net income	3,000	2,400	1,800
Retained earnings	3,000	2,400	1,800
Cash from operations[1]	(7,000)	(6,600)	(6,200)
Cash balance[2]	3,000	3,400	3,800
Closing inventory	10,000	9,000	8,000
Purchases	18,000	18,000	18,000

[1] Cash from operations = Sales − Other expenses − Purchases − Tax expense.

[2] Cash balance = $10,000 + Cash from operations

B. M & J Company

Balance Sheet, December 31, 20X0

	FIFO	Weighted Average	LIFO
Cash	$ 3,000	$ 3,400	$ 3,800
Inventory	10,000	9,000	8,000
Total assets	$13,000	$12,400	$11,800
Common stock	$10,000	$10,000	$10,000
Retained earnings	3,000	2,400	1,800
Total equities	$13,000	$12,400	$11,800

C. The advantages of LIFO are that it results in the highest cash flow (by reducing income taxes) and it best measures net income by matching the cost of sales with most recent costs to replace inventory sold. The disadvantage of LIFO is that inventory on the balance sheet is understated.

The advantage of FIFO is that inventory is measured at most recent costs. Its disadvantages are the reduced cash flow and overstatement of reported income.

Average cost has the disadvantage of misreporting both the balance sheet inventory and net income. Income taxes are higher than under the LIFO method (but lower than under FIFO). The "advantage" of average cost is that it is "less wrong" than LIFO on the balance sheet and "less wrong" than FIFO on the income statement.

4. {L} A.

Year	Zenab 20X1	(LIFO) 20X2	Faybech 20X1	(FIFO) 20X2
Current ratio	2.89	2.65	3.24	3.68
Inventory turnover		2.45		1.98
Gross profit margin		.339		.32
Pretax income/sales		.054		.045

B. Faybech's liquidity (as measured by the current ratio) appears to be better. Its inventory turnover is lower, however, implying lower efficiency. Faybech appears to be slightly less profitable as well.

C. i. Using the FIFO income statements below, we compute the following ratios:

Year	Zenab 20X1	(FIFO) 20X2	Faybech 20X1	(FIFO) 20X2
Current ratio[1]	3.20	3.04	3.24	3.68
Inventory turnover[2]		2.03		1.98
Gross profit margin		.355		.32
Pretax income/sales		.070		.045

[1] 20X1 = ($33,500 + $3,600)/$11,600
   20X2 = ($33,600 + $5,100)/$12,700

[2] $\dfrac{\$59,800}{(\$25,200 + \$5,100 + \$24,000 + \$3,600)/2}$

A comparision of both companies on a FIFO basis is presented below:

	Zenab	Faybech
Sales	$92,700	$77,000
Cost of goods sold	59,800	52,000
Gross profit	32,900	25,000
Selling and general expense	26,400	21,500
Pretax income	$ 6,500	$ 3,500

ii. Using the LIFO income statements below (using the Zenab statement after conversion to 100% LIFO), we compute the following profitability ratios:

Year	Zenab (100% LIFO) 20X2	Faybech (LIFO) 20X2
Gross profit margin	.332	.303
Pretax income/sales	.047	.024

Balance sheet adjustments are not possible for Faybech and the 30% of Zenab inventories on FIFO. Thus adjusted current and inventory turnover ratios cannot be computed.

A comparision of both companies on a LIFO basis is presented below:

	Zenab	Faybech
Sales	$92,700	$77,000
Cost of goods sold	61,300	53,675
Gross profit	31,400	23,325
Selling and general expense	26,400	21,500
Pretax income	$ 5,000	$ 1,825

iii. The current cost method of computing the inventory turnover ratio uses the FIFO measure of inventory and the LIFO measure of COGS. The ratios are:

	Zenab	Faybech
LIFO costs of goods sold	$61,943	$53,675
FIFO average inventory	29,400	26,300
Inventory turnover ratio	2.11X	2.04X

D. Balance sheet values are most meaningful when FIFO is used. For the income statement, however, LIFO should be used. Therefore for the current ratio, we use the FIFO amounts. For the gross profit margin, and pretax/sales we use the 100% LIFO amounts. For the inventory turnover ratio, the current cost approach is preferred. However that ratio and the FIFO based ratio are similar in this case:

		Zenab		Faybech	
Year		20X1	20X2	20X1	20X2
FIFO current ratio		3.20	3.04	3.24	3.68
FIFO inventory turnover			2.03		1.98
Current cost turnover			2.11		2.04
LIFO gross profit margin			.332		.303
LIFO pretax income/sales			.047		.024

Notice that, based on these ratios, Zenab is clearly more profitable than Faybech. The inventory turnover ratios are, however, virtually identical. While Faybech still has a higher current ratio, the difference is smaller than it appears based on the reported balance sheet data.

5. {M} A. The LIFO Reserve increased by $4,000. If the company used FIFO, its pretax income would be $4,000 higher. After-tax income would be higher by .65 × $4,000 = $2,600.

B. Inventory turnover is COGS/average inventory:

LIFO $3,800,000/[.5($748,000 + $696,800)] = 5.26X

FIFO $3,796,000/[.5($794,000 + $746,800)] = 4.93X

C. Since the firm's ROE is 4.6% and net income is $340,000, then average equity = $340,000/.046 = $7,391,304

If the company used FIFO, equity would be higher by the LIFO reserve amount adjusted for taxes. The average LIFO reserve is $48,000. Therefore, average equity should be higher by $31,200 (.65 × $48,000) after tax.

FIFO average equity = $7,391,304 + $31,200 = $7,422,504 ROE$_{FIFO}$ = $342,600/$7,422,504 = 4.62%

The adjustment of ROE is insignificant in this case because the increase in the numerator (income) and denominator (equity) are proportionate.

D. There are two reasons to make adjustments for accounting methods:

1. To more accurately measure the firm's operations

2. To facilitate comparisons of different firms on the same basis

For inventory turnover, the adjustment results in a more accurate measure of performance. However, the main purpose of the LIFO to FIFO adjustment is to enable the analyst to compare Zeta to other firms that use FIFO.

E. The current cost method (inventory and equity at FIFO, COGS and net income at LIFO) should be used for both inventory turnover and ROE. For inventory turnover, this method better approximates the actual (physical) turnover. The argument for ROE is that FIFO equity better reflects the Company's current value, while LIFO income reflects the current operating profits earned on that equity. For Zeta, these adjustments offset. In some cases, however, the current cost method ratios are quite different.

6. {M} A. The LIFO adjustment refers to the change in the LIFO reserve (or as Noland calls it 'Reduction to LIFO')

	1997	**1998**	**1999**
LIFO Reserve	$32,495	$32,876	$34,267
Change in LIFO reserve		381	1,391

B. COGS$_{FIFO}$ = COGS$_{LIFO}$ − change in LIFO reserve

For 1998: $372,033 − $381 = $371,652

For 1999: 385,892 − 1,391 = 384,501

C. Income would decline if prices in previous years were higher than current prices and the higher priced layer was liquidated.

D. i. 1998: COGS = $372,033 − $150 = $371,883

1999: COGS = 385,892 + 47 = 385,939

ii. For FIFO, COGS is the same as in part b—"liquidations" do not affect FIFO COGS

E. The most appropriate measure is the calculation computed in part d(i): LIFO COGS after eliminating effects of liquidation. That measure of COGS is closest to replacement cost.

F. By adding the LIFO reserve to equity: i.e. add $32,876,000 to 1998 equity and $34,267,000 to 1999 equity. Depending on the purpose of analysis, it may be appropriate to tax-adjust these values i.e. add [$32,876,000 × (1-tax rate)] to 1998 equity and [$34,267,000 × (1-tax rate)] to 1999 equity.

7. {S} A. The cost of inventory may have declined due to deflation.

B. 1. They might believe that the price decrease is temporary and in the future prices will increase again.

2. Since the LIFO reserve is large, a switch to FIFO would require a large tax expense (equal to tax rate times the LIFO reserve) immediately. Thus, even if they felt that prices would continue to decrease in the future, they are still better off paying the higher taxes slowly over time (as the LIFO reserve declines) rather than paying the full amount immediately.

8. {S}

		1997	1998	1999
A.	Sales	$515,728	$539,413	$572,696
	Gross margin	187,556	190,826	210,588
	Gross margin %	**36.4%**	**35.4%**	**36.8%**
B.	LIFO liquidation	$ 3,379	$ 1,733	none
	Pretax liquidation*	**5,198**	**2,666**	
	Adjusted			
	Gross margin	$182,358	$188,160	$210,588
	Gross margin %	**35.4%**	**34.9%**	**36.8%**

* Equals LIFO liquidation (net of tax)/.65

C. The adjusted gross margin percentage is more indicative of the longer-term trend of the company. By removing the effects of the LIFO liquidation(s), COGS and subsequently gross margin are more reflective of current cost income. Removing the effect of the liquidation shows that gross margins improved significantly from 1997–1998 to 1999.

9. {M} Contracts can provide strong incentives that affect the choice of inventory method. However different contracts may provide incentives for different choices. The following discussion assumes rising prices.

The management compensation plan provides a mixed incentive. Use of LIFO reduces income but increases cash from operations. Assuming a tax rate t, and a LIFO effect L, net income decreases by $(1-t)L$ while cash from operations increases by tL. The net effect $(2t-1)L$ is positive only at tax rates above 50%. Thus management contracts argue against use of LIFO.

Bond convenants also argue against LIFO. Working capital is reduced by the LIFO reserve less taxes saved. The annual amount is $(t-1)L$ which is always negative. Retained earnings are also lower under LIFO.

Union employee profit sharing payments are lower under LIFO, assuming that profits would exceed the minimum level. This would seem to argue for LIFO, to reduce compensation paid.

However, there are also second and third order effects that must be considered. Lower profit sharing payments, for example, increase net income (and cash from operations), increasing management compensation and easing the effect of bond covenants. These effects require complex calculations and are highly firm-specific.

Some effects are non-quantitative. Lower profit sharing payments may result in higher wage demands from workers. For management, use of FIFO may raise questions about why they failed to obtain tax savings by using LIFO.

Thus, while we can identify many of the factors that motivate the choice of inventory method, the controller's choice will depend on how these factors affect Sechne; there is no simple answer.

SOLUTIONS FOR READING 41

1. Depreciation computed:

	A	B	C	D	E
1	**Depreciation Method**	**Year**	**Computation**	**Depreciation**	**Carrying Value**
2	a. Straight-line	20x5	$13,500 ÷ 5	$2,700	$11,800
3		20x6	13,500 ÷ 5	2,700	9,100
4		20x7	13,500 ÷ 5	2,700	6,400
5		20x8	13,500 ÷ 5	2,700	3,700
6		20x9	13,500 ÷ 5	2,700	1,000
7					
8	b. Production	20x5	$13,500 × 1,500/7,500	$2,700	$11,800
9		20x6	13,500 × 2,625/7,500	4,725	7,075
10		20x7	13,500 × 2,250/7,500	4,050	3,025
11		20x8	13,500 × 750/7,500	1,350	1,675
12		20x9	13,500 × 375/7,500	675	1,000
13					
14	c. Double-declining-balance	20x5	$14,500 × .4	$5,800	$8,700
15		20x6	8,700 × .4	3,480	5,220
16		20x7	5,220 × .4	2,088	3,132
17		20x8	3,132 × .4	1,253*	1,879
18		20x9		879†	1,000
19					
20	* Rounded.				
21	† Remaining depreciation to reduce carrying value to residual value ($1,879 − $879).				

2. Balance sheet presentation on December 31, 20x5:

Property, plant, and equipment	
Cement mixer	$14,500
Less accumulated depreciation	2,700
	$11,800

3. The pattern of depreciation for the straight-line method differs significantly from the pattern for the double-declining-balance method. In the earlier years, the amount of depreciation under the double-declining-balance method is significantly greater than the amount under the straight-line method. In the later years, the opposite is true. The carrying value under the straight-line method is greater than under the double-declining-balance method at the end of all years except the fifth year. Depreciation under the production method differs from depreciation under the other methods in that it follows no regular pattern. It varies with the amount of use. Consequently, depreciation is greatest in 20x6 and 20x7, which are the years of greatest use. Use declined significantly in the last two years.

SOLUTIONS FOR READING 42

1. {M} Exhibit 42S-1 contains the calculations required.

EXHIBIT 42S-1   Chevron

Adjustments for Capitalization of Interest

Amounts in $ millions Year	1995	1996	1997	1998	1999	*part c 1999/95*
As reported						
Interest expense	$ 401	$ 364	$ 312	$ 405	$ 472	**1.18**
Pretax income	1,789	4,740	5,502	1,834	3,648	**2.04**
Net income	930	2,607	3,256	1,339	2,070	**2.23**
Capitalized interest	141	108	82	39	59	
Amortization of capitalized interest	47	24	28	35	9	
a. Calculations						
EBIT	$2,190	$5,104	$5,814	$2,239	$4,120	
Times interest earned	**5.46**	**14.02**	**18.63**	**5.53**	**8.73**	**1.60**
b. Adjusted						
Net capitalized interest	$ 94	$ 84	$ 54	$ 4	$ 50	
After 35% income tax	61	55	35	3	33	
Interest expense	542	472	394	444	531	**0.98**
EBIT	2,237	5,128	5,842	2,274	4,129	
i. Times interest earned	**4.13**	**10.86**	**14.83**	**5.12**	**7.78**	**1.88**
ii. % reduction from reported ratio	**−24.4%**	**−22.5%**	**−20.4%**	**−7.4%**	**−10.9%**	
Pretax income	$1,695	$4,656	$5,448	$1,830	$3,598	**2.12**
iii. Net income	**869**	**2,552**	**3,221**	**1,336**	**2,038**	**2.34**
% reduction from reported	−6.6%	−2.1%	−1.1%	−0.2%	−1.6%	

A. iv. Expensing all interest reduces net income for each year. However the effect diminishes over time.

B.   i. Because the amount of interest capitalized declined over time, restatement reduces the rate of increase in interest expense.

   ii. While the interest coverage ratio is lower after restatement, its trend improves due to the lower growth rate of interest expense.

   iii. Both pretax and net income are lower after restatement but their growth rate improves due to the lower growth rate of interest expense.

C. The restated data are more useful for financial analysis because they are based on actual interest expense. They provide better comparability with firms that do not capitalize interest.

2. {M} Exhibit 42S-2 contains the calculations required by parts a through c.

EXHIBIT 42S-2	Ericsson		

Amounts in SEK millions

	1997	1998	1999
A. *Under Swedish GAAP:*			
Net sales	167,740	184,438	215,403
Pretax income	17,218	18,210	16,386
Total assets	147,440	167,456	202,628
Stockholders' equity	52,624	63,112	69,176
Average total assets		157,448	185,042
Average stockholders' equity		57,868	66,144
Asset turnover		1.17	1.16
Pretax ROE		0.31	0.25
B. Adjustments:			
Development costs for software to be sold:			
Capitalization	5,232	7,170	7,898
Amortization	(3,934)	(3,824)	(4,460)
Write down			(989)
Net effect	1,298	3,346	2,449
Development costs for software for internal use:			
Capitalization			1,463
Amortization			(152)
Net effect	—	—	1,311
Total pretax effect	1,298	3,346	3,760
Adjusted pretax income	18,516	21,556	20,146
i. % change	**8%**	**18%**	**23%**
Year-end balances:			
Software to be sold	7,398	10,744	13,193
Internal use software			1,311
Total	7,398	10,744	14,504
Less: deferred tax @ 35%	(2,589)	(3,760)	(5,076)
Increase in equity	4,809	6,984	9,428

(Exhibit continued on next page ...)

EXHIBIT 42S-2	(continued)		
Adjusted total assets	154,838	178,200	217,132
ii. % change	5.0%	6.4%	7.2%
Adjusted equity	57,433	70,096	78,604
iii. % change	9.1%	11.1%	13.6%
C.			
Adjusted average assets		166,519	197,666
Adjusted average equity		63,764	74,350
i. Adjusted asset turnover		1.11	1.09
ii. Adjusted pretax ROE		0.34	0.27

D. The adjustments for Ericsson show that capitalization of software development costs can have a significant effect on reported income and equity, and on financial ratios. Therefore comparability requires that all firms be restated to the same basis.

E. The amounts capitalized highlight expenditures and enable the analyst to inquire about the new products under development. The amortization period used may be useful as a forecast of the useful life of the product. In both cases (capitalization and amortization) significant changes from prior periods may provide useful signals of impending change.

3. {S} A. The capitalization of the investment in displays delays their impact on income as compared with expensing. In addition, cash from operations is permanently increased as the expenditures are classified as cash flows for investment. Finally, if these expenditures are volatile, capitalization and amortization smoothes the impact on reported income.

B. **i.** In 2000, the capitalized amount increased by $1,648,000. Had promotional displays been expensed, net income would be $1,071,200 (after 35% tax) lower. Expensing would have reduced net income by 7.4% ($1,071.2/$14,467).

ii. Shareholders' equity would be reduced by 65% of $10,099,000 equal to $6,564,350 or 7.1%.

iii. Reported return on (average) assets equals $14,467[($166,656 + $140,609)/2] = 9.42%

Adjusted return on (average) assets equals ($14,467 − $1,071)/[($166,656 − $10,099) + ($140,609 − $8,451)/2] = 9.28% as assets must be reduced by the investment in promotional displays.

SOLUTIONS FOR READING 43

1. {M} i. Straight-line depreciation
ii. Sum-of-years' digits

	Depreciable base	$10,000,000	$10,000,000
	Sum-of-years' digits		15
Year		**Straight Line Method**	**Sum-of-Years' Digits**
1		$ 2,000,000	$ 3,333,333
2		2,000,000	2,666,667
3		2,000,000	2,000,000
4		2,000,000	1,333,333
5		2,000,000	666,667
Total		$10,000,000	$10,000,000

iii. Double declining balance

	Depreciable base	$12,000,000	Rate = 40%
		Double-Declining Balance	
Year		**Depreciation**	**Balance**
1		$ 4,800,000	$ 7,200,000
2		2,880,000	4,320,000
3		1,728,000	2,592,000
4		592,000	2,000,000
5			2,000,000
Total		$10,000,000	

2. {S} i. Straight-line methods report constant depreciation expense throughout the life of the asset. Accelerated methods result in higher depreciation expense initially, but a declining trend thereafter. The effect on total depreciation expense depends on the growth rate of capital spending (whether the effect of higher depreciation expense on new assets offsets the impact of declining depreciation expense on old ones). Using the same economic life, accelerated methods will report higher depreciation expense than the straight-line method during the early years and lower expense thereafter.

ii. The effect on net income is the reverse of the above. Net income is lower initially. Its reversal will depend on the level and growth of capital expenditures in the future.

iii. Accelerated depreciation methods report lower net income (higher depreciation expense), lower assets, and lower equity (higher accumulated depreciation) than the straight-line method. The numerator effect may dominate, producing lower return ratios. For a growing firm with increasing capital expenditures, the early years' depreciation expense difference will persist, resulting in lower return ratios.

iv. Accelerated depreciation methods report lower income in the first year but higher income in later years as depreciation expense declines. Reported assets are lower throughout. Companies with rapidly growing capital expenditures are likely to report lower ROA as the income effect dominates. As they mature, however, slowing capital expenditures and the growing effect of the reduced denominator (assets) is likely to result in higher ROA than under the straight-line method.

v. For financial reporting purposes, the choice of method has no effect on reported cash flows, as depreciation is a noncash expense. However, for tax purposes, the use of accelerated methods rather than the straight-line method reduces taxes paid, increasing cash from operations.

vi. As depreciation expense has no effect on revenues, accelerated depreciation methods increase reported asset turnover, as the denominator is lower.

3. {S} A. The present value of the cash flows, discounted at 10%, is $60 for each asset.

B. Asset A:

Year	Net Asset	Cash Flow	Depreciation Expense	Income	ROA
1	$60	$36	$30	$6	10%
2	30	23	20	3	10%
3	10	11	10	1	10%

Asset B:

Year	Net Asset	Cash Flow	Depreciation Expense	Income	ROA
1	$60	$26	$20	$6	10%
2	40	24	20	4	10%
3	20	22	20	2	10%

C. The pattern for Asset A is the sum-of-the-years' digits method. The pattern for Asset B is the straight-line method.

4. {S} A. Boeing uses accelerated depreciation methods: 150% declining balance for buildings and land improvements and sum-of-the-years digits for machinery and equipment. As a result early year depreciation resulting from capital expenditures is high keeping net plant and equipment low. The second reason is that, from 1995 to 1999, total depreciation expense was $6,286 while net additions to plant and equipment were $6,010 or $176 lower.

B. Accelerated depreciation methods result in low balance sheet carrying values for fixed assets, increasing the likelihood that asset sales will result in gains.

C. **i.** If Boeing adopted the straight-line method in 1999, depreciation expense for both 1998 and 1999 will most likely be reduced. Depreciation on assets acquired in recent years will be reduced although depreciation on older assets will be higher under the straight-line method. As 1998 capital spending was relatively high, the more recent year effects are likely to be greater than the older year effects of the accounting change. As 1999 capital spending was reduced, the effect on that year's depreciation will be less than on 1998.

ii. Stockholders' equity at December 31, 1999 will be higher due to lower prior year depreciation that increases net income and, therefore, retained earnings.

iii. Cash from operations is unaffected by the choice of depreciation method.

iv. Fixed asset turnover for 1999 will be decreased by the accounting change as lower prior year depreciation expense increases net fixed assets.

D. **i.** If Boeing adopted the straight-line depreciation method prospectively at January 1, 2000, net income for 2000 would increase as depreciation of current year capital additions is lower under the new method.

ii. Depreciation expense would be likely to decline due to the combined effect of lower depreciation expense on current year capital additions and the declining trend of depreciation expense on older assets for which accelerated methods remain in use.

E. As the accounting change would increase reported income without any effect on cash flows, an analyst might include that the company expects

i. future earnings trends to be negative

ii. capital spending to rise sharply

Either of these expectations might lead the company to change its accounting method to improve near-term reported earnings.

5. {M}A.–C. As shown in the table below, the accounting change improved the 2000 gross margin ratio by 0.5% and the operating ratio by 0.9%.

	As Reported		Accounting Change	Adjusted 2000
	1999	2000		
Net revenues	$1,452	$1,545		$1,545
Cost of sales	(835)	(845)	$ 8	(853)
Gross profit	$ 617	$ 700	$ 8	$ 692
S, D, & A expense	(575)	(625)	6	(631)
Operating income	$ 42	$ 75	$14	$ 61
% of Sales				
Net revenues	100.0%	100.0%		100.0%
Cost of sales	−57.5%	−54.7%	0.5%	−55.2%
Gross margin	**42.5%**	**45.3%**	**0.5%**	**44.8%**
S, D, & A expense	−39.6%	−40.5%	0.4%	−40.8%
Operating margin	**2.9%**	**4.9%**	**0.9%**	**3.9%**

D.   **i.** Fixed asset turnover is reduced as lower depreciation expense increases the net carrying amount of fixed assets.

ii. The accounting change improves the reported income trend as 2000 and following years benefit from the reduced depreciation expense.

iii. PBG's quality of earnings is reduced as the accounting change increases reported earnings.

iv. Cash from operations is unchanged as depreciation is a non-cash expense.

E. If the company believes that its performance is best measured using cash flow data, the accounting change has no benefit whatsoever. However reported income is increased, reducing the reported price-earnings ratio.

6. {M}A. Calculations below use the following definitions:

i. Average depreciable life (years) = Gross investment/depreciation expense

ii. Average age (years) = Accumulated depreciation/depreciation expense

iii. Average age (%) = Accumulated depreciation/gross investment

	1997	1998	1999
Buildings and land improvements			
i. Average depreciable life (years)	32.5	40.8	40.8
ii. Average age (years)	11.1	13.8	14.0
iii. Average age (%)	34.1%	33.9%	34.3%
Machinery and equipment			
i. Average depreciable life (years)	15.2	12.0	12.7
ii. Average age (years)	8.3	6.4	6.8
iii. Average age (%)	54.7%	53.6%	53.2%

B. The average depreciable life for buildings and land improvements is just over 40 years for 1998 and 1999, very close to the 40 years stated life. The 1997 ratio is much lower. The high depreciation for that year suggests that there was some special factor accounting for the discrepancy.

The average for machinery and equipment varies over the three-year period but is consistent with the 15-year maximum stated life. The ratio suggests that most assets in this category are depreciated over 15 years despite the stated policy of 5–15 years.

C. The average age (years) of buildings and land improvements has been increasing but is still low (and stable) compared with the average depreciable life (average age (%)). For machinery and equipment the average age fell in 1998 and was stable in 1999. These ratios suggest that Roche's physical facilities are modern, although it would be useful to compare the ratios with those of Roche competitors.

D. Questions worth asking include:

- Why was 1997 depreciation on buildings and land improvements abnormally high?
- Was 1997 depreciation on machinery and equipment abnormally low and, if so, why?
- What types of machinery and equipment are depreciated over 15 years versus shorter time periods?
- What is the breakdown of future capital expenditures between land improvements and machinery and equipment?
- Will future capital expenditures change the average depreciable life due to changes in the asset mix?

7. {S} A.
  i. Income before the effect of accounting changes was increased because intangible amortization was reduced.
  ii. Net income was reduced by the impairment charge, partly offset by reduced amortization.
  iii. Stockholders' equity was reduced by lower net income.
  iv. Cash from operations was unchanged as both the impairment charge and amortization are noncash expenses.

  B.
  i. 2001 net income will be increased as amortization of the reduced intangible assets is lower as a result of the accounting change.
  ii. Return on equity is increased by the accounting change as net income is increased and equity is reduced (see answer to A(iii)).
  iii. Cash from operations is unchanged as amortization is a noncash expense.

SOLUTIONS FOR READING 44

1. {S} Deferred taxes can be found in all of the categories listed. Examples are:

    i. Current liabilities may include deferred tax liabilities arising from an installment sale with cash payments expected within one year.

    ii. Deferred income tax credits resulting from the use of accelerated depreciation for tax purposes and straight line for financial reporting are reported in long-term liabilities.

    iii. The stockholders' equity account may include the deferred tax offset to the valuation allowance for available-for-sale securities or the cumulative translation adjustment account.

    iv. The deferred tax asset (debit) due to accrued compensation with cash payment expected within one year is a component of current assets.

    v. Long-term assets would include deferred tax assets (debits) recognized, (for example, for postretirement benefits or restructuring charges), but not expected to be funded within one year.

2. {S} i. Correct: Under SFAS 109, changes in tax laws must be reflected in the deferred tax liability in the period of enactment.

    ii. Correct: Answer to (i) also applies to deferred tax assets.

    iii. Correct: The tax consequences of events that have not been reflected in the financial statements (such as future earnings or losses) are not recognized.

    iv. Incorrect: See answers to (i) and (ii) above. This statement is true for the deferral method (see footnote 2 on text page 292).

    v. Incorrect: Changes in deferred tax assets and liabilities are included in income tax expense except for those charged directly to stockholders' equity.

3. {S} A. Permanent differences are items of income or expense that affect *either tax return income or financial income, but not both.* Examples include:

    ▶ Tax-exempt interest income (not reported on the tax return),

    ▶ Interest expense on amounts borrowed to purchase tax-exempt securities (not deductible on the tax return),

    ▶ Tax or other nondeductible government penalties (not reported on the tax return),

    ▶ Statutory mineral depletion in excess of cost basis depletion (not reported in the financial statements),

    ▶ Premiums on key-person life insurance policies (not deductible on the tax return),

    ▶ Proceeds from key-person life insurance policies (not reported on the tax return).

    B. Permanent differences, depending on their nature, either increase or decrease the firm's effective tax rate relative to the statutory rate. For example, tax-exempt interest income (the first example listed) reduces the effective tax rate as there is no tax expense associated with this income.

4. {S} A. i. If the deferred tax liability is not expected to reverse, there is no expectation of a cash outflow and the liability should be considered as equity.

ii. If the deferred tax liability is the result of a temporary difference that is expected to reverse, with consequent tax payment, it should be treated as a liability.

B. Because both the amounts and timing of tax payments resulting form the reversals of temporary differences are uncertain, deferred taxes should be excluded from both liabilities and equity.

C. The portion of the deferred tax liability that represents (the present value of) expected payments should be treated as debt. Accounting-based timing differences that are not expected to reverse should be treated as equity.

5. {M} We begin by determining the cost of each asset using the information about asset L. Year 2 depreciation under the sum-of-the-years' digits method with a five-year life is 4/15ths. Therefore, the depreciable base (cost − salvage value) must be $12,000/(4/15) = $45,000 and the cost must be $48,000 because salvage value is $3,000. We can now prepare a depreciation schedule for each method:

Depreciation Expense

Year	Asset K Straight-line[1]	Asset L SYD[2]	Asset M DDB[3]
1	$ 9,000	$15,000	$19,200
2	9,000	12,000	11,520
3	9,000	9,000	6,912
4	9,000	6,000	4,147
5	9,000	3,000	3,221
Total	$45,000	$45,000	$45,000

[1] Base = $45,000 (cost − salvage value); expense = $45,000/5 = $9,000.
[2] Base = $45,000; expense = 5/15ths, 4/15ths, 3/15ths, etc.
[3] Base = $48,000 (salvage value ignored); rate = 40%
Year 1 expense = .40 × $48,000 = $19,200, leaving $28,800
Year 2 expense = .40 × $28,800 = $11,520, leaving $17,280
Year 3 expense = .40 × $17,280 = $6,912, leaving $10,368
Year 4 expense = .40 × $10,368 = $4,147, leaving $6,221
Year 5 expense = $3,221 leaving $3,000

A. The double declining balance method is used on the tax return for all three assets; year 2 depreciation expense under that method is **$11,520.**

B. Financial statement depreciation expense in year two (from table above) is:

Asset K (straight line)	**$ 9,000**
Asset M (double declining balance)	**11,520**

C.   **i.** At the end of year two, accumulated depreciation equals (from table on previous page):

Asset K (straight line)	$18,000
Asset L (SYD)	27,000
Asset M (DDB)	30,720
Tax return (DDB)	30,720

Therefore, the deferred tax liability is:

Asset K: .34 ($30,720 − $18,000) = **$4,324.80**

Asset L: .34 ($30,720 − $27,000) = **1,264.80**

Asset M: No deferred tax as the same method is used for financial and tax reporting.

ii. At the end of year five, accumulated depreciation is the same under all methods and there is no deferred tax asset or liability.

6. {S} A.B. Assuming that Mother Prewitt continues to buy machines in the future, the depreciation timing difference will never reverse and there is no expected cash consequence. In this case, the deferred tax can be treated as equity.

If the installment sale is not expected to recur, the tax on that sale will be paid in 2001 and will require cash. For that reason, the $27,200 of deferred taxes should be considered a liability when calculating liquidity, solvency, and leverage ratios.

If, on the other hand, installment sales are expected to recur, such sales are no different from the depreciation case. The cash consequences of deferred tax items depend on the probability of their reversal, not on their nature.

C. Under SFAS 109 (liability method), enacted changes in tax rates are recognized, and the deferred tax liabilities must be restated to amounts based on the 40% tax rate. The incremental liability is recorded as a component of income tax expense regardless of when (or if) paid.

7. {S}

	Years Ended June 30			
Amounts in $millions	**1997**	**1998**	**1999**	**2000**
Deferred tax assets due to depreciation	$57.7	$40.3	$49.2	$37.7
Effect on fixed assets of:				
Impairment of long-lived assets		47.0		
Write-downs of operating assets		47.0	4.2	26.6
Write-downs of capitalized software		—	16.0	—
Total effect on fixed assets		$94.0	$20.2	$26.6
Tax rate		34%	35%	35%
a. Expected effect on deferred tax asset		$32.0	$ 7.1	$ 9.3
Reported change in deferred tax asset		(17.3)	8.9	(11.6)
Difference between expected effect and reported change in deferred tax asset		$49.3	$(1.8)	$20.9

Write-downs reduce the carrying amount of the assets on the financial statements but have no effect on the tax basis. Even if the company uses the straight-line depreciation method for both tax and financial reporting, tax depreciation would be higher than book depreciation after a write-off, generating deferred tax liabilities (credits) or lowering deferred tax assets (debits). In each year, therefore, write-downs increase the deferred tax asset but depreciation expense tends to reduce it.

In the table on the previous page, we compute the effect of the asset changes on the deferred tax asset for each year by multiplying the impairment plus the write-off amount by the tax rate for that year. We then compare that effect with the reported change in the deferred tax asset related to depreciation.

For 1998, the non-cash impairment of long-lived assets and the write-down of operating assets would generate a $32 million *increase* in deferred tax assets. However, the company reported a *decrease* of $17.3 million in deferred tax assets due to depreciation. The difference is much too high to result from current year depreciation expense. The most likely explanation is that the company sold fixed assets during the year, eliminating the book-tax difference relating to those assets. If those assets had a higher tax basis than book basis, sale would reduce the deferred tax asset by that difference multiplied by the tax rate.

In 1999, the difference is smaller and in the right direction, since we have an expected $7.1 million increase due to write-downs and a reported increase of $8.9 million. Regardless of whether internal-use software was capitalized on the tax return, its write-off should generate a deferred tax debit. This difference is probably due to a combination of current year depreciation (reducing the deferred tax asset) and asset sales (increasing the deferred tax asset).

In 2000, instead of an increase of $9.3 million, the company reports a decrease of $11.6 million in deferred tax assets. As for 1998, asset sales provide the most likely explanation.

8. {L} A. The first step converts the effective tax rate analysis from Exhibit 44-1 into a pretax income-based reconciliation, following the format of Exhibit 44-3. Exhibit 44S-2 shows the results for each year and three-year totals.

B. The reconciliation in Exhibit 44S-2 shows the following:

   i. Net changes in the valuation allowance increased tax expense by ¥36,593 (37,915 − 1,322) million over the three-year period increasing from ¥5,725 (¥6,246 − ¥521) million in 1999 to ¥19,634 (¥20,019 − ¥385) in 2001.

   ii. Changes in tax law decreased 1999 income tax expense by ¥21,861 million. There were no changes in tax laws and rates for other years.

   iii. Honda's disclosures are unclear. It appears that the decision not to recognize deferred taxes on reinvested subsidiary earnings decreased 2001 tax expense by ¥856 million [5,987 − 5,131] or 0.2% of pretax income. However the reported amounts are extremely low relative to the reported reinvested earnings (¥663,540 million at 3/31/01). A better understanding of this issue is required before meaningful adjustments can be made.

EXHIBIT 44S-2   Honda Motor

Reconciliation of Effective and Statutory Rates

In ¥ Millions Except Percentages	Years Ended March 31			3 Year Total
	1999	2000	2001	
Pretax income — Japanese	199,848	127,562	133,166	460,576
Pretax income — Foreign	320,663	288,501	251,810	860,974
Pretax income — Total	520,511	416,063	384,976	1,321,550
Statutory tax rate	48.0%	41.0%	41.0%	43.3%
Valuation allowance	1.2	2.8	5.2	
Difference in normal foreign tax rates	(3.0)	(1.3)	(1.0)	
Changes in tax laws and rates	(4.2)	0.0	0.0	
Reversal of valuation allowance	(0.1)	(0.1)	(0.1)	
Other	2.2	(1.4)	1.3	
Effective tax rate	44.1%	41.0%	46.4%	43.8%
Income tax expense at statutory rate	249,845	170,586	157,840	578,271
Effects of:				
Valuation allowance	6,246	11,650	20,019	37,915
Difference in tax rates of foreign subsidiaries	(15,615)	(5,409)	(3,850)	(24,874)
Changes in tax laws and rates	(21,861)	0	0	(21,861)
Reversal of valuation allowance due to operating loss carryforwards	(521)	(416)	(385)	(1,322)
Other	11,451	(5,825)	5,005	10,631
Income tax expense*	229,545	170,586	178,629	578,760
Calculation below required for part c.				
Pretax income — Foreign	320,663	288,501	251,810	860,974
Foreign tax expense**	(138,303)	(112,877)	(99,392)	(348,215)
Foreign net income	182,360	175,624	152,418	512,759
Foreign tax rate	43.1%	39.1%	39.5%	40.4%

* Numbers differ from Exhibit 44P-1 due to rounding

** Calculated as (statutory rate × foreign pretax income) − differences in tax rates of foreign subsidiaries. Using 1999 as an example: (48% × $320,663) − $15,615 = $138,303

C. i. Although lower non-Japanese tax rates reduced Honda's tax expense in each year, 1999–2001, that reduction declined from 1999 to 2001.

   ii. As Japanese tax rates declined from 48% in 1999 to 41% in 2000 and 2001, they are now closer to non-Japanese rates reducing the difference.

D. Factors an analyst must consider when forecasting Honda's effective tax rate for 2002 include the following:

   ▶ The mix of Japanese and foreign pretax income,

   ▶ Any possible changes in Japanese and foreign tax rates,

   ▶ The impact of the valuation allowance, and

   ▶ The composition of and trends in "other" tax differences.

9. A.

	1991 Tax Rate	1992 Tax Rate
Q1	$1,224/$4,797 = 25.5%	$232/$1,123 = 20.7%
Q2	$624/$2,600 = 24.0	$934/$3,723 = 25.1
Q3	$848/$3,244 = 26.1	$583/$98 = (594.9)

B. Using a tax rate of 17% for 1992 Q3 alone, tax expense would have been $16,660. The actual tax credit for Q3 was $583,000, for a difference of $600,000.

C. On a pretax basis, 1992 Q3 declined by 97% from 1991 Q3 ($98 versus $3,224). Net income, however, declined by only 72% ($681 versus $2,396) because 1992 Q3 included the tax benefit of revising the tax rate on earnings already reported for the first two quarters of 1992.

D. One possibility is to make comparisons only on a pretax basis to avoid distortions due to changes in the estimated tax rates. Another approach would use post-tax data to analyze the trends by applying the change to each quarter of 1992.

E. i.

	1992		
	Q1	Q2	Q3
Pretax income	$1,123	$3,723	$98
Income tax expense @17%	(191)	(633)	(17)
Net income	$ 932	$3,090	$81

   ii. The assumption has a marginal effect on Q1; it continues to reflect a significant decline relative to 1991 Q1. For Q2, we see the improvement in performance augmented by a lower tax rate (17% compared to 25%, but presumably a better indicator of future tax rates). The analyst should attempt to determine the causes of the decline in income in Q1 and Q3, the recovery in Q2 and better understand the implications for future performance.

SOLUTIONS FOR READING 45

1. {S} A. When full-coupon debt is issued, interest paid reduces cash from operations (CFO). When zero-coupon debt is issued, however, no cash interest is paid. CFO is unaffected, and is therefore higher than when full-coupon debt is issued. In addition, when imputed interest on zero-coupon debt is tax deductible, CFO is further increased by the tax benefit.

B. When full-coupon debt is issued, the proceeds are included in cash from financing (CFF). When that debt matures, the amount paid reduces CFF. Assuming the debt is issued and redeemed at par, the net effect on CFF is zero over the life of the debt.

Zero-coupon debt is issued at a discount; CFF is below the full-coupon case. However at maturity the full face amount is paid (same as full-coupon case). The net amount of CFF (outflow) is therefore greater than when full-coupon debt is issued.

C. No effect.

D. Interest on the zero-coupon bond rises each year as the carrying amount rises, increasing the base on which each year's interest expense is computed. All other things being equal, net income declines each year.

2. {M} A. Proceeds equal $100,000/(1.12)^5 = $ **$56,742**

B.

	2000	2001	2002	2003	2004
EBIT	$50,000	$50,000	$50,000	$50,000	$50,000
CFO before interest & taxes	60,000	60,000	60,000	60,000	60,000
Interest expense	6,809	7,626	8,541	9,566	10,714
CFO	60,000	60,000	60,000	60,000	60,000
Times interest earned	7.34	6.56	5.85	5.23	4.67
Times interest earned (cash basis)	[Infinite, since no interest is paid. In 2004, when the bond is retired, the payment will be reported as a financing cash outflow.]				

C. For a full-coupon bond, annual interest expense paid in cash would
be $56,742 \times .12 = \$6.809$

	2000	2001	2002	2003	2004
EBIT	$50,000	$50,000	$50,000	$50,000	$50,000
CFO before interest & taxes	60,000	60,000	60,000	60,000	60,000
Interest expense	6,809	6,809	6,809	6,809	6,809
CFO	53,191	53,191	53,191	53,191	53,191
Times interest earned	7.34	7.34	7.34	7.34	7.34
Times interest earned (cash basis)	8.81	8.81	8.81	8.81	8.81

D. Cash flow form operations is higher when zero-coupon bonds are
issued because interest is never reported as an operating cash outflow.
[Note the infinite cash-basis coverage ratio.] Interest coverage, however, is lower after the first year, and declines as interest expense
increases over time, reflecting the steadily increasing principal
amount. Full-coupon bonds (if sold at par) result in a constant cash
outflow from operations and constant interest expense. Given the
Null Company's "steady state," the interest coverage ratio is constant
on both accrual and cash flow bases.

E. Given the tax deductibility of accrued but unpaid interest on zero-
coupon bonds, cash flow form operations will be higher for both
cases. The reported cash flow differences will remain unchanged.
For the zero-coupon case, cash flow form operations is even more
misleading as the firm must generate sufficient cash from operations to repay the debt at maturity. The obligation must be repaid,
regardless of its cash flow classification.

3.{M}A. The $US carrying amount = 1,282/1.37 = **$936 million.**

B. Because the notes have no coupon, they were issued at a discount.
The difference between the face amount and the amount computed
in part a must be unamortized discount.

C. Interest expense (CHF millions) would be $7\% \times 1,282 = $ **CHF 90**

D. Adding the 1999 interest computed in part c to the carrying amount
at December 31, 1998: $90 + 1,282 = $ **CHF 1,372 million**

E. The most obvious explanation is the change in the exchange rate
from 1.37 to 1.60.

In $US, 1999 interest expense = $7\% \times \$936 = \$65$ million, making
the carrying amount at December 31, 1999 equal to $1,001 million
[$936 + $65]. This is much closer to the carrying amount computed
at 1,618/1.60 = $1,011 million.

A second factor is that interest expense in CHF is computed quarterly, based on average rates for each period. The CHF carrying
value at December 31, 1999 equals the 1998 carrying value + 1999
interest expense + translation loss [Swiss franc decline increases the
CHF debt amount].

F. **i.** Cash from operations is higher each year when zero coupon notes are issued because there is no cash interest.

ii. Interest expense rises each year (excluding the effect of exchange rates) because it is based on a (rising) $US carrying amount.

G. The rise in the value of the dollar (decline in Swiss franc) increases interest expense in CHF.

4. {S} **i.** Interest expense = Interest paid + change in bond discount

$$\$8,562 \quad = \quad \$7,200 \quad + \quad \$1,362$$

ii. = Market rate × [face value − discount]
= .12 × [face value − $8,652]

Therefore, face value = ($8,562/.12) + $8,652 = **$80,000**

iii. Coupon rate = interest paid/face value
= $7,200/$80,000 = **9%**

5. {S} A. and **B.** *In ¥ millions*

Years		1998	1999	% Increase
Issue				
2.14%	2005	6,248	6,356	1.72%
1.73%	2003	6,134	6,356	3.61%

The yen amounts were obtained by multiplying the dollar amounts by the exchange rate. For example, for the 2.14% bond at December 31, 1998, $55 × 113.60 = 6,248. [*Note:* the yen amounts are rounded.]

C. It appears that both bonds were issued at a discount, creating amortization that increases the carrying amount each year. If we add the 1999 increase to the coupon rate, it appears that the effective interest rates are 3.86% and 5.34% respectively.

D. One possible motivation is to finance Japanese operations that are conducted in yen. A second is that, as a well-known company, BMY may be able to borrow more cheaply by borrowing in yen and swapping the yen proceeds into US dollars.

6. {S} A. The advantage is that, when Takeda's share price rose, the debt was converted into equity, strengthening the balance sheet. As convertible notes are issued with a conversion price that exceeds the then market price, the company effectively sold common shares at a premium. In addition, because of the conversion feature, the interest rate would have been below the rate required by nonconvertible notes.

The disadvantage is that the debt was converted into common shares at a time when Takeda could have sold new shares at a much higher price, obtaining the same capital at a lower cost.

B. Reported data (Yen millions)

	1998	1999
Total debt	44,482	21,338
Equity	829,381	907,373
Total capital	873,863	928,711
Debt/total capital	5.1%	2.3%

The more than 50% debt decrease was the largest factor reducing the debt total capital ratio.

C. As the market price of Takeda shares was well above the conversion price in 1998, the convertible debt should be classified as equity. After that adjustment (subtracting 22,000 from debt and adding the same amount to equity) Takeda's debt was virtually unchanged from 1998 to 1999 and the decline in the debt/total capital ratio was small:

Adjusted Data (Yen millions)

	1998
Total debt	22,482
Equity	851,381
Total capital	873,863
Debt/total capital	2.6%

This analysis underscores the discussion in the reading; the analyst must classify convertible debt based on market considerations. Proper classification results in a more appropriate leverage measure.

7. {S} A. The market value of AMR's fixed rate debt issues fell relative to book value at December 31, 1999, implying that interest rates must have risen. Higher rates reduce the present value of payments associated with fixed rate debt.

B. The interest rate must have been below 10.2% as the present value exceeds book value.

C. Because the interest rate on variable rate debt floats, fair value should not change except as a result of changes in credit quality.

8. {S} A. An argument for inclusion is that, for Fannie Mae, the issuance and retirement of debt are recurring operating activities whose consequences should be included in operating earnings.

An argument for exclusion is that gains or losses from debt repurchase reflect economic changes during the entire period the debt was outstanding and should not be included in operating earnings for the period in which management chose to realize the gain.

B. An argument for including the hedging loss is that hedging activities are part of Fannie Mae's normal operating activities.

An argument for exclusion is that the hedging loss was unusually large and inclusion distorts the trend of operating earnings.

C. We believe that gains and losses from debt retirement should be excluded from operating earnings for most firms. These gains and losses result form management decisions and because (as discussed in the reading) refinancing may not yield any economic gain or loss despite the accounting gain or loss. Hedging results should be included in operating earnings as hedging gains and losses should offset other economic effects that are also included.

However, Fannie Mae may be an exception. As stated in part a, the company routinely issues and retires debt, suggesting that gains and losses should be included in operating earnings. Before doing so, the analyst should try to determine whether the gains or losses for the particular quarter are unusual or reflect interest rate changes over multiple periods, suggesting that the gains or losses should (analytically) be spread over several quarters.

9. {S} A. The calculated dividend capacity equals:

Minimum shareholders' equity, 12/31/93	$650.0 million
50% of 1994 net income of $48 million	24.0
Minimum shareholders' equity, 12/31/94	$674.0 million
Actual shareholders' equity, 12/31/94	717.3
Unrestricted amount	$ 43.3 million

B. Without any increase in income, the current dividend can be maintained for only two years:

	1995	1996	1997
Estimated Stockholders' Equity ($millions)			
Opening	$717.3	$723.3	$729.3
Income	48.0	48.0	48.0
Dividend	(42.0)	(42.0)	(42.0)
Closing	$723.3	$729.3	$735.3*

*Below minimum stockholders' equity required.

Minimum Stockholders' Equity ($millions)			
Opening	$674.0	$698.0	$722.0
Addition (50% of income)	24.0	24.0	24.0
Closing	$698.0	$722.0	$746.0

As the table above shows, in 1997 the minimum equity requirement will be violated.

C. To maintain dividend payments at the 1994 level through 1998, income would have to increase. The required income for 1997 and 1998 is $69.4 million and $84.0 million respectively.[1] These amounts result in the following table for those years:

	1997	1998
Estimated Stockholders' Equity ($millions)		
Opening	$729.3	$756.7
Income	69.4	84.0
Dividend	(42.0)	(42.0)
Closing	$756.7	$798.7
Minimum Stockholders' Equity ($millions)		
Opening	$722.0	$756.7
50% of income	34.7	42.0
Closing	$756.7	$798.7

[1] These amounts can be calculated as follows:

1997: Increase = 2 × shortfall in equity = 2 × ($746.0 − 735.3)
= 2 × $10.7 = $21.4 million

1998: Income must equal $84 million, twice the dividend, to maintain equity at the required level.

D. The answer would depend on the shareholder's view of the market price of NorAm's shares. Issuance of new shares to maintain the current dividend makes no sense given finance theory, which states that the two are equivalent. In an imperfect world, however, NorAm's shares may have been fully valued but the shareholder may not have wished to sell and incur capital gains taxes. If NorAm had attractive investment opportunities not reflected in its stock price, then issuing new shares to increase the firm's borrowing capacity would have been desirable.

SOLUTIONS FOR READING 46

1. {S}   **i.** Interest expense = 12% × $10,000 (beginning balance of lease obligation) = $1,200.

ii. The lease obligation will be reduced by $100 ($1,300 − $1,200) leaving an obligation of $9,900.

iii. Cash form Operations will be reduced by the interest payment of $1,200. Cash from investing activities will not be affected. (However, the firm will report the capital lease as a "noncash investment and financing activity.") Cash from financing will be reduced by the amount of the principal payment of $100.

iv. Under an operating lease there is no lease obligation on the balance sheet. The only effect on income is Rent Expense of $1,300. Similarly, CFO is reduced by $1,300. (CFI and CFF are not affected).

2. {M} A. The following states the effects of Tolrem using the capital lease method as compared with the operating lease method.

i. Cash from operations is higher as only the interest portion of lease expense is deducted from operating cash flows; total lease expense is deducted for operating leases.

ii. Financing cash flow is lower for capital lease, as part of lease rental is treated as amortization of liability and classified as financing cash outflow.

iii. Investing cash flow is not affected by the lease treatment. However, the firm will report capital leases in the statement of cash flows (or a footnote) as noncash investment activities.

iv. Net cash flow reflects the actual rental payment and is unaffected by the financial reporting treatment of the lease.

v. Debt/equity ratio is higher for capital lease, as it records the present value of minimum lease payments as debt *and* reduces net income (and therefore equity) in first year.

vi. Interest coverage ratio is usually (not always) lower for capital lease method, which reports interest expense but also higher EBIT, see (vii). For coverage ratios well above 1.0, the ratio will decline. If the increase in interest expense exceeds the increase in EBIT, the ratio will decline even for firms with very low coverage ratios.

vii. Operating income is lower for operating lease because the total lease payment is an operating expense; for capital lease, interest portion of lease expense is nonoperating.

viii. Net income is higher for operating lease; total lease expense (interest plus depreciation) is higher for capital lease.

ix. Deferred tax assets are higher for capital lease; as lease treatment for tax purposes is unaffected by accounting choice, capital lease will generate a deferred tax asset as taxable income (operating lease) exceeds pretax income (capital lease).

x. Taxes paid are unaffected by choice of method.

xi. Pretax return on assets is higher for operating leases as pretax income is higher and no assets are reported as the result of the lease; a capital lease reduces income and reports lease assets. Post-tax return on assets is higher for the same reasons.

xii. Pretax return on equity: both pretax income and equity are higher for operating than for capital leases. The higher pretax income should increase the ratio in all but exceptional cases. Post-tax return on equity should be higher for same reason. However as increase in post-tax income equals (for first year) increase inequity, there may be more exceptional cases.

B. Net income (viii) will be lower for the operating lease after the "crossover" point. As total net income over the life of the lease is unaffected by the accounting choice, higher net income (operating lease) in the early years must be offset by lower net income in later years.

C. Consistent use of the operating lease method in place of capitalization will not change the direction of the effects shown in part A, but will increase their magnitude. In aggregate, new leases will keep Tolrem from reaching the crossover point for net income, keeping net income and return ratios higher than if the leases were capitalized.

3. {M} A. Since it is the first year:

Capital lease obligations	$2,596,031
Repayment of capital lease obligations	3,969
Capital lease at inception	$2,600,000

B. Amortization expense = $2,600,000 − $2,479,570 = $120,430

Assuming the asset is being amortized on a straight line basis over the lease term, the lease term = $2,600,000/$120,430 = 21.6 or 22 years

Total expense = interest + amortization = $120,430 + $223,733 = $344,163

C. CFO was reduced by the interest expense of $223,733 and CFF was reduced by the "repayment of capital lease obligations" of $3,969

D. Free cash flows should be reduced by $2,600,000 − the "cost" of the leased asset.

E. **i.** Lease expense would be lease payment = $223,733 + $3,969 = $227,702

 ii. CFO would be reduced by lease payment of $227,702

F. Using 1999 payment only: $223,733/$2,600,000 = 8.6%

Using all the payments, we have exact MLP's for the six years 1999–2004. The "thereafter" MLP's totaling $4,596 thousand are spread over 16 years; i.e., $287.25 thousand/year. Equating this stream to the present value of $2,600,000 yields a rate (IRR) of 9.3%.

The two methods yield rates within "range" of each other especially when we consider that the rate derived from the first method is typically downward biased.

4. {M} A. The adjustment involves the addition of the interest component of minimum lease payments to stated interest expense. The adjustment reflects a partial, *de facto* capitalization of operating leases.

i. Unadjusted Ratio of Earnings to Fixed Charges:

Pretax earnings	$2,363,646
Interest on indebtedness	68,528
Earnings before interest and taxes (EBIT)	$2,432,174
Fixed Charges:	
Interest on indebtedness	$68,528
Unadjusted Ratio of Earnings to Fixed Charges	35.5X

ii. The unadjusted ratio is almost four times the adjusted ratio. *Note:* The SEC rule that governs this calculation assumes that the interest component is one-third of the MLP. The true interest component may be higher or lower, changing the coverage ratio.

B. Reported debt-to-equity = $550,000/$2,233,303 = **0.25**

C. Calculation of amounts adjusted for lease capitalization:

The Limited, Inc.
1999 Working Capital Position and Capitalization Table

	Reported	Adjusted
i. Working capital	**$1,070,249**	**$633,579**[1]
Capitalization:		
Long-term debt	550,000	550,000
Add: Capitalized lease payments		3,452,628[2]
ii. Adjusted long-term debt		**$4,002,628**
Shareholders' equity	2,233,303	2,233,303
Total capitalization	$2,783,303	$6,235,931
iii. Debt-to-equity	**0.25**	**1.80**

[1] Working capital is reduced by the principal component of the 2000 MLPs calculated as

$$\$436,670 = [\$643,828 - (0.6 \times \$3,452,628)],$$

where $3,452,628 is the present value calculated in note 2 below.

[2] Present value of MLPs using an interest rate of 6%. The "thereafter" MLPs are spread using the constant rate assumption; ($502,880 in 2005 and 2006 and $422,102 in 2007).

5. {M} A. All amounts in $ millions

	1997	1998	1999
Receivables reported	$664.0	$ 720.0	$ 739.0
Receivables sold	—	38.4	50.0
Adjusted receivables	$664.0	$ 758.4	$ 789.0
Average receivables			
as reported		692.0	729.5
adjusted		711.2	773.7
Sales		$4,537.0	$3,867.0
Receivable turnover			
Reported		6.56	5.30
Adjusted		6.38	5.00
# of days receivable			
Reported		56 days	69 days
Adjusted		57 days	73 days
Cash cycle effect		**1 day**	**4 days**

The sale of receivables allowed the company to show an improved receivable turnover and cash cycle; the improvement was more significant for 1999 as the amount of receivables sold increased and sales declined.

B. The effect on the current ratio is minimal as the same amount is added to both numerator and denominator of the ratio and that ratio is close to 1. The debt-to-equity ratio adjustment is more significant in 1999 due to the increase in receivables sold and the lower equity amount.

	1998	1999
Current assets	$1,673.0	$1,615.0
Current liabilities	1,492.0	1,472.0
Current ratio	**1.121**	**1.097**
Adjusted (add receivables sold)		
Current assets	$1,711.4	$1,665.0
Current liabilities	1,530.4	1,522.0
Current ratio adjusted	**1.118**	**1.094**
Debt reported	$ 963.0	$ 961.0
Debt adjusted	1,001.4	1,011.0
Equity	572.0	376.0
Debt-to-equity reported	**1.68**	**2.56**
Debt-to-equity adjusted	**1.75**	**2.69**

C. As the calculation below indicates, both the level and trend in CFO are overstated as a result of the sale of receivables.

	1997	1998	1999
CFO as reported	$(113.0)	$(59.0)	$ (6.0)
Change in receivables sold	—	38.4	11.6
CFO adjusted	$(113.0)	$(97.4)	$(17.6)

6. {M} A. Debt should be increased by:

$20 million	(present value of operating lease)
5	(guarantee)
7	(present value of take-or-pay agreement)
$32 million	

There is no effect on equity as each obligation is offset by a corresponding asset:

> Leased assets for operating lease
> Receivable for Crockett's obligation to repay debt
> Supply agreement

The recomputed debt-to-equity ratio is:

($12 + $32)/$20 = **2.2X** as compared to .6X before adjustment

B. Additional interest expense is:

Lease (effective interest rate is about 18%)

.18 × $20 = $3.6 million

Bond guarantee	.10 × 5 =	0.5
Total		$4.1 million

Before adjustment, the interest expense is $1.0 million and the times interest earned ratio is 5.0, implying EBIT of $5.0 million.

After adjustment, the ratio is:

($5.0 + $4.1)/($1.0 + $4.1) = **1.78X**

No adjustment has been made for the take-or-pay contract, as it does not affect 1993 interest expense. Adjustments in future years will be based on the implicit interest rate of 21%.

C. Reasons for entering into off-balance-sheet obligations:

1. Avoidance of or mitigation of the risk of violating debt covenant restrictions.
2. Leased assets revert to lessor after eight years, limiting risk of obsolescence.
3. Guarantee of Crockett's debt may lower interest costs, increasing profitability of investment.
4. Contract with PEPE secures source of supply and possibly advantageous pricing.

D. Additional information needed for full evaluation:

1. (Lease) Useful life of leased assets; conditions under which lease can be canceled; nature of leased assets.

2. (Guarantee) Financial condition of Crockett; bond covenants.

3. (Take-or-pay) Alternate sources of supply; quantity to be purchased relative to total needs; price provisions of contract.

7. {M}

	1st Year	9th Year
i. Assets	Higher	Higher
ii. Revenues	Higher	Lower
iii. Expenses	Higher	Lower
iv. Asset turnover ratio	Higher	Lower
v. Interest income	Higher	Higher
vi. Cost of goods sold	Higher	No effect
vii. Net income	Higher	Lower
viii. Retained earnings	Higher	Higher
ix. Taxes paid	No effect	No effect
x. Post-tax ROA	Higher	Lower
xi. Cash from operations	Higher	Lower
xii. Investment cash flow	Lower	Higher

Assets are higher because inventory is replaced with (higher) receivables because of the recognition of manufacturing profit. Assets remain higher throughout the lease term.

Revenues are higher in Year 1 as the sales-type lease recognizes a sale whereas the operating lease method does not. In later years, interest revenue from the sales-type lease should be lower than lease revenue for the operating lease. This effect is more pronounced over time; in year 9, interest income is low given the small remaining receivable. The revenue effect increases the asset turnover ratio in the first year. But the revenue effect reduces turnover in the ninth year.

Expenses are higher in year 1 due to the recognition of cost of goods sold. In later years, there is no expense for the sales-type lease; the operating lease method reports depreciation expense in every year, however.

Initial period income and income-related ratios are higher for the sales-type lease because the sale (and income) is recognized at the inception of the lease. In later years, however, income is higher for the operating lease.

Income taxes paid are the same since the lease cannot be considered a completed sale for tax purposes.

Cash from operations is higher for the first year due to recognition of the sale (the investment in the lease is classified as an investing cash outflow). In later years the operating lease method shows higher cash from operations as rental income exceeds the interest income recorded for the sales-type lease (income taxes paid are the same).

[See Exhibit 46-8 and the accompanying text for further explanation of these effects.]

8. {L} **A.** The present value of the minimum lease payments receivable of $170,271 (at 10%, the lower of lessee and lessor rates) is more than 90% of the fair market value of $185,250. Therefore, the lessee, Baldes, should capitalize the lease. It would be useful to know whether the lessee has guaranteed the residual value of the leased asset.

B.

Leased assets	$170,271
Long-term lease obligation	167,298
Current portion of lease obligation	2,973
Total lease obligation	$170,271

Note that there are no income or cash flow statement effects at the inception of the lease.

C.   **i.** Balance sheet effects of capital lease:

	01/01/01	12/31/01	12/31/02
Leased assets	$170,271	$170,271	$170,271
Accumulated depreciation	0	(8,514)	(17,028)
Leased assets (net)	$170,271	$161,757	$153,243
Current portion of lease obligation	$ 2,973	$ 3,270	$ 3,597
Long-term portion of lease obligation	167,298	164,028	160,431
Total lease obligation	$170,271	$167,298	$164,028

No impact on balance sheet if operating lease method applied. [Deferred tax assets reflecting the difference between total expense under the two methods would also be reported.]

ii. Income statement effects of capital lease:

Years ended December 31	2001	2002
Interest expense[1]	$17,027	$16,730
Depreciation expense[2]	8,514	8,514
Total expense	$25,541	$25,244

[1] Interest expense for: 2001 = .10 × $170,271
                            2002 = .10 × $167,298

[2] Depreciation expense = $170,271/20 for each year

The income statement would show lease expense of $20,000 each year under the operating lease method.

iii. Statement of cash flow effects of capital lease:

Years Ended December 31	2001	2002
Cash from operations	$(17,027)	$(16,730)
Financing cash flow	(2,973)	(3,270)

The operating lease method reports $20,000 cash outflow from operations for each year.

D. As in part A, the PV of the MLPs is more than 90% of the fair market value, permitting capitalization. However, for the lessor to capitalize the lease, revenue recognition criteria must be satisfied as well. These conditions are:

i. Collectibility of MLPs is reasonably assured, and

ii. There are no significant uncertainties regarding the amount of costs yet to be incurred by the lessor or other obligations under the provisions of the lease agreement.

To evaluate these issues, information would be needed regarding the financial condition of Baldes and any remaining obligations of Malbec.

E. The operating lease method has no effect on Malbec's balance sheet at the inception of the lease since the lessor has merely entered into a rental arrangement—an executory contract.

F. Sales-type lease reporting by lessor:

Malbec's gross investment in the lease:

MLPs ($20,000 × 20)	$400,000
Unguaranteed residual value	5,500
Gross investment	$405,500

Net investment:

Present value of 20 payments at 10%	$170,271
PV of $5,500, 20 periods hence at 10%	818
Net investment	$171,089
Unearned income: $405,500 − $171,089 =	$234,411

Journal entry at inception (1/1/01):

Gross investment	$405,500	
Cost of goods sold	149,182	
Sales revenue		$170,271
Inventory		150,000
Unearned income		234,411

Balance Sheet Effects, January 1, 2001:

Inventory (reduction due to sale)	$(150,000)
Gross investment in sales-type lease	$405,500
Less: unearned interest income	(234,411)
Net investment	$171,089

Income Statement Effects, Year Ended December 31, 2001:

Sales revenue	$170,271
Cost of goods sold	(149,182)
Income effect	$ 21,089

G.

Balance Sheet Effects:	**12/31/01**	**12/31/02**
Sales-type lease:		
Net investment in lease, current	$ 3,180	$ 3,498
Net investment in lease, long-term	159,518	156,020
Operating lease:		
Assets under lease	$ 150,000	$150,000
Accumulated depreciation	(7,225)	(14,450)
Net assets	$142,775	$135,550

Income Statement Effects:	**12/31/01**	**12/31/02**
Sales-type lease:		
Sales revenue	$ 170,271	$ —
Cost of goods sold	(149,182)	—
Sales profit	$ 21,089	—
Interest income	17,109	$ 16,820
Pretax income	$ 38,198	$ 16,820
Operating lease:		
Rental income	$ 20,000	$ 20,000
Depreciation expense	(7,225)	(7,225)
Pretax income	$ 12,775	$ 12,775

Cash Flow Statement Effects:	12/31/01	12/31/02
Sales-type lease:		
Cash from operations:		
Sales profit	$ 21,089	$ —
Inventory reduction	150,000	—
Interest income	17,109	16,820
Cash from operations	$ 188,198	$ 16,820
Investment cash flow:		
Net investment in lease	$(171,089)	$ —
Reduction in net investment	2,891	3,180
Investment cash flow	$(168,198)	$ 3,180
Net cash flow	$ 20,000	$ 20,000
Operating lease:		
Rental income	$ 20,000	$ 20,000
Cash from operations	$ 20,000	$ 20,000

Note: There is no effect on investment cash flow when the operating lease method is used.

CFO—Indirect Method:	12/31/01	12/31/02
Sales-type lease:		
Pretax income	$ 38,198	$16,820
Inventory reduction	150,000	—
Cash from operations	$ 188,198	$ 16,820
Operating lease:		
Pretax income	$12,775	$12,775
Depreciation expense	7,225	7,225
Cash from operations	$ 20,000	$ 20,000

$4\frac{5}{8}$ $4\frac{11}{16}$

$5\frac{1}{2}$ $5\frac{1}{2}$ $-$ $\frac{3}{8}$

$5\frac{1}{2}$ $21\frac{3}{16}$ $-$ $1\frac{1}{16}$

$20\frac{5}{8}$ $18\frac{1}{8}$ $+$ $\frac{7}{8}$

$17\frac{3}{8}$ $18\frac{1}{8}$ $+$ $\frac{7}{8}$

$6\frac{1}{2}$ $6\frac{1}{2}$ $-$ $\frac{1}{2}$

$7\frac{1}{4}$ $6\frac{1}{2}$

$15\frac{1}{16}$ $3\frac{1}{32}$ $-$ $\frac{1}{8}$

$9\frac{1}{16}$ $9\frac{1}{16}$

$1\frac{1}{32}$ $7\frac{13}{16}$ $7\frac{15}{16}$

$7\frac{15}{16}$

$2\frac{5}{8}$ $2\frac{11}{32}$ $2\frac{1}{2}$ $+$

$2\frac{3}{4}$ $2\frac{1}{4}$ $2\frac{1}{4}$

$6\frac{1}{8}$ $12\frac{1}{16}$ $11\frac{3}{8}$ $11\frac{3}{4}$ $+$

87 $33\frac{3}{4}$ 33 $33\frac{1}{8}$ $-$

602 $25\frac{5}{8}$ $24\frac{9}{16}$ $25\frac{3}{8}$ $+$

833 12 $11\frac{5}{8}$ $11\frac{7}{8}$ $+$

16 $10\frac{1}{2}$ $10\frac{1}{2}$ $10\frac{1}{2}$ $-$

78 $15\frac{7}{8}$ $15\frac{13}{16}$ $15\frac{7}{8}$ $-$

4538 $9\frac{1}{16}$ $8\frac{1}{4}$

430 $11\frac{1}{4}$ $10\frac{1}{8}$

GLOSSARY

Abnormal rate of return The amount by which a security's actual return differs from its expected rate of return which is based on the market's rate of return and the security's relationship with the market.

Above full-employment equilibrium A macroeconomic equilibrium in which real GDP exceeds potential GDP.

Absolute dispersion The amount of variability present without comparison to any reference point or benchmark.

Absolute frequency The number of observations in a given interval (for grouped data).

Accelerated method A method of depreciation that allocates relatively large amounts of the depreciable cost of an asset to earlier years and reduced amounts to later years.

Accrual accounting The system of recording financial transactions as they come into existence as a legally enforceable claim, rather than when they settle.

Accrued interest (1) Interest earned but not yet due and payable. This is equal to the next coupon to be paid on a bond multiplied by the time elapsed since the last payment date and divided by the total coupon period. Exact conventions differ across bond markets. (2) Interest earned but not yet paid.

Additional information Information that is required or recommended under the GIPS standards and is not considered as "supplemental information" for the purposes of compliance.

Addition rule for probabilities A principle stating that the probability that A or B occurs (both occur) equals the probability that A occurs, plus the probability that B occurs, minus the probability that both A and B occur.

Additions Enlargements to the physical layout of a plant asset.

Add-on interest A procedure for determining the interest on a bond or loan in which the interest is added onto the face value of a contract.

Administrative fees All fees other than the trading expenses and the investment management fee. Administrative fees include custody fees, accounting fees, consulting fees, legal fees, performance measurement fees, or other related fees. These administrative fees are typically outside the control of the investment management firm and are not included in either the gross-of-fees return or the net-of-fees return. However, there are some markets and investment vehicles where administrative fees are controlled by the firm. (See the term "bundled fee.")

Aggregate demand The relationship between the quantity of real GDP demanded and the price level.

Aggregate hours The total number of hours worked by all the people employed, both full time and part time, during a year.

Aggregate production function The relationship between the quantity of real GDP supplied and the quantities of labor and capital and the state of technology.

Allocative efficiency A situation in which we cannot produce more of any good without giving up some of another good that we value more highly.

Alpha A term commonly used to describe a manager's abnormal rate of return, which is the difference between the return the portfolio actually produced and the expected return given its risk level.

Alternative hypothesis The hypothesis accepted when the null hypothesis is rejected.

American Depository Receipts (ADRs) Certificates of ownership issued by a U.S. bank that represent indirect ownership of a certain number of shares of a specific foreign firm. Shares are held on deposit in a bank in the firm's home country.

American option An option contract that can be exercised at any time until its expiration date. (1) An option contract that can be exercised at any time until its expiration date. (2) An option that can be exercised on any day through the expiration day. Also referred to as American-style exercise.

American terms With reference to U.S. dollar exchange rate quotations, the U.S. dollar price of a unit of another currency.

Amortization The periodic allocation of the cost of an intangible asset to the periods it benefits.

Amortizing and accreting swaps A swap in which the notional principal changes according to a formula related to changes in the underlying.

Analysis of variance (ANOVA) The analysis of the total variability of a dataset (such as observations on the dependent variable in a regression) into components representing different sources of variation; with reference to regression, ANOVA provides the inputs for an F-test of the significance of the regression as a whole.

Annual percentage rate The cost of borrowing expressed as a yearly rate.

Annuity A finite set of level sequential cash flows.

Annuity due An annuity having a first cash flow that is paid immediately.

Anomalies Security price relationships that appear to contradict a well-regarded hypothesis; in this case, the efficient market hypothesis.

A priori probability A probability based on logical analysis rather than on observation or personal judgment.

Arbitrage (1) The simultaneous purchase of an undervalued asset or portfolio and sale of an overvalued but equivalent asset or portfolio, in order to obtain a riskless profit on the price differential. Taking advantage of a market inefficiency in a risk-free manner. (2) A trading strategy designed to generate a guaranteed profit from a transaction that requires no capital commitment or risk bearing on the part of the trader. A simple example of an arbitrage trade would be the simultaneous purchase and sale of the same security in different markets at different prices. (3) The condition in a financial market in which equivalent assets or combinations of assets sell for two different prices, creating an opportunity to profit at no risk with no commitment of money. In a well-functioning financial market, few arbitrage opportunities are possible. Equivalent to the law of one price. (4) A risk-free operation that earns an expected positive net profit but requires no net investment of money.

Arbitrage pricing theory (APT) A theory that posits that the expected return to a financial asset can be described by its relationship with several common risk factors. The multifactor APT can be contrasted with the single-factor CAPM.

Arithmetic mean (AM) The sum of the observations divided by the number of observations.

Arrears swap A type of interest rate swap in which the floating payment is set at the end of the period and the interest is paid at that same time.

Asian call option A European-style option with a value at maturity equal to the difference between the stock price at maturity and the average stock price during the life of the option, or $0, whichever is greater.

Asset allocation The process of deciding how to distribute an investor's wealth among different asset classes for investment purposes.

Asset class Securities that have similar characteristics, attributes, and risk/return relationships.

Asset impairment Loss of revenue-generating potential of a long-lived asset before the end of its useful life; the difference between an asset's carrying value and its fair value, as measured by the present value of the expected cash flows.

Assets under management (AUM) The total market value of the assets managed by an investment firm.

At-the-money option An option for which the strike (or exercise) price is close to (at) the current market price of the underlying asset.

Automatic fiscal policy A change in fiscal policy that is triggered by the state of the economy.

Automatic stabilizers Mechanisms that stabilize real GDP without explicit action by the government.

Autonomous expenditure The sum of those components of aggregate planned expenditure that are not influenced by real GDP. Autonomous expenditure equals investment, government purchases, exports, and the autonomous parts of consumption expenditure and imports.

Average cost pricing rule A rule that sets price to cover cost including normal profit, which means setting the price equal to average total cost.

Average fixed cost Total fixed cost per unit of output—total fixed cost divided by output.

Average product The average product of a resource. It equals total product divided by the quantity of the resource employed.

Average tax rate A person's total tax payment divided by his or her total income.

Average total cost Total cost per unit of output.

Average variable cost Total variable cost per unit of output.

Backwardation A condition in the futures markets in which the benefits of holding an asset exceed the costs, leaving the futures price less than the spot price.

Balance of payments (1) A summary of all economic transactions between a country and all other countries for a specific time period, usually a year. The balance-of-payments account reflects all payments and liabilities to foreigners (debits) and all payments and obligations received from foreigners (credits). (2) A record of all financial flows crossing the borders of a country during a given time period (a quarter or a year).

Balance of payments accounts A country's record of international trading, borrowing, and lending.

Balance of trade *See* Trade balance.

Balance sheet A financial statement that shows what assets the firm controls at a fixed point in time and how it has financed these assets.

Balanced budget A government budget in which tax revenues and expenditures are equal.

Balanced budget multiplier The magnification on aggregate demand of a *simultaneous* change in government purchases and taxes that leaves the budget balance unchanged.

Balanced fund A mutual fund with, generally, a three-part investment objective: (1) to conserve the investor's principal, (2) to pay current income, and (3) to increase both principal and income. The fund aims to achieve this by owning a mixture of bonds, preferred stocks, and common stocks.

Bank discount basis A quoting convention that annualizes, on a 360-day year, the discount as a percentage of face value.

Barriers to entry Legal or natural constraints that protect a firm from potential competitors.

Barter The direct exchange of one good or service for other goods and services.

Basic earnings per share Total earnings divided by the weighted average number of shares actually outstanding during the period.

Basis The difference between the spot price of the underlying asset and the futures contract price at any point in time (e.g., the *initial* basis at the time of contract origination, the *cover* basis at the time of contract termination).

Basis swap (1) An interest rate swap involving two floating rates. (2) A swap in which both parties pay a floating rate.

Bayes' formula A method for updating probabilities based on new information.

Bear spread An option strategy that involves selling a put with a lower exercise price and buying a put with a higher exercise price. It can also be executed with calls.

Behavioral finance Involves the analysis of various psychological traits of individuals and how these traits affect how they act as investors, analysts, and portfolio managers.

Below full-employment equilibrium A macroeconomic equilibrium in which potential GDP exceeds real GDP.

Benchmark An independent rate of return (or hurdle rate) forming an objective test of the effective implementation of an investment strategy.

Benchmark bond A bond representative of current market conditions and used for performance comparison.

Benchmark error Situation where an inappropriate or incorrect benchmark is used to compare and assess portfolio returns and management.

Benchmark portfolio A comparison standard of risk and assets included in the policy statement and similar to the investor's risk preference and investment needs, which can be used to evaluate the investment performance of the portfolio manager.

Bernoulli random variable A random variable having the outcomes 0 and 1.

Bernoulli trial An experiment that can produce one of two outcomes.

Beta A standardized measure of systematic risk based upon an asset's covariance with the market portfolio.

Betterments Improvements that do not add to the physical layout of a plant asset.

Bid-ask spread The difference between the quoted ask and the bid prices.

Big tradeoff A tradeoff between equity and efficiency.

Bill-and-hold basis Sales on a bill-and-hold basis involve selling products but not delivering those products until a later date.

Binomial model A model for pricing options in which the underlying price can move to only one of two possible new prices.

Binomial option pricing model A valuation equation that assumes the price of the underlying asset changes through a series of discrete upward or downward movements.

Binomial random variable The number of successes in n Bernoulli trials for which the probability of success is constant for all trials and the trials are independent.

Binomial tree (1) A diagram representing price movements of the underlying in a binomial model. (2) The graphical representation of a model of asset price dynamics in which, at each period, the asset moves up with probability p or down with probability $(1 - p)$.

Black market An illegal trading arrangement in which the price exceeds the legally imposed price ceiling.

Black-Scholes option pricing model A valuation equation that assumes the price of the underlying asset changes continuously through the option's expiration date by a statistical process known as *geometric Brownian motion*.

Bond A long-term debt security with contractual obligations regarding interest payments and redemption.

Bond-equivalent basis A basis for stating an annual yield that annualizes a semiannual yield by doubling it.

Bond-equivalent yield The yield to maturity on a basis that ignores compounding.

Bond option An option in which the underlying is a bond; primarily traded in over-the-counter markets.

Bond price volatility The percentage changes in bond prices over time.

Book value of equity (or book value) (1) Shareholders' equity (total assets minus total liabilities) minus the value of preferred stock; common shareholders' equity. (2) The accounting value of a firm.

Book value per share   Book value of equity divided by the number of common shares outstanding.

Box spread   An option strategy that combines a bull spread and a bear spread having two different exercise prices, which produces a risk-free payoff of the difference in the exercise prices.

Brady bonds   Bonds issued by emerging countries under a debt-reduction plan named after Mr. Brady, former U.S. Secretary of the Treasury.

Brand name   A registered name that can be used only by its owner to identify a product or service.

Broker   (1) An agent who executes orders to buy or sell securities on behalf of a client in exchange for a commission. (2) *See* Futures commission merchants.

Budget deficit   A government's budget balance that is negative—expenditures exceed tax revenues.

Budget surplus   A government's budget balance that is positive—tax revenues exceed expenditures.

Bull spread   An option strategy that involves buying a call with a lower exercise price and selling a call with a higher exercise price. It can also be executed with puts.

Bundled fee   A fee that combines multiple fees into one "bundled" fee. Bundled fees can include any combination of management, transaction, custody, and other administrative fees. Two specific examples of bundled fees are the wrap fee and the all-in fee.

All-in fee   Due to the universal banking system in some countries, asset management, brokerage, and custody are often part of the same company. This allows banks to offer a variety of choices to customers regarding how the fee will be charged. Customers are offered numerous fee models in which fees may be bundled together or charged separately. All-in fees can include any combination of investment management, trading expenses, custody, and other administrative fees.

Wrap fee   Wrap fees are specific to a particular investment product. The U.S. Securities and Exchange Commission (SEC) defines a wrap fee account (now more commonly known as a separately managed account or SMA) as "any advisory program under which a specified fee or fees not based upon transactions in a client's account is charged for investment advisory services (which may include portfolio management or advice concerning the selection of other investment advisers) and execution of client transactions." A typical separately managed account has a contract or contracts (and fee) involving a sponsor (usually a broker or independent provider) acting as the investment advisor, an investment management

firm typically as the subadvisor, other services (custody, consulting, reporting, performance, manager selection, monitoring, and execution of trades), distributor, and the client (brokerage customer). Wrap fees can be all-inclusive, asset-based fees (which may include any combination of management, transaction, custody, and other administrative fees).

Business cycle   The periodic but irregular up-and-down movement in production.

Business risk   The variability of operating income arising from the characteristics of the firm's industry. Two sources of business risk are sales variability and operating leverage.

Butterfly spread   An option strategy that combines two bull or bear spreads and has three exercise prices.

Buy-and-hold strategy   A passive portfolio management strategy in which securities (bonds or stocks) are bought and held to maturity.

Call   An option that gives the holder the right to buy an underlying asset from another party at a fixed price over a specific period of time.

Call market   A market in which trading for individual stocks only takes place at specified times. All the bids and asks available at the time are combined and the market administrators specify a single price that will possibly clear the market at that time.

Call option   Option to buy an asset within a certain period at a specified price called the *exercise price*.

Call premium   Amount above par that an issuer must pay to a bondholder for retiring the bond before its stated maturity.

Call provisions   Specifies when and how a firm can issue a call for bonds outstanding prior to their maturity.

Cap   (1) A contract on an interest rate, whereby at periodic payment dates, the writer of the cap pays the difference between the market interest rate and a specified cap rate if, and only if, this difference is positive. This is equivalent to a stream of call options on the interest rate. (2) A combination of interest rate call options designed to hedge a borrower against rate increases on a floating-rate loan.

Capital   The tools, equipment, buildings, and other constructions that businesses now use to produce goods and services.

Capital account   (1) The record of transactions with foreigners that involve either (a) the exchange of ownership rights to real or financial assets or (b) the extension of loans. (2) A component of the balance of payments that reflects unrequited (or unilateral) transfers corresponding to capital flows entailing no compensation (in the form of goods, services, or assets). Examples include investment capital given (without future repayment) in favor of poor countries, debt forgiveness, and expropriation losses.

Capital accumulation The growth of capital resources.

Capital appreciation A return objective in which the investor seeks to increase the portfolio value, primarily through capital gains, over time to meet a future need rather than dividend yield.

Capital asset pricing model (CAPM) A theory concerned with deriving the expected or required rates of return on risky assets based on the assets' systematic risk relative to a market portfolio.

Capital budgeting The process of planning expenditures on assets whose cash flows are expected to extend beyond one year.

Capital Employed (Real Estate) The denominator of the return expressions, defined as the "weighted-average equity" (weighted-average capital) during the measurement period. Capital employed should not include any income or capital return accrued during the measurement period. Beginning capital is adjusted by weighting the cash flows (contributions and distributions) that occurred during the period. Cash flows are typically weighted based on the actual days the flows are in or out of the portfolio. Other weighting methods are acceptable; however, once a methodology is chosen, it should be consistently applied.

Capital expenditure An expenditure for the purchase or expansion of a long-term asset, recorded in an asset account.

Capital market line (CML) The line from the intercept point that represents the risk-free rate tangent to the original efficient frontier; it becomes the new efficient frontier since investments on this line dominate all the portfolios on the original Markowitz efficient frontier.

Capital preservation A return objective in which the investor seeks to minimize the risk of loss; generally a goal of the risk-averse investor.

Capital return (real estate) The change in the market value of the real estate investments and cash/cash equivalent assets held throughout the measurement period (ending market value less beginning market value) adjusted for all capital expenditures (subtracted) and the net proceeds from sales (added). The return is computed as a percentage of the capital employed through the measurement period. Synonyms: capital appreciation return, appreciation return.

Capital stock The total quantity of plant, equipment, buildings, and inventories.

Capital structure A company's specific mixture of long-term financing.

Caplet Each component call option in a cap.

Capped swap A swap in which the floating payments have an upper limit.

Carried interest (private equity) The profits that general partners earn from the profits of the investments made by the fund (generally 20–25%). Also known as "carry."

Carrying value The unexpired part of an asset's cost. Also called *book value*.

Cartel A group of firms that has entered into a collusive agreement to restrict output and increase prices and profits.

Carve-Out A single or multiple asset class segment of a multiple asset class portfolio.

Cash For purposes of the statement of cash flows, both cash and cash equivalents.

Cash equivalents Short-term (90 days or less), highly liquid investments, including money market accounts, commercial paper, and U.S. Treasury bills.

Cash flow additivity principle The principle that dollar amounts indexed at the same point in time are additive.

Cash-generating efficiency A company's ability to generate cash from its current or continuing operations.

Cash price or spot price The price for immediate purchase of the underlying asset.

Cash settlement (1) A procedure for settling futures contracts in which the cash difference between the futures price and the spot price is paid instead of physical delivery. (2) A procedure used in certain derivative transactions that specifies that the long and short parties engage in the equivalent cash value of a delivery transaction.

CD equivalent yield *See* Money market yield.

Central bank A bank's bank and a public authority that regulates a nation's depository institutions and controls the quantity of money.

Central limit theorem A result in statistics that states that the sample mean computed from large samples of size n from a population with finite variance will follow an approximate normal distribution with a mean equal to the population mean and a variance equal to the population variance divided by n.

Certificates of deposit (CDs) Instruments issued by banks and S&Ls that require minimum deposits for specified terms and that pay higher rates of interest than deposit accounts.

Ceteris paribus Other things being equal—all other relevant things remaining the same.

Change in demand A change in buyers' plans that occurs when some influence on those plans other than the price of the good changes. It is illustrated by a shift of the demand curve.

Change in supply A change in sellers' plans that occurs when some influence on those plans other than the price of the good changes. It is illustrated by a shift of the supply curve.

Change in the quantity demanded A change in buyers' plans that occurs when the price of a good changes but all other influences on buyers' plans remain unchanged. It is illustrated by a movement along the demand curve.

Characteristic line Regression line that indicates the systematic risk (beta) of a risky asset.

Cheapest to deliver A bond in which the amount received for delivering the bond is largest compared with the amount paid in the market for the bond.

Classical A macroeconomist who believes that the economy is self-regulating and that it is always at full employment.

Clean price The price of a bond obtained as the total price of the bond minus accrued interest. Most bonds are traded on the basis of their clean price.

Closed-end fund (private equity) A type of investment fund where the number of investors and the total committed capital is fixed and not open for subscriptions and/or redemptions.

Closed-end investment company An investment company that issues only a limited number of shares, which it does not redeem (buy back). Instead, shares of a closed-end fund are traded in securities markets at prices determined by supply and demand.

Coefficient of variation (CV) The ratio of a set of observations' standard deviation to the observations' mean value.

Collar (1) A combination of a cap and a floor. (2) An option strategy involving the purchase of a put and sale of a call in which the holder of an asset gains protection below a certain level, the exercise price of the put, and pays for it by giving up gains above a certain level, the exercise price of the call. Collars also can be used to provide protection against rising interest rates on a floating-rate loan by giving up gains from lower interest rates.

Collateralized mortgage obligation (CMO) A debt security based on a pool of mortgage loans that provides a relatively stable stream of payments for a relatively predictable term.

Collateral trust bonds A mortgage bond wherein the assets backing the bond are financial assets like stocks and bonds.

Collusive agreement An agreement between two (or more) producers to restrict output, raise the price, and increase profits.

Combination A listing in which the order of the listed items does not matter.

Command system A method of organizing production that uses a managerial hierarchy.

Commercial bank A firm that is licensed by the Comptroller of the Currency in the U.S. Treasury or by a state agency to receive deposits and make loans.

Commercial paper Unsecured short-term corporate debt that is characterized by a single payment at maturity.

Commission brokers Employees of a member firm who buy or sell securities for the customers of the firm.

Committed capital (private equity) Pledges of capital to a venture capital fund. This money is typically not received at once but drawn down over three to five years, starting in the year the fund is formed. Also known as "commitments."

Common stock An equity investment that represents ownership of a firm, with full participation in its success or failure. The firm's directors must approve dividend payments.

Comparative advantage A person or country has a comparative advantage in an activity if that person or country can perform the activity at a lower opportunity cost than anyone else or any other country.

Competitive bid An underwriting alternative wherein an issuing entity (governmental body or a corporation) specifies the type of security to be offered (bonds or stocks) and the general characteristics of the issue, and the issuer solicits bids from competing investment banking firms with the understanding that the issuer will accept the highest bid from the bankers.

Competitive environment The level of intensity of competition among firms in an industry, determined by an examination of five competitive forces.

Competitive market A market that has many buyers and many sellers, so no single buyer or seller can influence the price.

Competitive strategy The search by a firm for a favorable competitive position within an industry within the known competitive environment.

Complement A good that is used in conjunction with another good.

Complement With reference to an event S, the event that S does not occur.

Completely diversified portfolio A portfolio in which all unsystematic risk has been eliminated by diversification.

Composite Aggregation of individual portfolios representing a similar investment mandate, objective, or strategy.

Composite creation date The date when the firm first groups the portfolios to create a composite. The composite creation date is not necessarily the earliest date for which performance is reported for the composite. (See composite inception date.)

Composite definition Detailed criteria that determine the allocation of portfolios to composites. Composite definitions must be documented in the firm's policies and procedures.

Composite description General information regarding the strategy of the composite. A description may be more abbreviated than the composite definition but includes all salient features of the composite.

Compounding The process of accumulating interest on interest.

Computer-Assisted Execution System (CAES) A service created by Nasdaq that automates order routing and execution for securities listed on domestic stock exchanges and involved on the Intermarket Trading System (ITS).

Conditional expected value (1) Expected value of a variable conditional on some available information set. The expected value changes over time with changes in the information set. (2) The expected value of a stated event given that another event has occurred.

Conditional probability The probability of an event given (conditioned on) another event.

Conditional variance (1) Variance of a variable conditional on some available information set. (2) The variance of one variable, given the outcome of another.

Confidence interval A range that has a given probability that it will contain the population parameter it is intended to estimate.

Consistency A desirable property of estimators; a consistent estimator is one for which the probability of estimates close to the value of the population parameter increases as sample size increases.

Consistent With reference to estimators, describes an estimator for which the probability of estimates close to the value of the population parameter increases as sample size increases.

Consolidated Quotation System (CQS) An electronic quotation service for issues listed on the NYSE, the AMEX, or regional exchanges and traded on the Nasdaq InterMarket.

Constant maturity swap or CMT swap A swap in which the floating rate is the rate on a security known as a constant maturity treasury or CMT security.

Constant maturity treasury or CMT A hypothetical U.S. Treasury note with a constant maturity. A CMT exists for various years in the range of 2 to 10.

Constant returns to scale Features of a firm's technology that leads to constant long-run average cost as output increases. When constant returns to scale are present, the *LRAC* curve is horizontal.

Consumer Price Index (CPI) An index that measures the average of the prices paid by urban consumers for a fixed "basket" of the consumer goods and services.

Consumer surplus The value of a good minus the price paid for it, summed over the quantity bought.

Consumption expenditure The total payment for consumer goods and services.

Contango A situation in a futures market where the current contract price is greater than the current spot price for the underlying asset.

Contestable market A market in which firms can enter and leave so easily that firms in the market face competition from potential entrants.

Continuously compounded return The natural logarithm of 1 plus the holding period return, or equivalently, the natural logarithm of the ending price over the beginning price.

Continuous market A market where stocks are priced and traded continuously by an auction process or by dealers when the market is open.

Continuous random variable A random variable for which the range of possible outcomes is the real line (all real numbers between – and +) or some subset of the real line.

Continuous time Time thought of as advancing in extremely small increments.

Contract price The transaction price specified in a forward or futures contract.

Convenience yield (1) An adjustment made to the theoretical forward or futures contract delivery price to account for the preference that consumers have for holding spot positions in the underlying asset. (2) The nonmonetary return offered by an asset when the asset is in short supply, often associated with assets with seasonal production processes.

Conversion value The value of the convertible security if converted into common stock at the stock's current market price.

Convertible bonds A bond with the added feature that the bondholder has the option to turn the bond back to the firm in exchange for a specified number of common shares of the firm.

Convexity (1) A measure of the change in duration with respect to changes in interest rates. (2) A measure of the degree to which a bond's price-yield curve departs from a straight line. This characteristic affects estimates of a bond's price volatility for a given change in yields.

Cooperative equilibrium   The outcome of a game in which the players make and share the monopoly profit.

Copyright   A government-sanctioned exclusive right granted to the inventor of a good, service, or productive process to produce, use, and sell the invention for a given number of years.

Correlation   A number between −1 and +1 that measures the co-movement (linear association) between two random variables.

Correlation analysis   The analysis of the strength of the linear relationship between two data series.

Correlation coefficient   A standardized measure of the relationship between two variables that ranges from − 1.00 to + 1.00.

Cost averaging   The periodic investment of a fixed amount of money.

Cost of carry   (1) The cost associated with holding some asset, including financing, storage, and insurance costs. Any yield received on the asset is treated as a negative carrying cost. (2) The net amount that would be required to store a commodity or security for future delivery, usually calculated as physical storage costs plus financial capital costs less dividends paid to the underlying asset. (3) The costs of holding an asset.

Cost of carry model   A model for pricing futures contracts in which the futures price is determined by adding the cost of carry to the spot price.

Cost-push inflation   An inflation that results from an initial increase in costs.

Council of Economic Advisers   The President's council whose main work is to monitor the economy and keep the President and the public well informed about the current state of the economy and the best available forecasts of where it is heading.

Counterparty   A participant to a derivative transaction.

Country risk   Uncertainty due to the possibility of major political or economic change in the country where an investment is located. Also called *political risk*.

Coupon   Indicates the interest payment on a debt security. It is the coupon rate times the par value that indicates the interest payments on a debt security.

Covariance   (1) A measure of the degree to which two variables, such as rates of return for investment assets, move together over time relative to their individual mean returns. (2) A measure of the extent to which the returns on two assets move together. (3) A measure of the co-movement (linear association) between two random variables.

Covariance matrix   A matrix or square array whose entries are covariances; also known as a variance–covariance matrix.

Covered call   An option strategy involving the holding of an asset and sale of a call on the asset.

Credit analysis   An active bond portfolio management strategy designed to identify bonds that are expected to experience changes in rating. This strategy is critical when investing in high-yield bonds.

Credit risk or default risk   The risk of loss due to nonpayment by a counterparty.

Credit union   A depository institution owned by a social or economic group such as firm's employees that accepts savings deposits and makes mostly consumer loans.

Creditor nation   A country that during its entire history has invested more in the rest of the world than other countries have invested in it.

Cross elasticity of demand   The responsiveness of the demand for a good to the price of a substitute or complement, other things remaining the same. It is calculated as the percentage change in the quantity demanded of the good divided by the percentage change in the price of the substitute or complement.

Cross-sectional analysis   An examination of a firm's performance in comparison to other firms in the industry with similar characteristics to the firm being studied.

Cross-sectional data   Observations over individual units at a point in time, as opposed to time-series data.

Crowding-out effect   The tendency for a government budget deficit to decrease in investment.

Cumulative distribution function   A function giving the probability that a random variable is less than or equal to a specified value.

Cumulative relative frequency   For data grouped into intervals, the fraction of total observations that are less than the value of the upper limit of a stated interval.

Currency   The bills and coins that we use today.

Currency appreciation   The rise in the value of one currency in terms of another currency.

Currency depreciation   The fall in the value of one currency in terms of another currency.

Currency drain   An increase in currency held outside the banks.

Currency option   An option that allows the holder to buy (if a call) or sell (if a put) an underlying currency at a fixed exercise rate, expressed as an exchange rate.

Current account A record of the payments for imports of goods and services, receipts from exports of goods and services, the interest income, and net transfers.

Current account (1) The record of all transactions with foreign nations that involve the exchange of merchandise goods and services, current income derived from investments, and unilateral gifts. (2) A component of the balance of payments covering all current transactions that take place in the normal business of the residents of a country, such as exports and imports, services, income, and current transfers.

Current credit risk The risk associated with the possibility that a payment currently due will not be made.

Current income A return objective in which the investor seeks to generate income rather than capital gains; generally a goal of an investor who wants to supplement earnings with income to meet living expenses.

Current P/E *See* Trailing P/E.

Current yield A bond's yield as measured by its current income (coupon) as a percentage of its market price.

Customer list A list of customers or subscribers.

Cyclical businesses Businesses with high sensitivity to business- or industry-cycle influences.

Cyclical company A firm whose earnings rise and fall with general economic activity.

Cyclical stock A stock with a high beta; its gains typically exceed those of a rising market and its losses typically exceed those of a falling market.

Cyclical surplus or deficit The actual surplus or deficit minus the structural surplus or deficit.

Cyclical unemployment The fluctuations in unemployment over the business cycle.

Daily settlement *See* Marking to market.

Data mining The practice of determining a model by extensive searching through a dataset for statistically significant patterns.

Day trader A trader holding a position open somewhat longer than a scalper but closing all positions at the end of the day.

Deadweight loss A measure of inefficiency. It is equal to the decrease in consumer surplus and producer surplus that results from an inefficient level of production.

Debentures Bonds that promise payments of interest and principal but pledge no specific assets. Holders have first claim on the issuer's income and unpledged assets. Also known as *unsecured bonds*.

Debtor nation A country that during its entire history has borrowed more from the rest of the world than it has lent to it.

Deciles Quantiles that divide a distribution into 10 equal parts.

Declining-balance method An accelerated method of depreciation in which depreciation is computed by applying a fixed rate to the carrying value (the declining balance) of a tangible long-lived asset.

Declining trend channel The range defined by security prices as they move progressively lower.

Deep in the money Options that are far in-the-money.

Deep out of the money Options that are far out-of-the-money.

Default risk The risk that an issuer will be unable to make interest and principal payments on time.

Default risk premium An extra return that compensates investors for the possibility that the borrower will fail to make a promised payment at the contracted time and in the contracted amount.

Defensive competitive strategy Positioning the firm so that its capabilities provide the best means to deflect the effect of the competitive forces in the industry.

Defensive stock A stock whose return is not expected to decline as much as that of the overall market during a bear market (a beta less than one).

Deflation A process in which the price level falls—a negative inflation.

Degree of confidence The probability that a confidence interval includes the unknown population parameter.

Degrees of freedom (df) The number of independent observations used.

Delivery A process used in a deliverable forward contract in which the long pays the agreed-upon price to the short, which in turn delivers the underlying asset to the long.

Delivery option The feature of a futures contract giving the short the right to make decisions about what, when, and where to deliver.

Delta The change in the price of the option with respect to a one dollar change in the price of the underlying asset; this is the option's *hedge ratio*, or the number of units of the underlying asset that can be hedged by a single option contract.

Delta hedge (1) A dynamic hedging strategy using options with continuous adjustment of the number of options used, as a function of the delta of the option. (2) An option strategy in which a position in an asset is converted to a risk-free position with a position in a specific number of options.

The number of options per unit of the underlying changes through time, and the position must be revised to maintain the hedge.

Demand   The relationship between the quantity of a good that consumers plan to buy and the price of the good when all other influences on buyers' plans remain the same. It is described by a demand schedule and illustrated by a demand curve.

Demand curve   A curve that shows the relationship between the quantity demanded of a good and its price when all other influences on consumers' planned purchases remain the same.

Demand for labor   The relationship between the quantity of labor demanded and the real wage rate when all other influences on firm's hiring plans remain the same.

Demand-pull inflation   An inflation that results from an initial increase in aggregate demand.

Dependent   With reference to events, the property that the probability of one event occurring depends on (is related to) the occurrence of another event.

Dependent variable   The variable whose variation about its mean is to be explained by the regression; the left-hand-side variable in a regression equation.

Depletion   The exhaustion of a natural resource through mining, cutting, pumping, or other extraction, and the way in which the cost is allocated.

Depository institution   A firm that takes deposits from households and firms and makes loans to other households and firms.

Depreciable cost   The cost of an asset less its residual value.

Depreciation   The decrease in the capital stock that results from wear and tear and obsolescence.
The periodic allocation of the cost of a tangible long-lived asset (other than land and natural resources) over its estimated useful life.

Derivatives   (1) Securities bearing a contractual relation to some underlying asset or rate. Options, futures, forward, and swap contracts, as well as many forms of bonds, are derivative securities. (2) A financial instrument that offers a return based on the return of some other underlying asset.

Derivatives dealers   The commercial and investment banks that make markets in derivatives. Also referred to as market makers.

Derivative security   An instrument whose market value ultimately depends upon, or derives from, the value of a more fundamental investment vehicle called the underlying asset or security.

Derived demand   The demand for a productive resource, which is derived from the demand for the goods and services produced by the resource.

Descriptive statistics   The study of how data can be summarized effectively.

Diff swaps   A swap in which the payments are based on the difference between interest rates in two countries but payments are made in only a single currency.

Diluted earnings per share   Total earnings divided by the number of shares that would be outstanding if holders of securities such as executive stock options and convertible bonds exercised their options to obtain common stock.

Diminishing marginal returns   The tendency for the marginal product of an additional unit of a factor of production is less than the marginal product of the previous unit of the factor.

Diminishing marginal utility   The decrease in marginal utility as the quantity consumed increases.

Direct method   The procedure for converting the income statement from an accrual basis to a cash basis by adjusting each item on the income statement.

Discount   (1) A bond selling at a price below par value due to capital market conditions. (2) To reduce the value of a future payment in allowance for how far away it is in time; to calculate the present value of some future amount. Also, the amount by which an instrument is priced below its face value.

Discounting   The conversion of a future amount of money to its present value.

Discount interest   A procedure for determining the interest on a loan or bond in which the interest is deducted from the face value in advance.

Discouraged workers   People who are available and willing to work but have not made specific efforts to find a job within the previous four weeks.

Discrete random variable   A random variable that can take on at most a countable number of possible values.

Discrete time   Time thought of as advancing in distinct finite increments.

Discretionary fiscal policy   A policy action that is initiated by an act of Congress.

Discretionary policy   A policy that responds to the state of the economy in a possibly unique way that uses all the information available, including perceived lessons from past "mistakes."

Diseconomies of scale   Features of a firm's technology that leads to rising long-run average cost as output increases.

Dispersion   (1) The variability around the central tendency. (2) A measure of the spread of the annual returns of individual portfolios within a composite. Measures may include, but are not limited to, high/low, inter-quartile range, and standard deviation (asset weighted or equal weighted).

Disposable income Aggregate income minus taxes plus transfer payments.

Distinct business entity A unit, division, department, or office that is organizationally and functionally segregated from other units, divisions, departments, or offices and retains discretion over the assets it manages and autonomy over the investment decision-making process. Possible criteria that can be used to determine this include: (a) being a legal entity; (b) having a distinct market or client type (e.g., institutional, retail, private client, etc.); (c) using a separate and distinct investment process

Dividend discount model (DDM) A technique for estimating the value of a stock issue as the present value of all future dividends.

Dominant strategy equilibrium A Nash equilibrium in which the best strategy of each player is to cheat (deny) regardless of the strategy of the other player.

Double-declining-balance method An accelerated method of depreciation in which a fixed rate equal to twice the straight-line percentage is applied to the carrying value (the declining balance) of a tangible long-lived asset.

Down transition probability The probability that an asset's value moves down in a model of asset price dynamics.

Dumping The sale by a foreign firm of exports at a lower price that the cost of production.

Duopoly A market structure in which two producers of a good or service compete.

DuPont system A method of examining ROE by breaking it down into three component parts: (1) profit margin, (2) total asset turnover, and (3) financial leverage.

Duration (1) A measure of an option-free bond's average maturity. Specifically, the weighted average maturity of all future cash flows paid by a security, in which the weights are the present value of these cash flows as a fraction of the bond's price. More importantly, a measure of a bond's price sensitivity to interest rate movements (*see* Modified duration). (2) A measure of the interest rate sensitivity of a bond's market price taking into consideration its coupon and term to maturity. (3) A measure of the size and timing of the cash flows paid by a bond. It quantifies these factors by summarizing them in the form of a single number. For bonds without option features attached, duration is interpreted as a weighted average maturity of the bond.

Dutch Book Theorem A result in probability theory stating that inconsistent probabilities create profit opportunities.

Dynamic comparative advantage A comparative advantage that a person or country possesses as a result of having specialized in a particular activity and then, as a result of learning-by-doing, having become the producer with the lowest opportunity cost.

Earnings momentum A strategy in which portfolios are constructed of stocks of firms with rising earnings.

Earnings multiplier model A technique for estimating the value of a stock issue as a multiple of its earnings per share.

Earnings surprise A company announcement of earnings that differ from analysts' prevailing expectations.

Earnings yield Earnings per share divided by price; the reciprocal of the P/E ratio.

EBITDA Earnings before interest, taxes, depreciation, and amortization.

Economic depreciation The change in the market value of capital over a given period.

Economic efficiency A situation that occurs when the firm produces a given output at the least cost.

Economic growth The expansion of production possibilities that results from capital accumulation and technological change.

Economic information Data on prices, quantities, and qualities of goods and services and factors of production.

Economic model A description of some aspect of the economic world that includes only those features of the world that are needed for the purpose at hand.

Economic profit A firm's total revenue minus its opportunity cost.

Economic rent The income received by the owner of a factor of production over and above the amount required to induce that owner to offer the factor for use.

Economics The social science that studies the *choices* that individuals, businesses, governments, and entire societies make and how they cope with *scarcity* and the *incentives* that influence and reconcile those choices.

Economic theory A generalization that summarizes what we think we understand about the economic choices that people make and the performance of industries and entire economies.

Economic value added (EVA) Internal management performance measure that compares net operating profit to total cost of capital. Indicates how profitable company projects are as a sign of management performance.

Economies of scale Features of a firm's technology that leads to a falling long-run average cost as output increases.

Economies of scope Decreases in average total cost that occur when a firm uses specialized resources to produce a range of goods and services.

Effective annual rate The amount by which a unit of currency will grow in a year with interest on interest included.

Effective annual yield (EAY) An annualized return that accounts for the effect of interest on interest; EAY is computed by compounding 1 plus the holding period yield forward to one year, then subtracting 1.

Effective duration Direct measure of the interest rate sensitivity of a bond (or any financial instrument) based upon price changes derived from a pricing model.

Efficiency A desirable property of estimators; an efficient estimator is the unbiased estimator with the smallest variance among unbiased estimators of the same parameter.

Efficient capital market A market in which security prices rapidly reflect all information about securities.

Efficient frontier The set of portfolios that has the maximum rate of return for every given level of risk, or the minimum risk for every potential rate of return.

Efficient market A market in which the actual price embodies all currently available relevant information. Resources are sent to their highest valued use.

Elastic demand Demand with a price elasticity greater than 1; other things remaining the same, the percentage change in the quantity demanded exceeds the percentage change in price.

Elasticity of demand The responsiveness of the quantity demanded of a good to a change in its price, other things remaining the same.

Elasticity of supply The responsiveness of the quantity supplied of a good to a change in its price, other things remaining the same.

Empirical probability The probability of an event estimated as a relative frequency of occurrence.

Employment Act of 1946 A landmark Congressional act that recognized a role for government actions to keep unemployment, keep the economy expanding, and keep inflation in check.

Employment-to-population ratio The percentage of people of working age who have jobs.

Ending market value (private equity) The remaining equity that a limited partner has in a fund. Also referred to as net asset value or residual value.

Entrepreneurship The human resource that organizes labor, land, and capital. Entrepreneurs come up with new ideas about what and how to produce, make business decisions, and bear the risks that arise from their decisions.

Equation of exchange An equation that states that the quantity of money multiplied by the velocity of circulation equals GDP.

Equilibrium price The price at which the quantity demanded equals the quantity supplied.

Equilibrium quantity The quantity bought and sold at the equilibrium price.

Equity forward A contract calling for the purchase of an individual stock, a stock portfolio, or a stock index at a later date at an agreed-upon price.

Equity options Options on individual stocks; also known as stock options.

Equity swap A swap transaction in which one cash flow is tied to the return to an equity portfolio position, often an index such as the Standard and Poor's 500, while the other is based on a floating-rate index.

Error term The portion of the dependent variable that is not explained by the independent variable(s) in the regression.

Estimate The particular value calculated from sample observations using an estimator.

Estimated (or fitted) parameters With reference to regression analysis, the estimated values of the population intercept and population slope coefficient(s) in a regression.

Estimated rate of return The rate of return an investor anticipates earning from a specific investment over a particular future holding period.

Estimated useful life The total number of service units expected from a long-term asset.

Estimation With reference to statistical inference, the subdivision dealing with estimating the value of a population parameter.

Estimator An estimation formula; the formula used to compute the sample mean and other sample statistics are examples of estimators.

Eurobonds Bonds denominated in a currency not native to the country in which they are issued.

Eurodollar A dollar deposited outside the United States.

European option An option contract that can only be exercised on its expiration date.

European-style option or European option An option exercisable only at maturity.

European terms With reference to U.S. dollar exchange rate quotations, the price of a U.S. dollar in terms of another currency.

European Union (EU) A formal association of European countries founded by the Treaty of Rome in 1957. Formerly known as the EEC.

Event study Research that examines the reaction of a security's price to a specific company, world event, or news announcement.

Ex-ante Before the fact.

Excess kurtosis Degree of peakedness (fatness of tails) in excess of the peakedness of the normal distribution.

Excess reserves A bank's actual reserves minus its required reserves.

Exchange for physicals (EEP) A permissible delivery procedure used by futures market participants, in which the long and short arrange a delivery procedure other than the normal procedures stipulated by the futures exchange.

Exchange rate risk Uncertainty due to the denomination of an investment in a currency other than that of the investor's own country.

Exchange-traded fund (ETF) A tradable depository receipt that gives investors a pro rata claim to the returns associated with a portfolio of securities (often designed to mimic an index, such as the Standard & Poor's 500) held in trust by a financial institution.

Exercise (or exercising the option) The process of using an option to buy or sell the underlying.

Exercise price The transaction price specified in an option contract; also known as the *strike price*.

Exercise price (or strike price or striking price, or strike) (1) The transaction price specified in an option contract. *See also* Strike price. (2) The fixed price at which an option holder can buy or sell the underlying.

Exercise rate or strike rate The fixed rate at which the holder of an interest rate option can buy or sell the underlying.

Exhaustive Covering or containing all possible outcomes.

Expansion A business cycle phase between a trough and a peak—phase in which real GDP increases.

Expected rate of return The return that analysts' calculations suggest a security should provide, based on the market's rate of return during the period and the security's relationship to the market.

Expected return The rate of return that an investor expects to get on an investment.

Expected utility The average utility arising from all possible outcomes.

Expected value The probability-weighted average of the possible outcomes of a random variable.

Expenditure A payment or obligation to make future payment for an asset or a service.

Expiration date The date on which a derivative contract expires.

Expiry The expiration date of a derivative security.

Exports The goods and services that we sell to people in other countries.

Extended DuPont System A method of examining *ROE* by breaking it down into five component parts.

External benefits Benefits that accrue to people other than the buyer of the good.

External cash flow Cash, securities, or assets that enter or exit a portfolio.

External costs Costs that are not borne by the producer of the good but borne by someone else.

External diseconomies Factors outside the control of a firm that raise the firm's costs as the industry produces a larger output.

External economies Factors beyond the control of a firm that lower the firm's costs as the industry produces a larger output.

Externality A cost or a benefit that arises from production and falls on someone other than the producer of or cost of a benefit that arises from consumption and falls on someone other than the consumer.

External valuation (real estate) An external valuation is an assessment of market value performed by a third party who is a qualified, professionally designated, certified, or licensed commercial property valuer/appraiser. External valuations must be completed following the valuation standards of the local governing appraisal body.

Extraordinary repairs Repairs that affect the estimated residual value or estimated useful life of an asset thereby increasing its carrying value.

Face value (1) The amount paid on a bond at redemption and traditionally printed on the bond certificate. This face value excludes the final coupon payment. Sometimes referred to as par value. (2) The promised payment at maturity separate from any coupon payment.

Factors of production The productive resources that businesses use to produce goods and services.

Federal budget The annual statement of the expenditures and tax revenues of the government of the United States together with the laws and regulations that approve and support those expenditures and taxes.

Federal funds rate The interest rate that banks charge each other on overnight loans of reserves.

Federal Open Market Committee The main policymaking organ of the Federal Reserve System.

Federal Reserve System The central bank of the United States.

Feedback-rule policy　A rule that specifies how policy actions respond to changes in the state of the economy.

Fee Schedule　The firm's current investment management fees or bundled fees for a particular presentation. This schedule is typically listed by asset level ranges and should be appropriate to the particular prospective client.

Fiduciary　A person who supervises or oversees the investment portfolio of a third party, such as in a trust account, and makes investment decisions in accordance with the owner's wishes.

Fiduciary call　A combination of a European call and a risk-free bond that matures on the option expiration day and has a face value equal to the exercise price of the call.

Financial account　A component of the balance of payments covering investments by residents abroad and investments by nonresidents in the home country. Examples include direct investment made by companies, portfolio investments in equity and bonds, and other investments and liabilities.

Financial innovation　The development of new financial products—new ways of borrowing and lending.

Financial risk　(1) The variability of future income arising from the firm's fixed financing costs, for example, interest payments. The effect of fixed financial costs is to magnify the effect of changes in operating profit on net income or earnings per share. (2) Risk relating to asset prices and other financial variables.

Financing activities　Business activities that involve obtaining resources from stockholders and creditors and providing the former with a return on their investments and the latter with repayment.

Firm　(1) For purposes of the GIPS standards, the term "firm" refers to the entity defined for compliance with the GIPS standards. See the term "distinct business entity." (2) An economic unit that hires factors of production and organizes those factors to produce and sell goods and services.

Fiscal imbalance　The present value of the government's commitments to pay benefits minus the present value of its tax revenues.

Fiscal policy　The government's attempt to achieve macroeconomic objectives such as full employment, sustained economic growth, and price level stability by setting and changing taxes, making transfer payments, and purchasing goods and services.

Fixed exchange rate　An exchange rate that is set at a determined amount by government policy.

Fixed exchange rate regime　A system in which the exchange rate between two currencies remains fixed at a preset level, known as official parity.

Fixed-income forward　A forward contract in which the underlying is a bond.

Fixed-income investments　Loans with contractually mandated payment schedules from firms or governments to investors.

Fixed-rule policy　A rule that specifies an action to be pursued independently of the state of the economy.

Flat trend channel　The range defined by security prices as they maintain a relatively steady level.

Flexible exchange rates　Exchange rates that are determined by the market forces of supply and demand. They are sometimes called floating exchange rates.

Flexible exchange rate system　A system in which exchange rates are determined by supply and demand.

Floating-rate loan　A loan in which the interest rate is reset at least once after the starting date.

Floor　(1) A contract on an interest rate, whereby the writer of the floor periodically pays the difference between a specified floor rate and the market interest rate if, and only if, this difference is positive. This is equivalent to a stream of put options on the interest rate. (2) A combination of interest rate put options designed to hedge a lender against lower rates on a floating-rate loan.

Floor brokers　Independent members of an exchange who act as brokers for other members.

Floored swap　A swap in which the floating payments have a lower limit.

Floorlet　Each component put option in a floor.

Flow　A quantity per unit of time.

Foreign bond　A bond issued by a foreign company on the local market and in the local currency (e.g., Yankee bonds in the United States, Bulldog bonds in the United Kingdom, or Samurai bonds in Japan).

Foreign exchange expectation　A relation that states that the forward exchange rate, quoted at time 0 for delivery at time 1, is equal to the expected value of the spot exchange rate at time 1. When stated relative to the current spot exchange rate, the relation states that the forward discount (premium) is equal to the expected exchange rate movement.

Foreign exchange market　The market in which the currency of one country is exchanged for the currency of another.

Foreign exchange rate　The price at which one currency exchanges for another.

Forward contract An agreement between two parties in which one party, the buyer, agrees to buy from the other party, the seller, an underlying asset at a later date for a price established at the start of the contract.

Forward discount A situation where, from the perspective of the domestic country, the spot exchange rate is smaller than the forward exchange rate with a foreign country.

Forward P/E *See* Leading P/E.

Forward premium A situation where, from the perspective of the domestic country, the spot exchange rate is larger than the forward exchange rate with a foreign country.

Forward price or forward rate The fixed price or rate at which the transaction scheduled to occur at the expiration of a forward contract will take place. This price is agreed on at the initiation date of the contract.

Forward rate A short-term yield for a future holding period implied by the spot rates of two securities with different maturities.

Forward rate agreement (FRA) A forward contract calling for one party to make a fixed interest payment and the other to make an interest payment at a rate to be determined at the contract expiration.

Four-firm concentration ratio A measure of market power that is calculated as the percentage of the value of sales accounted for by the four largest firms in an industry.

Franchise The right or license to an exclusive territory or market.

Franchise factor A firm's unique competitive advantage that makes it possible for a firm to earn excess returns (rates of return above a firm's cost of capital) on its capital projects. In turn, these excess returns and the franchise factor cause the firm's stock price to have a *P/E* ratio above its base *P/E* ratio that is equal to $1/k$.

Free cash flow to equity This cash flow measure equals cash flow from operations minus capital expenditures and debt payments.

Free-rider problem The absence of an incentive for people to pay for what they consume.

Frequency distribution A tabular display of data summarized into a relatively small number of intervals.

Frequency polygon A graph of a frequency distribution obtained by drawing straight lines joining successive points representing the class frequencies.

Frictional unemployment The unemployment that arises from normal labor turnover—from people entering and leaving the labor force and from the ongoing creation and destruction of jobs.

Full-costing A method of accounting for the costs of exploring and developing oil and gas resources in which all costs are recorded as assets and depleted over the estimated life of the producing resources.

Full-costing method A method of accounting for the costs of exploring and developing oil and gas resources in which all costs are recorded as assets and depleted over the estimated life of the producing resources.

Full employment A situation in which the quantity of labor demanded equal the quantity supplied. At full employment, there is no cyclical unemployment—all unemployment is frictional and structural.

Full price (or dirty price) (1) The total price of a bond, including accrued interest. (2) The price of a security with accrued interest.

Futures commission merchants (FCMs) Individuals or companies that execute futures transactions for other parties off the exchange.

Futures contract A variation of a forward contract that has essentially the same basic definition but with some additional features, such as a clearinghouse guarantee against credit losses, a daily settlement of gains and losses, and an organized electronic or floor trading facility.

Future value (FV) The amount to which a payment or series of payments will grow by a stated future date.

Game theory A tool that economists use to analyze strategic behavior—behavior that takes into account the expected behavior of others and the mutual recognition of independence.

Gamma A numerical measure of how sensitive an option's delta is to a change in the underlying.

GDP deflator One measure of the price level, which is the average of current-year prices as a percentage of base-year prices.

General Agreement on Tariffs and Trade An international agreement signed in 1947 to reduce tariffs on international trade.

Generally accepted accounting principles (GAAP) Accounting principles formulated by the Financial Accounting Standards Board and used to construct financial statements.

Generational accounting An accounting system that measures the lifetime tax burden and benefits of each generation.

Generational imbalance The division of the fiscal imbalance between the current and future generations, assuming that the current generation will enjoy the existing levels of taxes and benefits

Generic *See* Plain-vanilla.

Geometric mean (GM) A measure of central tendency computed by taking the nth root of the product of n non-negative values.

Goods and services The objects that people value and produce to satisfy their wants.

Goodwill The excess of the cost of a group of assets (usually a business) over the fair market value of the assets if purchased individually.

Government budget deficit The deficit that arises when federal government spends more than it collects in taxes.

Government budget surplus The surplus that arises when the federal government collects more in taxes than it spends.

Government debt The total amount of borrowing that the government has borrowed. It equals the sum of past budget deficits minus budget surpluses.

Government purchases Goods and services bought by the government.

Government purchases multiplier The magnification effect of a change in government purchases of goods and services on aggregate demand.

Government sector surplus or deficit An amount equal to net taxes minus government purchases of goods and services.

Great Depression A decade (1929–1939) of high unemployment and stagnant production throughout the world economy.

Gross domestic product (GDP) The market value of all the final goods and services produced within a country during a given time period—usually a year.

Gross-Of-Fees Return The return on assets reduced by any trading expenses incurred during the period.

Gross investment The total amount spent on purchases of new capital and on replacing depreciated capital.

Group depreciation The grouping of similar items to calculate depreciation.

Growth company A company that consistently has the opportunities and ability to invest in projects that provide rates of return that exceed the firm's cost of capital. Because of these investment opportunities, it retains a high proportion of earnings, and its earnings grow faster than those of average firms.

Growth stock A stock issue that generates a higher rate of return than other stocks in the market with similar risk characteristics.

Harmonic mean A type of weighted mean computed by averaging the reciprocals of the observations, then taking the reciprocal of that average.

Hedge A trading strategy in which derivative securities are used to reduce or completely offset a counterparty's risk exposure to an underlying asset.

Hedge fund An investment vehicle designed to manage a private, unregistered portfolio of assets according to any of several strategies. The investment strategy often employs arbitrage trading and significant financial leverage (e.g., short selling, borrowing, derivatives) while the compensation arrangement for the manager typically specifies considerable profit participation.

Hedge ratio The number of derivative contracts that must be transacted to offset the price volatility of an underlying commodity or security position.

Herfindahl-Hirschman Index A measure of market power that is calculated as the square of the market share of each firm (as a percentage) summed over the largest 50 firms (or over all firms if there are fewer than 50) in a market.

High-yield bond A bond rated below investment grade. Also referred to as *speculative-grade bonds* or *junk bonds.*

Histogram A bar chart of data that have been grouped into a frequency distribution.

Holding period return (HPR) The return that an investor earns during a specified holding period; a synonym for total return.

Holding period yield (HPY) (1) The total return from an investment for a given period of time stated as a percentage. (2) The return that an investor earns during a specified holding period; holding period return with reference to a fixed-income instrument.

Human capital The value of skills and knowledge possessed by the workforce.

Hurdle rate The discount rate (cost of capital) which the IRR must exceed if a project is to be accepted.

Hypothesis With reference to statistical inference, a statement about one or more populations.

Hypothesis testing With reference to statistical inference, the subdivision dealing with the testing of hypotheses about one or more populations.

Implicit rental rate The firm's opportunity cost of using its own capital.

Implied repo rate The rate of return from a cash-and-carry transaction implied by the futures price relative to the spot price.

Implied volatility The volatility that option traders use to price an option, implied by the price of the option and a particular option-pricing model.

Imports The goods and services that we buy from people in other countries.

Incentive A reward that encourages or a penalty that discourages an action.

Incentive system A method of organizing production that uses a market-like mechanism inside the firm.

Income effect The effect of a change in income on consumption, other things remaining the same.

Income elasticity of demand The responsiveness of demand to a change in income, other things remaining the same. It is calculated as the percentage change in the quantity demanded divided by the percentage change in income.

Income statement A financial statement that shows the flow of the firm's sales, expenses, and earnings over a period of time.

Incremental cash flows The changes or increments to cash flows resulting from a decision or action.

Indenture The legal agreement that lists the obligations of the issuer of a bond to the bondholder, including payment schedules, call provisions, and sinking funds.

Independent With reference to events, the property that the occurrence of one event does not affect the probability of another event occurring.

Independent variable A variable used to explain the dependent variable in a regression; a right-hand-side variable in a regression equation.

Index amortizing swap An interest rate swap in which the notional principal is indexed to the level of interest rates and declines with the level of interest rates according to a predefined schedule. This type of swap is frequently used to hedge securities that are prepaid as interest rates decline, such as mortgage-backed securities.

Indexing An investment strategy in which an investor constructs a portfolio to mirror the performance of a specified index.

Indirect method The procedure for converting the income statement from an accrual basis to a cash basis by adjusting net income for items that do not affect cash flows, including depreciation, amortization, depletion, gains, losses, and changes in current assets and current liabilities.

Individual transferable quota (ITQ) A production limit that is assigned to an individual who is free to transfer the quota to someone else.

Induced taxes Taxes that vary with real GDP.

Industry life cycle analysis An analysis that focuses on the industry's stage of development.

Inelastic demand A demand with a price elasticity between 0 and 1; the percentage change in the quantity demanded is less than the percentage change in price.

Infant-industry argument The argument that it is necessary to protect a new industry to enable it to grow into a mature industry that can compete in world markets.

Inferior good A good for which demand decreases as income increases.

Inflation A process in which the price level is rising and money is losing value.

Inflationary gap The amount by which real GDP exceeds potential GDP.

Inflation rate The percentage change in the price level from one year to the next.

Information An attribute of a good market that includes providing buyers and sellers with timely, accurate information on the volume and prices of past transactions and on all currently outstanding bids and offers.

Informationally efficient market A more technical term for an efficient capital market that emphasizes the role of information in setting the market price.

Information ratio Statistic used to measure a portfolio's average return in excess of a comparison, benchmark portfolio divided by the standard deviation of this excess return.

Initial margin requirement The margin requirement on the first day of a transaction as well as on any day in which additional margin funds must be deposited.

Initial public offering (IPO) A new issue by a firm that has no existing public market.

Intangible assets Long-term assets with no physical substance whose value is based on rights or advantages accruing to the owner.

Intellectual property rights Property rights for discoveries owned by the creators of knowledge.

Interest The income that capital earns.

Interest-on-interest Bond income from reinvestment of coupon payments.

Interest rate A rate of return that reflects the relationship between differently dated cash flows; a discount rate.

Interest rate call An option in which the holder has the right to make a known interest payment and receive an unknown interest payment.

Interest rate cap or cap A series of call options on an interest rate, with each option expiring at the date on which the floating loan rate will be reset, and with each option having the same exercise rate. A cap in general can have an underlying other than an interest rate.

Interest rate collar A combination of a long cap and a short floor, or a short cap and a long floor. A collar in general can have an underlying other than an interest rate.

Interest rate floor or floor A series of put options on an interest rate, with each option expiring at the date on which the floating loan rate will be reset, and with each option having the same exercise rate. A floor in general can have an underlying other than the interest rate.

Interest rate forward   *See* Forward rate agreement.

Interest rate option   An option in which the underlying is an interest rate.

Interest rate parity   The relationship that must exist in an efficient market between the spot and forward foreign exchange rates between two countries and the interest rates in those countries.

Interest rate put   An option in which the holder has the right to make an unknown interest payment and receive a known interest payment.

Interest rate risk   The uncertainty of returns on an investment due to possible changes in interest rates over time.

Interest rate swap   An agreement calling for the periodic exchange of cash flows, one based on an interest rate that remains fixed for the life of the contract and the other that is linked to a variable-rate index.

Intergenerational data mining   A form of data mining that applies information developed by previous researchers using a dataset to guide current research using the same or a related dataset.

Intermarket Trading System (ITS)   A computerized system that connects competing exchanges and dealers who trade stocks listed on an exchange. Its purpose is to help customers find the best market for these stocks at a point in time.

Internal liquidity (solvency) ratios   Financial ratios that measure the ability of the firm to meet future short-term financial obligations.

Internal rate of return (IRR)   The discount rate that makes net present value equal 0; the discount rate that makes the present value of an investment's costs (outflows) equal to the present value of the investment's benefits (inflows).

Internal Rate of Return (Private Equity) (IRR)   IRR is the annualized implied discount rate (effective compounded rate) that equates the present value of all the appropriate cash inflows (paid-in capital, such as drawdowns for net investments) associated with an investment with the sum of the present value of all the appropriate cash outflows (such as distributions) accruing from it and the present value of the unrealized residual portfolio (unliquidated holdings). For an interim cumulative return measurement, any IRR depends on the valuation of the residual assets.

Internal Valuation (Real Estate)   An internal valuation is an advisor's or underlying third-party manager's best estimate of market value based on the most current and accurate information available under the circumstances. An internal valuation could include industry practice techniques, such as discounted cash flow, sales comparison, replacement cost, or a review of all significant events (both general market and asset specific) that could have a material impact on the investment. Prudent assumptions and estimates must be used, and the process must be applied consistently from period to period, except where a change would result in better estimates of market value.

International Fisher relation   The assertion that the interest rate differential between two countries should equal the expected inflation rate differential over the term of the interest rates.

Interval   With reference to grouped data, a set of values within which an observation falls.

Interval scale   A measurement scale that not only ranks data but also gives assurance that the differences between scale values are equal.

In the money   An option that has positive intrinsic value.

In-the-money option   (1) An option that has a positive value if exercised immediately. For example, a call when the strike price is below the current price of the underlying asset, or a put when the strike price is above the current price of the underlying asset. (2) An option that has positive intrinsic value. (3) Options that, if exercised, would result in the value received being worth more than the payment required to exercise.

Intrinsic value   The portion of a call option's total value equal to the greater of either zero or the difference between the current value of the underlying asset and the exercise price; for a put option, intrinsic value is the greater of either zero or the exercise price less the underlying asset price. For a stock, it is the value derived from fundamental analysis of the stock's expected returns or cash flows.

Inverse floater   A floating-rate note or bond in which the coupon is adjusted to move opposite to a benchmark interest rate.

Inverse relationship   A relationship between variables that move in opposite directions.

Invested Capital (Private Equity)   The amount of paid-in capital that has been invested in portfolio companies.

Investing activities   Business activities that involve the acquisition and sale of marketable securities and long-term assets and the making and collecting of loans.

Investment   The current commitment of dollars for a period of time in order to derive future payments that will compensate the investor for the time the funds are committed, the expected rate of inflation, and the uncertainty of future payments.

Investment The purchase of new plant, equipment, and buildings and additions to inventories.

Investment Advisor (Private Equity) Any individual or institution that supplies investment advice to clients on a per fee basis. The investment advisor inherently has no role in the management of the underlying portfolio companies of a partnership/fund.

Investment company A firm that sells shares of the company and uses the proceeds to buy portfolios of stock, bonds, or other financial instruments.

Investment decision process Estimation of intrinsic value for comparison with market price to determine whether or not to invest.

Investment demand The relationship between investment and real interest rate, other things remaining the same.

Investment horizon The time period used for planning and forecasting purposes or the future time at which the investor requires the invested funds.

Investment management company A company separate from the investment company that manages the portfolio and performs administrative functions.

Investment Management Fee The fee payable to the investment management firm for the on-going management of a portfolio. Investment management fees are typically asset based (percentage of assets), performance based (based on performance relative to a benchmark), or a combination of the two but may take different forms as well.

Investment Multiple (TVPI Multiple) (Private Equity) The ratio of total value to paid-in-capital. It represents the total return of the investment to the original investment not taking into consideration the time invested. Total value can be found by adding the residual value and distributed capital together.

Investment strategy A decision by a portfolio manager regarding how he or she will manage the portfolio to meet the goals and objectives of the client. This will include either active or passive management and, if active, what style in terms of top-down or buttom-up or fundamental versus technical.

IRR The discount rate which forces the PV of a project's inflows to equal the PV of its costs.

IRR rule An investment decision rule that accepts projects or investments for which the IRR is greater than the opportunity cost of capital.

January effect A frequent empirical anomaly where risk-adjusted stock returns in the month of January are significantly larger than those occurring in any other month of the year.

Job search The activity of looking for acceptable vacant jobs.

Joint probability The probability of the joint occurrence of stated events.

Keynesian An economist who believes that left alone, the economy would rarely operate at full employment and that to achieve full employment, active help from fiscal policy and monetary policy is required.

Kurtosis The statistical measure that indicates the peakedness of a distribution.

Labor The work time and work effort that people devote to producing goods and services.

Labor force The sum of the people who are employed and who are unemployed.

Labor force participation rate The percentage of the working-age population who are members of the labor force.

Labor productivity Real GDP per hour of work.

Labor union An organized group of workers whose purpose is to increase wages and to influence other job conditions.

Laffer curve The relationship between the tax rate and the amount of tax revenue collected.

Land The gifts of nature that we use to produce goods and services.

Law of demand Other things remaining the same, the higher the price of a good, the smaller is the quantity demanded of it.

Law of diminishing returns As a firm uses more of a variable input, with a given quantity of other inputs (fixed inputs), the marginal product of the variable input eventually diminishes.

Law of one price The condition in a financial market in which two financial instruments or combinations of financial instruments can sell for only one price. Equivalent to the principle that no arbitrage opportunities are possible.

Law of supply Other things remaining the same, the higher the price of a good, the greater is the quantity supplied of it.

Leading indicators A set of economic variables whose values reach peaks and troughs in advance of the aggregate economy.

Leading P/E (or forward P/E or prospective P/E) A stock's current price divided by next year's expected earnings.

Learning-by-doing People become more productive in an activity (learn) just by repeatedly producing a particular good or service (doing).

Leasehold A right to occupy land or buildings under a long-term rental contract.

Leasehold improvements Improvements to leased property that become the property of the lessor at the end of the lease.

Legal monopoly A market structure in which there is one firm and entry is restricted by the granting of a public franchise, government license, patent, or copyright.

Leptokurtic   Describes a distribution that is more peaked than a normal distribution.

License   The right to use a formula, technique, process, or design.

Likelihood   The probability of an observation, given a particular set of conditions.

Limit down   A limit move in the futures market in which the price at which a transaction would be made is at or below the lower limit.

Limited Partnership (Private Equity)   The legal structure used by most venture and private equity funds. Usually fixed life investment vehicles. The general partner or management firm manages the partnership using the policy laid down in a partnership agreement. The agreement also covers terms, fees, structures, and other items agreed between the limited partners and the general partner.

Limit move   A condition in the futures markets in which the price at which a transaction would be made is at or beyond the price limits.

Limit order   An order that lasts for a specified time to buy or sell a security when and if it trades at a specified price.

Limit pricing   The practice of setting the price at the highest level that inflicts a loss on an entrant.

Limit up   A limit move in the futures market in which the price at which a transaction would be made is at or above the upper limit.

Linear association   A straight-line relationship, as opposed to a relationship that cannot be graphed as a straight line.

Linear interpolation   The estimation of an unknown value on the basis of two known values that bracket it, using a straight line between the two known values.

Linear regression   Regression that models the straight-line relationship between the dependent and independent variable(s).

Linear relationship   A relationship between two variables that is illustrated by a straight line.

Liquid   Term used to describe an asset that can be quickly converted to cash at a price close to fair market value.

Liquidity premium   A premium added to the equilibrium interest rate on a security if that security cannot be converted to cash on short notice and at close to "fair market value."

Liquidity risk   Uncertainty due to the ability to buy or sell an investment in the secondary market.

Living wage   An hourly wage rate that enables a person who works a 40-hour week to rent adequate housing for not more than 30 percent of the amount earned.

Locked limit   A condition in the futures markets in which a transaction cannot take place because the price would be beyond the limits.

London InterBank Offer Rate (LIBOR)   (1) The rate at which international banks lend on the Eurocurrency market. This is the rate quoted to a top-quality borrower. The most common maturities are one month, three months, and six months. There is a LIBOR for the U.S. dollar and a few other major currencies. LIBOR is determined by the British Banking Association in London. *See* also Euribor. (2) The Eurodollar rate at which London banks lend dollars to other London banks; considered to be the best representative rate on a dollar borrowed by a private, high-quality borrower.

Long   The buyer of a derivative contract. Also refers to the position of owning a derivative.

Longitudinal data   Observations on characteristic(s) of the same observational unit through time.

Long position   The buyer of a commodity or security or, for a forward contract, the counterparty who will be the eventual buyer of the underlying asset.

Long run   A period of time in which the quantities of all resources can be varied.

Long-run aggregate supply curve   The relationship between the real GDP supplied and the price level in the long run when real GDP equals potential GDP.

Long-run average cost curve   The relationship between the lowest attainable average total cost and output when both capital and labor are varied.

Long-run industry supply curve   A curve that shows how the quantity supplied by an industry varies as the market price varies after all the possible adjustments have been made, including changes in plant size and the number of firms in the industry.

Long-run macroeconomic equilibrium   A situation that occurs when real GDP equals potential GDP—the economy is on its long-run aggregate supply curve.

Long-run Phillips curve   A curve that shows the relationship between inflation and unemployment when the actual inflation rate equals the expected inflation rate.

Long-term assets   Assets that have a useful life of more than one year, are used in the operation of a business, and are not intended for resale. Less commonly called *fixed assets*.

Long-term equity anticipatory securities (LEAPS)   Options originally created with expirations of several years.

Look-ahead bias   A bias caused by using information that was unavailable on the test date.

Lower bound   The lowest possible value of an option.

Lucas wedge   The accumulated loss of output that results from a slowdown in the growth rate of real GDP per person.

M1   A measure of money that consists of currency and traveler's checks plus checking deposits owned by individuals and businesses.

M2   A measure of money that consists of M1 plus time deposits, savings deposits, and money market mutual funds and other deposits.

Macroeconomic long run.   A time frame that is sufficiently long for real GDP to return to potential GDP so that full employment prevails.

Macaulay duration   A measure of the time flow of cash from a bond where cash flows are weighted by present values discounted by the yield to maturity.

Macroeconomics   The study of the performance of the national economy and the global economy.

Macroeconomic short run   A period during which some money prices are sticky and real GDP might be below, above, or at potential GDP and unemployment might be above, below, or at the natural rate of unemployment.

Maintenance margin   The required proportion that the investor's equity value must be to the total market value of the stock. If the proportion drops below this percent, the investor will receive a margin call.

Maintenance margin requirement   The margin requirement on any day other than the first day of a transaction.

Management fee   The compensation an investment company pays to the investment management company for its services. The average annual fee is about 0.5 percent of fund assets.

Margin   (1) The percent of cost a buyer pays in cash for a security, borrowing the balance from the broker. This introduces leverage, which increases the risk of the transaction. (2) The amount of money that a trader deposits in a margin account. The term is derived from the stock market practice in which an investor borrows a portion of the money required to purchase a certain amount of stock. In futures markets, there is no borrowing so the margin is more of a down payment or performance bond.

Margin account   The collateral posted with the futures exchange clearinghouse by an outside counterparty to insure its eventual performance; the *initial* margin is the deposit required at contract origination while the *maintenance* margin is the minimum collateral necessary at all times.

Marginal benefit   The benefit that a person receives from consuming one more unit of a good or service. It is measured as the maximum amount that a person is willing to pay for one more unit of the good or service.

Marginal benefit curve   A curve that shows the relationship between the marginal benefit of a good and the quantity of that good consumed.

Marginal cost   The opportunity cost of producing one more unit of a good or service. It is the best alternative forgone. It is calculated as the increase in total cost divided by the increase in output.

Marginal cost pricing rule   A rule that sets the price of a good or service equal to the marginal cost of producing it.

Marginal probability   *See* Unconditional probability.

Marginal product   The increase in total product that results from a one-unit increase in the variable input, with all other inputs remaining the same. It is calculated as the increase in total product divided by the increase in the variable input employed, when the quantities of all other inputs are constant.

Marginal product of labor   The additional real GDP produced by an additional hour of labor when all other influences on production remain the same.

Marginal propensity to consume   The fraction of a change in disposable income that is consumed. It is calculated as the change in consumption expenditure divided by the change in disposable income.

Marginal revenue   The change in total revenue that results from a one-unit increase in the quantity sold. It is calculated as the change in total revenue divided by the change in quantity sold.

Marginal revenue product   The change in total revenue that results from employing one more unit of a resource (labor) while the quantity of all other resources remains the same. It is calculated as the increase in total revenue divided by the increase in the quantity of the resource (labor).

Marginal social benefit   The marginal benefit enjoyed by society—by the consumer of a good or service (marginal private benefit) plus the marginal benefit enjoyed by others (marginal external benefit).

Marginal social cost   The marginal cost incurred by the entire society—by the producer and by everyone else on whom the cost falls—and is the sum of marginal private cost and the marginal external cost.

Marginal tax rate   The part of each additional dollar in income that is paid as tax.

Margin call   A request by an investor's broker for additional capital for a security bought on margin if the investor's equity value declines below the required maintenance margin.

Marked to market   The settlement process used to adjust the margin account of a futures contract for daily changes in the price of the underlying asset.

Market demand   The relationship between the total quantity demanded of a good and its price. It is illustrated by the market demand curve.

Market failure   A state in which the market does not allocate resources efficiently.

Market order   An order to buy or sell a security immediately at the best price available.

Market portfolio   The portfolio that includes all risky assets with relative weights equal to their proportional market values.

Market power   The ability to influence the market, and in particular the market price, by influencing the total quantity offered for sale.

Market risk   The risk associated with interest rates, exchange rates, and equity prices.

Market risk premium   The amount of return above the risk-free rate that investors expect from the market in general as compensation for systematic risk.

Market Value   The current listed price at which investors buy or sell securities at a given time.

Market Value (Real Estate)   The most probable price that a property should bring in a competitive and open market under all conditions requisite to a fair sale, the buyer and seller each acting prudently and knowledgeably, and assuming the price is not affected by undue stimulus. Implicit in this definition is the consummation of a sale as of a specified date and the passing of title from seller to buyer under conditions whereby: (a) Buyer and seller are typically motivated. (b) Both parties are well informed or well advised and each acting in what they consider their own best interests. (c) A reasonable time is allowed for exposure in the open market. (d) Payment is made in terms of currency or in terms of financial arrangements comparable thereto. (e) The price represents the normal consideration for the property sold unaffected by special or creative financing or sales concessions granted by anyone associated with the sale.

Market value added (MVA)   External management performance measure to compare the market value of the company's debt and equity with the total capital invested in the firm.

Marking to market   (1) Procedure whereby potential profits and losses on a futures position are realized daily. The daily futures price variation is debited (credited) in cash to the loser (winner) at the end of the day. (2) A procedure used primarily in futures markets in which the parties to a contract settle the amount owed daily. Also known as the daily settlement.

McCallum rule   A rule that adjusts the growth rate of the monetary base to target the inflation rate but also to take into account changes in the trend productivity growth rate and fluctuations in aggregate demand.

Mean absolute deviation   With reference to a sample, the mean of the absolute values of deviations from the sample mean.

Mean excess return   The average rate of return in excess of the risk-free rate.

Means of payment   A method of settling a debt.

Mean–variance analysis   An approach to portfolio analysis using expected means, variances, and covariances of asset returns.

Measurement scales   A scheme of measuring differences. The four types of measurement scales are nominal, ordinal, interval, and ratio.

Measure of central tendency   A quantitative measure that specifies where data are centered.

Median   The value of the middle item of a set of items that has been sorted into ascending or descending order; the 50th percentile.

Mesokurtic   Describes a distribution with kurtosis identical to that of the normal distribution.

Microeconomics   The study of the choices that individuals and businesses make, the way those choices interact, and the influence governments exert on them.

Minimum efficient scale   The smallest quantity of output at which the long-run average cost curve reaches its lowest level.

Minimum wage   A regulation that makes the hiring of labor below a specified wage rate illegal.

Modal interval   With reference to grouped data, the most frequently occurring interval.

Mode   The most frequently occurring value in a set of observations.

Modified duration   (1) Measure of a bond's price sensitivity to interest rate movements. Equal to the duration of a bond divided by one plus its yield to maturity. (2) A measure of Macaulay duration divided by one plus the bond's periodic yield used to approximate the bond's price volatility. (3) An adjustment of the duration for the level of the yield. Contrast with Macaulay duration.

Monetarist   An economist who believes that the economy is self regulating and that it will normally operate at full employment, provided that monetary policy is not erratic and that the pace of money growth is kept steady.

Monetary base   The sum of the Federal Reserve notes, coins, and banks' deposits at the Fed.

Monetary policy   The Fed conducts the nation's monetary policy by changing in interest rates and adjusting the quantity of money.

Money   Any commodity or token that is generally acceptable as a means of payment.

Money market The market for short-term debt securities with maturities of less than one year.

Money market fund A fund that invests in short-term securities sold in the money market. (Large companies, banks, and other institutions also invest their surplus cash in the money market for short periods of time.) In the entire investment spectrum, these are generally the safest, most stable securities available. They include Treasury bills, certificates of deposit of large banks, and commercial paper (short-term IOUs of large corporations).

Money market mutual fund A fund operated by a financial institution that sells shares in the fund and holds liquid assets such as U.S. Treasury bills and short-term commercial bills.

Money market yield (or CD equivalent yield) A yield on a basis comparable to the quoted yield on an interest-bearing money market instrument that pays interest on a 360-day basis; the annualized holding period yield, assuming a 360-day year.

Money multiplier The amount by which a change in the monetary base is multiplied to determine the resulting change in the quantity of money.

Moneyness The relationship between the price of the underlying and an option's exercise price.

Money price The number of dollars that must be given up in exchange for a good or service.

Money wage rate The number of dollars that an hour of labor earns.

Monopolistic competition A market structure in which a large number of firms compete by making similar but slightly different products.

Monopoly A market structure in which there is one firm, which produces a good or service that has no close substitute and in which the firm is protected from competition by a barrier preventing the entry of new firms.

Monte Carlo simulation A risk analysis technique in which probable future events are simulated on a computer, generating estimated rates of return and risk indexes.

Mortgage bonds Bonds that pledge specific assets such as buildings and equipment. The proceeds from the sale of these assets are used to pay off bondholders in case of bankruptcy.

Moving average The continually recalculating average of security prices for a period, often 200 days, to serve as an indication of the general trend of prices and also as a benchmark price.

Multifactor model An empirical version of the APT where the investor chooses the exact number and identity of the common risk factors used to describe an asset's risk-return relationship. Risk factors are often designated as *macroeconomic* variables (e.g., inflation, changes in gross domestic product) or *microeconomic* variables (e.g., security-specific characteristics like firm size or book-to-market ratios).

Multiplication rule for probabilities The rule that the joint probability of events A and B equals the probability of A given B times the probability of B.

Multiplier The amount by which a change in autonomous expenditure is magnified or multiplied to determine the change in equilibrium expenditure and real GDP.

Multivariate distribution A probability distribution that specifies the probabilities for a group of related random variables.

Multivariate normal distribution A probability distribution for a group of random variables that is completely defined by the means and variances of the variables plus all the correlations between pairs of the variables.

Must A required provision for claiming compliance with the GIPS standards.

Mutual fund An investment company that pools money from shareholders and invests in a variety of securities, including stocks, bonds, and money market securities. A mutual fund ordinarily stands ready to buy back (redeem) its shares at their current net asset value, which depends on the market value of the fund's portfolio of securities at the time. Mutual funds generally continuously offer new shares to investors.

Mutually exclusive events Events such that only one can occur at a time.

Nasdaq InterMarket A trading system that includes Nasdaq market makers and ECNs that quote and trade stocks listed on the NYSE and the AMEX. It involves dealers from the Nasdaq market and the Intermarket Trading System (ITS). In many ways, this has become what had been labeled the third market.

Nash equilibrium The outcome of a game that occurs when player A takes the best possible action given the action of player B and player B takes the best possible action given the action of player A.

National saving The sum of private saving (saving by households and businesses) and government saving.

Natural monopoly A monopoly that occurs when one firm can supply the entire market at a lower price than two or more firms can.

Natural rate of unemployment The unemployment rate when the economy is at full employment. There is no cyclical unemployment; all unemployment is frictional and structural.

Natural resources Long-term assets purchased for the economic value that can be taken from the land and used up.

Near-term, high-priority goal A short-term financial investment goal of personal importance, such as accumulating funds for making a house down payment or buying a car.

Needs-tested spending Government spending on programs that pay benefits to suitably qualified people and businesses.

Negative relationship A relationship between variables that move in opposite directions.

Negotiated sales An underwriting arrangement wherein the sale of a security issue by an issuing entity (governmental body or a corporation) is done using an investment banking firm that maintains an ongoing relationship with the issuer. The characteristics of the security issue are determined by the issuer in consultation with the investment banker.

Neoclassical growth theory A theory of economic growth that proposes that real GDP grows because technological change induces a level of saving and investment that makes capital per hour of labor grow.

Net asset value The market value of the assets owned by a fund.

Net borrower A country that is borrowing more from the rest of the world than it is lending to it.

Net exports The value of exports minus the value of imports.

Net investment Net increase in the capital stock—gross investment minus depreciation.

Net lender A country that is lending more to the rest of the world than it is borrowing from it.

Net-of-Fees Return The gross-of-fees return reduced by the investment management fee.

Net present value The present value of the future flow of marginal revenue product generated by capital minus the cost of the capital.

Net present value (NPV) A measure of the excess cash flows expected from an investment proposal. It is equal to the present value of the cash *inflows* from an investment proposal, discounted at the required rate of return for the investment, minus the present value of the cash *outflows* required by the investment, also discounted at the investment's required rate of return. If the derived net present value is a positive value (i.e., there is an excess net present value), the investment should be acquired since it will provide a rate of return above its required returns.

Net taxes Taxes paid to governments minus transfer payments received from governments.

Netting When parties agree to exchange only the net amount owed from one party to the other.

New issue Common stocks or bonds offered by companies for public sale.

New Keynesian A Keynesian who holds the view that not only is the money wage rate sticky but that prices of goods and services are also sticky.

Node Each value on a binomial tree from which successive moves or outcomes branch.

No-load fund A mutual fund that sells its shares at net asset value without adding sales charges.

Nominal GDP The value of the final goods and services produced in a given year valued at the prices that prevailed in that same year. It is a more precise name for GDP.

Nominal risk-free interest rate The sum of the real risk-free interest rate and the inflation premium.

Nominal scale A measurement scale that categorizes data but does not rank them.

Nominal yield A bond's yield as measured by its coupon rate.

Noncash investing and financing transactions Significant investing and financing transactions involving only long-term assets, long-term liabilities, or stockholders' equity that do not affect current cash inflows or outflows.

Nonlinear relation An association or relationship between variables that cannot be graphed as a straight line.

Nonparametric test A test that is not concerned with a parameter, or that makes minimal assumptions about the population from which a sample comes.

Nonrenewable natural resources Natural resources that can be used only once and that cannot be replaced once they have been used.

Nontariff barrier Any action other than a tariff that restricts international trade.

Normal backwardation The condition in futures markets in which futures prices are lower than expected spot prices.

Normal contango The condition in futures markets in which futures prices are higher than expected spot prices.

Normal good A good for which demand increases as income increases.

Normal profit The expected return for supplying entrepreneurial ability.

North American Free Trade Agreement An agreement, which became effective on January 1, 1994, to eliminate all barriers to international trade between the United States, Canada, and Mexico after a 15-year phasing in period.

Notes Intermediate-term debt securities with maturities longer than 1 year but less than 10 years.

Notional principal The principal value of a swap transaction, which is not exchanged but is used as a scale factor to translate interest rate differentials into cash settlement payments.

NPV rule An investment decision rule that states that an investment should be undertaken if its NPV is positive but not undertaken if its NPV is negative.

Null hypothesis The hypothesis to be tested.

Objective probabilities Probabilities that generally do not vary from person to person; includes a priori and objective probabilities.

Objectives The investor's goals expressed in terms of risk and return and included in the policy statement.

Obsolescence The process of becoming out of date, which is a factor in the limited useful life of tangible assets.

Offensive competitive strategy A strategy whereby a firm attempts to use its strengths to affect the competitive forces in the industry and, in so doing, improves the firm's relative position in the industry.

Official reserves The amount of reserves owned by the central bank of a government in the form of gold, Special Drawing Rights, and foreign cash or marketable securities.

Official settlements account A record of the change in a country's official reserves.

Off-market FRA A contract in which the initial value is intentionally set at a value other than zero and therefore requires a cash payment at the start from one party to the other.

Offsetting A transaction in exchange-listed derivative markets in which a party re-enters the market to close out a position.

Okun gap The gap between real GDP and potential GDP, and so is another name for the output gap.

Oligopoly A market structure in which a small number of firms compete.

One-sided hypothesis test (or one-tailed hypothesis test) A test in which the null hypothesis is rejected only if the evidence indicates that the population parameter is greater than (smaller than) θ_0. The alternative hypothesis also has one side.

Open-End Fund (Private Equity) A type of investment fund where the number of investors and the total committed capital is not fixed (i.e., open for subscriptions and/or redemptions).

Open market operation The purchase or sale of government securities—U.S. Treasury bills and bonds—by the Federal Reserve System in the open market.

Operating activities Business activities that involve the cash effects of transactions and other events that enter into the determination of net income.

Operating efficiency ratios Financial ratios intended to indicate how efficiently management is utilizing the firm's assets in terms of dollar sales generated per dollar of assets. Primary examples would be: total asset turnover, fixed asset turnover, or equity turnover.

Operating leverage The use of fixed-production costs in the firm's operating cost structure. The effect of fixed costs is to magnify the effect of a change in sales on operating profits.

Operating profitability ratios Financial ratios intended to indicate how profitable the firm is in terms of the percent of profit generated from sales. Alternative measures would include: operating profit (EBIT)/net sales; pretax profit (EBT)/net sales; and net profit/sales.

Opportunity cost The highest-valued alternative that we give up to something.

Optimal portfolio The portfolio on the efficient frontier that has the highest utility for a given investor. It lies at the point of tangency between the efficient frontier and the curve with the investor's highest possible utility.

Option A financial instrument that gives one party the right, but not the obligation, to buy or sell an underlying asset from or to another party at a fixed price over a specific period of time. Also referred to as contingent claims.

Option-adjusted spread A type of yield spread that considers changes in the term structure and alternative estimates of the volatility of interest rates.

Option contract An agreement that grants the owner the right, but not the obligation, to make a future transaction in an underlying commodity or security at a fixed price and within a predetermined time in the future.

Option premium The initial price that the option buyer must pay to the option seller to acquire the contract.

Option premium (or option price or premium) (1) The price of an option. (2) The initial price that the option buyer must pay to the option seller to acquire the contract. (3) The amount of money a buyer pays and seller receives to engage in an option transaction.

Ordinal scale A measurement scale that sorts data into categories that are ordered (ranked) with respect to some characteristic.

Ordinary annuity An annuity with a first cash flow that is paid one period from the present.

OTC Electronic Bulletin Board (OTCBB) A regulated quotation service that displays real-time quotes, last-sale prices, and volume information for a specified set of over-the-counter (OTC) securities that are not traded on the formal Nasdaq market.

Outcome A possible value of a random variable.

Out-of-sample test A test of a strategy or model using a sample outside the time period on which the strategy or model was developed.

Out-of-the-money option (1) An option that has no value if exercised immediately. For example, a call when the strike price is above the current price of the underlying asset, or a put when the strike price is below the current price of the underlying asset. (2) An option that has no intrinsic value. (3) Options that, if exercised, would require the payment of more money than the value received and therefore would not be currently exercised.

Overnight index swap (OIS) A swap in which the floating rate is the cumulative value of a single unit of currency invested at an overnight rate during the settlement period.

Overweighted A condition in which a portfolio, for whatever reason, includes more of a class of securities than the relative market value alone would justify.

Paid-In Capital (Private Equity) The amount of committed capital a limited partner has actually transferred to a venture fund. Also known as the cumulative drawdown amount.

Paired comparisons test A statistical test for differences based on paired observations drawn from samples that are dependent on each other.

Paired observations Observations that are dependent on each other.

Pairs arbitrage trade A trade in two closely related stocks involving the short sale of one and the purchase of the other.

Panel data Observations through time on a single characteristic of multiple observational units.

Parameter A descriptive measure computed from or used to describe a population of data, conventionally represented by Greek letters.

Parameter instability The problem or issue of population regression parameters that have changed over time.

Parametric test Any test (or procedure) concerned with parameters or whose validity depends on assumptions concerning the population generating the sample.

Par value *See* Principal. The principal amount repaid at maturity of a bond. Also called face value.

Patent A government-sanctioned exclusive right granted to the inventor of a good, service, or productive process to produce, use, and sell the invention for a given number of years.

Patent An exclusive right granted by the federal government for a period of 20 years to make a particular product or use a specific process.

Payback The time required for the added income from the convertible security relative to the stock to offset the conversion premium.

Payer swaption A swaption that allows the holder to enter into a swap as the fixed-rate payer and floating-rate receiver.

Payment date The date on which a firm actually mails dividend checks.

Payoff The value of an option at expiration.

Payoff matrix A table that shows the payoffs for every possible action by each player for every possible action by each other player.

Pegged exchange rate regime A system in which a country's exchange rate in relation to a major currency is set at a target value (the peg) but allowed to fluctuate within a small band around the target.

Percentiles Quantiles that divide a distribution into 100 equal parts.

Perfect competition A market in which there are many firms each selling an identical product; there are many buyers; there are no restrictions on entry into the industry; firms in the industry have no advantage over potential new entrants; and firms and buyers are well informed about the price of each firm's product.

Perfectly elastic demand Demand with an infinite price elasticity; the quantity demanded changes by an infinitely large percentage in response to a tiny price change.

Perfectly inelastic demand Demand with a price elasticity of zero; the quantity demanded remains constant when the price changes.

Perfect price discrimination Price discrimination that extracts the entire consumer surplus.

Performance appraisal (1) The assessment of an investment record for evidence of investment skill. (2) The evaluation of risk-adjusted performance; the evaluation of investment skill.

Performance measurement The calculation of returns in a logical and consistent manner.

Permutation An ordered listing.

Perpetuity (1) An investment without any maturity date. It provides returns to its owner indefinitely. (2) A perpetual annuity, or a set of never-ending level sequential cash flows, with the first cash flow occurring one period from now.

Personal trust An amount of money set aside by a grantor and often managed by a third party, the trustee. Often constructed so one party receives income from the trust's investments and another party receives the residual value of the trust after the income beneficiaries' death.

Phillips curve A curve that shows a relationship between inflation and unemployment.

Physical deterioration A decline in the useful life of a depreciable asset resulting from use and from exposure to the elements.

Plain-vanilla Refers to a security, especially a bond or a swap, issued with standard features. Sometimes called generic.

Plain vanilla swap An interest rate swap in which one party pays a fixed rate and the other pays a floating rate, with both sets of payments in the same currency.

Platykurtic Describes a distribution that is less peaked than the normal distribution.

Point estimate A single numerical estimate of an unknown quantity, such as a population parameter.

Policy statement A statement in which the investor specifies investment goals, constraints, and risk preferences.

Pooled estimate An estimate of a parameter that involves combining (pooling) observations from two or more samples.

Population All members of a specified group.

Population mean The arithmetic mean value of a population; the arithmetic mean of all the observations or values in the population.

Population standard deviation A measure of dispersion relating to a population in the same unit of measurement as the observations, calculated as the positive square root of the population variance.

Population variance A measure of dispersion relating to a population, calculated as the mean of the squared deviations around the population mean.

Portfolio An individually managed pool of assets. A portfolio may be a subportfolio, account, or pooled fund.

Position trader A trader who typically holds positions open overnight.

Positive relationship A relationship between two variables that move in the same direction.

Potential GDP The quantity of real GDP at full employment.

Posterior probability An updated probability that reflects or comes after new information.

Potential credit risk The risk associated with the possibility that a payment due at a later date will not be made.

Poverty A situation in which a household's income is too low to be able to buy the quantities of food, shelter, and clothing that are deemed necessary.

Power of a test The probability of correctly rejecting the null—that is, rejecting the null hypothesis when it is false.

Predatory pricing Setting a low price to drive competitors out of business with the intention of setting a monopoly price when the competition has gone.

Preferences A description of a person's likes and dislikes.

Preferred stock An equity investment that stipulates the dividend payment either as a coupon or a stated dollar amount. The firm's directors may withhold payments.

Premium A bond selling at a price above par value due to capital market conditions.

Present value The amount of money that, if invested today, will grow to be as large as a given future amount when the interest that it will earn is taken into account.

Present value (PV) (1) The current worth of future income after it is discounted to reflect the fact that revenues in the future are valued less highly than revenues now. (2) The current worth of a future cash flow. Obtained by discounting the future cash flow at the market-required rate of return. (3) The current (discounted) value of a future cash flow or flows.

Price ceiling A regulation that makes it illegal to charge a price higher than a specified level.

Price continuity A feature of a liquid market in which there are small price changes from one transaction to the next due to the depth of the market.

Price discovery A feature of futures markets in which futures prices provide valuable information about the price of the underlying asset.

Price discrimination The practice of selling different units of a good or service for different prices or of charging one customer different prices for different quantities bought.

Price/earnings (P/E) ratio The number by which expected earnings per share is multiplied to estimate a stock's value; also called the *earnings multiplier.*

Price effect The effect of a change in the price on the quantity of a good consumed, other things remaining the same.

Price elasticity of demand A units-free measure of the responsiveness of the quantity demanded of a good to a change in its price, when all other influences on buyers' plans remain the same.

Price floor A regulation that makes it illegal to charge a price lower than a specified level.

Price level The average level of prices as measured by a price index.

Price limits Limits imposed by a futures exchange on the price change that can occur from one day to the next.

Price momentum A portfolio strategy in which you acquire stocks that have enjoyed above-market stock price increases.

Price multiple The ratio of a stock's market price to some measure of value per share.

Price relative A ratio of an ending price over a beginning price; it is equal to 1 plus the holding period return on the asset.

Price risk The component of interest rate risk due to the uncertainty of the market price of a bond caused by changes in market interest rates.

Price taker A firm that cannot influence the price of the good or service it produces.

Price-weighted index An index calculated as an arithmetic mean of the current prices of the sampled securities.

Primary market The market in which newly issued securities are sold by their issuers, who receive the proceeds.

Principal-agent problem The problem of devising compensation rules that induce an agent to act in the best interest of a principal.

Prior probabilities Probabilities reflecting beliefs prior to the arrival of new information.

Private Equity Private equity includes, but is not limited to, organizations devoted to venture capital, leveraged buyouts, consolidations, mezzanine and distressed debt investments, and a variety of hybrids, such as venture leasing and venture factoring.

Private information Information that is available to one person but is too costly for anyone else to obtain.

Private placement A new issue sold directly to a small group of investors, usually institutions

Private sector surplus or deficit An amount equal to saving minus investment.

Probability A number between 0 and 1 describing the chance that a stated event will occur.

Probability density function A function with non-negative values such that probability can be described by areas under the curve graphing the function.

Probability distribution A distribution that specifies the probabilities of a random variable's possible outcomes.

Probability function A function that specifies the probability that the random variable takes on a specific value.

Producer surplus The price of a good minus the opportunity cost of producing it, summed over the quantity sold.

Product differentiation Making a product slightly different from the product of a competing firm.

Production efficiency A situation in which the economy cannot produce more of one good without producing less of some other good.

Production function The relationship between real GDP and the quantity of labor when all other influences on production remain the same.

Production method A method of depreciation that assumes depreciation is solely the result of use and that allocates depreciation based on the units of use or output during each period of an asset's useful life.

Production possibilities frontier The boundary between the combinations of goods and services that can be produced and the combinations that cannot.

Production quota An upper limit to the quantity of a good that may be produced in a specified period.

Productivity growth slowdown A slowdown in the growth rate of output per person.

Profit The income earned by entrepreneurship.

Property rights Social arrangements that govern the ownership, use, and disposal of resources or factors of production, goods, and services that are enforceable in the courts.

Prospective P/E *See* Leading P/E.

Protective put An option strategy in which a long position in an asset is combined with a long position in a put.

Public good A good or service that is both nonrival and nonexcludable—it can be consumed simultaneously by everyone and from which no one can be excluded.

Purchasing power parity The equal value of different monies.

Purchasing power parity (PPP) A theory stating that the exchange rate between two currencies will exactly reflect the purchasing power of the two currencies.

Pure discount instruments Instruments that pay interest as the difference between the amount borrowed and the amount paid back.

Put An option that gives the holder the right to sell an underlying asset to another party at a fixed price over a specific period of time.

Put option A contract giving the right to sell an asset at a specified price, on or before a specified date.

Put–call–forward parity The relationship among puts, calls, and forward contracts.

Put-call parity The relationship that must exist in an efficient market between the prices for put and call options having the same underlying asset, exercise price, and expiration date.

p-**Value**   The smallest level of significance at which the null hypothesis can be rejected; also called the marginal significance level.

Quality financial statements   Financial statements that most knowledgeable observers (analysts, portfolio managers) would consider conservatively prepared in terms of sales, expenses, earnings, and asset valuations. The results reported would reflect reasonable estimates and indicate what truly happened during the period and the legitimate value of assets and liabilities on the balance sheet.

Quantile (or fractile)   A value at or below which a stated fraction of the data lies.

Quantity demanded   The amount of a good or service that consumers plan to buy during a given time period at a particular price.

Quantity of labor demanded   The labor hours hired by the firms in the economy.

Quantity of labor supplied   The number of labor hours that all households in the economy plan to work.

Quantity supplied   The amount of a good or service that producers plan to sell during a given time period at a particular price.

Quantity theory of money   The proposition that in the long run, an increase in the quantity of money brings an equal percentage increase in the price level.

Quartiles   Quantiles that divide a distribution into four equal parts.

Quintiles   Quantiles that divide a distribution into five equal parts.

Quota   A quantitative restriction on the import of a particular good, which specifies the maximum amount that can be imported in a given time period.

Random number   An observation drawn from a uniform distribution.

Random number generator   An algorithm that produces uniformly distributed random numbers between 0 and 1.

Random variable   A quantity whose future outcomes are uncertain.

Random walk theory   (1) The theory that current stock prices already reflect known information about the future. Therefore, the future movement of stock prices will be determined by surprise occurrences. This will cause them to change in a random fashion. (2) A theory stating that all current information is reflected in current security prices and that future price movements are random because they are caused by unexpected news.

Range   The difference between the maximum and minimum values in a dataset.

Range forward   A trading strategy based on a variation of the put-call parity model where, for the same underlying asset but different exercise prices, a call option is purchased and a put option is sold (or vice versa).

Rational expectation   The most accurate forecast possible, a forecast that uses all the available information, including knowledge of the relevant economic forces that influence the variable being forecasted.

Ratio scales   A measurement scale that has all the characteristics of interval measurement scales as well as a true zero point as the origin.

Real business cycle theory   A theory that regards random fluctuations in productivity as the main source of economic fluctuations.

Real Estate   Real estate Investments include: (a) Wholly owned or partially owned properties, (b) Commingled funds, property unit trusts, and insurance company separate accounts, (c) Unlisted, private placement securities issued by private real estate investment trusts (REITs) and real estate operating companies (REOCs), and (d) Equity-oriented debt, such as participating mortgage loans or any private interest in a property where some portion of return to the investor at the time of investment is related to the performance of the underlying real estate.

Real estate investment trusts (REITs)   Investment funds that hold portfolios of real estate investments.

Real income   A household's income expressed as a quantity of goods that the household can afford to buy.

Real interest rate   The nominal interest rate adjusted for inflation; the nominal interest rate minus the inflation rate.

Realization Multiple (Private Equity)   The realization multiple (DPI) is calculated by dividing the cumulative distributions by the paid-in-capital.

Realized capital gains   Capital gains that result when an appreciated asset is sold; realized capital gains are taxable.

Real options   Options embedded in a firm's real assets that give managers valuable decision-making flexibility, such as the right to either undertake or abandon an investment project.

Real rate of interest   The money rate of interest minus the expected rate of inflation. The real rate of interest indicates the interest premium, in terms of real goods and services, that one must pay for earlier availability.

Real risk-free rate (RRFR)   The basic interest rate with no accommodation for inflation or uncertainty. The pure time value of money.

Real wage rate   The quantity of goods ands services that an hour's work can buy. It is equal to the money wage rate divided by the price level.

Receiver swaption   A swaption that allows the holder to enter into a swap as the fixed-rate receiver and floating-rate payer.

Recession   There are two common definitions of recession. They are (1) A business cycle phase in which real GDP decreases for at least two successive quarters. (2) A significant decline in activity spread across the economy, lasting for more than a few months, visible in industrial production, employment, real income, and wholesale-retail trade.

Recessionary gap   The amount by which potential GDP exceeds real GDP.

Reference base period   The period in which the CPI is defined to be 100.

Registered competitive market makers (RCMMs)   Members of an exchange who are allowed to use their memberships to buy or sell for their own account within the specific trading obligations set down by the exchange.

Registered traders   Members of the stock exchange who are allowed to use their memberships to buy and sell for their own account, which means they save commissions on their trading but they provide liquidity to the market, and they abide by exchange regulations on how they can trade.

Regression coefficients   The intercept and slope coefficient(s) of a regression.

Regulation   Rules administrated by a government agency to influence economic activity by determining prices, product standards and types, and conditions under which new firms may enter an industry.

Regulatory risk   The risk associated with the uncertainty of how derivative transactions will be regulated or with changes in regulations.

Relative dispersion   The amount of dispersion relative to a reference value or benchmark.

Relative frequency   With reference to an interval of grouped data, the number of observations in the interval divided by the total number of observations in the sample.

Relative price   The ratio of the price of one good or service to the price of another good or service. A relative price is an opportunity cost.

Renewable natural resources   Natural resources that can be used repeatedly without depleting what is available for future use.

Rent   The income that land earns.

Rent ceiling   A regulation that makes it illegal to charge a rent higher than a specified level.

Rent seeking   Any attempt to capture a consumer surplus, a producer surplus, or an economic profit.

Replacement value   The market value of a swap.

Required rate of return   The return that compensates investors for their time, the expected rate of inflation, and the uncertainty of the return.

Required reserve ratio   The ratio of reserves to deposits that banks are required, by regulation, to hold.

Reserve ratio   The fraction of a bank's total deposits that are held in reserves.

Reserves   Cash in a bank's vault plus the bank's deposits at Federal Reserve banks.

Ricardo-Barro effect   The equivalence of financing government purchases by taxes or by borrowing.

Residual value   The estimated net scrap, salvage, or trade-in value of a tangible asset at the estimated date of its disposal. Also called *salvage value* or *disposal value.*

Resistance level   A price at which a technician would expect a substantial increase in the supply of a stock to reverse a rising trend.

Return prediction studies   Studies wherein investigations attempt to predict the time series of future rates of return using public information. An example would be predicting above-average returns for the stock market based on the aggregate dividend yield—e.g., high dividend yield indicates above average future market returns.

Revenue bond   A bond that is serviced by the income generated from specific revenue-producing projects of the municipality.

Revenue expenditure   An expenditure for ordinary repairs and maintenance of a long-term asset, which is recorded by a debit to an expense account.

Rising trend channel   The range defined by security prices as they move progressively higher.

Risk averse   The assumption about investors that they will choose the least risky alternative, all else being equal.

Risk-free asset   An asset with returns that exhibit zero variance.

Risk management   The process of identifying the level of risk an entity wants, measuring the level of risk the entity currently has, taking actions that bring the actual level of risk to the desired level of risk, and monitoring the new actual level of risk so that it continues to be aligned with the desired level of risk.

Risk-neutral probabilities Weights that are used to compute a binomial option price. They are the probabilities that would apply if a risk-neutral investor valued an option.

Risk-neutral valuation The process by which options and other derivatives are priced by treating investors as though they were risk neutral.

Risk premium (1) The difference between the expected return on an asset and the risk-free interest rate. (2) The increase over the nominal risk-free rate that investors demand as compensation for an investment's uncertainty. (3) The expected return on an investment minus the risk-free rate.

Risk premium (RP) The increase over the nominal risk-free rate that investors demand as compensation for an investment's uncertainty.

Risky asset An asset with uncertain future returns.

Rival A good or services or a resource is rival if its use by one person decreases the quantity available for someone else.

Robust The quality of being relatively unaffected by a violation of assumptions.

Runs test A test of the weak-form efficient market hypothesis that checks for trends that persist longer in terms of positive or negative price changes than one would expect for a random series.

Safety-first rules Rules for portfolio selection that focus on the risk that portfolio value will fall below some minimum acceptable level over some time horizon.

Sample A subset of a population.

Sample excess kurtosis A sample measure of the degree of a distribution's peakedness in excess of the normal distribution's peakedness.

Sample kurtosis A sample measure of the degree of a distribution's peakedness.

Sample mean The sum of the sample observations, divided by the sample size.

Sample selection bias Bias introduced by systematically excluding some members of the population according to a particular attribute—for example, the bias introduced when data availability leads to certain observations being excluded from the analysis.

Sample skewness A sample measure of degree of asymmetry of a distribution.

Sample standard deviation The positive square root of the sample variance.

Sample statistic or statistic A quantity computed from or used to describe a sample.

Sample variance A sample measure of the degree of dispersion of a distribution, calculated by dividing the sum of the squared deviations from the sample mean by the sample size (n) minus 1.

Sampling (1) A technique for constructing a passive index portfolio in which the portfolio manager buys a representative sample of stocks that comprise the benchmark index. (2) The process of obtaining a sample.

Sampling distribution The distribution of all distinct possible values that a statistic can assume when computed from samples of the same size randomly drawn from the same population.

Sampling error The difference between the observed value of a statistic and the quantity it is intended to estimate.

Sampling plan The set of rules used to select a sample.

Sandwich spread An option strategy that is equivalent to a short butterfly spread.

Saving The amount of income that households have left after they have paid their taxes and bought their consumption goods and services.

Savings and loan association (S&L) A depository institution that receives checking deposits and savings deposits and that makes personal, commercial, and home-purchase loans.

Savings bank A depository institution, owned by its depositors, that accepts savings deposits and makes mortgage loans.

Saving supply The relationship between saving and the real interest rate, other things remaining the same.

Scalper A trader who offers to buy or sell futures contracts, holding the position for only a brief period of time. Scalpers attempt to profit by buying at the bid price and selling at the higher ask price.

Scarcity Our inability to satisfy all our wants.

Scatter diagram A diagram that plots the value of one economic variable against the value of another.

Scatter plot A two-dimensional plot of pairs of observations on two data series.

Scenario analysis A risk management technique involving the examination of the performance of a portfolio under specified situations. Closely related to stress testing.

Search activity The time spent looking for someone with whom to do business.

Seasoned equity issues New equity shares offered by firms that already have stock outstanding.

Seats Memberships in a derivatives exchange.

Secondary market The market in which outstanding securities are bought and sold by owners other than the issuers. Purpose is to provide liquidity for investors.

Sector rotation strategy An active strategy that involves purchasing stocks in specific industries or stocks with specific characteristics (low *P/E*, growth, value) that are anticipated to rise in value more than the overall market.

Security market line (SML)   The line that reflects the combination of risk and return of alternative investments. In CAPM, risk is measured by systematic risk (beta).

SelectNet   An order-routing and trade-execution system for institutional investors (brokers and dealers) that allows communication through the Nasdaq system rather than by phone.

Self-interest   The choices that you think are the best for you.

Semideviation   The positive square root of semivariance (sometimes called semistandard deviation).

Semilogarithmic   Describes a scale constructed so that equal intervals on the vertical scale represent equal rates of change, and equal intervals on the horizontal scale represent equal amounts of change.

Semivariance   The average squared deviation below the mean.

Separation theorem   The proposition that the investment decision, which involves investing in the market portfolio on the capital market line, is separate from the financing decision, which targets a specific point on the CML based on the investor's risk preference.

Settlement date or payment date   The date on which the parties to a swap make payments.

Settlement period   The time between settlement dates.

Settlement price   The price determined by the exchange clearinghouse with which futures contract margin accounts are marked to market.

Settlement risk   When settling a contract, the risk that one party could be in the process of paying the counterparty while the counterparty is declaring bankruptcy.

Shareholders' equity   Total assets minus total liabilities.

Sharpe measure   A relative measure of a portfolio's benefit-to-risk ratio, calculated as its average return in excess of the risk-free rate divided by the standard deviation of portfolio returns.

Sharpe ratio   (1) The ratio of mean excess return (return minus the risk-free rate) to standard deviation of returns (or excess returns). (2) The average return in excess of the risk-free rate divided by the standard deviation of return; a measure of the average excess return earned per unit of standard deviation of return.

Shortfall risk   The risk that portfolio value will fall below some minimum acceptable level over some time horizon.

Short hedge   A short position in a forward or futures contract used to offset the price volatility of a long position in the underlying asset.

Short position   The seller of a commodity or security or, for a forward contract, the counterparty who will be the eventual seller of the underlying asset.

Short run   The short run in microeconomics has two meanings. For the firm, it is the period of time in which the quantity of at least one input is fixed and the quantities of the other inputs can be varied. The fixed input is usually capital—that is, the firm has a given plant size. For the industry, the short run is the period of time in which each firm has a given plant size and the number of firms in the industry is fixed.

Short-run aggregate supply curve   A curve that shows the relationship between the quantity of real GDP supplied and the price level in the short run when the money wage rate, other resource prices, and potential GDP remain constant.

Short-run industry supply curve   A curve that shows the quantity supplied by the industry at each price varies when the plant size of each firm and the number of firms in the industry remain the same.

Short-run macroeconomic equilibrium   A situation that occurs when the quantity of real GDP demanded equals quantity of real GDP supplied—at the point of intersection of the *AD* curve and the *SAS* curve.

Short-run Phillips curve   A curve that shows the tradeoff between inflation and unemployment, when the expected inflation rate and the natural rate of unemployment remain the same.

Short sale   The sale of borrowed securities with the intention of repurchasing them later at a lower price and earning the difference.

Should   Encouraged (recommended) to follow the recommendation of the GIPS standards but not required.

Shutdown point   The output and price at which the firm just covers its total variable cost. In the short run, the firm is indifferent between producing the profit-maximizing output and shutting down temporarily.

Signal   An action taken by an informed person (or firm) to send a message to uninformed people or an action taken outside a market that conveys information that can be used by that market.

Simple interest   The interest earned each period on the original investment; interest calculated on the principal only.

Simple random sample   A subset of a larger population created in such a way that each element of the population has an equal probability of being selected to the subset.

Simulation trial A complete pass through the steps of a simulation.

Single-price monopoly A monopoly that must sell each unit of its output for a same price to all its customers.

Sinking fund (1) Bond provision that requires the bond to be paid off progressively rather than in full at maturity. (2) Bond provision that requires the issuer to redeem some or all of the bond systematically over the term of the bond rather than in full at maturity.

Skewed Not symmetrical.

Skewness A quantitative measure of skew (lack of symmetry); a synonym of skew.

Slope The change in the value of the variable measured on the *y*-axis divided by the change in the value of the variable measured on the *x*-axis.

Small-firm effect A frequent empirical anomaly where risk-adjusted stock returns for companies with low market capitalization (i.e., share price multiplied by number of outstanding shares) are significantly larger than those generated by high market capitalization (large cap) firms.

Small-Order Execution System (SOES) A quotation and execution system for retail (nonprofessional) investors who place orders with brokers who must honor their prevailing bid-ask for automatic execution up to 1,000 shares.

Social interest Choices that are the best for society as a whole.

Soft dollars A form of compensation to a money manager generated when the manager commits the investor to paying higher brokerage fees in exchange for the manager receiving additional services (e.g., stock research) from the broker.

Software Capitalized costs associated with computer programs developed for sale, lease, or internal use and amortized over the estimated economic life of the programs.

Sovereign risk The risk that a government may default on its debt.

Spearman rank correlation coefficient A measure of correlation applied to ranked data.

Specialist The major market maker on U.S. stock exchanges who acts as a broker or dealer to ensure the liquidity and smooth functions of the secondary stock market.

Speculative company A firm with a great degree of business and/or financial risk, with commensurate high earnings potential.

Speculative stock A stock that appears to be highly overpriced compared to its intrinsic valuation.

Spending phase Phase in the investment life cycle during which individuals' earning years end as they retire. They pay for expenses with income from social security and returns from prior investments and invest to protect against inflation.

Spot price Current market price of an asset. Also called cash price.

Spot rate The required yield for a cash flow to be received at some specific date in the future—for example, the spot rate for a flow to be received in one year, for a cash flow in two years, and so on.

Spread An option strategy involving the purchase of one option and sale of another option that is identical to the first in all respects except either exercise price or expiration.

Spurious correlation A correlation that misleadingly points towards associations between variables.

Stagflation The combination of recession and inflation.

Standard deviation A measure of variability equal to the square root of the variance.

Standardizing A transformation that involves subtracting the mean and dividing the result by the standard deviation.

Standard normal distribution (or unit normal distribution) The normal density with mean (μ) equal to 0 and standard deviation (σ) equal to 1.

Stated annual interest rate or quoted interest rate A quoted interest rate that does not account for compounding within the year.

Statement of cash flows A financial statement that shows how a company's operating, investing, and financing activities have affected cash during an accounting period.

Statistic A quantity computed from or used to describe a sample of data.

Statistical inference Making forecasts, estimates, or judgments about a larger group from a smaller group actually observed; using a sample statistic to infer the value of an unknown population parameter.

Statistically significant A result indicating that the null hypothesis can be rejected; with reference to an estimated regression coefficient, frequently understood to mean a result indicating that the corresponding population regression coefficient is different from 0.

Statistics The science of describing, analyzing, and drawing conclusions from data; also, a collection of numerical data.

Stock A quantity that exists at a point in time.

Stock dividend A dividend paid in the form of additional shares rather than in cash.

Stock split An action taken by a firm to increase the number of shares outstanding, such as doubling the number of shares outstanding by giving each stockholder two new shares for each one formerly held.

Storage costs or carrying costs The costs of holding an asset, generally a function of the physical characteristics of the underlying asset.

Straddle An option strategy involving the purchase of a put and a call with the same exercise price. A straddle is based on the expectation of high volatility of the underlying.

Straight-line method A method of depreciation that assumes depreciation depends only on the passage of time and that allocates an equal amount of depreciation to each accounting period in an asset's useful life.

Strangle A variation of a straddle in which the put and call have different exercise prices.

Strap An option strategy involving the purchase of two calls and one put.

Strategies All the possible actions of each player in a game.

Stratified random sampling A procedure by which a population is divided into subpopulations (strata) based on one or more classification criteria. Simple random samples are then drawn from each stratum in sizes proportional to the relative size of each stratum in the population. These samples are then pooled.

Stress testing A risk management technique in which the risk manager examines the performance of the portfolio under market conditions involving high risk and usually high correlations across markets. Closely related to scenario analysis.

Stress testing/scenario analysis A set of techniques for estimating losses in extremely unfavorable combinations of events or scenarios.

Strike price Price at which an option can be exercised (same as exercise price).

Strip An option strategy involving the purchase of two puts and one call.

Structural change Economic trend occurring when the economy is undergoing a major change in organization or in how it functions.

Structural surplus or deficit The budget balance that would occur if the economy were at full employment and real GDP were equal to potential GDP.

Structural unemployment The unemployment that arises when changes in technology or international competition change the skills needed to perform jobs or change the locations of jobs.

Structured note (1) A bond or note issued with some unusual, often option-like, clause. (2) A bond with an embedded derivative designed to create a payoff distribution that satisfies the needs of a specific investor clientele. (3) A variation of a floating-rate note that has some type of unusual characteristic such as a leverage factor or in which the rate moves opposite to interest rates.

Style analysis An attempt to explain the variability in the observed returns to a security portfolio in terms of the movements in the returns to a series of benchmark portfolios designed to capture the essence of a particular security characteristic such as size, value, and growth.

Subjective probability A probability drawing on personal or subjective judgment.

Subsidy A payment that the government makes to a producer.

Substitute A good that can be used in place of another good.

Substitution effect The effect of a change in price of a good or service on the quantity bought when the consumer (hypothetically) remains indifferent between the original and the new consumption situations—that is, the consumer remains on the same indifference curve.

Successful efforts accounting A method of accounting for the costs of exploring and developing oil and gas resources in which successful exploration is recorded as an asset and depleted over the estimated life of the resource and all unsuccessful efforts are immediately written off as losses.

Sunk cost The past cost of buying a plant that has no resale value.

Supplemental Information Any performance-related information included as part of a compliant performance presentation that supplements or enhances the required and/or recommended disclosure and presentation provisions of the GIPS standards.

Supply The relationship between the quantity of a good that producers plan to sell and the price of the good when all other influences on sellers' plans remain the same. It is described by a supply schedule and illustrated by a supply curve.

Supply curve A curve that shows the relationship between the quantity supplied and the price of a good when all other influences on producers' planned sales remain the same.

Supply of labor The relationship between the quantity of labor supplied and the real wage rate when all other influences on work plans remain the same.

Supply-side effects The effects of fiscal policy on employment, potential GDP, and aggregate supply.

Support level A price at which a technician would expect a substantial increase in price and volume for a stock to reverse a declining trend that was due to profit taking.

Survivorship bias The bias resulting from a test design that fails to account for companies that have gone bankrupt, merged, or are otherwise no longer reported in a database.

Sustainable growth rate A measure of how fast a firm can grow using internal equity and debt financing and a constant capital structure. Equal to retention rate _ ROE.

Swap (1) A contract whereby two parties agree to a periodic exchange of cash flows. In certain types of swaps, only the net difference between the amounts owed is exchanged on each payment date. (2) An agreement between two parties to exchange a series of future cash flows.

Swap spread The difference between the fixed rate on an interest rate swap and the rate on a Treasury note with equivalent maturity; it reflects the general level of credit risk in the market.

Swaption (1) An option to enter into a swap contract at a later date. (2) An option to enter into a swap.

SWOT analysis An examination of a firm's *S*trengths, *W*eaknesses, *O*pportunities, and *T*hreats. This analysis helps an analyst evaluate a firm's strategies to exploit its competitive advantages or defend against its weaknesses.

Symmetry principle A requirement that people in similar situations be treated similarly.

Synthetic call The combination of puts, the underlying, and risk-free bonds that replicates a call option.

Synthetic forward contract The combination of the underlying, puts, calls, and risk-free bonds that replicates a forward contract.

Synthetic put The combination of calls, the underlying, and risk-free bonds that replicates a put option.

Systematic risk The variability of returns that is due to macroeconomic factors that affect all risky assets. Because it affects all risky assets, it cannot be eliminated by diversification.

Systematic sampling A procedure of selecting every *k*th member until reaching a sample of the desired size. The sample that results from this procedure should be approximately random.

Tangible assets Long-term assets that have physical substance.

Tangible book value per share Common shareholders' equity minus intangible assets from the balance sheet, divided by the number of shares outstanding.

Tap Procedure by which a borrower can keep issuing additional amounts of an old bond at its current market value. This procedure is used for bond issues, notably by the British and French governments, as well as for some short-term debt instruments.

Target semideviation The positive square root of target semivariance.

Target semivariance The average squared deviation below a target value.

Tariff A tax that is imposed by the importing country when an imported good crosses its international boundary.

Tax incidence The division of the burden of a tax between the buyer and the seller.

Tax multiplier The magnification effect of a change in taxes on aggregate demand.

Tax wedge The gap between the before-tax and after-tax wage rates.

Taylor rule A rule that adjusts the federal funds rate to target the inflation rate and to take into account deviations of the inflation rate from its target and deviations of real GDP from potential GDP.

Technical analysis Estimation of future security price movements based on past price and volume movements.

Technological change The development of new goods and better ways of producing goods and services.

Technological efficiency A situation that occurs when the firm produces a given output by using the least amount of inputs.

Technology Any method of producing a good or service.

***t*-Distribution** A symmetrical distribution defined by a single parameter, degrees of freedom, that is largely used to make inferences concerning the mean of a normal distribution whose variance is unknown.

Temporary New Account A tool that firms can use to remove the effect of significant cash flows on a portfolio. When a significant cash flow occurs in a portfolio, the firm may treat this cash flow as a "temporary new account," allowing the firm to implement the mandate of the portfolio without the impact of the cash flow on the performance of the portfolio.

Termination date The date of the final payment on a swap; also, the swap's expiration date.

Terms of trade The quantity of goods and services that a country exports to pay for its imports of goods and services.

Term structure of interest rates The relationship between term to maturity and yield to maturity for a sample of comparable bonds at a given time. Popularly known as the *yield curve*.

Term to maturity Specifies the date or the number of years before a bond matures or expires.

Test statistic A quantity, calculated based on a sample, whose value is the basis for deciding whether or not to reject the null hypothesis.

Theta The rate at which an option's time value decays.

Third market Over-the-counter trading of securities listed on an exchange.

Thrift institutions Thrift institutions include savings and loan associations, savings banks, and credit unions.

Tick The minimum price movement for the asset underlying a forward or futures contract; for Treasury bonds, one tick equals 1/32 of 1 percent of par value.

Time-period bias The possibility that when we use a time-series sample, our statistical conclusion may be sensitive to the starting and ending dates of the sample.

Time-series analysis An examination of a firm's performance data over a period of time.

Time-series data Observations of a variable over time.

Time-series graph A graph that measures time (for example, months or years) on the *x*-axis and the variable or variables in which we are interested on the *y*-axis.

Time to expiration The time remaining in the life of a derivative, typically expressed in years.

Time value decay The loss in the value of an option resulting from movement of the option price toward its payoff value as the expiration day approaches.

Time-weighted rate of return (1) The compound rate of growth of one unit of currency invested in a portfolio during a stated measurement period; a measure of investment performance that is not sensitive to the timing and amount of withdrawals or additions to the portfolio. (2) Calculation that computes period-by-period returns on an investment and removes the effects of external cash flows, which are generally client-driven, and best reflects the firm's ability to manage assets according to a specified strategy or objective.

Total cost The cost of all the productive resources that a firm uses.

Total Firm Assets Total firm assets are all assets for which a firm has investment management responsibility. Total firm assets include assets managed outside the firm (e.g., by subadvisors) for which the firm has asset allocation authority.

Total fixed cost The cost of the firm's fixed inputs.

Total probability rule for expected value A rule explaining the expected value of a random variable in terms of expected values of the random variable conditional on mutually exclusive and exhaustive scenarios.

Total product The total output produced by a firm in a given period of time.

Total return A return objective in which the investor wants to increase the portfolio value to meet a future need by both capital gains and current income reinvestment.

Total revenue The value of a firm's sales. It is calculated as the price of the good multiplied by the quantity sold.

Total revenue test A method of estimating the price elasticity of demand by observing the change in total revenue that results from a change in the price, when all other influences on the quantity sold remain the same.

Total variable cost The cost of all the firm's variable inputs.

Tracking error (1) The standard deviation of the difference in returns between an active investment portfolio and its benchmark portfolio; also called tracking error volatility. (2) The condition in which the performance of a portfolio does not match the performance of an index that serves as the portfolio's benchmark. (3) A synonym for tracking risk and active risk; also, the total return on a portfolio (gross of fees) minus the total return on a benchmark.

Tracking risk The standard deviation of the differences between a portfolio's returns and its benchmark's returns; a synonym of active risk.

Trade balance The balance of a country's exports and imports; part of the current account.

Trade Date Accounting The transaction is reflected in the portfolio on the date of the purchase or sale, and not on the settlement date. Recognizing the asset or liability within at least 3 days of the date the transaction is entered into (Trade Date, T + 1, T + 2 or T + 3) all satisfy the trade date accounting requirement for purposes of the GIPS standards. (See settlement date accounting.)

Trademark A registered symbol that can be used only by its owner to identify a product or service.

Tradeoff An exchange—giving up one thing to get something else.

Trading effect The difference in performance of a bond portfolio from that of a chosen index due to short-run changes in the composition of the portfolio.

Trading Expenses The costs of buying or selling a security. These costs typically take the form of brokerage commissions or spreads from either internal or external brokers. Custody fees charged per transaction should be considered custody fees and not direct transaction costs. Estimated trading expenses are not permitted.

Trading rule A formula for deciding on current transactions based on historical data.

Trading turnover The percentage of outstanding shares traded during a period of time.

Trailing P/E (or current P/E) A stock's current market price divided by the most recent four quarters of earnings per share.

Tranche Refers to a portion of an issue that is designed for a specific category of investors. French for "slice."

Transaction cost The cost of executing a trade. Low costs characterize an operationally efficient market.

Transaction Expenses (Private Equity) Include all legal, financial, advisory, and investment banking fees related to buying, selling, restructuring, and recapitalizing portfolio companies.

Transactions costs The costs that arise from finding someone with whom to do business, of reaching an agreement about the price and other aspects of the exchange, and of ensuring that the terms of the agreement are fulfilled. The opportunity costs of conducting a transaction.

Treasury bill A negotiable U.S. government security with a maturity of less than one year that pays no periodic interest but yields the difference between its par value and its discounted purchase price.

Treasury bond A U.S. government security with a maturity of more than 10 years that pays interest periodically.

Treasury note A U.S. government security with maturities of 1 to 10 years that pays interest periodically.

Tree diagram A diagram with branches emanating from nodes representing either mutually exclusive chance events or mutually exclusive decisions.

Trend The general tendency for a variable to move in one direction.

Trimmed mean A mean computed after excluding a stated small percentage of the lowest and highest observations.

t-Test A hypothesis test using a statistic (t-statistic) that follows a t-distribution.

Two-sided hypothesis test (or two-tailed hypothesis test) A test in which the null hypothesis is rejected in favor of the alternative hypothesis if the evidence indicates that the population parameter is either smaller or larger than a hypothesized value.

Type I error The error of rejecting a true null hypothesis.

Type II error The error of not rejecting a false null hypothesis.

Unbiasedness Lack of bias. A desirable property of estimators, an unbiased estimator is one whose expected value (the mean of its sampling distribution) equals the parameter it is intended to estimate.

Uncertainty A situation in which more than one event might occur but it is not known which one.

Unconditional probability (or marginal probability) The probability of an event not conditioned on another event.

Uncovered interest rate parity The assertion that expected currency depreciation should offset the interest differential between two countries over the term of the interest rate.

Underlying (1) Refers to a security on which a derivative contract is written. (2) An asset that trades in a market in which buyers and sellers meet, decide on a price, and the seller then delivers the asset to the buyer and receives payment. The underlying is the asset or other derivative on which a particular derivative is based. The market for the underlying is also referred to as the spot market.

Underweighted A condition in which a portfolio, for whatever reason, includes less of a class of securities than the relative market value alone would justify.

Unemployment rate The percentage of the people in the labor force who are unemployed.

Unit elastic demand Demand with a price elasticity of 1; the percentage change in the quantity demanded equals the percentage change in price.

Unit normal distribution *See* Standard normal distribution.

Univariate distribution A distribution that specifies the probabilities for a single random variable.

Unrealized capital gains Capital gains that reflect the price appreciation of currently held unsold assets.

Unsystematic risk Risk that is unique to an asset, derived from its particular characteristics. It can be eliminated in a diversified portfolio.

Unweighted index An indicator series affected equally by the performance of each security in the sample regardless of price or market value. Also referred to as an *equal-weighted series*.

Unwind The negotiated termination of a forward or futures position before contract maturity.

Up transition probability The probability that an asset's value moves up.

U.S. interest rate differential A gap equal to the U.S. interest rate minus the foreign interest rate.

U.S. Official reserves The government's holdings of foreign currency.

Utilitarianism A principle that states that we should strive to achieve "the greatest happiness for the greatest number of people."

Utility The benefit or satisfaction that a person gets from the consumption of a good or service.

Utility of wealth The amount of utility that a person attaches to a given amount of wealth.

Value The maximum amount that a person is willing to pay for a good. The value of one more unit of the good or service is its marginal benefit.

Valuation The process of determining the value of an asset or service.

Valuation analysis An active bond portfolio management strategy designed to capitalize on expected price increases in temporarily undervalued issues.

Valuation process Part of the investment decision process in which you estimate the value of a security.

Value at risk (VaR) (1) A money measure of the minimum loss that is expected over a given period of time with a given probability. (2) A probability-based measure of loss potential for a company, a fund, a portfolio, a transaction, or a strategy over a specified period of time. (3) A money measure of the minimum value of losses expected during a specified time period at a given level of probability.

Value chain The set of transformations to move from raw material to product or service delivery.

Value stocks Stocks that appear to be undervalued for reasons besides earnings growth potential. These stocks are usually identified based on high dividend yields, low *P/E* ratios, or low price-to-book ratios.

Value-weighted index An index calculated as the total market value of the securities in the sample. Market value is equal to the number of shares or bonds outstanding times the market price of the security.

Variance The expected value (the probability-weighted average) of squared deviations from a random variable's expected value.

Variation margin Profits or losses on open positions in futures and option contracts that are paid or collected daily.

Vega The relationship between option price and volatility.

Velocity of circulation The average number of times a dollar of money is used annually to buy the goods and services that make up GDP.

Venture Capital (Private Equity) Risk capital in the form of equity and/or loan capital that is provided by an investment institution to back a business venture that is expected to grow in value.

Vintage Year (Private Equity) The year that the venture capital or private equity fund or partnership first draws down or calls capital from its investors.

Volatility (1) A measure of the uncertainty about the future price of an asset. Typically measured by the standard deviation of returns on the asset. (2) As used in option pricing, the standard deviation of the continuously compounded returns on the underlying asset.

Voluntary export restraint An agreement between two governments in which the government of the exporting country agrees to restrain the volume of its own exports.

Wages The income that labor earns.

Warrant An instrument that allows the holder to purchase a specified number of shares of the firm's common stock from the firm at a specified price for a given period of time.

Weak-form efficient market hypothesis The belief that security prices fully reflect all security market information.

Wealth The market value of all the things that people own.

Weighted-average cost of capital A weighted average of the after-tax required rates of return on a company's common stock, preferred stock, and long-term debt, where the weights are the fraction of each source of financing in the company's target capital structure.

Weighted mean An average in which each observation is weighted by an index of its relative importance.

Winsorized mean A mean computed after assigning a stated percent of the lowest values equal to one specified low value, and a stated percent of the highest values equal to one specified high value.

Working-age population The total number of people aged 16 years and over who are not in jail, hospital, or some other form of institutional care.

Working capital management The management of a company's short-term assets (such as inventory) and short-term liabilities (such as money owed to suppliers).

World Trade Organization An international organization that places greater obligations on its member countries to observe the GATT rules.

Yankee bonds Bonds sold in the United States and denominated in U.S. dollars but issued by a foreign firm or government.

Yield The promised rate of return on an investment under certain assumptions.

Yield spread The difference between the promised yields of alternative bond issues or market segments at a given time relative to yields on Treasury issues of equal maturity.

Yield to maturity   The total yield on a bond obtained by equating the bond's current market value to the discounted cash flows promised by the bond. Also called actuarial yield.

Yield to worst   Given a bond with multiple potential maturity dates and prices due to embedded call options, the practice is to calculate a yield to maturity for each of the call dates and prices and select the lowest yield (the most conservative possible yield) as yield to worst.

Zero-cost collar   A transaction in which a position in the underlying is protected by buying a put and selling a call with the premium from the sale of the call offsetting the premium from the purchase of the put. It can also be used to protect a floating-rate borrower against interest rate increases with the premium on a long cap offsetting the premium on a short floor.

4⅝ 4¹¹/₁₆ — ⅜

5½ 5½ — ⅜

20⅝ 21³/₁₆ — ¹/₁₆

17⅜ 18⅛ + ⅞

6½ 6½ — ½

7¼ 3¹/₃₂ — ⅛

15/16

9/16 9/16

7¹/₁₆ 7¹³/₁₆ 7¹⁵/₁₆

2⅝ 2¹¹/₃₂ 2½ +

2¾ 2¼ 2¼

12¹/₁₆ 11⅜ 11¼ +

87 33¾ 33 33¼ —

25⅝ 24⁹/₁₆ 25⅝ +

12 11⅝ 11⅞ +

16 10½ 10½ 10½ —

78 15⅝ 15¹³/₁₆ 15

9¹/₁₆ 8¼

11¼ 10⅛

INDEX